Jewish Liturgy: A Comprehensive History

Translated by Raymond P. Scheindlin

Based on the original 1913 German edition,
and the 1972 Hebrew edition
edited by Joseph Heinemann, et al.

Jewish Liturgy

A Comprehensive History

by Ismar Elbogen

 5753 - 1993
The Jewish Publication Society   Philadelphia – Jerusalem

 The Jewish Theological Seminary of America   New York – Jerusalem

Previously published in German under the title
Der jüdische Gottesdienst in seiner geschichtlichen Entwicklung, 1913
and in Hebrew under the title *Hatefila beyisra'el behitpathutah hahistorit,* 1972

This edition © 1993 by The Jewish Publication Society
and by The Jewish Theological Seminary of America
Translated by Raymond P. Scheindlin
First English edition   All rights reserved
Manufactured in the United States of America

Library of Congress Cataloging-in-Publication Data

Elbogen, Ismar, 1874–1943.
  [Jüdische Gottesdienst in seiner geschichtlichen Entwicklung,
English]
  Jewish liturgy : a comprehensive history / by Ismar Elbogen ;
translated by Raymond P. Scheindlin.
      p.   cm.
  "Based on the original 1913 German edition and the 1972 Hebrew
edition edited by Joseph Heinemann, et al."
  Includes bibliographical references and index.
  ISBN 0-8276-0445-9
  1. Judaism—Liturgy—History.   I. Title.
BM660.E513   1993
296.4—dc20
                                                    93–18401
                                                    CIP

Typeset in Goudy Old Style and Novarese by Graphic Sciences, Inc.

Designed by Adrianne Onderdonk Dudden

The publishers express their gratitude to
Herman Elbin, son of Ismar Elbogen,
for his dedication and support of this project
over a period of many years.
We trust that the publication will be a fitting tribute
both to him and to the erudition
and scholarship of his father, *z"l.*

The publishers wish to acknowledge the generosity of
The Lucius N. Littauer Foundation
in support of the research and translation of the work.

Contents

CHAPTER TWO

Prayers for Special Days   91

CHAPTER THREE

The Reading of the Torah and the Sermon   129

PART THREE
THE ORGANIZATION OF THE JEWISH LITURGY

Foreword

Seventy years after its first appearance, Ismar Elbogen's *Der jüdische Gottesdienst in seiner geschichtlichen Entwicklung* remains the only academic study of the Jewish public liturgy in its entirety. It is a monument to the historical and philological approach that characterized Jewish studies—and humanistic studies generally—in the last half of the nineteenth century. It is an ambitious work, covering the areas traditionally treated by liturgical scholars and going far beyond them to deal also with synagogue organization, architecture, and music. Though Elbogen's reconstruction of liturgical history and the book's intellectual matrix are somewhat outdated, his work remains the most exhaustive compendium of factual information about the Jewish liturgy, and it is likely to remain so for some time.

Elbogen's book can be read in two ways: as a scientific history and description of the Jewish liturgy; or as a monument to the outlook of a religious Jewish intellectual in nineteenth- and early twentieth-century Germany.

Elbogen's book is very much a product of turn-of-the-century German Jewish scholarship. Like many works of the period, it impresses the contemporary reader with its sheer erudition, its delight in facts, and its bravura citation of sources. It breathes confidence that, given patience, common sense, objectivity, and exhaustive knowledge of the sources, the truth can be found. Yet, for all its objectivity and despite its marshaling of evidence for every claim, it is also an engaged book—engaged sometimes to the point of lyricism, and sometimes to the point of crankiness.

Liturgy was a living issue for Elbogen, for he saw the challenge facing the liturgy as a miniature version of the challenge facing Judaism in general. For Elbogen, the question of whether the liturgy could adjust to modernity while retaining its authentic character was a test case for the ability of Judaism as a whole to survive in a manner that would do justice to its past.

Writing soon after a period of radical experimentation with all forms of Jewish life, Elbogen was sympathetic to the need for reform. He saw the orthodox refusal to diagnose accurately the dangers faced by Judaism as a symptom of atrophy. He denounced the orthodox rabbis of Germany for refusing to participate with other rabbis who attempted to confront these dangers more actively. He was convinced that the fossilized orthodoxy of his age would strangle Jewish religiosity unless the spirit of life could be salvaged from its ritualism. He knew that the true spirit of Judaism did not lie in blind traditionalism; yet he had faith that beneath the petrified religious institutions a real religious spirit was still alive, waiting to be blown to life. In our age of fundamentalist revival, Elbogen needs to be heard again, for he reminds us that the path of uncompromising traditionalism leads nowhere.

But Elbogen was not complacent about the Reform movement, for he did not believe in radical upheaval. He believed that the ancient liturgy gave voice to simple, eternal truths, and that these truths could be recovered not by radical change but by careful, scientific restoration. He held that an awareness of the history of the liturgy could provide the discipline that would prevent reform from turning into anarchic experimentation. He sought legitimate rather than indiscriminate change; restoration and refurbishing rather than revolution.

Thus, Elbogen's history of the Jewish liturgy is a work of pure scholarship, yet at the same time it is a contribution to the urgent debate on the future of Jewish religious life. In treating matters of fact, Elbogen is rigorously objective, marshaling sources and weighing evidence down to the finest minutiae. But the objective data are in service of a larger religious vision, and in matters of opinion bearing on this vision Elbogen is passionate. Precious traces of the man behind the book and of the intellectual climate of his times are scattered throughout these pages: the author's polemics against what he saw as superstition, rigidity, and illogic; his lyrical effusions on the synagogue poetry of the Golden Age; and his pride in Judaism's contribution as the first Western religion to devise a verbal means of communication with God.

Elbogen's Judaism was traditional, yet rational and anti-mystical. His warm feelings about tradition are couched in language that today may ring too sweet for some; yet in these expressions he is quite as sincere as he is in his harsh condemnations of both radical reform and blind traditionalism. His anger at liturgical changes made out of ignorance is as vehement as is his anger at hidebound orthodoxy.

His opposition to mysticism reflects a nineteenth-century perspective that some of today's religious liberals might find odd. Insofar as mysticism represents a religion of the heart and a rebellion against rigidity, Elbogen is inclined to describe it favorably; accordingly, his tone grows agreeably warm at the beginning of his chapter on the influence of mysticism on the liturgy. But when mysticism crosses a certain intellectual line he sees it as superstition, not only because of its inherently irrational character, but also because of its association with socially reactionary forces. Here Elbogen provides us with a badly needed corrective. For in our desperate late twentieth-century quest for spirituality we tend to forgive mysticism its ties to intellectual reaction and superstition, which Elbogen could still observe in full bloom.

Thus, Elbogen's peculiarly objective yet engaged work has wisdom for our own time.

HISTORY OF PUBLICATION

Elbogen's magisterial work first appeared in German in 1913; second and third editions appeared in 1924 and 1931, respectively, each edition being revised and supplemented with additional notes. An abridged Hebrew translation of Part 1 by B. Krupnick appeared in 1924. In the course of the fifty years following the original publication of the book, Judaic scholarship made considerable progress in several fields related to the liturgy. Materials discovered in the Cairo geniza contributed to knowledge of the ancient Palestinian rite and of medieval liturgical poetry. Developments in archeology enhanced the knowledge of the ancient synagogue. The study of Jewish mysticism became a full-fledged academic discipline. By the time the work began on a new, complete Hebrew translation, it was felt that it was necessary not merely to translate but to update Elbogen's work.

Accordingly, a team of scholars was formed under the general supervision of Professor Ḥayim Schirmann to provide supplementary material for the new Hebrew translation of Elbogen's book. Professor Joseph Heinemann served as coordinator and editor for this new Hebrew edition, which appeared in 1972. Professor Heinemann also added the supplementary material for the sections dealing with the wording and history of the statutory prayers, the reading of the Torah, and the liturgical customs of the synagogue—that is, §§6–30, §§34–38, and perhaps §§43–44. Professor Schirmann edited the chapters of the book bearing on Hebrew sacred poetry, its development, genres, and forms (§§31–33, 39–42). Professor Jakob Petuchowski wrote the supplementary remarks to the chapters on the history of the Reform movement and its prayer books (§§45–47); Dr. Abraham Negev brought up to date the treatment of ancient synagogue buildings (§§48–49); and Dr. Israel Adler summarized the consensus of scholarship on the history of synagogue music (§54).

All the supplementary material in the new Hebrew edition was enclosed in square brackets so that it could be distinguished from Elbogen's original text. Longer additions were also indented. Every effort was made to preserve Elbogen's intentions, even where the scholar in charge of a section disagreed strongly with his views. But the contributing scholars did point out significant changes in the consensus since Elbogen's time, citing sufficient bibliographical data so that the serious student would have no trouble getting a completely rounded picture of any aspect of the book.

The combined efforts of so many scholars resulted in a comprehensive, up-to-date, but somewhat idiosyncratic book. Elbogen frequently personalizes his writing by using such expressions as "in our rites," meaning the German version of the Ashkenazic rite; or "in these territories," meaning Germany. Some of the 1972 contributors also used the first person to refer to their own scholarly writings. The Hebrew translator, Joshua Amir, here and there inserted a correction or a note of his own.

The present English version of Elbogen retains all the idiosyncrasies of the Hebrew version and adds to them the presence of yet another figure, the English translator, the author of this Foreword, who occasionally makes an appearance in a bracketed note.

THE PRESENT TRANSLATION

The first draft of the present translation was made from the Hebrew edition of 1972. This draft was compared word-for-word with the German edition of 1931 (the reprint of Georg Olms Verlagsbuchhandlung, Hildesheim, 1967) and revised in accordance with my understanding of Elbogen's intentions. This revision resulted in a number of places where the English does not agree with the Hebrew in meaning or emphasis. Accordingly, this book may be regarded as an independent translation from the German, incorporating all the supplementary material found in the Hebrew. The Hebrew supplementary material in this translation appears within square brackets and is set in a different typeface from that used for Elbogen's text.

In translating I tried to keep three kinds of reader in mind: the student of religion who possesses little or no familiarity with Hebrew or the Jewish liturgy, and who reads the book in quest of an authoritative picture of the Jewish liturgy; the specialist who knows Hebrew and other ancient languages, who uses the book in order to gain access to the problems of the liturgy and the history of scholarship relating to these problems; and the Jewish reader who has some familiarity with the liturgy and knows the Hebrew alphabet, but has little experience with the historical study of Jewish texts. Since both the German and the Hebrew editions demand of the reader a good deal of prior knowledge, I have had to provide some help, particularly in the manner of referring to liturgical texts.

Elbogen nearly always refers to particular prayers in the traditional way, by quoting their opening words (incipit) in Hebrew, using the Hebrew alphabet. Following this style exactly would have made the book unusable by the student of religion and most Jewish laypersons. I have devised a compromise that should make the book accessible to both groups.

Prayers and other Hebrew words that are sufficiently familiar to have entered standard English dictionaries, like Kaddish, Kedushah, and Mishnah, appear in their standard English spellings.

The Hebrew name in transliteration is used for common prayers whose names have not been naturalized in English, like ʿAmida and Shemaʿ. Technical terms and the genres of liturgical poetry like seliha and qerova are treated similarly. It should be pointed out that for the prayer that today is generally called ʿAmida, Elbogen consistently uses the word *tefila*, but I have followed the Hebrew translation in using the more familiar term. Benedictions of the ʿAmida are usually given by number.

The bulk of the prayers, which have no name, are cited by their incipits. The incipit is given in Hebrew script on its first appearance, together with a translation of the incipit. Thereafter, the English translation of the incipit is used throughout the book. Thus, non-Hebraists can follow the discussion, while Hebraists have the actual Hebrew words. Both readers can also locate the prayer in a standard prayer book, though of course the English translation in any given prayer book will not be identical with mine. Because of differences in the natural word order of Hebrew and English, the English version of an incipit is not always exactly equivalent to the words of the Hebrew.

Two indexes of incipits—Hebrew and English—are provided. Their main purpose is to enable the reader to locate all references to a particular prayer. But they may also be used by the Hebraist to identify the exact Hebrew incipit of a prayer given in the text in English.

I used English as much as possible, reasoning that Hebraists will have an easier time with English than non-Hebraists will have with Hebrew. When a Hebrew word must be used repeatedly in the text, I have provided a transliteration on its first occurrence. But I have ordinarily not provided transliteration in the notes, which were written mostly with the scholar in mind.

Religious services and festivals are given wherever possible in English, in order to make the book accessible to the largest possible circle of readers. Furthermore, using Hebrew for prayers, services, and festivals, in addition to other technical terms, would have resulted in an unpleasant jargon style. When in doubt, I was guided by the principle that, wherever practical, a translator should translate. But in the notes, where the discussion is often rather technical, foreign terms are translated far less often. Here I felt that translation would impede the specialist without helping the nonspecialist.

I restricted myself to translating and resisted the temptation to edit. I did not tone down Elbogen's style or eliminate his repetitions. Nor did I eliminate his references to "this country," "our time," and the like, for such intrusions of the personal element serve to remind the reader that this is an engaged book, and that its seemingly impersonal positivistic scholarship was motivated by personal commitment to the subject.

One of the impressive features of the book is its extraordinary wealth of references to books and articles, both general and specialized. Thanks to these references the book can be used to trace the entire history of scholarship on any particular point. In the German editions, Elbogen gave these references in a very crabbed and incomplete form, rarely citing a title in full, giving an author's first name only on occasion, and almost never providing complete publication data. Furthermore, the German editions have no alphabetized bibliography (and the Hebrew has only a very incomplete one). But Elbogen is not entirely to blame; standards of citation have become much more rigorous in our time than they were in an age when a book like this one was read only by academic specialists. This deficiency was improved somewhat in the Hebrew edition. I have done my best to guide the reader through the thicket of bibliographical data by making a number of changes in the manner of presentation, as follows:

I have filled in the publication data for many of the books and articles cited incompletely by Elbogen, but I have not done so for every source cited. Such an attempt would have involved vast bibliographical research and would have increased the length of the book substantially. Moreover, in many cases it was not possible to identify a work or locate an obscure local German periodical. But when the data were available I have provided them, and in most cases enough information is now given to enable the nonspecialist or the student to locate the works cited.

In the dates of books and articles, the style 1954/5 indicates the Hebrew year 5715; I used this style because the Hebrew years begin in September or October, so that each Hebrew year stretches over parts of two Gregorian years. The style 1954–55 indicates a sequence of two Gregorian years.

As in all the previous editions, the book is divided into sections numbered from §1 to §54. Each section beginning with §7 is broken down further into subsections, which are numbered consecutively within each section. The beginning of a subsection is designated by a number in parentheses.

In addition, each section beginning with §7 in the German and Hebrew editions is preceded by a bibliography of works dealing with the specific subject of that section. I have removed these "section bibliographies" from the section beginnings and reproduced them in an appendix at the end of the book. There the specialist may consult them, and they will not impede or intimidate the general reader.

Books and articles that are mentioned repeatedly are cited in a short form. These short forms are listed alphabetically in the section entitled "Selected Bibliography," where full titles and the necessary bibliographical data are provided. This list, designed originally as merely a listing of abbreviated titles, is not a complete bibliography—such a bibliography would have occupied a whole volume—but it is so extensive that it is a useful guide to the literature on the field of Jewish liturgy.

The reader should bear in mind that occasionally the authors of the supplementary notes of 1972 also occasionally speak in the first person. A note indicating that a work is "still not available" or "publication is expected" reflects the situation in 1972. In some cases the publication has occurred; in others, lamentably, it is still awaited.

The process of translating, revising, and editing uncovered many small errors in references to both primary and secondary sources, some made by Elbogen and others introduced by the Hebrew translator. Also, thanks to the persistence of the copy editor, I have filled in Elbogen's ibid.-references with exact page numbers wherever I felt secure in doing so, and the process of identifying these ibid.-references uncovered many other small errors. I mean no disrespect to my predecessors. This book contains thousands of references to books ancient and modern; in such a plethora of references it is frighteningly easy to make mistakes. I only hope that in the process of correcting the slips of the German and Hebrew editions I have not introduced any of my own.

A peculiarity of the notes is Elbogen's occasional use of the long dash instead of paragraphing to separate discussion of different topics.

I have not updated the bibliographies or the discussion to reflect the developments in the field of Jewish liturgy since 1972. The twenty intervening years have brought some discoveries, some revisions of opinion. The new material has not yet been completely absorbed and integrated, and it will most likely be a long time before a new synthesis of the history of the Jewish liturgy will be written. My hope is that the existence of this translation may inspire someone to take up the field, to master the sources and the new disciplines, and to devote a career to this new synthesis. Such a successor to Elbogen would ideally update his work and go beyond it to deal with the religious meaning of the liturgy, a meaning Elbogen felt keenly but had not the tools to describe. Such an outcome would be a real reward for the time and effort that have gone into this endeavor.

Raymond P. Scheindlin
New York, April 1992

Acknowledgments

The initiative for this project came from Ismar Elbogen's son, Mr. Herman Elbin, who first approached Chancellor Gerson D. Cohen of the Jewish Theological Seminary in 1981 with the idea of sponsoring the translation as a memorial to his father. Mr. Elbin recalls that in their last conversation, one day before Professor Elbogen's passing in August 1943, his father confided to him the intention of issuing an updated English version of the book. The project had apparently been on Elbogen's mind since his lecture tour in the United States in 1922/3. It is extremely gratifying that the English edition is appearing in 1993, the year of the author's fiftieth Jahrzeit. I have taken much personal satisfaction in serving as the translator of this classic, having made extensive use of it over the years both as a teacher of liturgy at the Seminary and as a specialist in medieval Hebrew literature.

Mr. Herman Elbin provided the funds for the translation and publication of the book. Additional funding came from the Abbell Fund of the Jewish Theological Seminary. A supplementary grant was also provided by the Lucius Littauer Foundation.

Many individuals provided help at various stages of this project. Professor Jack Wertheimer of the Seminary read and critiqued a draft of §§45–47, dealing with the Reform movement; Susan Braunstein, Associate Curator of the Jewish Museum, read and critiqued a draft of §49, dealing with synagogue construction, and made a very useful correction to the text. Boaz Tarsi, assistant professor at the Cantors Institute of the Jewish Theological Seminary, read and critiqued a draft of §54, dealing with synagogue music. Two graduate students at the Seminary, Jeff Rubenstein and Amy Goldstein, did essential library research. Naomi Lewin and Jay Sales helped with the word processing. Alice Tufel, the copy editor, grappled heroically with a difficult manuscript and contributed sound advice toward the solution of many problems. My wife, Janice Meyerson, proofread the manuscript with patience, skill, and good humor. To all I extend my sincere thanks.

Special thanks are due to Chancellor Ismar Schorsch, who provided me with much personal encouragement in his accustomed generosity of spirit and friendship. Thanks to his erudition in matters pertaining to German Jewry he was able instantly to clarify a technical term that had eluded me and baffled my other consultants.

Finally, thanks are due to Vice-Chancellor of the Seminary, John Ruskay, and to Seminary Counsel Ann Appelbaum for devising and pressing for the adoption of the complex arrangement among all parties that made publication possible.

Abbreviations

Bible

Gen.	Genesis	Nah.	Nahum
Ex.	Exodus	Hab.	Habakkuk
Lev.	Leviticus	Zeph.	Zephaniah
Num.	Numbers	Hag.	Haggai
Deut.	Deuteronomy	Zech.	Zechariah
Josh.	Joshua	Mal.	Malachi
Judg.	Judges	Ps.	Psalms
I Sam.	I Samuel	Prov.	Proverbs
II Sam.	II Samuel	Job	Job
I Kgs.	I Kings	Song of Songs	Song of Songs
II Kgs.	II Kings	Ruth	Ruth
Is.	Isaiah	Lam.	Lamentations
Jer.	Jeremiah	Qoh.	Qohelet (Ecclesiastes)
Ezek.	Ezekiel	Esth.	Esther
Hos.	Hosea	Dan.	Daniel
Joel	Joel	Ezra	Ezra
Amos	Amos	Neh.	Nehemiah
Obad.	Obadiah	I Chron.	I Chronicles
Jonah	Jonah	II Chron.	II Chronicles
Mic.	Micah		

Rabbinic Texts

Avot	Avot	Bik.	Bikurim
ʿA.Z.	ʿAvoda Zara	Dem.	Demai
B.	Babylonian Talmud	Deut. r.	Deuteronomy raba
B.B.	Bava Batra	ʿEd.	ʿEduyot
B.M.	Bava Meṣia	ʿEruv.	ʿEruvin
B.Q.	Bava Qama	Ex. r.	Exodus raba
Bekh.	Bekhorot	Git.	Gitin
Ber.	Berakhot	Gen r.	Genesis raba
Beṣ.	Beṣa	Ḥag.	Ḥagiga

Rabbinic Texts (cont.)

Hal.	Hala	Pes.	Pesaḥim
Hor.	Horayot	Qid.	Qidushin
Kel.	Kelim	R.H.	Rosh hashana
Ker.	Keritot	Sanh.	Sanhedrin
Ket.	Ketubot	Shab.	Shabat
Kil.	Kilaim	Shevu.	Shevuʿot
Lev. r.	Leviticus raba	Sheq.	Sheqalim
M.	Mishnah	Song of Songs r.	Song of Songs raba
Ma.	Maʿaserot	Sifre Deut.	Sifre to Deuteronomy
Mak.	Makot	Sifre Num.	Sifre to Numbers
Makhsh.	Makhshirim	Sota	Sota
Meg.	Megila	Suk.	Suka
Me.	Meʿila	T.	Tosefta
Mekhilta	Mekhilta derabi	Ta.	Taʿanit
	ishmaʿel	Tam.	Tamid
Men.	Menaḥot	Tem.	Temura
Mid.	Midot	Ter.	Terumot
Miq.	Miqvaʾot	Toh.	Tohorot
M.Q.	Moʿed qatan	T.Y.	Tevul yom
Naz.	Nazir	ʿUqs.	ʿUqsin
Ned.	Nedarim	Y.	Yerushalmi
Neg.	Negaʿim	Yad.	Yadaim
Nid.	Nida	Yev.	Yevamot
Num. r.	Numbers raba	Yoma	Yoma
Ohal.	Ohalot	Zab.	Zabim
ʿOrl.	ʿOrla	Zer.	Zeraʿim
Par.	Para	Zev.	Zevaḥim
Pe.	Peʾa		

Non-rabbinic Texts

I Macc.	I Maccabees	Philo (cont.)	
II Macc.	II Maccabees	Legat.	Legatio ad Gaium
Praep. Ev.	Praeperatio Evangelica	Mos.	De vita Mosis
Philo		Spec.	De specialibus legibus
Flacc.	In Flaccum		
Hypoth.	Hypothetica		
	(Apologia pro Iudaeis)		

Medieval Texts

Abudarham	Sefer Abudarham	Pardes	Sefer hapardes
Eshkol	Sefer haʾeshkol	S.A.	Shulhan ʿarukh
ʿItim	Sefer haʿitim	S.L.	Shibole haleqet
Manhig	Sefer hamanhig	Sapir	Even sapir
M.T.	Mishne tora	Tur	Arbaʿa turim
O.H.	Oraḥ hayim	Vitry	Mahzor Vitry
O.Z.	Or zaruʿa	Y.D.	Yore Deʿa
Orhot	Orhot hayim		

Journals and Other Publications

AJSL	*American Journal of Semitic Languages and Literatures*
ARW	*Archiv für Religionswissenschaft*
AZDJ	*Allgemeine Zeitung des Judentums*
E.J.	*Encyclopaedia Judaica*
HUCA	*Hebrew Union College Annual*
J.E.	*Jewish Encyclopaedia*
JJS	*Journal of Jewish Studies*
JQR	*Jewish Quarterly Review*
MGWJ	*Monatsschrift für Geschichte und Wissenschaft des Judentums*
OLZ	*Orientalische Literaturzeitung*
PAAJR	*Proceedings of the American Academy for Jewish Research*
REJ	*Revue des Études Juifs*
Riv. Isr.	*Rivista Israelita*
SRIHP	*Studies of the Research Institute for Hebrew Poetry*
ZAW	*Zeitschrift für die Alttestamentliche Wissenschaft*
ZDMG	*Zeitschrift der Deutschen Morgenländischen Gesellschaft*
ZGJD	*Zeitschrift zur Geschichte des Juden in Deutschland*
ZHB	*Zeitschrift für hebräische Bibliogra*
ZNW	*Zeitschrift für die Neutestamentliche Wissenschaft*

Jewish Liturgy: A Comprehensive History

Introduction

§ 1 Delimitation of the Subject

The purpose of this book is to describe the liturgy as it developed in the Jewish communities. The word *liturgy* makes us think today mostly of prayer and worship. But because the reading of the Torah and its exposition occupy such an important place in the synagogue service, we shall have to deal not only with the prayers but also with study; not only with the service of the heart but also with the propagation of the Torah. Furthermore, public worship is tied to certain external requisites, presupposing organization, places of assembly, functionaries, and particular ways of performing the service. We intend to deal with all of these matters and to examine their development and historical evolution. On the other hand we shall not deal with the theological questions connected to prayer, or the details of ritual law that apply to it. We shall also exclude from our discussion two other areas: first, the sacrificial cult, though it was ordinarily accompanied by prayers; and, second, the broad area of individual prayer, including prayers entirely within the individual sphere, such as Grace after Meals or the Bedtime *Shemaᶜ*, and religious ceremonies of a somewhat public nature, such as circumcisions, weddings, and funerals.

§ 2 The Historical Development of the Liturgy[1]

Jewish liturgy has unparalleled importance in the history of religions,[2] for it was the first to free itself completely from the sacrificial cult, thus deserving to be called "The Service of the Heart."[3] Likewise, it freed itself of all external paraphernalia, such as worship sites endowed with special sanctity, priests, and other incidentals, and became a completely spiritual service of God. Because its performance required no more than the will of a relatively small community, it was able to spread easily throughout the world. It was also the first public liturgy to occur with great regularity, being held not only on Sabbaths and festivals, but on every day of the year, thus bestowing some of its sanctity upon all of life. This effect was all the more enduring in that the daily morning and evening services, originally the practice of the community, soon became the customary practice of individuals, even when they were not with the community.

The format of Jewish prayer was not always the one that is familiar to us today; at first it was neither as long nor as complex. Both the order of prayer as a whole and the individual prayers have changed in the course of time, so that "the liturgy of today is the fruit of a thousand years' development" (Zunz, *Haderashot*, 180). At first there was no fixed liturgy, for the prayers were not set down in writing; only the gist of their content was fixed, while their formulation was provided by the precentor in his own words. Public prayer was brief, and when it came to an end, the individual worshiper laid out his own petition in silence. But the prayer of the individual was displaced little by little until it vanished completely from public worship. The ancient prayers could not be lengthy, and their content had to be clear and simple; there was no room for convoluted language or structure. But once these prayers had become entrenched, they were subject to continual unconscious expansion, resulting from the need for innovation, changes in taste, outside influences, and the practice of individual holy men. These expansions consisted of wordier development of the existing themes, the insertion of biblical verses and verse-fragments into the text, and poetic embellishment of the established text. They were small in scale, simple in form, and clear in their manner of expression. Thus, there crystallized little by little a stock of prayers that was in use every day of the year, though with minor changes on particular days; and since these prayers were closely attached to the old nucleus of the prayers, we call them "statutory prayers" (*Stammgebete*).

[2]

Beginning in the [fourth,] fifth, or sixth century, soon after the recording of prayers in writing was permitted, there arose another type of expansion—free poetic compositions based on religious teachings, particularly on the themes of the festivals. These were called *piyyutim* [singular, piyyut—*Engl. trans.*], a term derived from Greek.[4] The piyyut brought into the liturgy a dynamic element that lent it variety. Its character was formed and its content fixed by artistic taste and religious outlook, which varied considerably by country and period. The piyyut was entirely optional; its content and form were not subject to regulation or limitation. Because of it, public worship became long and involved, resulting in the great variations between countries and communities that we designate by the term *rites* (מנהג). No sooner had the wanderings of the Jews and the invention of printing begun to reduce these differences somewhat when along came mysticism, which introduced a new influence into the service, one that was deep and not always beneficial. It brought new outlooks, additions, and expansions; it occasioned a shift in the conception of prayer, emphasizing the secondary and obscuring the essential. From this point on, the quantity of prayers was taken more seriously than the correctness of their wording. Late additions and petty usages were cultivated industriously, while the statutory prayers were treated casually, and the behavior of the worshipers became undisciplined. Only the critique of Mendelssohn's circle and the Reform movement one hundred years ago brought about an effort to elevate and refine worship in the synagogue. The newly revived taste for simplicity, sublimity, and solemnity found in the realm of prayer a rich and rewarding field. Since then all movements have worked to improve and simplify public worship. And while the early attacks had to do with the external form of prayer, the transformation of the Jewish people's civil status and the advances in theological study soon gave rise to other demands. Ample room was demanded for the vernacular, both in the prayers and in sermons. Like the tradition as a whole, the statutory prayers became subject to critical judgment; to the extent that their content or style did not suit the spirit of the times, they were altered or eliminated. The prayer books of the Reform congregations adopted a fundamentally different form from the one that had preceded them. Since these books were first composed, prayer has been the subject of intense struggles that are waged passionately to this very day.

§ 3   *Terminology*

The regularity of public prayer among the Jews necessitated an order of prayer and occasioned the establishment of liturgy. The word λειτουργεῖν is used by the Septuagint to translate the Hebrew word שרת, "to serve," and in the later biblical books, λειτουργία serves as the equivalent of עבודה, "service."[5] *Liturgy* thus means the service of the Temple and, above all, the service of the priests—that is, the bringing of sacrifices. In the course of time the meaning of the word underwent the same evolution as did its Hebrew equivalent, being transferred from the material to the spiritual cult.[6] As the Midrash says:

[3]

> *And to serve Him* (Deut. 11:13): This refers here to prayer. You might say, "This refers to prayer (according to you), but might it not refer to (Temple) service?" (The answer is *no*.) Since Scripture says, *With all your heart and with all your soul* (Deut. 11:13), is there such a thing as (Temple) Service in one's heart? Therefore, what does the verse mean by *and to serve Him?* It refers to prayer (*Sifre* Deut., 80a, §41).[7]

Thus, as used by the talmudic rabbis, the word עבודה remained the general word for liturgy; the noun λειτουργία passed over to Christian theology, and only recently has been used in the confines of the synagogue, though, for the most part, only in the narrow sense of the prayers that are said by the rabbi, rather than by the precentor.

The Bible is rather rich in words for *prayer* and *to pray,*[8] but in the literature dealing with liturgical matters, not one of these is used in quite the same way as in the Bible, nearly all having acquired different meanings in the course of time. No comprehensive word exists for the entire liturgy, but every part is called by its own name, corresponding to its content. In the Talmud, and to some extent in the geonic period, the terms are precisely distinguished, whereas later they are often used interchangeably.

The basic element of the statutory prayer is called ברכה (*berakha*), "benediction." This expression comes from II Chron. 20:26: ". . . the Valley of Blessing, for there they blessed the Lord"; in Neh. 9:5, "benediction" occurs alongside תהלה, "praise," already in its new technical sense. *Berakha* is derived from the root ברך,[9] which originally meant "to bend one's knee," but it developed to mean "to pray for someone's welfare," "to invoke upon one blessings from heaven," until it eventually arrived at the meaning "to praise and extol God" (*pi'el* and *qal* passive participle). Likewise, "benediction" designates the prayer of praise and thanksgiving, and its character is almost always hymnic. The benediction has a fixed form, which is called טופס ברכות, or מטבע של ברכה, "the formula of the benedictions" (Y. *Ber.* 1:8, 3d). It was modeled on the many expressions of praise in the Psalms, and especially on the doxologies at the end of the books of Psalms (Pss. 41:14, 72:18, etc.). The first of the amoraim (third century C.E.) established rules for the formulation of the benediction, ordaining that each one must include the mention of God's name (שם), while some added that it must also mention God's kingdom (מלכות). In this way, the form for the opening of the benediction that is familiar today came into being: "Blessed are You, Lord our God, King of the universe . . ."[10] Some benedictions, such as the Enjoyment Benedictions and the Benedictions for Religious Obligations, are in the "short form"—that is, מטבע קצר (Y. *Ber.*, ibid.), which is but a single sentence. Such benedictions only begin with "blessed" (פותחות בברוך). Alongside them a "long form" (מטבע ארוך) exists—for the most part, prayers in the narrow sense, which not only begin with "blessed" but which also have a חותם, "seal" (M. *Ber.* 9:5) or חתום (B. *Ber.* 12b; Y. *Ber.*, ibid.) with "blessed." This ending too, when taken by itself, is called ברכה (Greek εὐλογία, as the Septuagint translates ברכה in the verse from II Chronicles quoted above), and has the form ברוך אתה ה', "Blessed are You, Lord." Thus, a biblical verse can also be turned into a benediction with the simple addition of a concluding eulogy (for example, the verses from Psalm 120 and others that are cited in M. *Ta.*, chap. 2).[11] Such eulogies are also found as the conclusion of petitions, and accordingly the name of the main petitionary prayer is the "Eighteen Benedictions." When benedictions occur consecutively, it is the rule that only the first opens with "blessed," while a benediction that follows a preceding one in a series (ברכה הסמוכה לחברתה) does not begin with "blessed." But like the preceding rule, this one, too, has many exceptions; it seems to be later than many of the prayers of this type, and thus does not apply to them (see Y. *Ber.*, ibid.). If the text of a prayer is long, and its train of thought wanders from its starting point, the rule is that the sentence preceding the eulogy must return to the starting point (סמוך לחתימה מעין החתימה).

[4]

Alongside the term *berakha* stands the term תפלה (*tefila*), which means "petitionary prayer," originally "to turn to God as to a judge."[12] להתפלל, "to pray," occurs in the Bible both in connection with petitions and in connection with thanksgiving. In the Talmud התפלל and תפלה, together with Aramaic צלי and צלותא, are applied particularly to the 'Amida, which is the petitionary prayer (εὐχαί) par excellence [in its weekday form], whereas in the post-talmudic period *tefila* denotes any petition or prayer for someone's welfare, for which in the Talmud the words רחמים, "mercy," and תחנונים, "supplications," serve. To be sure, the word *tefila* occasionally serves, as in the Bible, for any kind of prayer, including prayers of praise and thanksgiving; thus, the benedictions and prayers (*berakhot* and *tefilot*) established, according to the tradition, by the men of the Great Assembly (B. *Ber.* 33a), designate prayers of every type. The title of the oldest extant order of prayers is סדר תפילות וברכות, "The Order of Prayers and Benedictions," or, more briefly, סדר תפילה or סידור תפילה. From this was derived the term for a prayer book, which is called סדור (*sidur*) or, in some places, תפלה (*tefila*).

The word סדר (*seder*) means "a fixed arrangement," "a specified order," and in exact usage, also "a fixed quantity."[13] All of these meanings are relevant to our context, but in rabbinic Hebrew and in the Targumim this word occurs frequently in connection with a great complex, to denote a concatenation of things, as in Gen. 1:16, where the Palestinian Targum renders the scriptural words ואת הכוכבים as וית סדר כוכביא. In the first known place where the word *seder* occurs with reference to prayers (B. *R.H.* 17b), סדר תפלה designates the contents of a single prayer. Likewise, סדר and סדרא, without any addition, occur in the meaning of "prayer as a whole." Similarly, in the context of prayer, *piꜥel* and *hifꜥil* derivatives of the Hebrew and Aramaic verb *seder* occur with the meaning "to recite prayers aloud" or "to compose prayers." There is a special reason for this close connection between this root and the idea of prayer. The biblical root ערך, which the Targum everywhere renders as סדר, is connected with, among other things, the direct object מלין, "words" (Job 32:14); likewise in Ps. 5:4, בקר אערוך לך ואצפה, "At daybreak I plead before You and wait," where the verb occurs without a direct object, we can deduce from the context that its meaning is "to pray." The same semantic shift occurred to the root סדר and all of its derivatives, until an inseparable bond was formed between it and expressions for prayer. In this way, *seder* and *sidur* became terms for the order of prayers.

Another collection of prayers is customarily called מחזור (*mahzor*). The root חזר, "to recur in a particular sequence," was originally used in connection with the calendar. The *mahzor* of the moon is the cycle of a single year, or the great astronomical cycle of nineteen years. Since the word *mahzor* referred originally to the cycle of the year, it is also applied to a book that deals with calendrical matters. We first find it transferred to the book of prayers in the Syriac church, which calls its books of prayers *Mahzarta*. In Jewish literature this word designates the recurring order of the service of the synagogue. The original *mahzorim* may have been calendars in which laws of the prayers were given in accordance with the cycle of the year. But with the expansion of the piyyut, all traces of the calendar were displaced, leaving only the name that derived from them, while the *mahzor* contained mainly the statutory prayers and the piyyutim. When one wanted to speak precisely he would call this collection "*mahzor* of prayers." The words *sidur* and *mahzor* are not mutually exclusive, but rather *mahzor* is the comprehensive term. In a *sidur*, only the statutory prayers are found for the most part, while the *mahzor* contains poetic additions, as well. Also, in a *sidur* the instructions and comments about the prayers are brief; in the *mahzor* they are more detailed and are expanded into discussions of various related matters. Eventually, standard usage limited the word *mahzor* to the festival prayers (statutory prayers with piyyutim), while the collection of all the statutory prayers was called *sidur*. In recent times, the piyyutim for special Sabbaths are occasionally appended to the *sidur*.

Collections of prayers are a relatively late phenomenon in Judaism; originally the dominant view was that it is forbidden to reduce the prayers to writing, and that "those who write benedictions are like those who burn the Torah" (T. *Shab.* 14:4).[14] Only after the close of the Talmud, when necessity compelled that the other parts of the Oral Law be written down, were the prayers also reduced to writing, and only after the sixth century were collections of prayers compiled. "In the time of the compilation of Tractate *Soferim* there is no doubt that collections of prayers existed."[15] But even these are not prayer books in the present-day sense, because many points in them remained unsettled and subject to local variation. This situation was changed by the sages who composed the orders of prayer. The latter were constructed on the basis of the dictum

[5]

of Rabbi Meir (ca. 150 C.E.) that "One is obliged to recite one hundred benedictions every day" (B. *Men.* 43b; Y. *Ber.* 9:2, 13b). Thus, for some time prayer books were composed according to the principle of one hundred benedictions. The oldest composition of this type, the much-quoted *One Hundred Benedictions* of Natronai Gaon (ca. 860 C.E.), was recently discovered and published by Louis Ginzberg.[16] As for complete prayer books, the most ancient is the one that Rav Amram Gaon (ca. 875 C.E.) sent to Spain, called *Seder rav ʿamram gaʾon* or *Yesod haʿamrami*; it was published in Warsaw in 1865. Its text was corrected and completed on the basis of manuscripts by Alexander Marx. Alongside it the prayer book of R. Saadia Gaon (882–942 C.E.) deserves mention. It originally enjoyed much attention, but was later forgotten and recently rediscovered [and published in Jerusalem in 1951]. Thus for several centuries it was common for distinguished sages to compose their own individual prayer books, resulting in the emergence of the comprehensive prayer collections. The most famous and richest is *Maḥzor Vitry*, by R. Simḥa b. Samuel of Vitry (ca. 1100), emanating from the circle of Rashi. It provides the most reliable evidence for the old French rite. It was discovered by Samuel David Luzzatto and printed in Berlin (1889–93). Rashi's own prayer book, which contains regulations concerning prayer but not the text of the prayers themselves, was published in Berlin (1911).[17]

Several smaller literary genres separated themselves out of the abundant contents of the holiday prayer book and became independent pamphlets, such as the books of *seliḥot* and *qinot*. As the piyyut came to occupy a larger place in synagogue prayer, these collections expanded greatly, and the piyyut came to comprise most of the contents of the holiday prayer book. Since it was used in the communities in a great number of variations, it led to tremendous variety in the liturgy. It was mainly the spread of the piyyut that brought about the differentiation of the rites,[18] for every individual community clung faithfully to its own usage (מנהג). Minor variations were already found in the statutory prayers, but they were so slight that only the eye of an expert could detect them. But the addition of poetic insertions led to a noticeable distinction among the prayer books of the various lands, particularly in the holiday prayers. The communities chose piyyutim solely on the basis of their own tastes and their own desires, so that it is possible to find different rites even in adjacent locales; migrations and expulsions sometimes made a unity out of entirely disparate elements, and it was not uncommon for compositions of a poet that were neglected in his homeland to achieve fame in some distant place. It would take us too far afield to enumerate all the rites and their local variations (Zunz counts more than sixty), especially since, in the course of time, and partly under the influence of printing, most of them have been lost. We shall content ourselves with mentioning the most important of them, those whose prayer books are continually before our eyes in these studies.

Two basic groups of rites must be distinguished, the Palestinian and the Babylonian. These were already rather different in their statutory prayers, and traces of both are found in the talmudic literature, but neither has been preserved in its original form. The Palestinian rite has been almost completely suppressed. Like all the institutions and traditions of the Jewish people, the prayers were decisively influenced by Babylonia, to such an extent that even the rites that are reckoned among the Palestinian group bear for the most part a Babylonian stamp on their basic prayers. Witnesses for the Palestinian rite are Tractate *Soferim* (edited by Joel Müller, Leipzig, 1878), the prayer book of R. Saadia Gaon, and many fragments found in the Cairo geniza and published since the beginning of this century.[19] Likewise, the following belong to the Palestinian group:

1. The Germanic rite (Ashkenaz in the broad sense) is divided into the western branch (Ashkenaz in its narrow sense) and the eastern branch (Polish rite), with the Elbe River as the boundary. But it must be remembered that the Jews who were expelled or who migrated from Germany or Poland took their prayer book with them to their new homeland. Thus, we find it in such places as Italy, England, the Middle East, and America [and Israel]. The first editions of the Ashkenazic rite (in its narrow sense) come from Italy in the year 1490; of the Polish rite, from Prague in 1512–22. Related to the Ashkenazic rite is the old French rite, which is represented by *Maḥzor Vitry*; because of the expulsion of the Jews from France in the fourteenth century, this rite early fell into desuetude and survived only in the three Italian communities of Asti, Fossano, and Moncalvo (Apam).

2. The Italian, or the Roman rite, also called the *Rite of the Loazim* (Rome), may be the earliest offshoot of the Palestinian rite, the first prayer book in a diaspora country. For it we possess a superior edition containing the fine analysis of S. D. Luzzatto (Luzzatto, *Mavo*). The first edition appeared in the cities of Soncino and Casalmaggiore (1485–86). This rite has come to be limited to Italy and a few communities in Turkey.

[7]

3. The Romaniot,[20] or more exactly Romali or Greek rite (also known as the Romanian rite), was originally current throughout the Balkan countries, and is still in use in a few synagogues on the Island of Corfu; in the statutory prayers it is very close to the Roman rite. Complete copies are extremely rare. The first extant edition appeared in Venice in 1524, and the second in Constantinople in 1574.

The Babylonian rite has also not been preserved in its original form. The prayer book of R. Amram Gaon, its first representative, deviates frequently from the Talmud.

4. The version of R. Amram reached Spain, and therefore the rite of this land—the Sephardic rite[21]—is the main witness for the Babylonian order of prayer, though it has undergone numerous changes and it was not uniform in all times and in all communities. Since after the expulsion most of the Jews of Spain migrated to Portugal, they are called Portuguese, and their rite is called the Portuguese rite. Through their subsequent migration to various lands on three continents they disseminated their rite in many places, and suppressed completely the ancient eastern rite of the Oriental countries, which was closest to the ancient Babylonian rite. The first edition of the Sephardic prayer book appeared in Venice in 1524. A special branch of this rite is that of Yemen,[22] whose prayer book (*Tiklāl*) was greatly influenced by Maimonides; a good edition appeared in Jerusalem in 1901.

5. Intermediate between the two above-mentioned groups are the communities of Provence:[23] Avignon, Carpentras, and Montpelier (known as the Provençal rite). As in the other branches of Jewish literature these Jews were influenced in their liturgical traditions both by France and by Spain.

§ 4 *Sources*

The sources for the history of prayer are meager. From the ancient period no prayers have been preserved in writing, and the oldest extant collections of prayers have come down to us only in late reworkings, none earlier than the twelfth century. For the most ancient period, we are dependent on scattered data in the two Talmuds, the midrashim, and their commentators; in the responsa literature; and in works on synagogal institutions. These data are neither extensive nor coherent; [statutory daily] prayers are never reported to us in their entirety in the Talmud, nor are we able always to fix their date with certainty. The period of the true development of the statutory prayers is relatively brief, and nearly all outside the limits of our sources. By the time our written documentation begins, the prayer book is already basically fixed. The most ancient extensive source is Tractate *Soferim*, composed around 600 C.E. From the following centuries we have the above-mentioned prayer collections. From the High Middle Ages the *Mishne tora* of Maimonides (1180) must be singled out, as it contains not only the laws of the prayers, but also, at the end of its first book, "The Order of Prayers for the Entire Year." From that period we have the *Manhig ʿolam* or the *Sefer hamanhig* by Abraham b. Nathan Hayarḥi of Lunel (*Manhig*), who was well informed because of his travels, and who reports much information about the rites of northern France and Spain. The same may be said of several halakhic treatises of great value to us from the following two centuries, the *Shibole haleqet* by R. Zedekiah b. Abraham Anav (ca. 1250) of Rome, *Orḥot ḥayim* by Aaron Hakohen (ca. 1300) of Narbonne, and *Oraḥ ḥayim*, the first of the four *Turim*, by R. Jacob b. Asher (ca. 1330) of Toledo (here cited as the *Tur*). To these may be added the detailed commentary by R. David Abudarham (1340) of Seville. All of the above-mentioned works serve as important testimony for the prayer books and the prayer texts of their countries, as well as those of other lands, of which they frequently cite details for comparative purposes. The rite books of the following century transmit but little information about the text of the prayers; on the other hand, they are rich in material bearing on the organization of public worship. The same is true of the *Shulḥan ʿarukh*. In the following period, so marked by the influence of the Kabbalah, the rites of R. Isaac Luria and his disciples were influential. Among the modern editors of the prayer book, the first place belongs to Wolf Heidenheim of Frankfurt, the first to strive for exactness and simplicity in the prayer book. The critical work begins with the notes of S. L. Rapoport in his sketch of the life of Rabbi Eleazar Kallir. This is the foundation for the classic works of Leopold Zunz, who made use of an enormous quantity of manuscript material, thereby becoming the guide for all the scholars who followed in his footsteps.

[8]

§ 5 *The Organization of the Material*

Our presentation is divided into three sections. First we provide a description of Jewish prayer as it is observed on weekdays, the Sabbath, and the festivals. Here we treat consecutively the prayers, the reading of the Torah, the readings of the Prophets and Hagiographa, and the poetic additions; in every case we reconstruct the most ancient form known to us and follow its development through the course of time and through the various rites until our day. For this purpose our starting point is the Ashkenazic prayer book according to the text in the edition of Baer ('*Avodat*). The second part is the consecutive narration of the history of Jewish prayer as it developed from its beginnings to our time; it is divided into three periods: the period of the statutory prayers (to 600), the period of the piyyut (600–1800), and the period of critical scholarship (1800–1900). The third part is devoted to the liturgical institutions of the Jewish people. It deals with the external framework of prayer: the synagogue building and its furnishings; the congregation, its administration, and its officers; and the officers' functions in the prayer service.

PART ONE

Description of
the Jewish Liturgy

CHAPTER ONE

The Weekday Prayers

A. THE MORNING SERVICE

§ 6 *The Morning Service of Weekdays*

Called שחרית (M. *Ber.* 1:3),[1] the Morning Service is also בשחר (M. *Ber.* 1:4), יוצר or תפילה של יוצר (*Midrash tehilim* 65b, §17), תפילת השחר (*Midrash tehilim* 163b, §72), צלותא דצפרא,[2] צלוה יוצר תמיד, אלתמיד,[3] Greek ἕωθεν (Josephus, *Antiquities*, 8.8.3) and ἀρχομένης τῆς ἡμέρας (Epiphanius, *Haereses*, 29:9). It is divided into five parts:

1. ברכות השחר, "Morning Benedictions," from the beginning of the prayer book down to, but not including, ברוך שאמר, "Blessed is He Who Spoke" (Baer, *ʿAvodat*, 33–54).

2. פסוקי דזמרה, "Verses of Song," or זמירות, "Psalms," from "Blessed is He Who Spoke" to ישתבח, "May Your Name Be Blessed," inclusive (Baer, *ʿAvodat*, 58–75).

3. יוצר, "Creator," or קריאת שמע, "Recitation of the *Shemaʿ*," a group of prayers beginning with and grouped around שמע ישראל, "Hear, O Israel" (Baer, *ʿAvodat*, 76–86).

4. עמידה, "*ʿAmida*"; literally, "Standing"; also called תפילה, "Prayer," or שמונה עשרה, "The Eighteen" (Baer, *ʿAvodat*, 87–104).

5. תחנון, "Supplication"; this name includes all the prayers that occur after the *ʿAmida* (Baer, *ʿAvodat*, 112–32, 162).

The Morning Service did not always have its present form. The individual parts were not always so long, nor were all of them originally included in the synagogue service. In the ancient period the Supplication (**5**, above) was a prayer of the individual worshiper, offered in silent devotion at the end of the public service. The only prayer that the precentor recited standing in a particular place was the *ʿAmida* (**4**, above), for even during the recitation of the *Shemaʿ* he did not leave the ranks of the congregation. In a later development, the precentor recited the Supplication as well, and he took up his post already with the recitation of the *Shemaʿ*, but in *Seder rav ʿamram* we still find the old view that he should come before the Ark only for the ʿAmida and that Supplication is not a public prayer. The Verses of Song (**2**, above) were originally said by each individual to himself. It is still very common today for there to be no precentor at all until the end of the Verses of Song, or at least not the same one as the one who executed the main prayers (**3** and **4**, above). The first section was not said in the synagogue at all, but at home, and served as preparation for public prayer. In Amram and as late as Maimonides we find regulations along these lines; Rabbi Meir of Rothenberg (after 1250)[4] (Responsa of *Tashbes*, no. 217) introduced this section in the synagogue in the Ashkenazic rite, and eventually it was accepted in other lands as a result; but the memory of the original practice was never completely lost.

[12]   In the circles of the kabbalists, the four sections of the Morning Service (counting the ʿAmida and Supplications as a single section) were considered a unit, built according to the rule of ascending importance.[5] The four sections of the service were supposed to correspond to the four ranks of the cosmos—that is, the lower world, the sefirotic world, the world of the angels, and the world of the godhead. Others identified the four parts with the parts of the human organism, with the first part corresponding to the body and the three remaining parts corresponding to the three parts of the soul—the vegetative, the animal, and the rational. Yet, though this division lends itself to heightening and intensifying the devotion of the worshiper with the increasing significance of each individual section, the entire structure is untenable; for the prayers were not edited according to a plan, by a single person at a single point in time, but came into being and joined each other at different times.

The most ancient and important of the prayers are the Recitation of the *Shemaʿ* (**3**, above) and the ʿAmida (**4**, above).

The *Shemaʿ* contains the confession of faith, the core of Israel's belief, while the ʿAmida consists of a number of petitions touching the chief needs of the individual and the community. Theoretically, it may be correct that one should not solicit favors of the Lord; it is an ancient belief among the Jews that He knows our needs before we express them to Him. Yet, in real life, nearly everyone experiences the longing to clothe his heart's desire in words and to lay them out before his Father in Heaven. The confession of faith and the petition are thus the most ancient parts of the prayer service. It is not difficult to explain why this section was prefaced with a section of hymns. But we must not make the present-day sequence of prayers into the basis of far-reaching conclusions as to the original intention of the prayers. We begin our discussion with sections 3, 4, and 5, and then we return to sections 2 and 1.

§ 7   *The* Shemaʿ *and Its Benedictions*

(1)   The third section of the weekday Morning Service is called קריאת שמע, "The Recitation of the *Shemaʿ*," after its main content, or יוצר, "Creator," because it begins [13]   with the benediction יוצר אור, "Creator of Light"; in fact, from this latter the entire Morning Service has acquired the name תפלת יוצר, which is still in use in Eastern lands.[1] Likewise, the poems inserted in the fixed prayers are called יוצר (plural, יוצרות), because the first of them is inserted in this benediction.

At the heart of this section stand three passages from the Torah, שמע (Deut. 6:4–9), והיה אם שמע (Deut. 11:13–21), and ויאמר (Num. 15:37–41); the three sections together are called "*Shemaʿ*" or "The Recitation of the *Shemaʿ*" because of the first word of the first passage. The Mishnah already fixes the structure of the entire section: "In the morning two benedictions are said before [the *Shemaʿ*] and one after it" (M. *Ber.* 1:4), meaning that one must preface the *Shemaʿ* with two benedictions and follow it with one. The first benedictions are named for their beginnings, יוצר אור, "Creator of Light"; sometimes—as, for example, in Abudarham—also ברכת המאורות, "Benediction of the Luminaries," and אהבה רבה, "With great love"; the concluding benediction is אמת ויציב, "True and certain," with the eulogy גאל ישראל, "Who redeemed Israel." This prayer was often prefaced with yet another special benediction, or with the verse והוא רחום, "And He, being merciful" (Ps. 78:38; thus *Manhig*, "Laws of Prayer," §26); but these two additions have not been preserved in any rite.

(2)   This section begins with ברכו, "Bless the Lord." Already in the Mishnah (M. *Ber.* 7:3), R. Ishmael (ca. 120) cites it in the current wording, though this wording was even then the object of a dispute that remained unresolved until the end of the amoraic period.[2] The ancient orders of prayer make no mention of the custom that while the precentor says ברכו the congregation recites the hymn יתברך, "May the Name of the King be blessed,"[3] which is composed of fragments of the Kaddish (§12a) and other biblical phrases. Apparently, in ancient times no reply to "Bless the Lord" was expected,[4] but this call served as the invitation to begin the public worship. Only later, when the call was taken to be part of the prayer, did the custom arise for the congregation to answer it with the special response ברוך יי המבורך, "Blessed is the Lord, Who is blessed." This custom was generally established by the second century (*Sifre* Deut., §306).

(3)   The current text of the Creator benediction contains rhymes, an alphabetical acrostic (in some rare versions, even further developed than in the current one), and other signs of relatively late origin.[5] In accordance with the benediction's function as a morning prayer, it begins with praises based on Is. 45:7, with a slight alteration at the end of the verse to suit it for the service. The daily renewal of light is briefly praised as a renewal of the act of creation. The beginning and the end, twelve words in all, are quoted in B. *Ber.* 11b and 12a; and of what follows, the words המחדש בכל יום מעשה בראשית, "Who renews every day the act of creation," occur in B. *Hag.* 12b, though not in connection with our prayer. Parallel to the opening of the benediction is the eulogy יוצר המאורות, which is prefaced by the verse "Who made the great lights" (Ps. 136:7). This verse, too, may still be reckoned as part of the original stock of the prayer,[6] but with these words everything has been said that needed to be said in this place. Indeed, the version of the prayer prescribed by Saadia for individual worship is in this short form, which is also found in several geniza fragments without special remark.[7]

The rest of the material between the opening and the conclusion in the current version adds nothing new to the ideas that were meant to be expressed; it is merely an artificial expansion that might be deleted without loss to the content. The beginning, מה רבו, "How numerous," is drawn from Ps. 104:24, and the conclusion has a petition, רחם עלינו, "Have mercy upon us," which is out of place here; the intervening words form an unnecessarily wordy transition to it. The words "have mercy upon us" themselves

[14]

belong to the following series of rhymes, which Saadia quotes in a slightly altered form. Its content and form betray it as a later addition to the original base; yet, it may be older than the expansions that follow it. The fragment, אל ברוך גדול דעה . . . תמיד, "Blessed God, great in knowledge," is an alphabetical acrostic, which apparently was meant to include the letters that have special final forms (מנצפ״ך);[8] it originated at the very earliest at the end of the talmudic period. In the geonic period such acrostics were not yet incorporated into the prayer; several were available to be inserted as alternatives. Saadia, for example, recommends a longer one in which every letter is represented by at least two words, and fragmentary prayer books provide additional examples. Another acrostic is found toward the end of this benediction: כולם אהובים . . . ברורים . . . גבורים . . . עושים . . . פותחים, "All are beloved . . . pure . . . mighty . . . perform . . . open. . . ." The acrostic is not complete, but that need not mean that our tradition is defective, for the poets did not always work out the acrostics to their completion. We do find more of this acrostic in the Crimean rite than in the other rites (ותיקים זכים חפצים . . . לובשים עוז ותפארת), but this is very likely a late addition.[9]

The thirteen following words, תתברך, "Be blessed," to סלה, "*Sela*," return to the theme of the benediction (the luminaries) and were therefore considered by Zunz to belong to the original benediction; but they do not fit there and serve only to pick up again the subject's broken thread. The words קדושים, "holy ones," and משרתים, "servants," open a new theme, leading to the Kedushah. All scholars agree that this Kedushah in its present form is not ancient, but they are divided as to whether the Kedushah itself originally belonged here or not. Many hold that this in fact was its original place, and that from here it entered the 'Amida, while others believe that it originated in the 'Amida and was transferred here. We deal with this problem below in §9a. The verbose character of our text, which serves as a transition and which appears in Saadia in a very abbreviated form, is apparently no older than the geonic period, having originated in the circles of the Merkava mystics,[10] who strove mightily in their prayers to comprehend the godhead. They longed for visions; and the heaping up of hymns is a tried and true means of achieving ecstasy that was practiced by mystics in every age. From the circles of the mystics we have many prayers of marvelous beauty, but also many in which verbiage overwhelms feeling and thought. According to information in *Seder rav 'amram*, the Kedushah was one of the most beloved prayers of the mystics of that period. Evidence has lately come to light that in the first century of the geonic period the mystics made great efforts to disseminate their ideas, thereby arousing much opposition.[11] They were especially eager to spread the recitation of the Kedushah. In Palestine the Kedushah was recited [in the 'Amida] only on Sabbaths and festivals, while the mystics demanded that it be introduced on weekdays as well; despite bitter opposition they did not let up until they had achieved their purpose. About the year 750 this movement spread from Babylonia to Palestine. It would seem that at that time the Kedushah entered Creator, while the ancient Palestinian rite did not know it at all. [This matter is still in dispute; see the supplementary notes to §9a, pp. 59–61, below.]

The section beginning לאל ברוך, "To the Blessed God," is directly connected to the reference to the angelic choirs that preceded and thus cannot predate it. It, too, contains several rhymes (פועל גבורות, עושה חדשות, and so forth). In accordance with the ancient rule (see above, p. 16), it returns to the theme of the opening, in fact, to the very words: המחדש בטובו בכל יום תמיד מעשה בראשית, "Who renews in His goodness every day the work of creation"; and as a biblical prooftext, כאמור, "as it is said," it cites: לעושה אורים גדולים, "Who made the great lights" (Ps. 136:7). But the word "lights" proved to be a stumbling block, for poetic souls (perhaps the mystics mentioned above) attached to it a petition for the light of the messianic redemption: אור חדש על ציון תאיר, "Cause a new light to shine upon Zion." Saadia, whose prayer book does not even have "Who made the great lights," campaigned against this addition,[12] but in Babylonia his effort was to no avail; yet, it is absent from the Sephardic, Romaniot, and Italian rites, while in the sphere of the French-Ashkenazic rite, Rashi expressed his opposition to it. In Germany it became known early on and was defended by R. Eliezer ben Nathan of Mayence (ca. 1100). The dispute is reflected in the manuscripts as well, some of them citing the sentence and others omitting it; in the printed editions of the Ashkenazic rite it is found since the first edition. Where "Cause a new light" is lacking, a different conclusion is found. The Italian and Romaniot rites have, after Ps. 136, ובחסדו נתנם [להאיר] על הארץ, "and in His mercy He set them [Romaniot: to give light] over the earth"; and the Sephardic rite, והתקין מאורות לשמח (את) עולמו אשר ברא, "and He established luminaries to rejoice His world that He created." It appears that this was the original conclusion until the messianic conclusion replaced it.[13] The version "Cause a new light" itself is apparently a shortened version of a more elaborate messianic petition. In southern France it was the custom to follow "Cause a new light" with Is. 60:1 and Ps. 118:27. This might be a vestige of a Palestinian tradition, as is often the case with this rite; in the geniza fragments we frequently find between the two parts of the sentence "Cause a new light to shine" and "that we may all be worthy," alongside the above-mentioned verses, ונר משיחך תאיר לנו, "And cause the lamp of your anointed one to shine for us."[14] The eulogy יוצר המאורות, "Creator of the luminaries," is found already in B. *Ber.* 12a, Y. *Ber.* 1:8, 3b. The Reform prayer books have abridged the benediction in various ways; at first objections were raised only to "Cause a new light," but later the references to angels ("Be blessed, our Rock") were eliminated, and ultimately the short version found in Saadia was restored.

(4)   The second benediction is called ברכת התורה, "The Benediction of the Torah," in Y. *Ber.* 1:8, 3c. In our rite it begins with the words אהבה רבה, "With great love," while in the Sephardic and Italian rites it begins אהבת עולם, "With eternal love," alluding to Jer. 31:2. This variation is ancient; it goes back to the Talmud, B. *Ber.* 11b, and may be rooted in the different practices of Babylonia and Palestine. It continued in various times and places and even caused the text of the Talmud to be transmitted in alternate versions. In the geonic academies, Pumbedita had "With eternal love," while Sura read "With great love" in the Morning Service but assigned "With eternal love" to the Evening Service. This compromise was accepted by Amram and by the Ashkenazic and Romaniot rites as well, while Saadia has "With eternal love" in both services, as do the Sephardic and Italian rites.

The content of this benediction, as attested by its ancient name, is gratitude for the revelation. This becomes clear through comparison with the Evening Service and with the ancient versions, for as it stands before us the original purpose of the benediction is evident only from its first part. In its content this benediction is identical in all the rites. In most of them the text is longer than in Ashkenaz, but the variants are numerous only in the second part. As in the first benediction, a petition of messianic

[16]

content was inserted here, sometimes longer, sometimes shorter; already in Amram and Saadia it is longer than in Ashkenaz. An important variation in this petition is that whereas Ashkenaz and Rome have a petition for the assembling of the diaspora communities, והביאנו לשלום בארבע כנפות הארץ, "Bring us in peace from the four corners of the earth," Amram, Saadia, and, following them, Sepharad express the petition for the messianic redemption in very general terms: [מהר ו] הבא עלינו ברכה (ישועה) ושלום מארבע כנפות הארץ, "[quickly] bring upon us blessing, [salvation,] and peace from the four corners of the earth." It is noteworthy that the messianic petition is found only in geniza fragments that begin "With eternal love" and not in those that begin "With great love." The introduction of the messianic petition was probably occasioned by the sentence ויחד לבבנו, "and unite our hearts," which concluded the first part and served as a transition to the proclamation of the divine unity. In its source, Ps. 86:11, this sentence was a petition for unbounded devotion to God, but it was then linked to the later conception of יחוד השם (The Confession of the Unity of God's Name)—the acknowledgment of God even at the moment of death, and especially in martyrdom, bringing it into connection with thoughts of the world to come and the messianic age. Even in the present version it can still be seen that the benediction originally ended with "and unite our hearts," for the conclusion—"and bring us (our King) to Your great Name"—leads back to the thought represented by these words. Already in Amram, Saadia, and following them all the other rites, the conclusion goes on: להודות לך וליחדך באמת [ו] באהבה Rome], "to give thanks to You and to declare Your unity (Rome: in truth and) in love"; in the Romaniot rite the formulation is even more elaborate: וליחדך ולאהבה ולאהוב את שמך הגדול, "to declare Your unity and to love Your great Name"—showing how the development of individual words could lead to an expansion of the wording as a whole. As already mentioned, Ashkenaz and Rome have the shortest and simplest version of "With great Love."[15] The eulogy, הבוחר בעמו ישראל באהבה, "Who chooses His people Israel in love," is identical in all the rites;[16] its nucleus may be found already among the benedictions of the high priest on the Day of Atonement (Y. *Yoma* 7:1, 44b). For the Reform prayer books, the model is the version introduced in the Temple of Hamburg in 1818; there the messianic petition was much abridged and reworded after the version quoted above from the Sephardic rite.

(5)   For the passages from the Torah in the Recitation of the *Shema* itself, see page 17. For private worship, Ashkenaz adds before the *Shema* the words אל מלך נאמן, "God, faithful King"; they exemplify the typical way in which misunderstandings arise and acquire religious significance. The three words are simply the word *amen* treated as an acronym. This word is found before the *Shema* in Amram, Saadia, and even in *Mahzor Vitry*;[17] in Palestine it was the practice to say "amen" after the benediction "With great Love," though this custom was early prohibited (Y. *Ber.* 5:5, 9c). Now in the Talmud (B. *Shab.* 119b) we find: "What does 'amen' mean? Said R. Ḥanina: God, faithful King." When the kabbalists came along and began to count the words of the prayers, seeking the mysteries concealed in numbers, they found that the three biblical passages contain 245 words, so that by adding the three words, "God, faithful King," they reached the mystical number 248, corresponding to the number of limbs in the human body or the number of the positive commandments. The precentor does not say, "God, faithful King," but he reaches the same total number by concluding aloud, "the Lord your God is true."[18]

After the verse "Hear O Israel" the recitation is interrupted by the response, ברוך שם כבוד מלכותו לעולם ועד, "Blessed be the Name of His majestic glory forever." This formula is borrowed from Ps. 72:19; the middle words are equivalent to "The Lord our God." This response formula was used in the Temple in answer to the pronouncing of the ineffable name by the high priest (M. *Yoma* 3:8 and elsewhere). Its insertion in the *Shemaᶜ* is related to the customary manner of reciting this passage in the most ancient period.[19] On this subject, see page 24.

[17]

(6)   As a conclusion to the recitation of the biblical passages comes the benediction, אמת ויציב, "True and Certain." This name is found already in Mishnah (*Tam.* 5:1) in the Morning Service of the priests during the offering of the daily sacrifice. Because of its antiquity, R. Yehuda asserts (B. *Ber.* 21a) that the obligation of reciting it is toraitic. The eulogy of this extremely long benediction is גאל ישראל, "Who redeemed Israel," whence its other name, "Redemption" (compare B. *Ber.* 9b; Y. *Ber.* 1:1, 2d). The two names point to two stages in the development of the prayer. "True and Certain" is a confirmation of the declaration of faith; it fits well with the first two passages of the *Shemaᶜ* and confirms the validity of these ancient verses for every age. The name "Redemption" arose through the introduction of the third biblical passage; its present content has its source in the Tosefta (*Ber.* 2:1; Y. *Ber.* 1:9, 3d): "One who recites the *Shemaᶜ* [in the morning] must mention the exodus from Egypt in 'True and Certain.' Rabbi says: 'In it one must mention [God's] sovereignty.' Others say: 'In it one must mention the smiting of the firstborn [in Egypt] and [the miracle of] the splitting of the sea.' "[20] This dispute is resolved at the end: "R. Joshua b. Levi says, 'One must mention them all and must also say, "The rock of Israel and its redeemer".' "

Also regarding the wording, a number of points deserve mention. "True and Certain" contains Hebrew and Aramaic words side by side, a frequent occurrence in ancient prayers. In addition, there is a large number of synonyms; Rashi requires eighteen, while in the prayer book there are altogether sixteen, and these words are exactly the same in all the rites, a sign of their antiquity. The sentence is thereupon resumed with אמת, "true," and developed rather wordily in midrashic style. The text is the same in all the versions except for minor stylistic variants, though Romaniot has a completely different conclusion; Ashkenaz contains the surprising reading יוצרנו צור ישועתנו, "Our Creator, the Rock of our salvation," instead of the expected צורנו צור ישועתנו, "Our Rock . . .," which is found in all the other rites, including *Vitry*, and which matches the parallelism of the other phrases. When piyyutim are inserted, Ashkenaz employs a shortened version with the same content; the conclusion—למען שמך מהר לגאלנו, "For the sake of Your Name hurry to redeem us"—seems like an expansion, but is apparently only a summary of the Redemption benediction. Romaniot preserved this conclusion in the weekday service, and in the geniza fragments the short "True and Certain" is found in the weekday prayers; once again we have here a remnant of the Palestinian liturgy preserved in the Ashkenazic rite in connection with piyyut, a phenomenon we will frequently meet again.

With עזרת אבותינו, "Help of our fathers" (*Vitry* reads "helper") begins the second part, the Redemption, in the form of a vigorous hymn. It is in the nature of this style that in the course of time certain phrases in it were altered or replaced with longer ones; in some geniza manuscripts it is still evident how parts of the text were deleted and

[18] added. But for these changes, which scarcely affect the content, the text is the same in all rites. It leads to the two quotations from the Song of the Sea, Ex. 15:11 and 15:18. But toward the end the variations are more numerous. Amram simply concludes here, rejecting any additions explicitly and absolutely. Nevertheless such additions are present in every rite. The simplest version is that of Sepharad, which adds only גואלנו, "Our Redeemer" (Is. 47:4). In all the other rites there is inserted at this point, again contrary to the original plan, a petition that God repeat the act of Redemption. Amram mentions בגלל אבות תושיע בנים, "For the sake of the fathers save the sons," but he rejects it; nevertheless, it is in use in the weekday prayers of Romaniot and Rome, as well as in Ashkenaz on Passover in connection with the piyyut ברח דודי, "Flee, my beloved." It is likely that this wording, too, derives from the Palestinian rite. In Ashkenaz the language of the petition in the weekday prayers is צור ישראל קומה בעזרת ישראל, "Rock of Israel, arise for the help of Israel," with the addition, to which some Ashkenazic scholars objected, of "Our Redeemer"; this version was known also in southern France. Romaniot has "Our Redeemer" together with "For the sake of the fathers." Very lengthy concluding formulas, completely different from the above versions, are found in fragments from the Oriental countries. After Ex. 15:11 comes: מפי עוללים ויונקים שירה שמעת, "From the mouths of babes and sucklings you heard song," and as a response, Ex. 15:18, together with an extensive hymn and a petition:

ה' מלכנו מלך אל חי וקיים שמך עלינו ה' יוצרנו ה' הושיענו חוס ורחם עלינו ברחמים הרבים כי אל חנון ורחום
טוב אתה ה' מלך ה' מלך ה' ימלוך לעולם ועד קיים ועד עולם עלינו ה' אלהינו מלכותו וכבודו גדלו ותפארתו וקדושתו
וקדושת שמו הגדול הוא ה' אלהינו ירחם עלינו וירוח לנו מכל צרתינו ויגאל' גאולה שלמה וימלך עלינו מהרה
לעולם ועד בא"י צור ישראל וגואלו אמן.

"O Lord our King, King and God living and eternal, Your Name is upon us. O God, our Creator, O God, save us; spare us and have mercy on us in Your great love, for You are a kind, merciful, and good God. The Lord reigned, the Lord reigns, the Lord will reign forever. The Lord our God is eternally over us. His kingdom and His glory, His greatness and His splendor, His sanctity, and the sanctity of His great Name—He, the Lord our God, will have mercy upon us and relieve us of all our troubles, and redeem us with a perfect redemption, and rule over us speedily and forever.[21] Blessed are You, O Lord, Rock of Israel and its Redeemer. Amen."

The eulogy formula, "Who redeemed Israel," originated in Babylonia in the fourth century (B. *Pes.* 117b): "Rava said: '[The ending of the benediction following] the recitation of the *Shemaʿ* . . . is, "Who redeemed Israel".' "[22] In Palestine R. Joshua b. Levi (third century) prescribed the wording: צור ישראל וגואלו, "Rock of Israel and its Redeemer" (Y. *Ber.* 1:9, 3d). This eulogy is in use today only in Ashkenaz for the evening service of festivals in connection with piyyut, but it was once in use in Palestine on weekdays, as the above-cited version attests.

(7) The combining of the biblical passages and the benedictions into the Recitation of the *Shemaʿ* occurred in stages. As far back as our sources go, the three passages are mentioned as a single unit; nevertheless, there is reason to think that they found their way into the liturgy successively. A declaration of faith was to be made at this point; this purpose was met by the first passage, with its expression of the community's

attachment to the one God, and of wholehearted love for Him as a commandment binding in every time and condition.[23] The Septuagint provides this passage with a solemn introduction. Of the three passages, the Nash Papyrus cites only it, together with the Ten Commandments, which also originally served in public worship. The second passage matches the first at its beginning and conclusion, and probably it was appended to it for this reason. Its main content, the Torah's simple doctrine of reward and punishment, still suited the faith of the ancient period when the two passages were combined. There are several indications that the passage ויאמר, "And the Lord said," was the last of the three, in time as well as in order. First, since it is taken from Numbers, it should not have come after the two passages from Deuteronomy. Second, we have a reliable tradition that, in Palestine, as late as the ninth century, it was not recited in the Evening Service. It seems that originally only the concluding verse, Num. 15:41, was part of the liturgy, for here that central event in Jewish history—the exodus from Egypt—particularly its religious significance, is emphasized with a degree of clarity unmatched in Scripture. And when the first two passages acquired a halakhic interpretation, and the laws of *tefilin* and *mezuza* were derived from them, the beginning of "And the Lord said" was also brought into the liturgy, and the commandment of fringes was given the significance attributed to it in the halakhic conception. The Mishnah (*Ber.* 1:2) and Josephus (*Antiquities,* 4.8.13, §218) know the three passages only as a unit, and in this form they have come down through the centuries.

[19]

Like the biblical passages themselves, the framework prayers are not from a single period. Here, the first in order is the latest in time. It was unthinkable to proclaim God's unity in the public worship without a proper liturgical framework. An introduction was needed that would prepare the worshiper for its content. This function was filled by the second benediction, "With great love," which accordingly was called "The Benediction of the Torah," containing as it does thanksgiving for the revelation [and the giving of the Torah and the commandments]. That originally this was the only benediction before the biblical passages is attested by the liturgy of the priests, reported in M. *Tam.* 5:1—"One blessing" (compare B. *Ber.* 11b). "True and Certain," in which every community in its time affirms its acceptance of the ancient revelation, served as a conclusion to the expression of faith. After the solemn declaration of God's unity was joined to the Morning Service, an expression of gratitude for the physical light and for the continual daily renewal of nature was added; appropriately, it took the first place.

In the most ancient period, public worship concluded with the recitation of "True and Certain." Its content was solely the declaration of faith. It did not contain any petitions, these being left for individual worship, which was their special province. The problem of the relationship between public and individual worship was resolved by setting aside a place after the public prayer for the individual and his petitions (*devarim, tahanunim*). With the later expansion of the liturgy, this practice was no longer appropriate; hence, the stringent prohibition against uttering individual prayers after "True and Certain": "One does not utter words of private petition and supplication after 'True and Certain' but he may utter words [of petition] after the *'Amida,* even [if the petition is] as [long as] the order [another version says 'something like the order'] of the confession on Yom Kippur" (T. *Ber.* 3:6).

(8)   The Recitation of the *Shema* and its benedictions was performed as follows: One of the members of the congregation served as precentor; the congregation would sit on the ground and the precentor would remain among them. The recitation was antiphonal, with the congregation and the precentor alternating. From this practice the recitation of this prayer was referred to by the peculiar term פרס על שמע—that is, to recite the *Shema* by dividing it.[24] The head of the congregation would turn to one of its members and say to him: פרוס על שמע. The one thus invited served as precentor, reciting the beginning of the verse—for example, "Hear O Israel." The congregation would repeat his words and finish the verse: "Hear O Israel, the Lord our God, the Lord is One." When the precentor heard them uttering the divine name, he would respond: "Blessed be the Name of His majestic glory forever," exactly as the patriarch Jacob did, according to the story in Targum Jonathan and the midrash, when his sons declared to him their faith, saying, "Hear, O Israel." At Mt. Sinai too, according to the midrash, the Israelites recited this verse, and Moses responded: "Blessed be the Name of His majestic glory forever." This ancient manner of recitation gave rise to the practice, still current, of interrupting the first two verses of the *Shema* with "Blessed is the Name of His majestic glory forever." As then, so in all generations it is recited silently (B. *Pes.* 56a), the only exception being on Yom Kippur. Another manner of reciting the *Shema* is called כרך את שמע, "to wrap the *Shema*" (M. *Pes.* 4:8). This method is said to have been usual in Jericho; it consisted of the precentor reciting the entire verse from beginning to end, and the congregation repeating it after him word for word. In this system there was no room for "Blessed be the Name of His majestic glory forever"; and the absence of this response is in fact mentioned as typical of the rite of Jericho.

[20]

It may be that only the biblical passages were recited antiphonally, for only they could be assumed to be known perfectly by the congregation, while the benedictions were said originally only by the *pores*—that is, the precentor. In the Mishnah we find that the term *pores et* (or *'al*) *Shema* already refers to the entire complex, including the benedictions; hence, a blind man is excluded from fulfilling this function. This would also explain the false opinion that the word *pores* has to do with prayer or blessing. The Talmud does not give any direct explanation for this term, while in the post-talmudic period it was not properly understood since the procedure was no longer in use.

§ 8   The *'Amida: Composition and Structure*

(1)   Unlike the first section, the second section of the weekday Morning Service contains petitions—hence its traditional name, תפלה, Aramaic צלותא, Greek εὐχαί, or simply, "The Petitionary Prayer." This, too, is the meaning of the verbs התפלל and צלי (*pa''al*); whenever the terminology is used with precision, as in the Mishnah and the Talmud, these verbs refer to the *'Amida* and never to other prayers. These petitions are recited standing—hence the name *'Amida*, which is current to this day among Portuguese and Oriental Jews. The most common name is שמונה עשרה, meaning "the eighteen (benedictions)"; this refers to the number of benedictions that the prayer contained when it was composed (M. *Ber.* 4:3). Though a nineteenth benediction was later added, the name remained unchanged; it has become so deeply rooted that it is used popularly

[21]

for every 'Amida, even those of the Sabbath and festivals, which have only seven benedictions.[1]

When the time came to recite this prayer, the congregation would rise and the precentor would take his place before the holy ark. Hence, the performance of this prayer is designated by the expression, עבר לפני התיבה, Aramaic עבר קומי תיבותא, "pass before the ark." Later, when the precentor would recite all the prayers from a special place, this expression was misused to mean all of his activity; but in the ancient sources it is applied exclusively to this prayer. In Babylonia, where the precentor's place was lower than that of the congregation, they would say ירד לפני התיבה or "go down before the ark"; in manuscripts this expression frequently replaces the former. Sometimes they would omit the designation of the place and say simply עבר, "to pass"; the expression ירד, "to descend," is even more frequently used in this way, and still more frequent is the Aramaic equivalent נחת in the Babylonian Talmud, so that the expression, ההוא דנחית, "he who descends," designates the precentor who recites the 'Amida.[2]

(2)   The 'Amida was originally intended for public worship; it was recited by the precentor acting as the representative of the congregation (שליח צבור). The congregation answered "amen" after every benediction, thus making the prayer its own. R. Gamaliel II ruled that every individual in the community must say the 'Amida by himself. So as not to diminish the 'Amida's character as a public prayer, the repetition (חזרה) was introduced; from then on the congregation would first recite the 'Amida in silence, and then the precentor would repeat it aloud.[3]

(3)   The 'Amida is divided into three sections: The first three benedictions form a hymnic introduction; the final three are a conclusion with thanksgiving; and the thirteen middle ones contain petitions.[4] The first and the last section are in use every day of the year without change (in the Mishnah they are provided with special names); the middle section is in use only on weekdays, while on Sabbaths and festivals the petitions are replaced by a different passage.

(4)   Various traditions have come down to us about the age and origin of the 'Amida, some legendary and some to be taken seriously. Putting aside the legends, we have, first of all, the tradition that "The men of the Great Assembly instituted for Israel ... prayers ..." (B. *Ber.* 33a). No contradiction exists between this statement and "One hundred and twenty elders, among them several prophets, drew up the eighteen benedictions in a fixed order" (B. *Meg.* 17b; Y. *Ber.* 2:4, 4d). Both traditions view the 'Amida as a very ancient prayer.[5]

On the other hand, there is the report that "Simon the Flaxworker[6] formulated the eighteen benedictions in the presence of R. Gamaliel II in the proper order in Yavneh" (B. *Meg.*, ibid.). This creates a discrepancy of several centuries in fixing the time of the prayer's composition. Furthermore, one source speaks of creating the prayer anew (תקנו), while the other speaks of formulating it (הסדיר). The Talmud attempts to resolve the contradiction by postulating that the 'Amida was forgotten and then was created anew (B. *Meg.* 18a). This solution is unacceptable because it cannot be harmonized with the course of the nation's history; it is merely an attempt at harmonization that runs completely counter to both history and common sense.

[22]

(5)   Thus, we are compelled to examine the 'Amida itself to see if it contains any hints as to its time of composition; and for the starting point we must not use the version current today, but rather the most ancient form of the text to which we can reach back.[7] Benediction 10 speaks of the dispersion of the community. This is not compelling evidence that the 'Amida was composed after the destruction of Jerusalem by Titus, for even during the Second Temple period there was a significant diaspora; the words of Ben Sira (51:12, 6), "Give thanks to Him who has assembled the scattered people of Israel," show that even in ancient times the ingathering of the diaspora of Israel was the subject of prayer. [The quotation is an expanded form of 51:12, and can be found in English in *The Wisdom of Ben Sira*, trans. Patrick W. Skehan, with an introduction and commentary by Alexander A. Di Lella (New York: Doubleday & Co., 1987), 568–69—*Engl. trans.*] In Benediction 14, it would appear that the petition "and build it" alludes to the destruction of the city, and many scholars see here an addition from the period after 70 C.E.; but from the fact that in the hymn of Ben Sira just cited we find: "Give thanks to Him who builds His city and His sanctuary" (51:12, 7) we can see that the petition is not necessarily for the rebuilding of a destroyed city. To be sure, the petition "restore the Temple service" in Benediction 16 suits only the period after the Temple service had already lapsed; however, immediately thereafter comes the petition, "Accept the fire offerings of Israel and their prayer speedily in love," which testifies to the opposite, for it assumes the existence of the Temple service. Thus, the language of this benediction contains echoes of two different periods side by side. Benediction 9 assumes in its general content a period when the majority of the Jews dwelt on their land and rejoiced in the produce of their fields, which does not fit the period when the Romans were in control of Palestine. As for the influence of particular religious and political movements on the prayer, it is difficult to find any certain foothold. To be sure, the atmosphere of the prayer is generally the same as the pietistic tone of the *Anavim*, "The Humble Ones," in Psalms and Proverbs, but we have no tangible facts with which to fix the period of the literature that deals with these groups. One clear mark of identification is the stress on resurrection of the dead in Benediction 2; though in the much simpler Palestinian version of the 'Amida it is not mentioned as frequently as in the current version, there too the eulogy speaks of it, and one senses clearly that the wording of the prayer gives particular stress to the theme. Such emphasis on one of the articles of faith in the prayer cannot have come about unintentionally, for this doctrine was one of the points in dispute between the Sadducees and the Pharisees, and the victorious Pharisaic party demanded acknowledgment of its view in the worship. Thus, if we seek evidence in the wording of the prayer itself, we are saying only that it contains various elements from various periods.

Similarly, the order of the benedictions can only be understood on the basis of this assumption. The present order displays problems in several spots. Benediction 7 has no connection with either what comes before or after; though located among the petitions of the individual, it deals with the needs of the nation, and besides, it is very similar to the petitions that are to follow: "The seventh benediction now seems partly redundant and partly out of place" (Zunz, *Haderashot*, 179). After Benediction 9, unexpectedly and without any transition, come petitions with national content; these are rather miscellaneous and neither their order nor their classification is completely logical. Thus it is hard to understand why Benediction 16, a general or personal petition, should come after the national petitions. Finally, it is surprising that Benediction 17 and Benediction 19 contain petitions, though, according to the division described above, the third part ought to have been devoted exclusively to thanksgiving. The attempts made in the Talmud to explain the current order by conjectures or by biblical paradigms (B. *Meg.* 17b; Y. *Ber.* 2:4, 4d) are unsatisfactory; the order and organization can be understood only on the assumption that the parts of the prayer come from different periods. If we then reexamine the two statements transmitted to us in the sources cited above, we come to the conclusion that both are very likely correct; the prayer may have been put in final form by R. Gamaliel II, but its origins go back to the far earlier pre-Hasmonean period, the age of the Great Assembly.

(6)   Among the petitions of the 'Amida are components of various types and periods: remnants from the liturgy of the Temple, benedictions and petitions of general content, petitions for national affairs, and finally, prayers that may be designated 'occasional prayers' that were adopted because of particular circumstances and were then preserved forever. From the Temple service come the two petitions at the end of the 'Amida. Benediction 17 was mentioned above for its peculiar wording. Already in the early Middle Ages[8] it was realized that the version in our possession had been reworked, and that originally this was a prayer for the acceptance of the daily sacrifices brought by the priests. The high priest, too, upon finishing the Yom Kippur ritual, would recite a prayer, על העבודה, "for the Service," with the eulogy שאותך לבדך ביראה נעבד, "You Whom alone we worship in awe" (Y. *Soṭa* 7:6, 22a; Y. *Yoma* 7:1, 44b), exactly like the eulogy of Benediction 17 [in the ancient Palestinian wording, and], which is in use to this day in the Additional Service of all the festivals [in Ashkenaz]. Likewise, the Mishnah relates that the priests in the Temple would interrupt the offering of the daily morning sacrifice in order to hold prayers, and that there too a prayer called עבודה (that is, Benediction 17) was recited: "They pronounced three benedictions . . . עבודה and ברכת כהנים" (M. *Tam.* 5:1).[9] Another prayer that was recited there was the Benediction of the Priests (ברכת כהנים), the prayer for peace with which the congregation responded to the Priestly Blessing; it was linked to the last word of the Blessing. Likewise, Benediction 14, the petition for Jerusalem, derives from the liturgy of the Temple, not, of course, in its present form, which refers to the destruction of the city, but in the same spirit in which Ben Sira[10] and the high priest prayed on the Day of Atonement for Jerusalem and the Temple. The eulogy of the prayer of the high priest was השוכן בציון, "Who dwells in Zion" (Y. *Soṭa* 7:6, 22a),[11] and this version was probably customary in the daily prayers as well.

(7)   These are the petitions that were taken over ready-made when public worship had to be fitted out with petitionary prayers. First, a framework had to be created that suited the view of the nature of prayer. The petitions had to be prefaced with a hymnic section and followed with thanksgiving. Thus, the first three benedictions arose, as well as Benediction 18 (הודאה, "Thanksgiving"), which lent its name to the entire concluding section and which was inserted between Benedictions 17 and 19 (עבודה and ברכת כהנים), so that the petition for peace could continue to come at the end. In fact, the first three and the last three benedictions of the 'Amida have a special status of their own. Only they are in use unchanged throughout the year in every 'Amida, and only

[24]

they have fixed names mentioned already in the Mishnah: "The order of the benedictions is that one says, אבות, גבורות ה', קדושת ה' . . . עבודה, הודאה, and ברכת כהנים" (M. *R.H.* 4:5). Their language, especially in their most ancient formulation (§9), justifies attributing them to an ancient period, and their content does not afford any contradiction to this assumption if we overlook the introduction of the theme of the resurrection of the dead in Benediction 2.

The question now arises whether there ever was a time when the ʿAmida consisted of only the elements just named [that is, the first three and the last three benedictions].[12] This assumption is most unlikely, for the daily prayers would hardly have been incorporated in their entirety into the Sabbath and festival services. Furthermore, such a prayer would not have been a *tefila* of the kind that could properly be called "mercy and favor." As far back as we are able to trace the sources, we always find the opening and concluding benedictions accompanied by a middle section containing petitions. This does not mean that the original ʿAmida contained petitions in the same number and organization as that in which they are found today, but nothing prevents us from assuming that the petitions of a general nature were present in their entirety. These petitions are for personal, even material, needs—Benediction 8 and Benediction 9—yet they are for things that are vital for every person without distinction, things whose value would not have been subject to differences of opinion or of self-interest. Health and prosperity are the foundations of our existence. Insight and understanding (Benediction 4) are considered, as shown by Psalms and Proverbs, to be prerequisites of religious life; the petitions for repentance (Benediction 5) and forgiveness (Benediction 6) are connected with these, and they point to the spiritual attitude of the circles that created the ʿAmida. The combining of these two groups of petitions, those concerned with material and those concerned with spiritual needs, the welfare of body and of soul, reflects a healthy outlook on life; far from negating or fleeing worldly things, it nevertheless remains continually cognizant of responsibility before divine judgment. The prayer for the hearing of prayer (Benediction 16) is a natural conclusion. All of the above-mentioned petitions—seven in number, together with the petition for Jerusalem—were consecutive and uninterrupted. It does not seem likely that they were originally divided, each with its own eulogy; more probably they were all united in a single benediction. In the formula הביננו, "Give Us Understanding," we still have such a condensation of the petitions, and the formulation of the middle section of the ʿAmida was probably similar.

(8)   Now the national petitions were added. No longer the natural subjects of prayer arising out of the worshiper's inner needs, these petitions presuppose reflections concerning the nature of prayer and a particular national experience that gave prayer new direction. This event was the religious persecution by Antiochus, the Maccabean uprising, and the establishment of an independent Judean kingdom together with the sects that arose therein. These were violent shocks that diverted the attention of the Jewish people more and more away from the present and toward hope for the ideal future. Apocalypse dominated all thought and all hope. Apocalyptic images of the messianic age stirred every heart, and the realization of these dreams had to become the subject of public worship. The source from which all of the apocalypses drew their inspiration was Ezekiel. One of the recurring images of the end of days in his visionary

speeches is the assembling of the scattered people of Israel and the divine judgment that will separate the chaff from the wheat, punishing the wicked and uniting the righteous into a new nation. This is the train of thought followed by the national benedictions. The first of them is the petition for the assembling of the exiled communities (Benediction 10). We have already said that there is no reason to assume that this benediction was composed against the background of the destruction of Jerusalem. A Jewish diaspora was in existence in ancient times, even before the Babylonian exile; during the Second Commonwealth, especially from the beginning of the Hellenistic period, these communities became very numerous. In Babylonia, Egypt, and Asia Minor, perhaps in other Mediterranean countries as well, many Jewish colonies existed. But this was not seen as a national misfortune; on the contrary, this peaceful infiltration provided the nation with a sense of renewed well-being and strength that was a cause for satisfaction in the homeland. Only during the hellenizing movement, when it became clear how the number of Jews speaking and thinking only in Greek had increased, was the Diaspora recognized as a danger; from that point on the ancient promises about the assembling of the scattered communities became a subject for prayer. As in Ezekiel, the petition for the bringing of the day of judgment was added to the petition for uniting the people; almost no trace of this motif remains in the present-day version of the 'Amida, but originally it was the subject of Benediction 11. In the present version the starting point of this benediction is the complaint about unjust judges [and about the judiciary being in control of foreigners] and the petition to God that He appoint once again in every place righteous judges as of old. But it is almost impossible to find any period in which such a prayer could have been composed. Neither the Hasmonean kings nor the princes of the House of Herod, and certainly not the Roman procurators, would have tolerated such seditious statements about their judicial activity. The notion that no one paid any attention to what the Hasidim did, that everyone was aware of their stubbornness and their recklessness, and therefore avoided challenging them, is not borne out by history. Nor would it have been compatible with the security of the state, for the party of the Hasidim was too strong. In a land where civil war and rebellion were everyday events and were conducted with such violence, the daily attack on the judicial system would have been a severe danger that not even the most pious government could have tolerated. The petition's content must originally have been different, as is suggested both by the text and its sources. The unexpected transition from a supposed complaint about the judges to the petition for the realization of the kingdom of heaven ("and rule over us") would be too abrupt, and hence points more toward the world to come than toward the present age. But above all the conclusion וצדקנו במשפט, "and show us innocent in judgment," [which, however, has been preserved only in Ashkenaz and Romaniot] cannot refer to a mundane civil judgment but must refer to the messianic judgment. These final words were considered so important that in the condensed version they were used to summarize this benediction, thus providing a key to its original intention: a petition that God bring His judgment over the world in the messianic era. The purpose of this eschatological day of judgment is to separate the righteous from the wicked and punish the wicked. This theme, too, was covered in the original benediction, for in the condensed version, "Give us understanding," it is represented by the sentence "And may those who are in error be judged according to Your will," or, according to another version "And shake

[26]

Your hand over the wicked." In the brief summary of the ʿAmida in the Talmud it says at this place, ". . . and when judgment is executed against the wicked. . . ." From all of these texts we are forced to conclude that the original content of Benediction 11 was the punishment of the wicked in the last judgment. It should also be borne in mind that the biblical version from which the words "Restore our judges" derive is a description of the messianic age (Is. 1:26); it seems likely that here, too, it was used for the same purpose. The description in Ezek. 20:34ff. of the messianic era, when God will be Israel's king, is as follows: First, the scattered Jews will be gathered from among the nations, then they will be brought together for the day of judgment, and finally the wicked will be separated out so that they will not enter the land of Israel. This is the sequence of ideas that determined the arrangement of the national benedictions.[13] Benediction 10 prays for the assembling of the exiled communities; Benediction 11, for the divine judgment and the punishment of the wicked; and Benediction 13, for the reward of the righteous.[14] These three benedictions were consecutive, and they were inserted in the ʿAmida at the point where the general petitions ended, after Benediction 9. Probably the reference to the Davidic messiah in Benediction 14, the blessing for Jerusalem, belongs to that eschatologically minded period.

(9)   At this point the ʿAmida was, for all intents and purposes, complete, and only because of particular circumstances were a few more petitions added. It is hard to explain the addition of Benediction 7; the problems in its contents and location are noted above. By position it ought to have been a petition for deliverance from personal hardship, such as captivity or the like, but the wording contradicts this. Prayer for deliverance from national troubles occurs in the later benedictions and does not belong with the personal petitions; besides, it is hard to infer from the general language just what national disaster is meant. The way out of all these difficulties is to turn to the most ancient sources. These speak of a special liturgy for fast days; on such occasions one would recite the petitions of the weekday ʿAmida and add to them seven more. The first of the petitions intended for fast days began "Look at our misery," and ended "redeemer of Israel," exactly like the Benediction 7 of our ʿAmida. The similarity of the text was observed early on, and the Talmud was able to explain it only by assuming that not seven but six new benedictions were added, the first of the seven being merely an expansion of the weekday Benediction 7. (B. *Ta.* 16b: "It is the seventh of the longer benedictions. As it has been taught: [the benediction] 'Who redeemest Israel' is prolonged.") Meanwhile, the daily sufferings of Israel increased to the point that "Look at our misery" was made part of the weekday service. And if the source of this benediction is the liturgy of fast days, then its place in the ʿAmida is automatically explained, for the fast-day prayers were attached to the benediction for forgiveness: Thus, Benediction 7, "Look at our misery," stands immediately after Benediction 6, "Forgive us." In this way the ʿAmida reached the number of seventeen benedictions.[15]

[M. *Ta.* 2:2–4 says, on the one hand, that on fast days the precentor recites the eighteen daily benedictions and adds six more; but it goes on to say, "And he says their eulogies. The first he concludes with 'May He Who answered Abraham . . . answer you . . . Blessed are You, O Lord, Redeemer of Israel.' The second [benediction—*Engl. trans.*] . . . The seventh (!) he concludes with . . .," yielding altogether seven additional benedictions. But the contradiction is only an apparent one, for the number of benedictions added on fast days is six; while the number of special eulogies is seven, since a eulogy in this special style was added to Benediction 7 of the daily ʿAmida, as is already explained in the Babylonian Talmud (ad loc.); see Albeck, *Mishnah*, 2:492. Thus, this seeming contradiction cannot serve as the basis to conjecture that at an early stage "Redeemer of Israel" was one of the (seven) fast-day benedictions. Furthermore, the style of this benediction attests clearly that it does not belong to the special group of fast-day benedictions. It is formulated in the style common to the other benedictions of the ʿAmida, whereas in the other benedictions of the fast-day group the body of the benediction consists only of biblical verses. As for the problem of the position of Benediction 7, already S. D. Luzzatto (Luzzatto, *Mavo*, 18; Goldschmidt ed., 18) conjectured that this benediction was not originally for national messianic redemption, "but for the redemption of individuals in captivity or prison"; thus "this benediction was placed appropriately after the benediction for forgiveness," in conformity with Ps. 107:10–11. Luzzatto finds support for his opinion in the words of *Sifre* Deut., §343: "And also in the eighteen benedictions that the ancient sages established . . . they did not begin with the needs of Israel first, but started with the praise of God, as it is said, 'God, the great, the mighty and the terrible,' 'Holy are You and terrible is Your name,' and after that 'Who releases the bound,' and after that 'Who heals the sick,' and after that 'we give thanks to You.' " The words "Who releases the bound" can only refer to our Benediction 7, which in one of its early versions must have contained a specific reference to the freeing of captives and the like.[16]]

(10) The ʿAmida became "The Eighteen Benedictions" when R. Gamaliel II ordered its redaction and introduced into it Benediction 12 (the Benediction against the Sectarians),[17] in order to separate the Christians from the Jewish community (B. *Ber.* 28b; "The Benediction against the Sectarians was instituted in Yavneh"). This benediction originally began not with ולמלשינים, "And to the informers," but with למינים ולמשומדים, "to the sectarians and the apostates," and it employed the epithets זדים or מלכות זדון, "the arrogant" or "the arrogant kingdom," פושעים, "sinners," and apparently also נוצרים, "Christians."

The Hebrew word מין has the basic meaning "species" and can denote any special or exceptional group—hence, all those who separate themselves from the way of the Torah, heretics. Any heresy could be called מינות; the term embraces the views of the Sadducees, Samaritans, Christians, and Gnostics. Accordingly, considerable debate has occurred as to what particular heresy this benediction was intended to attack, and whether it did not exist already before Christianity. The church fathers, Justin Martyr and Jerome, report that the Jews curse the Christian believers three times a day in their synagogues, and Epiphanius says explicitly that they pray for God to destroy the Christians. Thus, hardly any doubt exists that this prayer was directed against the Christians and that it served as a means of bringing about the total separation of the two religions.

Originally the Christians did not have any special prayers or any particular public worship of their own. They held assemblies for whatever rites were peculiar to Christianity, like the Lord's Supper, but they did not have a coherent liturgy; hence, no Christian liturgy from the first century exists.[18] The Jewish Christians continued to pray with the Jews. At first no one prevented them from doing so, and they had no reason to avoid the synagogue. In one sense the synagogue offered them too little, because it did not take into consideration their particular type of messianic faith and made no

[28]

room for its expression in the prayers; they found expression for it in their assemblies. Yet, by the same token, nothing in the service conflicted with their own religious views. Thus, they participated in public worship and even served as precentors. The fact that they were Jews who believed in Christ did not make any difference at all, and only gradually did the synagogue attempt to protect itself against heterodox phenomena. Little by little tension arose between Judaism and Judeo-Christianity. The natural development of Christianity led to the increasing deification of Jesus and to the growing tendency to address him in prayer as a miracle worker. Therefore, the sages ruled that when a sectarian recites a benediction, one does not answer "amen" unless he has heard the benediction in its entirety. This makes perfect sense to anyone who has read the ancient Christian prayer texts. Add to this the fact that the Christians came to be enemies of the Jewish nation, for in their desire to curry favor with the Romans, they denounced their former coreligionists—hence, the words דילטורין and מוסרים (informers) became synonyms for Christians.[19] The hope and the longing of the Jews was for the rebuilding of the Temple in Jerusalem. For the Christians, the destruction of the Temple was a principal propaganda point; for them, God—by putting an end to the sacrifices—had in effect proclaimed His will that the law of Moses be abrogated. They would not let themselves be deprived of this proof. It was a matter of principle to the Christians that the word of the gospel would be fulfilled, and that Jerusalem would remain in total subjugation until the end of time. Whether and when the Jews acquired any serious, well-founded hopes for the fulfillment of their desires before the rebellion in the time of the Emperor Trajan we do not know. Such hopes may have been connected with the journey to Rome of some tannaim, led by R. Gamaliel during the brief reign of the Emperor Nerva. In any case, the beginning of the total break between Jews and Jewish Christians must be fixed at this period. An important step in accomplishing the separation was the expulsion of the Christians from the synagogue. The synagogue was a convenient base for missionary activities. It provided occasion for discussions of matters of faith and opinion, and excellent opportunities for disseminating propaganda. The Jewish Christians were among the most eager synagogue-goers, and they even served as precentors [as mentioned above—*Engl. trans.*].[20] It was necessary to make this function distasteful to them and to pressure them out of the synagogue. To achieve this end, Benediction 12 was introduced into the ʿAmida, and Samuel the Lesser established it according to the instructions of R. Gamaliel, "Samuel the Lesser arose and composed it" (B. *Ber.*, ibid.). The petition for the annihilation of the sectarians was intended to expel them from the synagogue. This follows clearly from the words of the Midrash:

> If one passes before the ark and makes a mistake in any of the benedictions, he is not made to repeat it; but in the benediction concerning the sectarians he must be made to repeat it against his will. The reason that he must repeat it is that, if he has in him any element of heresy, he will be cursing himself and the congregation will respond "amen" (*Tanhuma* B., Leviticus, 2a).

Errors in the course of prayer were an everyday occurrence, and for the most part they were passed over with indulgence and in silence;[21] only in Benediction 12 was strict attention paid that the precentor not drop or change a word from the prayer text.

Here no leniency was granted in case of an error; the precentor either followed the ordained ritual or he was removed, for the whole purpose was to test him to see whether he was inclined to Jewish Christianity or not. A Jewish Christian could not recite this prayer if he did want not to curse himself and to make the congregation join in by saying "amen." Even if he was among the worshipers, he would not be able to listen quietly while the precentor recited the petition for the eradication of his community and the congregation endorsed this petition with its "amen." Thus, Benediction 12 became a touchstone for the presence of Jewish Christians in the synagogue and for their partici-pation in prayer. Unwilling to listen to this prayer on a daily basis, they left the syna-gogue, and the purpose was achieved.

[29]

A foothold for the new petition was found in Benediction 11, which speaks of the punishment of the wicked. Moreover, attitudes toward eschatology had changed. The details of the former vision of the future had acquired new meaning, and the petitions in the 'Amida that were connected to them were no longer understood as they had for-merly been. Accordingly, the passage dealing with the punishment of the wicked was removed from Benediction 11 and inserted in a new petition ending "Who humbles the arrogant." This benediction now included an imprecation against all who betray the Jewish religion: "One inserts the benediction for the heretics and sinners in the benediction 'Who humbles the arrogant'" (M. *Ber.* 3:25; Y. *Ber.* 2:4, 5a; 4:3, 8a).[22] Benediction 11 now spoke only of the restoration of the former judges and the coming of the kingdom of heaven. On the other hand, parallel to the curse against the apos-tates in Benediction 12, a special petition on behalf of those converted to Judaism was introduced as Benediction 13. The number of converts who had accepted the law of Moses was not negligible in those days; the increased number of conversions, even among the highest levels of society, had the effect of exacerbating the bitterness against those who had abandoned the ancestral religion, though it was also a certain comfort in a time of troubles. The juxtaposition of the petition in behalf of the converts (Bene-diction 13) alongside the curse against the wicked (Benediction 12) gave expression to the sorrow over the wicked and the satisfaction over the converts. Thus, Benediction 12 was, to a certain degree, a response to particular events, and with the elimination of its cause it too might have been eliminated, had the editing of the 'Amida not occurred at the very time when Benediction 12 was introduced.[23]

(11) By order of R. Gamaliel II, the 'Amida, which, with Benediction 12, counted eighteen benedictions, was now redacted and made an obligatory daily prayer for every Jewish person: "R. Gamaliel says, 'Every day a man should say eighteen bene-dictions'" (M. *Ber.* 4:3). Because of the number of benedictions it contains, the prayer is now called the "Eighteen Benedictions,"[24] and this name became fixed for all genera-tions. As we have seen above, the eighteen sections came together at various times, and thus their number is completely arbitrary. However, in order to attach to this number a higher significance—canonical significance, so to speak—it was provided with a sym-bolic explanation; precedent for it was sought in biblical prayers and stories. Yet, it might be that the number eighteen was picked intentionally, and once it was reached the prayer was closed. For its symbolic significance is found already in tannaitic sources; furthermore, opportunities arose to add to the number of benedictions but advantage was not taken of them. But since the number of petitions was greater than the number

of benedictions, it was necessary to combine some of them: "One combines the benediction of the sectarians and of the sinners in the benediction 'Who humbles the arrogant,' and of the elders and of proselytes in the benediction 'Stronghold of the
righteous,' and of David in the benediction 'Who builds Jerusalem' " (T. *Ber.* 3:25).
Nevertheless, it was not prohibited to separate the benedictions that had been combined, thus increasing their number: "If he recited them separately he has fulfilled his
obligation" (ibid.). In one case such a separation was made a regular practice, thereby
adding to the *'Amida* a nineteenth benediction.

[30]

(12)   No sooner had the amoraic period begun and Babylonian Jewry felt itself
independent of the Palestinian authorities under the exilarchs, who were direct descendants of the House of David, when a special prayer was introduced for the appearance
of the Messiah of the House of David. The eulogy of this benediction was "Who makes
the horn of salvation flourish." The first to mention it in the Talmud is Rabba Bar Shila
(ca. 250, B. *Pes.* 117b). At one time the dominant opinion was that this Benediction
15 was part of the original *'Amida*, and that the benediction against the sectarians was
added as the nineteenth benediction; but, in fact, the benediction against the sectarians brought the number to eighteen, while Benediction 15 is the additional nineteenth.
The proof for this is given in detail in Elbogen, *Achtzehngebets*, 24ff. (see also *MGWJ*
46 [1902]: 348ff.); only the main proofs are summarized briefly here. The Palestinian
Talmud and the Midrashim that originated in Palestine know of no special benediction
for the Messiah; the sources that list the *'Amida*'s contents mention only Benediction
14, never Benediction 15, and the reference to David occurs only in the eulogy
intended for Benediction 14: "God of David, Builder of Jerusalem" (while in Babylonia
the phrase "God of David" is explicitly rejected); when the benedictions of the *'Amida*
are listed, Benediction 16 is reckoned as fifteenth, since the present Benediction 15
is missing. Indeed, long after the close of the Talmud, the Palestinian rite did not know
the eulogy, "Who makes the horn of salvation flourish"; the payyetanim, who match
their stanzas to the eulogies of the *'Amida*, do not mention it. R. Eleazar Kallir
(ca. 750?), for example, never composed stanzas for Benediction 15, in his *qerovot*
(§23) for fast days and Purim; his piyyutim presuppose the eulogy "God of David,
Builder of Jerusalem." Also, in the Palestinian version of the *'Amida*, known from the
Cairo geniza, Benediction 15 is lacking, and the eulogy of Benediction 14 is "God of
David, Builder of Jerusalem." The solution proposed by R. Isaiah de Trani
(ca. 1280)—that, in Palestine, the two consecutive and thematically related Benedictions 14 and 15 were combined into a single benediction when the benediction against
the sectarians was introduced, in order not to exceed the number eighteen—is not
acceptable, for the sources explicitly testify the exact opposite, that Benediction 15 was
introduced later. In discussing the number of the benedictions, the Yerushalmi (*Ber.*
4:3, 8a) says, "If someone says to you that they are seventeen, reply to him: 'The benediction against the sectarians was already established by the sages in Yavneh.' " This
shows that before the introduction of Benediction 12 there were but seventeen benedictions and the new benediction was the eighteenth. A clear picture of the process
of the combining of the benedictions is given in the Midrash, *Num. R.*, 18:21:

טוב has the numerical value of seventeen, and the *'Amida* has nineteen benedictions.

Deduct from these the benediction against the sectarians, which was instituted in Yav-neh, and 'The Plant of David', which was instituted after that.

This shows that the number of nineteen benedictions in the Babylonian rite (the Palestinian rite never had this number) arose when Benediction 12 and, only later, Benediction 15 were added.[25] Eventually the Babylonian rite remained as the only rite, and with it Benediction 15 was adopted everywhere as one of the benedictions of the ʿAmida; in the course of time it was grafted onto the *qerovot*, which, as we have seen, presuppose the Palestinian rite and do not recognize this benediction at all. When this nineteenth benediction was added, the name שמונה עשרה, "Eighteen," was no longer appropriate, but since it had been fixed by the Mishnah, it continued to be used with no further thought. With this the history of the ʿAmida came to an end; the reworkings that it underwent and its further developments have to do with alterations to the text, which are treated in detail in the following paragraph.

[The above description of the development of the ʿAmida requires correction with respect to certain points. The conception that from time to time new benedictions were devised and added to those already current among the people, until the total number eventually reached eighteen or nineteen benedictions, cannot be accepted. To be sure, the ʿAmida was not created at once, but rather in stages. However, it was not created by institutional edicts, but grew and took shape in many different circles of worshipers. Only regarding Benediction 12 do we have testimony that it was enacted by R. Gamaliel of Yav-neh and his court as a reaction to contemporary needs. But the other benedictions emerged in various communities out of the practices of different circles. In this formative period there certainly existed side by side alternative orders of prayer differing from each other in the number of benedictions, their content, their organization and, of course, their wording. Such varied rites as were in use in different times and places can still be seen reflected, for example, in the morning prayer of the priests in the Temple (M. *Tam.* 5:1), in the eight benedictions of the High Priest on Yom Kippur (M. *Yoma* 7:1), in the six special benedictions for fast days (M. *Ta.* 2:2–4), apparently in the hymn in the Hebrew Ben Sira (51:12), and in the series of petitions there (chap. 36). All of these include prayers or bene-dictions matching some, but not all, of the benedictions of the ʿAmida known today. On the other hand, every one of these rites is lacking some of the contents or benedictions of the ʿAmida. Thus it might be assumed that toward the end of the Second Temple period a more or less uniform rite of eighteen benedictions took shape, based on selection from and combination of the various rites previously current; this rite acquired official, binding status through its "formulation" by Simon the Flaxworker. Thus, it is impossible to establish an exact chronological order for the first appearance of each of the various benedictions, and there is no way of knowing what "state" the ʿAmida had reached at the various stages of its development. Even after the "redaction" in Yavneh, variant customs still remained respecting particular benedictions and as to whether they were to be combined or sepa-rated, as attested by the Tosefta (*Ber.* 3:25 and parallels): "One combines the benediction of the sectarians with that of the separatists, of the proselytes with that of the elders, and of David with 'Who builds Jerusalem'; and if he recites them separately he has fulfilled his obligation."

Thus, the Benediction against the Sectarians introduced at Yavneh cannot be viewed as an addition to the number of the benedictions; for according to the passage in the To-

[31]

sefta cited above, this benediction was inserted into another that was already in use—that is, the benediction of the 'separatists' (meaning "those who separate themselves from the ways of the community of Israel at large"), or the benediction "Who humbles the wicked" (Y. *Ber.* 2:4, 5a). It thus seems that even before it was introduced, the practice of most worshipers was to recite exactly eighteen benedictions. The two sources cited above, from which it might seem possible to conclude that the number of benedictions was at some time only seventeen, cannot be taken as historical evidence, for they are of an aggadic nature, and seek to find numerical analogies at all costs. (Compare Heinemann, *Prayer*, 142, n. 20. As for the passage in the Yerushalmi mentioned above, "If someone says to you that they are seventeen," see also Lieberman, *Tosefta* 1:54.) The innovation of the sages of Yavneh in enacting the Benediction against the Sectarians was not in the adding of a new benediction to the number already in use, but in lending a new meaning to an already current benediction. This was the explicit mention of the heretics who denied the faith of Israel, and particularly of the Christians (as attested by the geniza versions) in a blessing-curse, formerly directed against Jews who separated themselves from the Jewish community (and collaborated with the foreign conqueror), and against the arrogant wicked (that is, the 'arrogant kingdom,' which is none other than the Roman Empire; see Lieberman, *Tosefta* 1:54).

Likewise, Benediction 15 is not to be seen as an innovation introduced in Babylonia at a late period; for even in Palestine a minority existed who recited the benediction of David separately, as attested by the above-cited Tosefta. This benediction is also reflected in Ben Sira 51: "Give thanks to Him Who makes the horn of the House of David flourish." The existence of a prayer of this type is attested also by the wording preserved in Luke [32] (1:68–69): "Blessed is the Lord God of Israel, Who has remembered and redeemed His people, and lifted a horn of salvation for us in the House of David, His servant," except that in the Christian source the petition for the coming of the redeemer is replaced by thanksgiving for his having come (see David Flusser, *Hazon haqeṣ vehageʾula* [Jerusalem: Mifʿal hashikhpul, 1961/2], 31). But in Palestine itself the recitation of this benediction as an independent one did not become the majority practice; and in prayer fragments of the Palestinian rite from the Cairo geniza, and in the *qerovot* of the Palestinian payyetanim, we have innumerable pieces of evidence that in fact the number of benedictions in the Palestinian *ʿAmida* was always eighteen, and that it never contained a separate benediction for the restoration of the Davidic dynasty. But this very practice that had been rejected in Palestine and had become a minority practice did reach to Babylonia, yielding the nineteen benedictions in the *ʿAmida* of the Babylonian version, and the versions of the communities derived from it. There is no way of knowing whether the Babylonian Jews also had an ideological motivation for accepting this practice, which lays particular stress on the longing for the restoration of the Davidic monarchy.

The source of the widespread erroneous opinion that Benediction 12 is the additional benediction, the adoption of which turned the prayer of eighteen benedictions into a prayer of nineteen, is B. *Ber.* 28b: "These eighteen are actually nineteen! Rabbi Levi said, 'The benediction against the sectarians was introduced in Yavneh. . . .' " But this is nothing more than a late Babylonian effort to explain the custom in use there; and clearly the words of Rabbi Levi (a Palestinian amora!) were not said as a reply to the Talmud's question. (The wording "The benediction against the Sadducees" found in the printed editions of the Babylonian Talmud in the above quotation and elsewhere is merely an "emendation" of the censorship; see *Diqduqe soferim*.)

Even though we have no explicit information about the existence of the ʿAmida of eighteen benedictions in the time of the Second Temple—as we do have concerning the ʿAmida of seven benedictions for Sabbaths and festivals (T. *Ber.* 3:13 and parallels)—there can be no doubt that the nucleus of this prayer took shape as early as the Second Temple period; and it seems likely that the number of benedictions was already eighteen, at least in the practice of most communities, before the "formulating" of this prayer in Yavneh. This view is nearly universally accepted today.]

§ 9 *The* ʿAmida: *Text*

(1)   The redaction discussed in the preceding section affected only the contents of the benedictions and the eulogies determined by those contents, as well as their division and sequence: "Simon the Flaxworker formulated the eighteen benedictions in the presence of Rabban Gamaliel in the proper order in Yavneh" (B. *Meg.* 17b). But the text of the benedictions itself was not fixed; it remained free and flexible, subject to the spontaneous inspiration of the precentor. Thus, for a long period numerous versions existed side by side, and certain variations were possible that had to be prohibited as signs of sectarianism.[1] Frequently, the precentors recited a text that deviated from the usual one, or that even contained obvious mistakes, and they would occasionally fall into confusion through forgetting what came next in the prayer. Deviations in the recitation of the prayer are reported to us from as late as the fourth century, and as long as the text was not reduced to writing they must have continued to occur. Even later the ʿAmida had no uniform text but was transmitted by the prayer books of the various rites in various versions, some longer and some shorter. Even within the boundaries of a single country it was possible to hear variant readings in neighboring communities. R. David Abudarham did not exaggerate when he said, at the end of his commentary on the prayer book (Abudarham, 59a), that in all the world no two communities exist in which the ʿAmida is recited with exactly the same wording. The invention of printing reduced the great number of variants, for many prayer books intended only for the use of small groups were not reproduced by the press; but the variants were not thereby eliminated. The Reform movement of the modern period again occasioned considerable division. It is impossible to establish one particular text as the archetype of the ʿAmida, for even the most ancient versions have come down in numerous variations containing some expressions that have to be of later origin. Thus, any theory of the ʿAmida based on a particular wording or on the enumeration of the words of the individual benedictions is untenable;[2] their only value is as evidence of the textual tradition. Equally unacceptable is the attempt of Joseph Dérenbourg to derive the ʿAmida from benedictions of three lines each—two parallel petitions and a short motivation clause—and a two-word eulogy.[3] The ʿAmida was not made by one person or of one piece in such a way as to result in this kind of uniformity, and only through willful interference with the text, sometimes necessitating even the elimination of biblical quotations, can such a scheme be achieved. The extent to which the ʿAmida was influenced by the Bible can be observed particularly clearly in the Palestinian version, which has only recently come to be known, and which deviates in many important passages from the current text.[4]

[33]

(2)   Turning now to an examination of the text of the ʿAmida, we mention only the main variations among the different rites;[5] to mention all of them would take us beyond the limits of this general survey, without yielding any particular benefit. Some of the Oriental rites indicate a particular fondness for embellishing the text of the ʿAmida without any specific authority in the sources. One of the favorite and simplest means of doing so is to introduce the word(s) *king* or *our king* into nearly every benediction.

(3)   R. Yoḥanan (third century) placed Ps. 51:17, "O Lord, open my lips," at the head of the silent ʿAmida, and in the Middle Ages other verses were sometimes prefaced to this,[6] such as Deut. 32:3 or Ps. 65:3. Despite the opposition of great legal authorities, these verses have been preserved here and there; they are still absent in Amram. At a later stage the biblical verses were distributed among the various ʿAmidot.

Benediction 1: The ʿAmida begins with a hymnic introduction: "The three first benedictions are the praise of God" (Y. *Ber.* 2:4; compare B. *Ber.* 34a). The first benediction is called אבות, "Patriarchs" (M. *R.H.* 4:5), because it refers to the three patriarchs; in the Middle Ages the payyetanim and legal authorities also called it מגן, "shield," after its eulogy מגן אברהם, "shield of Abraham." Its beginning is quoted by the *Mekhilta*, 19a (to Ex. 13:3); the words האל הגדול הגבור והנורא, "the great, mighty, and terrible God," are a quotation from Deut. 10:17 and Neh. 9:32. The heaping-up of divine epithets other than these biblical expressions is severely prohibited by the Talmud (B. *Ber.* 32b; B. *Meg.* 25a; Y. *Ber.* 9:1, 12d; *Midrash tehilim*, 82b to Ps. 19). The words אל עליון, "highest God," derive from Gen. 14:19; in Palestine the following words קונה שמים וארץ, "possessor of heaven and earth," were also quoted.[7] In the current texts we find this clause only in the ʿAmida for Friday night, while elsewhere the phrase "heaven and earth" is combined into a single word, הכל, "everything," preceded by the additional phrase גומל חסדים טובים, "Who bestows freely acts of kindness." The words וזוכר חסדי אבות, "He remembers the kindnesses of the patriarchs," lead to the theme, for the covenant between God and the patriarchs is the basis of all of the petitions to follow; the words are absent in the Palestinian version, as is the clause, ומביא גואל לבני בניהם, "and He brings a redeemer to their children's children." Nor is there any real need to mention here the eschatological hope; perhaps this emphasis on the future redemption came here in order to counter the Christian belief that the redemption has already come. Saadia's version reads: לזרעם אחריהם, "to their seed after them" instead of לבני בניהם, "to their children's children." The words מלך עוזר ומושיע ומגן, "king, helper, salvation, and shield," serve as a transition to the eulogy, which concludes with the word, מגן, "shield"; in Palestine they said at this point, מגננו ומגן אבותינו מבטחנו בכל דור ודור, "our shield and the shield of our ancestors, our hope in every generation," while Rome and Sepharad each have one further epithet (for additional variants, see Elbogen, *Achtzehngebets*, 49f.). The eulogy *shield of Abraham* is attested in Ben Sira 51:12, 7, as opposed to the version of Friday night (§15), which has מגן אבות, "shield of the patriarchs";[8] the version *shield of Abraham* is derived by the Talmud (B. *Pes.* 117b) and midrash from Gen. 12:2. On the Ten Days of Repentance, the sentence זכרנו לחיים, "Remember us for life," is inserted here. The Talmud does not know of it (or of any of the other additions for the Days of Repentance); nor does it even belong here, since it contains a petition. It is first men-

[34]

tioned in the ninth century; Amram (44b) already has it, but R. Hai Gaon (died 1038) still rejected it. Maimonides (*M.T.*, "Laws of Prayer," 2:9) recognizes it as the practice of individuals, and *Manhig* lists it only as the usage of northern France. Eventually it was declared obligatory.[9] The text is found in Amram (51b) with insignificant variants.

Benediction 2: גבורות, "Might" (M. *R.H.* 4:5) praises God's might. The name is derived from the opening words, אתה גבור, "You are mighty," to which there may originally have been the corresponding eulogy, האל הגבור, "the mighty God."[10] It is also called תחית המתים, "the Resurrection of the Dead," after the eulogy, "Who revives the dead," and the repeated references to resurrection (M. *Ber.* 5:2); in the Middle Ages it was called מחיה, "He Who revives." The emphasis on one of the doctrines of the faith cannot be accidental, as was mentioned above. The repeated references to resurrection in the present version are not original, and the Palestinian rite does not know them. The simplest version of the benediction reads: אתה גבור ואין כמוך חזק ואין זולתך משיב הרוח ומוריד הגשם מכלכל חיים מחיה המתים ורב להושיע, "You are mighty and there is none like You; strong, and there is none but You; You make the wind blow and rain fall; You sustain life, resurrect the dead, and are mighty to save." The basic text probably read אתה גבור מחיה המתים ורב להושיע, "You are mighty, reviving the dead, and mighty to save." All the other versions contain expansions; even the Palestinian rite knows a second version that is considerably longer. The present version is rather lengthy, making use of biblical material to detail God's acts of kindness and of might. The biblical allusions in this benediction are especially numerous; they are modeled on Ps. 146:7ff. and similar passages. For expansions of the text [ending with the additional phrase, ומשען לאביונים, "and support of the poor," while lacking other phrases], see Saadia in *Osar tov*. The eulogy מחיה המתים, "Who revives the dead," is found in *Pirqe derabi eli'ezer*, at the end of chapter 31.[11]

In this benediction, in accordance with M. *Ber.* 5:2, the words משיב הרוח ומוריד הגשם, "Who makes the wind blow and the rain fall," are inserted. This phrase is called גבורות גשמים, "The Might of the Rain," by Rabbi Eliezer (first century) in the Mishnah (*Ta.* 1:1). According to the accepted rule, this addition is recited from the Additional Service of the Eighth Day of Assembly until the Morning Service of the first day of Passover (M. *Ta.* 1:2) [inclusive]. Originally the congregation would begin reciting it only at the Afternoon Service (Amram), but later they began to announce it before the Additional Service, and the congregation would begin saying it immediately in the Additional Service (*Pardes*, 45c). Apparently, in Palestine other similar sentences connected with natural phenomena were known, but none was accepted into the liturgy: "The sages did not make it obligatory to refer to dew and wind" (Y. *Ta.* 1:1, 63d; B. *Ta.* 3a). In the amoraic period we first encounter (with Rabbi Yohanan) the custom of saying, מוריד הטל, "Who makes the dew fall," in summer (Y. *Ta.*, ibid.). This insertion is thus found in the Palestinian rite, but it was unknown in Babylonia, perhaps because of climatic conditions. Amram does not know it, though it is written spuriously in the texts of his rite. From Palestine the custom migrated to Italy and, surprisingly, also to Spain. It never spread to Germany; in France it was lacking in the early centuries (*Vitry*; *Eshkol*), but apparently it did eventually take root (*Manhig*). Some worshipers there seem to have recited "Who brings down the dew" both summer and winter, as in the Castilian custom.[12]

[35]

On the Ten Days of Repentance, מי כמוך, "Who is like You, Father of mercy?" is inserted in this second benediction. The same may be said about its origin as about "Remember us," above. Instead of אב הרחמים, "Merciful Father," *Vitry* and Maimonides read אב הרחמן, "Father of mercy."[13]

Benediction 3: קדושת השם, "Sanctification of the Name" (M. *R.H.* 4:5); קדושות, "Sanctifications" (B. *R.H.* 32a); קדושה, "Sanctification" (B. *Meg.* 17d); these names are based on the contents of the third benediction, which in medieval poetry was called simply משלש, "The Third." After the praise of God's might comes praise of His sanctity. In the earliest period the opening words were קדוש אתה ונורא שמך, "Holy are You and terrible is Your name," as they are today in Ashkenaz and Sepharad only on the New Year and the Day of Atonement. This formula, confirmed by Sifre Deut., 142b, §343, is found also in Palestine. We cannot be far from the truth if we suppose that Is. 6:3 was cited here as a prooftext, and that from this the Kedushah developed (see below, §9a). The current use of Is. 5:16, for this purpose, is not found in Palestine, although it is already attested in *Pirqe derabi eliᶜezer* (chap. 35, end); it is particularly appropriate for the Days of Awe because they are days of judgment.

Amram reads:

לדור ודור המליכו לאל כי כי הוא לבדו מרום וקדוש ושבחך אלהינו מפינו לא ימוש לעולם ועד כי אל מלך גדול
וקדוש אתה

"From generation to generation proclaim God king, for He alone is exalted and holy; and may Your praise, our God, never depart from our mouths, for You are the great and holy king."

This same version is found in the manuscripts of Rome, except for the variant נמליך, "We shall proclaim God king," instead of המליכו, "proclaim God king." For the New Year and the Day of Atonement, Amram has also "Holy are you," while Rome adds here only the prooftext, Is. 5:6. In the printed editions of Rome, Romaniot and Carpentras, the opening reads לדור ודור נגיד גדלך ולנצח נצחים קדושתך נקדיש, "From generation to generation we will tell of Your greatness, and forever and ever we will declare Your sanctity," and the conclusion is, "and may Your praise . . . ," as above. Rome has "From generation to generation we will tell . . ." throughout the year, while Romaniot has in this place on the New Year and the Day of Atonement, "From generation to generation we will proclaim God King." Sepharad has a completely new version, with אתה קדוש, "You are holy," whose concluding sentence וקדושים בכל יום יהללוך "and holy ones will praise You every day," alludes to the Kedushah; but on the New Year and the Day of Atonement after "You are holy" there comes also "From generation to generation declare God King" (as in Amram, but without "and Your praise"), and also "Holy are You and terrible is Your name." None of these rites distinguishes between the silent ᶜAmida and the precentor's repetition. Such a distinction is made in Ashkenaz (already in *Vitry*), for there the silent ᶜAmida has "You are holy," while the precentor, after concluding the Kedushah, says "From generation to generation we will tell of Your greatness"; on the New Year and the Day of Atonement he says in addition, "Holy are You and terrible is Your name."

On the text of "You are Holy," it should be noted that Saadia adds וכרך קדוש, "And Your fame is holy"; Persia adds also ומשרתיך קדושים, "and Your servants are holy"; Sepharad adopted these plus the concluding sentence from the prayer, "From generation to generation," כי אל מלך גדול וקדוש אתה, "For You are a great and terrible God." Abudarham complained in vain that ignorant persons neglect this sentence, for it is not said to this day. Comparison with the text of the following benedictions makes it likely that the sentence is of ancient origin.

The eulogy is האל הקדוש, "the Holy God" (Y. *R.H.* 4:6, 59c; B. *Ber.* 12b); but on the Ten Days of Repentance one says המלך הקדוש, "the Holy King" (B. *Ber.*, ibid.). In Palestine this Babylonian variant did not obtain, and in all of the geniza fragments, without exception, we find "the holy God."[14] In the precentor's repetition, the Kedushah is inserted here; see below, §9a.

(4)   We now come to the intermediate benedictions (אמצעיות), containing the petitions for "the people's needs" (Y. *Ber.* 2:4, 4d). The sources do not specify any particular number, since their number fluctuated, and since the employment of separate eulogies was permitted in places where several of them were ordinarily combined in a single benediction. (Compare, for example, Benedictions 14 and 15.) It was also said that their order is not binding (B. *Ber.* 34a): "The intermediate benedictions have no order." Nor do they have fixed names; the names of some vary, and others are not named in the Talmud at all.

Benediction 4: In the Mishnah (*Ber.* 5:2) called חונן הדעת, "Who bestows knowledge," because of its eulogy. In the Talmud it is called בינה, "Understanding" (B. *Meg.* 17b) or דעה, "Knowledge" (Y. *Ber.* 2:4, 4d), and the "Benediction of Wisdom" (B. *Ber.* 33a), because of its contents.

The first petition is thus for wisdom or enlightenment (compare the prayer of Solomon, I Kgs. 3:9–12, or II Chron. 1:10). The Talmud (Y. *Ber.*, 2:4, 4d) quotes from this petition the words חננו דעה, "Bestow upon us knowledge," and in fact the Palestinian version reads חוננו דעה מאתך בינה והשכל מתורתך, "Bestow upon us knowledge from Yourself, understanding and wisdom from Your Torah." In all the other sources this is preceded by the superfluous hymnic introduction אתה חונן, "You bestow"; and in place of השכל and בינה one often finds חכמה (compare Amram and Baer). Persia has here, as in most of the following petitions, the concluding formula: כי אל דעות ורחמן אתה, "For You are a God of wisdom and mercy." The eulogy, "Who bestows knowledge," is mentioned already by the Mishnah (see above).

On Saturday night the *Havdala*, "Separation," prayer is introduced here (M. *Ber.* 5:2) through the insertion of אתה חוננתנו, "You have bestowed upon us," between the first two sentences. For the origin of the *Havdala* see §19. Its content follows from Y. *Ber.* 5:2, 9b and B. *Pes.* 104a. Of its actual wording, we find in Y. *Ber.*, 5:2, 9c,

> Rabbi Jeremiah and Rabbi Zeora in the name of Rabbi Hiyya b. Ashi: It is necessary to say, החל עלינו את הימים ששת ימי המעשה הבאים לקראתנו לשלום, "Cause the days, the six days of work which are approaching us, to descend upon us in peace."

This text is not found verbatim anywhere else, but it does occur with a few variants in Ashkenaz (Baer, *'Avodat*, 301); Amram, Maimonides, Sepharad, Rome and Romaniot have a different one (of Babylonian origin?): . . . וכשם שהבדלתנו מעמי הארצות כן תטהרנו, "And just as You have separated us from the nations of the world . . . so purify us . . ."; the wording is slightly expanded in Sepharad. The insert in Amram, Rome and Romaniot begins אתה הבדלת, "You have distinguished." In Ashkenaz this sentence, which is the *Havdala* itself, begins ותבדל, "And You separated," for before it one would repeat the first sentence of the benediction in a different form—אתה חוננתנו, "You have bestowed upon us." Whether this repetition was necessary was long disputed, and despite the opposition of the chief legal authorities, the two sentences were preserved. This custom entered even the Sephardic rite, though it is not yet found in Abudarham.[15]

[37]

Benediction 5: תשובה, "Repentance" (B. *Meg.* 17b and Y. *Ber.* 2:4, 4d). The eulogy is הרוצה בתשובה, "Who desires repentance," *Midrash tehilim* 29:2 (116b), and this is attested also by the summarizing formula, רצה בתשובתנו, "accept our repentance," in Y. *Ber.*, 2:4, 4d and 4:3, 8a. After the petition for knowledge comes one for religious renewal. The text in the Palestinian rite consists only of Lam. 5:21: "Return us, O Lord, to You, and we shall return; renew our days as of old." The current text has three petitions, which recur in all the prayer rites. All early medieval sources have a fourth petition ודבקנו במצוותיך, "And make us cling to Your commandments," as is still the custom in Rome and Romaniot. Saadia adds to this last also כי פשענו, "for we have sinned," as in Benediction 6.

Benediction 6: סליחה, "Forgiveness" (same sources as Benediction 5) follows consecutively upon "Repentance" and is closely related to it. The content is summarized in the words, סלח לנו, "Forgive us" (Y. *Ber.* 2:4, 4d and 4:3, 8a). The Palestinian text is closer to the words of Scripture, for the second petition reads, מחה והעבר פשעינו מנגד עיניך, "Efface and remove our sins from before You," as in Ps. 51:3, and the motivating clause, כי רבים רחמיך, "for Your mercies are abundant," recalls Ps. 119:156.[16] In the current text the latter reads: כי אל טוב וסלח אתה, "For You are a good and forgiving God,"[17] and only in Ashkenaz is it כי מוחל וסולח אתה, "For You are a forgiving and pardoning God" (*Vitry:* "For You are a forgiving God and King"), apparently a shortened form of Ps. 86:5, as is noted in *Oṣar ṭov*. Persia displays a surprising conflation of the Palestinian version and the current one. The eulogy reads מרבה לסלוח, "Who forgives abundantly," as in Y. *R.H.* 4:6, 59c, and in the piyyut (by Kallir?), מי אל כמוך, "Who is a God like You,"[18] for the Day of Atonement. Likewise, the Palestinian version is המרבה לסלוח, "Who forgives abundantly," whereas the current eulogy, חנון המרבה לסלוח, "The merciful One Who forgives abundantly," is found already in *Midrash tehilim* 29:2 and in all the rites; for חנון ומרבה לסלוח, "Merciful and forgiving abundantly," see *REJ* 53 (1907).

On fast days other than the Ninth of Av poems called *seliḥot* are inserted in this benediction (compare §33) already in Amram; on such occasions the transition to the eulogy reads, ואל יעכב חטא ועון את תפילתנו סלח ומחל לכל עוונותינו, "And may sin and transgression not block our prayer; forgive and pardon all our sins."[19] In this case even the Ashkenazic rite has the old concluding formula, "For You are a good and forgiving God."

Benediction 7: גאולה, "Redemption" (B. *Meg.* 17b and Y. *Ber.* 2:4, 4d and 4:3,

8a). For the meaning of this petition see above, §8:9. The opening comes from Ps. 119:153ff.,[20] altered to the plural, as is appropriate for public worship. In Palestine the eulogy follows immediately; the current version adds כי גואל חזק אתה, "For You are a mighty Redeemer"; while *Vitry* and Yemen add כי אל מלך גואל וחזק אתה, "For You are a redeeming and mighty King." Sepharad reads, ומהר לגאלנו גאולה שלמה למען שמך, "Redeem us quickly with a perfect redemption for Your name's sake"; similarly, *Midrash tannaim*, 209, reads גאלנו ה' אלהינו גאולה שלמה מלפניך, "Redeem us, O Lord our God, with a perfect redemption from You"; in place of this, *Sifre* Deut., §343 has מתיר אסורים, "Who releases the bound," a most astonishing variant. [See above, page 31.] Saadia and Maimonides have additionally ודון דיננו, "and judge our case." *Oṣar ṭov* contains a great expansion. The current eulogy, גואל ישראל, "Redeemer of Israel" (Is. 49:7), is found already in Ben Sira 51:12, 5; compare M. *Ta.* 2:4; B. *Pes.* 117b; and Y. *Ber.* 2:4, 4d.

On fast days the precentor adds here the Prayer for Fast Days (B. *Ta.* 11b), namely, עננו, "Answer us."[21] The ancient version is quoted in Y. *Ber.* 4:3, 8a; Y. *Ta.* 2:2, 65c, but not one of the current versions is exactly identical to this. The closest is Ashkenaz, which is the only one that still retains the talmudic conclusion of "Answer us," but even here the reference to Ps. 107:28 is lacking, appearing only in Romaniot. However, all the versions have a different conclusion: טרם נקרא אתה תענה, "Before we call You will answer" (Rome, Sepharad) or טרם נקרא אליך תענה, "Before we call to You, answer" (Ashkenaz as early as *Vitry*), with reference to Is. 65:24, which, in the Talmud (B. *Ber.* 29a; Y. *Ber.* 4:3, 8a), is the conclusion of the short *'Amida*, "Give Us Understanding." The eulogy העונה בעת צרה, "Who answers in time of trouble," is found already in the Mishnah (*Ta.* 2:4).

Benediction 8: רפואה, "Health" (B. *Meg.*, ibid.), ברכת חולים, "the benediction of the sick" ('*A.Z.* 8a); רופא חולים, "Who heals the sick" (Y. *Ber.* 2:4)—a petition for physical strength, and the first petition for material needs. In the current version the opening is taken from Jer. 17:14, altered to the plural, as is appropriate for public worship. But the Palestinian rite, which ordinarily follows more closely the language of Scripture, reads here: רפאנו ה' אלהינו ממכאוב לבנו [ויגון ואנחה העבר ממנו] והעלה רפואה למכותינו, "Heal us, O Lord our God, from the sickness of our heart [and remove from us misery and sighing], and bring about healing for our wounds"; or, as in *REJ* 53 (1907), רפאנו ה' ונרפא והעלה רפואה לכל מכותינו, "Heal us, O Lord, and we shall be healed; and bring about healing for all of our wounds." We are at present unable to determine whether this surprising deviation from the usual style is original, or whether it is a later change. [Compare the discussion of this version in *Tarbiz* 34 (1964/5): 363ff.] The concluding petition, "and bring about," recurs in all the current versions, but with the addition of the word שלמה, "complete," to the word רפואה, "healing"; Sepharad (but not Abudarham) reads here ארוכה ומרפא, "healing and cure." Alongside לכל מכותינו, "for all of our wounds," Amram, Vitry, Rome, Sepharad, and Romaniot have לכל תחלואינו, "for all of our sicknesses," in accordance with Ps. 103:3. Maimonides (Yemen) has only this last word, while Sepharad adds לכל מכאובינו, "for all of our pains."[22] The motivating clause כי אל רופא רחמן אתה, "for You are a merciful and healing God," is found everywhere from Amram on, usually with the addition of the word נאמן, "faithful," and in Ashkenaz מלך, "King." The eulogy in Y. *Ber.* 2:4; *Eshkol* 1:19 reads רופא חולים, "Who heals the sick"; but all the known versions agree in using the language found in B. *Shab.* 12a, reading רופא חולי

[38]

עמו ישראל, "Who heals the sick of His people Israel." The prayer books of the Reform movement have restored the original version. In the amoraic period, permission was given to insert private prayers on behalf of the sick before כי אל מלך, "For You are a healing King" (B. ʿA.Z. 8a; B. *Ber.* 31a); a version of an individual prayer of this type may be found in Baer, ʿAvodat, 91.

Benediction 9: ברכת השנים, "Benediction of the years" (*Ber.* 5:2); מברך השנים, "Who blesses the years" (Y. *Ber.* 2:4). This is a petition for blessing in agriculture and for the success of the harvests. Ashkenaz has preserved the shortest and simplest version (already in *Vitry*). Rome has expanded the conclusion somewhat, starting from the word ושבענו, "and satisfy us." Palestine already introduces the idea, foreign to the context, of redemption through the petition וקרב מהרה שנת קץ גלותנו, "and bring near speedily the ordained year of our Redemption." In accordance with M. *Ber.* 5:2, the prayer for rain, known as שאלה (Petition), is inserted into this benediction.[23] The day of the year on which this addition is first made may vary, according to the Talmud (B. *Ta.* 14b, and compare Elbogen, *Achtzehngebet*, 44 and *Halakhot gedolot*, 175); in our time it is recited, in accordance with B. *Ta.* 10a, from the Evening Service of the fourth or fifth of December [in Palestine from the seventh of Marheshvan on], until Passover. In Rome the petition is accomplished by simply adding the word ומטר, "and rain," in the winter to the words ותן טל לברכה, "and give dew for a blessing"; in Ashkenaz one says in summer ותן ברכה, "and give blessing," and in winter ותן טל ומטר לברכה, "give dew and rain for a blessing." According to *Leqaḥ ṭov*, 29b (to Gen. 12:3), it appears that all these words belong to the prayer for the whole year, and so it was in Palestine; but in winter this version added ותן גשמי רצון על פני האדמה, "and give rains of satisfaction to the surface of the earth." In all the above versions the petition for rain is contained in a slight variation of the usual benediction, which doubtless conforms to the Mishnah's stipulation. Only Sepharad, and already Amram, at least in the printed editions[24] [and Saadia], have two completely different versions, a short one for summer similar to the one in use in Rome, and another very long version for winter. The text is found in Maimonides's "The Order of the Prayers" [see *SRIHP* 7 (1957/8): 196ff.]; but Amram cannot have known such a distinction, to judge by the rule that he cites (*Amram* 8a). Against this distinction see also *Manhig*, "Laws of Prayer," §56; it may have been occasioned by the talmudic concession (B. ʿA.Z. 8a, third century): "If one is in need of sustenance he may speak of it in the Benediction of the Years"; and, in fact, similar additions have been preserved containing special petitions for the success of the individual's livelihood. The eulogy מברך השנים, "Who blesses the years," is the same in all texts, in accordance with Y. *Ber.* 2:4.[25]

Benediction 10: קבוץ גליות, "The Assembling of the Exiled Communities" (B. *Meg.* 17b). The petitions for material needs having ended, those for national needs follow, beginning with the petition for the assembling of the Diaspora. The text follows the words of Scripture (Is. 27:13, 11:12). Palestine concludes, לקבץ גליותינו, "to assemble our exiled communities"; *REJ* 53 (1907), לקבצנו, "to assemble us"; in both [as well as in Saadia], the last sentence, וקבצנו, "and assemble us," is lacking. All of the versions except Ashkenaz (but including *Vitry*) read at the end לארצנו, "to our land." This word is lacking also in the manuscripts of Amram,[26] which read: ושא נס לקבץ גליותינו (אוצר טוב

[39]

ותקרא דרור לחירותנו) וקרא דרור לקבצנו יחד מארבע כנפות הארץ, "And lift up a standard to assemble our exile communities, and proclaim freedom [*Oṣar ṭov*: "and You will proclaim our freedom"] to assemble us together from the four corners of the earth." The eulogy מקבץ נדחי ישראל, "Who assembles the scattered people of Israel," based on Is. 56:8, is found already in Ben Sira 51:12, 6; compare Y. *Ber.* 2:4. All prayer books, including Palestine, read נדחי עמו ישראל, "the scattered ones of his people Israel," in accordance with *Midrash tehilim*, 29:2. In the Reform prayer books this and the following national petitions have been radically altered to express a completely spiritual conception of the messianic redemption.

Benediction 11: This benediction has no particular name; in the Talmud (B. *Meg.*, 17b) it is named for its beginning: השיבה שופטינו, "Restore our judges," and only in a late source (Ḥananel, ad loc.) do we find the name ברכת משפט, "The Benediction of Judgment." The content is described in the expressions "judge us fairly" and "judgment is executed" (Y. *Ber.* 2:4), or "judgment is executed against the wicked" (B. *Meg.* 17b), or, as in the prayer "Give us understanding": "and it is for You to judge those who are in error" (Y. *Ber.* 4:3, 8a), or "those who are in error will be judged in accordance with Your will" (B. *Ber.* 29a). The current versions contain nothing about the judgment of the wicked, and the petition is only for the appointment of righteous judges and freedom from the oppression of this world. Only Romaniot has the conclusion, ואל נא תרשיענו בדין, "and do not judge us to be guilty," which recalls the ancient version. The wording of the first petition, "Restore our judges," is based on Is. 1:26. Saadia and *REJ* 53 (1907): 327 [and Saadia, *Siddur*, 18] have only this verse, but already in Palestine there is added, ומלך (ותמלך) עלינו אתה לבדך, "and rule (and You will rule) alone over us." The petition והסר ממנו, "and remove from us," which is inserted in the middle in Ashkenaz (already in *Vitry*) and Sepharad, disturbs the context, and in fact is lacking in Rome, Romaniot, and Amram. At the end, Rome and Amram add בחסד וברחמים בצדק ובמשפט, "in grace, loving kindness, righteousness, and judgment" (*in loving kindness* is lacking in Sepharad); compare Hos. 2:21. Romaniot and Ashkenaz (already in *Vitry*) read בחסד וברחמים וצדקנו במשפט, "in loving kindness and mercy, and justify us in judgment." The eulogy in Palestine is אוהב המשפט, "Who loves judgment" (according to Alfasi האל המשפט, "the God of judgment")[27] while all prayer books have the version of the Babylonian Talmud (*Ber.* 12b; compare Ps. 33:5)—מלך אוהב צדקה ומשפט, "King Who loves righteousness and judgment."

On the Ten Days of Repentance the eulogy is changed, in accordance with B. *Ber.* 12b, to המלך המשפט, "The King of judgment." As for the grammatical difficulty in this phrase, compare Josh. 3:14, 8:11; II Kgs. 16:17; Jer. 31:39 (Rashi to *Ber.* 12b).

[40]

Benediction 12: ברכת המינים, "The Benediction Against the Sectarians" (B. *Ber.* 28b; compare above, §8[10]). No benediction has undergone as many textual variations as this one,[28] some through the natural effect of changing times, and others through censorship. It is most doubtful that we will ever be in a position to recover its original text. Throughout the Middle Ages, through the time of the Reuchlin-Pfefferkorn disputation,[29] its beginning is always cited as ולמשומדים, "To the apostates." This word has been preserved in only one prayer book still in use, that of Yemen; it is found also in the very rare edition of the Ashkenazic rite, Salonika, 1580, and in

Romaniot, but is common in manuscripts.[30] Further, the word מינים, "sectarians," from which the benediction's name derives, must also have appeared in it. From the church fathers, it may be conjectured that it also contained the word נוצרים, "Christians," which in fact does occur in the Oxford manuscript of Amram. From the eulogy מכניע זדים, "Who humbles the arrogant," it may be assumed that similar language occurred also in the body of the petition, and in fact the Sulzberger manuscript of Amram, and Rome, Romaniot, and Yemenite read: ומלכות זדון במהרה תעקר, "and may the arrogant kingdom speedily be uprooted."[31] All of these elements occur together in the Palestinian version: ולמשומדים אל תהי תקוה ומלכות זדון מהרה תעקר בימינו והנוצרים והמינים כרגע יאבדו, "May there be no hope for the apostates, and may the arrogant kingdom be speedily uprooted in our days, and may the Christians and sectarians instantly perish"; as a conclusion the verse from Ps. 69:29 is added: "May they be wiped out from the Book of the Living and not written with the righteous." The version published in *REJ* 53 (1907): 238 [that is, Saadia's version; compare Saadia, *Siddur*, 18] is identical [at its beginning] with this one.

In the course of time this version was no longer understood; it was therefore changed and partly reworked out of consideration for the Christian accusations. Typical is the addition in the Oxford Amram manuscript, אם לא ישובו לבריתך, "if they do not return to Your covenant," which is known from the prayer "Give us Understanding." Similarly, the names of the ancient opponents in the benediction were eliminated, and replaced with general designations of Israel's many historic enemies: וכל אויבינו, "and all our enemies"; ואויביהם וקמיהם וכל, "and all the enemies of Your people"; וכל אויביך, "and their enemies and those who rise against them and all Your enemies"; וכל צוררי עמך ישראל, "and all the opponents of Your people Israel"; and various other expressions such as can be found in Baer. Among these new epithets is also ולמלשינים, "and to the informers," which today is the first word of the current versions; this is a biblical word (compare Prov. 31:10) equivalent to מסורות or מוסרים, which occur frequently in connection with מינים, "sectarians." מלשינים cannot have been devised by expanding the word מינים to serve as a replacement for it in the face of censorship, since the two words occur side by side in uncensored books and manuscripts.[32] The eulogy according to the Yerushalmi and the midrashim is מכניע זדים, "Who humbles the arrogant," and so it is in Palestine and in the piyyut for Yom Kippur, מי אל כמוך, "Who is a God like You." *Midrash tehilim* 29:2 has instead: שובר אויבים, "Who breaks the enemies" (that is, the Babylonian version). From the time of Amram, both expressions are found together in all known prayer books, except Amram, Saadia, Maimonides, and Yemen, which have שובר רשעים, "Who breaks the wicked." In modern prayer books the text has been subjected to many alterations, but the most sensible change is to eliminate it entirely, as was done in the Berlin prayer book.

Benediction 13: The name ברכת הצדיקים, "Benediction of the Righteous," occurs first in Hananel on B. *Meg.* 17b. This benediction, the converse of the preceding one, is a petition on behalf of the righteous ("the horn of the righteous is lifted up," B. *Meg.* 17b; "the righteous rejoice," Y. *Ber.* 2:4), and on behalf of the proselytes who had joined the Jewish people. In its most ancient version the benediction mentions, alongside the proselytes, also the elders, representing the administrative authorities (T. *Ber.* 3:25; Y., ibid.). In Palestine the version of the benediction is brief: על גרי הצדק יהמו רחמיך

ותן לנו שכר טוב עם עושי רצונך בא"ה מבטח לצדיקים, "For the righteous proselytes may Your mercy be stirred up, and give us a good reward along with those who do Your will. Blessed are you, O Lord, the trust of the righteous," but surprisingly the word *elders* required by the sources is lacking here. Likewise, it is lacking in medieval sources, Rome and Romaniot, and only in Ashkenaz (for example, *Vitry*) and in later editions of Sepharad does it reappear. An innovation in Ashkenaz and Sepharad is the reference to the scribes, already known to Rashi. In place of ועל פלטת (בית) סופריהם, "And for the survivors (of the house) of their scribes,"[33] Rome reads ועל פליטת עמך בית ישראל, "And for the survivors of Your people, the house of Israel"; and for this the Oxford manuscripts of Amram, Maimonides, and Sepharad read, ועל שארית עמך בית ישראל, "And for the remnant of Your people, the house of Israel." Ashkenaz and Sepharad (as early as Abudarham) add also the word ועלינו, "And upon us." Romaniot opens על החסידים, "For the pious," and then reads only על הצדיקים ועל גרי הצדק ועלינו, "for the righteous and for the righteous proselytes and for us." The second petition, ותן שכר טוב, "And give a good reward," is also expanded: *Us* has been replaced by an expression corresponding to the eulogy— לכל הבוטחים בשמך באמת, "for all those who truly trust in Your name." The personal petition was expressed in the words ושים חלקנו עמהם, "And make our portion with theirs," and at the end, again under the influence of the eulogy, came the conclusion, ולעולם לא נבוש כי בך בטחנו, "and may we never be put to shame, for in You do we trust." Against the ancient tradition, the late Ashkenazic versions connect the word *forever* with what preceded. The conclusion derives from Pss. 22:6 and 25:2. Its conclusion shows how arbitrarily this spot was expanded: Rome adds the words מלך עולמים, "eternal king," and France, Sepharad, and Romaniot add ועל חסדך (הגדול באמת) נשעננו, "and upon Your (great and true) mercy do we rely." The eulogy reads in T. *Ber.* 3:25, מבטח לצדיקים, "the trust of the righteous,"[34] and likewise in Palestine and in the above-mentioned piyyut, "Who is a God like You"; the current version reads, in accordance with *Midrash tehilim* 29:2, משען ומבטח לצדיקים, "The reliance and trust of the righteous."

Benediction 14: It has no ancient name, but the petition itself is ancient; its original eulogy was הבוחר בציון, "Who chooses Zion" (Ben Sira 51:12, 40), or השוכן בציון, "Who dwells in Zion" (Y. *Yoma* 7:1, 44b), but it was later changed to a petition for the ruined city and the rebuilding of the Temple (Y. *Ber.* 2:2: "Build Your house"). To it the petition for the Messiah, the descendant of David, was attached (Y. *Ber.* 4:5, 8c), and the eulogy read אלהי דוד ובונה ירושלים, "God of David and Builder of Jerusalem" Y. *R.H.* 4:5, 59c, and the Palestinian midrashim). The Palestinian version of this benediction, which, but for the eulogy, is still preserved almost verbatim in Saadia, but in simpler and more original wording, matches this eulogy:

רחם ה' אלהינו עלינו ועל ישראל עמך ועל ירושלים עירך ועל ציון משכן כבודך (ועל היכלך ועל מעונך) ועל מלכות בית דוד משיחך. ..בא"ה אל' דוד בונה ירושלם

"Have mercy, O Lord our God, upon us and upon Israel Your people, and upon Jerusalem Your city, and upon Zion, the dwelling place of Your glory (and upon your Temple and your dwelling place) and upon the Kingdom of the House of David, Your annointed one ... Blessed are you, O Lord, God of David, Builder of Jerusalem."[35]

This formula is preferable to the current one, if only because it is very similar to other prayers with the same content, where the same list occurs verbatim [for example, the text of the benediction "Who builds Jerusalem" in Grace after Meals in all rites; compare also the abbreviation of this benediction in the short form of Grace after Meals: רחם . . . על ישראל עמך ועל ירושלים עירך ועל ציון משכן כבודך ועל מזבחך ועל היכלך, "Have mercy . . . upon Israel Your people and upon Jerusalem Your city and upon Zion, the dwelling place of Your glory, and upon Your altar and upon Your Temple."] In the ellipsis there is a petition in which we can already sense reworking; in Palestine it reads, בנה ביתך שכלל היכלך, "Build Your Temple and restore Your house," a formula that has clear parallels elsewhere; while in Saadia the reading is in the spirit of the later version: ובנה ברחמים את ירושלים, "and build Jerusalem in mercy." The most extreme reworking is in the current version, where almost no echo of the original is found, and where only the sentence וכסא דוד מהרה לתוכה תכין, "and quickly establish the throne of David within it," in Ashkenaz and Sepharad (but not in Abudarham) alludes to the original unity of benedictions 14 and 15. Benediction 14 was diverted into an eschatological direction, to the theme of the return of the divine presence to Jerusalem. It reads, ולירושלים עירך ברחמים תשוב, "and to Jerusalem, Your city, return in mercy" (Rome and Ashkenaz), or תשכון בתוך ירושלים עירך, "dwell in the midst of Jerusalem, Your city" (Sepharad and Yemen); this last recalls Zech. 8:3. Amram and Romaniot begin על ירושלים עירך, "upon Jerusalem Your city," which apparently derives from a version beginning with רחם, "Have mercy."

This version beginning "Have mercy" has been preserved verbatim in an insert for the Ninth of Av quoted in the Y. *Ber.* 4:3, 8a, and taken up in Amram, Rome, and Romaniot, which, however, insert into the middle of the text from the Yerushalmi a petition for the building of the ruined city: נערה ה' אלהינו מעפרה והקיצה מארץ דויה, "Shake off its dust, O Lord our God, and awaken it from the wretched land." This petition is inserted into all three of the daily ʿAmidot in these versions. As against this, the completely reworked version of "Console" is found in one manuscript of Amram, in Sepharad and Ashkenaz; its source is Saadia, according to whom it is to be said only in the Afternoon Service. [In Saadia, *Siddur*, 318–19 the text begins רחם ה' אלהינו על ישראל עמך ועל ירושלים עירך . . . ועל העיר האבדה האבלה ושוממה, "Have mercy, O Lord our God, upon Israel Your people and upon Jerusalem Your city . . . and upon the lost, mournful, and ruined city." Before citing it the Gaon notes: "Some add this in the ʿAmida of the Ninth of Av in the benediction 'Who builds Jerusalem'," and then: "There is nothing wrong with saying it."] A peculiar combination of the two versions is quoted by Maimonides: on the Ninth of Av he completely eliminates Benediction 14 and replaces it with a version of "Have mercy," the beginning of which resembles Amram and the end, Sepharad. In the Middle Ages it was customary in many places to recite "Have mercy" in the Evening Service and in the Morning Service, and "Console" in the Afternoon Service.[36] The eulogy, מנחם ציון ובונה ירושלים, "Who consoles Zion and builds Jerusalem,"[37] which is customary in Rome and Ashkenaz in combination with this text, also comes from a Palestinian source. In Rome the *qerovot* of the Ninth of Av are expanded in Benediction 14, and all of the *qinot* are introduced here (§32), while "Have mercy" serves as the conclusion of the *qinot*.[38]

Benediction 15: ברכת דוד, "The benediction of David." The name is not found until R. Ḥananel to *Meg.*, 18a. "The Plant of David" is the latest of the benedictions of the *'Amida*. In Palestine it is not found at all (see above, §8[12]). Since Amram the text of the petition is identical everywhere. Ashkenaz, Rome and Romaniot read דוד עבדך, "David Your servant"; Amram, in one manscript, has וקרננו, "and our horn"; the motivating clause כי לישועתך, "because for Your salvation,"[39] is lacking in Saadia [,Maimonides] and Yemen. The eulogy comes from B. *Pes.* 117b; a similar eulogy is found already in Ben Sira 51:12, 8. The wording, which recurs verbatim in similar prayers, derives from Ps. 132:17. In the prayer books of the Reform movement, alterations have been introduced to both benedictions 14 and 15, corresponding to the modern spiritual conception of the messianic idea.

Benediction 16: This is the last of the middle benedictions; it is called תפלה, "prayer," in B. *Meg.* 18a, and שומע תפלה, "Who listens to prayer," in Y. *Ber.* 2:4. A very short version is found in Palestine: שמע [בקולנו] ה' א-ל' בקול תפלתנו ורחם עלינו כי אל חנון ורחום אתה בא"ה שומע תפלה, "Hear O Lord our God [our voice] the voice of our prayer, and have mercy upon us, for You are a kind and merciful God. Blessed are You, Lord, Who hears prayer."[40] As against this basic version, all the current rites have versions that expand the petition by means of parallel clauses, adding their own individual style to the motivation. After the first motivating clause, which reads everywhere כי אל שומע תפלות ותחנונים אתה, "for You are a God Who hears prayers and supplications," comes the additional petition ומלפניך מלכנו ריקם אל תשיבנו, "and do not turn us aside empty-handed from before You," which in Spain, and especially in Romaniot, has a much expanded form. Its motivating clause in Amram and Sepharad is כי אתה שומע תפלת כל פה, "for You hear the prayer of every mouth," an expression that has been reduced in Ashkenaz (already in *Vitry*) to תפלת עמך ישראל, "the prayer of Your people Israel." The additional word ברחמים, "in mercy," is a vestige of the wording כי אב מלא רחמים רבים אתה, "for You are a father full of many mercies," found in Rome, Romaniot, and *Osar tov*, and agreeing with the version of the Amram manuscripts. The prayer books of the Reform movement have restored the universalistic version of the motivation clause. The eulogy is שומע תפלה, "Who hears prayer" (M. *Ber.* 4:4; *Ta.* 2:4; compare Y. *Ber.* 2:4). Already in ancient times it was permitted to insert here private petitions during the silent recitation of the *'Amida*: "A person may ask for his own needs in the benediction, 'Who hears prayer' " (B. *Ber.* 31a; B. *'A.Z.* 8a); by the beginning of the third century Rav relies upon this rule as authoritative, and it apparently was what led to the creation of the new petition, ומלפניך מלכנו, "and from before us, our King . . . ." In kabbalist circles, full use was made of the permission to do this, and a number of similar petitions were formulated for insertion at this point. Likewise, the worshiper was permitted to recite here additions for particular days that he had forgotten to recite at the appropriate point (such as *Havdala*). Here the individual worshiper would insert "Answer us" on fast days, without a eulogy, in all the *'Amidot*; eventually this custom was restricted to the Afternoon Service, and dropped in the other services.

[43]

(5)   Benedictions 17 to 19: שלש אחרונות, the three final benedictions. The final benedictions, corresponding to the first three, were intended to be of hymnic character, "praise of the Omnipresent" (Y. *Ber.* 2:4; B. *Ber.* 34a), and particularly to express thanksgiving. This characterization does not fit either the first or the last of them, and yet there is no doubt that when the above-mentioned inner division of the *'Amida* was

advanced, the content of these benedictions was no different from their content today. In any event, these two benedictions do not speak about the needs of the individual but about the individual's relationship to God.

Benediction 17: עבודה, "Temple Service" (M. *R.H.* 4:5; *Tam.* 5:1), is probably the most ancient part of the ʿAmida; accordingly, no part has undergone as many changes in the course of time as this benediction. This is the petition that was recited in the Temple at the time of the offering of the sacrifices, and its subject is that God accept them with favor. The most ancient version preserved is [perhaps], רצה אלהינו ושכון בציון מהרה יעבדוך בניך [פסיקתא: בירושלים], "Desire, O Lord, to dwell in Zion; soon may Your children worship You [*Pesiqta derav kahana*: in Jerusalem]" (*Lev. R.*, §7:2; *Pesiqta derav kahana, Shuva*, 158b), forming the entire text in Palestine. Provence has the several additional sentences borrowed from Sepharad. It is very unlikely that this short version alone formed the whole of "Temple Service"; the sentence that recurs in all the current versions, ואשי ישראל ותפלתם [מהרה] באהב' תקבל ברצון ותהי לרצון תמיד עבודת ישראל עמך, "and the fire-offerings of Israel and their prayer [speedily] in love accept with favor, and may the service of Your people Israel always be acceptable to You," was certainly already included in the most ancient version, for it cannot have been added after the cessation of sacrifices. The present text goes on as if there were no contradiction with a petition for the restoration of the sacrifices: והשב [את] העבודה לדביר ביתך, "and restore the Temple service to the inner court of Your house." This is a (Babylonian?) adaptation of the ancient version to the new circumstances. Nor is it the only one, for in *Midrash tehilim*, 64a (to Ps. 17:4), we read, "Therefore the pious men of old ordained that one should pray three services every day, and they ordained [the following prayer]: 'O Merciful One, in Your great mercy restore Your presence to Zion and order of the Temple Service to Jerusalem.'" This version has been preserved in actual use; in Ashkenaz it occurs in the Additional Service of all the festivals, alongside "Accept," when the priests perform their blessing (Baer, ʿAvodat, 358), and in *Vitry* it is used even in the weekday prayers.

As in Palestine, the current versions begin with רצה, "Accept," but the object בעמך ישראל, "Your people, Israel," is added. Rome, Romaniot, and Sepharad have, instead of the following word, ובתפלתם, "and their prayer," as in Amram, Saadia, and Ashkenaz, the words ולתפלתם שעה, "and accept their prayer."[41] The concluding sentence of petition, "Dwell in Zion," resembling Benediction 14, has been inserted: ותחזינה עינינו בשובך [תימן: לנוך] לציון [רומה: ולירושלים עירך] ברחמים [רומה: כמאז; רומניה :וכשנים קדמוניות], "May our eyes behold Your return [Yemen: to Your home] to Zion [Rome: to Jerusalem Your city] in mercy [Rome: as of old; Romaniot: as in ancient years]." The brackets show how many additions have occurred here. Before "may our eyes behold,"[42] there is a further addition in *Vitry*, Sepharad, and Provence, in the petition ואתה ברחמיך הרבים תחפץ בנו ותרצנו, "And You in Your great mercy be pleased with us and accept us," an expansion of Saadia's ותרצה בנו כמו אז, "and accept us as of old." In *Oṣar tov*, Romaniot, and Yemen, further expansions are found in nearly every sentence. With all of the forms that we have cited we have still not exhausted the variety of versions. Maimonides was asked if it is permitted to say, as recommended by a certain sage, בהר מרום ישראל שם נעבדך ושם נדרוש את כל אשר צויתנו כריח ניחוח תרצה אותנו ותחזינה, "In the mountain of the height of Israel, there we will serve You and there we will seek out everything that You commanded us; You will accept us like fragrant incense, and our eyes will behold, etc.,'' and he ruled that this version is permitted.[43] Such flexibility still prevailed at the end of the twelfth century, and it may be assumed that poetic embellishments of this kind, added *ad libitum*, were widespread.

R. Saadia Gaon ruled—and in this R. Sherira Gaon yielded, although in general he did not accept Saadia's deviations from the accepted text—that the first sentence of "Accept"[44] is to be recited only when the priests raise their hands in blessing (§ 9a); thus, it must have been omitted in the Afternoon and Evening services at all times except fast days. This was still the custom in Toledo[45] in the fourteenth century; that is, they began with "the fire-offerings of Israel." This opinion was based upon an interpretation of the word עבודה not accepted elsewhere; in Provence and northern France they began already around the year 1200 to begin with the word *accept* at all times, and around 1500 Joseph Caro knew only this custom;[46] since then it has prevailed everywhere.

In Palestine the eulogy, in accordance with Y. *Yoma* 7:1, 44b and Y. *Sota* 7:6, 22a, is שאותך ביראה נעבוד, "Whom we worship in awe"; similarly in Rome on fast days, when the *qerovot* of Kallir are recited (§32), and in Ashkenaz in the Additional Service of festivals, when the blessing of the priests is said: שאותך לבדך ביראה נעבוד, "Whom alone we worship in awe." In the current version the eulogy reads, המחזיר שכינתו לציון, "Who restores His presence to Zion"; Rome adds ברחמיו, "in His mercy"; Romaniot has a version different from all the others: המשיב שכינתו, "Who restores His presence." The prayer books of the Reform movement have mostly reverted to the ancient version, "Whom alone we worship in awe"; likewise they changed the reference to the Messiah and eliminated the reference to the bringing of sacrifices, as they did in Benediction 14.[47]

Before "and may our eyes behold"—that is, after the former conclusion of the benediction—"Ascend and Come" is added on New Moons and the intermediate days of festivals; this text is called קדושת היום, "The Sanctification of the Day," in the sources (T. *Ber.* 3:10), or מעין המאורע, "Reference to the Occasion" (B. *Shab.* 24a). The opening words are first mentioned in *Soferim* 9:7, 11; with the exception of the Palestinian rite, in which the lists are more detailed, all texts known today are identical but for minor variants. This fact suggests that the prayer is ancient, though its style points rather to the beginning of the period of piyyut. It is worth mentioning a statement of R. Paltoy Gaon (ca. 850),[48] according to which the original location of the "Ascend and Come" was in the Remembrance verses of the Additional Service of the New Year (§24); this would explain the frequent repetition of the words זכרון and פקדון, "memory" and "remembrance."

Benediction 18: תודה, הודייה, הודיה, הודאה, "Thanksgiving" (M. *R.H.* 1:5; *Ber.* 2:4; B. *Meg.* 17b, respectively), contains thanksgiving for the kindness that God bestows upon humanity at all times. This benediction, also very ancient, has undergone a great many changes and additions in the course of time.[49] Its opening, מודים אנחנו לך, "We give thanks to you," is found in *Sifre* Deut., 142b, §333; *Midrash tannaim*, 209 quotes instead, ועתה א' מודים אנחנו לך, "And now O Lord, we give thanks to You." A short and simple version is found in Palestine; its concluding reference to Ps. 94:18 should be noted. A similar version, attached to the piyyutim of Kallir, is quoted by Luzzatto from Rome.[50] Saadia and Romaniot also have short texts. Additions to it were apparently

[45]

in use already in ancient times. The Mishnah cites two, which it rejects; their meaning and purpose are no longer clear to us, apparently because they are connected with gnostic beliefs. They are the repetition of the word מודים, "We give thanks," at the beginning; the sentences על קן צפור יגיעו רחמיך ועל טוב יזכר שמך, "Your mercy extends to the nests of the birds, and may Your name be mentioned for good"; and יברכוך טובים, "The good will bless You," which apparently were placed at the end. But, even after the year 300, despite the prohibition, occasional precentors permitted themselves to insert similar sentences (B. *Ber.* 33b). The expanded current text, the nucleus of which is already found in Amram, is identical in Ashkenaz, Rome, and Sepharad. It is made up of biblical phrases, so that understandably it kept continually growing. Amram, Romaniot, and Rome conclude, ולא הכלמתנו ה' אלהינו לא עזבתנו ולא הסתרת פניך ממנו, "And You have not put us to shame, O Lord, Our God; You have not abandoned us; You have not hidden Your face from us," words that are lacking in Sepharad and Ashkenaz.

The current text adds two further short sections, ועל כלם, "And for all of them," and וכל החיים, "And all the living" (Saadia has only the former), which summarize the contents of Thanksgiving, and which should be seen as its doublets. (They may have been introduced because of the additions that were inserted in the middle; see below.) The later texts of Ashkenaz and Sepharad have further additions: האל ישועתנו, "God, our salvation"; Sepharad, האל הטוב, "the good God"; Romaniot, חי עולמים ונודה לך, "You live forever, and we give thanks to You"; Saadia, כי יחיד אתה ואין בלתך, "For You are unique, and there is none except You." [Saadia, *Siddur*, 19 actually reads ואין זולתך.] The eulogy in Palestine is, following Y. *Yoma* 7:1, 44b, הטוב לך להודות, "You to Whom it is good to give thanks"; the current texts have הטוב שמך וכו', "You Whose name is good," which is found for the first time in *Midrash tehilim*, 29d.

On Hanukkah and Purim, a special prayer of gratitude, a "Reference to the Occasion," is added in accordance with T. *Ber.* 3:10. A short version of this prayer of thanksgiving is found in *Soferim*, 20:8, וכניסי פלאות ותשועות כהניך שעשית . . . כן עשה עמנו, "And like the wondrous miracles and the acts of salvation of Your priests which You performed . . . so do for us," which fits very well into the Palestinian version of Thanksgiving.[51] The current texts are composed of two sentences, one an introduction applicable to both festivals, על הנסים, "For the miracles" ("for" goes back to "We give thanks"), and one recounting the story of the holiday: בימי מתתיהו, "In the days of Mattathias," and בימי מרדכי, "In the days of Mordecai." Since Amram the texts have been identical except for minor and unavoidable variants. It is worth mentioning that Abudarham reads,[52] in opposition to all other texts, על הנחמות, "For the consolations," instead of המלחמות, "the wars." Numerous variants are found in place of להשכיחם (לשכחם) [מ]תורתך, "to make them forget your Torah"; compare Abudarham and *Rivista Israelita* 5 (1908): 125. At the end Amram, followed by Rome and Sepharad, reads, כשם שעשית עמהם כן עשה עמנו פלא ונסים וגו', "Just as You did for them, so do for us wonders and miracles . . . ," a vestige of the version of *Soferim* mentioned above. Already Hai Gaon and the Tosafists objected to this sentence, for this is not the right place for petitions;[53] in Romaniot and Ashkenaz it is lacking. Probably after the long interruption of "For the miracles" it was felt necessary to get back to the theme of "We give thanks" through the words "and for all of them," and that is how this sentence entered the prayer.

On the Ten Days of Repentance, since the time of the geonim, the petition וכתוב לחיים טובים כל בני בריתך, "And write for a good life all the children of Your covenant,"[54] has been inserted in Ashkenaz before "And all the living," and in the other rites, as well as Amram, after the first occurrence of the word *sela* in it. Romaniot has yet another petition, which is longer and perhaps later—זכר רחמיך, "Remember Your mercy." This occurs in *Vitry* only on the New Year and the Day of Atonement. From here it also entered Ashkenaz, but only in the repetition of the 'Amida on the Day of Atonement and in the Additional Service of the New Year.

[46]

In the amoraic period, the custom (originating in Babylonia?) was that when the precentor said, "We give thanks" in the repetition of the 'Amida, the congregation would also say, "We give thanks." The opening is by Rav, in whose name several short sentences for this purpose are reported in B. *Soṭa* 40a and Y. *Ber.* 1:5, 3d; other sages recommended other sentences, and eventually the custom arose of saying them all. The text in Baer comes from B. *Soṭa* 40a (compare Amram 11b); the passage is known as מודים דרבנן, "*Modim* of the Sages,"[55] apparently for the amoraim who combined the various statements.

The Priestly Benediction: When the 'Amida is repeated, the priests lift their hands in blessing at this point. (Compare §9b.)

Benediction 19: ברכת כהנים, "The Benediction of the Priests." The same name is used for the final benediction because it follows directly upon the words of the Priestly Benediction (M. *R.H.* 4:5; *Tam.* 5:1). With the words שים שלום, "Grant Peace" (the benediction's name in B. *Meg.* 18:1), it echoes the concluding words of the priests; it ends with the eulogy עושה השלום, "Who makes peace" (*Lev. R.*, §9, end; *Midrash tehilim*, 29b). A short form is found in Palestine. The present version includes expansions, the texts of which have been identical since Amram save for minor variations. Peculiar to Ashkenaz is the short version, שלום רב, "Great peace,"[56] said only when the Priestly Benediction does not precede this benediction. The first to mention it is Eliakim of Speyer (eleventh century); it is not yet found in *Vitry*, but later R. Meir of Rothenburg reintroduced it into the rite, and it spread to all of Germany. It is also said in the Afternoon Service in Yemen. [There is no evidence for this in the prayer books or among members of the community.] The current eulogy is המברך את עמו ישראל בשלום, "Who blesses His people Israel with peace," though Amram 18a has "Who makes peace" for the Afternoon Service.[57] This ancient eulogy is found in Ashkenaz only on the Ten Days of Repentance, together with the addition בספר חיים, "In the Book of Life"; it has vanished completely from the other rites. In the text of "In the Book of Life," Rome, Romaniot, and Sepharad are slightly expanded compared with Ashkenaz, but the addition itself is a late one.

After the conclusion of the 'Amida, "amen" is said in the Roman and Sephardic rites, as a sign that it is over.

(6)   The prayer of the precentor ends here, but several additions were made for the individual worshiper over the course of time. Just as R. Yoḥanan recommended that a biblical verse open the 'Amida, so he recommended one for its conclusion: "May the words of my mouth" (Ps. 19:15). But before this verse comes the prayer that Mar b. Ravina used to say when he concluded his 'Amida: אלהי נצור, "My God, protect" (B. *Ber.* 17a, with one sentence omitted); after this comes in Ashkenaz and Sepharad (but

not yet in Abudarham) . . . עשה למען שמך, "act for the sake of Your name . . . ."[58] This section, with its payyetanic style, is simply an abridgement of a longer petition, מלכנו אלהינו יחד שמך בעולמך, "Our King, our God, make Your name One in Your world," which is found in Amram, Saadia, [not in the current version of Saadia, *Siddur*, 19;] *REJ* 53 (1907); *Vitry*; *Manhig*, "Laws of Prayer," §63); *Tur*, *O.H.*, §122, but has again vanished from the printed prayer books. Since this addition was not considered to be an obligatory prayer, it was treated with great freedom; thus, we find other additions in Amram, like the private prayer of Rava, B. *Ber*. 17a: אלהי עד שלא נוצרתי, "My God, before I was created," and ופתח לי שערי בינה, "and open for me gates of understanding." Rome skips this last prayer, together with "My God, protect." Abudarham lists only the talmudic "My God, protect," and as the minority practice at that; in Romaniot the entire addition is lacking except for "May the words of my mouth." After Ps. 19:15 we find already in *Vitry*, and then in Ashkenaz and Sepharad, עושה שלום במרומיו הוא יעשה שלום עלינו ועל כל ישראל, "May He Who makes peace in His high places make peace for us and for all Israel" (based on Job 25:2). Rome has both of these before "My God, protect," from which we learn that the latter is a later addition.

In general, much freedom was allowed for individual prayer at this point, and generous space was allotted for expansions as long as their content was appropriate to that of the benediction (B. ʿA.Z. 8a).

(7) In an emergency it was also permitted to abridge the ʿAmida—that is, to recite מעין שמונה עשרה, "the short form of the ʿAmida." Such an abridgement is הבינו, "Give us understanding," by Mar Samuel, who reduced the thirteen middle benedictions to a single one with the eulogy שומע תפלה, "Who hears prayer"; this benediction was placed between the first three and the last three. The text is given in Y. *Ber*. 4:3, 8a and B. *Ber*. 29a in two different versions. The Babylonian text prevailed with negligible variations. Among medieval authors the texts differ in details; see, for example, *Halakhot gedolot*, 30, and *Eshkol*, 1:59. But even in public worship these abridged forms were in use. The beginning of such an abridgement in the form that the Talmud calls י"ח מעין י"ח, "Eighteen, the Gist of Eighteen" (Y. *Ber*., ibid.), composed in the geonic period (in the eighth century at the earliest), is found in *Eshkol*, 1:55, while the complete prayer is preserved in one geniza manuscript in Cambridge. This piece shows that poetic reworkings of the ʿAmida were in use that did not follow the language of the prayer, but preserved only the contents and the eulogies of the various benedictions. Especially in Palestine, the homeland of liturgical poetry, such poetically embellished texts were favored; many compositions of this type were preserved and used in the synagogue.

§ 9a *The Kedushah*

(1) When the precentor repeats the ʿAmida in the Morning, Afternoon, and Additional services, the Kedushah, "Sanctification," is inserted in the third benediction, "The Sanctification of the Name."[1] Its name comes from Is. 6:3, the 'trishagion', which has special status in the ancient Christian liturgy as well.[2] Alongside this verse,

[47]

the Kedushah is also composed of the verses, "Blessed is the Glory" (Ezek. 3:12) and "May God reign" (Ps. 146:10), while the Kedushah of the Additional Service [in most communities, but not Yemen or Maimonides] contains also "Hear, O Israel" (Deut. 6:4) and "I am the Lord, your God" (Num. 15:41). This Kedushah, which is inserted into the ʿAmida, is called קדוש של עמידה, " 'Holy' of the ʿAmida" (*Soferim* 16:12, end). Besides it, there are two other Kedushahs in the prayer service: one in the benediction "Creator," which has only the verses from Isaiah and Ezekiel (see p. 18), and the קדושה דסדרא, " 'Sanctification' of the Lesson" (B. *Sota* 49a; see §10), which has besides these two verses Ex. 15:18 and the Targum of all three.

[48]

The Kedushah of "Creator" and of the ʿAmida have a connecting text between the verses from Isaiah and Ezekiel, and the Kedushah of the ʿAmida has a special introduction.[3] Both represent the biblical verses as an antiphonal song sung by the angelic choirs. The Kedushah of the Lesson juxtaposes the verses without a connecting link. Only it is mentioned in the Talmud by name, while the names of the other Kedushahs come only from the post-talmudic Tractate *Soferim*. Later, in Amram, we find the texts in the versions known today.

(2)   The origin of the Kedushah is most obscure;[4] the ancient sources leave us in the lurch. The oldest relevant report is found in T. *Ber.* 1:9: "One does not respond to someone who recites a benediction; R. Judah used to respond to one who recited a benediction, 'Holy, holy, holy is the Lord of Hosts. . . . ,' and 'Blessed is the glory in His place'; all this would R. Judah respond to one who recited a benediction." What kind of precentor is meant here, and why is he called "One who recites a benediction"[5]—a term found nowhere else? Where did he recite these biblical verses? Did the other sages agree with R. Judah's practice, or did they oppose it? This meager source does not answer any of these questions. Likewise, when R. Joshua b. Levi (ca. 230) speaks about the Kedushah[6] of the precentor (B. *Ber.* 21a: "until the precentor reaches the Kedushah"), it cannot be determined whether he is referring to the third benediction of the ʿAmida as it is, or to an addition to it. We learn no more from the passage in Y. *Ber.* 5:3, 9c, end:

> Batyty became silent at the "wheels" (אופנייה). They went and asked R. Abun (what to do). R. Abun said to them:[7] "The one who passes before the Ark to replace him should begin from the point where he stopped."[8] They said to him: "But have we not learned in the Mishnah, 'from the beginning of the benediction where the error occurred'?" He said to them: "Since you have responded with the Kedushah, it is equivalent to the beginning of a benediction."

Here, too, the prayer under discussion is not named explicitly. But we may infer that in R. Abun's time (before 354), the connecting text already existed, and that it contained a reference to the choirs of angels called אופנים (literally *wheels*; see Ezek. 1:19, etc.). Such a text is found in the traditional prayer book in every Kedushah of "Creator," while in the Kedushah of the ʿAmida one like it is found, though only on special occasions. From this it has been concluded that the Kedushah of *Yoser*, which is a representation of the daily morning song of the Hosts of Heaven, preceded the Kedushah of the ʿAmida in time, and that the latter developed from the former.

But this conclusion is erroneous, for the language of the Talmud, "the one who passes before the Ark to replace him," and the entire context make it impossible to presuppose any other prayer but the ʿAmida. Furthermore, according to the reliable collection *Ḥiluf minhagim* (*Variant Customs between the Babylonians and the Palestinians*), the Kedushah was customary in Palestine only on the Sabbath, while in Babylonia it was recited every day (*Ḥiluf minhagim*, §59);[9] it appears that even around the year 800 this was not customary in Palestine in any place where immigrants from Babylonia did not constitute a majority.[10] It is entirely possible that the Kedushah should have been dropped from the weekday ʿAmida, where it simply was an addition, but we cannot explain at all how it could have been dropped from "Creator" if it was an important part of the structure of the Morning Service. We have no direct evidence that the Kedushah was originally connected to "Creator," but the third benediction of the ʿAmida provides an excellent foothold for it, both by its name and content.

[49]

(3)   The most ancient form of this benediction was קדוש אתה ונורא שמך, "Holy are You and awesome is Your name," and it is very likely that Is. 6:3 was cited as a biblical prooftext: "As it is written, 'Holy, holy, holy is the Lord of Hosts' "; given the predilection for the language of Scripture in the ancient ʿAmida, the possibility may not be excluded that this verse constituted the entire text of the benediction. The original context of this verse refers explicitly to the angels' song of praise in heaven; from verses such as Enoch 39:12 and Revelation 4:8 we learn that the mystically inclined knew how to exploit this allusion. Similar in content is Ezek. 3:12, for the "sound of great quaking" that reaches the prophet's ears from the fluttering wings of the angels also concludes with a hymn; furthermore, both passages alike refer to the "glory" of God. All of this gave rise to the idea of joining the two passages and forming them into the lively picture of the antiphonal song of the angelic choirs. The cherubim of Isaiah and the wheels and the sacred beasts of Ezekiel who intone the hymn are brought together in the Kedushah to sing praise to the Lord. These are the ideas that provided the early mystics and the medieval kabbalists rich material with which to work—hence, the many and varied openings and connecting sentences that arose over the course of time.

Only the two verses from Isaiah and Ezekiel belong to the original Kedushah. The verse "May God reign" in the Kedushah of the ʿAmida is always connected very loosely to the preceding verses as a prooftext from the Hagiographa, sufficient evidence that it is a late addition. And why was this verse exchanged in the Kedushah of the Lesson for Ex. 15:18? Because in this Kedushah an Aramaic translation was also needed, but no authorized translation of the Hagiographa existed; therefore, it was necessary to choose a verse of similar content from a book for which an Aramaic translation existed. It is impossible to say exactly why "May God reign" entered the Kedushah; it may have been transferred from the ʿAmida of the New Year; or perhaps the intention was to express here, as in many other prayers, the idea of the kingdom of heaven. On the other hand, we know more about the manner in which "Hear O Israel" entered the Kedushah.[11] During the religious persecutions in the Byzantine Empire, various Jewish prayers were prohibited, among them the declaration of God's unity, and also "Holy, holy, holy," which for the church was a prooftext for the doctrine of the Trinity. The synagogues, which on weekdays were probably completely locked, were guarded on the Sabbath until the time for reciting the proscribed prayers had passed. Therefore, as a temporary measure, the Kedushah was inserted into the Additional Service, with the beginning and the end of the *Shema*ᶜ, "Hear O Israel . . . to be your God; I am the Lord your God," worked into it. Even after persecution subsided and religious freedom was restored, the addition to the Kedushah of the Additional Service on Sabbaths and festivals was left in its place. It is possible that the adoption of "Hear O Israel" was the occasion for the introduction of "May God reign"; for once verses from the prophets and the Torah had acquired a place in the Kedushah, it was only fitting that the Hagiographa also be represented. The first evidence for the presence of "Hear O Israel" in the Kedushah is *Pirqe derabi eli*ᶜ*ezer*, chapter 4, end, but "May God reign" is not mentioned there.

(4)   The text of the Kedushah in the narrow sense of the word—that is, the biblical verses—was preserved by the Masora from alteration; variants arose in the connecting texts and in the introductions of the Kedushah of the ᶜAmida.[12] The following are the variants.

[50]

a. Introductions

These are intended to introduce the Kedushah recited in the congregation as an imitation of the praise of God by the angels.

1.   The most ancient introduction known to us is נעריצך ונקדישך, "We shall declare your awesomeness and holiness" (*Soferim* 16:12). In Ashkenaz it is used in the Additional Service. With the order of the words reversed we find it in Sepharad and, since the sixteenth century, in Rome, in all services except the Additional Service; in Romaniot, we find it on weekdays. The verse Is. 29:23 provides strong support for this latter word order. The version of Maimonides, נקדישך ונמליכך, "We shall declare Your holiness and kingship"[13] [Goldschmidt ed., 199: נקדישך ונעריצך] differs from all others. All the rites except Ashkenaz mention in one form or another the three-part form of the Kedushah (שלוש קדושה); the manner in which the reference is made to the praise of the angels varies in the different texts. It should be mentioned that in one Kedushah, a variant for the Morning Service of Passover in Romaniot, the verses Is. 6:1–2 are also attached to the introduction.

2.   A similar introduction is נקדש, "Let us sanctify," which is used in Ashkenaz for all services except for the Additional Service, and in Romaniot for the Morning Service of Sabbaths and festivals. This is the simplest form of the Kedushah; it does not mention even the angels explicitly. No trace of it is found in the ancient sources.

3.   כתר, "A crown,"[14] in Amram for all services without exception, is found in the other rites in the ᶜAmidot of the Additional Service. Ashkenaz does not know it, though the ancient French rite used it in the Additional Service. *Vitry* calls it *Kedushah Rabba*. Rome originally had it daily, like Amram, until, under the influence of the Kabbalah, it was exchanged for "We shall declare Your holiness." It may be that the source of "A crown" is the circles of mystics in Babylonia; in any case, both the idea and the vocabulary were familiar to them.

b. Connecting Sentences

These serve as a transition from verse to verse.

1. Between *Holy* and *Blessed*:

a. The shortest version has only the words, לעומתם ברוך יאמרו, "Those standing opposite them say, 'Blessed' "; in Rome this is used in all services except for the Additional Service, and in Ashkenaz it or לעומתם משבחים ואומרים, "Those standing opposite them praise and say," is in use on weekdays. This last is customary in Romaniot and Sepharad at all times except for the Additional Service. This transition does not make clear what the words *those opposite them* refer to, and thus it seems to be merely an abridged form of the following version.

b. אז בקול רעש גדול, "Then with the sound of great quaking,"[15] assigned for daily use by Amram, and for the Morning Service of Sabbaths and festivals by Ashkenaz (already in *Vitry*). The content is in every way similar to "the wheels and the holy beasts" of the Kedushah of "Creator." Since the Talmud already mentions the wheels in connection with the Kedushah, it may be surmised that this connection, or at least the idea behind it, is very ancient.

c. כבודו (וגדלו) מלא עולם, "His glory (and His greatness) fill the world": in all rites in the *'Amida* of the Additional Service; in Maimonides and Yemen every day, and in Germany in all the services of the Day of Atonement, since the fifteenth century. Its source is unknown. Its form is payyetanic, since the sentence begins with the concluding word of the verse, "His glory" [in the manner of the payyetanic device of שרשור, "linking"].

2. Between *Blessed* and *Hear* in the Additional Service of Sabbaths and festivals. The simplest version is in Romaniot: פעמים בכל יום אומרים, "Twice each day they say,"[16] according to the ancient sources, to be concluded with באהבה, "with love." But even Romaniot has the expanded text, the beginning of which is linked to the last word, "from His place," of the biblical verse. It is essentially the same version as in Rome, Sepharad and Ashkenaz, though all of these have slight expansions.

[51]

3. Between *Hear* and *to be your God*, Romaniot has no connecting sentences, and if in fact these verses served the purpose mentioned above, they must originally have been recited without interruption. But later, when the reason for the adoption of the *Shema'* in the Kedushah was forgotten, they too were connected with lines of piyyut, אחד הוא אלהינו, "One is our God," which are also linked to the last word of the verse, and which stylistically appear relatively late. The versions of Rome and Ashkenaz are identical; in Sepharad another addition is found toward the end, containing a petition for redemption—הן גאלתי אתכם אחרית כראשית, "Behold, I have redeemed you at the end as at the beginning"—which entered here through total misunderstanding of the original significance of the words.

4. To אני ה' אלהיכם, "I am the Lord, Your God," Ashkenaz attaches on festivals אדיר אדירנו, "O mighty One, our mighty One," which strongly emphasizes the kingdom of heaven; the other rites do not know it. It is, thus, Ashkenazic in origin and its wording appears to be influenced by a piyyut of R. Meshulam b. Kalonymus (d. Mainz, ca. 1000). Originally, it was customary to recite it only on the Days of Awe,[17] but since 1100 it began to be transferred also to the festivals. Rome has, in turn, a petition on festivals, אלהיכם אל עליון, "Your God, the highest," which apparently is connected with the same idea; its language and rhymes attest that it is relatively late.

5. Before "May God reign," we find in most texts the same formula, וּבְדִבְרֵי קָדְשְׁךָ, "And in Your holy writings it is written as follows," which is merely a citation reference with no inner relationship to the Kedushah. But Amram, Maimonides and Yemen have in the daily service, and Ashkenaz has in the Sabbath and festival Morning Service, מִמְּקוֹמְךָ מַלְכֵּנוּ תּוֹפִיעַ, "From Your place, O King, appear," instead of these neutral transitional words. This is a petition for the bringing of the messianic age, when God alone will rule. Once again the petition is attached to "from His place," the last word of the verse, and the citation reference ("as it is written") comes at the end.

The external form, the train of thought, and the wording of most versions of the Kedushah justify the assumption that they were composed close to the time of the closing of the Babylonian Talmud.[18] The few exceptions have been noted above. The variety of forms can apparently be explained by the fact that different archetypes came from Palestine and Babylonia. The texts changed only in minor details with the changing of times and places. In the modern Reform prayer books the references to angels have been mostly eliminated, and the connecting texts have been provided with a number of poetic reworkings in German and English.[19]

(5)   The Kedushah of "Creator" appears to be considerably later than that of the *'Amida*; it seems to be the creation of the mystics in the geonic period.[20] It is a foreign body in "Creator"; the ancient text (above, §7:3) does not contain it, and even in the present texts it is evident that the topic of the angels and their praise has been introduced by force. From the vestiges of mystical literature we know what great importance the mystics attached to the recitation of the Kedushah, and there is firm reason to assume that it was they who caused its introduction into "Creator." But this could not have occurred later than the composition of *Soferim*, in which the Kedushah of "Creator" is mentioned several times. Perhaps by accepting the Kedushah into "Creator" the mystics hoped to give those who did not worship with the congregation the opportunity to recite the verses of the Kedushah. The various substitutes for the Kedushah in Amram do not belong to the original text; but they all originate in the mystical literature, and they express clearly the goals of these circles. The Kedushah of "Creator" has been provided with an introduction describing the ministering angels. The connecting words between the two verses, *Holy* and *Blessed*, are "And the wheels and the sacred beasts," which are common to all the rites; in Ashkenaz they are replaced with "And the beasts sing," when accompanied by piyyut.

[The origins of the Kedushah and the stages of its development are still a thorny problem which has been treated by many scholars, including: Louis Finkelstein, "La Kedouscha et les bénédictions du schema," *REJ* 93 (1932): 1–26; Adolf Baumstark, *Comparative Liturgy* (London: A.R. Mowbray, 1958), 49ff.; Eric Werner, "The Doxology in Synagogue and Church: A Liturgico-Musical Study," *HUCA* 19 (1945–46): 293ff.; E. Werner, *The Sacred Bridge: The Interdependence of Liturgy and Music in Synagogue and Church During the First Millennium*, vol. 1 (London: D. Dobson, 1959), 308 and n. 68; Sh. A. Altmann, "Shire qedusha besifrut hahekhalot haqeduma," *Melila* 2 (1945/6): 1–24; Heinemann, *Prayer*, 145ff.

Opinions are still divided as to the antiquity of the Kedushah, whether it originated in Babylonia or Palestine, and especially whether both Kedushahs—of "Creator" and of the *'Amida*—are ancient and whether they come from the same time and place. In light of the above Yerushalmi passage, which refers unambiguously to the Kedushah of the *'Amida*, there can be no doubt that this Kedushah was customary in Palestine in the amoraic period, and perhaps even earlier (if the words of R. Judah in the above Tosefta also refer to this Kedushah), and therefore very likely was composed there. However, this does not prove that the Kedushah of "Creator" did not also exist in the same period, for there is no reason to assume that only one of the Kedushahs and not the other was known then. And because the Kedushah of "Creator" is also reflected in early Christian sources, it seems likely that it was in use in Palestine in the first centuries of the common era. A source of decisive importance in this respect is the *Apostolic Constitutions* 8:12, where the Kedushah of the angels ("Holy, holy, holy," together with "Blessed art Thou forever") is inserted in a lengthy prayer, the main subject of which is the description of the act of creation. This union of the Kedushah of the angels with praise for the creation of the world points clearly to the Kedushah of "Creator" as the prayer's Jewish source. (On the other hand, the Kedushah found in the *Apostolic Constitutions* 7:35 is clearly based on that of the *'Amida*, *pace* Altmann in his above-mentioned article, 5ff.; compare also K. Kohler, *HUCA* 1 [1924]: 410ff., and the translation of this Kedushah given there.) Several of the above-mentioned scholars even raise reasonable arguments to show that the inclusion of the Kedushah in "Creator" is even earlier, and that it actually originated in the Temple.

In light of the latest studies of G. Scholem (*Jewish Gnosticism, Merkabah Mysticism and Talmudic Tradition* [New York: The Jewish Theological Seminary of America, 1960]; see also the Hebrew appendix by S. Lieberman in Scholem, and the above-mentioned article by Altmann), the relationship of the Kedushah to the circles of Merkava mystics and to the *hekhalot* literature is clear; from these studies we learn also that these doctrines have ancient roots in the thinking of the amoraim, and perhaps even in that of the tannaim. Astonishing, therefore, would seem the fact established by I. Elbogen (*Studien*, 21ff.), J. Mann (*HUCA* 2 [1925]: 289ff.), and others (such as M. Zulay, *Qoves 'al yad* 3 [1887]: 11), that the Kedushah of "Creator" is not mentioned in the geniza texts or in the ancient Palestinian piyyut. However, besides the reference to the Kedushah of "Creator" in *Soferim*, which in any case reflects essentially one of the rites in use in Palestine at the beginning of the geonic period, a number of liturgical poems for "Creator" have been published that refer to the Kedushah or that contain it explicitly—for example, the "Creator" for the New Year attributed to Kallir, printed in Luzzatto, *Mavo*, 1:33a, and in the Romaniot prayer book; the "Creator" for the New Year by Haduta, published by M. Zulay in *SRIHP* 5 (1938/9): 119; Haduta's "Creator" for *Sukkot* published in *Tarbiz* 22 (1952/3): 32ff.; the "Creator" of Yosef b. R. Nissan, *Tarbiz* 22 (1952/3): 163ff.; and others.

[53]

Furthermore, among the as yet unpublished geniza fragments, a number include the Kedushah of "Creator" or allude to it—for example, T.-S. 8 H9/4, 8H 11/13, 8H 10/12, 8 H10/7, 10 H2 [the foregoing are manuscript numbers—*Engl. trans.*], all in Cambridge. Even if it can be argued that among these fragments are some belonging to prayer books of the Babylonian rite (or a version close to it), still at least some of them must represent the ancient Palestinian version, especially 8 H21/1, in which a Kedushah in a poetic version has been inserted, the Palestinian origin of which cannot be doubted.

Particularly important for our purposes is fragment 8 H/7, which contains at the beginning a "Creator" for the New Year with the following wording:

ברוך אתה ה' אלהינו מלך העולם יוצר אור ובורא חשך עושה

שלום ובורא את הכל אור עולם אוצר חיים אורות מאופל אמר ויהי
יתברך מלך מלכי המלכים
הנערץ והנקדש בצבאות מלאכים
לו מרוממים וממליכים
למלך וקדוש וכולם עומדים וגו׳
מקבלים ואומרים ק׳ק׳ וגו׳
כבודו מלא עולם ומשרתיו שואלים אי זה מקום כבודו לעומתם
משבחים ואומרים
ברוך כבוד ה׳ ממקומו
ונ׳ קומי אורי כי בא אורך וכבוד ה׳ עליך זרח
ברוך אתה ה׳ יוצר המא[ורות]

"Blessed are You, Lord our God, King of the universe, Creator of light, Creator of darkness, Who makes peace and creates everything. Eternal Light/ The treasury of life/ Light out of darkness/ He spoke, and it was./ Praised be the King of kings,/ The dreaded and Holy One among the hosts of angels./ He is exalted and acclaimed as King,/ the King and Holy One. And all stand, etc./ They accept and say, 'Holy, holy, holy etc. . . . /His glory fills the world. His ministering angels ask each other: 'Where is the place of His glory?' Those standing opposite them praise and say: /'Blessed is the glory of God from His place.' And it is said: 'Arise and shine, for your light has come, and the glory of the Lord has shone upon you./ Blessed are You, Lord, Creator of the lumin(aries).' "

There cannot be any doubt that this fragment reflects essentially the Palestinian version; this follows clearly from the eulogies of the other benedictions that follow: "Who loves Israel," and "Rock of Israel."

It seems likely, however, that the Kedushah of "Creator" was recited in Palestine only on Sabbaths and festivals, but not on New Moons, Hanukkah, Purim, or the intermediate days of festivals. The practice does not seem to have been uniform; there were even places where the Kedushah of "Creator" was not recited at all. On the other hand, the Kedushah of the ʿAmida was in use in Palestine on Sabbaths, festivals, New Moons, and Hanukkah and even on the intermediate days of festivals—compare *Masekhet Soferim*, ed. Michael Higger (New York: Deve rabanan, 1937), 20:5—but only in the Morning Service, as proved by the many *qerovot* of the Palestinian liturgical poets known today. At the same time, the Kedushah seems to have been recited in the Additional services of the New Year and doubtless in the Additional, Afternoon, and Closing services of Yom Kippur.

I wish to express my gratitude to Dr. Ezra Fleischer, who called my attention to these geniza sources; see his detailed article, "On the Dissemination of the Kedushahs of the ʿAmida and 'Creator' in the Palestinian Prayer Rites" (Hebrew), *Tarbiz* 38 (1958/9): 255ff.

Thus, there can be no doubt that the two Kedushahs were known in Palestine and were used there in the prayers of certain days in most places. And even though we find that the Kedushah was more widely used in geonic Babylonia, for the custom there was to say both Kedushahs even in the daily prayers, this does not obviate the conclusion that the birthplace of the Kedushah was in Palestine, and in a rather early period. This is not the only case in which a prayer composed in Palestine failed to become the majority custom there, but did in Babylonia. The Plant of David is a perfect example!]

[54]

(6)   As for the origin of the Kedushah of the lesson, see §10. It is older than the

Kedushah of "Creator," and it, too, seems to be of Babylonian origin. [But compare below.] When the *Targum sheni* to Esth. 5:1 says that Israel recites "Holy, Holy, Holy" before God "three times each day," it appears that the author is thinking of this Kedushah and the Kedushah in the repetition of the ʿAmida in the Morning and Afternoon services. On the other hand, the late collection, *Midrash hagadol*, mentions thirty Kedushahs in a week—that is, four on every one of the six weekdays and six more on the Sabbath: three in the ʿAmida, one in "Creator," and two in the Kedushah of the Lesson of the Afternoon Service and the service on the conclusion of the Sabbath.

§ 9b *The Priestly Blessing*

(1)   The Priestly Blessing (ברכת כהנים) is a vestige of the Temple cult; it was part of the daily sacrifice. Every morning and afternoon before the bringing of the whole-offering the priests would pronounce over the people the blessing in Num. 6:24–26. At the appropriate moment the priests would ascend the steps of the porch from which they used to address the people, and would pronounce the blessing. The Tosefta (*Soṭa* 7:7) explains the reference in the Mishnah (*Soṭa* 7:1) to the Priestly Blessing as follows: "The Priestly Blessing is that which the priests recite on the steps of the portico."[1] In amoraic times, the place where the priests stood was called דוכן (*dukhan*), a word that in the Mishnah ordinarily has a different meaning; thus, this function of the priests came to be called "to ascend to the *dukhan*"[2] (for example, B. *Shab.* 118a). The word has been preserved in Yiddish to this day in the form *dukhenen* for the Priestly Blessing.

While performing the Blessing the priests would lift up their hands as Aaron had done at the dedication of the Tent of Meeting (Lev. 9:22). The expression נשא את ידיו, "He lifted his hands," is still in use in the Hebrew Ben Sira (50:20), but in tannaitic literature it is replaced by נשא את כפיו, "He lifted his palms"—hence, the noun נשיאות כפים, "the lifting of the hands," (*Sifre* Num., 11b, §39), which is the usage from then on in all halakhic literature. Finally, the Babylonian Talmud and Targum use the expression פרס ידיו (ידו), "he stretched out his hands" (for example, *Targum Yonatan* on Num. 6:23), because the priests spread their hands when they recite the Blessing. But alongside all these the simple biblical *blessed* taken from Num. 6:23 ("The priests blessed the people") still survived (compare M. *Soṭa* 7:6 and B. *Soṭa* 39a), and together with "the lifting of the hands,"[3] the expression *the Priestly Blessing* continues to occur.

(2)   Originally the Priestly Blessing, as mentioned, was part of the Temple service. According to the mishnaic tradition (*Ta.* 4:1), the Blessing was sometimes recited as many as four times a day: Besides the Morning and Afternoon services, it was also recited at noon during the Additional Service (called *noon* in T. *Ta.* 4[3]:1), and also toward evening at the time of the 'Locking of the Gates.' This occurred on the Day of Atonement, on public fast days, and during the services of the *Maʿamadot* (§34). This is our first encounter with the Priestly Blessing not connected with the offering of a sacrifice. Accordingly, already in the time of the Temple, this blessing was transferred to the synagogues outside the Temple (called מדינה or גבולין): "Just as there is the lifting of the hands in the Temple, so there is lifting of the hands in the province"

(T. *Soṭa* 7:8; compare *Sifre zuṭa*, 250).[4] But several distinctions were observed: In the Temple, the Priestly Blessing was recited in its entirety without interruption ("a single benediction"), while outside the Temple it was recited "as three blessings" (whence eventually derived the expression "the threefold blessing"), interrupted, apparently, by the congregational response "Amen." In the Temple the tetragrammaton was used, while outside the Temple it was not. In the Temple the priests would lift their hands to the level of their heads, while outside the Temple they would lift them only to the level of their shoulders (M. *Tam.* 7:2; M. *Soṭa* 7:6; *Sifre* and *Sifre zuṭa* to the verse). There is no doubt that in antiquity the priests would rise spontaneously to recite the Blessing when their turn came; it does not appear that the Blessing had an organic connection with the ʿAmida. Every priest, irrespective of age, was authorized to pronounce the Blessing, whether his course was in service at that time or not; the only exceptions to this rule were priests with physical deformities,[5] and even this rule was not absolute and without exception (B. *Meg.*, end).

(3)   With the Temple's destruction, the original site of the Priestly Blessing was eliminated and only the place to which it had been transferred—that is, the synagogue service—remained. Here, too, the descendants of Aaron were obligated to recite the Priestly Blessing (Y. *Ber.* 5:5–6, 9d):[6] It was incorporated into the ʿAmida. The point when this occurred cannot be established with certainty; the Mishnah already assumes that the Priestly Blessing is pronounced aloud during the recitation of the ʿAmida (*Ber.* 5:4). Regulations dating from that period also point to a change in the place of the Priestly Blessing; in the Temple such regulations were unnecessary, for their purpose was achieved through conditions that anyway obtained there. R. Yoḥanan b. Zakkai ruled that the priests should remove their shoes when they blessed the people (B. *Soṭa* 40a); R. Joshua b. Levi insisted on the washing of the hands before the blessing (B. *Soṭa*, 39a); R. Eleazar b. Shamua, his younger contemporary, also required a special blessing over the performance of the commandment (B. *Meg.* 29b). It must have been roughly at the same time that the practice was introduced of having the priests spread their fingers when reciting the blessing (compare *Targum Yerushalmi* on Num. 6:27), and that the congregation should stand facing them ("face to face"), and at times this was connected with strange conceptions about the magic activity inherent in the blessing (compare B. *Soṭa* 38b). R. Akiva prohibited looking at the priests when they blessed the people (compare B. *Ḥag.* 16a).[7] The priests did not begin on their own, but the precentor had to call out the blessing before them, and this custom has become so deeply rooted that it is regarded as a law of the Torah (*Sifre* Num., §39). Perhaps this was when the custom was introduced of having the precentor summon the priests to take their places before the congregation and recite the blessing;[8] in any case, this was the practice in amoraic times. The amoraim already made distinctions in the procedure according to whether one priest or several were present (B. *Soṭa* 38a; Y. *Ber.* 5:5–6, 9d). Besides the blessing on the commandment mentioned above, the text of which is first reported to us in the name of R. Hisda (B. *Soṭa* 39a), the Talmud also is aware of a silent petition of the priests when they leave their place [to go up to recite the Blessing—Engl. trans.], and another when they conclude the Blessing and turn away from the congregation. Since the congregation did not wish to remain idle during the Blessing, certain verses were designated for them to recite while the priests were pronouncing

[56]

it.[9] But the amoraim were divided as to how these verses should be recited, because they did not want the Priestly Blessing to be interrupted in an unseemly way; some even wished to eliminate the verses altogether: "Can there be a servant who does not listen when his master blesses him?" (compare Y. *Ber.* 1:1–2, 2c; B. *Soṭa* 39b ff.). The introduction of numerous verses led to the unfortunate consequence that, by the post-talmudic period, the congregation had a verse for every single word that the priests pronounced. Distinguished authorities admonished the congregations to say the verses only while the precentor was calling out the words, and to listen in silence when the priests repeated them; but the hubbub of the verses drowned out the words of the Blessing in spite of all reproaches. Another equally bad and equally severe practice arose from the terror of nightmares common in Babylonia. An amora (ca. 400) advised that if one had forgotten his dream he should stand before the priests during the Blessing and pray that it should have been a good one, or that God in His mercy turn it into a good one; he should conclude his prayer together with the Priestly Blessing so that the congregation's "Amen" would apply to his as well (B. *Ber.* 55b). This prayer, too, רבונו של עולם חלום חלמתי, "Master of the World, I have dreamed a dream . . . ," was eventually attached to the Priestly Blessing, and all the worshipers recited it, not just once, but at the end of each of the Blessing's three verses. In a later period, under the influence of the Kabbalah, a much longer prayer was introduced at the end of the third verse of the blessing, יהי רצון, "May it be Your will . . . ,"[10] and, oddly enough, it was connected with the "divine name of twenty-two letters that emerges from the verses of the Priestly Blessing." All these bad practices were possible only because the priests no longer recited the Blessing, but sang it, drawing the melodies out at length.[11] But in this way the original significance of the prayer was completely lost. This was one of the reasons that it aroused extreme opposition in the modern period, frequently leading to its elimination or simplification.

(4)   The Priestly Blessing is recited in the synagogue only when a full quorum is present (M. *Meg.* 4:4). The ancient rule was that it must accompany every ʿAmida recited aloud, but it came early to be restricted to the Morning Service and eliminated from the Afternoon Service (B. *Ta.* 26b). Fast days, when the recitation of the Blessing at the Closing Service was permitted, are the exception; in Palestine it was recited four times on the Day of Atonement, as it was in antiquity, while in Babylonia, and therefore in all Diaspora communities, only three times (*Ḥiluf minhagim*, §22). The custom for the priests to lift their hands daily was long retained only in the Oriental countries, and it is observed in Yemen [and in Palestine, especially Jerusalem] down to this very day.[12] It seems to have fallen into desuetude in Europe very early, apparently because it made the prayer too lengthy, and also because priests were not always present in the synagogue. Therefore, in Sepharad the Priestly Blessing was restricted to Sabbaths and festivals, and in other countries to festivals alone. Even on festivals the Priestly Blessing was limited in Ashkenaz to the Additional Service, and when R. Jacob Möllin (ca. 1400) permitted its recitation in the Morning Service as well, this was an exception. A deviation from the regular practice was introduced only in Amsterdam during the Sabbatean hysteria;[13] in honor of the arrival of the messianic age, the Priestly Blessing was again recited every Sabbath, a custom preserved in the Portuguese Synagogue until the present.

If no priests are in the synagogue, or in those places and services where the priests themselves do not pronounce the Blessing, the precentor must say it in the repetition of the ʿAmida. In Babylonia, as in the entire Diaspora, the precentor would say the Priestly Blessing after an introduction; in Palestine he was not permitted to recite the verses themselves,[14] but had to content himself with reciting the concluding verse: "And they shall place My name on the people of Israel and I shall bless them" (Num. 6:27). This substitute was introduced for all the ʿAmidot in which the priests were supposed to recite the Blessing—that is, in the Morning and Additional services, in the Afternoon Service of fast days,[15] and on the Day of Atonement in the Concluding Service as well. The rites differed as to the Afternoon Service of the Day of Atonement.

[57]

(5) Where the priests themselves recite the Blessing, they leave their places at the beginning of Benediction 17, "Accept." In ancient times they would do so on their own, but later, the sexton would summon them. In this case, in Ashkenaz the benediction begins not only with "Accept," but also with an older formula, ותערב, "May our prayer be sweet" (see page 50). According to Saadia, "Accept" is said only where the Priestly Blessing may be said (see page 51). The Blessing itself is inserted between the eighteenth and nineteenth benedictions of the ʿAmida. Where several priests are present, the precentor summons them to pronounce the Blessing by calling out "Priests"; but Jacob Tam took vigorous exception to this interruption in the prayer. After the priests recite the blessing on the commandment in accordance with the talmudic ruling, the precentor begins the verses of the Blessing itself, and they repeat it after him word by word. In the Oriental countries it was still the practice in Maimonides' time for the precentor to begin with the second word, and for the priests to say the first word, יברכך, "May the Lord bless you," on their own. Where the precentor recites the Priestly Blessing alone, he adds as an introduction the petition: ברכנו בברכה, "Bless us with the threefold blessing." And since in the Middle Ages it was only rarely that the Blessing came to be recited by the priests themselves, the custom of reciting "Bless us with the threefold blessing" became rooted even when the Priestly Blessing was said. Rabbi Meir of Rothenburg[16] would say this introduction silently down to the words, "by Aaron and his sons," and then he would call out the word "priests," at which the priests would join in, "Your holy people, as it is said." This remained the custom in Ashkenaz, while in Sepharad and Rome the entire formula "Bless us" was retained. After the Blessing of the Priests comes the nineteenth benediction of the ʿAmida, "Grant Peace." In Ashkenaz, wherever the Priestly Blessing is not recited, this is replaced by the short formula, "Great peace."

(6) The text of the Priestly Blessing stands as fixed in the Torah. The text of the introductory formula, "Bless us with the threefold blessing," is identical in all rites, proof of its great antiquity. A remarkable variant is found once (but not consistently) in Romaniot, where it says בתורה הכתובה על ידי נביאך האמורה לאהרן ולבניו כהנים לעם קדושך, "in the Torah written by Your prophet, recited to Aaron and to his sons the priests to Your holy people," and R. Joseph Kimḥi suggested, on stylistic grounds, the version כהנים בעם קדושך, "The priests among Your holy people."[17] In Palestine, instead of the Priestly Blessing, the precentor would say only, "And they shall place My name . . . ." Amram

and Saadia also cite this verse after the Blessing itself, and so it was also in Sepharad and southern France, while in northern France, Germany, and Italy this was not customary. By the decision of an assembly of rabbis in Frankfurt in 1845, the recitation of the Blessing by the priests was eliminated completely in Reform congregations in Germany and America,[18] and only its recitation by the precentor was retained. This became the practice even in conservative congregations; or at the very least, the simplest form of the Blessing was restored, and all the wild growths, particularly the superfluous singing, were eliminated.

[58]

§ 10 *The Supplications*

(1)   Immediately after the ʿAmida comes the last part of the Morning Service, called תחנונים (Dan. 9:3 and elsewhere), תחינה (Dan. 9:20), תחנון, תחינות, תחנות [all meaning "supplication(s)"].[1] It embraces everything in the prayer book after the ʿAmida. Today it is a varied mosaic of biblical verses and prayers from different periods, a group of prayers that has completely lost its original character and that can only be understood by retracing its origins. In the halakha the technical term for this prayer is נפילת אפים, "Falling upon the Face," or נופלים על פניהם, "They Fall upon their Faces." This expression comes from the Talmud, and is explained in B. *Meg.* 22b, where it says that נפל על אנפיה (אפיה), "He fell upon his face," or נפול אאנפייהו, "They fell upon Their faces," are equivalent to the biblical expression, ויקוד, while the biblical השתחוה is explained as פשוט ידים ורגלים, "spreading out the arms and legs." Both types of prostration were customary in Babylonia at the beginning of the third century during the recitation of the Supplications after the ʿAmida, and Maimonides still knew both from experience. These terms can help us to ascertain the origin of the prayer. The Mishnah says:

> The Levites recited the psalm. When they reached the end of the section they blew the shofar, and the people prostrated themselves. For every section the shofar was blown, and for every blowing of the shofar there was a prostration (*Tam.* 7:3).

During the Levites' singing that immediately followed the daily sacrifice, the people present in the Temple would prostrate themselves. What we find in the Mishnah as a prescription of religious law becomes vivid in the narrative of Ben Sira 50:16–21. There it says that at the sound of the shofar and later, after the Priestly Blessing, the people would fall upon their faces several times as an expression of reverence. This was the moment when the people worshiped in the full sense of the word, when each individual expressed in his private prayer the desires that at that moment moved his own heart. This custom was transferred from the Temple to the synagogue, so that the prayer of the individual was no longer annexed to the public sacrifice but to the public prayer.[2] At the end of the ʿAmida the opportunity was given to every individual to pour out his heart and to conduct a dialogue with his Creator without any external pressure. Thus, the most difficult problem of all public worship was resolved, and an appropriate balance achieved between the demands of the community for congregational prayer and the justified desire of the individual for personal prayer independent of and uninfluenced by the community. The community laid claim to the first place, but once its own prayer was concluded, it left the individual worshipers to satisfy their inner needs. When the public worship consisted simply of the confession of faith, ending with "True and Certain," the individual prayer came immediately after the latter; later it was transferred from there to the end of the ʿAmida.

(2)   The oldest name that we find for the individual prayer is דברים, "Words": "One says 'words' (that is, private prayer) after the ʿAmida" (T. *Ber.* 3:6), and these "words" may be as long as desired, as long as the longest prayer known to us, which is "the order (or confession) of the Day of Atonement." Very characteristic, though incorrect, is the reading that we find in B. *Ber.* 31a: "One does not say any word of petition after 'True and Certain'. . . ," where *words* is equated with *petition*.

[59]

The posture during this prayer remained in some countries as it had been in the Temple. Maimonides still knows only that one falls upon the ground—whether with the face alone or with the entire body—and the Jews of Yemen, true to him, fall upon the ground to this very day.[3] Whenever the Talmud describes real-life practice, it always speaks about "falling upon the face"; thus, it is said that the wife of R. Eliezer (ca. 120; B. B.M. 59b), Ima Shalom, did not permit him "to fall upon his face," and the same expression was used of Rav in Nehardea (B. *Meg.* 22a). For men of high rank the sages were satisfied with their turning their faces to one side—מצלי אצלויי (B. *Meg.* 23a); רבע על סטריה (Y. ʿA.Z. 4:1 ff., 43d top)—hence, the expression נטייה על הצד of the legal authorities. The custom that has spread to the synagogues is that one inclines to one side or leans one's head on something and covers it; nevertheless, the expression *falling upon the face* continued in use. The meaning of this expression became so attenuated that we even find expressions like "One does not say 'falling upon the face.' "[4] Maimonides uses the expression מתחננים, "to supplicate."

(3)   Since the petitions were of a personal nature, their contents were not fixed, but were as varied as the talents and expressive abilities of the worshipers, and as the moods and needs of the people. Several prayers of this type by sages have been preserved for us in B. *Ber.* 16b, 17a and Y. *Ber.* 4:2, 7d. They are appropriately referred to as בעי רחמי, "he requested mercy." The geonim were still fully aware that this is a private prayer. R. Natronai Gaon sees "the falling upon the face" as an optional prayer. R. Amram says that those who wish to recite the confession after the ʿAmida or to express a petition may do so, and he permits all to pray as they wish.[5] Only in one point is there any innovation here as against the Talmud, namely, that the prayers reported as individuals' prayers after the ʿAmida are distinguished from those of "the falling upon the face," while it is most likely that these are actually the same prayers. The Supplications retained their optional character, in that they were considered merely customary (מנהג) throughout the Middle Ages and down to the *Shulhan ʿarukh*.[6] Furthermore, they have remained to this day a silent prayer, at least for their first part, and in most places the precentor sits while they are being said, so that he leaves the congregation to itself, as it were.

(4)   Once the Supplications became a fixed part of the liturgy their original purpose was forgotten and they, too, acquired a text. For this purpose, biblical models were

followed, prayers such as Ezra 9:6, Neh. 1:5, and particularly Dan. 9:3ff., the classic example of a "prayer of petition and supplication." This petition is preceded by a confession of sin, stressing the worshiper's unworthiness; God's favors are sought as a freewill gift of grace. This train of thought has been preserved in all the Supplications, with all the variations in form in which they have been transmitted. All express the idea of the sinfulness and unworthiness of man, recalling the liturgy of fast days, from which they have borrowed much. Their form varies. While Amram offers a selection of prayers recalling the Supplications in the Talmud, Saadia has a confession with Dan. 9:5 as its starting point. Maimonides adds Dan. 9:18 and Ezra 9:6, but he says that everyone may add or delete verses at will. *Vitry*, too, has a freely composed petition that recalls the *Selihot* service in form and content, but preceded by Pss. 25 and 3. Individual psalms were retained as supplication texts—in Ashkenaz, Ps. 6 without its heading, and in other rites, Ps. 25.[7] The psalms are prefaced by the sentence, רחום וחנון חטאתי רחם עלי וקבל תחנוני, "Merciful One, I have sinned; have mercy upon me and accept my supplication,"[8] a sentence first found in Saadia, and apparently the beginning of ancient litany for the forgiveness of sin. Ashkenaz prefaces this today with II Sam. 24:14, "David said to Gad," but this verse is not found before the eighteenth century.

(5)   It is in the nature of the Supplications that they are only recited silently; but once they became part of the public synagogue service, it was inevitable that the precentor would claim a part in them. Thus, a second part of the Supplications came into being, in which the congregation would rise from the ground and the precentor would speak aloud ("The people have the custom of supplicating with the following verses after falling upon their faces, when they lift their faces from the ground"— Maimonides). In Saadia the supplication ends with the sentence אבינו מלכנו חננו ועננו, "Our Father, our King, have mercy upon us and answer us," which R. Akiva had once said during a public fast. Beginning with Amram this sentence opens the second part of the supplications, which is said aloud, and which contains several other verses, most of them from Psalms, beginning ואנחנו לא נדע, "And we do not know." Probably this collection, too, originally belonged to the *Selihot* ritual. Some additions have been made to it. In Ashkenaz it is preceded by the rhymed piece שומר ישראל, "Guardian of Israel,"[9] which is used in other rites only on fast days and on the days of *Selihot*, and which seems to have found a permanent place in the weekday prayer book only in the last century; it was adopted further also in Sepharad and Rome. The present text has obviously been considerably abridged; from manuscripts a few additional verses are known. Sepharad, under the influence of the kabbalists, introduced the confession of sins every day, consisting of אשמנו, "We have sinned," and the Thirteen Attributes (Ex. 34:6–7);[10] these sections seem to have been transferred from the prayers of Mondays and Thursdays.

(6)   Mondays and Thursdays have been fast days since ancient times. *Megilat ta'anit*, at the end of chapter 12 (compare B. *Ta.* 12a),[11] refers to "one who has taken upon himself Monday and Thursday of the entire year." The Pharisee in the Gospel of Luke 18:12 boasts that he fasts twice a week, and the Didache 8:1 explicitly names these days as Monday and Thursday.[12] As the reason for the fast, the apocryphal conclusions of *Megilat ta'anit* and *Soferim* 21:3 note: "And furthermore our sages decreed that they should fast on Mondays and Thursdays for three reasons: because of the

destruction of the Temple, because the Torah was burnt, and because of the disgrace of God's name," a motivation too late for the Christian sources. The fasts in time of drought or for other disasters also begin on Monday, continue on Thursday, and so on.[13] Monday and Thursday are market and court days, "days of assembly" (ימי כניסה);[14] therefore, the Torah reading is held then. This fact alone is sufficient to explain the lengthier liturgy of these two days. But that they became fast days with a penitential liturgy must apparently find its explanation in the ancient chronological work *Seder ʿolam*.[15] According to its reckoning, the Seventeenth of Tammuz, when Moses broke the tablets (Ex. 32:19), occurred on a Thursday, and the Tenth of Tishre [the day when the Israelites were forgiven for the sin of the calf], on a Monday; this is the day of the Thirteen Attributes, which form the nucleus of the fast day liturgy (compare B. *R.H.* 17b, and below, §33).

[61]

(7)   In Amram and Rome,[16] the Thirteen Attributes and the confession "We have sinned" are assigned to Monday and Thursday; and in Sepharad the Attributes are even repeated several times (a practice not yet known to Abudarham). Rome gives Dan. 9:15–19 as an introduction; Amram gives a choice between these and similar passages, among them והוא רחום, "And He, being merciful,"[17] the long prayer familiar from Ashkenaz and Sepharad. Medieval manuscripts tell the following story about the origin of this prayer: After the destruction of the Temple, Vespasian sent a number of Jews to be set adrift on the sea on three vessels with no rudder. Thus, the three ships reached three different places, apparently all in southern France. There the travelers were at first received hospitably, but when the prince who had favored them died they were oppressed and robbed of their goods. They then declared a fast, for which two brothers, Joseph and Benjamin, and their uncle, Samuel, composed the prayer, "And He, being merciful." The text of the prayer was transmitted to other communities, which also accepted it. On the basis of this story, Zunz fixes the composition of the prayer in the seventh century, and sees it as a cry of rage in a period of oppression by the Franks and the Goths. The stories of the origin of "And He, being merciful" were embellished with legends and augmented by miracle stories. In other sources the names of the authors are Amitai, Shefatia, and Yosifia; these names would point to southern Italy, but they do not appear to be correct. "And He, being merciful" is mentioned for the first time in *Pardes* (eleventh century); in the text of Amram it is a late addition lacking in the two manuscripts. The style and content attest to its antiquity; the language is mostly biblical. It contains many literal quotations, especially at the beginning, and many biblical allusions. Likewise, its freely composed parts are distinguished by the purity and simplicity of their language. The attribution of the prayer's composition to three different authors may allude to its having been compiled from several petitions that were originally independent. Their mood varies: While the beginning expresses mainly consciousness of sin, there are toward the end clear allusions to persecution. Probably these were originally separate supplications for fast days. The text in the manuscripts diverges from the printed text only in non-essentials. In Sepharad it is considerably shorter than in Ashkenaz, so that later additions may be present, but these have been so well matched to the main body of the prayer that the foreign elements cannot be detected. These additions expanded the prayer considerably; in popular parlance one speaks of "the long 'And He, being merciful,'" and in modern prayer books the text has been

abridged in various ways. Berliner proposes dividing the text between the two weekdays. Other than the additional prayer for forgiveness, the daily silent Supplication remains unchanged on Mondays and Thursdays. The prayers that follow it are all drawn from the *Seliḥot* liturgy. In Amram and Rome there comes next an alphabetical petition with the refrain זכור ברית אברהם ועקדת יצחק . . . והושיענו למען שמך, "Remember the covenant of Abraham and the binding of Isaac . . . and save us for the sake of Your name," and also a litany with the recurring word חטאנו ("we have sinned"), followed by Pss. 120 and 130, all of which are used also on fast days. Ashkenaz, France, and Sepharad insert after the daily psalm of supplication ה' אלהי ישראל שוב מחרון אפך, "Lord, God of Israel, turn aside from Your anger,"[18] a sentence made up of Ezek. 9:15 and Ex. 32:12. Originally, this verse stood alone, but later it became the refrain for elaborate liturgical poems, many of which are contained in the printed edition of Amram, though they are lacking in the manuscript.[19] The poem in Ashkenaz, containing complaints about severe persecution, is obviously preserved only in part (acrostic: החזק).[20] After the supplication, Ashkenaz and Sepharad have אל ארך אפים, "God, the patient." Ashkenaz, already in *Vitry*, has two slightly different versions, which *Vitry* divides between the precentor and the congregation; Abudarham also quotes both. On stylistic grounds, "God, the patient" must have been composed at the beginning of the geonic period.[21]

[62]

(8) Supplication is not recited on any day that has a festive character; the number of such days increased in the course of the Middle Ages, while their recognition spread gradually.[22]

After Supplication, Half-Kaddish is recited (§12a) as a sign that the service is over. On Monday and Thursday the Torah is read at this point (§25:3–4).

(9) On weekdays, there are attached to the Supplication, in the narrow sense of the word, other passages that have no particular name and that we therefore include under this heading. One of this group in all rites is ובא לציון גואל, "A Redeemer will come to Zion," a collection of verses known as קדושא דסדרא, "Kedushah of the Lesson," and in Maimonides' Hebrew, סדר היום or סדר קדושה, "the order of the Kedushah" or "the order of the day." It is mentioned already in the Talmud, B. *Soṭa* 49a, where the highest significance is attached to it. The name tells us that it is the Kedushah that comes after the public Torah lesson. As to its origin, there are a number of unsubstantiated hypotheses; we owe the correct solution to a responsum of R. Natronai Gaon.[23] According to this responsum, early in the morning, immediately after the service, Torah lessons were held. At the end of the lesson, several verses from the Prophets were recited, ending with the verses of the Kedushah; as was customary in these sermons, the verses were translated into Aramaic. As the struggle for survival became harder and there was no longer time for study, the lesson was reduced and eventually eliminated altogether, but the verses remained standing at the end of the Morning Service. Several pieces of evidence as to the authenticity of this information may be cited. First, wherever in the liturgy we find the Kedushah of the Lesson, we find also evidence for didactic sermons and readings from the Prophets or the Hagiographa. Second, after the entire series of verses comes the benediction ברוך אלהינו שבראנו לכבודו, "Blessed is God Who created us for His glory," which contains a clear allusion to the preceding study of Torah ("and gave us the Torah of truth"). Finally, the two introductory verses, Is. 59:20–21, though

they are sometimes omitted, contain an allusion to the messianic vision with which such sermons customarily concluded.

Already in the Babylonian rite it was customary to preface Ps. 20 ("May God answer you in time of trouble") to the Kedushah of the Lesson. This is another psalm used originally for the Supplication, and it is therefore omitted whenever this is not recited; it is customary in Ashkenaz and Sepharad but not in Saadia, Rome and Romaniot. Preceding this psalm in Ashkenaz and Sepharad, also pursuant to Babylonian instructions, is אשרי, "Happy"—that is, the combination of Ps. 84:5 with 144:15–145:21, in fulfillment of the talmudic maxim, "Whoever recites 'A Psalm of David' three times a day is assured of belonging to the world to come" (B. *Ber.* 4b; third century). Romaniot and Rome have it only on Mondays and Thursdays, or on days when Supplication is not recited.

[63]

(10)   Now the full Kaddish is recited and the service comes to an end; according to *Vitry*, at this point the precentor goes off and sits down. This did not prevent the addition of other supplements, but these were rather unstable and were not considered obligatory (Maimonides: "Some of the people have the practice . . ."). They are already found in Amram, but how many belong to the original text is questionable; in any case, only in the course of time did they become as numerous as they are today. Nor do they follow the same order everywhere. Common to all prayer books is the daily psalm of the Levites, from the end of Tractate *Tamid*; usually several biblical verses are attached to them, including "May the Lord our God be with us" (I Kgs. 8:57–58). In *Vitry*, Psalm 83 replaces these psalms; hence, Ashkenaz has both the psalm of the day and Psalm 83. All rites but Ashkenaz have אין כאלהינו, "There is none like our God," in the daily service, and several quotations from the Talmud, including the concluding Aggadah of B. *Ber.*; Sepharad has also the end of B. *Nid.*, and Rome, פטום הקטורת, "The compounding of the incense" (B. *Ker.* 6a, Y. *Yoma* 4:5).[24]

(11)   Since about 1300, עלינו, "It is our duty," is named as the conclusion of the daily service. In all rites it stands at the very end; only Ashkenaz cites it as the first in the group of additions now to be mentioned, and adds to it also על כן נקוה, "Therefore we hope." "It is our duty" is taken from the New Year service, where it serves as the introduction to the Kingship verses (§24), which deal with the theme of the kingdom of heaven on earth. It was of high religious significance that the lofty ideal of the future union of all mankind in the world to come in the service of the one God became part of the daily service.

The acceptance into the daily service of *It is our duty* was the cause of repeated indictments of the Jewish religion, which did not subside in Germany for centuries and even brought about the alteration of the prayer text in Ashkenaz. Today we read שלא שם חלקינו כהם וגורלנו ככל המונם ואנחנו, "Who has not made our portion like theirs, nor our lot like that of their masses; and we bow . . . ." But the ancient manuscripts and Sepharad [and the versions of all other communities] read to this day after the second clause, שהם משתחוים להבל וריק ומתפללים אל אל לא יושיע, ". . . nor our lot like that of their masses. For they bow to something vain and empty, and pray to a god who cannot save; but we bow . . . ." About 1400 a Jewish apostate informed on the Jews, saying that these words refer to Jesus, as proved by the fact that the word וריק, "and empty," is numerically equivalent to 316, the same as יש״ו, "Jesus." Even though Lippman-Mühlhausen, in his book *Niṣaḥon*, protested immediately, the accusation was frequently repeated, and wherever censorship was applied to the books of the Jews, the sentence "For they bow . . ." was altered by means of excisions of greater or lesser extent. But even this was no help; the enemies of Israel, above all, of course, Eisenmenger, were always seeking cause to renew their accusations. In Prussia a particularly severe accusation was leveled against the Jews on account of this prayer in 1702. A thorough investigation resulted, which we can follow thanks to a thick extant legal dossier. Its outcome was the "Edict concerning the Jewish prayer, 'It is our duty'; that they must eliminate certain words, not spit, and not hop during its recitation" of August 28, 1703. The edict was probably the reason that this sentence was finally eliminated from the prayer books in Germany. It rules that the precentor must recite "It is our duty" aloud, and officials were appointed whose job it was to visit the synagogue and supervise the enforcement of the edict's provisions. Since there was not a single occasion for police action, the edict was quickly forgotten.[25]

[64]

(12) Likewise the שיר היחוד, "Song of Unity," was introduced in Ashkenaz, the mystic-speculative hymn that originated in the circle of R. Judah the Pious (§44). R. Solomon Luria (ca. 1540) protested on the grounds that such an exalted prayer should not be allowed to become hackneyed through overuse—a principle that would have benefited the entire liturgy had it been applied on other occasions. However, despite this opposition, which arose from other quarters as well, the conclusion of the Song of Unity, אנעים זמירות, "I shall sing hymns," known as the Song of Glory, was annexed to the weekday Morning Service.[26] Since the appearance of the Venice prayer book in 1549, "I shall sing hymns" has been found in all prayer books of the Ashkenaz and Poland. All the additions mentioned in sections 10–12 are not used in the same way in all communities. They are separated by the Mourners' Kaddish (§12a), and increased because of the favor enjoyed by Kaddish. In the Reform prayer books they have been limited mostly to "It is our duty."

§ 11   *The Morning Psalms*

(1) We now turn from the main parts of the service to the later elements of the liturgy; we deal first with the פסוקי דזמרה, "Morning Psalms." They are also called הלל (B. *Shab.* 118b and in the writings of Natronai Gaon), or זמירות (Psalms). This term derives from the main and most original contents of this section, which goes from ברוך שאמר, "Blessed is He Who spoke,"[1] to the end of ישתבח, "May Your name be praised." Misunderstandings, incorrect synagogue procedures, and particularly the custom, originating in the Middle Ages (and attested already in *Vitry*), that here the precentor steps to the pulpit, created the impression and favored the opinion that this section concludes before "May Your name be praised," but this view is wrong.

(2) The nucleus of this section comprises the six psalms, Pss. 145 to 150, which are the Morning Psalms proper. To these, one benediction was added before and one

after, as in Hallel. The passage *Blessed is He Who spoke* served as an introduction, and *May Your name be praised* served as a conclusion. These psalms are first mentioned as part of the daily prayer in the dictum of R. Yosi b. Ḥalafta: "May my lot be that of those who complete the Hallel every day [from 'A Psalm of David' to 'Every soul']" (B. *Shab.* 118b;[2] *Soferim* 17:11). This shows that in his time—that is, in the middle of the second century—the practice of adding these psalms to the weekday service was not yet universal; it was recognized as the preferred practice, but was not yet obligatory. On the other hand, we are informed that in the Temple the Levites would sing every morning after the sacrifice from הודו to אל תגעו במשיחי, "Praise the Lord" to "Do not touch my anointed ones" Ps. 105:1–15) and every evening, שירו לה׳ שיר חדש, "Sing to the Lord a new song," Ps. 96). These two passages were united and provided with a liturgical conclusion from I Chron. 16:8–36 (*Seder ʿolam* 14). It appears that a great number of other psalms belonged to the Temple liturgy. The songs of the Levites during the sacrifices were partially transferred to the synagogue, and of these, the last chapters of the Book of Psalms, all of which begin and end with "hallelujah," were selected for use. As is customary almost everywhere in the liturgy, a benediction was attached before the recitation of the psalms, and one afterwards. This is the framework of the section, into which all the pieces it contains today were inserted, and in the light of which the whole is to be explained.

[65]

(3)   Today this section usually begins with Ps. 30;[3] this is the latest addition and is found only since the seventeenth century. In Sepharad this psalm is designated for Hanukkah, and it was incorrectly taken from there without the designation; in many places it is even recited without the heading. "Blessed is He Who spoke" is a hymn of lovely content; its first part praises the creator's power and providence, a subject irrelevant here. Only the second part, המהלל בפי עמו, ". . . praised by the mouth of His people," leads to the subject, the recitation of the psalms. We may conclude that only the second part was originally intended for this spot. Ancient texts lacking the first part verify this assumption; we may almost definitely call these versions Palestinian and say that the Palestinian rite began only with the second part of "Blessed is He Who spoke." Such texts are very common in the geniza, and they so resemble the blessings before and after Hallel, even in their wording, that this seems a guarantee of their originality. Likewise, Romaniot, which so often preserves Palestinian traditions, includes in the Sabbath service, among the Morning Psalms, the Benediction of the Song, which corresponds in content to the second part of "Blessed is He Who spoke," and greatly resembles the above-mentioned texts. But how did the present version develop? In Ashkenaz, "Blessed is He Who spoke" is relatively short, with ten lines beginning with the word "Blessed"; in Sepharad it is longer, with substantial variants in the different editions. If we trace the origins of "Blessed is He Who spoke," we must note Nathan of Babylonia's account of the festive service on the occasion of the installation of the Babylonian exilarch. According to him, the choir and the precentor would sing responsively, and for every short sentence that begins with "Blessed," the choir would respond, "Blessed is He." Therefore, Rapoport conjectured that the manner of recitation was always the same—that is, that "Blessed is He" was added as a refrain after every half-line. However, this does not seem likely; it is more probable that "Blessed is He Who spoke" is an abbreviated version of a prayer that was originally considerably longer and elabo-

rated in poetic style. Its beginning is derived from several benedictions in the Mishnah, *Ber.* 9 (see also B. *Ber.* 57b, 59a–b; Y. *Ber.* 12d; M. *Ta.* 2). The part from the beginning to ברוך עושה בראשית, "Blessed is He Who made the creation," is quoted as a single unit already in *Tana deve eliayahu zuṭa*, chapter 4. The stringing together of these unrelated sentences was apparently determined by the section that precedes it in the prayer book, אתה הוא ה׳ אלהינו, "You are the Lord our God," which ends with Zeph. 3:20. The sentence ברוך אומר ועושה ברוך גוזר ומקים, "Blessed is He Who promises and fulfills/Blessed is He Who decrees and performs," is connected to the future salvation promised by the prophet, and praises God as He Who fulfills the promise given through His prophets. Thus, the entire hymn would have messianic significance. If so, only the short version of Ashkenaz, Romaniot, and Rome can be original, and not the long one in Sepharad that here amasses all kinds of descriptions of God's attributes. Confirmation for this view may be found in Rome, where "You are the Lord our God" is included among the Morning Psalms, though it is separated from "Blessed is He Who spoke" by a group [66] of verses that are to be discussed presently. If this is the case we must go one step further and assume that originally the first part of "Blessed is He Who spoke" had no connection to the second part, but that it was closely connected with the preceding complex of prayers (§12). It is hard to say when these heterogeneous elements were joined; they are found this way in the most ancient extant version. "Blessed is He Who spoke" is first mentioned by R. Moses Gaon (ca. 825). Zunz, probably correctly, attributes its composition to the period of the saboraim.[4]

(4)   If "Blessed is He Who spoke" is the introduction to the Morning Psalms,[5] then the Psalms belonging to this section should follow immediately. But this is not the case, for at least in Ashkenaz, הודו לה׳ קראו בשמו, "Praise the Lord, call upon His name," has been interposed. The composition and source of this prayer have been explained above. To I Chron. 16:36 about another twenty biblical verses, most of them from Psalms, have been added, and in Romaniot and Rome, Ps. 19 besides. The selection of verses varies greatly in the Middle Ages,[6] but verses put forward in the Talmud or the midrash as having particular significance are favored. Some of these are already mentioned in ancient sources, such as Pss. 46:8 and 84:13, recommended by Y. *Ber.* 5:1, 8d,[7] and Ps. 106:47–48, recommended by *Soferim* 17:11, but only for the New Moon; and after all, this prayer, like the passages that follow, up to but not including Ps. 145, belonged originally to the liturgy of the festive days. Amram does not have it, and it is lacking also in the geniza fragments, and in the Middle Ages it was treated freely, as said. In all rites except Ashkenaz, its place is before "Blessed is He Who spoke," so that it does not break the necessary connection; yet, even there they did not hesitate to insert the following [that is, the prayer described in the next two paragraphs—*Engl. trans.*]:

First, Ps. 100,[8] which is also probably a vestige of the Temple liturgy, is inserted. In Rome it originally used to be said only on the Sabbath, but in France and Germany it was eliminated on the Sabbath. In Romaniot it comes before "Blessed is He Who spoke"; Amram has Ps. 20 instead.

יהי כבוד, "May the glory," is found in all known prayer books, though originally it too was meant only for special days. It is made up of a series of verses that all contain the tetragrammaton, most of them from the Psalms: Pss. 104:31, 113:2–4, 135:13, and so forth. ישמחו השמים, "May the heavens rejoice," is borrowed from I Chron. 16:31, but it is easy to see why this version was given preference over Ps. 96:11. There is no verse in the Bible that contains the three clauses ה' מלך ה' מלך ה' ימלך וגו', "The Lord reigns, the Lord has reigned, the Lord will reign forever,"[9] but each individual part is a fragment of a biblical verse. It appears that this sentence too is one of those intended for the festival liturgy. Together with "May the glory," it is mentioned in *Soferim* 17:11 and 18:2 among those to be said standing, unlike all the other psalms. It is not to be assumed that the reference is to the prayer "May the glory" known to us. In Romaniot and Rome, the Morning Psalms begin to this day with a group of verses headed by "The Lord reigns" and "May the glory." In Sepharad, too, one says with special solemnity "The Lord reigns," accompanied by several verses between "Give thanks" and "Blessed is He Who spoke." The source of all these additions must be sought in the holiday liturgy, as is still evidenced in the manuscripts. In Romaniot and Rome, yet more biblical passages were added.

[67]

(5)   Only now come the Morning Psalms proper—that is, Pss. 145 to 150, or, to be more precise, 144:15 to 150. The additional verse is prefaced by yet another verse beginning with "Happy": "Happy are those who dwell in Your house" (Ps. 84:5).[10] These two verses grew to be such a part of Ps. 145 that the entire psalm is often called after them, אשרי, "Happy." Reciting Ps. 84:5 makes sense only when it is done immediately upon entering the synagogue, as is the case, for example, in the Afternoon Service (§13). Incidentally, not every place was content with only two verses beginning with "Happy"; Rome adds also Ps. 119:1, and *Vitry* adds four other verses beginning with the same word. At the end of Ps. 145 another foreign verse is added on, Ps. 115:18, so that the psalm now ends with "hallelujah," the word that begins and ends each of the following psalms. This addition is found already in Amram. Now come the other five psalms verbatim. The last verse of Ps. 150 is repeated, because it is the end of the book of Psalms. Ashkenaz and Sepharad follow it with the doxologies from the ends of the individual books of the Psalms, plus Ps. 135:21.

(6)   Here the Morning Psalms should end with ישתבח, "May Your name be praised," and so they do in the older prayer books; but today in all rites come David's song of thanksgiving (I Chron. 29:10–13), then Nehemiah's song of praise (Neh. 9:6–11), and finally the Song of the Red Sea (Ex. 14:30–15:18). As late as the geonic period only the first of these pieces is known, and it alone is found in Amram. The last piece is more recent; originally intended only for Sabbaths, it was recited after "May Your name be praised," so that it did not interrupt the Morning Psalms. The reason for its adoption is to be sought in the talmudic tradition (B. *R.H.* 31a) according to which it used to be divided among three Sabbaths and recited in the Afternoon Service. *Vitry* cites a Roman responsum supporting its recitation on weekdays, with only the Ninth of Av and the house of a mourner named as exceptions; but the contemporaneous R. Judah b. Barzilai still recognizes its use only on the Sabbath, absolutely rejecting any interruption of the Morning Psalms by improper additions. It seems that the Romaniot lands were the first to introduce it in the weekday services; Maimonides places it after "May Your name," but *Vitry* places it before. Eventually it was adopted everywhere, and then the Nehemiah passage was added, ending with the splitting of

the Red Sea, apparently as a connecting link with David's song of thanksgiving ויברך דוד, "And David blessed." Finally, to round off the entire section, some verses in which the word *king* appears were attached to the final, repeated verse (Ex. 15:18). Thus, the sections of psalms were inordinately expanded. In some modern prayer books the psalms have been divided among several days of the week in order to reduce the length of this entire section.[11]

(7)   The end of the Morning Psalms is "May Your name be praised," which is very similar in its contents to the benediction that concludes Hallel. The heaping up of synonyms is not an original part of it, but mystical attitudes seem to have been at play here.[12] Abudarham found in this passage the acrostic שלמה (Solomon), and assumed this to have been the name of the author. Rapoport, on the basis of the Sephardic texts, found the name אברהם (Abraham). But already in Amram this piece has the same text as that current today, and it therefore probably predates the period when acrostics were introduced; if so, there is no point in searching after the name of the author. The Morning Psalms are closed by the Half-Kaddish (§12a), which, however, was attracted to the following section in the order of the prayer, and thus came to be attached to "Bless the Lord" (§7[2]).

[68]

(8)   There are various indications that the Morning Psalms are still not considered part of the actual service: They may be recited even when there is no quorum in the synagogue. According to *Vitry*, the phylacteries are put on only after their conclusion; according to Amram, and as late as Abudarham, and sometimes to this day, it is only here that the precentor passes before the Ark; in Sepharad the one who recites the Morning Psalms before the congregation is called the מזמר, "Psalm-singer," to distinguish him from the precentor.[13] In any case, even according to Amram these psalms were recited in the synagogue, while the sections preceding them are designated as belonging to home worship. Maimonides does not mention either in connection with public prayer. [But compare the edition of Goldschmidt, in *SRIHP* 5 (1938/9), 190.]

§ 12 *The Morning Benedictions*

(1)   Even less does the beginning of our prayer book, known as the Morning Benedictions, belong to the original synagogue service. Maimonides still knows it only as the practice of individuals, though Amram cites the custom of having the precentor say it in the synagogue in order to fulfill the duty on behalf of the ignorant.[1]

(2)   Since the first printed editions, Ashkenaz opens with מה טובו, "How good" (Num. 24:5); according to an ancient interpretation, the "tents of Jacob" and the "dwelling places of Israel" are the synagogues and the houses of study (B. *Sanh.* 105b). The passage is composed of biblical verses, especially verses beginning with the word ואני, "and I."[2] שחר אבקשך, "At dawn I seek You," is a rhymed and metrical poem by Solomon Ibn Gabirol (1050), which is distinguished by reverence of rare intensity. It is not found in all prayer books. These two passages are not actually part of the Morning Ser-

vice, but are rather overall preparation for prayer. The other rites provide other pieces for the same purpose; Romaniot and Rome have lengthy petitions.

(3)   In this country the service begins with יגדל, "The living God be exalted," while in the western German rite it comes only after the Morning Benedictions. It is a poem monorhymed in -to and composed of thirteen metrical stanzas; Sepharad has one more stanza at the end, but it does not fit the meter, and is probably not original. The rhyme and meter testify to its late origin.[3] The content, as explicitly stated in the concluding sentence in Sepharad, is a reworking of the thirteen principles that Maimonides placed at the end of the great theological introduction to his commentary on chapter 10 of Tractate *Sanhedrin*. These articles of the Jewish faith were taken up into the prayer book,[4] usually at the end of the Morning Service for weekdays in the form אני מאמין, "I believe . . ."; they were also attached to our prayer book in poetic form in "The living God be exalted." Some have thought Maimonides himself the author of this reworking, but there is no proof of this or similar claims. All tracks lead to Italy as the poem's homeland; a prayer book of 1383 contains a note indicating that it was composed by the owner's grandfather, Daniel b. Judah Dayan of Rome. The poem also echoes one of the poems of Emanuel b. Solomon,[5] a contemporary of the putative author. Furthermore, we know that at that time there was in Rome a large circle of Jewish scholars that applied itself to the study of philosophy, and that zealously disseminated the teachings of Maimonides. Thus, we cannot be far off the mark if we accept the report, and regard the poem as having been composed in Rome ca. 1300. In the prayer book it first appears at the beginning of the Morning Service in the edition of Cracow, 1578.[6] In the synagogue the poem was used originally only in the Evening Service of the Sabbath or at the end of the Additional Service. Ashkenaz was the first rite to adopt it for the weekday Morning Service and also for the Evening Service of the Day of Atonement. The poem was transferred for these purposes also to Sepharad, while in Rome it remained restricted to the Friday Evening Service.

[69]

(4)   One of the most beautiful pieces in the prayer book—אדון עולם, "Eternal Lord"—is also not very old. Like the preceding poem, it contains metrical monorhymed verses, rhyming in -ra; here too Sepharad has two verses more than Ashkenaz, but they are probably authentic, since they fit neatly into the poem's rhythm.[7] As a prayer of purest poetry and universal religious content, "Eternal Lord" has been attributed to the greatest of the medieval sacred poets, Solomon Ibn Gabirol.[8] It is in fact worthy of him, but there is no compelling proof of his authorship. The end of the poem suggests that it originated as a night-time prayer, and it was actually incorporated into the bedtime recitation of the *Shemaʿ*; but the synagogue adopted it for the Evening Service only on Sabbath evening and the night of the Day of Atonement. In Worms it is recited to this day only on the Day of Atonement, while in Morocco, for example, it is customarily said at weddings, before the bride is led to the canopy. "Eternal Lord" appears in manuscripts shortly before the invention of printing, and then passes with the printed books into all the rites, usually opening the weekday Morning Service.

(5)   With the complex of benedictions that follows, the Morning Benedictions in the narrow sense begin. In Ashkenaz they have been uprooted from their original

context and can only be understood by considering B. *Ber.* 60b, the source of most of them. There the Talmud speaks of a person's morning activities upon rising and dressing, and counsels the pious, who see God's presence and help everywhere, to give thanks to Him for each individual act, even the most insignificant. The entire discussion there was meant merely as good counsel for the pious, and as guidance for the proper attitude toward every act that comes one's way. There was absolutely no thought of making the short benedictions listed there obligatory, nor was there the slightest intention of fixing them in the daily public service.[9] Nevertheless, they were formulated as benedictions, to be taken over in the geonic period into the domestic weekday prayers, and finally to be transferred to the synagogue service. The benediction על נטילת ידים, "on the washing of hands," the passages אשר יצר, "Who created" and אלהי נשמה, "My God; the Soul," and the short benedictions down to גומל חסדים טובים לעמו ישראל, "Who bestows acts of lovingkindness upon His people Israel"—to which יהי רצון, "May it be Your will," from B. *Ber.* 16b, was added, probably because their beginnings are similar—all come from the above-named passage; except for the benediction on the washing of the hands, they even occur in the same order. Likewise in Natronai, Amram and Rome they come in unbroken succession; Sepharad omits the first two, and thus does not once deviate from the talmudic order.[10] The short benedictions, of which only eleven are attested in the Talmud, were expanded when they entered the prayer book. Some said fewer, and some said even more; Ashkenaz added to those in the Talmud הנותן ליעף כח, "He Who gives strength to the weary," a benediction not found in any other prayer book, but which did infiltrate the later editions of Sepharad. To the above collection three further benedictions from B. *Men.* 43b were added; their original text read שעשאני ישראל, שלא עשאני אשה, שלא עשאני בור, "Who made me a Jew," "Who has not made me a woman," "Who has not made me an ignoramus." In T. *Ber.* 7:18, and Y. *Ber.* 9:2, 12b, the first benediction read "Who has not made me a gentile"; a completely nonapologetic motivation is given on the spot. In Palestine only these three benedictions were taken into the daily service. This was the practice of Saadia and was still that of Maimonides, though both designated these passages for private worship and not for the community; in place of "ignoramus" they read, against Palestine and with B. *Men.*, 43b, bottom, עבד, "slave." These three benedictions did not come together by accident. However they may relate to similar statements in late Greek literature attributed to Plato or Socrates, they are strikingly parallel to the Persian prayer to Ormuzd, which blesses the Creator for having made the worshipers Iranians, adherents of the good religion, free men and not slaves, men and not women. A parallel that deserves even greater attention because it comes from a Jewish source is a verse in the Epistle of Paul to the Galateans, which says that because of the death of Jesus all distinction between Jews and Greeks, slaves and free men, men and women, has become void (3:19).[11]

(6)   But this passage, which in the sources is continuous, is interrupted by a rather long section that goes from לעסוק בדברי תורה, "To occupy ourselves with the words of the Torah," to ותלמוד תורה כנגד כולם, ". . . the study of Torah is equivalent to all of them." Here we find first a benediction over the Torah, or, more exactly, three benedictions with the identical content. In B. *Ber.* 11b, three third-century amoraim recommend them, not for daily prayer but as an introduction to daily Torah study, and R. Papa (fourth century) combines them, in accordance with his customary means of resolving

disputes. After these benedictions comes, appropriately, a passage of Torah study. In Amram, Romaniot, and Rome this consists of the passages about the daily sacrifice, the recitation of which was long seen as a replacement for the sacrifice itself, which could no longer be offered.[12] On the other hand, there is a talmudic principle that one is obliged to devote a certain amount of time daily to the study of the Bible, the Mishnah, and the Talmud.[13] The combining of these two views resulted in the introduction here of Num. 28:1–8, M. *Zev.* 5, and the baraita "R. Ishmael says, 'The Torah is expounded by thirteen rules.'" This ordinance permitted free expansion by the addition of other selections from the Torah or from the Talmud dealing with the daily sacrificial service (such as Ex. 30:17–20, 34–36; B. *Ker.* 6a; B. *Yoma* 33a).[14] These sections are found first in Natronai Gaon and in the works of other geonim. Ancient prayer books preserve the logical order, with the study selections immediately after the benedictions. But as they have come down in Ashkenaz and Sepharad, with the Bible and Talmud selections at the very end of the Morning Benedictions, far from their proper benediction, the sequence is incomprehensible.

Alongside the group of study materials just mentioned, there existed also another considerably shorter (perhaps Palestinian?) group, consisting of the Priestly Blessing (Num. 28:1–8), Num. 6:24–26, M. *Pe.* 1:1,[15] and several other short baraitas. When in the French rite and Ashkenaz the benedictions of the Torah were moved to the place before "My God, the soul," some study material from the sources was needed there, too; the Priestly Blessing and the following selections were placed after the benedictions, with the result that these rites now have a duplication of study materials.

[71]

(7)   With לעולם יהא אדם, "A person should always," begins a new complex of ideas, a composite of the most miscellaneous quotations.[16] The entire context is given in *Tana deve eliyahu*, 118 (chapter 19, end): "Therefore they said: 'A person should fear God, acknowledge the truth, and speak the truth in his heart, every day rising and saying, "Lord of the world, not for our righteousness do we lay our supplication before You . . . ." And he should say: "At that time I will bring you and at that time I will assemble you . . . ."'" *S.L.* already mentions this source, and traces back to it the introduction into the prayer book of the entire passage. Its individual sentences are found separately in the talmudic sources. רבון כל העולמים, "Lord of the Worlds,"[17] and מה אנו מה חיינו, "What are we? What is our life?" are the confessions of R. Yoḥanan and of Mar Samuel in B. *Yoma* 87b: לא על צדקותינו, "Not for our righteousness," is based on Dan. 9:18; אבל אנחנו, "But we," comes from the *Mekhilta*, 44a (to Ex. 15:18), אתה הוא עד שלא נברא כעולם, "You existed before the world was created," from Y. *Ber.* 9b.[18] Because opinions were long divided as to whether the introductory words, "A person should always," should be recited as part of the service, the custom in Ashkenaz is to print them in small letters. R. Benjamin b. Abraham Anav (ca. 1240) may possibly have been right in maintaining that the recitation of the *Shemaʿ* at this point originated in a time of persecution, but more likely it was introduced here simply so that one would not miss the correct time for its recitation.[19] The passage אתה הוא ה' אלהינו, "You are the Lord our God," serves as a conclusion; it is a mosaic of biblical quotations concluding, in accordance with the *Tana deve eliyahu*, with a petition for the redemption. In Amram it is evident from the text before us that this section is simply a late addition. The medieval rite books and *Vitry* confirm the order found in Amram. In Rome before "A person

should always" there already appears the heading "Psalms for weekdays";[20] and we have already noted above (§11) that "Blessed is He Who spoke" is attached directly to the conclusion of the preceding passage בשובי את שבותיכם, "When I restore your exile . . . ."

(8)   To summarize this exposition, we may conclude that the first part of the Morning Service is essentially composed of the following subsections: (1) various benedictions derived from B. *Ber.* 60b; (2) material for study and introductory benedictions deriving from B. *Ber.* 11b; (3) a prayer for messianic redemption derived from *Tana deve eliyahu*, chapter 19. Later these three sections were no longer understood in their original order; extraneous prayers were inserted in them, to the point that in Ashkenaz they became so mixed up that they no longer made any sense. We do not know when they were assembled; there is no doubt that the entire section did not originally belong to the public liturgy, but belonged to private devotion. It did not find a place in the synagogue before the ninth century, and long thereafter it was still not universally accepted everywhere.[21]

[72] # § 12a *Kaddish*

(1)   As is clear from its being so frequently mentioned, Kaddish serves as a conclusion to the entire service, or the main sections of the service, and the Torah reading; it is also recited by mourners at the end of the service. But its liturgical use does not correspond to its original meaning; this has led to its reinterpretation and to the expansion of its text. But the original text has undergone considerable expansion for other reasons as well.

(2)   The nucleus of the Kaddish is the blessing, יהא שמה רבא מברך לעלם ולעלמי עלמיא, "May His great name be blessed forever and ever," in which can be heard clearly the echo of Dan. 2:20; the Hebrew equivalent is found in Ps. 113:2 and in the blessing that was customary in the Temple: ברוך שם כבוד מלכותו לעולם ועד, "Blessed be the name of His majestic glory forever." All of the references to Kaddish in talmudic literature relate to this sentence, to which they attribute extreme importance. "May His great Name be blessed" is, to the rabbis of the Talmud, the hymn of hymns. The first tana to mention this verse is R. Yose b. Ḥalafta (ca. 150) in *Sifre* Deut., 132b, §306, and B. *Ber.* 3a; while among the amoraim, Rava designates " 'May the great Name' of the Aggadah" as one of the things upon which the world stands (B. *Soṭa* 49a).[1] Now what we find in Rava's language as a unified concept points to the origin of this prayer; it was originally used at the end of sermons on Aggadah (§29).[2] The rule was that every sermon had to conclude with words of consolation—that is, with references to the messianic age—and some preachers added another short prayer to these eschatological conclusions. This prayer may at first have had no fixed formula, but was freely worded by the preacher. One such prayer that became established in the course of time was the Kaddish. Its first sentence contains the two eschatological petitions for the sanctification of the name of God and for the coming of the kingdom of God. To these petitions belongs the blessing "May His great name be blessed," or, in its Hebrew

formulation, יהא שמה רבא מברך (B. *Ber.* 3a). The connection with Ezek. 36–38 and especially with the wording of 28:23 is obvious. This is the core and the original meaning of Kaddish.

We do not know when the petitions were composed, but the very simple form of their eschatology, their simple wording, and their lack of any allusion to the destruction of the Temple are signs of their antiquity. Besides, their similarity to the Christian Lord's Prayer is well known;[3] the first three petitions of the latter in Matthew (6:9–10) fully parallel the first sentence of the Kaddish. It follows from all of these considerations that the nucleus of Kaddish is very ancient. It appears that besides these petitions and the blessing, the Aramaic clause לעלא מן כל ברכתא, "above all blessings . . . ,"[4] also belongs to the first stratum, because it contains a clear reference to the aggadic sermon and its eschatological conclusion (נחמתא). The connection with the Aggadah also explains the Aramaic language of Kaddish, for this was the language spoken by the sages. Kaddish was not composed in the dialect of the common people but in the artificial dialect used in the house of study,[5] and familiar from the officially recognized Targums (§28). Just as the Targum tradition was transplanted from Palestine to Babylonia, so the Kaddish, which originated in Palestine, was preserved and developed thanks to Babylonia, where it also achieved recognition as one of the "pillars of the world."

[73]

(3)   As a liturgical prayer we find Kaddish first in a Palestinian source, Tractate *Soferim*, composed around 600; there it comes at the end of the Torah reading (21:6) in connection with "Bless the Lord" (10:8), and at the conclusion of the service (19:1). Later in Amram the usage is identical with that customary today. For these liturgical purposes the Kaddish was expanded. At its end a petition was appended for the acceptance of the prayer: תתקבל צלותהון וגו׳, "May their prayer be accepted . . . ," while before "Bless the Lord" (§7), before the Kedushah of the Lesson (§10), and after the reading of the Torah (§25) in the Morning Service, as well as before the *'Amida* in the other services, the ancient form of Kaddish without "May their prayer" remained in use.[6] But the first part too sustained two additions: The Aramaic blessing "May His great Name" was supplemented by a Hebrew paraphrase of the same idea; and after each petition an invitation to the congregation, ואמרו אמן, "and say Amen," was added. We also find Kaddish connected with the week of mourning already in *Soferim*. There it says that after the Additional Service of the Sabbath, the mourners are visited at home, a benediction is recited, and then Kaddish is recited (19:12).[7] It is quite likely that on such occasions the blessing formula יהא שלמא רבא, "May great peace . . . ," was added to the existing Kaddish. We have no information as to when or why the same idea was later added again in Hebrew in the words עושה שלום במרומיו, "He Who makes peace in the heavens" (compare Job 25:2). When a scholar died, the beginning of Kaddish would be expanded with the words בעלמא דעתיד לאתחדתא, "In the world that will one day be renewed," but later this formula came to be used only at funerals [and also in the Kaddish after the conclusion of the study of a tractate; in Maimonides and Yemen it is used in every rabbinical Kaddish]. But the sentences that conclude the mourner's Kaddish, "May great peace . . . ," and "He Who makes peace" were appended also to the liturgical Kaddish and remain unchanged whenever it is recited.

(4)   The reason that Kaddish is used in the liturgy is the blessing that it contains

and the fact that the words ברכתא שירתא תשבחתא, "Blessings, songs, and praises," were understood as referring to the prayers. It was considered to be appropriate for mourning ceremonies because of the eschatological petition at its beginning; the sanctification of the name of God and the coming of God's kingdom are intimately connected, especially in the prophet Ezekiel, with resurrection; and doubtless the word *consolations* was understood as relating to the comforting of mourners. To these real connections was added the mystical conception that the recitation of Kaddish has magic powers over the living and the dead (compare B. *Shab.* 119b and *Tana deve eliyahu*, chap. 20), and even the response "Amen" after the Kaddish was supposed to have power to influence the divine decree. To this was added the idea that sons are obliged to act in behalf of the welfare of their parents' souls. This can be accomplished through participation in public worship and the reciting of certain prayers in the presence of the congregation, and according to the mystical legend of R. Akiva,[8] especially through the reciting of certain hymnic prayers like Kaddish and "Bless the Lord." Now these traditions have to do only with the liturgical Kaddish, but out of it the custom gradually arose that sons recite Kaddish for a full year after the death of their parents.[9] This custom originated in Germany during the great persecutions. It is still completely foreign to Vitry, and R. Eleazar of Worms (ca. 1200) still expresses himself very cautiously about it. But R. Isaac Or Zarua[10] (1220) already relates that in Bohemia and in the Rhineland the orphans recite Kaddish at the end of the service, while in France no care is given as to who recites it. He decries this indifference, pointing to the version of the legend according to which R. Akiva saved a father who had been sentenced to punishment in Gehenna by teaching his son Kaddish and having him say it in the synagogue. Two centuries later we find for the first time in the writing of R. Jacob Möllin the concept of *Jahrzeit* (Memorial Day),[11] the commemoration of the anniversary of the parents' death by the reciting of Kaddish. The custom of reciting Kaddish during the year of mourning and on the anniversary of the death was gradually adopted, together with its German/Yiddish designation by world Jewry. None of the early law codes, including the *Shulḥan ʿarukh*, knows of any binding precepts in connection with it; but what religious law left optional, religious feeling made sacred, and the Mourner's Kaddish became one of the most widespread and faithfully observed religious institutions.[12] Protests against the conception of Kaddish as a means of salvation have been raised continually.

[74]

(5)   Out of the various usages three types of Kaddish have developed: Complete Kaddish (קדיש שלם, קדיש גמור, or קדיש בתרא) is the one that includes תתקבל צלותהון, "May the prayer be accepted," together with יהא שלמא רבא, "May great peace"—that is, the Kaddish at the end of the service; Half-Kaddish (קדיש חסר, חצי קדיש, and קדיש זוטא), which goes only up to the words דאמירן בעלמא, ". . . which are said in the world"; and Mourner's Kaddish (קדיש יתום or קדיש אבל), which is the whole Kaddish minus the sentence "May their prayer be accepted," said following the conclusion of the service after such later additions as "It is our duty." A particular type of this Kaddish [which is in fact the Kaddish in its original function] is called Rabbinical Kaddish (קדיש דרבנן); it is recited by mourners after a Talmud lesson, and it is formed by the insertion of the paragraph beginning על ישראל, "For Israel . . ." before "May great peace." This addition, too, is no older than the closing of the Talmud.[13] Because the Kaddish came to be used in

the synagogue liturgy, congregational responses were added to it. [It appears that the congregational response is actually an integral part of the Kaddish following the public homily.] According to *Sifre*, 132b, §306, the manner of the prayer's recitation is that after the words "May His great name be blessed" the congregation should respond "forever and ever"; but later this custom fell into disuse, and instead the congregation would repeat the entire sentence. Already in the Talmud the mystics attributed extraordinary powers to this response. In later centuries its prestige increased to the point that substitute prayers were devised for each service for the sake of people who were unable to attend the public service and who therefore could not hear the Kaddish, which could be recited only in the presence of a quorum;[14] in these versions the sentence "May the great name" was cunningly inserted by the authors. To this was added the repeated response of "amen" by the congregation. It was not said everywhere in the same places, and this is [perhaps] evidence that it is a late custom.

(6) The full text of Kaddish first appears in Amram. It goes without saying that the text of a prayer so much in use undergoes considerable variation over the course of time, but it must be noted that the first half of the text, the part known as the Half-Kaddish, shows fewer variants than the second half; this, too, shows that the second half is a later addition. The text of Amram is preserved almost without variants in Ashkenaz and Rome, while the other rites have many. These variants have been carefully collected, sentence by sentence, by de Sola Pool; we shall mention only those that have general significance. The messianic petition at the beginning was further developed in Sepharad, Romaniot, and Yemen, and in its fullest version reads, ויצמח פורקניה [וישכלל היכליה] ויקרב משיחיה, "and may He make His salvation flourish [and rebuild His Temple] and bring near His messiah." The words in brackets are sometimes lacking in one rite or another; the variety in the wordings of the text (Pool, *Kaddish*, 26–38) proves [perhaps] that these sentences are late additions. Similarly, יתברך, "May it be blessed," itself a development of the preceding blessing, has seen changes in the word order and a slight increase in the synonymous verbs, which are abundant to begin with (Pool, *Kaddish*, 54);[15] the same goes for תתקבל, "May the prayer" (Pool, *Kaddish*, 65f.). The additions to the two final petitions are, however, more numerous, because of decorative and expansive elaborations (Pool, *Kaddish*, 69f., 75f.); in Sepharad and Romaniot many other favors are requested, mostly in Hebrew, besides "life." In a text dominated by Aramaic, this fact alone would show that this is a late addition. The variations in על ישראל, "For Israel," (Pool, *Kaddish*, 89) are few in number and importance. על ישראל ועל צדיקיא, "For Israel and for the righteous," taken from the prayer for the soul of the dead called השכבה in Sepharad, may be considered a variant to it; in Reform prayer books[16] it is inserted in the text of the Mourner's Kaddish, because this provides a direct link with the dead, which is lacking in the traditional text.

(7) Alongside the variants, the expansions of Kaddish must be mentioned. At the beginning, in the petition for the speedy bringing of the kingdom of God "in the lifetime of all Israel," holders of high offices were specially named. In an ancient report of the installation of a Babylonian exilarch[17] it is said that during the formal prayer-service the formula was inserted into the Kaddish בחיי נשיאנו ראש גלות ובחייכון ובחיי דכל בית ישראל, "in the life of our prince, the exilarch, and in your life and in the life of all the

[75]

house of Israel." In the Cairo geniza, fragments have been found indicating that this custom was followed regularly, and that in every recitation of Kaddish the name of the exilarch together with those of the heads of the great academies in Babylonia and Palestine were mentioned. One source reads בחיי נשיאנו ראש הגולה ובחיי ראש הישיבה של גולה ובחייכון . . ., "in the life of our prince the exilarch and in the life of the head of the academy of the Diaspora and in your life . . ." and another, בחיי אדוננו אביתר הכהן ראש ישיבת גאון יעקב, ובחיי רבנו שלמה הכהן אב הישיבה ובחיי רבנו צדוק השלישי בחבורה ובחייכון . . ., "in the life of our master Abiathar the Priest, Head of the Academy of the Splendor of Jacob, and in the life of Solomon the Priest, Father of the Academy, and in the life of R. Ṣadok, the Third in the Fellowship. . . ." This custom did not end in the eleventh century, for a century later we are told that the communities of Yemen would show their reverence for Maimonides by naming him in the Kaddish: . . . בחיי דרבנא משה בר מיימון, "in the life of our master Moses b. Maimon . . . ."[18] Typical is the fact that this addition remained in Hebrew inside an Aramaic text. Incomparably more numerous are the additions at the end, most of them elaborations of the three final sentences, and most of them in Aramaic, interrupted occasionally by Hebrew words. Most of these additions[19] have been preserved in the Cochin rite: (1) תתבני קרתא, "May the city be rebuilt" (Pool, *Kaddish*, 108); (2) תשלח אסותא, "Send healing" (ibid., 13, n. 12); (3) ייתון שמעין, "May good tidings come" (ibid.); (4) תענו ותעתרו, "May you be answered and responded to"; (5) תכתבו כלכם, "May you all be inscribed"; (6) a rhymed passage יהי רצון, "May it be Your will" after "May their prayer be accepted," and finally a verbose "May He Who makes peace" and דכירין לטב, "Remembered for good."

Also, in a few Sephardic communities, "May you be answered and responded to" is said at the end of festivals.

[76]

B. OTHER WEEKDAY PRAYERS

§ 13 *The Afternoon Service*

(1) The name of the Afternoon Service, תפלת מנחה (*Tefilat minha*) (M. *Ber.* 4:1), Aramaic צלותא דמנחה, points to the service's origin in the Afternoon Sacrifice. In connection with the service, as with the sacrifice, a distinction is made between "the great *minha*," which begins at six and one-half hours, and "the lesser *minha*," beginning at nine and one-half hours (compare M. *Pes.* 5:1; B. *Ber.* 26b). To derive this distinction from the Bible, one must think of צהרים, "noon" (Ps. 55:18) and מנחת ערב, "evening offering" (Ps. 141:2) as times of prayer. The usual time of this service in the Temple was the ninth hour (Acts 3:1: ἡ ὥρα τῆς προσευχῆς ἡ ἐνάτη). In some lands the great *minha* was recited, and this is today the practice nearly everywhere on Sabbaths and festivals; in Rome and in the Orient it is often cited on weekdays, as well. But already in early times the Afternoon Service was moved, out of consideration for working conditions, to a point very close to the beginning of nighttime and joined with the Evening Service.[1] This was always the practice at the beginning of Sabbaths or festivals.

(2)   The prayer for the Afternoon Service is the ʿAmida, which, as in the Morning Service, is first recited silently, then repeated aloud.[2] Changes occur only in two points. First, in some communities, it was customary to delete the beginning of Benediction 17, "Accept." Second, there was no Priestly Blessing, and therefore in Ashkenaz "Great peace" was said instead of "Grant peace." According to the unanimous testimony of all sources, the ʿAmida was preceded by the recitation of Ps. 145 in its customary form.[3] R. Jonah of Gerona (thirteenth century) introduced the passage of the daily sacrifice (Num. 28:1–8) and "The Compounding of the Incense." Sepharad and Rome adopted this practice, adding Ps. 84 before it. *Vitry* precedes it with Ps. 5:8, "And I, in Your great kindness"; in Ashkenaz none of these was adopted for the public service, but were recited only by individuals.

(3)   After the ʿAmida, Supplications are said, as in the morning. *Vitry* contains several special supplication prayers for this purpose, and these are identical with those in Amram for the Morning Service. Since the Afternoon Service was often recited only just before dark, there was not always time to recite it properly. In such cases the geonim already recommended deleting it and, if time was very short, even to abridge the repetition of the ʿAmida.[4]

On the eve of Sabbaths and festivals, Supplications are not said at the Afternoon Service. From Catalonia it is reported as a special custom that on Sabbath eve Kaddish was said immediately after the silent ʿAmida; it can no longer be determined if the reason for this practice was that the repetition of the ʿAmida was originally omitted. In places where the Afternoon Service is recited apart from the Evening Service, it is concluded with "It is our duty."

§ 14   *The Evening Service*

(1)   תפלת הערב (M. *Ber.* 4:1), ערבית (M. *Ber.* 1:1), מעריב [in post-talmudic sources]: This service cannot be derived from the institutions of the Temple, for the Temple was closed in the evening, and no ceremonies took place at night. But the natural need for a night prayer gave rise to the Evening Service. The biblical authority for it is the phrase "when you lie down" (Deut. 6:7); its time is, in Josephus's words, ὁπότε πρὸς ὕπνον ὥρα τρέπεσθαι, "when time turns toward sleep." By the beginning of the Common Era, the service had been introduced everywhere; but no public worship was held in the evenings, for this was rather a private night prayer. When public prayer was introduced for the evenings, the service was held at the onset of evening, and for the convenience of the congregation it was combined with the Afternoon Service. It was most rare to wait until night had fully fallen.[1]

[77]

(2)   The nucleus of the service is the Recitation of the *Shemaʿ* with two benedictions before it, as in the Morning Service, and, unlike the Morning Service, with two benedictions after it (M. *Ber.* 1:4).[2]

In all known texts since Amram, the Evening Service begins with Pss. 78:38 and 20:10, והוא רחום, "And He, being merciful."[3] The most plausible of the reasons offered is that they wanted to fill the time until nightfall as well as to preface this service, like the others, with a few biblical verses. *Vitry* cites, besides these verses, Deut. 4:31, and stipulates for all verses that they be recited responsively between the precentor and the congregation.[4] Since the seventeenth century these verses have sometimes been preceded by Ps. 134,[5] and, according to the kabbalists, by another group of verses; so it is in Sepharad and Rome, but in Ashkenaz it is done this way only when the service is actually recited at night.

(3)   The first passage before *Shemaʿ* parallels "Creator of light," and it is not impossible that in ancient times the text of both was the same. In B. *Ber.* 11b, Abaye (fourth century) quotes from this text גולל אור מפני חשך וחשך מפני אור, "Who rolls away the light before the darkness and the darkness before the light," and in B. *Ber.* 12a the eulogy is cited (anonymously) as מעריב ערבים, "Who makes the evening fall." The texts are identical in all versions except for a few minor variants; Amram, Ashkenaz (already in *Vitry*), Romaniot, and Rome read at the end ה' צבאות שמו אל חי וקיים, "the Lord of Hosts is His name, the living and everlasting God," a version rejected totally by Abudarham, and which, in fact, is lacking in Sepharad.[6] A much shorter versified version was published in *REJ* 53 (1907): 234f.

(4)   For the beginning of "With eternal love," see above, §7:4. Here too the versions are identical except for the end, and the variants are insignificant.[7] The content is much more unified than in "With great love" of the Morning Service. It speaks only about revelation, thereby justifying its name, "the benediction of the Torah." See above, ibid.

(5)   Originally the third of the three passages of the *Shemaʿ* was not recited at night: " 'And the Lord spoke' is only customary in the daytime" (M. *Ber.*2:2).[8] In Palestine this was still the practice in amoraic times (Y. *Ber.* 1:9, 3d; B. *Ber.* 14b), and it remained the practice in many communities for centuries afterwards (*Halakhot gedolot*, 23). The contents of the last verse, the commemoration of the exodus from Egypt, were also expressed at night, as attested by Josephus (ibid.) and his younger contemporary, R. Eleazar b. Azariah (M. *Ber.* 1, end). For this purpose, the following texts are reported:

מודים אנחנו לך שהוצאתנו ממצרים ופדיתנו מבית עבדים להודות לשמך, "We give thanks to You for bringing us out of Egypt and redeeming us from the house of bondage to give thanks to Your name" (Y. *Ber.* 1:9, 3d) or מודים אנחנו לך ה' אלהינו שהוצאתנו מארץ מצרים ופדיתנו מבית עבדים ועשית לנו נסים וגבורות על הים ושרנו לך, "We give thanks to You, Lord our God, for bringing us out of the land of Egypt and redeeming us from the house of bondage and performing for us miracles and wonders on the sea; and we sang to You . . ." (B. *Ber.* 14b).

Probably the last phrase served as a transition to "Who is like You" and the Redemption Benediction. But Babylonia, as early as ca. 300, did not know anything of the omission of "And the Lord spoke"; therefore, the transition to Redemption was different and was matched to that of the Morning Service. Earlier, Rav[9] had introduced

"True and Faithful" into the Evening Service.[10] The text is identical in all rites since Amram, most of it being drawn from verses in Psalms. The transition from "Who is like You" to "The Lord will reign" in Amram is identical to that of Palestine for the Morning Service;[11] but today the same text is used everywhere with slight variants. Sepharad has יחד כולם הודו והמליכו, "together all of them gave thanks and gave homage," like the text in the Morning Service. Saadia has a version different from all others; yet another version, possibly Palestinian in origin, and versified, is in *REJ* 53 (1907): 234f.

(6) Unlike the Morning Service, the Evening Service has a fourth passage, השכיבנו, "Make us lie down," which the Talmud calls "a long Redemption" (B. *Ber.* 4b). The basic text in Amram was expanded in all the rites to a greater or lesser extent, the shortest being that of Rome and the longest that of Sepharad. A short text consisting of nothing more than a reworking of Ps. 4:9, "Safe and sound I lie down and sleep" is found in *REJ* 53 (1907): 234f. The eulogy in all prayer books is שומר עמו ישראל לעד, "Who guards His people Israel ever"; the source is *Midrash tehilim* to Ps. 6:1, but the text there is not above suspicion. In Palestine, the eulogy reads הפורס סוכת שלום עלינו ועל כל עמו ישראל (ועל ירושלים) [מנחם ציון ובונה ירושלים], "Who spreads the tabernacle of peace over us and over all Israel (and over Jerusalem) [who consoles Zion and builds Jerusalem]," a version current today only on the Sabbath and festivals.[12] This version could be deduced from Y. *Ber.* 4:5, 8c and its many parallels in the midrash: "R. Abun said, בנוי לתלפיות' (Song of Songs 4:4) means the hill toward which all mouths pray with benedictions, the Recitation of the *Shemaꞌ*, and the *ꞌAmida* . . . . In the Recitation of the *Shemaꞌ* (they say), 'Who spreads the tabernacle of peace over us and over all Israel and over Jerusalem.' "[13] Texts newly discovered in the geniza quoting this version in the weekday service make this conjecture a certainty.[14]

(7) The reason for the introduction of a petition in this unusual place is that this passage was intended as a replacement for the *ꞌAmida*. As long as the Evening Service was a true night prayer, there was no room in it for any petition but one for protection through the night; the other petitions served no purpose. But the service was soon shifted to the early evening, and, as in the two other services, the *ꞌAmida* was introduced, perhaps after the destruction of the Temple, as a replacement for the *ꞌAmida* that was recited in the temple for the "Closing of the Gates" (§34). But the *ꞌAmida* of the Evening Service was seen as optional, not obligatory: "The evening prayer has no fixed obligation" (M. *Ber.* 4:1); "The evening service is optional" (B. *Ber.* 27b; Y. *Ber.* 4:1–2, 7d). Though R. Gamaliel set off a mighty conflict with R. Joshua on this account (ca. 100),[15] the opinion that the *ꞌAmida* of the Evening Service is optional prevailed both on that occasion and later, despite continually renewed opposition. It is therefore separated from the prayers that precede it by Kaddish and is not repeated aloud.[16] But for a long time it was not recited in public at all, and a replacement was devised for it.

(8) A similar substitute is the passage, ברוך ה' לעולם אמן ואמן, "Blessed is the Lord forever, Amen, Amen." This is a collection of verses, mostly from Psalms, containing the tetragrammaton and intended to replace the eighteen benedictions of the *ꞌAmida*. All sources agree that it was meant to substitute for the *ꞌAmida*, but opinions are

divided as to why it was instituted.[17] According to some, the passage comes from Baby-lonia[18] and was introduced because the synagogues were far outside the city (cf. §48),[19] so that latecomers to the service who had not finished praying would not be left alone in the dark. Others say that the passage was introduced during a time of persecution,[20] when the recitation of the ʿAmida was prohibited, but nowhere can such a persecution be demonstrated with any certainty. There is even an opinion that "Blessed is the Lord forever" was introduced to save the time that would otherwise have been necessary for the ʿAmida;[21] there are, in fact, arrangements elsewhere that are intended to reduce the unnecessary prolongation of the weekday prayers. Finally, we must mention an opinion, though it is given without reference to any source, according to which the passage origi-nated in Palestine.[22] It may be that in one of the two lands the ʿAmida was said, and in the other, a substitute was said. This would explain the fact that in all rites from Amram on we find both together, the ʿAmida preceded by its substitute. To be sure, in most rites, "Blessed is the Lord forever" is recited silently, a final indication that it was not originally part of the service. [Most congregations in the Land of Israel in our time do not recite this prayer.]

Likewise, everyone is in agreement as to the time of the prayer's composition. All available sources, except such as can be discounted at a glance, attribute it to the post-talmudic period, specifically the saboraic period.[23] Its contents suit this period very well, for other prayers containing collections of biblical verses come from the same period.

If we examine the text closely, we find that all rites have the same verses, though not always in the same order, but not one extant text actually has eighteen verses;[24] most have only fifteen or sixteen. Whether and how to fill in the missing ones cannot be known; it is worth mentioning here that manuscript versions like the prayer book of R. Saadia [and its printed version], have the verses Obad. 21; Pss. 120:2, 15:6; Is. 45:17; and I Kgs. 8:57. Perhaps the sentences, "Blessed is the Lord forever" and "The Lord reigns" are also to be counted, for, though not actually biblical verses, they are stylistically close. Furthermore, it must be stressed that the prayer as it now stands has two endings. The series of verses is followed immediately by אלהינו שבשמים, "Our God in Heaven" and then by יראו עינינו, "May our eyes see," a second conclusion similar in content and expressing messianic hopes. In Rome "May our eyes see" is lacking, and the end is shorter: תהילה נביע לרובך בערבות לאל המפואר במקהלות קדושים בא״ה מלך אל חי לעד וקיים לנצח, "We express praise to the One who rides upon the heavens, to the God Who is extolled in the choirs of the angels. Blessed are You, O Lord, King, God, living forever and lasting forever." In Romaniot the choice is given between "May our eyes see" and the conclusion יהללוך ה' אלהינו כל פה וכל לשון, "May every mouth and every tongue praise you, O God,"[25] which, though identical in content to the ending in Rome, is longer. The eulogy, as well, has notable variants. R. Samuel b. Meir (ca. 1130)[26] was of the opinion that it is forbidden altogether to conclude a prayer with a eulogy not authorized by the ancient sources, and many thirteenth and fourteenth century French and Span-ish authorities agreed with him. Maimonides reportedly also held this opinion,[27] and we find clearly that Persia has, in fact, no eulogy at the end of this prayer.[28] But Romaniot has two: After "May our eyes see" there is the familiar eulogy, המלך בכבודו חי וקיים תמיד הוא ימלוך עלינו לעולם ועד ועל כל מעשיו לנצח, "The King in His glory, living and eternal, will reign over us forever and ever and over all of His works," which occurs in a shorter form in Amram, Ashkenaz, and Sepharad; after "May they praise," there is a different eulogy, similar to that of Rome. In Rome the wording is brief: מלך אל חי לעד וקיים לנצח, "King, God, living forever and lasting eternally," a literal quotation of the beginning of the eulogy in Saadia, מלך אל חי לעד וקיים לנצח משובח שמו תמיד ימלוך לעולם ועד אמן, "King, God, living forever and lasting eternally; praised is His Name; forever may He reign, forever and ever, Amen." But in Saadia there is also a second eulogy, for in his prayer book, "Blessed is the Lord forever" is said not only on weekdays, but, in opposition to the opinions of the other Babylonian geonim, on Friday night as well; and he concludes המולך בכבודו תמיד לעולם ועד אמן, "Who reigns in His glory forever and ever, Amen."[29] A version completely deviating from all rites is offered by Maimonides. After "Make us lie down" comes "Blessed is the Lord forever," with Ps. 31:6: "In Your hand I commend my spirit." But he goes on to say that some people have the custom of including a series of verses in the middle of the benediction; there follow five verses found also in "Blessed is the Lord forever," with the conclusion אלהינו שבשמים יחד שמך הקרוי עלינו, "Our God in heaven, make Your Name, which is called upon us, One"; after that come yet another nine verses followed by ברוך ה' ביום . . . ברוך ה' בקומנו תמיד נהלך סלה ונשיח בחוקיך ובאמונתך, "Blessed is the Lord in the Day . . . Blessed is the Lord when we rise up. We will always praise You and speak of Your Laws and Your Faithfulness," and at the end, . . . המלך בכבודו חי וקיים תמיד ימלוך, "The King in His glory, living and eternal, will reign forever. . . ." Given the poor state in which Maimonides's prayer text has been transmitted to us it is unclear how the addition quoted by him is to be understood: whether the eulogy at its end belongs only to the addition, or whether it is to be used even when the benediction is not expanded. [But see now the Goldschmidt edition in *SRIHP* 5 (1938/9): 195.] It should be mentioned that in Persia the series of verses also begins as in Maimonides, with I Kgs. 18:39, and that Yemen, which faithfully preserves Maimonides's tradition, prefaces this verse only with "Blessed is the Lord forever" and "The Lord will reign forever."

An attempt to account for this prayer based on all the characteristics that we have found in it leads to the following conclusion. Two prayers of completely different kinds seem to have been combined. First, there was a night prayer.[30] One series of verses definitely relates to a petition, whether preceding or following, for God's protection at night; this can be seen clearly in the arrangement of the material in Maimonides and in Saadia's manuscript prayer book. This nighttime prayer would have had no connection with the Evening Service itself. It would be a late composition from the time when the Evening Service was held just after nightfall, and would have been introduced as a nighttime prayer to be said just before going to sleep. The second part of the prayer, on the other hand, is a petition expressing messianic hopes;[31] the entire content of "May our eyes see" relates to the revealing of the kingdom of heaven. From this point of view we understand why, according to Saadia, this section should be recited even on Friday nights, independently of the verses that precede it, and why the oldest sources for this prayer speak about "Blessed is the Lord forever" and not "May our eyes see." The introduction of a messianic petition in this unusual place may perhaps be explained by the fact that in ancient Palestine the eulogy of "Make us lie down" was, as mentioned above, "Who consoles Zion and builds Jerusalem" or "Who spreads . . . and over Jerusalem." Likewise *Midrash tehilim* on Ps. 14:7 reports that schoolchildren used to recite in the evenings the verse, "Would that the redemption of Israel come

[80]

from Zion." But when that eulogy was eliminated in Babylonia and replaced by "Who guards His people Israel forever," a replacement was sought for the messianic prayer that had been eliminated. We would be able to view "May our eyes see" as this replacement, but we must not overlook the fact that its eschatology is formulated in such a classic style that the date of composition cannot be set very late. Until we discover ancient texts that quote the two parts of the prayer separately, we will not be able to get beyond such conjectures. In any case, we can see how R. Isaac ibn Ghiyath (eleventh century)[32] could still view "May our eyes see" as a foreign element, and would not authorize the interruption of the service on its account.

[81]

(9)   The ʿAmida of the Evening Service was also followed by Supplications in ancient times. This fact confirms somewhat the claim above that Supplications is the prayer of an individual that is recited after the public service. The Babylonian geonim,[33] to be sure, merely authorized, without requiring, its recitation; but the custom of the exilarch and R. Saadia's prayer book prescribe the Supplications also for the evening. [In Saadia, *Siddur*, 28, Saadia only permits the recitation of Supplications in the evening.] In our prayer books it no longer appears, but its traces have been preserved here and there. Thus, *Vitry* has here, as at the end of the Morning Service, "The compounding of the incense" and Gen. 1:5,[34] but lacks the daily psalm, found in Rome and Sepharad at the beginning of the Evening Service. Others quote Ps. 83 or 124 as a conclusion, alongside "There is none like our God" and "The compounding of the incense." All of these additions are lacking in some prayer books. In recent centuries Ashkenaz introduced arbitrarily various psalms after "It is our duty to praise,"[35] mainly out of consideration for the Mourner's Kaddish.

Prayers for Special Days

A. SABBATH PRAYERS

§ 15   *Friday Night*

(1)   In the most ancient period, no public service was held at the beginning of the Sabbath any more than on other evenings, but religious "fraternities" (חבורות) would celebrate the day by holding a common festive meal.[1] These meals would begin while it was still daylight; they were interrupted at nightfall, when the leader of the fraternity would recite the "Sanctification of the Day" over a cup of wine. Otherwise, each individual would recite his own night prayer separately as on every day, with some adding special words in honor of the Sabbath. An example has come down in the name of R. Zadok:

מאהבתך ה' אלהינו שאהבת את ישראל עמך ומחמלתך מלכנו שחמלת על בני בריתך נתת לנו ה' אלהינו את יום השביעי הגדול והקדוש הזה באהבה

"And because of Your love, O Lord our God, with which You loved Israel Your people, and because of Your kindness, our King, which You bestowed on the children of Your covenant, You gave us, O Lord, our God, this great and holy seventh day in love" (T. *Ber.* 3:7).[2]

Only from the beginning of the amoraic period, first in Babylonia and later in Palestine, was a service held in the synagogue on Friday night as well, with Kiddush—that is, the Sanctification of the Day—at the end. Furthermore, the tendency was to prolong the service more than on other days. Because of the distance that separated the Babylonian synagogues from the cities, and because of the superstitions prevalent there, people were afraid to remain alone in the dark or in a small number in a synagogue. Many pursued their work on Fridays until the latest permissible minute, arrived late at the synagogue, and therefore had to catch up with the congregation in reciting their prayers. So that these latecomers would not remain alone in the synagogue after the service, it was lengthened by a number of additions. Accordingly, to mention only the most familiar rule, the practice was introduced of repeating the *ʿAmida* on Friday nights, something that was not customary on weekdays. Thus was laid the foundation of the Friday night service, which is similar in all the rites.

[83]

(2)   The Sabbath service is introduced by an element not known in the Middle Ages, the Welcoming of the Sabbath (קבלת שבת). It originated in the circle of kabbalists in Safed at the end of the sixteenth century,[3] whose influence on Jewish life was a lasting and unhappy one. The Talmud (B. *Shab.* 111a) reports that certain sages would receive the Sabbath by saying: "Come, let us go out to greet the Sabbath Queen"; in these circles this poetic expression was taken literally. They would go out to the fields in groups reciting it and singing Pss. 95–99 and Ps. 29, followed by a song with the refrain, "Come my friend" and ending "Come O bride, come O bride, in peace, Sabbath Queen." There were several 'come my friend' songs of this type. The one that was generally adopted is that of R. Solomon Alkabez Halevi[4] (ca. 1540), which pleased R. Isaac Luria (the Ari, 1534–72); through the latter's influence it penetrated the congregations, despite opposition. Romaniot, for example, never accepted this innovation. The kabbalistic rite of welcoming the Sabbath, first described in *Seder hayom* by R. Moses b. Makhir (1599), was not performed everywhere in exactly the same manner. Only Ashkenaz has all of the Psalms; Sepharad has only Ps. 29, and Rome, none. Common to all is the song, "Come my friend"; and all rites adopted the custom that during the last sentence the congregation turns to the door, in commemoration of the originally customary walk outdoors. "Come my friend" is thus the latest element in the entire prayer book and, by dint of its poetic verve (Johann Gottfried Herder[5] and Heinrich Heine translated it into German), it was naturalized in the Jewish tradition. The introduction to the Sabbath prayers was shortened by the Reform movement, which generally reduced the number of psalms to one or two, and kept only the first, middle and final stanzas of "Come my friend."

The opening of the Sabbath service with Pss. 92 and 93 is older, though we do not know its origin. Maimonides was already asked whether their recitation is permitted.[6] They too are found in all rites, even though the *Shulḥan ʿarukh*, for example, is still silent about them. Romaniot and Persia added to them a whole series of biblical passages, including Pss. 100 and 150; before Ps. 92 Romaniot has a text that is based on I Kgs. 8:56: ברוך ה' אשר נתן מנוחה לעמו ישראל ביום השבת, "Blessed is the Lord Who has given rest to His people Israel on the Sabbath day."

(3)   The Evening Service is structurally the same as that of weekdays. A number of comments may be made about its text. According to Amram, the Friday night service begins also with "And He, being merciful"; this was the custom also in Spain, as, in Germany, it was long customary in Worms. In Sepharad the original Spanish practice has not survived.[7] In Rome, the texts of the benedictions before and after the *Shemaʿ* include the ancient Palestinian additions: אשר כלה מעשיו ביום השביעי ויקראהו שבת קדש, "Who concluded His work on the seventh day and called it the holy Sabbath," for "Who makes the evening fall," and the alphabetical בשביעי גזרת (קיימת) דברת, "On the seventh day You decreed (fulfilled) and spoke," for "True and Faithful." Saadia has the analo-

gous piyyutim for "With eternal love" and "Make us lie down."[8] These were opposed by Amram and are therefore lacking in Sepharad and Ashkenaz. The eulogy of "Make us lie down" was originally the same on Sabbath as on weekdays, "Who guards His people Israel forever," and Abudarham still knows this custom from Seville and Toledo; but today all the rites follow the Babylonian academies in saying, ופרוס עלינו סוכת שלומך, "and spread over us the tabernacle of Your peace," with the eulogy הפורס סוכת שלום וכו׳, "Who spreads the tabernacle of peace . . . ."[9] The expression "Who consoles Zion," also Palestinian, was rejected by the Babylonian geonim, and was therefore not preserved anywhere. One difference is that already in Saadia, Romaniot, and to this day also in Sepharad the words והגן בעדנו וכו׳, "and protect us . . ." are skipped, while in Rome and Ashkenaz they are recited even on Friday night, including the sentence, ושמור צאתנו ובואנו, "And guard our going out and our coming in," which is lacking in Provence and France, and therefore also in *Vitry*. In the academy of Sura, Kaddish was recited immediately after this benediction, which was followed by the ʿAmida, while in other synagogues Ex. 31:16–17, "And the children of Israel will observe . . ." was added.[10] Saadia reads besides this, כי המלכות שלך היא, "for the kingdom is Yours," and יראו עינינו, "May our eyes see," with the eulogy המולך בכבודו, "Who rules in His glory." According to R. Judah b. Barzilai and Abudarham, this was the general custom in Spain, but that, not as on weekdays, they would say, "May the heavens rejoice" (I Chron. 16:31) instead of "May our eyes behold." R. Judah b. Barzilai[11] and other authorities[12] criticized this custom. In France,[13] Ashkenaz, and Italy[14] they said only "And the children of Israel will observe" without additional verses and without a eulogy, as is the practice in all rites today.[15]

[84]

(4)   The ʿAmida of the Sabbath differs from that of weekdays in that the thirteen middle benedictions drop out and are replaced by a single benediction; it thus becomes ברכת שבע, "Seven Benedictions": "On the Sabbath . . . one recites Seven, with the Sanctification of the Day in the middle" (T. *Ber.* 3:12). The name of the middle benediction is "The Sanctification of the Day" (compare M. *R.H.* 4:5), and in a later period קלוס, "Praise" (*Soferim* 19:7);[16] its structure parallels that of the ʿAmida as a whole in that it always begins in a hymnic style, goes on to speak of the meaning of the day, and ends with the petition that the worshiper be enabled to fulfill the day in a way fully appropriate to its sanctity. In antiquity the formula may have been the same for all the day's ʿAmidot of the Sabbath, and on festivals in all rites this is still the case (except for the Additional Service); on Sabbaths, as well, at least the concluding petition או״א רצה במנוחתנו, "Our God and God of our fathers, accept our rest," is shared by all the ʿAmidot. From this benediction the sentence קדשנו במצוותיך, "Sanctify us by Your commandments," and the eulogy מקדש השבת, "Who sanctifies the Sabbath"[17] are found already in the Talmud (B. *Pes.* 117b). The full text is first found in Amram, but with the conclusion: וישמחו בך ישראל אוהבי שמך, "and may Israel, who love Your name, rejoice in You,"[18] which is preserved in Rome and which resembles the Ashkenazic text for festivals. But even though the benediction is mentioned in the Talmud and appears in all the rites, it is probably more recent than the short petition in Amram: הנח לנו כי אתה אבינו, "Give us rest, for You are our Father."[19] Certainly ancient is the introduction in Amram: ומאהבתך ה׳ אלהינו, "And because of Your love, O Lord, our God"; this is an expanded version of the prayer of R. Zadok, found also in Saadia and Rome.[20] To be

sure, in Rome and in the Oxford manuscript of Amram we already find alongside it: אתה קידשת את יום השביעי לשמך, "You sanctified the seventh day for Your name,"[21] by which it was eventually displaced. "You sanctified" must be ancient, for its language is simple, and it appears with uncommon unanimity in all rites [except for the above-mentioned]. At the end of "You sanctified" all rites today have Gen. 2:1–3 as a prooftext. The manuscript of Amram begins with 2:2, recorded also by R. Asher, and Abudarham even knows the custom of saying only 2:3.[22] Persia[23] has the entire creation story, Gen. 1:1–2:3. In Spain and Provence, and Sepharad today, this was followed immediately by: ישמחו במלכותך, "May they rejoice in Your kingdom,"[24] or at least the last sentence, ובשביעי רצית בו וקדשתו, "On the seventh day You were pleased with it and sanctified it." This must originally have appeared also in *Vitry*,[25] though perhaps not in its correct place. By analogy with the Sabbath Morning Service, the sentence must be in its correct place here. For the petition, "Accept our rest," see above.

The three opening and three closing benedictions of the ʿAmida have no differences from the weekday text; any additions are identical on weekdays and Sabbaths. Amram inserts in all the ʿAmidot, as an addition to Benediction 1, before למען שמו באהבה, "For His Name's sake in love," the words ורצה והנחל לבניהם שבתות למנוחה, "Accept and let their children inherit Sabbaths for rest,"[26] but we do not know the source of this tradition. This addition is somewhat astonishing, for it was declared invalid in geonic circles already in ancient times.[27] R. Judah b. Barzilai rightly opposed this petition as unsuitable to its place, and no vestige of it has remained in any rite.[28]

(5)   After the silent ʿAmida, in accordance with an amoraic edict (B. *Shab.* 119b) Amram has Gen. 2:1–3, which is said to this day, though today these verses are already included in the ʿAmida. Then comes the ברכה אחת מעין שבע, "One Benediction Replacing Seven," the substitute for the repetition of the ʿAmida mentioned above. The composition of this benediction is peculiar: The middle section, מגן אבות, "Shield of the fathers," constitutes a summary of all the seven benedictions—hence the name—and it should have sufficed. But it is preceded by the opening of the ʿAmida, in its Palestinian version, with קונה שמים וארץ, "Possessor of heaven and earth"; and it is followed by the complete text of the petition "Our God and God of our fathers, accept our rest."[29] The text is identical in all rites. The full Kaddish then shows that here the service ends.

(6)   Kiddush[30] and the recitation of the second chapter of M. *Shab.*,[31] together with an aggadic conclusion, serve as a kind of appendix appearing already in Amram. The case of Kiddush is discussed above. Originally it belonged to the meal, and was only later transferred to the synagogue, where we find it since the time of the first Babylonian amoraim. Babylonia did not know the custom of common fraternal meals for religious purposes, nor were vineyards generally cultivated. Therefore, where no wine was available, Kiddush was transferred to the synagogue, where it remained as the conclusion of the service. Knowing that Kiddush belonged only in a private house, by the family table, they [presumably the amoraim—*Engl. trans.*] excused the practice on the grounds that the synagogue served also as a hostel for travelers, who took their meals there. In the course of time, when the synagogue ceased serving this purpose, doubts were expressed about the propriety of saying Kiddush there, but no one dared to act on those doubts. Here is a classic example of how religious rites, once they have taken

root, cannot be removed by the force of logic. Kiddush remained an integral part of the Friday night service [in the Ashkenazic rite outside of the land of Israel]—in fact one of the high points of that service, a moment of extraordinary reverence and religious feeling. No community today, whether traditional or reform, would be prepared to give it up.

The text of Kiddush is identical but for minor variations in all rites, proof that it rests on good and ancient tradition. In the Reform prayer books the words מכל העמים, "From all the nations," have been eliminated from the Kiddush, as have all references to the election of Israel, though the most recent Reform prayer books have restored the traditional text.

"With what does one kindle?" (M. *Shab.* 2) was introduced in order to keep the congregation in the synagogue as long as possible, out of consideration for those who had come late to the service. This chapter was chosen because it has to do with the eve of the Sabbath. In Amram and the medieval codes it stands at the very end. In *Vitry*[32] and thus in Ashkenaz, it precedes Kiddush, while in Sepharad it was moved to the place before the Evening Service by reason of its conclusion.[33] There it is found to this day in Sepharad, and thence it was taken into Romaniot and Rome. In some congregations it was even recited before the Afternoon Service. Only when a festival falls on the Sabbath, or during a festival period, is it omitted. In recent times it has been dropped, not only by synagogues of the Reform rite, but even in traditional synagogues. After "It is our duty," Rome has "The living God be exalted" and Ashkenaz has "Eternal Lord"; and here the service ends. Persia concludes the Evening Service with "There is none like our God." Whatever else is found here in the prayer books comes from the kabbalistic תקוני שבת, "Sabbath rites,"[34] and these, too, were intended for the home Sabbath observances.

[86]

§ 16 *The Sabbath Morning Service*

(1)   The Morning Service is composed of the same elements as on weekdays (§6). The morning benedictions are augmented already in Amram as in all the later prayer books with biblical passages about the Sabbath sacrifice (Num. 28:9–10), which are rejected by Saadia.[1] The number of psalms in the Morning Psalms is also greatly increased already in Amram;[2] some elements in the daily liturgy originated in the Sabbath service. After the verses ה' מלך, "The Lord is king," etc., Amram has Pss. 100 and 136, I Chron. 16:8–26, Ps. 19, and then individual verses containing the name of God—most of them identical with the verses following הודו לה' קראו בשמו, "Praise the Lord, call upon His Name" (Ps. 135). Then come "Blessed is He Who spoke" (Pss. 92 and 93), "May the glory," and so on. This is what we find to this day in Rome. To all of these, Pss. 33, 34, 90, and 91, and in Sepharad also Pss. 95 and 121–124 were later added. The order of the sections was also changed. There were disagreements with regard to Ps. 100. In Italy, Spain, and Provence it was added only on Sabbaths, not on weekdays; in northern France and Germany the custom was the reverse, and so it has remained in Ashkenaz and Sepharad. We have already indicated that the Song of the Sea belonged originally only to the Morning Psalms of the Sabbath. Romaniot has many more psalms than all the other rites, as well as a special benediction for them.

Just as the number of psalms increased on the Sabbath, so their conclusion length-ened. All rites make use here of the hymn, נשמת כל חי, "The breath of everything that lives,"[3] whose antiquity is proved by the fact that its language is by and large identical in all rites, and by its lovely and poetic style. In fact, its beginning is mentioned already in the Talmud; R. Yoḥanan (B. *Pes.* 118a) understood this to be the "Blessing of the Song" required by the Mishnah as the conclusion to Hallel. And the same R. Yoḥanan quotes in connection with the prayer for rain a complete sentence that is found in our version of "The breath": אלו פינו מלא שירה כים, "If our mouths were full of song as the sea" (B. *Ber.* 59b). Likewise, his older contemporary, Bar Kapara, quotes in his prayer of thanksgiving sentences that are also found in this prayer (Y. *Ber.* 1:8, 3d): לך תכרע כל ברך, "To You every knee will bend." In the Middle Ages the legend was widely dis-seminated (in France and Germany) that the author of "The breath" was the Apostle Peter;[4] Rashi rejected this opinion forcefully. Another widespread assumption was that the author's name was Isaac, and the sentences near the end, ... בפי ישרים תתהלל, "By the mouth of the righteous You will be praised ... ," were arranged one under the other so as to form the acrostic יצחק.[5] We have mentioned above similar conjectures in con-nection with "May your name be praised"; all are pointless because in the ancient time when "The breath" originated, authors did not yet indicate their names in acrostics. There is room to doubt whether "The breath" has been preserved in its original form; in some places the synonyms are so heaped up that it seems to betray later reworking.[6] There is no overlooking the similarity between it and the benediction at the end of Hal-lel, the prayer "All Your deeds will praise You," which is also mentioned in the Talmud (B. *Pes.*, 118a), and which at one point even has a similar abundance of words. Thus, there is something to be said for the opinion of R. Samuel b. Meir in his commentary on the Talmud, that "The breath" is merely an addition to "All Your deeds will praise You." The end of "The breath" is "May Your name be praised," with the same eulogy as in the weekday service.

[87]

(2)   The benedictions of the *Shemaᶜ* (§7) resemble those of weekdays;[7] only the first is expanded significantly in all rites. It is composed of three parts: (1) הכל יודוך, "All give thanks to You"; (2) אל אדון על כל המעשים, "God, Lord of all creation"; and (3) לאל אשר שבת, "To the God Who rested." The first of these is a poetic piece turning on the word הכל, "everything," that concludes the preceding sentence. Then it incorporates המאיר לארץ, "Who illuminates the world," down to the words משגב בעדנו, "fortress pro-tecting us," and concludes in midrashic style with אין כערכך, or, as in Rome, Romaniot, and Sepharad, אין ערוך לך,[8] "There is none like You." "God, the Lord of all creation" is a reworking of the acrostic poem "Blessed God" in the weekday service, with a whole sentence instead of a single word for each letter of the alphabet.[9] "To the God Who rested" is perhaps a Palestinian piyyut, the only extant vestige of a genre originally developed for each of the days of the week.[10] These were hymns extolling the work of creation of each individual day; in each the day would appear and praise its creator in the words of that day's psalm (B. *R.H.* 31a). "To the God Who rested" is cited in the Middle Ages in the name of R. Natronai Gaon; but though he may be the first to men-tion the poem, it seems that the actual author lived several centuries earlier. All of the additions of this type must have been composed no later than the end of the talmudic period, for they have been adopted in all rites. In the geniza fragments they are not

always found; even Saadia[11] does not know them, and he mentions "To the God Who rested" only as the custom of individuals. In Spain R. Judah b. Barzilai protested vigorously against such "erroneous" and unfounded alterations of the weekday service as the insertion of "All give thanks to You," but his protest was unavailing, for only Toledo[12] is reported to have actually dropped "To the God Who rested."

(3)   The ʿAmida of the Sabbath Morning Service is structured exactly like that of the Evening Service; undoubtedly the texts of both were originally identical, as shown by the analogy of the festival ʿAmida. That the insertions were altered has a natural explanation in the fact that the Sabbath recurs far more frequently than the festivals, so that repeating the same text four times every Sabbath would have been too monotonous. In all the rites the Morning Service has ישמח משה, "Moses rejoiced";[13] the text is the same everywhere. The wording would lead one to expect the Ten Commandments as the biblical prooftext, but in all known texts since the time of Amram we find instead Ex. 31:16–18, apparently because the Ten Commandments are too long. The beginning of ישמחו במלכותך, "Those who observe the Sabbath," which should have come here, was expanded into ולא נתתו, "And You did not give it." Maimonides, differing from all other rites, has this addition in the Additional Service, while Abudarham does not mention it at all. The text has undergone various alterations to avoid misinterpretation; one geniza fragment reads, ובצלו לא ישבו גויים וגם במנוחתו לא ישכנו ערלים, "The gentiles do not sit in its shade, nor do the uncircumcised enjoy its rest," which produces good parallelism. The whole piece is probably based on a midrash. Because of the expansion, only the second part of "Those who observe the Sabbath" remained, beginning with the words עם מקדשי שביעי, "the people who sanctify the seventh day," though Sepharad preserved the entire text of both, whereas Romaniot, though lacking "And You did not give it," kept only the concluding sentence, חמדת ימים, "most delightful of days."

[88]

For the Kedushah, see §9a.

After the Morning Service comes the reading of the Torah; for this and the prayers surrounding it, from the taking out of the Torah to its return to the Ark, see §§25, 26, and 30.

§ 17   *The Additional Service*

(1)   מוסף, תפלת המוספין (*musaf*): The word *musaf* means "something additional," whether a prayer or a sacrifice—something in addition to the one offered every day. In fact, the Additional Service is known in connection with the Additional Sacrifice, and it is generally viewed as a replacement for the latter. But the earliest sources know of an Additional Service even without a sacrifice. It is reported of the *maʿamadot* (§34) that they would hold services four times on each weekday; one of these services was called Additional (compare M. *Ta.* 4:1,4).[1] Perhaps it is to this service that the dictum of R. Eleazar b. Azariah refers: "The Additional Service takes place only in a town assembly" (M. *Ber.* 4:7),[2] according to which the institution of this service is conditioned upon the existence of a communal association—that is, one that participated in the *maʿamad*. It would follow that originally the Additional Service had nothing to

do with the Additional Sacrifice. But all the other sources in our possession know of an Additional Service only on days when the Additional Sacrifice was brought (compare Num. 28, 29). It is first mentioned by first century tannaim (T. *Ber.* 3:3; compare 3:10–11; T. *Suk.* 4:5). The time of the Additional Service was between the Morning and Afternoon services.[3]

(2)   As for the Sabbath Additional Service, it is reported that in the Temple the poem in Deut. 32 was read. It was divided among six weeks, at the end of which it was begun anew (B. *R.H.* 31a).[4]

The text of the *'Amida* of the Additional Service was probably identical with that of the others. Only at the beginning of the amoraic period was it changed by the addition of a reference to the Additional Sacrifice:[5]

> Rav said, "One must say something new in it," and Samuel says, "There is no need to say something new in it." R. Zeera asked in the presence of R. Yose: "Must one say something new in it?" He said to him: "Even if he said 'And we shall perform before You our obligatory sacrifices, the daily sacrifice, and the additional sacrifice,' he has done his duty" (Y. *Ber.* 4:6, 8c).

A similar sentence to the one mentioned is found to this day in all Additional services. But the reference to the sacrifice did not long remain isolated. It received— probably early—an introduction, the content of which was prescribed by the conclusion, a petition for the restoration of Israel and the renewal of the Temple service. This is the passage common to all rites: יהי רצון מלפניך שתעלנו, "May it be Your will to bring us up."[6] It is prefaced by another short passage, doubtless also originally intended as an introduction, containing not a petition for the fulfillment of eschatological hopes, but a historical recounting of the establishment of the Sabbath and its sacrifices. In [89] Sepharad (Maimonides and Abudarham), its wording is very simple: למשה צוית על הר סיני מצות שבת זכור ושמור ובו צויתנו . . . להקריב לך קרבן מוסף כראוי, "You bade Moses on Mt. Sinai to remember and observe the Sabbath day; and on it You commanded us . . . to offer suitably the Additional Sacrifice." The other rites have instead the complex text: תיקנת שבת רצית קרבנותיה, "You instituted the Sabbath and accepted its sacrifices." The words in this passage begin with successive letters of the alphabet in reverse alphabetical order (תשרק); in the best versions, after the word אז comes פעליה כראוי נצטוו מסיני so that the acrostic embraces also the letters that have special forms when they come at the end of a word (מנצפך), though the last three words are found only in ancient sources, having vanished from the prayer books. Yet another change from the ancient text must be mentioned: instead of מוסף יום שבת, "The Additional Sabbath Service," Amram, *Vitry*, Maimonides, and Romaniot have מוסף יום המנוח הזה, "The Additional Service of this day of rest," apparently the original expression. It should also be mentioned that in the geniza fragments[8] alongside the two above-mentioned introductions, another, wordier one is found. In all the Reform prayer books the entire passage has been eliminated and replaced with one referring to the Sabbath rest.[9]

To the mention of the Additional Sacrifice belongs the recitation of verses from the Torah about the Sabbath Sacrifice (Num. 28:9–10). Only Maimonides [and following him, Yemen] seems to avail himself of the permission given in the Talmud to skip the sacrificial verses. After them, all the rites have "Those who observe the Sabbath" and "Accept our rest." Romaniot deletes the former; Maimonides has "And You did not give it" and only the conclusion of "Those who observe the Sabbath"—namely, "The people who sanctify the seventh day." The final benedictions of the ʿAmida are the usual ones, and in the Additional Service, as in the others, the Priestly Blessing is recited in the penultimate benediction [actually, in the final benediction—*Engl. trans.*].

(3)   After the ʿAmida Amram has nothing, while the other rites have "There is none like our God." In Sepharad (according to the *Manhig*,[10] also in France), it is preceded by a chapter of the Mishnah with an aggadic conclusion, and followed by *Tana deve eliyahu*, as on weekdays (compare §10). In Rome and Ashkenaz, the ʿAmida is followed by "The compounding of the incense" and "It is our duty"; in Rome it is followed also by Yigdal and ברוך יי אשר נתן מנוחה, "Blessed is the Lord, Who gave rest"; in Ashkenaz, it is followed by Psalm 92. But Psalm 92 is preceded in a great many communities by the Song of Glory, and in a few, mostly Polish communities, also by אז ביום השביעי נחת, "Then on the seventh day You rested," from the Song of Unity (on both, compare §10:12).

In modern prayer books the ʿAmida is followed only by "There is none like our God" and "It is our duty."

§ 18   *The Afternoon Service*

(1)   We know that in the Temple the Sabbath Afternoon Service had a particular poem designated for it: the Song of the Sea, divided into two parts (Ex. 15:1–10; 11–18), and the Song of the Well (Num. 21:17–18). These were sung on Sabbath afternoons alternately in a three-week cycle.[1] Even in that early time, most of the Sabbath was devoted to edifying sermons,[2] followed, around noon, by the Afternoon Service. In later centuries the sermons and the service were moved to the afternoon hours, and in some places they were extended to nightfall. The liturgy preserves a vestige of the former link between the popular sermons and the Afternoon Service: After "Happy," with which the weekday service ordinarily begins (§13), "A redeemer will come to Zion" is recited, the prayer that always serves to conclude the study of the Torah (§10). The Talmud speaks of readings from the Prophets at the Sabbath Afternoon Service (B. *Shab.* 24b), and such readings were retained in Persia until the eleventh century (§26); it is reported that in the amoraic period readings from the Hagiographa were held in Nehardea (B. *Shab.*, 115b). R. Natronai Gaon no longer knew this custom from his own experience, but he did know from older geonic sources that before the Sabbath Afternoon Service they used to read a freely chosen selection from that week's Torah reading and from the Haftara; at the end the precentor would read the final verse of the Torah reading, which was repeated by the congregation, and then he would continue with ואתה קדוש, "And You, the Holy One"—that is, "A redeemer will come to Zion" minus the first two verses. This custom has been retained in the old Portuguese synagogue in London[3] until today. In Romaniot and Rome,[4] the

Afternoon Service begins with several verses of messianic content, such as Is. 58:13–14; 52:7; Zech. 9:9; Mal. 3:1, 23–24, and so on, altogether making up ten verses, exactly the number that has to be read according to geonic responsa. This is probably a vestige of the sermons of antiquity.

After "And a redeemer will come to Zion," Kaddish is said as well as Ps. 69:14. In Amram[5] this verse is not yet present, except in the Oxford manuscript. The oldest known source for it is apparently Rashi, whose homily on it entered the codes. No reasonable historical explanation is known;[6] the most satisfactory one is that the expression עת רצון, "a propitious time," refers to the time of the Afternoon Service. In Rome the verse is recited three times; in Spain and Sepharad today, twice; eventually the repetition was eliminated in Rome, and replaced with Ps. 86:10 as a congregational response. For the reading of the Torah and the former readings from Hagiographa and the Prophets, see §§25, 26, and 27.

(2) In the middle benediction of the ʿAmida, Amram reads הנח לנו כי אתה אבינו, "Give us rest, for You are our Father," a version found also in geniza fragments.[7] These ancient sources already cite as a variant, אתה אחד, "You are one," which has become universal, though in manuscript sources[8] it has the addition למשה עבדך בסיני אמרת לו פני ילכו והניחותי לך מנוחה שלימה, "To Moses Your servant You said at Sinai, 'My face will go and lead you to perfect rest' "; this last at least partially explains the rather surprising words אברהם יגל יצחק ירנן יעקב ובניו ינוחו בו, "Abraham rejoices, Isaac sings, Jacob and his sons rest thereon."[9] Common to both versions is the conclusion, מנוחת אהבה ונדבה, "rest of love and free-will," identical in all rites but Romaniot, which is much briefer; but the manuscripts show many variants, hardly surprising when so many synonyms are present. The language appears to derive from a midrash. Then follows "Accept our rest . . ." to the end of the ʿAmida. Romaniot prefaces this with the three words זכר למעשה בראשית, "In remembrance of the work of creation," apparently a vestige of "Those who observe the Sabbath."

(3) Next come already in Amram Pss. 119:142, 71:19 and 36:7; in Sepharad the order is reversed, corresponding to the order in the book of Psalms (Abudarham even claims that this order is found already in Amram and Saadia), and this was the medieval practice in France and Provence as well. The custom of inserting the verses here is certainly very ancient. The explanation given in the geonic period was that Moses died on a Sabbath afternoon, and that therefore, as in any case of mourning, God's justice must be praised (צידוק הדין).[10] For the same reason, according to this tradition, *Avot* (including the apocryphal sixth chapter) is read in the Sabbath Afternoon Service, though it is unclear whether the entire tractate was read or only a chapter each week. The reading of chapters 1 and 3 of *Derekh eretz zuṭa*, also mentioned in Amram, is not confirmed by the manuscripts or any rite. That this reason is not satisfactory was often raised already in the Middle Ages, nor are we any more satisfied with the explanation offered instead, that the torments in Gehenna cease on the Sabbath and are renewed at its conclusion. The only reasonable explanation is the one already given in *Vitry*,[11] that the moralistic content of *Avot* is what led to its inclusion in the prayer book. For the Sabbath was always a day of religious instruction. When actual sermons ceased, the study of books replaced oral teaching, and, because of its abundance of

moral dicta, *Avot* was particularly suited as instructional material. This explains why it was chosen for reading on Sabbath afternoons. But this practice did not obtain universally throughout the year, for the rites vary greatly in this respect. For the most part it was customary to read a chapter every Sabbath throughout the summer months, and in some places only on the six Sabbaths between Passover and the Pentecost. The customs also varied in that some read the chapter before the Afternoon Service. Every chapter of *Avot* is preceded with M. *Sanh.* 10:1 and is concluded with the last mishnah of *Makot*. For the winter, Ashkenaz has Pss. 104 and 120 to 134 (fourteenth century; *Vitry* does not know the custom); in Sepharad this role is filled by Pss. 119 to 134 and 91, which were also chosen because of their uplifting contents. In Sepharad, both *Avot* and Psalms are recited before the Afternoon Service, and afterwards only Ps. 111 is recited.

§ 19   *The End of the Sabbath*

(1)   The end of the Sabbath, אפוקי שבתא, מוצאי שבת (B. *Pes.* 105d; Y. *Ta.* 1:6, 64c), was also observed in ancient periods by fraternal meals. At nightfall, light was brought and, as at the end of every meal, incense on coals, מוגמר (M. *Ber.* 6:6); a benediction was recited for both. In the Grace a benediction, called Havdala, was inserted for the conclusion of the Sabbath.[1] Havdala is exceedingly ancient and, like Kiddush, was attributed to the men of the Great Assembly. This benediction was inserted (no later than the second generation of tannaim) also in the ʿAmida recited by individuals. Eventually the meals fell out of use; indeed the view arose that it was forbidden to taste any food or drink during the twilight hour.[2] In the twelfth century the explanation, not found in the Talmud, was given that this is harmful to the dead, who break their thirst at that time. The odd notion arose that the souls of the dead have respite from punishment throughout the Sabbath and after it, עד שהסדרים שולמים[3]—that is, until the service and the Torah study connected with it come to an end—and then prepare at twilight to return to Gehenna. Likewise it is noted that it is best for the women to refrain from work until that time. From the fact that the time was defined by the conclusion of the service, it may be surmised that the liturgy for the end of the Sabbath was rather lengthy; besides the fact that it was considered meritorious to lengthen the sacred time at the expense of the profane time, and to prolong the period of rest, they also sought to prolong the service as much as possible. The prayers were supposed to be recited slowly, in a melodious and solemn fashion. To the regular Evening Service sermons were added; no trace of them is left in the books of rites, but we have a vestige of them in the Kedushah of the Lesson. The expression עד שהסדרים שולמים also alludes to them, and the Oxford manuscript of Amram says explicitly:

[92]

> The scholars recite the Mishnah and read the Talmud, each as much as he wishes, and when they finish studying the law one of the scholars stands and says, ברוך אלהינו, "Blessed is our God," and the others respond, . . . ברוך אלהינו שבראנו לכבודו, "Blessed is our God who created us for His glory."[4]

From this it is clear that homilies were offered at that time just as they were offered every morning.

It is possible that in this connection the scriptures were read; the psalms that today precede the Evening Service in all rites could be a vestige of this practice.

(2) All rites concur in the recitation of Pss. 144 and 67 before the Evening Service, though no trace of this practice is found in the Middle Ages. While Ashkenaz is generally satisfied with these two psalms, sometimes in western Germany other psalms are added, and in Sepharad Ps. 75 is added. The service itself is identical with the weekday service. Only Saadia's prayer book quotes in the benedictions preceding and following the *Shemaʿ* the ancient Palestinian additions:[5] in the first benediction, אל המבדיל בין קודש לחול, "God, Who distinguishes between the sacred and the profane"; in the second, אותנו הבדלת להיות לך לעם, "You distinguished us to be Your people"; and in the first benediction after the *Shemaʿ*, אמת ואמונה אמרה איומה הבדילני, " 'True and faithful' the Awesome Nation said"—which were rejected by Natronai and R. Amram. [These are not additions but poetic versions of the above-mentioned benedictions, replacing the usual versions; compare Saadia, *Siddur*, 123 ff.]

In the fourth benediction of the ʿAmida, Havdala is inserted before the petition. It is not only a farewell benediction, but also a prayer for warding off moral dangers. The text in Rome and Sepharad, as in Amram,[6] is אתה הבדלת, "You distinguished," and כשם שהבדלתנו, "As You distinguished us," but is somewhat expanded in Sepharad. The wording in Ashkenaz is completely different. Connecting with the introductory words "You bestow," it begins אתה חוננתנו, "You bestowed on us," continues with ותבדל, "and You distinguished," and borrows the petition החל עלינו, "make descend on us" from the Talmud (Y. *Ber.* 5:2 end, 9c): החל עלינו את הימים ששת ימי המעשה הבאים לקראתנו לשלום, "Make the six days of work, that are coming towards us, descend upon us in peace." The addition חשוכים מכל חטא, "Guarded from all sin" comes close to Amram's version. The double introduction in Ashkenaz and Sepharad, "You bestow" alongside "You bestowed on us" remained in place, despite all protests of authorities.[7]

(3) The ʿAmida is followed already in Amram by Ps. 91, called by the Talmud "The Song of Disasters"; *Vitry* calls it "The Psalm of Blessing." This second conception of the psalm is what led to its introduction by the verse immediately preceding, Ps. 90:17.[8] This is followed by the Kedushah of the Lesson, just as in the Afternoon Service, except that the first verses are omitted so that the prayer begins with Ps. 22:4. If one of the major festivals falls during the coming week, both pieces are omitted; only in Sepharad is "And You, being holy" retained. In Sepharad, this ends the service, but in Rome, Romaniot, and Ashkenaz (since *Vitry*[9]), ויתן לך, "May God give you"[10] is appended, a collection of biblical verses signifying good fortune and blessing, in which nearly all the blessing-formulas of the Pentateuch are contained. A distinct unit is constituted by "Three (biblical verses) of reversing, three of redeeming, three of peace," ordained by the Talmud to calm one made anxious by a bad dream and incorporated here (B. *Ber.* 55b). In details there are numerous differences between Rome and Ashkenaz; in western Ashkenaz a few passages are omitted that are customary in the East; but common to all is the intention of collecting verses that promise good fortune. Also common to all is the conclusion, the aggadah from the end of B. *Ber.*, "Scholars increase peace in the world."

(4)   Havdala follows, consisting of individual blessings over wine, spices, and light, and one over the "distinguishing." This prayer originated at the meal, as shown especially by the spices; its transfer to the synagogue can be explained by the cessation of the ancient table customs and the lack of wine in certain regions of Babylonia (compare §15[6]). In Sepharad and Rome the benedictions are preceded by biblical verses containing petitions for blessing in the coming week, and in Sepharad, a part of the poem אליהו הנביא, "Elijah the Prophet," besides. In Ashkenaz, already in Vitry,[11] these passages are only for the home ceremony. There they multiplied without limit, each person adding whatever he liked, and superstition often had a role in the heaping-up of prayers for the new week. In general, the intention was to pray as much as possible for blessing on the work of the coming week.

B. WEEKDAYS OF FESTIVE NATURE

§ 20   *The New Moon*

(1)   Among the special days is the one that recurs most often in the year, ראש חדש, νουμηνία. Already in the Bible it plays a great role as a solemn feast-day, a day of rest from work, liturgical assembly, and prophetic instruction.[1] In the post-biblical period the New Moon lost its festive character; it was demoted to the rank of secondary feasts, and the prohibition of labor was removed. The establishing of the beginning of a New Moon was one of the most important functions of the Sanhedrin and one of the main prerogatives of its authority. This was designated קדוש החודש, the sanctification of the New Moon, a vestige of the day's sanctity in biblical times. *Soferim* 19:9 has preserved an ancient report about a solemn session for the determination of a New Moon, in connection with which a festive meal was held, and a special solemn grace was recited. After the introduction of a fixed calendar, after 360, the central authorities[2] gave brief notice of the main signs according to which anyone sufficiently knowledgeable could easily draw up a calendar. In the synagogues, after the Torah reading on the Sabbath of the week preceding the New Moon, the occurrence of the New Moon was proclaimed, מזכירין החדש. The proclamation is found in all rites. The oldest formula is in Romaniot:

הקול כל עמא הבו דעתכון למשמע קל קדוש ירחא הדין כמה דגזרו מרנן ורבנן חבורא קדישא דהוו יתבין בארעא
דישראל אית לך ריש ירחא ד . . . בכך וכך בשבת חושבניה ומניניה בכך בשבת

"Hear, all the people! Pay attention to hear this proclamation of the New Moon, as decreed by our masters, the sages, the holy council that used to sit in Palestine. We have the New Moon of the month of . . . on the . . . day of the week."

It recalls the ancient time when the authorities of the Holy Land had to inform the communities of the beginning of the month in Aramaic. In a somewhat modified form and now in Hebrew the statement reads in Rome:

כך גזרו רבותינו המכובדים שנכריז בפני הקהל הקדוש הזה שיהיו יודעים גדולים וקטנים שיש לנו ראש חדש . . .
בחשבון רבותינו יום . . . ויום . . .

"Thus our honored sages decreed that we announce to this holy congregation for old and young to know that we have the New Moon of . . . on . . . and . . . ."[3]

Here, too, the proclamation appears as the most natural means to provide exact information about the date of the New Moon and the occurrence of festivals in an age poor in calendars. To the proclamation, as with any happy announcement, a prayer for welfare in the coming month was added: מלכא דעלמא יעברניה לסימנא טבא לנא ולכל עמיה בית ישראל, "May the King of the world make it a good sign for us and for all His people the house of Israel," is the formula in Romaniot. Out of this developed later the longer stylized petition יחדשהו, "May God renew it," customary in Ashkenaz and Sepharad, following the brief proclamation formula . . . ראש חדש . . . יהיה ביום "The New Moon of . . . will be on . . . ." In all rites save Romaniot, the proclamation is preceded by a petition of eschatological content, מי שעשה נסים, "He Who performed miracles," which is everywhere the same in content despite many variants in the text; Romaniot has a petition for the restoration of the Temple when the New Moon coincides with the Sabbath. The connection seems to be that when the announcement of the New Moon is made, the destruction of the central point from which it was formerly made should be mourned and God should be petitioned to restore it. Of this a vestige remains today in the longer or shorter prayers for the bringing of the messianic age. To the prayer for the future redemption, Rome and Sepharad erroneously added אחינו ישראל ואנוסי ישראל, "Our brethren, Israel, and the oppressed of Israel," a prayer for the freeing of the brethren in faith from present oppression recited weekly by many congregations.

This is the old form of the New Moon proclamation, to which Sepharad and Ashkenaz have prefaced more prayers in modern times: Ashkenaz for about the last century and a half has had the supplication that Rav used to attach to his daily ʿAmida (B. *Ber.* 16b), put into the plural and with the beginning modified to suit the occasion, יהי רצון מלפניך שתחדש עלינו את החדש הזה לטובה ולברכה, "May it be Your will to renew this month for us in prosperity and blessing." Sepharad has the petitions beginning "May it be Your will" that in Rome and Ashkenaz are recited after the reading of the Torah.

The original function of the New Moon proclamation as a replacement for the calendar fell into the background with time, and the petitions came to be seen as the main thing; thus, the designation מזכירין החדש, "The proclamation of the month," was changed to מברכין החדש, "The blessing of the month," ראש חדש בענטשן in Yiddish; the more recent term is *Neumondsweihe.*

(2)   Since the end of the sixteenth century the custom has arisen, first in Palestine, of fasting on the day before the New Moon. This fast day is called יום כפור קטן, "Minor Day of Atonement"; a special liturgy was composed for it, assembled from the penitential prayers of the Day of Atonement. Indications providing some basis for such a fast day are found in the literature of preceding centuries, even in the biblical fast for the day of the New Moon. But the fast became widespread through the circle of kabbalists influenced by Isaac Luria. Moses Cordovero brought it to Italy, and thence

it found its way to the northern lands, but it never struck deep roots and has been mostly forgotten in modern times.[4] For the customary *seliḥot*, see below, §33.

(3)   At the Afternoon Service on the eve of the New Moon and on the day itself, Supplications are omitted, and on the Sabbath צדקתך צדק, "Your righteousness is eternal" (Psalms verses mentioned in §18:3) are omitted. In other respects the services are hardly different from those of weekdays. In Benediction 17 of the ʿAmida, after "Accept," since the time of the early tannaim, a piece referring to the solemn character of the day (מעין המאורע)[5] is inserted, which the amoraim called הזכיר של ראש חודש. The beginning, יעלה ויבא, "Ascend and come," is cited in *Soferim* 19:11; this must refer to the piece current today, as it is the same, but for insubstantial variants, in all rites since Amram. Palestine has a version that is much expanded, compared with the familiar text.

[95]

(4)   After the Morning Service the psalms of Hallel (Pss. 113–118, known as הלל המצרי, "the Egyptian Hallel") are recited with the omission (דלוג)[6] of the beginning (verses 1–11) of Pss. 115 and 116. Hallel on the New Moon is unknown to tannaitic sources. It was customary in many parts of Babylonia, to the astonishment of Rav.[7] Since the peculiar manner in which it was recited made the impression on him that it was an ancient custom, he authorized it, and thus Hallel was introduced for the New Moon in its shortened form. Hallel is introduced by a special benediction, לקרוא את ההלל, "to recite the Hallel,"[8] and concluded by another, called "the Benediction of the Song." This function is filled in all rites by "All Your deeds will praise You," mentioned already in the Talmud (B. *Pes.* 118a); in Rome it has a very simple text, expanded in Ashkenaz and Sepharad by the heaping-up of synonyms, while Amram[9] and Romaniot have four short rhymes: יהללוך מעשיך ישבחוך עמוסיך יודוך חוסיך כפי גודל נסיך, "Your deeds will praise You, Your borne-people will laud You, Your sheltered ones will give thanks to You, in accordance with Your great miracles," accompanied by the last verse of Psalms.[10] The eulogy מלך מהולל בתשבחות, "King lauded with praises," is universal. For the Torah reading that follows, see §25.

(5)   The New Moon has, at least since the time of Hillel,[11] an Additional Service, constructed in the same manner as that of the Sabbath. In Palestine, the Additional Service ʿAmida seems to have had the same text as that of festivals.[12] In Y. *Ber.* 9:2, 13d, the question is discussed whether "And grant us" (§28) is to be recited, and ברוך מחדש חדשים, "Blessed is He Who renews the months," is given as the eulogy. In manuscript fragments, the introduction, like that of festivals, is אתה בחרת, "You chose" (§23). In all rites today we have a later version.[13] It contains, like the Additional Service ʿAmida for the Sabbath, (1) an introduction, dealing with the significance of the sacrifice (Num. 28:15) and the festival (Num. 10:9, 10) as atonement; (2) petition for the restoration of the sacrificial cult, citing Num. 28:11–15; and (3) petition of blessing for the new month, חדש עלינו את החדש הזה, "Renew this month for us," with the eulogy מקדש ישראל וראשי חדשים, "Who sanctifies Israel and the New Moons."

If the New Moon falls on a Sabbath, all insertions and omissions are the same. In the Additional Service, the introduction is אתה יצרת, "You created,"[14] a longer version than that used on weekdays, in more elevated language, closer to the Palestinian version mentioned above. Before the biblical verses on the sacrifice, Num. 28:9, 10 are recited, and afterwards "Those who observe the Sabbath." The eulogy is מקדש השבת וישראל וכו', "Who sanctifies the Sabbath and Israel . . . ." The text of the ʿAmida of the Additional Service is, since Amram, everywhere identical[15] but for unavoidable slight differences, indicating high antiquity. In the modern [Reform] prayer books it has, like all other ʿAmidot of Additional services, been altered by the elimination of the reference to the sacrifices. Likewise, the old view of the New Moon as a day of atonement has also fallen aside.

(6) Since antiquity the New Moon has had its own psalm, but the tradition does not tell us which.[16] Ps. 104 is customary. The oldest source that names it is *Orhot* 1:69c; Romaniot has here, as is usual with this rite, several psalms (Pss. 93, 96, 137, and so on).

[96]

§ 21 *Fast Days*

(1) On "public fast days" (תענית צבור, νηστεία) the liturgy undergoes certain changes. Such fast days were instituted for public disasters (compare I Kgs. 21:9; Joel 1:14, 2:15), especially frequently occurring ones like drought (תענית גשמים; compare M. *Ta.* 1, 3).[1] Such fasts had a special ceremony with its own liturgy (M. *Ta.* 2). In Babylonia the regulations for these fasts were not in force (B. *Ta.* 11b: "There is no public fast day in Babylonia") and with the cessation of Jewish authority in Palestine (ca. 350), they fell completely out of use; nevertheless, the fast day liturgy was used around 1000 in times of dire necessity. Alongside the fast days, instituted on a case-by-case basis, were also historical fast days commemorating unfortunate events in Jewish history. Most of these also have fallen into desuetude, although the Scroll of Fasts (last chapter) says that they are of toraitic origin. The four biblical fasts remained (Zech. 8:19): the Seventeenth of Tammuz, the Ninth of Av, the Third of Tishre, the Tenth of Tevet; to them the Thirteenth of Adar was added. Thus, one spoke of five fasts[2]—or of four, since either the Ninth of Av or the Third of Tishre was sometimes accorded special status and given separate prayer books, "The Order of the Four [Five] Fasts." To these Ashkenaz added (apparently not before 1250) the fasts of Monday, Thursday, and Monday that fall after Passover and Tabernacles at the beginning of the months Iyyar and Marheshvan. A ground for this was found in Ps. 2:11 and Job 1:5, but actually they were probably instituted in the dark days of persecution. In a few countries and communities, expulsions and pogroms led to the establishment of local fast days, on which the liturgy was treated exactly as on other fast days.

(2) In Spain and France the fasts, like the New Moons, would be proclaimed during the service on the preceding Sabbath,[3] while in our countries only the fasts of Monday, Thursday and Monday are announced in the synagogue; this proclamation takes the form of a special blessing for those who observe them. In modern prayer books, the "five fasts" are announced together with the Blessing for the New Moon, but no special attention is paid to the others. The liturgy of fast days is altered by the introduction

of prayers. In the ʿAmida, "Answer us" is inserted (צלותא דתעניתא, של תענית, "the prayer of the fast day"); see above, §8(9).

(3)   During the repetition of the ʿAmida, at least since the geonic period, the precentor inserts *seliḥot* in Benediction 6. Fast days commemorate disasters, which occur, in the ancient and medieval view, on account of sin; therefore, on fast days the petition for forgiveness is expanded. Already in antiquity the expansion of the ʿAmida was prescribed for fast days. Attached to the petition for forgiveness (Benediction 6), six or seven benedictions were added, most of them psalms or other biblical verses dealing with community disasters; they conclude with a petition in the pattern, מי שענה ל . . . , הוא יענה אתכם, "May He Who answered . . . answer you," with a eulogy. As late as 1000, fasts for drought were still being held in the Oriental countries, with a prayer pleading for the removal of the disaster being added to the Morning Service within the framework of the ancient liturgy.[4] Together with long passages from the Bible, freely composed prayers or liturgical poems were incorporated. According to our sources, the service was so long that it must have occupied nearly the whole day. But on historical fast days this liturgy was not used; rather the regular weekday ʿAmida was retained, and was only interrupted in the middle of Benediction 6 by the recitation of *seliḥot*. The *seliḥot* themselves, which do not belong to the statutory prayers, are treated below, in §33; here we mention only that the "Thirteen Attributes" (Ex. 34:6–7) are their constantly repeating refrain. At the end of the *seliḥot* the ʿAmida would be resumed by means of the transition formula, used only on this occasion, ואל יעכב, "and may sin not block our prayer." Romaniot and Rome have, on the biblical fast days, *qerovot* besides, which are inserted in each of the benedictions of the ʿAmida (§32).

[97]

Finally, the Torah is read on fast days, both in the Morning Service and Afternoon Service; in the Afternoon Service there is also a reading from the Prophets—see §§25 and 26. Unlike all other days, on fast days the Priestly Blessing is recited in the Afternoon Service; therefore, in the last benediction one says, even in Ashkenaz, "Grant peace." In places where on other days the custom was to omit the beginning of "Accept" in Benediction 17, it was recited on fast days. On the Third of Tishre, other changes occur because it is one of the Ten Days of Repentance; see §24.

A special place among the fast days is occupied by the Ninth of Av, when the changes in the liturgy are more extensive because it is a kind of day of mourning. *Soferim* and Amram[5] ordain rites of mourning as if on the death of a close relative, customs that have been partially preserved till this day. The same outlook was operative in the prayer book; an examination of the sources shows that it was responsible for constant change in the liturgy in the course of the centuries. *Soferim* does not know of any special prayers for that day, but only a few verses for recitation in the evening, Jer. 14:19–22; Pss. 79 and 137; Romaniot kept these verses and added Ps. 74. The only change in Amram is the insertion of the prayer רחם, "Have mercy" in Benediction 14 of the ʿAmida, a change that applies to all three ʿAmidot of the day. The text is identical with that of Y. *Ta.* 65c,[6] but toward the end there is an additional petition: נערה ה' אלהינו מעפרה והקיצה מארץ דויה נטה עליה כנהר שלום וכנחל שוטף שלל גוים, "Shake off her dust, O Lord, our God, awaken her from the land of sickness; turn toward it peace like a river, and the booty of the enemy like a flowing spring." The entire text has been preserved verbatim also in Romaniot and Rome. Already manuscript 'S' of Amram has the text beginning with "Comfort,"[7] which is probably Babylonian in origin, and which passed into Sepharad and Ashkenaz. The eulogy today is everywhere as in Amram מנחם ציון ובונה ירושלים, "Who consoles Zion and builds Jerusalem,"[8] while in the Middle Ages various versions with מנחם אבלי ציון, "Who consoles the mourners of Zion," were also in use. In all of medieval France (and perhaps also in Spain?),[9] "Have mercy" was said in the Evening and Morning services, and "Console" in the Afternoon Service, so that both versions were preserved concurrently. Later, only Romaniot retained this custom; in Ashkenaz and Sepharad only "Console" was said in the Afternoon Service, and only Rome has "Have mercy" in all three services.

In other respects, the liturgy in Amram is the same as for other fast days. In the Kedushah of the Lesson, Is. 59:21 is omitted, and if the night of the Ninth of Av falls on a Saturday, Ps. 91 is skipped. For the Evening Service, Amram mentions also the reading of Lamentations. In *Soferim* it is not yet definitely established whether Lamentations is read in the evening or the morning. This reading is followed by the Kedushah of the Lesson, as is the custom after all other such readings.

But that is not all. *Soferim* states that in the Evening Service "Bless the Lord" is omitted, and further, that the Kedushah and Kaddish are omitted until the Afternoon Service; this has not been accepted by any rite. The practice was early adopted that on the Ninth of Av itself and on the eve of the Ninth of Av, Supplications are not recited,[10] and this custom has become universal. From Rome came the initiative of skipping the Song of the Sea on that day,[11] and apparently this custom did spread everywhere in the Middle Ages, though eventually it was restored and again recited everywhere but Rome; in Romaniot it was replaced by Deut. 32. Likewise, other parts were omitted, such as Ps. 100 and even "Praise the Lord, call upon His name," and the verses about the sacrifices after the introductory benediction [i.e., Morning Benedictions].[12] In Kaddish, too, "May it be accepted" was dropped.[13] Not all of these customs have been preserved, and the practice varied in the different communities. The recitation of *selihot* mentioned by Amram was eliminated, and it was replaced by poetic *qerovot* and *qinot* (compare §33).[14] These are recited in Romaniot and Rome within the ʿAmida, before the eulogy of Benediction 14: "God of David and Builder of Jerusalem"; in Spain, they come immediately after the ʿAmida; and in Ashkenaz they are recited only after the reading of the Torah. In some places the *qinot* were recited not in the synagogue but at home,[15] and elsewhere people would assemble to read the Book of Job in the synagogue.[16] In the modern period [in the Reform congregations] the attitude toward the Ninth of Av has changed considerably, and so, accordingly, has its order of prayers. Among these changes it should be mentioned that usually only the Book of Lamentations or a selection from it is read, and one or two *qinot* added.

On the reading of the Torah and Haftara, see §§25 and 26.

§ 22 *Hanukkah and Purim*

a. Hanukkah

(1)   Hanukkah (*Megalit ta'anit*, chap. 9), ἐγκαινισμός (I Macc. 4:59), ἐγκαίνια (John 10:22), was celebrated for eight days, from the Twenty-fifth of Kislev on, in commemoration of the dedication of the Temple under Judah Maccabee. The influence of this holiday on the liturgy is not especially great. The changes in the statutory prayers are limited to the insertion of the reference to the event in the penultimate benediction of the 'Amida;[1] the contents of this passage have already been discussed above, in §9:5. The passage is first reported in *Soferim* 20:8 in abbreviated form; the present text is very faulty, but clearly very different from the one found in all rites. It ends with the petition: עשה עמנו ה' אלהנו ואלהי אבותנו נסים ונפלאות ונודה לשמך נצח, "Do for us, Lord our God and God of our fathers, miracles and wonders, and we will give thanks to Your name forever," which has passed into Amram, Sepharad, and Rome, with a minor change: כשם שעשית עמהם נס כן עשה, "Just as You did a miracle for them, so do. . . ." There was considerable disagreement about the appropriateness of having a petition in this place in the 'Amida, and thus Romaniot and Ashkenaz do not have it. The introductory sentence, על הנסים, "For the miracles" is first mentioned by R. Aha (ca. 750);[2] the conclusion, וקבעו שמנת ימי חנכה אלו בהלל והודאה, "and they fixed these eight days of Hanukkah with songs of praise and thanksgiving" (*Megalit ta'anit*, chap. 9; Amram), corresponds to I Macc. 4:59: καὶ ἔστησεν Ἰούδας . . . ἵνα ἄγωνται αἱ ἡμέραι ἐγκαινισμοῦ τοῦ θυσιαστηρίου . . . μετ' εὐφροσύνης καὶ χαρᾶς.[3]

[99]

(2)   On Hanukkah, Supplications are not recited, while the recitation of Hallel (in its unshortened form) has been customary since antiquity (T. *Suk.* 3:2); the benediction on this occasion in all rites except Ashkenaz is לגמור את ההלל, "to recite the full Hallel."[4] Hanukkah has its own psalm, Ps. 30 (*Soferim* 18:2); the psalm may derive its heading, "A Song for the Dedication of the House," from this fact. For the reading of the Torah, compare §25.

(3)   Lamps are the symbol of the Hanukkah holiday; hence Josephus calls the holiday φῶτα (*Antiquities*, 12.7.7). The lamps were originally lit only in the home, but later also in the synagogue. Already in the time of the first amoraim special benedictions were recited during their kindling—three on the first day and two on the others; but there was also an opinion that benedictions should be recited only on the first day. The wording of the first benediction is reported in B. *Shab.* 23a[5] in the form customary everywhere to this day, להדליק נר של חנוכה, "to kindle the Hanukkah lamp," while a different version is found in Y. *Suk.* 3:4, 53d. The text of the two other benedictions, שעשה נסים, "Who performed miracles," and שהחיינו, "Who has kept us alive," appears to have been omitted from the Talmud editions by a printer's error, but it is no less ancient than the first. In *Soferim* 20:6 the hymn הנרות הללו, "These lamps," is also quoted, apparently in the wrong place; it should be recited after the benedictions. Lately the custom has arisen in Ashkenaz to sing, afterwards, the poem מעוז צור ישועתי, "Fortress, Rock of my Salvation"[6] or a Hanukkah song in the vernacular. In Rome and Sepharad, Ps. 30 is recited after the benedictions instead of "These lamps," while in Romaniot nothing is added at all.

b. Purim

(1)   It is scarcely possible to reach a historically grounded conclusion about the time and the reason for the origin of the festival of Purim (Fourteenth of Adar) and the fast preceding it (Thirteenth of Adar). The fast cannot have existed as long as the Day of Nicanor was being celebrated (*Megalit ta'anit*, chap. 12). *Soferim* 21:1 reports that in Palestine the "days of the Fast of Mordecai and Esther" were observed for three days (Monday, Thursday, and Monday) after Purim.[7] All other sources know the fast only as "the fast of Esther," on the Thirteenth of Adar. It was never considered as important as the biblical fasts, but its effect on the liturgy is the same. Compare §21.

(2)   On Purim, as on Hanukkah, "For the miracles" is inserted in the 'Amida (compare *Soferim* 20:8, end), and a special psalm is designated for the day. According to *Soferim* 18:2, it is Ps. 7, but this is found only in Romaniot, while the other rites have Ps. 22, which the Midrash connects with the story of Esther. Hallel is not recited on Purim, and therefore Amram retains the Supplications;[8] in the Middle Ages the Supplications were again eliminated. For the Torah reading, see §25.

(3)   On Purim the Scroll of Esther is read, a custom that the Mishnah already regards as established, and which in fact must have existed centuries before its redaction (compare *Meg.*, beginning).[9] Since the time of the amoraim the reading is held twice (B. *Meg.* 4a), at night after the 'Amida and in the morning after the reading of the Torah. The reading of Esther is prefaced by three benedictions: על מקרא מגילה, "concerning the reading of the Scroll"; שעשה נסים, "Who performed miracles"; and שהחיינו, "Who has kept us alive," which the Talmud summarizes with the acronym מנ"ח (B. *Meg.* 21b).[10] After the reading comes the benediction הרב את ריבנו, "Who fought our cause,"[11] after which, according to the Talmud, come the following additional sentences: ארור המן, ברוך מרדכי, "Cursed is Haman, blessed is Mordecai," which later was usually reworked in poetic form.[12] After the reading, the Kedushah of the Lesson is recited. There was much debate as to whether to recite "Who has kept us alive" in the morning as well. Amram already mentions that certain verses in the scroll are recited together by reader and congregation;[13] the number of such verses was later increased. Often the reading of the scroll was accompanied by customs intended to release the overwhelming feelings of joy, and these not infrequently took on wild form;[14] see Abrahams, *Jewish Life*, 33, 262. In Reform congregations the reading of the Scroll of Esther has mostly been limited to the Morning Service, while in the evening it is replaced by a selection in the vernacular. The noisy disturbances have been eliminated in every civilized country.

[100]

C. FESTIVALS

§ 23 *The Three Pilgrim Festivals*

(1)   The festivals, ימים טובים ומועדים (Amram),[1] are a single unit from a liturgical point of view. The structure of the services, with one exception,[2] is the same for all; the differences have their origin in the meaning of each festival. In accordance with their character they have been divided, since antiquity, into two categories: שלש רגלים, "The Three Pilgrim Festivals," and הימים הנוראים, "The Days of Awe." In tannaitic sources the usual names are פסח (Passover), עצרת (Pentecost), and חג (Tabernacles) (M. *Suk.* 3:5 and T., ibid.) [Elbogen's original is incorrect here; the correct references are M. *Meg.* 3:5 and T. *Meg.* 3:5—*Engl. trans.*]; in Aramaic פסחא, עצרתא, and חגא, later also חגא דפטיריא and חגא דמטללתא [Tabernacles and Passover, respectively—*Engl. trans.*]. The Mishnah presupposes everywhere one day of each festival, while the Babylonian Talmud also deals with the יום טוב שני של גלויות, "the second festival day of the Diaspora."[3] In Palestine, to this day, only one day is observed, except for the New Year.

(2)   The services parallel those of the Sabbath. As with the latter, the ʿAmida is composed of seven benedictions, of which the first three and the last three are the same as on weekdays, while the seventh contains in its petition the passage קדשנו במצותיך, "Sanctify us by Your commandments," familiar from the Sabbath. They are distinguished in that on the Sabbath each service has a different introductory formula, while on the festivals there is a single text for the Evening, Morning, and Afternoon services,[4] and that of the Additional Service, like that of the Sabbath, is an expansion of this text. The number of seven benedictions goes back to the days of the early tannaim, as shown by the dispute between the House of Shammai and the House of Hillel on the manner in which the festival ʿAmida should be expanded on the Sabbath.[5] Our text dates from the beginning of the amoraic period, and is the work of Rav and Samuel; only slight and insignificant additions point to later centuries. Ula bar Rav (ca. 330) mentions אתה בחרתנו, "You chose us," in Yoma 87b as a well-known prayer; ותתן לנו, "And You gave us," is mentioned in B. *Ber.* 33b in connection with the "pearl" (מרגניתא) of Mar Samuel (230). The same author mentions והשיאנו, "And grant us"; from this petition comes the sentence "Sanctify us by Your commandments," as well as the eulogy מקדש ישראל והזמנים, "Who sanctifies Israel and the seasons," which, however, was still being disputed in the fourth century (see B. *Pes.* 117b.) If the festival falls on the Sabbath, the tanna R. Nathan (ca. 160) already requires the wording, מקדש השבת וישראל והזמנים, "Who sanctifies the Sabbath and Israel and the seasons" (T. *Ber.* 3:13).

[101]

(3)   All of the above citations come from Babylonian authorities, but there is no doubt that another, Palestinian version of the ʿAmida existed as well, vestiges of which are found in *Soferim* 19:3. There it is required that a festival be named with the words יום טוב מקרא קדש הזה הזה יום חג הזה, "the festival, this day of holy assembly, this festival day"; among the known prayer books we find exactly this version only in Maimonides. Fur-

ther, *Soferim* 19:7 mentions as components of the three festival ʿAmidot the passages: גלה, "Reveal"; "Arise and come"; and "And bestow upon us." This, too, has no parallel in our prayer books; in them, "Reveal" occurs only as part of the Additional Service, while "Arise and come" is in all the ʿAmidot except the Additional Service. The wild attempts that have been made to alter this source in order to harmonize it with the known prayer books have all failed. As a eulogy, *Soferim* offers: מקדש עמו ישראל והזמנים ומקראי קדש, "Who sanctifies His people Israel and the seasons and the days of holy assembly"; this abundance of words is not found in any of the extant liturgies. But fragments in the Cairo geniza with all the above-mentioned characteristics were published and discussed in *MGWJ* 55 (1911), 443–46 and 586–93. They are vestiges of the ancient Palestinian rite, and are referred to below as Palestinian.

(4)   In the Additional Service of all festivals, the middle benediction is expanded by the insertion of ומפני חטאינו, "And because of our sins," between "You gave us" and "And grant us"; "Arise and come" is omitted. Since Amram the structure and text of these additions are identical in all services. "And because of our sins" is intended as an introduction to the verses of sacrifices; it starts with the destruction of the Temple and the impossibility of bringing sacrifices, and goes on with a plea for the coming of the messianic era and the rebuilding of the Temple. Then come the verses from Num. 28 and 29 with details of the sacrifices, followed by the petition אלוהנו ואלוהי אבותינו מלך רחמן רחם עלינו, "Our God and God of our fathers, merciful King, have mercy upon us," about the restoration of the pilgrimage. Palestine also had for the ʿAmida of the Additional Service quite different and much simpler texts than the current ones; there the Additional Service differs from the others only in the words actually necessary for the reference to the sacrifices. Immediately after "And You gave us" comes להקריב בו קרבן מוסף ככתוב בתורתך, "to offer on it the Additional Sacrifice as it is written in Your Torah," with the appropriate biblical verses as a prooftext. After "Reveal" comes a brief reference to the restoration of the pilgrimage, and at the end of "And grant us" the prayer returns to its starting point with the words, ונעשה לפניך את חובותינו תמידי יום וקרבן מוסף, "and we will perform our obligations before You, the daily sacrifices and the Additional Sacrifice," known from Y. *Ber.* 4:6. Other than this, everything is the same, and even "Arise and come" is present.

(5)   As for the text of the festival prayers, the following details must be noted. Instead of "You chose us," Palestine has אתה בחרת as the introduction to a hymnic section with more poetic flair than the current one.[6] In "And You gave us," Palestine follows *Soferim* exactly, while Amram[7] and, following him, Sepharad, give the name of the festival before the words "the festival, this day of holy assembly"; in all the other rites these words are completely lacking. Palestine has only מועדים לשמחה, "seasons for joy"; Amram and the others add חגים וזמנים לששון, "feasts and seasons for happiness"; R. Isaac Ibn Ghiyath[8] and Romaniot add also the words ימים טובים לישועה, "holidays for salvation." Since the time of Amram all the rites have added a reference to the significance of the festival—for example, זמן חרותנו, "the season of our freedom." Palestine adds to "And You gave us" verses from Lev. 23 about the festival, adding after them verses from the Hagiographa and the Prophets, as the other rites do only in the Additional Service of Rosh Hashana. The petition אלוהנו ואלהי אבותנו גלה, "Our God and God of our fathers,

reveal . . .," is concluded in Palestine with the sentence ‫ואמרו מעשיך ה' אלהי ישראל מלך‬ ‫ומלכותו בכל משלה‬, "and all of Your creatures will say: the Lord God of Israel is King, and His kingdom has dominion over everything," known also from the New Year service. The theme of the kingdom of heaven enjoys expression in its pure classical form in Palestine on every one of the festivals.[9] "Arise and come" begins in Pal. and *Soferim*, with ‫אנא אלהינו‬, "O our God"; the text was expanded in various ways, the list of things to be called to mind becoming much longer. At the end comes a petition for redemption, ‫ויהי יום מקרא קודש הזה יום . . . הזה סוף וקץ לכל צרותינו תחילה וראש לישועתנו‬, "and may the day of this holy assembly, this day of . . . be an end and a conclusion to all our troubles and the beginning and start of our salvation," known otherwise only from Sepharad for the New Moon (above, page 105), and preserved in Romaniot and Rome also for the festivals. "And grant us"[10] is known from Y. *Ber.* 9:2, which, however, cites only the beginning. At the end all rites except Ashkenaz read ‫כן תברכנו סלה‬, "so may You bless us forever"; support for this reading is found in Palestine, which has ‫כאשר אמרת ורצית‬ ‫כן תברכנו סלה‬, "as You have said and have desired, so may You bless us forever." The petition "sanctify us by Your commandments" is not found in the known texts from Palestine. It was probably not deleted by the copyists, but was actually not an original part of the text. In its version of the eulogy, Palestine, as said, stands completely alone (compare B. *Pes.* 117b).

(6)   ‫ומפני חטאינו‬, "And because of our sins," for the Additional Service begins ‫אלהינו ואלהי אבותינו‬, "Our God and God of our fathers," in Amram,[11] hence in Sepharad; otherwise, it is identical in all the rites but for the usual insignificant variations. Only in *Vitry* is it somewhat expanded at the end. As is well known, the verses of the sacrifices are lacking in Spain, though they are found in Amram. Their omission is sanctioned on the basis of a talmudic dictum (B. *R.H.* 35a).[12] Among the geonim, Sar Shalom, in opposition to Natronai and Saadia, insisted that they be recited. Since prayer books were rare, and since the copies were abbreviated as much as possible, the verses were not very familiar, and thus had to be skipped. Rashi was greatly astonished by this custom, which he saw as a complete innovation. Nevertheless the verses are found in all rites except Sepharad, and even there they were widespread in the Middle Ages. The pilgrimage is mentioned in Palestine in the words, ‫עינינו תאיר בבית מאויינו ושם‬ ‫נראה לפניך בשילוש פעמי רגלינו‬, "And make our eyes shine in the house for which we long, and there we will appear before You on the three pilgrimages," a text deriving from Deut. 16:16–17.

(7)   When a festival falls on the Sabbath, the middle benediction is not changed, but in the appropriate places a reference to the Sabbath is added. It is doubtful whether this is exactly in accordance with the enactment of the House of Hillel (T. *Ber.* 3:13), "One begins with the Sabbath and concludes with the Sabbath"[13] but it is hard to determine exactly to what this baraita refers. In "And You gave us," before the reference to the festival, ‫שבתות למנוחה‬, "Sabbaths for rest," and ‫את יום המנוח הזה‬, "and this day of rest," are added. Ashkenaz reads, instead, ‫את יום השבת הזה‬, "this Sabbath day," and adds after the reference to the festival, ‫באהבה‬, "in love," which is lacking in Ashkenaz on festivals coinciding with weekdays. The appropriate supplements from the Sabbath petition "Accept our rest" are added to "sanctify us with Your commandments." In

the Additional Service ʿAmida, the verses of the Sabbath sacrifices are inserted before the verses of the festival sacrifices, and after them, "Those who observe the Sabbath." The Palestinian text for the Sabbath is not extant. The eulogy is already quoted by R. Nathan: "מקדש השבת וישראל והזמנים," "Who sanctifies the Sabbath and Israel and the festivals," but Ravina (fifth century) still had to combat deviations from this text.

[103]   (8)   When a festival falls at the end of the Sabbath, the "pearl" of Mar Samuel, beginning ותודיענו, "And You proclaimed to us" (B. *Ber.* 33b),[14] is inserted in the ʿAmida of the Evening Service before "And You gave" to replace Havdala (§19[2]).

(9)   As with the ʿAmida, the same basic material is common to all three festivals. The Evening Service is the same as on weekdays, except that in Sepharad and Ashkenaz, "Make us lie down" is recited in the form customary on the Sabbath.[15] As a biblical verse Rome and Sepharad have Lev. 23:4, while Ashkenaz, since *Vitry*, has Lev. 23:44; in Romaniot each festival has a special verse.[16] Palestine knows nothing of the relatively late custom of reciting these verses. Sepharad and Romaniot preface the Evening Service with a psalm, as they do on weekdays, and they have another at the end, as on the Sabbath. These psalms are listed below. After the ʿAmida, Kiddush is said over wine; the text has much in common with the middle benediction of the ʿAmida.[17]

At the Morning Service, after the Morning Benedictions, the psalms are recited. *Soferim* 18:2–3 and 9:2 specify a psalm for each festival,[18] to be recited at the beginning of the Verses of Song; afterwards, "May the Glory" and the various daily psalms are recited. But this practice did not survive. Rather, in all rites the order of the psalms customary on the Sabbath is retained: in Ashkenaz without change; in Rome, with the insertion of Ps. 97; in Sepharad and Romaniot, with the psalm for that particular festival and, as in Amram, with the omission of the first verse of Ps. 92. As on the Sabbath, the Song of the Sea—in Amram, all the way to Ex. 15:26—and "The breath" are recited. Then follows the "Creator" of weekdays, in the form "All give thanks to You" on the Sabbath; but it seems that Palestine had special liturgical poems for the "Creator" of festivals. Then comes the ʿAmida, which has been covered.

Common to all three festivals is the recitation of Hallel,[19] Pss. 113–118, which was established already in the tannaitic age; in that period Hallel was assigned to only one day of Passover (two in the Diaspora), and the shortened Hallel to the other days. In the Middle Ages the custom was revived (at first in France?) of reading one of the five scrolls on each of the festivals;[20] in Romaniot this reading is divided among several days.

For the reading of the Torah, see §25; for the Additional Service, see above, §23(4). For the Additional Service a particular psalm, not the same one as mentioned above, was recited in the Temple.[21]

(10)   On the intermediate days (חול המועד) of Passover and Tabernacles the service is the same as on weekdays, with "Ascend and come" inserted into the ʿAmida and Supplications omitted. The Additional Service, which, as on the New Moon, is introduced by "Happy" and "And a redeemer will come to Zion," is that of the festival. In the reference to the festival in "Ascend and come" or in "And You gave us" the

words יום טוב מקרא קודש, "festival, solemn assembly,"[22] are omitted, in accordance with *Soferim* 19:3, and this was the practice in Palestine; among the known rites a change is found only in Sepharad, which skips the word טוב, "good," and reads only את יום מקרא קודש הזה, "this day of solemn assembly." Hallel and the Torah reading also form part of the liturgy of the intermediate days of the festival.

(11)   For the individual festivals the following details must be noted:

a.   Passover is called in the prayers, חג המצות, "the festival of unleavened bread," and also זמן חרותנו, "the season of our freedom."[23] *Soferim* 19:3 and Palestine do not use the expression "festival, solemn assembly" on the intermediate days of the festival. The seventh day is called יום שביעי עצרת, "the seventh day of assembly," in *Soferim*; in the rites this distinction is not known; only Sepharad omits the word "good." In *Soferim* 18:2 the psalm for the Morning Service of Passover is Ps. 135; according to others, it is Ps. 83 for the first and intermediate days of the festival, Ps. 136 for the seventh day. Sepharad has Ps. 107 as the "song," and Ps. 114 after the evening service. Romaniot has Ps. 92, as on the Sabbath, and afterwards Ps. 135 or 106, and 136 and 150; on the seventh day it has Ps. 18 instead of Ps. 135. On the first and second nights of Passover, Kiddush is not recited over wine in the synagogue, and when it occurs on the Sabbath the One Benediction Replacing Seven is omitted (above, §15).[24] It is reported that in Spain and in Babylon, the Seder was held in the synagogue[25] because the masses were ignorant and did not know how to read the Haggadah. According to Sepharad, Hallel is recited on the first two nights in the synagogue as well, and this custom was adopted also in Poland[26] and in the Balkans [and in Palestine on the first night]. According to the Talmud, Hallel is recited in the Morning Service only on the first day of Passover, but later it was instituted on the other days of Passover in the same form as on the New Moon.[27] From among the five scrolls, the Song of Songs is read on the seventh day of Passover or on the Sabbath of the intermediate days.[28] The verses of the sacrifice in Palestine and in Romaniot are Num. 28:16 or 19–24 or 25, depending on the day; in Ashkenaz and Rome, Num. 28:16–19 or 19 alone, while 20–24 were telescoped into a text applicable to all festivals, ומנחתם ונסכיהם, "And their meal offerings and their wine offerings." The eulogy in the 'Amida is in Palestine, מקדש ישראל וחג המצות ומועדי שמחה והזמנים ומקראי קדש, "Who sanctifies Israel and the festival of unleavened bread and the appointed times of joy and the seasons and the holy assemblies." In the Additional Service of the first day of Passover, the recitation of "Who makes the wind blow" comes to an end. In Sepharad, Rome and Romaniot "Who makes the dew fall" is added from then on, while in Ashkenaz no mention is made of dew at all. [In Palestine even the Ashkenazim include the reference to dew.] Out of this, a special prayer developed eventually, the prayer for dew attached to the Additional Service.

For the Torah reading, see §25.

b.   Pentecost is called חג השבועות, "The Festival of Weeks," in the prayers, and already in *Soferim* 19:4, and is celebrated as the feast of the revelation, זמן מתן תורתנו, "the season of the giving of our Torah," which has no authority at all in the Bible. The psalm assigned to it according to *Soferim* 18:3 is Ps. 29. Sepharad and Romaniot have Ps. 68;[29] Rome has it before the Torah reading, but, after the Evening Service, Ps. 122.

[104]

Of the scrolls, the Book of Ruth is read.[30] For the reading of the Torah, see §25. The biblical verses of the Additional Service are Num. 28:26–27 (in Romaniot, 26–31), and afterwards "and their meal offerings and their wine offerings," as above; Romaniot has Num. 28:26 here as well as in the evening, in place of the fixed verse from Leviticus (see above).

c.   Tabernacles is called חג הסכות, "the Festival of Booths," and, in accordance with Deut. 16:14–15, זמן שמחתנו, "the season of our joy." In *Soferim*, there is no indication here at all due to the damaged state of our texts. In Palestine the eulogy in the *Amida* is מקדש ישראל וחג הסכות ומועדי שמחה והזמנים והרגלים ומקראי קדש, "Who sanctifies Israel and the festival of Tabernacles and the appointed times of joy and the seasons and the pilgrimage festivals and the holy assemblies." As the psalm for the Morning Service, *Soferim* 19:2, and likewise, Romaniot, has Ps. 76.[31] The order of the psalms of the Additional Service for the intermediate days is given in B. *Suk.* 55a: on the first day, Ps. 29; on the second, Ps. 50:16–?; on the third, Ps. 94:16–?; on the fourth, ibid. 8–16?; on the fifth, Ps. 81:7–?; and on the sixth, Ps. 82:5–?. In Sepharad, Pss. 42 and 43 are used, and after the Evening Service, Ps. 122. On all days of Tabernacles, the complete Hallel is recited. The verses for the Additional Service are selected from Num. 29:12–39 according to the day. Peculiar to the festival of Tabernacles are the Processions (הקפות)[32] with palm branches after the Additional Service [or after the Morning Service]. During the procession prayers are recited concluding each time with הושענא (Hosanna), "O, save!" and which are therefore called *hosha‘not* (see §32). The seventh day, which the Talmud calls יומא דערבתא, "The Day of the Willow" (in Romaniot and Rome, יום הערבה), is called יום הושענא, "Day of Hosanna," and later, הושענא רבא, "The Great Hosanna," because of the many processions and the numerous repetitions of these prayers.[33] The day was declared a day of judgment, apparently based on M. *R.H.* 1:2; in Italy, France, and Germany it was especially singled out by the early Middle Ages (going back to the twelfth century). Already in *Vitry*,[34] the psalms of the Sabbath, "The Soul," the "great" Kedushah, and various other holiday prayers were assigned to it. In the later kabbalistic period (from the fourteenth century onward), it was considered comparable in importance to the Day of Atonement,[35] and a great number of the customs of that day were transferred to it, with some people even fasting. Sepharad, especially, shows signs of this penitential view of the day. In Romaniot, the first and last benedictions of the *Amida* were recited according to the version customary in the Closing Service of the Day of Atonement (§25). Early in the Middle Ages, it seems that the processions were held not only in the Morning Service but also in the Afternoon Service[36] after the *Amida*. From the tenth century we have reliable information that on Tabernacles, or at least on the seventh day, processions were held around the Mount of Olives in Jerusalem.[37] Many pilgrims came from a great distance to participate in them; on this occasion the calendrical regulations for the New Year would be proclaimed.

d.   The eighth (and ninth) day of Tabernacles, called שמיני עצרת, "The Eighth Day of Assembly," is considered a separate festival: "The eighth day is a festival on its own account."[38] In the *Amida* it is referred to as יום השמיני [חג] העצרת, "the eighth day [the festival] of the assembly." Nevertheless it is called, like Tabernacles, "the season of our

[105]

joy." Its psalm, according to *Soferim* 19:2,[39] is Ps. 12 (apparently by virtue of its heading), and this was the custom in Spain; the Romaniot custom, apparently based likewise on an external factor, was to say Ps. 6. *Soferim* gives the choice of Ps. 111, as well, which we find in Palestine. Before the ʿ*Amida* of the Evening Service, Romaniot has Num. 29:35. As the verses for the ʿ*Amida* we find in Palestine Lev. 23:36–39, I Kgs. 8:66, Neh. 8:18 and Ezek. 43:27. The wording of the eulogy is מקדש ישראל ויום שמיני עצרת ומועדי שמחה והזמנים ומקראי קדש, "Who sanctifies Israel and the Eighth Day of Assembly and the appointed times of joy and the holidays and the days of assembly."[40] The verses of the Additional Service are Num. 29:35–36 and in Palestine, also, 29:37–39, and 30:1. The scroll of Tabernacles is Ecclesiastes,[41] which is read on the eighth day, because of 11:2 [or on the Sabbath of the intermediate days]; in Romaniot it is divided among the days of the festival. In the Additional Service on the Eighth Day of Assembly the reciting of "Who makes the wind blow" begins,[42] and this is announced before the silent ʿ*Amida*; out of this practice developed a special prayer called גשם, "Rain."[43] Since ca. 1000, the second day of the Eighth Day of Assembly has borne in the literature, though not in the prayers, its own name of שמחת תורה, "The Joy of the Torah."[44] The reason is that, on this day, the last chapter of the Torah is read, and according to a custom dating back to geonic times, the first chapter is read as well (see §25). The Torah reading of that day is accordingly accompanied by a great number of festive prayers (§30), though the statutory prayers are not distinguished in any way from those of the day before. [In Palestine the Joy of the Torah is celebrated on the Eighth Day of Assembly, and the above-mentioned Torah readings are performed then.]

§ 24 *The Days of Awe*[1]

[106]

a. New Year

(1) The New Year,[2] ראש השנה (*Rosh Hashana*), on the First of Tishre (the name is used in Ezek. 40:1 for the Tenth of Tishre), is so called because on it the reckoning of the new year begins. Both the name of the festival and its duration over two days can be traced back to the time of the Mishnah; no less ancient is the view that the two days together are a single institution of the highest antiquity: "The two festival days[3] of the New Year are among the institutions of the first prophets" (Y. ʿ*Eruv.* 3, end, 21c). In the Torah, the First of Tishre is called יום תרועה, "a day of blowing the shofar" (Num. 29:1), זכרון תרועה, "a commemoration of blowing of the shofar" (Lev. 23:24), whence in the prayers the terms יום הזכרון, "the day of commemoration," and יום תרועה, "the day of blowing the shofar," are used. If the first day of the New Year occurs on the Sabbath, the expression "day of blowing the shofar" is replaced by "a commemoration of blowing the shofar." Only in Palestine was the term "New Year" preserved in the language of the prayers as well.[4]

(2) The external sign that distinguishes the services of the New Year from those of the other days and comes to expression in the day's liturgical name is the blowing of the shofar. The Talmud reports that originally the shofar was blown early, during

the Morning Service, but that once, apparently during a time of political unrest, the Romans interpreted these sounds as a call to rebellion and fell upon the Jews and massacred them. From then on, the blowing of the shofar was moved to the Additional Service,[5] because by that late hour there could be no doubt as to the festive character of the ceremony (Y. *R.H.* 4:8, 59c). The Mishnah, *R.H.* 4:7, takes this new arrangement into account when it rules that the shofar should be blown while the second precentor officates—that is, during the Additional Service, "The second one blows the shofar." This innovation had a double consequence. First, as to the shofar blowing: In order that the congregation not be forced to wait for the shofar blowing until such a late hour, the shofar blowing of the Morning Service[6] ("when they are sitting") was introduced before the shofar blowing of the Additional Service ("when they are standing"); by the year 300 the reason was already forgotten. The second consequence had to do with the order of the prayers, as we shall see presently.

(3)   Already in ancient times it was said that the New Year services are longer than those of the other days of the year: "What benedictions are made long? The benedictions of the New Year" (T. *Ber.* 1:6). Likewise, the advice to the precentor—"One should always think through his prayers and then recite them" (B. *R.H.* 35a)—was applied to the services of the New Year because they are long. The idea of the kingdom of heaven[7] determined the character of these prayers, for the New Year gives religious expression to the acknowledgment of God's dominion over all people; God as king unites all of humanity in one bond; he judges them, remembers all their deeds, and decrees their sentence. Though in the present the kingdom of heaven has not yet been realized, in the time to come God will extend His dominion over everything, and all creatures will acknowledge His dominion.

These ideas are expressed in three groups of prayers that are peculiar to the New Year. The 'Amida is expanded by the addition of מלכיות, "Kingship verses," which celebrate God as king of the world; זכרונות, "Remembrance verses," which celebrate Him as judge; and שופרות, "Shofar verses," which celebrate Him as redeemer. Though three new benedictions were added, the total was only nine, for the Kingship verses were joined with one of the existing benedictions. In the north of Palestine it was attached to Benediction 3, the Sanctification of the Name, and this at a later time was still the practice of R. Yohanan b. Nuri; in the south of Palestine it was joined to the fourth benediction, the Sanctification of the Day, this later being the custom of R. Akiva.[8] It was his practice that prevailed. A third opinion, that the Remembrance verses ought to be connected with the Sanctification of the Day,[9] did not gain acceptance anywhere. To this day the third benediction, the Sanctification of the Name, is greatly expanded, with the addition of three passages beginning ובכן, "And so": (1) ובכן תן פחדך, "And so set Your fear"; (2) ובכן תן כבוד, "And so give glory"; (3) ובכן [ואז] צדיקים, "And so [and then] the righteous,"[10] plus ותמלך, "And You will rule," and concluding with Ps. 146:10. Apparently all this is a vestige of the joining of the Remembrance verses with the Sanctification of the Name, in the manner of R. Yohanan b. Nuri. In Palestine, even the eulogy known from Y. *R.H.* 4:6, 59c, אדיר המלוכה האל הקדוש, "Mighty in kingdom, the holy God,"[11] was preserved, which attests to the same manner of combining the benedictions, and which, according to the Talmud, was intended only for the Additional Service on the New Year. The three passages peculiar to the festival are inter-

[107]

rupted by the blowing of the shofar, and are therefore called תקיעתא, "Shofar blowing." The Mishnah (*R.H.* 4:5), the oldest source on the composition of the New Year service, leaves no doubt that the same 'Amida was used for all the services of the New Year. But when, as mentioned, the blowing of the shofar was shifted to the 'Amida of the Additional Service, the Kingship, Remembrance, and Shofar verses[12] became especially connected with it, but the "And so" passages, the original purpose of which was forgotten, remained in all the services. Thus, one form of the Kingship verses appears in all services, and two appear in the Additional Service.

(4)   The three passages of Kingship, Remembrance, and Shofar were originally composed of groups of biblical verses;[13] they ended with a eulogy, probably prefaced by a petition. It is doubtful whether in ancient times the kind of introductions that came into use later were known. Every individual verse was called a Kingship, Remembrance, or Shofar verse. The number of verses that had to be combined is fixed in the Mishnah as no fewer than ten per section. R. Yoḥanan b. Nuri disagreed, maintaining that three of each were sufficient,[14] and there is an Amora who holds that even one verse from the Torah for each of the three sections suffices. Ashkenaz accepted ten verses each for the Kingship and Shofar verses, and nine for the Remembrance verses [there is a tenth verse but it occurs close to the eulogy], while the other rites have ten for each section.[15] The verses are taken from each of the three parts of the Bible, starting with the Torah, then the Hagiographa, and finally the Prophets. The rule of closing with a verse from the Torah was observed only in the case of the Kingship verses, while in the other two the concluding Torah verse occurs only right before the eulogy; this is the practice of Palestine[16] even with regard to the Kingship verses as well. No verses were included that threaten punishment. The Talmud discusses which verses are suitable and which unsuitable; surprisingly, not one of the verses with פקד, "to visit, remember," which the Talmud permits for the Remembrance verses, was adopted, though the number of appropriate verses was not great. It is noteworthy that the tannaim in the Restoration period[17] (ca. 140) were of different opinions as to the choice of verses, and that in general the composition of the New Year service was much discussed at that time, showing that only then did it take on a definite form. The verses included in the prayer books are identical, including only a few of those discussed in the Talmud; Palestine has a few verses more than the rites in use today.

[108]

(5)   Each group of verses is today preceded by a hymnic introduction: the Kingship verses by "It is our duty" and "Therefore we hope"; the Remembrance verses by אתה זוכר, "You remember"; and the Shofar verses by אתה נגלית, "You revealed Yourself."[18] These introductions are identical in all rites since Amram. We have no information as to when they were composed; the legends about the antiquity of "It is our duty" that circulated in the Middle Ages have no value for us. From the beginning of "You remember," the words זה היום תחילת מעשיך . . . להזכירם לחיים ולמות, "This day is the beginning of Your work . . . to remember them for life or death," are quoted in Y. *R.H.* 1:3, 57a; Y. 'A.Z. 1:2, 39c (and compare B. *R.H.* 27a). The source of the quotation is given as תקיעתא דרב, "the shofar blowing of Rav," and there is no doubt that not only the one sentence but the entire prayer is attributed to Rav or someone of his school.[19] We are told nothing about the origin of the other two introductions; but since the style and

the form of expression of all three passages are very similar, and since Rav's energetic activity in matters of liturgy is otherwise attested, it would not be too daring to suppose that the three introductions are all from his hand. This supposition does not exclude the possibility that here and there these passages have been subject to reworking. In any case this must have occurred before Amram, because since then all versions are identical but for the usual minor variations in wording.

[The attribution of the three introductions common to all communities to the amora Rav is not certain. The expression דבי רב, ''of the school of the master,'' occurs in other connections where it refers in a general way to the schools of the sages. The sources of the amoraic period, quoted above, already thought that the expression referred to the amora Rav. Yet, it appears that these prayers, which, with their elevated style and pure Hebrew diction are among the finest early poetic compositions, were composed in Palestine, perhaps already in tannaitic times. Likewise, some doubt exists, for a variety of reasons, over whether the introduction to the Kingship verses, ''It is our duty,'' was composed by the author of the prayer as a whole: Its first part includes stylistic elements that have no parallel in the other parts of the introductions to the shofar blowing or in the other statutory prayers; the reference to God in the third person; the use of epithets such as אדון הכל, ''Lord of all''; מלך מלכי המלכים, ''King, King of Kings''; and so forth. Therefore there is some basis for the conjecture that the prayer is more ancient, and that the author of the introduction to the shofar blowing found it ready-made and incorporated it; compare Heinemann, *Prayer*, 173ff.; L.J. Liebreich, *HUCA* 34 (1963): 162; and the bibliography listed there. Liebreich maintains that even the petitionary prayers at the conclusion of Kingship, Remembrance, and Shofar antedate Rav.

Despite the antiquity of the introductions to the shofar blowing accepted in all rites, other versions were used alongside them. The best known of these are the poetic compositions of Yose ben Yose, אהללה אלהי אשירה עוזו, ''I shall praise the Lord and sing of His might,'' and of Kallir, אנסיכה מלכי, ''I shall proclaim my King King,'' which are found to this day in Ashkenaz (in the precentor's repetition) alongside the standard introductions. See further below, §40(3).]

[109]

The author did not succeed equally in all the parts of this prayer; the introduction to the Kingship verses excels in its cohesiveness and elevated theme, and no less by its beauty of expression. Possibly earlier models were used; certainly the petition מלוך על כל העולם, ''Rule over all the world,'' is taken from the Palestinian rite, where it was used for all the festivals. The conclusion, ודברך [מלכנו] אמת, ''and Your word [our King] is true,'' makes sense only if preceded by a biblical verse; the eulogy מלך על כל הארץ, ''King over all the world,'' depends on the joining of the Sanctification of the Day and the Kingship verses. Likewise, in ''You remember,'' the splendid opening hymn deserves praise, though it repeats the same theme too many times. The transition to the biblical verses is an obvious failure; the whole passage about Noah and the flood seems to be founded in a dilemma, and serves only to attach the first of the biblical verses (Gen. 8:1) to the body of the introduction, and it does not match at all what follows.[20] Likewise, the reference to the binding of Isaac in the petition seems not to belong to the original text; the verse Lev. 26:45 cited after it is completely unrelated, but could connect easily to the preceding sentence. No less strange are the words following the verse, ועקדת יצחק לזרעו היום ברחמים תזכור, ''and remember Isaac's binding to the credit of his seed in mercy,'' which also disturb the transition to the eulogy. Perhaps originally

"Arise and come" served as the petition; this would make its frequent repetition of the words זכר and פקד, which both mean "remember," more intelligible. There is, in fact, an explicit ancient report that this prayer was included only in the Remembrance verses of the New Year. "You revealed Yourself" deals only with the revelation on Mount Sinai, but most of the verses, the petition, and the eulogy lead one to think that the Shofar verses were meant rather to apply to the messianic era. The beginning of the petition תקע בשופר גדול, "Blow the great Shofar," is simply a verbatim copy of Benediction 10 of the weekday 'Amida. In what follows, the words את קרבנות חובותינו, "our obligatory offerings," are completely meaningless and lead away from the subject; in fact, ancient texts have only ושם נעשה לפניך כמצוה עלינו, "and there we shall do before You what we are commanded,"[21] . . . בתורתך . . . גליותינו וקים לנו ה' אלהינו את הדבר שהבטחתנו, ". . . our exilic communities; and fulfill for us, Lord our God, what You promised in your Torah . . . ." The eulogy in Rome is as in M. *Ta.* 2:4, שומע תרועה, "Who hears the blowing of the Shofar."[22]

(6) In view of the great length of this prayer, it was impossible to impose it as an obligation upon the individual worshiper. R. Gamaliel ruled that the recitation of the prayer by the precentor fulfills the individual worshiper's obligation; his opinion prevailed despite vigorous opposition. Accordingly, the custom in Babylonia was for the congregation to recite in the silent 'Amida only the seven benedictions of the other 'Amidot of the New Year, and to hear the Kingship, Remembrance, and Shofar verses from the precentor. All the geonim agree that this report is correct, and they express their approval of it.[23] Nevertheless, it was not usual in Europe; here, whoever said his own prayers said all nine benedictions even in the silent prayer, and those who relied upon the precentor did not recite the silent 'Amida at all. But since, in the course of the Middle Ages, prayer came to be more and more diligently cultivated, the custom became entrenched that each individual recited the complete 'Amida, in spite of the difficulty in obtaining a copy of such an extensive text in a time when prayer books were rare.

(7) This great addition does not exhaust the uniqueness of the 'Amida. Even the Sanctification of the Day, which is common to all festivals, has some peculiarities deriving from antiquity and connected with several changes in the prayer text. For one thing, the New Year is also a New Moon, raising the question whether this should be especially mentioned in the service. In the Mishnah ('Eruv. 3:9), R. Dosa b. Hyrcanus (before 100) reports from the precentor's prayers on the New Year the words, החליצנו ה' אלהינו את יום ראש החדש החדש הזה, "Give us strength, O Lord our God, on this first day of the month."[24] One may doubt whether this text is correct, but clearly it calls for a reference to the New Moon. The Babylonian amoraim wanted none of this; they ruled unanimously that there is no need to call attention specially to the New Moon: "One reference counts for both" (Rabba in the presence of R. Huna, B. 'Eruv. 40a). In the Yerushalmi, also, the opinion rejecting any reference to the New Moon is represented, though there is still some dispute there about it (Y. Shevu. 1:7, 33b). But *Soferim* (19:5), which reflects the Palestinian rite, says explicitly: "On the New Year one must mention ביום טוב מקרא קודש הזה ובראש החדש הזה וביום ראש השנה הזה וביום תקע שופר הזכרון הזה, 'on this festival, this day of solemn assembly, this New Moon, this New Year, this day of

[110]

the blowing of the shofar of memorial' ";[25] and in Palestinian fragments the text of the eulogy is מקדש ישראל וראשי שנים ומחדש חדשים וזכרון תרועה ומועדי שמחה והזמנים ומקראי קדש, "Who sanctifies Israel and the New Years [sic], and Who renews the months and the commemoration of the blowing of the shofar and the festivals of joy and the seasons and the days of holy assembly."[26] Accordingly, in Palestine the reference to the New Moon was common, and thus the verses of the sacrifice were also preceded by the verses dealing with the New Moon sacrifice, Num. 28:11–15. Prayer books of this type must have existed in Italy, and from there they must have reached Ashkenaz; but they did not preserve the Palestinian 'Amida and did not mention the New Moon either in "And You gave us" or in the eulogy. They did accept the verses of the sacrifice. This was in contradiction to the tradition, which extended the omission of the reference to the New Moon to the sacrifice verses of the Additional Service. The dispute over this question in eleventh- and twelfth-century Germany and northern France was carried on heatedly and sometimes bitterly.[27] In France the custom was not to recite any verses of the sacrifices on festivals, while in Germany they were introduced in 1050 by R. Isaac Halevi, the rabbi in Worms. But it was only consistent that it was now made obligatory to add Num. 29:1–6 to the verses of the sacrifices on the New Year. Traditionalists objected to any manner of reference to the New Moon, and they eventually prevailed. At first, R. Isaac Halevi did have supporters. Rashi, who was his disciple, agreed to the innovation, but he also approved omitting them, as had till then been the practice. His grandson, R. Tam[28] (died 1171) omitted the New Moon verses, but he also changed the conclusion of the verses, reading מלבד עלת החדש ומנחתה . . . ושני שעירים . . . ושני תמידים כהלכתם, "Besides the whole offering of the month and its meal offering . . . and *two* goats . . . and the two daily sacrifices in accordance with their rule." This text was adopted in some countries, such as western Germany, but generally the reference to the New Moon remained limited to the words מלבד עולת החדש ומנחתה, "Besides the whole offering of the month and its meal offering."

(8)   On other festivals, the Sanctification of the Day concludes with "And grant us."[29] Was there a reason to deviate from this text on the New Year? Many pens have been broken over this question. Since *Soferim*, all authorities agree that it should be recited; in fact, it is found in all rites except Ashkenaz, which also had it until R. Isaac Halevi eliminated it as appropriate only for the three pilgrim festivals. Out of a similar motivation, the custom of omitting "And grant us" spread to all France and Germany. There can be no argument with those who have pointed out that, in contradistinction to the festivals, the word והזמנים, "and the seasons," has fallen out of the eulogy on the New Year; but we do find it in Palestine.

At bottom this question is connected with another: Is the New Year properly called יום טוב (Yom ṭov), "a festival"? The Mishnah leaves no doubt about the matter, for it says יום טוב של ראש השנה, "the festival day of the New Year" (*R.H.* 4:1; *'Eruv.* 3, end). Likewise, *Soferim* 19:5 and Amram use Yom ṭov, and Rome and Sepharad do not deviate from the language customary on the other festivals; but Ashkenaz and Romaniot omit the words מועדים לשמחה, "seasons for joy," customary on the festivals.[30] The view came to the fore that Rosh Hashana, as a day of judgment,[31] is more a day for repentance than a festival day.

(9)   The changes in the first three and the last three benedictions, in particular the many versions in which Benediction 3 appears, have already been discussed in §8. The eulogy of Benediction 3 is changed to המלך הקדוש, "the holy king," in accordance with the Babylonian rule (B. *Ber.* 12b), while in Palestine we read האל הקדוש, "the holy God," which appears frequently together with אדיר המלוכה, "mighty in kingdom,"[32] and so it is also in Romaniot. We have already discussed the conjectured manner in which "And so" arose. Also peculiar to this ʿAmida are the insertions זכרנו לחיים, "Remember us for life," in Benediction 1; מי כמוך, "Who is like You," in Benediction 2; וכתוב, "and write," in the penultimate benediction; and בספר החיים, "In the Book of Life," in the last benediction. All of these come only from the post-talmudic period. *Soferim* 19:8 reports that they were permitted only with difficulty, and throughout the Middle Ages they were subject to constant attack, because petitions do not belong in the first and last benedictions; but the geonim asserted themselves on their behalf, so that they were eventually sanctioned.[33] Since the time of Amram they appear in all prayer books. In Amram,[34] "And write" is introduced by the petition אבינו מלכנו זכור רחמיך, "Our Father, our King, remember Your mercy"; this appears also in Romaniot and Rome. In Sepharad, on the other hand, "And write" always occurs alone, and in Ashkenaz "Our Father, our King, remember" has been adopted only in the repetition of the ʿAmida of the Additional Service. This is all the more astonishing, in that *Vitry* gives it for all ʿAmidot. As the eulogy of "In the Book of Life," Hai Gaon[35] has המלך עושה השלום, "the King Who makes peace,"[36] while everywhere else only עושה השלום, "Who makes peace," is known.

(10)   The changes just discussed (subsections 8 and 9) occur, of course, not only in the Additional Service but in all the other services. "And so set Your fear," despite its unmistakable connection with the Kingship verses, is retained also in the ʿAmidot that have no Kingship verses. Likewise, in the Sanctification of the Day, the petition מלוך על כל העולם, "Rule over all the world," is recited, which also belongs to the Kingship verses, but which, as has been shown elsewhere (§23:5) is used in Palestine on all the festivals. In the prayer book of R. Saadia,[37] "Arise and come" is found only in the Remembrance verses in the Additional Service, with some justification, as we have seen. This custom was known also in Babylonia, though not everywhere, while in Europe, as far as we know, it was followed only in Toledo.

(11)   All other components of the New Year liturgy are identical to those of the other festivals, with the exception, of course, of the Psalms [, Hallel,] and the biblical verses. The psalm according to *Soferim* 19:2 is Ps. 47; for the Additional Service (B. *R.H.* 30b), Ps. 81; for the Afternoon Service, Ps. 29.[38] Before the ʿAmida of the Evening Service, Rome has, as on all festivals, Lev. 23:4; Sepharad has Num. 10:10; Romaniot has Num. 29:1; and Ashkenaz has Ps. 81:4. In the evening, Kiddush is recited over the wine; the text differs from the Kiddush of festivals in the same phrases that change in the ʿAmida, as well. After the Morning and Afternoon services, אבינו מלכנו, "Our Father, our King," is recited; it is omitted on the Sabbath. This litany, every line of which begins with the words "Our Father, our King," goes back to a prayer that R. Akiva once recited on a fast that had been proclaimed on account of extended drought: "R. Akiva went down before the ark and said: 'Our Father, our King, we have sinned before You,

Our Father, Our King, though we have no good deed among us, perform for us acts of generosity and save us' " (B. *Ta.* 25b). These two sentences still form the prayer's beginning and end. Given the open structure of the litany, it was easy to insert sentences into it, and this happened extensively. Already Amram contains twenty-five sentences; the same number, though with slight differences, is found in Sepharad, with a few more in Romaniot and Rome. Ashkenaz has the most; here in the last centuries the martyrs for the faith have been memorialized.[39] In the Middle Ages, "Our Father, our King" was not said in Sepharad.[40] But there, as in Amram, it was customary to insert היום תאמצנו, "Today strengthen us," toward the end of the repetition of the 'Amida.[41] This is an alphabetical litany of which Amram has preserved only the first half. The Ashkenazic communities preserved only a few lines from the beginning and the end, and they recited it only in the Additional Service. Romaniot and Rome do not know it at all.

On the reading of the Torah, see §25.

Connected with the idea of the New Year as a day of repentance is the practice of many persons in the early Middle Ages of fasting.[42] Though this was later prohibited on the first day, it remained permitted on the second until it was finally prohibited, then too out of consideration for Neh. 8:10. But in the conduct of prayer, the character of the day as a day of judgment was to a large extent retained; in the southern lands even the *selihot* customary on days of fasting and repentance were transferred to the New Year.[43]

(12)   The days between the New Year and the Day of Atonement are called the Ten Days of Repentance. On them the additions to the first two and the last two benedictions of the 'Amida are in use, as are the changes in the eulogies of Benedictions 3, 11, and 19, and "Our father, our King" after the repetition of the 'Amida. It was also customary already in the geonic period to hold vigils at night and to recite *selihot*,[44] as on fast days (see §33). Already ca. 1000 such early services were held every morning, in some places from the First of Elul and in other places from the Fifteenth of Elul. The customs varied greatly: In Ashkenaz it was customary to begin on the Sunday before the New Year if that day was at least four days before the festival—otherwise, a week earlier. Lately the number of *selihot* days and the length of the prayers have been considerably reduced. The custom of beginning the service while it is still nighttime has disappeared in western lands, even in the most traditional communities. As with the *selihot*, the blowing of the shofar is begun already at the First of Elul.[45] This custom has found general acceptance and has only recently been abandoned by the Reform communities. The blowing of the shofar is performed at the end of the Morning Service without a benediction; in Ashkenaz the congregation then recites Ps. 27.

[113]   ## b. Day of Atonement

(1)   יום הכפורים, "The Day of Atonement" (צומא רבא, "the Great Fast") is a day with an exceedingly lengthy liturgy. Philo already reports that the congregation would linger the whole day in prayer. In Palestine, too, the service of the Day of Atonement was considered the longest known service, and when one wanted to portray a prayer as very

long, one would compare it with the Day of Atonement liturgy: "Even like the order of Yom Kippur." We cannot determine exactly when the practice began of extending the prayers over the entire day, but as early as R. Akiva's time we are told that he would interrupt the service so that the people might go home. From the amoraic period, too, we hear of such recesses, permitting the inference that generally the day was entirely filled with prayer. Thus already in the most ancient period the Day of Atonement liturgy was counted among those that were extended to an extraordinary degree: "These are the benedictions that are made lengthy . . . the benedictions of the Day of Atonement."[46] The service of the Day of Atonement is different from that of other days also in that it includes a service that occurs nowhere else, the Closing Service.

(2)   The characteristic prayer of the Day of Atonement is the Confession.[47] This has undergone great changes both in form and content. In the Torah it is found in connection with the ceremony of atonement of the high priest (Lev. 16:21); the tannaim discussed the text of this Confession, and they established a text based on biblical usage. But the simple version arrived at in this way, חטאתי, עויתי, פשעתי, "I have erred, I have sinned, I have transgressed," is used only in the description of the service of the high priest in the Temple. A different confession is recited within the ʿAmida of the precentor and as an appendix to it by the individual worshiper. This Confession, belonging to the ʿAmida, was known already to the tannaim, and some of them require even a detailed enumeration of sins;[48] but, as with many liturgical passages, it is only from the early amoraim that we hear of a text of the Confession.[49] In B. *Yoma* 87b several third-century sages cite by their incipits some formulas that were then in use; some can no longer be tracked down, but others are in use today, whether on other occasions, or in other parts of the service for the Day of Atonement. Two pieces introduced by Rav and Mar Samuel remain in the Confession: אתה יודע רזי עולם, "You know the secrets of the world," and אבל אנחנו חטאנו, "Indeed we have sinned." But the passages named in the Talmud have been expanded greatly in the course of time, also not an uncommon phenomenon. "But we have sinned," which Mar Samuel saw as a very important part of the Confession, and which apparently is its actual core, is now the conclusion of the introduction, the petition תבא לפניך תפלתנו, "May our prayer come before You."[50] After it comes the alphabetical confession, אשמנו בגדנו גזלנו, "We have sinned, we have betrayed, we have stolen." Already in Amram we find the wording in use today; the text is identical in all the rites, though here and there a word or two has been added. This uniformity and the alphabetical acrostic make it likely that the passage comes from the last century of the amoraic period. It is followed in the prayer books by סרנו ממצותיך, "We have gone astray from Your commandments,"[51] and ואתה צדיק על כל הבא עלינו, "And You are righteous, whatever happens to us," both reworkings of biblical verses. Only now comes the passage mentioned by Rav, "You know the secrets of the world," with another petition for the atonement of sins, transferred apparently from Y. *Yoma*, end (45c).[52] This is followed by another list of sins, the litany על חטא, "For the sin,"[53] which, to judge from its structure, should also be assigned to the fifth century. In Amram we find only a very few "For the sin" lines, eight altogether, which speak in the most general terms about the sins committed: בזדון, בשוגג, בגלוי, בסתר, "intentionally, unintentionally, openly, covertly." In a later version, but not much later, as it is identical in all rites, this formula too turns into an alphabetical list of sins; not

satisfied with this, Ashkenaz doubled the alphabet. To the oldest stock of prayers belong the passages that in all liturgies after Amram come after the acrostic, על חטאים, "For sins," which sort the sins according to the type of punishment or sacrifice required for their atonement. The Confession ends with the prayer of R. Hamnuna in B. *Yoma* 87b, עד שלא נוצרתי איני כדאי, "Before I was created I was worthless." While in the other rites the alphabetical sequence is unbroken, in Ashkenaz the petition ועל כלם, "And for all of them," is inserted after the letters *yod*, *ʿayyin*, and *tav*.[54] In modern prayer books [i.e., Reform], the Confession has been considerably abridged and reduced to the few general sentences found in Amram.

The Confession is prescribed for all of the ʿAmidot of the Day of Atonement, even for that of the Afternoon Service of the eve of the Day of Atonement (T. *Yoma* 5:14). In the Middle Ages, "We have sinned" was called ודוי זוטא, "Lesser Confession," and "For the sin," ודוי רבא, "Greater Confession."[55] Apparently in the early Middle Ages a special eulogy, האל הסלחן, "the forgiving God" was provided for the Confession; Saadia knew and opposed it, and in fact it is not found in any rite. As already mentioned, while the congregation would recite the Confession after the end of the ʿAmida, the precentor would insert it in the ʿAmida, before the conclusion of the Sanctification of the Day.[56]

(3)   Except for the Confession, the ʿAmida has the same character as that of the New Year. It includes the additions in the first two and the last two benedictions, and surprisingly also "And so"[57] in the third. The reference to the festival follows *Soferim* 19:6, and so in Palestine:[58] ביום מקרא קדש הזה ביום צום העשור הזה ביום מחילת העון הזה, "On this day of holy assembly, on this day of the fast of the tenth day, on this day of forgiveness of sin." The eulogy of the Sanctification of the Day is modeled on the prayer of the high priest after the conclusion of the Temple service. One of his petitions concluded: מוחל עונות עמו ישראל ברחמים, "Who forgives the sins of His people Israel in mercy (B. *Yoma* 7:1, 44b). Longer than this is the text in *Soferim*: מוחל וסולח לעונותינו ולעונות עמו ישראל ברחמים ומכפר על פשעיהם מלך על כל הארץ מקדש ישראל וצום הכפורים והזמנים ומקראי קדש, "Who forgives and pardons our sins and the sins of His people Israel in mercy, and provides atonement for their sins; King over all the world, Who sanctifies Israel and the fast of atonement and the seasons and the holy assemblies." Amram[59] abbreviated both: His reference to the festival reads יום הכפורים יום מקרא קדש יום סליחת העון, "The day of Atonement, the day of holy assembly, the day of forgiveness of sin"; the eulogy reads מלך מוחל וסולח לעונותינו ולעונות עמו ישראל ומעביר אשמותינו בכל שנה ושנה מלך על כל הארץ מקדש ישראל ויום הכפורים, "the King Who forgives and pardons our sins and the sins of His people Israel and Who effaces their guilt every year, King over all the world, Who sanctifies Israel and the Day of Atonement." This was adopted by all rites; but since, in the meantime, "And You gave us" had been changed with respect to all the festivals, the reference was changed on this festival as well. The beginning of the petition that concludes the Sanctification of the Day was long contested. All agreed that "And grant us" should be skipped;[60] the question was whether the petition should open with מלוך, "Rule," or מחל, "Forgive." Amram does not read "Rule,"[61] while Ibn Ghiyath, apparently relying on Saadia, does. The source of the dispute seems to be a difference between Palestine and Babylonia; in Palestine, "Rule" was said on the Day of Atonement as on all festivals, while in Babylonia it was omitted. Later ages followed Babylonia and adopted "Forgive." Whether to say "Ascend and come" in the ʿAmida was also contested. Again

Amram does not have it. The source of the difference may have been the same, but the consequence was the opposite, for "Ascend and come" has remained in all rites. Sepharad has all the disputed passages, first "Forgive," then "Ascend and come," finally "Rule." In the beginning of the *Amida*, before מגן אברהם, "Shield of Abraham," Amram has, by analogy with the Sabbath, the additional sentence רצה והנחל לבניהם את יוה״כ הזה, "Be pleased to bestow upon their children this Day of Atonement,"[62] but this addition was not preserved in any rite. After the *Amida* there comes, as on the New Year, "Our Father, our King"; at the Afternoon Service many communities skip it.

(4)   In every other respect the prayers are no different from those of the other festivals. Amram begins the Evening Service, as always, with "And He, being merciful." *Soferim* 19:2 designates Ps. 103 and Ps. 130.[63] In the Morning Service, Amram adds many psalms besides those of the Sabbath; all may be called Psalms of Repentance: Pss. 17, 25, 32, 65, 51, 67, 103, and 104.[64] Later, the additional psalms were inserted alternately among the regular ones. Before the *Amida* of the Evening Service, Rome has, as on the festivals, Lev. 23:4; Sepharad and Ashkenaz have Lev. 16:30; Romaniot has Num. 29:7 and Lev. 16:30 or Lev. 23:32.

(5)   One peculiarity of the Day of Atonement is the fifth service, נעילה, "the Closing Service." In the most ancient times, it was also a daily service. The *ma'amad* in the Temple would assemble for prayer four times a day, and the last service, called נעילת שערים, "the Closing of the Gates," was recited when the gates of the Temple were closed. The name of the service comes from its time. Outside the Temple this service was known only on public fast days. But while every trace of the Closing Service has disappeared from the rest of the liturgy, it has been retained on the Day of Atonement. It acquired a particularly solemn character from its place at the end of the great day, at the actual moment of the forgiveness of sins. The ancient conception[65] that at the time of the Closing Service man's fate is sealed led to a few alterations in the text of the *Amida*. Wherever the other prayers read כתבנו, "write us," one now says חתמנו, "seal us." Otherwise the text of the *Amida* is identical with that of the Afternoon Service that preceded it. The only change is in the Confession. At the Closing Service, the litany "For the sin" is not recited, and after "You know the secrets of the world" comes the prayer "You give Your hand."[66] The nucleus of this passage, מה אנו מה חיינו, "What are we, what is our life?" also comes from B. *Yoma* 87b. In fact, Maimonides and, to this day, Sepharad begin with these words; but all other rites have also the lofty introduction, "You give Your hand." Its text is identical everywhere, and we are probably not far off if we fix the date of its composition close to that of the additions to the New Year *Amida*. It is not impossible that "You give Your hand" is a doublet of "You distinguished man," which follows it, or that one is of Palestinian and the other of Babylonian origin. The *Amida* of the Closing Service is preceded by "Happy" and "And a redeemer will come to Zion,"[67] as usual at the Afternoon Service.

For the reading of the Torah of the Day of Atonement, see §§25 and 26.

(6)   Since the most ancient times, several elements have belonged to the liturgy of the Day of Atonement, which, though not statutory prayers, are common to all rites, though not always with the same text. The Day of Atonement is a fast day; accordingly

we find the inserts peculiar to fasts, the *Selihot*,[68] attached to all the five services. Likewise, since antiquity—at least since the fourth century—the *ʿAvoda* is attached to the *ʿAmida*, a description, more or less freely elaborated, of the sacrificial rite observed in the Temple. Originally connected to several *ʿAmidot*, the *ʿAvoda* was later limited to the Additional Service *ʿAmida*. Below (§32) we deal at length with the *ʿAvoda* literature.

(7) Finally, we must mention here the addition with which the Evening Service is introduced and which has lent the evening of the Day of Atonement its popular name, כל נדרי, "All vows."[69] It contains a declaration canceling all personal vows that a person has made in any form in the course of the year, and thus it has nothing at all to do with the themes and the liturgy of the Day of Atonement; only with great difficulty can a connection between them be found. We are no longer able to determine when this text was created, and when it passed from the individual domain to that of the public, to be incorporated into the liturgy. It must have originated in the first centuries of the geonic period and outside Babylonia, for from the ninth century on we have opinions of the Babylonian geonim, almost without exception opposing it, sometimes in strong words.[70] Nevertheless, it kept its place in the liturgy. While, however, the original text referred to the past—that is, to vows made during the preceding year (מיום כפורים שעבר עד יום כפורים זה, "from the Day of Atonement that has passed to this Day of Atonement")—it was changed through the initiative of R. Tam in the twelfth century to the future (מיום כפורים זה עד יום כפורים הבא, "from this Day of Atonement to the next Day of Atonement").[71] In this new form we find it in Ashkenaz, while Rome and Romaniot have retained the old form; in Sepharad both have been combined. The language of "All vows" in Ashkenaz and Sepharad is Aramaic, while in Rome and Romaniot, as in Amram and all the geonic quotations, it is Hebrew. It is well known how many baseless accusations the text of "All vows" has aroused against the Jews in the course of centuries. But nowhere in the sources can any interpretation of a morally offensive nature be found, for the authorities agree unanimously that the text has in view only obligations undertaken by an individual toward himself or obligations respecting cultic regulations of the community. Likewise, it is well known to what extent religious feelings and poetry have, in the course of centuries, been attached to "All vows," which doubtless arise not from the content of the passage but from its position at the beginning of the Day of Atonement service. It was the sanctity of this greatest festival that inspired the hearts and prompted the composition of the solemn melodies[72] that spread the fame of "All vows" far beyond Jewish circles. In the modern period the text of "All vows" has been replaced with other texts, either prayers for the forgiveness of sin (כל פשעי וחטאי, "All my transgressions and sins")[73] or Ps. 130.

"All vows" is preceded by the lines בישיבה של מעלה, "In the court of heaven." In them, following ancient custom, the ban of excommunication is lifted that had been imposed against members of the community who had transgressed its regulations and had been proclaimed עברינים, "sinners," permitting them to participate in public worship.[74]

CHAPTER THREE

The Reading of the Torah and the Sermon

§ 25   The Reading of the Torah

(1)   The reading of the Torah and the Prophets is one of the most ancient liturgical institutions; indeed, it is very likely that the reading of Scripture was the occasion for the first communal assemblies for the purpose of prayer. Like the prayers, the Torah reading has undergone change; this development occurred almost completely outside the sources available to us, and we can do no more than make conjectures about it.

In order to start on firm ground, let us examine the present-day situation.[1] The Torah is read regularly in the synagogue four times a week: at the Sabbath Morning and Afternoon Services, and in the Morning Service on Monday and Thursday. To this there are added the readings in the Morning Service on festivals and the intermediate days of festivals, on the New Moon, fast days, Hanukkah and Purim, and in the Afternoon Service of fast days. On Sabbaths and festivals, on the fast of the Ninth of Av, and in the Afternoon Service of all fasts there are readings from both the Torah and the Prophets; on the other days, readings are from the Torah only. For the purpose of the weekly reading the Torah is divided into fifty-four sections (סדרא, סדר, פרשה, pericope), which are read sequentially at the Sabbath Morning Service. Since there are not sufficient Sabbaths in every year, sometimes two pericopes are combined on one Sabbath. The last pericope of the Torah is read on the Eighth Day of Assembly [in the Diaspora, on its second day] and after the festival a new cycle begins. At the Afternoon Service on the Sabbath and on the following Monday and Thursday, the beginning of the pericope to be read on the following Sabbath is read. Special readings have been assigned to festivals, the intermediate days of festivals, and fast days, corresponding to the significance of the day. If a fast day or the intermediate day of a festival occurs on a Monday or Thursday, that day's selection, rather than the weekly pericope, is read. The festivals and the intermediate days of festivals take precedence over even the weekly pericope; only when the New Moon and Hanukkah coincide with the Sabbath is the weekly pericope read, followed by the reading of the day. Among the Sabbaths of the year, four special ones occur between the last Sabbath before the month of Adar and the last Sabbath before the month of Nisan (ארבע פרשיות, or ארבעה ערכים).[2] On these, an additional reading is customary, alongside the pericope of the consecutive reading. They are named for the first or the characteristic word of their pericopes: פרשת שקלים, פרה, זכור, and החדש, "Shekels," "Remember," "Heifer," "The Month." The length of the reading varies—short on weekdays, longer on festivals, and longest of all on the Sabbath. The reading is performed with the participation of the congregation, from which at least three, but sometimes seven or more people, are "called up" to the Torah, the number depending on the importance of the day.[3] For each, the reader reads a passage according to a traditional melody, "the manner of singing come down from antiquity, known as trope." [Elbogen did not provide a source for this quote—*Engl. trans.*] Before and after the reading, each of those called up recites a benediction. Taking the Torah out of the ark and replacing it, opening it, and rolling it up again are also done with congregational participation.

(2)   If we inquire as to the origin of this institution, the ancient sources tell us that Moses[4] introduced the reading on Sabbaths and festivals, and that Ezra[5] introduced the readings on Mondays and Thursdays, though according to another version it was "prophets and elders"[6] who instituted the weekly readings. As to the order of readings on fast days, Hanukkah, and Purim, we have no chronological tradition. Thus, even the tradition seems to assume that the introduction and expansion of the Torah reading occurred in stages. The Mishnah already knows of the Torah reading on all the days when it is still read today. It mentions fixed readings for the first days of festivals, for all the days of Tabernacles, for Hanukkah, Purim, the New Moon, fast days, and the four special Sabbaths. For the other Sabbaths, Mondays, and Thursdays, it presupposes a cycle (סדר, *seder*), without giving any details as to what it is, other than that only the Sabbath morning readings are included in it [that is, the passages read in the Afternoon Service of the Sabbath, on Mondays, and on Thursdays must be read again on the Morning Service of the following Sabbath] (B. *Meg.* 3:5–6). The Tosefta mentions the reading for all the days of the Passover festival, and cites different readings for most of the other days (T. *Meg.* 4:5–9). In both Talmuds further detail is found about the readings: the Bavli adds the readings of the second day of festivals for the Diaspora and additional pericopes (מוסף) from the chapters on the sacrifices (Num. 28–29; B. *Meg.* 31a–b). It also mentions that in Babylonia the annual cycle was in use, and the triennial cycle in Palestine (ibid. 29b). It may be said that the Babylonian Talmud generally assumes the same pattern of Torah readings as is customary in the synagogue today. Yet some of its details and its deviations from the regulations of the Mishnah, insignificant as they may be in themselves, demonstrate that the most ancient form of the Torah reading was quite different from our own. We will attempt to clarify what was originally read, and when.

(3)   The most ancient commandment concerning the reading of the Torah is found in Deut. 31:10 in connection with the Assembly (הקהל) during Tabernacles, immediately following the Sabbatical year (compare *Soṭa* 7:8). The first information about a Torah reading that actually took place is found in Neh. 8, in the story of the famous assembly of the people at which Ezra imposed the observance of the Torah upon the congregation (444 B.C.E.).[7] This gives us a *terminus a quo*; there can be no doubt that Ezra's reading is what led to the introduction of the Torah reading, and that

its particulars were imitated in the synagogue and their minutiae preserved. Ezra's first readings occurred on festival days, and so the first regular readings must certainly have been held on festivals. On those occasions the commandments in the Torah about the festival itself would be read and expounded: "Moses said, 'Be diligent to study the theme of the day and to expound it'" [another reading: "Moses urged Israel to be diligent at studying the Torah . . ."] (*Sifre* Deut., 100b, §127; *Midrash tanaim*, 89). If it is true that the first readings and explications of the Torah were instituted because the Samaritans gave the laws of the festivals a deviant interpretation,[8] this would also bring us to the period around the time of Ezra. The Talmud designates the pilgrim festivals as the ones whose laws must be expounded in public (B. *Meg.*, end). In fact it was these festivals that were at issue with the Samaritans—whence the need to explicate the law specifically on the pilgrim festivals. Further, the most ancient source, the Mishnah, knows of a separate reading for every day of Tabernacles, but only one single reading for the days of Passover;[9] the reason must lie in Ezra's regulation, for he held a reading in "The Book of the Law of God" on Tabernacles, on "every day from the first day to the last day" (Neh. 8:18). The reading on the Day of Atonement found its model in the service in the Temple, where the high priest would read from the Torah after completing the rites (M. *Yoma* 7:1; *Sota* 7:7).[10] Since each festival had its own reading, the New Year could not be the only exception; apparently, the reading on this day is later than all the readings of the festivals, and in fact it is the shortest of all.[11]

No one disagrees that the first Sabbath readings were the those of the four special Sabbaths.[12] Their origin, their circumstances, and the time of their institution are shrouded in mystery. But the Mishnah's simple report leaves no room for doubt about one point, namely that the reading on these Sabbaths was not in any way dependent on the other Sabbath readings. Never do the ancient sources mention a conflict between the readings of the special Sabbaths and a regular and consecutive weekly reading. On the contrary, the practice of reading the Torah on occasional Sabbaths is what led to the extension of the reading to all Sabbaths. A part may also have been played by the expression מקרא קודש, "holy assembly," which is applied to both Sabbath and festivals, for it was misinterpreted as meaning "a holy reading of the Torah."[13] Finally the reading was extended to the two "days of assembly," Monday and Thursday,[14] so that villagers who did not have synagogues or regular services would have the opportunity to hear the Torah read and expounded. The final stage is represented by the readings of Hanukkah, Purim,[15] and the fast days, the introduction of which reflects the view that there could be no solemn day without a Torah reading.

As long as the Torah reading was held only on festivals and special Sabbaths, only a few selected passages were read; but when the regular reading on the Sabbath was introduced, the Torah was read consecutively in its entirety. Furthermore it was ruled that in the Torah, as distinguished from the Prophets, only consecutive readings were permitted: "One may not skip in the Torah"[16] (M. *Meg.* 1:5; B. *Meg.* 24a). From this regulation and similar ones giving the Torah reading priority over the prophetic reading, we can infer as a *terminus ad quem* for the introduction of the regular Torah reading the date of the editing of the prophetic canon.[17] The leniencies permitted for the readings of the Prophets can be explained only on the assumption that they did not have canonical status. The Torah reading must therefore have been introduced before the middle of the third century [B.C.E.]. If the Greek translation of the Torah[18] owes its cre-

[120]

ation to the needs of the synagogue, that may also be seen as evidence for the high age of the Torah reading, though direct evidence for regular Torah readings is late. It is not certain that the expression ἀναγινώσκοντας, "readers," in the introductory words of Ben Sira's grandson,[19] alludes to a reading in Scripture, and it is likewise impossible to fix exactly the dates of certain regulations in the Mishnah that are doubtless considerably older than the closing of the Mishnah. Philo[20] and Josephus[21] speak of the reading in the Torah every Sabbath as an ancient custom; the Gospels,[22] too, mention it occasionally, and the Book of Acts (15:21) says that Moses had evangelists in every city since ancient times, for his words are read in the synagogue every Sabbath.

(4)   The ancient readings were not long. Among the festival readings mentioned in the Mishnah, the shortest, that of the New Year,[23] has only three verses, and among the special Sabbaths, "Remember"[24] also has only three verses. The longest of all the readings, chapter 16 of Leviticus, intended for the Day of Atonement, has no more than thirty-four verses, assuming that all of it was read. Nor were the Sabbath readings very long, for only a few verses were considered enough;[25] even in the later period, when the entire structure was already highly developed, a reading of twenty-one verses was considered to be absolutely normal.[26] Furthermore, it is quite probable that in the most ancient period the reading was not consecutive, but every Sabbath a passage (ענין) was freely chosen; even when this custom was prohibited "so that Israel should hear the Torah in order,"[27] there was still no conception of a regular order of readings—that is, a cycle. Even R. Meir,[28] supporting the idea of a consecutive reading, has in mind only that each reading should begin where the last had concluded—that is, that the Sabbath Afternoon Service reading would continue the morning reading, and that on Monday and Thursday the reading would continue where it had left off. If we posit this sort of division and the usual number of verses, then two and a third years would be required to complete the Torah reading; and if only the Sabbath readings are taken into account, reckoning twenty-one verses for each, the reading of the Torah would be completed in only five and a half years, especially if we take into account that on the New Moons and special Sabbaths the regular reading was interrupted. The Tosefta gives instructions regarding the smallest amount of text that may be left at the end of a book or at the end of the entire Torah,[29] and such a situation could not arise and would be meaningless if the present or any other cyclical division was known. Eventually, a regular cycle (*seder*) was established, about which we first hear in B. *Meg.* 29b, namely, that "The Westerners (that is, the Palestinians) complete the Torah in three years." The triennial cycle of the Palestinians, as has been shown, lies at the basis of many midrash collections, nearly all the Rabbot, and especially *Lev. R., Tanḥuma*, and others.[30] It is this division to which the Masora refers when it gives at the end of each book of the Torah the tally of pericopes;[31] the number fluctuates in the sources between 153 (154) and 167;[32] the Midrash alludes to 155,[33] the greatest number of Sabbaths that can occur in the course of three years. As against the triennial cycle, the Babylonian amoraim speak of a one-year cycle[34]—that is, on every Sabbath they would read three times what the Palestinians would read, and they divided the Torah as is customary today, into fifty-four pericopes,[35] or פרשות, later erroneously also called סדרא. As with all other matters of religious life, in the end the Babylonian authorities prevailed in this matter, and the one-year cycle replaced the triennial in all communities except a small,

diminishing number. One such was the Palestinian synagogue in Cairo. R. Benjamin of Tudela (ca. 1170) relates that in this synagogue they did not read a pericope every week, but that every pericope was divided into three *sedarim*, and the reading of the Torah took three years. Maimonides, too, says: "There are some who complete the Torah in three years, but this is not the common custom" (*M.T.*, "Laws of Prayer," 13:1). His son Abraham relates, exactly like R. Benjamin of Tudela, that in the synagogue of the Palestinians in Cairo only one *seder* was read each week.[36] This synagogue and this custom were still in existence in 1670, to be concluded from R. Joseph Sambari's report.[37] Otherwise, no further reference is made to the triennial cycle until the modern period. In the Rabbinical Assembly of Frankfurt am Main in 1845, this cycle was recommended in order to shorten the Torah reading, and some communities did adopt it. A chart describing the division of the Torah according to this principle was first published in the prayer book put out in 1845 by the Israelite Temple of Hamburg. But the fifteen hundred years' habit of reading the Torah in an annual cycle and designating each week by the name of its reading was so powerful that it was a decisive impediment to the new principle, for all the historical authority behind the latter. Therefore, in some Reform communities a new kind of triennial cycle came into being, in which the pericopes of the annual cycle were retained but only one-third of each was read. In a few communities the remainder of the reading is divided among the other three readings of the week, so that on the Sabbath the new pericope is begun, yet despite the abridgement of the reading on the Sabbath the entire Torah is read in the course of a single year. In others a different third is read each year, so that each pericope returns every year, but the reading of the entire Torah requires three. A few of these begin the readings in the second and third year of the cycle with a few verses from the beginning of the pericope to mark the weekly reading. But in some congregations, the annual cycle of readings is retained even though the Reform prayer book has been introduced. In the Reform Jewish Congregation in Berlin and in a large part of the Reform congregations in America, the reading is a freely chosen selection, taken, to the extent possible, from the traditional weekly pericope.[38]

It is said that alongside the triennial cycle there existed also a three-and-a-half-year cycle,[39] in which the Torah was read twice through in the course of a sabbatical cycle. This practice, too, is reportedly Palestinian, but we have no proof that it was ever in use anywhere. In its favor, an aggadah may be adduced that speaks of the Torah's 175 pericopes,[39*] and that is quoted in *Soferim* (16:10) as a model for the 175 pericopes for the weekly reading. If we count fifty weeks to a year, then that number of readings does correspond to the number of Sabbaths that occur in the course of three-and-a-half years. But this reckoning rests on an error, for in three years there is at least one intercalated month, and thus the number of Sabbaths is greater. Furthermore, some Sabbaths coincide with festivals, and so fall out of the cycle of readings. In fact, this aggadah does not really speak about pericopes of the Torah reading but about passages beginning with a particular expression (ויצו, ויאמר, וידבר). That a three-and-a-half-year cycle existed is not out of the question, for among the characteristic practices of the Palestinians it is reported that their cycle was not uniform in all communities, that the same thing was not read in every place, and that they did not complete the Torah on the same day. The truth of this last claim cannot be denied, since we read in the Midrash that the amora Hanina bar Abba (third century?) encountered a congregation in which

[122]

the words "And the remainder of the meal-offering" (Lev. 2:10) began a pericope.[39**]
This would be possible only if that community lacked a regular cycle.

(5)   The annual cycle began after Tabernacles, as did the triennial cycle as far as
we can tell; since, according to a statement in the Talmud, Num. 28 can be read in the
spring, it seems likely that the cycle began in the fall. The contrary assumption[40] is not
supported by any weighty arguments.

[According to the testimony of *Hiluf minhagim*, the Palestinian triennial cycle lasted
three and a half years, and thus the beginning of the new cycle did not occur at any fixed
time in the calendar. It does not appear that there were two cycles, one of three years and
one of three and a half years exactly, but a single cycle (with local variations), whose reading continued more than three years, or nearly three and a half years. There is no proof
of any relationship between this cycle and the period from the beginning of one sabbatical
year to another. Today it is known that such a cycle not aligned with the calendar was actually in use, for from the contents of the *qerovot* of Yannai, which are built upon the triennial pericopes, it is possible to tell whether they were recited in the summer or in the winter
(by means of the reference to dew or rain); and it turns out that adjacent pericopes could
occur—in different cycles, of course—one in the summer and one in the winter. In addition to the lists of 154 and 167 pericopes, we now know of another list of 141. All of these
lists have more pericopes than the average number of Sabbaths in three years; only the
list of 141 matches the number of Sabbaths if two out of three years are leap years. For,
according to the halakha that was practiced in Palestine, the weekly cycle of readings was
interrupted for the four special Sabbaths; see Yisakhar Yoel, " 'Keter' mishenat hameshet
alafim ve‹esrim liveri›at ha‹olam," *Qiryat sefer* 38 (1962/3): 122–32 and Heinemann in *Tarbiz* 33 (1963/4): 362–68.

In the tannaitic period, no uniform distribution of pericopes among Sabbaths was yet
in practice. This can be proven from R. Meir's statement in the baraita (*Meg.* 31b or T. *Meg.*
3[4]:10) and also from the Tosefta (*Meg.* 3[4]:4) [chap. 3 in the Vilna edition, chap. 4 in
Zuckermandel—*Engl. trans.*], which speaks, contrary to the baraita in the B. *Meg.* 29b,
about the possibility that each of the four special Sabbath readings could coincide in the
month of Adar with the pericope in the consecutive cycle of readings from which it derives.

[123]   This cannot be harmonized with any fixed, uniform cycle of readings lasting three years.
Incidentally, from the passage in the Babylonian Talmud mentioned above (B. *Meg.* 29b)
it cannot be deduced that "Shekels" would fall regularly in the month of Adar in accordance with the three-year cyle, but only that in this cycle anything is possible, since it is
not synchronized with the calendar. Compare, explicitly, R. Hananel, *Meg.* 29b: "For the
westerns. . . it is possible (!) that something of this type could occur."]

For the purposes of the reading, Genesis is divided [in the annual cycle] into twelve
pericopes, Exodus and Deuteronomy into eleven each, Leviticus and Numbers into ten
each. And since the last pericope of the Deuteronomy is designated for the Eighth Day
of Assembly, fifty-three pericopes are left over for the Sabbaths.[41] The division of these
pericopes was not exactly uniform in all places and in all times, but despite variations
here and there, the total number was everywhere the same.[42] The pericopes get their
names from their first word or from a key word; these names are not particularly
ancient. There are not as many Sabbaths in a year as pericopes, and some Sabbaths
are lost because they coincide with festivals. Therefore, two pericopes may be joined

(מחוברות). This can occur once in Exodus, once in Deuteronomy, three times in Leviticus and twice in Numbers. Not everywhere were the same pericopes joined. How many double pericopes were used depends both on the type of year and particular rules. Some of these rules come from ancient times. R. Simon b. Eleazar (ca. 170) mentions a rule of Ezra that the curses in Lev. 26 must be read before Pentecost, and those in Deut. 28 before the New Year (B. *Meg.* 31b). The pericopes had to be distributed to accord with these rules. In later centuries a formula was established that we first find among the widely circulated rules of R. Yehudai Gaon (ca. 750)[43]—and still authoritative: פקידו ופסחו מנו ועצרו צומו וצלו קומו ותקעו, meaning that in any ordinary year צו (Lev. 6) is read before Passover; במדבר (Num. 1) before Pentecost; ואתחנן (Deut. 3:23ff.) after the Ninth of Av; and נצבים (Deut. 29:99ff.) before the New Year. In a leap year the only change is that מצורע (Lev. 14) is read before Passover.

The sequence of the readings is interrupted by the special Sabbaths [that is incorrect in current usage—*Engl. trans.*], the festivals, the intermediate days of festivals, and fast days. In the most ancient period these were the only days when readings from the Torah were held at all, and even when the consecutive readings were introduced for every Sabbath, they gave way to these special readings. The Mishnah's statement leaves no doubt about this: "One interrupts for everything, for New Moons, Hanukkah, Purim, and fast days (*maʿamad* and Yom Kippur)."[44] The special Sabbaths bear the days of their pericopes, "Shekels" (Ex. 30:11–16), "Remember" (Deut. 25:17–19), "Heifer" (Num. 19:1–22), and "The Month" (Ex. 12:1–20). The opinion of Rav that "Shekels" is Num. 28:1–8 doubtless arose from a learned inference and not from a tradition.[45] One who reads the Mishnah without any prior opinion gets the impression that the four special readings follow each other without interruption, but already the Tosefta cites a late interpretation according to which the second and third readings must occur before and after Purim, and the fourth on the Sabbath prior to the New Moon of Nisan or on that New Moon itself (T. *Meg.* 4:1–4). On the Sabbaths between these dates one "interrupts" and so these days are called "interruption" (הפסקה). The sequence of these Sabbaths is also regulated by one of R. Yehudai's formulas mentioned above,[46] a rule that has passed into the calendar and is still in force. But while even the Tosefta leaves no doubt that these four pericopes were the exclusive reading of the four Sabbaths, a change occurred in the amoraic period;[47] the regular sequence was continued, and the special reading was done as a kind of addition (מוסף) to it.

The same happened when a New Moon or Hanukkah occurred on a Sabbath. Originally, Num. 28:11–15 was the reading for the New Moon, and a passage from the description of the chieftains' offerings (Num. 7) was the reading for Hanukkah,[48] but eventually both were read alongside the consecutive weekly reading. Complications could arise when the New Moon of Tevet, Adar, or Nisan occurred on the Sabbath. In this event, since amoraic times, three different readings have been performed one after the other: the weekly reading, the New Moon reading, and the special reading (B. *Meg.* 29b; Y. *Meg.* 3, 74b). The reading for the Afternoon Service of the Sabbath remained unchanged everywhere,[49] while the readings for Monday and Thursday[50] were cancelled on the New Moon, Hanukkah, and Purim, to be replaced by the special pericopes of these days. On fast days, according to the Mishnah, Lev. 26 and Num. 28 (the blessings and curses) were read; the Tosefta already knows of the Ninth of Av—on which Deut. 4:25–40 is read,[51] as an exception, and this reading has been retained. The geonim[51*] changed the reading for the other fast days: They restricted the reading stipulated in the Mishnah to fast days for rain, which in their time were no longer observed with the ancient ceremonies (§21:3), while for the historical fasts they selected Ex. 32:11–14, and 34:1–10, the sole nonconsecutive Torah reading (דלוג). For the Ninth of Av the Tosefta knows another reading, Lev. 26:14, which appears to have long been actually read in Palestine, for *Soferim* and *Lam. R.* also know it.[52] Finally, the same reading from the Book of Exodus was introduced to the Afternoon Service of fast days,[53] something unknown to the most ancient sources. On the Seventeenth of Tammuz in thirteenth-century Bohemia, they would read from Ex. 32:11 to 34:10 without skipping.

The pericopes for the festivals are listed in their most ancient form in the Mishnah (*Meg.* 3:5), but hardly one has remained exactly as given there: They were too short for the needs of later times,[54] and more were needed for the second festival day of the Diaspora.[55] For the festivals other than Pentecost the Mishnah designates the few verses dealing with each in Lev. 23, known as פרשת המועדות, "the pericope of the festivals," and for Pentecost—since Lev. 23:15 had to serve for Passover—Deut. 16:9–12. In the amoraic period, the entire chapter was assigned to every festival. Likewise, Lev. 22:26 to 23:44 was assigned [outside of Palestine] to the second day of Passover and the first two days of Tabernacles, while Deut. 15:19 to 16:17 was assigned to the last days of all holidays. On Passover the Mishnah knows of a reading only for the first day, with good reason, as we have seen above, while the Tosefta[56] already knows the readings for the other days that are taken from other references to Passover in the Torah. Abaye established an authoritative maxim: משך תורא קדש בכספא פסול במדברא שלח [125] בוכרא. This means that on the first day one reads "Draw" (Ex. 12:21 ff.; in the geonic period,[57] the reading began earlier, with 12:14); on the second day, "An ox" (Lev. 22:26); on the third day, "Sanctify every firstborn for Me" (Ex. 13:1ff.); on the fourth day, "If you lend money" (Ex. 22:24ff.); and on the seventh day the splitting of the Red Sea (Ex. 13:17 to 15:26), which occurred according to the traditional reckoning on the night of the twenty-second of Nisan.[58] For the Sabbath of the intermediate days of Passover and Tabernacles, "Lo, you say to Me" (Ex. 33:12 to 34:26) was fixed in Babylonia as the reading as early as the third century (B. *Meg.* 31:1).[59] On the first day of Pentecost, which in the meantime had become the festival of the giving of the Torah, the Tosefta already names Ex. 19 and 20.[60] Lev. 23:23–25, as a reading for the New Year did not suit the spirit of later times; hence, the Tosefta gives Gen. 21, since, according to the Midrash, God remembered Sarah on the New Year. The Babylonian Talmud fixes Gen. 22, the binding of Isaac, as the reading for the second day.[61] Only the Day of Atonement kept the reading originally set for it (Lev. 16).[62] For Tabernacles, readings for each day were already set in the Mishnah.[63] Num. 29:17–30:1 (the festival sacrifices) was to be divided among the intermediate days, and the Tosefta divides it in such a way that each day gets three verses.[64] Later, however, three were not enough; the reading had to be longer, and the question of where to get the additional verses arose. A solution was found in the fiction that [outside of Palestine] the fixing of the calendar is uncertain and that therefore a doubt exists about the actual reckoning of the days. This approach provided the excuse to combine the verses of the sacrifices of two days for each day of the festival. Thus, the second and third days are combined, as are the third and fourth, and so on. But twice the number of verses was still needed, so in the Middle Ages various systems were devised for expanding the readings by additions and supplements. Here Amram deviated from Yehudai, and all of Western Europe differs from both. Rashi devised his own method, which was at first rejected even in his own circle, but eventually achieved general recognition and, as far as we can tell, is now accepted everywhere. In this method, each day the sacrifices of three days are read (second, third, and fourth; third, fourth, and fifth; etc.), and afterwards the first two are repeated. But, also, in some communities only two days are read (two plus three, three plus four, etc.): First each is read separately, then the second is repeated, and finally the two are read together. [In Palestine each day's passage is read four times, one after the other.] These difficulties were caused by the lengthening of the Torah reading on days when the content of the pericope did not permit it. The seventh day caused special difficulty (Hoshana Rabba) because many hesitated to accord it the reading of the eighth day, a full-scale festival; but only in Ashkenaz was this hesitancy normative, not in the other rites.

For the Eighth Day of Assembly,[65] the Babylonian Talmud assigns Deut. 15:19ff., as for all other last days of the festivals, but it adds the note: מצות וחקים ובכור (B. *Meg.* 31a). The sages differed as to what passages are meant by these words, and so different rites have developed, some of great duration. In general it remained Deut. 15:19, though here, too, Rashi introduced an expansion:[66] while on the other festivals—only on the Sabbaths—when a longer reading was called for, one would begin by reading the preceding passage (Deut. 14:22),[67] he determined that on the Eighth Day of Assembly the reading should begin here no matter what the day of the week. At first there was opposition to this innovation, but eventually it was adopted in Ashkenaz and France, although not in Sepharad and Italy. In Italy they would begin even on the Sabbath only with Deut. 15:12.

On the second day of the Eighth Day of Assembly the Babylonian Talmud designates Deut. 33; it cannot be determined whether they meant to include chapter 34, also.[68] Likewise, we do not know whether Deut. 33 and 34 served also as a regular Sabbath reading; since the geonic period it has been an exception unto itself, the only festival pericope not read also on one of the Sabbaths of the year. It was assigned to the Eighth Day of Assembly so that the annual cycle might be completed on the last day of the festival. In this way the day came to be called "The Joy of the Torah," which, to be sure, is not attested before the year 1000. The conclusion of the cycle of readings was celebrated in the synagogue with homilies and prayers (see §30). To this was added another custom, that of following the conclusion of the Torah immediately with its beginning. R. Judah of Barcelona,[69] the first to report on it, says that Gen. 1:1–5 is often recited from memory and expounded or elaborated in poetic form. This custom, too, has its own history, for in the Babylonian academies the beginning of Genesis was recited from memory at the Afternoon Service on the Day of Atonement. Saadia even tells us that the Torah was read again at the Closing Service, and the verses read were again the first ones of Genesis; but after his time this custom was eliminated. It seems that underlying these customs is a different kind of cycle, to which the Talmud may allude. It may be that originally the end of the Torah, followed by its beginning, was read at the Afternoon Service of the Day of Atonement.[70] When, later, the festival of the Joy of the Torah was moved to the Eighth Day of Assembly, Gen. 1 was added to the end of Deuteronomy as a new reading. Though originally the verses were recited

[126]

only from memory, afterward they were actually read from the scroll, and though originally it was only the first few verses (in Rome only Gen. 1:1–5 are still read [from memory] as in ancient times), soon it became the entire story of creation down to Gen. 2:3. From the twelfth century on[71] this custom gradually took root, again, apparently, earlier in France and Germany than in the other countries. It was a great honor to be allowed to read the end or beginning of the Torah; the two men, usually the most distinguished and learned in the community, who were accorded this honor were given the titles חתן תורה, "bridegroom of the Torah," and חתן בראשית, "the bridegroom of Genesis."

[127]

All the readings discussed till now belong to the Morning Service. The Mishnah knows of an afternoon reading only for the Sabbath,[72] and the Talmud knows of one for the Day of Atonement, Lev. 18. What about the rest of the festivals? We have no evidence for such readings, which can be inferred only from one vague reference in the Talmud.[73] The only source that claims that such an afternoon reading existed is *Soferim* 11:5, but it is of very doubtful reliability. Only when a festival coincides with the Sabbath is the Torah read in the Afternoon Service, and then just as on any ordinary Sabbath, without any special attention being given to the festival. Fast days also have an afternoon reading, apparently the latest of all, for its existence cannot be proven before the geonic period.

Another institution not known to the early sources is the addition of festival pericopes from the description of the sacrifices, Num. 28:6–29.[74] On the Day of Atonement, the high priest would recite from memory Num. 29:7–10 (*Yoma* 7:1), and the Tosefta requires the same reading in the synagogue (T. *Meg.* 4:6). Thus, we find in the Talmud that the readings of the four special Sabbaths, for the New Moon, and for Hanukkah are read as a supplement to the Sabbath reading. Out of these roots sprang the custom, found in the literature universally since the time of Yehudai Gaon, of reading alongside the traditional pericope another one from Numbers describing the sacrifice of the day. This reading is also called מפטיר, "ending," because it comes immediately before the reading of the Haftara (§26). Frequently this passage was quite distant from the regular reading, necessitating considerable rolling of the scroll in order to find it. To avoid holding up the congregation (טרחא דצבורא),[75] the practice was introduced of reading from two scrolls: the regular pericope from the first and the additional reading from the second. When three pericopes were read, as on the Joy of the Torah, three scrolls were used; this was the case also when the New Month of Nisan, Tevet or Adar occurs on the Sabbath. The additional pericope is not attested before Yehudai Gaon, but thereafter it is widespread. Not every congregation owned three Torah scrolls;[76] especially in times of pogroms, expulsions, and plundering, few congregations were wealthy enough, and sometimes there was no way to avoid using only one or two scrolls, reading several passages from one.

In those days it might even happen that a congregation did not have a single scroll written according to regulation; in that case the authorities permitted overlooking the regulations so that the Torah reading would not be neglected.

(6) How was the reading of the Torah performed? There can hardly be any doubt that originally one person read the entire pericope. As the pericopes were never long, a single person could read them without effort. The reading, as we shall see, was not originally an end in itself, but preparation for the explanatory homily,[77] and it would

have been a disturbance if more than one person read the pericope. Little by little this changed; the reading acquired a significance of its own, and the congregation became a participant. At the leader's summons, several of the worshipers would come forward to read; their number increased with the sanctity of the day.[78] On weekdays, including Hanukkah, Purim, and fast days, and likewise on the afternoon of the Sabbath, three would come forward; on the New Moon and the intermediate days of festivals, four; on festivals, five; on the Day of Atonement, six; and on the Sabbath, seven. On Sabbaths and festivals the number could be increased, but on weekdays and the intermediate days of festivals it was not permitted to prolong the service unnecessarily. The minimum reading was set at three verses, and when three men read the total had to be no less than ten.[79] But there were ancient pericopes that were not long enough to satisfy these rules. They were changed or lengthened when possible, as on the festivals, but otherwise they had to be accepted as they were. Thus, the Purim reading, Ex. 17:8–16, with its mere nine verses, remained unchanged because no substitute passage could be found.[80] It was probably for this reason that the readings of the four special Sabbaths were reduced to the rank of additional readings, for two of them could not be brought up to the obligatory number of verses. Some readings had a traditional division; Deut. 32:1–43 was used like a psalm in the Temple, divided into six sections. When used as a Torah reading it was divided in exactly the same way,[81] though with time doubts arose as to the exact traditional division. Some passages had to be read consecutively without interruption, such as the curses of Lev. 26 and Deut. 28: "The curses are not to be interrupted" (M. *Meg.*, 3:6). At the end of every pericope of the Torah[82] (פיסקה, also called פרשה), no fewer than three verses could be left, and where this was likely to occur, the preceding divisions had to be made in such a way as to prevent it. Some amoraim permitted dividing a traditional verse in such cases (פוסק or חותך), which was probably an ancient practice. Others demanded that the verse be read twice (חוזר, דולג),[83] and that is how the reading of the New Moon is treated to this day: Num. 28:1–3 and then 3–5. With the introduction of the annual cycle, in which the pericopes and the individual readers' passages are rather long, a requirement was imposed that no reading should begin or end with a verse containing anything negative.[84] As to the details of the division, complete freedom obtained, yet over time a certain tradition developed for this too,[85] which has achieved general acceptance but has never become legally binding.

[128]

(7)   Those summoned by the leader would approach the Torah and read ἀνέστη ἀναγνῶναι, "He stood up to read" (Luke 4:16). An exception was made in Babylonia for the Exilarch; the scroll was brought to his place and he read from it there: "There they bring the Torah to the Exilarch" (Y. *Yoma* 7:1, 44a, bottom). This custom survived until at least the tenth century.[86] At first, anyone was permitted to read from the Torah without exception, including women,[87] minors,[88] and even slaves;[89] but already in tannaitic times women were excluded, and later, when the institution of Bar Mitzvah was introduced,[90] so were minors. Likewise, it was prohibited to call to the Torah people dressed in rags (פוחח)[91] as this was a disgrace to the community. No one could approach unsummoned, and even the head of the congregation (ראש הכנסת)[92] could go up only if invited by the congregation; when the sexton of the congregation (שמש) went up, someone had to take his place. Later—the custom is first mentioned in *Soferim*—the

people were called to the Torah by name; for this purpose the verb קרא was used, as it was for the reading itself.[93] Confusion thus arose between the "calling" of the readers and the "reading" of the Torah; those who were called to the Torah were called קרויים, קרואים, or קריות.

[129]   Those called to the Torah read by themselves without help.[94] Not every synagogue had the required number of worshipers who knew how to read the Torah. In such a case, those more learned[95] would read more than once; if only one such person was present, he would read seven times in a row. Naturally this happened most often in congregations where Hebrew was not the native language (בית כנסת של לועזות).[96] There they would read, if at all possible, at least the beginning and end of the pericope in Hebrew, and the rest in the local language, all of it if necessary. This may be why Philo speaks of only one person reading the Torah every Sabbath.[97] The principle that every individual reads his portion was adhered to as long as possible, but this could not be carried through permanently. In antiquity the individual portions were short, usually from three to five verses, and at the same time familiarity with the Torah was great, for children were taught the Torah from their earliest years (Philo): "They were better able to recite the Torah from memory than their own name" (Josephus, *Contra Apionem*, 2.18). But in the course of time the knowledge of the Torah diminished while the readings got longer, and at the same time a particular melody of recitation came to be required;[98] thus, it became difficult to find people who knew how to read their portion. In Babylonia,[99] they therefore turned to the precentor to help the reader, at first in an undertone, later louder, particularly for the sake of the melody. Eventually he replaced the congregant completely, and from then on the precentor or a reader specially appointed for this purpose would read alone, while the person called would stand by him in silence. This process did not happen everywhere at the same time; it seems that in Palestine, the Balkans, and Italy,[100] the congregants were still reading in the twelfth century, and the precentor standing idly by their side, while in other countries he was already helping them. In thirteenth-century Germany[101] and Bohemia the precentor was reading alone, and about that time this became customary also in Spain and France. It is characteristic that wherever Amram mentions the reading of the Torah,[102] the Oxford manuscript speaks of the precentor reading. So it remained, with the one exception that on his Sabbath a Bar Mitzvah boy reads his own portion or even the entire pericope.[103] The modern suggestion to shorten the weekly readings and have the congregation again do the reading itself has gained no attention anywhere.[104] In Reform congregations in America, and likewise in the Reform congregation in Berlin, no one is called to go up to the Torah; the preacher, who serves as a precentor, reads the portion without interruption.

(8)   The result was that nothing remained for the person called to the Torah to do but to recite the benedictions before and after the reading of the Torah (ברכות התורה, "The benedictions of the Torah").[105] In the most ancient period the custom was that one benediction was recited at the beginning of the entire reading, and one at the end: "The first and last reader of the Torah recites a blessing before and after" (M. *Meg.* 4:1).[106] This changed in the course of the amoraic period, "after the introduction of the regulation" (B. *Meg.* 22a). At first, a benediction was required to precede and follow only particular passages, such as the various songs, the Ten Commandments, and

the curses,[107] but in Babylonia they went further and had everyone called to the Torah recite the blessing before and after his passage. The most ancient Torah benediction known to us is: הבוחר בתורה, "He who chooses the Torah (Y. *Yoma* 7:1, 44d). As the beginning of the benediction in the synagogue the Talmud already cites ברכו, "Bless the Lord" (Y. *Ber.* 7:2: "This is the blessing of the Torah"). It cannot be determined whether the congregation responded, "Blessed is the Lord Who is blessed forever," but this may be inferred by analogy with the text of the prayers;[108] Saadia even requires that the reader himself repeat the response, and so the custom was fixed. As the blessing before the reading, אשר בחר בנו מכל העמים, "Who chose us from among all the nations," is in use everywhere; it is mentioned in B. *Ber.* 11b as the benediction preceding the study of Torah. *Soferim* 13:8 quotes instead a different benediction, הנותן תורה מן השמים, "Who gave the Torah from heaven," but this was probably intended only for the study of Torah at home, not for synagogue use, a matter that cannot be settled exactly because of the faulty text of *Soferim*.[109] It is also likely that the benediction in the Talmud is of Babylonian origin, and that in *Soferim* is of Palestinian origin. Another version of the benediction, also Palestinian, was put in the mouth of Moses: אשר בחר בתורה הזאת, "Who chose this Torah" (Deut. *r.*, §11); it recalls the above-quoted benediction of the high priest. The benediction after the reading is universally אשר נתן לנו תורת אמת, "Who gave us the Torah of truth." It is first found in *Soferim*, ibid., but it also may be much older. While the benediction before the reading was considered to be a rule of toraitic origin, the obligation of the second benediction was derived only by analogy with the Grace after Meals (B. *Ber.* 21a), showing that the former is much older. Through the elimination of the reading of the Torah by the congregants, the reciting of the benediction acquired inordinate significance.

[130]

(9)   The order in which people were called to the Torah was originally completely free and was governed by no regulations. As long as only a single person read, this honor was probably always accorded to one of the most prominent members of the community; thus according to Philo,[110] one of the priests or elders would read. Accordingly, later too the priestly aristocracy claimed the right of priority, which is conceded to them by the Mishnah. A priest reads from the Torah first, then it is read by a Levite, followed by a common Jew. "And all of this was said for the sake of peace" (M. *Git.* 5:9). If no priest is present, the Levite, too, loses his right. In the view of the amoraim, no one may precede a priest to the Torah; even if the priest is willing to cede his privilege, he is not permitted to do so.[111] At the beginning of the amoraic period, it was still possible for the leading authorities like Rav and R. Huna[112] to go up to the Torah first; later this practice came to a stop, and an unlettered or even an underage priest took precedence. The amoraim wanted to distribute the places after the priests and the Levites also in accordance with the rank of the one called (B. *Git.* 60a). Holders of high office, like the Exilarch[113] or the geonim, would read after the Levites. Thus, it came about that in the later centuries the rabbi would be the third one called to the Torah; in thirteenth-century France he was called seventh,[114] apparently so as to be last, which was also a position of honor, but this practice did not find general acceptance. In this matter, attitudes and customs varied, and only the regulation concerning the first two places remained in force until most of the Reform communities in the modern period eliminated this privilege as well. When someone was celebrating a per-

sonal event, whether of joy or of mourning, he saw himself as obliged to go up to the Torah.[115] Thus a young bridegroom was normally called to the Torah during the wedding week, and for this occasion a solemn ceremony evolved.[116] Up until the seventeenth century, it was customary everywhere for the precentor and the congregation to sing the story of Eliezer and Rebekah (Gen. 24), and in Oriental countries the custom continues to be observed until this day. In the late Middle Ages congregants would donate money for the welfare of the community to secure the right to be called to the Torah;[117] only the rabbi was called to the Torah regularly every Sabbath and festival. They also aspired to, and paid good cash for, the right to roll the Torah (גלילה), for which the Talmud accords priority to the most distinguished member of the community, and which in the Middle Ages was also often given to the rabbi. It was also considered an honor to bring forward the Torah ornaments (§30), to take the Torah scroll, and to put it back. Certainly this paying for ritual functions (later called מצות) was bound to lead to undesirable consequences,[118] especially since for a time, they were even sold at public auction to the highest bidder. But for the most part they remained reserved for the most deserving, for they were so highly valued that even when they were acquired by the less deserving they would be passed on to those who were more deserving, and the giver would consider that to be an honor for himself.

[131]

(10)   Only a Torah scroll (ספר) written in accordance with particular rules could be used for the reading in the synagogue.[119] It must contain the entire Torah and is invalid if it has only one or some of the five books (חומשין).[120] Every congregation thus had to have one or more Torah scrolls; only in the Middle Ages, in times of severe hardship, did a majority of the authorities permit the reading, in cases of extreme necessity, without a valid scroll. The scrolls of the Torah were kept in a special chest (תיבה), from which they were removed before the reading (הוצאה) and to which they were returned afterwards (הכנסה). The Mishnah tells us about the manner in which this was done in ancient times, when it describes the solemn reading by the high priest on the Day of Atonement and by the king on the Eighth Day of Assembly. The sexton would remove the Torah and hand it to the head of the congregation; he would pass it on to the vice high priest, who would pass it on to the high priest; and he would pass it on to the king.[121] Eventually, the chest was replaced by a Holy Ark (ארון הקדש), and the precentor removed and replaced the Torah. Since the twelfth century,[122] the worshipers strove for the right to participate in this ceremony; they removed the scroll from the Holy Ark and handed it to the precentor, and later they received it from the hands of the precentor and returned it. These activities turned into solemn ceremonies accompanied by special prayers, discussed in §30. After the Torah scroll is placed by the precentor on the reading desk, it is opened, unrolled, and lifted up to be shown to the congregation, which recites Deut. 4:44. In Ashkenaz this "lifting" (הגבהה) is done after the reading. One can get an idea of the great significance acquired by this ceremony over time from the lovely German poem *Hagbaha*, by M.H. Harbleicher.[123] In many places undressing the Torah scroll before and rolling it up after the reading is entrusted to a member of the congregation, and this, too, is considered a special honor.

§ 26 *The Haftara*

(1)   The Torah reading was supplemented by a reading from the Prophets, known as the Haftara (Aramaic, אפטרתא or אשלמתא); the one who reads from the Prophets is called in the Mishna מפטיר בנביא.[1] להפטיר means "to conclude." The question arises as to what object is understood for this verb. According to Rapoport, it means "to complete the service"; thus the reading from the Prophets would always have come at the very end of the entire liturgy, and would be called "conclusion," equivalent to "Missa" in the Christian liturgy. This explanation is not particularly convincing, nor is there any evidence that the service actually ended with the reading from the Prophets. Rather, the expression means to conclude the scriptural readings with a reading from the Prophets. They would read from the Torah and complete the reading with a chapter from the Prophets (קרא בתורה והפטיר בנביא). The same meaning is indicated also by the Talmud's Aramaic designation of the prophetic reading, אשלים (Y. *Sanh.* 1:2, 19a), for which *Pesiqta rabati* frequently has the Hebrew השלים בנביא; as said, the Haftara is called in Aramaic אשלמתא or שלמתא, "the completion," namely, "of the reading."

(2)   When was the reading from the Prophets introduced? About this we do not even have the kind of legendary accounts that we have about the Torah reading. Based on indications by several early authors, Elijah Levita (1469–1549)[2] says that in a time of persecution, when the Syrians banned, tore, and burned the Torah scrolls (compare I Macc. 1:56), the reading from the Prophets was introduced as a substitute. There is no ancient evidence for this assumption, and it has been properly countered with the argument that the Syrians could with equal malice have also prevented the reading of the Prophets. In the absence of any information from the ancient period, we must resort to conjectures. The reading from the Prophets is surely later than the reading of the Torah, but it must necessarily be earlier than the closing of the canon of the Prophets. The Prophets are not read in order, as is the Torah, but by freely chosen selections; within one prophet, two nonconsecutive passages are sometimes read,[3] and in ancient times it was even permitted to read from two different prophets. The books used for the reading from the Prophets are not subject to the stringent regulations that apply to Torah scrolls. The Torah that is used for reading must be complete and must contain all five books, while for the reading of the Prophets it is enough to have the book that is being read.[4] All this permits the conclusion that when the Haftara was introduced, the Prophets were not yet considered to be a closed canonical work. In any case, it is certain that the Haftara was introduced in pre-Christian times, because the earliest Christian sources already know the prophetic reading as an absolutely fixed institution (Luke 4:17; Acts 13:15). Also, the Mishnah, whose contents regarding this are much older than the date of its redaction, speaks about the reading of the Prophets in language that compels the conclusion that the institution had long been in existence.

(3)   The Mishnah (*Meg.* 4:2) stipulates that on Sabbaths and festivals the Prophets be read at the Morning Service. It is very doubtful that this was done originally. The Mishnah mentions only passages from the Prophets that it prohibits to be used as a Haftara. Haftarot actually in use are first named in the Tosefta (*Meg.* 4:2), for the four special Sabbaths, and in a baraita in the Babylonian Talmud, for the festivals, the Sab-

[132]

baths of the intermediate days of festivals, Hanukkah, the New Moon, and the Ninth of Av (B. *Meg.* 31a–b).[5] Probably what happened with the reading of the Torah happened also with the Haftara, namely that originally it was customary only on festivals and on some special Sabbaths, and eventually spread to all Sabbaths and to special days such as the Ninth of Av. After that the Haftara was extended only slightly further, being added only to the Afternoon Service of fast days. This is the only Haftara in an Afternoon Service, sufficient evidence of its lateness, and it is not customary in all rites.

[133] It has already been mentioned that that there is no cycle of prophetic readings, but that passages were read with no connection between them. Did the reader of the Haftara choose his own selection, or were certain passages prescribed? Luke (4:16ff.) relates that when Jesus came to the synagogue in Nazareth on the Sabbath, the Book of Isaiah was handed to him, and that when he opened the book he *found* Is. 61:1–2. Does "εὗρεν" in the narrative mean that Jesus found the verse for which he was looking, or was the book handed to him in such a way that he had to open it to this place?[6] The problem can probably never be solved, especially since the author of the gospel had to make Jesus find this particular verse. In any case, the fact that only the Book of Isaiah was handed to him shows some restriction in the choice of the passage. We have no evidence about fixed Haftarot in the period spoken of, and it seems that those for the festivals were fixed before those for the Sabbath.[7] The clearest proof that the Haftarot changed in the course of time is Ezek. 16. In the Mishnah, the use of this chapter as a Haftara is prohibited; we could deduce from the prohibition that it was formerly in use, and in this case we actually have an explicit report to this effect (T. *Meg.* 4:34). Similarly the Mishnah prohibits Ezek. 1 (the chariot vision), but the opposing opinion of R. Judah prevailed and this chapter has become the Haftara for the first day of Pentecost.

(4)   On what principle were Haftarot selected? The Talmud laconically formulates the sole condition: "[one] that resembles it" (B. *Meg.* 29b)—that is, there must be some relationship between the content of the Haftara and the content of the pentateuchal pericope that preceded it. In the Haftarot of the festivals and of the special Sabbaths, this relationship was always present; where it is not obvious, the aggadic exegesis of the Haftara or festival themes helps to clarify it.[8] But with the Sabbath Haftarot, the connection can be quite loose, sometimes no more than a single word. This can be easily understood if we consider the fact that more than 150 prophetic readings are needed for the readings of the triennial cycle.[9] When the annual cycle came into use, the congregations had to decide which of the three Haftarot to retain for the Torah readings. The choices of the various congregations were not uniform, and as demonstrated by the newly discovered Haftara lists, the variations between them reflect the Haftarot of the different portions of the triennial cycle that were combined into the annual cycle. The Karaites took the simplest solution by retaining in nearly every case the Haftara of the first portion; they may have been preceded in this by the old Babylonian rite.[10]

(5)   Whenever two weekly readings are combined, the Haftara is generally that of the second, though in Worms in the early Middle Ages it was always the first that was retained.[11] For minor reasons—as, for example, when a bridegroom is present in

the synagogue during the seven days of his feast, or a Sabbath coincides with the eve of the New Moon—the customary Haftara could be replaced with another one, "because the Haftarot are not so set that they cannot be replaced when necessary" (R. Hai Gaon).[12] A fixed cycle of Haftarot was formed for the Sabbaths between the Seventeenth of Tammuz and Tabernacles; these weeks were called תלתא דפרענותא, "the three weeks of admonishment," and the שבעה דנחמתא, "seven of consolation," and no other event can displace them. This series must have been compiled in ancient times, because the *Pesiqta midrashim* were organized around it, and all the rites, including that of the Karaites, adopted it. We cannot learn anything more about the time or the place when it was came into being. It probably came from Babylonia. [It is more likely that it comes from Palestine because the *Pesiqta* reflects Palestinian customs, and from an early time, at that.][13]

[134]

(6) Like the Torah readings, the Haftarot were also originally short, and no fixed number of verses was prescribed.[14] The Tosefta speaks of Haftarot of only four or five verses, and even of one Haftara that has no more than a single verse, Isaiah 52:3. In the amoraic period the length of a Haftara was fixed at twenty-one verses,[15] in line with the number of verses that must be read from the Torah. This number is completely theoretical, because it was immediately necessary to permit many exceptions. Whenever ancient Haftarot were in use that could not be lengthened because the prophet moves on to a new theme, דסליק עניינא, these were permitted even if they were shorter. Second, the Haftarot were not an end in themselves, but above all served as material for the homilies attached to them (many such examples are given in *Pesiqta rabati*, and compare Luke 4:21 ff.); where the translator (§28) interpreted the prophetic passages after they were read, it was permitted and may even have been necessary that the Haftara be short. Thus the rather late list of Haftarot for the triennial cycle contains not a few very short Haftarot, some of them with only two verses.

(7) The Haftarot were not always written, as described in Luke, out of a complete book of that prophet, and certainly not from scrolls containing all the Prophets, for such books were of the greatest rarity (see *Soferim* 3:5). But already in ancient times there were special Haftara scrolls,[16] in which all the Haftarot and only the Haftarot were written. In Babylonia, around 300, an attempt was made to prohibit the use of such scrolls in the synagogue, because the excerpting of the Holy Scripture was considered to be prohibited, but the Talmud rules in favor of such scrolls (B. Git. 60a). Despite opposition even in late centuries they actually prevailed for quite a long time. R. Hai Gaon knew of ancient Haftara scrolls that had been written in Sassanid times (that is, before 640),[17] and as late as a century afterward evidence was adduced from such ancient copies that were circulating in formerly Persian provinces. In Islamic countries the custom of reading the Haftara from special scrolls seems to have long survived,[18] while in Christian lands, once the book format was introduced, Haftarot were read from them. There were books of the Bible, in which the Haftarot were marked in the margin, as in the famous copy that came to Germany from Babylonia in the eleventh century,[19] as well as special books for the Haftarot. After the invention of printing, the Haftarot were read from printed books, and for the most part copies were used that contained the books of the Torah with their Haftarot. Reading from Haftara scrolls

is exceedingly rare;[20] even when the Haftarot are written in a scroll they are provided with vowel signs and the cantillation accents and in this way are distinguished from scrolls of the Torah. [But communities that follow the practice of the Gaon of Vilna are strict about reading the Haftara from scrolls written according to the same regulations as the Torah, without vowels or cantillation marks.]

(8)   The reading of the Haftara is also distinguished from the reading of the Torah in that only one person does the reading. Out of care that the prophetic reading not be taken more seriously than the reading of the Torah, the regulation was introduced that the person who reads the Haftara must read first from the Torah.[21] In the most ancient period, before the establishment of a regular cycle, the last reader continued where the preceding reader had left off; later, the pericope was divided among seven readers, and the one who was to read the Haftara went back and read the last verses again. On festivals and special Sabbaths, when there was a special additional reading, it was read by the one who was to read the Haftara. In any case, the Half-Kaddish (§12a) separates the reading of the weekly pericope from the Torah reading of the Haftara reader.

The lower status of the Haftara is reflected in the fact that even minors are permitted to read it, even where they were not permitted to read from the Torah.[22] In some places *only* minors were permitted to read the Haftara, except for a few special Haftarot[23] reserved for community notables, usually the rabbi. In the later centuries, when the institution of the Bar Mitzvah was developed,[24] it became customary for boys to read the Haftara on the Sabbath of their Bar Mitzvah.

(9)   The Haftara is read after the Torah scroll is rolled shut (B. *Soṭa* 39b). Like the Torah reading, the Haftara is preceded and followed by benedictions. They are probably of equal antiquity; the first reference to benedictions of the Haftara is found among the amoraim around the year 300.[25]

In the Talmud, מגן דוד, "The Shield of David," is named as the eulogy of one of the Haftara benedictions (B. *Pes.* 117b), and another is presupposed in which the appropriate festival was mentioned (B. *Shab.* 24a). As far as our sources go, the number of Haftara benedictions is five, one before and four after; whether this number was so great in the talmudic period as well cannot be shown. The benediction before the Haftara is similar to the one preceding the Torah reading, according to the version in *Deut. R.*, §11, אשר בחר בנבאים טובים, "Who chose good prophets." Noteworthy is the mention in this benediction of the Torah and Moses, again apparently with the intention of excluding too great veneration of the Prophets. Of the benedictions following the Haftara, the first has to do with the fulfillment of the promises contained in the words of the Prophets just read, and the last contains the sanctification of the day on which they were read. The two middle benedictions have national content: The first is a petition for Zion, and the second, for the Messiah. Probably, as in the 'Amida, they were originally only one benediction, which in Babylonia was divided out of consideration for the house of the Exilarch (§8:12). The benedictions following the Haftara are a special group built on the pattern of the larger prayers, especially that of the 'Amida. As an introduction we find a hymn, confident gratitude for the fulfillment of the promises for the future; the core is a petition for national restoration, and at the end, gratitude for granting the Holy Day. [Thus, it seems likely that these benedictions were in some ancient period the main prayer of the day; see Heinemann, *Prayer*, 143ff.] The most ancient text for the benedictions of the Haftara is found in *Soferim* 8:9–14, and the Palestinian tradition reported there corresponds in every essential way with our current texts; in the details on which it differs, Amram provides the model for our text. But Amram himself has a second tradition.[26] The benediction before the Haftara is identical, except for minor variations, in all texts. The first benediction after the Haftara is, according to the printed edition of Amram (but not the manuscripts), much shorter than in *Soferim*; but that cannot be the original text, because important sentences are missing in it. The benediction falls into two parts, which are separated even externally in both the manuscripts (compare Tosafot with *Ber.* 46b, s.v. והטוב) and the printed edition; at the beginning of the second part, נאמן אתה הוא, "You are faithful," the congregation would chime in aloud, and the Haftara reader would repeat the sentence and go on to its conclusion. In Palestine the congregation would rise to its feet at these words, while in Babylonia it remained seated. In the later rites (already in Amram) the custom of the congregation's breaking in has completely vanished, leaving no trace in our prayer books, but the repetition of the word נאמן, "faithful." *Vitry* testifies to the old custom, though it is not mentioned.[27] Between the Haftara and the first benediction, all the rites except Ashkenaz have the verse Is. 47:4. At the beginning of the next benediction, *Soferim* reads: נחם יי אלהנו על ציון, "Console [us], O Lord our God, for Zion." Amram reads: רחם על ציון, "Have mercy on Zion"—that is, the same variation as in the service of the Ninth of Av; "Have mercy" became customary (already in *Vitry*). In the following sentence the ancient texts read, ולעגומת נפש תנקום נקם במהרה בימינו, "And take vengeance on behalf of the sorrowful one soon in our days," but some editions of *Soferim* have the reading that has become usual: ולעלובת נפש, "for the miserable one." תנקום נקם, "take vengeance," was changed to תושיע, "save," apparently to avert misunderstanding. The eulogy מנחם ציון בבניה, "Who consoles Zion with her children," in *Soferim* became current in the form משמח ציון בבניה, "Who makes Zion rejoice with her children"; in Amram its text is the same as the parallel eulogy in the ʿAmida: בונה ירושלים, "Builder of Jerusalem." Only Romaniot has faithfully preserved the text of *Soferim*. The variants in the third benediction are surprising. In Amram its wording is the same as Benediction 15 of the ʿAmida: את צמח, "The plant of David"; but while *Soferim* has the eulogy that goes with this benediction, מצמיח קרן ישועה, "Who makes sprout the horn of salvation," Amram reads מגן דוד, "The Shield of David," in accordance with the Babylonian Talmud. The text of *Soferim* became customary (but without the concluding verse, Jer. 23:6, which only Romaniot has preserved) with the eulogy of Amram; we find this hybrid form already in *Vitry*.[27*] The text of the concluding benediction in Amram is the same as the middle benediction of the Sabbath Afternoon Service: הנח לנו, "Give us rest"; the current version is that of *Soferim*, but the end has been expanded slightly as compared to the latter. They are identical in their eulogy, which on the Sabbath is מקדש השבת, "Who sanctifies the Sabbath." Both sources alter the text of the eulogy when, for example, the New Moon coincides with the Sabbath:[28] מקדש השבת וישראל וראשי חודשים, "Who sanctifies the Sabbath and Israel and the new months," which is not attested in any later rite. On the other hand, it is customary everywhere to alter the benediction and the eulogy on festivals, and to use a different text on the Days of Awe from that of the pilgrim festivals. We have evidence for this

[136]

from the oldest known readings, for we find among the benedictions of the high priest, על מחילת העון, "for the forgiveness of sin"; and we read that on Tabernacles the king replaces "the forgiveness of sin" with the benediction for the festivals (M. *Soṭa* 7, end). Amram again follows the text of the ʿAmida in this matter, and reads: ותתן לנו "and You gave us...."[29] Only Ashkenaz lacks a reference to the festival, on the Sabbath of the intermediate days of Passover;[30] but on Tabernacles it has such a reference. On the Ninth of Av, the only weekday on which the Haftara is read in the morning, the concluding benediction was eliminated since the time of Natronai because it is a day of mourning.[31] Likewise it was omitted from the afternoon Haftara of fast days. For the Afternoon Service of Yom Kippur, *Vitry* prescribes the same benediction as in the Morning Service;[32] nevertheless, it has become customary everywhere to drop the final benediction.[33]

[137]

(10)   The subject of the Haftarot of the Afternoon Service demands further discussion. On the basis of a passage in the Talmud that has already been mentioned ("If it were not for the Sabbath there would be no prophetic reading in the Afternoon Service of a festival," B. *Shab.* 24a), we must assume that at one time Haftarot were customarily recited at the Afternoon Service of the Sabbath.[34] This report, which cannot be confirmed by concrete evidence, has caused medieval commentators great confusion. The view of the Babylonian academies,[35] which reached Germany, was that on Sabbath afternoons in ancient times chapters of consolation were read from Isaiah, that is, mainly from the second part of that book, until the Sassanians prohibited it. Others[36] believe that the report refers not to a reading from the Prophets but from the Hagiographa; this is in fact attested elsewhere (see below, §27:3). Yet others claim that the whole text has been corrupted in transmission, but they are unable to suggest an emendation. In fact, only one of two possibilities remains: Either this entire tradition is false, or we must assume that in the most ancient times there was a prophetic reading at the Afternoon Service of the Sabbath, though we find no other trace of it. The only Afternoon Service Haftara that can be proved from the Talmud to have existed is that of the Day of Atonement; by then, as now, the Book of Jonah was read (B. *Meg.* 31b). Following the example of the Day of Atonement, the afternoon Haftara was transferred also to fast days, but there is no evidence of this custom before the year 1000. Ibn Ghiyath is the first to mention Hos. 14 as a Haftara for the Ninth of Av, but he notes that this reading was completely optional.[37] In fact all the rites except Ashkenaz adopted Hos. 14 as the Haftarot for the afternoon of the Ninth of Av. The afternoon Haftarot for the other fast days seem even later; it is hard to determine exactly when and how they came into being. Sepharad never accepted them, and Romaniot knows but rejects them; only Rome and Ashkenaz read Is. 56:6–57:8 on fast day afternoons,[38] and Ashkenaz reads the same Haftara on the Ninth of Av as well.

The Haftara of the Afternoon Service can be recognized as a late institution also through the fact that the one who reads it is one of the three called to the Torah. The rule that the third serves also as Haftara reader led in the Middle Ages to a renewal of the incorrect view, already rejected by the Talmud, that "the Haftara reader counts as one of the seven,"[39]—that is, that at the Sabbath Morning Service, for example, only six others have to be called to the Torah. In fact, the contradiction can be resolved only by acknowledging that, historically, the Haftara of the Afternoon Service is a later institution, and that when it was introduced no attention was paid to the old rule that the one who reads the Haftara must also read in the Torah.

(11) A fundamental change was instituted in the prophetic reading in the modern period, on the basis of the discussions of the Rabbinical Assembly of Frankfurt am Main in the year 1845.[40] There it was decided to read the Haftara in the vernacular. In the synagogues that introduced this innovation, the beginning and the end are usually read in Hebrew, and in between the entire chapter is read in the language of the land. Likewise, the language of the benedictions in many places is the vernacular, and even when they are recited in Hebrew they are abridged considerably, and the national petitions omitted. Everywhere the Haftara is recited by the rabbi, and usually the benedictions as well. Where they are recited in Hebrew, this is done by the person called to the last section of the Torah reading. Even in traditional congregations, where the Haftara and its benedictions have in many places remained as they always were, the diminished knowledge of Hebrew on the part of the congregations has brought about the custom that the rabbi and only the rabbi always reads the Haftara. Another change is that in many congregations the Haftara is not chanted to the traditional melody, but it is read tunelessly.

[138]

§ 27 *The Reading from the Hagiographa*

(1) The Hagiographa do not serve for regular reading, if only because when the reading of Scripture was introduced they did not yet have canonical status.[1] The Mishnah knows only of the reading of the Scroll of Esther on Purim. We do not know whether originally the entire book was read. In the Mishnah this apppears to have been the rule of R. Meir, but his contemporary, R. Judah, wanted to read only beginning with Esth. 2:5, R. Yose from 3:1, and R. Simon, only from 6:1 (M. *Meg.* 2:3; T. *Meg.* 2:9). The decision in accordance with R. Meir is reported in the name of the early amoraim (Y. *Meg.* 2:3, 73b), and from then on the book has always been read in its entirety. Originally the scroll was read in the daytime. When it was introduced, it was not always read on Purim itself—that is, on 14 or 15 Adar—but in Palestine it was read also on the preceding "Day of Assembly" for the sake of the villagers who had no synagogue. This custom ceased with the destruction of the Jewish state, when the reading was restricted to the day of Purim itself; instead, two readings have been obligatory since the time of the first amoraim, in the evening and in the morning (B. *Meg.* 4a; Y. *Meg.* 2:3, 73b). The book is read from a special scroll containing no other biblical book (B. *Meg.* 19a); it therefore came to be called מגילה, "the Scroll." Originally even a minor was permitted to read the scroll, but at the end of the tannaitic period this practice was prohibited (M. *Meg.* 2:4). The scroll was read not only in the synagogue, but at home as well, and therefore the teachers (סדראי) would drill its reading in the synagogue in advance of Purim; half was read on Saturday night of the first two Sabbaths of the month of Adar (chaps. 1–5 and 6–10). But R. Meir rebuked those who divided the scroll in this fashion (*Soferim* 14:18). No benediction was absolutely required for the reading of the scroll, for the benediction was only a custom (M. *Meg.* 4:1). A benediction might be

recited before the reading or after it, or both, or it might even be omitted altogether, depending on local usage (T. *Meg.* 2:5). Only Abbaye ruled that the benediction before it is obligatory (B. *Meg.* 21b; compare Y. *Meg.* 4:1, 74d), while the benediction following it remained optional. Even though the benedictions were not yet considered obligatory, they were recited frequently, so that a fixed text evolved. The text of the benediction preceding the reading is reported by R. Ashi in B. *Meg.* 21b (compare *Soferim* 14:3 and 14:5); for the benediction after it we have an ancient version from R. Yoḥanan (Y. *Meg.*, 4:1, 74d) and a later version in B. *Meg.* 21a, which couches the same idea in different words, and which has been accepted everywhere. The text in *Soferim* 14:5 is influenced by both versions.[2]

[139]

(2)   The reading of the other scrolls is not yet known to the Talmud, while *Soferim* 14:3 mentions the reading of Ruth, the Song of Songs, and Lamentations. Ruth and the Songs of Songs—here *Soferim* follows the order of the books customary in the old manuscripts of the Bible[3]—were read in two halves, the one on Pentecost and the other on the last two days of Passover; in fact the Masora also divides the books into two parts,[4] and this division has for the most part been preserved by the congregations. In Ashkenaz each is read at once, Ruth on the second day of Pentecost and the Song of Songs on the Sabbath of the intermediate days of Passover or on the seventh day. While at one time the scrolls were read aloud and with special benedictions[5]—in Sepharad they are sung aloud to this day—in Ashkenaz every individual reads them to himself with no benediction [except for the congregations that follow the practice of the Vilna Gaon, according to which each book is read aloud from a scroll, preceded by a benediction.] The scroll of Lamentations is read on the Ninth of Av. The customary time of the reading varied in antiquity; today it is read in the Evening Service, but even then the benediction prescribed by *Soferim* 14:3 is not recited. *Soferim* does not mention the reading of Ecclesiastes on Tabernacles; yet medieval authors[6] claim that it is mentioned there, and it does not seem likely that this scroll alone would have been excluded from the synagogue readings, or that Tabernacles would have been left without a scroll of its own. The existence of rather ancient midrashim on them testifies to the relatively early introduction of the scrolls.

In the modern period the reading of the scrolls has been considerably reduced. In most [Reform] congregations, only Esther and Lamentations remain, and even these are read in Reform synagogues only partially and in the vernacular.

(3)   Were there also readings from other books of the Hagiographa (apart, of course, from the many psalms incorporated into the daily services)? *Soferim* 14:4 cites a special benediction for the reading of the Hagiographa, but it seems intended only for individual reading. During the most ancient period it was prohibited to read the Hagiographa *before* the Sabbath Afternoon Service;[7] but such a reading seems to have been held in connection with that service.[8] From Nehardea it is explicitly attested (B. *Shab.* 116b); despite the obscurity of the statement בנהרדעא פסקי סדרי בכתובים בשבתא במנחה, there can be no doubt that a regular reading of the Hagiographa is what is meant. It is not clear in what way this was done; probably a commentary was attached to each individual verse. Rapoport[9] pointed to the surprising fact that the proem verses of the midrashim on the Torah (see below, §29) are almost all taken from the Hagiographa;

he concluded from this that it was the custom to offer edifying homilies on the books of the Hagiographa at the Sabbath Afternoon Service, and that the midrashim that have come down to us are derived from those homilies. True, the midrashim are of Palestinian origin, while the testimony of the reading of the Hagiographa comes to us from Nehardea; but probably this city was the only one in Babylonia to observe this custom, while in Palestine it was universal. To this must be connected also the fact that the midrashic collection *Agadat bereshit*[10] contains for every Sabbath not only comments on the Torah reading and the Haftara, but also for a passage from the Hagiographa.

In the most recent period the *Hebrew Union Prayer Book* has adopted chapters from the Hagiographa as Haftarot. It should also be mentioned that, in the ancient period, the Book of Job was sometimes read on the Ninth of Av.

§ 28   *The Translation of the Reading*   [140]

(1)   Since the purpose of the reading is to advance knowledge and understanding of Scripture among the people, Scripture had to be read in a manner accessible to them. Knowledge of the Hebrew language among the masses declined continually. Even in Palestine, Nehemiah already complains of the suppression of Hebrew, while in the Diaspora it was hardly understood at all, so that in some places even the prayers were recited in the vernacular. But Scripture ought always to be read as it was at the Great Assembly in the time of Ezra the Scribe, "clearly, with the meaning explained" [Neh. 8:8—*Engl. trans.*]. Therefore, the translation, or *Targum* (תרגום), as the sources call it, was added to the reading.[1] In Palestine and Babylonia, the countries where the translation was first introduced and where it survived longer than anywhere else, the Bible was translated into Aramaic; hence, in our tradition, "Targum," with no further qualification, means the Aramaic translation. The word by itself could signify translation into any other language, but in such cases they would specify תרגום בכל לשון, "translation into any language" (M. *Meg.* 2:1), or, in the amoraic period, תרגמא בלעז, "translated it into a foreign language" (Y. *Meg.* 2:1, 73a). Obviously, the Greek translation was also a Targum: "They studied the matter and found that the Torah cannot be properly translated into any language but Greek"; "Aquila the proselyte translated [it]" (Y. *Meg.* 1:11, 71c). The Talmud also mentions translations into Egyptian, Elamite, and Median (B. *Shab.* 115a–b, B. *Meg.* 18a). Likewise, in later times translations into Arabic and Persian were used in the synagogue.[2] R. Zedekiah b. Abraham, in the name of his philosophically educated relative, Giuda Romano, correctly says, "Our translation into Italian is the same as their Targum."[3] That is, the vernacular language is to us what Aramaic was for our ancestors; thus, he is inclined to make the vernacular translation a full obligation. This was a very broad-minded opinion, which was taken up again and brought to realization—despite great struggles—only in the nineteenth century.

(2)   We are no longer able to determine the antiquity of the reading's regular translation; it is probably as old as the reading itself. All signs point to its having been introduced at the time when only one person would read the Torah. By the side of the

reader, the translator (מתורגמן, תורגמן, תורגמן, תרגמן) came up to the Torah.[4] He had to stand free and recite his translation without a text before him. In the most ancient period, a regularly appointed translator did not yet exist; anyone could fulfill that function, even a minor (M. *Meg.* 4:6).[5] We cannot tell from the sources whether one person had to translate the entire reading, or whether the translators changed as the readers did. In later times, the sexton of the synagogue, who also taught small children, probably served as a translator as well (compare Y. *Meg.* 4:1);[6] little by little, the translator became a regular functionary, for in later times when the readings were lengthy, not just any member of the community could be expected to have the ability to serve as the translator. This function was considered as much an honor as the reading itself, and on solemn occasions it was performed by community notables. When the exilarchs were installed in Babylonia a solemn service was held on the Sabbath; the Exilarch

[141] would read his portion from the Torah, and the Gaon of Sura would serve as his transla-tor.[7] Likewise, the Haftara was translated on the Sabbath by one of the community notables, who saw this religious function as a great honor. Where the Jews did not understand Hebrew (לעזות), the Torah was often read partially or not at all in Hebrew, and instead most or all of it was read straight away in the vernacular (T. *Meg.* 4:3; see above, §25[7]).

(3)   The translation was free, not only in that it had to be improvised,[8] but also in that it was not allowed to be literal.[9] It was not supposed to cling slavishly to the literal meaning of the Hebrew, but had to take into account the character of the new language and to translate according to the meaning; on the other hand, it was not per-mitted to expand the text and to turn it into an arbitrary paraphrase (T. *Meg.* 4:41). In fact, religious law allowed a certain freedom in paraphrasing, and it may have become rigid only when the deleterious consequence of paraphrasing had become manifest. The Septuagint apparently is an example of a translation that takes a middle course.[10] Among the Aramaic translations to be dealt with presently, the one attributed to Jona-than has preserved many ancient elements;[11] it shows that the style of translation was often free, even moralizing. Noteworthy is the apostrophe that frequently occurs in important places—"My people, my people, children of Israel"— suggesting that a simi-lar form of address was used in the synagogue. The extreme freedom that the translators permitted themselves led eventually to restrictions on their freedom[12] and the introduc-tion of an authorized translation. This was the one called Targum Onkelos, composed at the time of the first establishment of the amoraic academies in Babylonia (ca. 250).[13] In the realm of translations into Greek, that of Aquila is the parallel phe-nomenon;[14] it, too, was composed with the support and the authorization of sages, and was intended to displace the Septuagint from synagogue use. A certain similarity in method is evident between Aquila and Onkelos, so that it is not inappropriate that the name of the Greek translator was also attached to the Aramaic translation. But even the appearance of Onkelos did not solve all problems, for in Palestine and the lands that followed its rite, people did not want and were not able to accustom themselves to its dry style; thus, the ancient free method survived. The translation attributed to Jonathan and the fragmentary translation show that, for hundreds of years, free transla-tions with extensive aggadic additions continued to be used, introduced arbitrarily by precentors and translators.[15]

(4)   The purpose of the translation was to disseminate the understanding of the contents of Scripture: "to bring it closer to the ignorant (הדיוטות), the women, and the children";[16] but a translation unaccompanied by any explanation could also cause problems and lead to many misunderstandings. To prevent this from happening, literal translation was often avoided. The Septuagint, the Targumim, and the Peshiṭta employ certain fixed deviations from the text, out of the fear that certain expressions, stories, and laws would be improperly understood.[17] But the sages went further, and excluded certain whole chapters from being translated: "Some are read and not translated" (T. *Meg.* 4:31).[18] In the Torah, two stories are not translated—the story of Reuben (Gen. 35:22) and the second story of the calf (Ex. 32:21–25)—because they show their protagonists in a bad light; also, the Priestly Blessing (Num. 6:24–26) is not translated, apparently because it was familiar to all in the original text (M. *Meg.* 4, end).[19] But originally the number of passages that were not to be translated was certainly greater, for the Mishnah and the Tosefta enumerate passages of similar character that are to be translated; this would not have been necessary had doubt not been raised about them at some time. It also seems that agreement as to what passages to omit was reached only gradually, and that this agreement was not universally in force (see T. *Meg.* 4:35). We do not know how long these skips in the translation were retained; the Targumim as we have them include translations even of the prohibited passages. Yet, Saadia's prayer book[20] enumerates twenty-one verses in the Torah that may not be translated, a number considerably greater than that prescribed by the Talmud. The list has not always been transmitted exactly, and all kinds of doubts about it have arisen, but in Kairawan in North Africa the rule obtained until at least the year 1000.

[142]

(5)   The introduction of fixed translations was the death knell of the whole institution, which, having lost its purpose, died out with time. Though even later the rule was strictly observed that the translator should not read from a book, the translation itself had turned into nothing but a repetition of the reading. Once Targum Onkelos was canonized, it was ruled that it should be used everywhere, even where Aramaic was not the vernacular; but even where Aramaic was the vernacular, a completely different dialect was spoken, and Onkelos was understood no better than the Hebrew original. The Greek translations lost ever more ground with the decline of the number of Greek-speaking Jews. But as late as 553, the emperor Justinian had to decide a dispute within a congregation in which some of the members insisted on hearing the Greek translation alongside the Hebrew text: τὴν ἑλληνίδα φωνὴν πρὸς τὴν ἀνάγνωσιν προσλαμβάνειν. The emperor decided that the demand was justified, and recommended the Septuagint and Aquila.[21] But Justinian and his successors saw to it that the Jews in the Greek lands were reduced to total insignificance, and thereafter we hear nothing more about Greek translations. *Soferim*, composed at this time, recommends translation, but not in accordance with the ancient custom; rather, it recommends that the Torah passage and the Haftara be translated together after being read (*Soferim* 14:4).[22] With the Moslem conquest, the Arabic language spread throughout the Orient and considerably reduced the standing of the Aramaic translation. In addition, an opposition movement arose in Babylonia that demanded a translation into the vernacular instead of the תרגום דרבנן, "rabbinic translation." Natronai Gaon, a zealous opponent of any deviation from tradition, declared such a translation completely invalid, and the elimination of Targum

Onkelos as a grave sin.[23] From this we learn that in his time the reading was still being translated, but that the received Targum was being used only unwillingly. A generation later, R. Judah Ibn Quraish of Tahert complained that in the synagogue in Fez the Aramaic translation of the Bible was neglected and even in disfavor.[24] In Babylonia itself, we find that the Targum maintained its position until the end of the geonic period, but that afterward it seems to have been eliminated there too.[25] [The Yemenites continue to translate the Torah into Aramaic during the reading.] The Jews of Europe never seem to have used the Aramaic translation. R. Samuel the Nagid sought expressly to defend the Jews of Spain with the claim that each person reads the Targum for himself at home, and that the congregation was spared its reading only so as not to prolong the service. But only a century later, R. Judah b. Barzilai could no longer find any authority for either custom, though he personally was very inclined to retain the reading of the Targum. In Germany and France, the Targum was used only for the two most solemn readings: the splitting of the Red Sea on the seventh day of Passover (Ex. 13:17–26), and the revelation on Mt. Sinai (Ex. 19:20) on Pentecost. The text of the Targum, as transmitted in *Vitry* for these two days, is very peculiar, a conflation of Onkelos and the fragmentary translation.[26] To this translation poetic introductions (רשויות) in the Aramaic language were also composed; one of them, אקדמות מילין, "The beginning of words," has been preserved to this day in our holiday prayer book for the first day of Pentecost.[27] These poems were never intelligible, but now, with the elimination of the translation that they were intended to introduce, they have completely lost their significance and their right to exist.

[143] The use of the Aramaic translation declined, as was clear to everyone, because it was no longer understood.[28] Therefore, the natural desire arose to replace it with the vernacular. It thus appears that on the above-mentioned two days, vernacular versions of the Torah were commonly used in southern France.[29] But in general this remained a pious wish until 1845, when the rabbinical conference in Frankfurt (see below, §46) decided that the Torah reading should be followed by a translation into the vernacular; since then, such a translation has been introduced in many communities in Germany and America.

(6)   The translation of the Haftara is treated like the translation of the Torah; in fact, in the reading of the Haftara the translation is even more important. The prophetic writings were harder to understand, and therefore the translation had to be fuller, clarifying parables, allusions, and the like. Because in the Prophets not every verse contains a complete idea, the translator did not have to interrupt after every single verse, but was permitted to combine as many as three verses together (*Meg.* 4:4). The Haftara concluded the scriptural readings, and therefore there could be no harm in attaching to it lengthy disquisitions. Hence, it was permitted to abridge the Haftara considerably in favor of the translator, so that he could do his job unhampered (Y. *Meg.* 4:2, 75a; B. *Meg.* 23b). The memory of the significance of the Haftara translation retained such power that, in Babylonia as late as the year 1000, the Haftara would be omitted altogether if a translator could not be found who knew how to explain it.[30]

As with the Torah, the Prophets also contained passages that were not to be translated: The scandalous doings of the House of David were not to serve as matter for popular discussion, and Ezekiel's vision of the chariot was found by many to be unsuitable for reading;[31] in the time of gnosticism, Ezekiel's threats of punishment found translators opposed to the very existence of the Jewish people (compare M. *Meg.* 4:5; T. *Meg.* 4:32–38). With the Haftara, it was much easier to avert errors and misunderstandings; since the reading was not bound to a cycle, the more radical final resort was available of excluding these passages altogether from serving as the Haftara.

The translation method of the prophetic Targum has been well preserved in Targum Jonathan,[32] but in the ancient period this paraphrase, too, may have been accompanied by lengthy homilies; the above-mentioned apostrophe, "My people, my people, children of Israel," is encountered also in Targum Jonathan at the beginning of passages that served as Haftarot. The development was the same as with the Torah: The redaction of the Targum extinguished its vitality and led to its gradual decline. The Aramaic translation of the Haftara was eliminated even before the translation of the Torah vanished from the synagogue service. The reason was the same, with the additional problem in the case of the Prophets that the difficulty of the translation was considerably greater than in the case of the Torah. Only in connection with the festival Haftarot did the custom of the Aramaic translation of the Haftara prevail for some time.[33] *Vitry* contains a translation of all the Haftarot of the week of Passover and of Pentecost (*Vitry*, 165–171), and Rome, too, has them all with Targum; it is unlikely that a Targum was not recited at least also on Tabernacles, and it is probably lacking in *Vitry* only because of the carelessness of medieval copyists. Romaniot and Sepharad both have the Targum only for the last day of Passover: Sepharad has the usual Haftara,[34] which deserved special treatment because of its messianic content, and Romaniot has the Song of Deborah (Judg. 5), the Targum of which is probably to be explained merely as a survival of an ancient custom. Introductions were composed also for the reading of the Targum of the Haftara, of which *Vitry* transmits a great number; by chance one has been preserved in Ashkenaz, יציב פתגם, "Your word stands firm," for the second day of Pentecost.[35]

[144]

Peculiar to Spain is the translation of the Haftara into the vernacular for the Ninth of Av, which is customary to this day in most Portuguese communities. But its fate was the same as that of the ancient Targum: The communities hold on to the ancient translation even though the Portuguese language has long ceased to be their vernacular and is no longer understood by the worshipers at all.[36] The vernacular Haftara was also introduced by the rabbinical conference in Frankfurt [see §46—*Engl. trans.*]. Pursuant to the decisions made at the conference, the vernacular is used exclusively for the Haftara by many communities in Germany and America. Even in communities that consider this reform too extreme, the translation into German has been introduced alongside the Hebrew text (compare §26:11).

(7)   As for the Hagiographa, we must first mention here only the Scroll of Esther, which was recited in the vernacular in many communities that did not know Hebrew— "It is read to the foreign speakers in a foreign language" (M. *Meg.* 2:1; compare B. *Meg.* 18a)—but where it was read in Hebrew it was not translated. Opinions may have changed with time, and at least it seems that the Mishnah contains two opposing opinions.[37] The post-talmudic Tractate *Soferim* requires a translation along with the reading of Lamentations on the Ninth of Av, "so that the uneducated, the women and the children can understand" (18:4). It is impossible to tell whether this means only an Ara

maic translation or a translation into any language. Apparently this is the source of the Sephardic custom that the Haftara of the Ninth of Av, specifically, is translated into the vernacular.

[145] ## § 29 *The Sermon*

(1)   Reading the Torah in the vernacular was not enough to achieve the purpose of ensuring thorough knowledge of the Scripture's contents and disseminating its interpretation; its contents had also to be explained and synthesized. As early as the reading of the Torah by Ezra, the model to which we must continually return, we find the Levites "explaining the Scripture to the people" (Neh. 8:7); their function was to instruct the people in the Torah and to familiarize them with its contents. The book of Chronicles attributes a similar function to the messengers of King Jehosephat: "They went about in all the cities of Judea and taught among the people" (II Chron. 17:9).[1] The two expressions, הבין, "explained," and לימד, "taught,"[2] are the most ancient terms for the sermon, the liturgical exegesis of Scripture. לימד is equivalent to the Greek διδάσκειν; hence, Philo calls the synagogue "study places (διδασκαλεῖα) of all the virtues." Likewise, in the New Testament διδάσκειν is used for the sermon; thus the Sermon on the Mount begins ἐδίδασκεν αὐτούς, "He taught them" (Matthew 5:2). When Mark speaks of Jesus' sermons on the Sabbath in the synagogue, he uses the expressions τοῖς σάββασιν ἐδίδασκεν εἰς τὴν συναγωγήν, "He taught in the synagogue on the Sabbaths (1:21); and Luke says ῏Ην δὲ διδάσκων ἐν μιᾷ τῶν συναγωγῶν, "He was teaching in one of the synagogues" (13:10), or ἦν διδάσκων αὐτοὺς ἐν τοῖς σάββασιν, "He was teaching them on the Sabbaths" (4:31). לימד and its derivatives serve, in the technical language of the oldest Jewish exegetical literature, for attaching the explanation to the text of Scripture (Bacher). Alongside לימד and with the same meaning we find הגיד, and especially the participle מגיד; from this word is derived the term אגדה, the most important element in what was later to become the sermon.[3]

A later designation for the scriptural exegesis used throughout the ages is the root דרש (*darash*).[4] Ezra is the first of whom this word is used in connection with the study of the Torah (Ezra 7:10). Its derivative, the noun מדרש (*midrash*), is used in the Bible (II Chron. 13:22, 24:27) and in the most ancient sources of the tradition to denote a more wide-ranging kind of exegesis and reworking, where the direct connection with the actual words of Scripture themselves is not always clearly evident. Only in the period after the destruction of the Second Temple do the words *darash* and *midrash* denote a public lecture for the purpose of explicating Scripture—that is, a sermon. From these words, the person who delivers the lecture is called a דרשן (*darshan*); but this expression is found in the Mishnah only once, in a passage whose authenticity is contested (M. *Soṭa* 9:15).

(2)   The change in terminology seems to be connected with a change in the method of scriptural exegesis. The most ancient exegesis, the "explanation" of Ezra, followed directly upon the reading; it explained the short Torah passage just read, and may even have been identical with the translation that restated the contents of Scrip-

ture in a broad paraphrase. For the Haftara there is the rule that when a translator is present the selection may be quite short, apparently because the translation expanded the theme of the verse considerably. Our sources give no information as to whether the sermon followed immediately upon the reading of the Torah or of the Prophets, and when it was attached to the one or the other. [More exactly, they teach us that at different times and places the time of the sermon also varied.] An example of a sermon attached directly to the Haftara is offered by Luke 4:20ff. But two things must be noted: The exegesis cannot always have been connected to the Haftara,[5] and the reader cannot always have been the same as the preacher. From Philo's description of the liturgy, we can learn that the practice was not uniform, that sometimes the one who read Scripture also expounded it, while at other times one of the more learned would take over the sermon. We can no longer tell when the sermon was so rigorously connected to the reading. As the readings became longer, the area of freedom expanded, the material that could be selected increased, and the themes became freer and more loosely connected to the text. The sermons of Philo[6] are the oldest documents of the new kind of exegesis; likewise Paul, in his speeches in the synagogue in Damascus (Acts 9:19) and at Antioch in Pisidia (13:16), does not hew to the verse just read. It is probable that the new type of sermon spread in Palestine at the same time that it was spreading abroad. Shemaya and Avtalion, contemporaries of King Herod, were the first upon whom the honorary title of Great Homiletician was bestowed;[7] this, too, may testify to the independent status of the sermon in the synagogue service of that period. Even though the sermon was still attached to the verses that had been read (דרש בענינו של יום, "He gave a homily on the theme of the day"),[8] the verse was only the starting point, and the themes were treated freely and independently. In this new stage of its development, the homily, originally intended as instruction in the interpretation of Scripture, took on more the character of an edifying sermon. Eschatology became an important element in it, and the preachers would end with words of comfort (נחמת ציון, נחמה—λόγος παρακλήσεως).[9] The sermon in this sense could now be detached completely from the liturgy, and could be taught outside the synagogue in a public place (דרש ברבים).[10] The sermon was never an indispensable part of public worship; where no preacher was available, it was omitted. This probably occurred often enough, as long as there were no professional preachers. The sermon was delivered in the local language.[11] The manner of the sermon changed in the course of time with the changing fortunes of the Jewish people and with changing tastes; in some districts it was nearly completely neglected for centuries. The classical historian of the sermon was Leopold Zunz; his book, *Die gottesdienstliche Vorträge der Juden (Haderashot beyisraʾel [The Sermons in Israel])*, is one of the chief factors that enabled the sermon, in the course of the last century, to regain the place in the synagogue that it had in ancient times. Thanks to it, the last seventy years have seen regular liturgical instruction successfully reassert itself in Jewish communities, irrespective of religious inclination, in every civilized country, and the vernacular sermon has once again become an integral part of the Sabbath and festival service.

(3)   As with all the other functions in the synagogue, anyone sufficiently knowledgeable, without distinction of status or descent, could originally serve as the expositor of Scripture. Paul and his comrades appear in Antioch as unknown strangers, yet they

[146]

are invited to preach; in small diaspora communities liturgical religious instruction was often forgone for lack of appropriate teachers, and a sermon by a visitor was more than welcome. Later the sermon became the domain of scholars, to the point that the Sabbath was sometimes designated by the name of the preacher ("Whose Sabbath was it?"). Not all scholars were equally successful in this function: Sharp-witted halakhists were less favored by the congregation than aggadists. Likewise the craft of the sermon was not equally developed in all times: "When Ben Zoma died, there were no more preachers" (M. *Soṭa*, end); yet it was revived, though perhaps in a new form, and never completely died out even in the most difficult times. But it can hardly be doubted that since the second century the sermon has been restricted to the circle of professionals. The preacher of amoraic times bears the title *hakham*; later he is the rabbi. If the term *darshan* nevertheless remained in use, it did not refer to the office, but to the particular kind of activity, to a special skill in the aggadic exposition of Scripture.[12]

(4)   The sermon was recited in a seated posture. When Jesus had read the passage from the Prophets he rolled the scroll and returned it to the sexton; then he sat and began to speak: ἐκάθισεν . . . ἦρξατο δὲ λέγειν (Luke 4:20ff). So the custom remained for centuries: The preacher would ascend an elevated platform (עָאל ודרש), where he delivered his sermon in a seated position ("the sage sits and preaches"). But in Babylonia [and especially in Palestine], where great throngs listened to the sermon, the preacher did not speak directly to the congregation, but a speaker stood by his side (אמורא) who served as an intermediary (תורגמן, מתורגמנא) for his thoughts. The sage would whisper his leading themes and prooftexts to the speaker, whose duty it was to spin them out for the public so as to be intelligible and audible to all. The function of the speaker was a very respected one, and through it men who later acquired fame as great sages began their careers. At the end of the amoraic period, this function fell into desuetude, and since then the preacher has reverted to addressing the congregation directly. In fact, in the great synagogues of our time the problem often arises that one does not find individuals who combine intellectual capacity, vocal power, and rhetorical skill.

§ 30   *Prayers Before and After the Reading of the Torah*

The most ancient sources do not know of any special prayers before, during, or after the reading of the Torah. The Torah was removed and replaced without any special ceremony, and the reading was not interrupted by prayers. This changed completely in the course of time. Removing the Torah and returning it to the Ark turned into solemn ceremonies with special prayers; the reading itself was accompanied by prayers, and, following the reading, several prayers were inserted before the Torah was returned to the ark. We will familiarize ourselves with these prayers in the above sequence, according to their historical evolution.

(1)   The taking out of the Torah (הוצאה, יציאה) is described in the Mishnah, *Yoma*

7:1 and *Soṭa* 7:7, but without mention of any special prayers, nor does the Talmud know
of such. In a later source we are told that the pious of Jerusalem used to go out to greet
the Torah in order to receive it with honor (*Soferim* 14:14);[1] and elsewhere it is reported
that the Palestinians would accompany the Torah ceremoniously both when it was
taken out and when it was put back, but the Babylonians would do so only when it was
replaced (*Ḥiluf minhagim*, §49). Only *Soferim* gives a detailed description, though not
an entirely clear one, of the taking out of the Torah and of an elaborate liturgy connected to it (*Soferim* 14:8–14). On this model all prayer books since Amram provide
the taking out of the Torah with prayers that lend it pomp and majesty. With all the
notable differences among the various rites, the principle is everywhere the same; hymnic verses and thanksgiving verses, mostly taken from the Bible, are used to embellish
the appearance of the Torah. It is no longer only the words read from the Torah that
are honored, but the Torah itself. Consciously or unconsciously the biblical account
of the bringing the Ark of the Covenant by King David (II Sam. 6:5; I Chron. 13:8,
15:28ff.) had a decisive influence on the formation of this ceremony. The liturgy of the
taking out of the Torah is divided into three parts. First, a group of verses is recited
before it is removed; as early as *Soferim* there are nine, but later some were eliminated
and others added as desired by each community. While everywhere else only selections
of verses were used, in Rome the "song"—that is, the chapter of Psalms designated
for that day— was introduced. The Ashkenazic custom of opening the ceremony with
Num. 10:35 is mentioned in southern France already in the middle of the thirteenth
century, but it has been universal in Ashkenaz only since the middle of the sixteenth
century.[2] The preceding group of verses, אין כמוך, "There is none like You," comes from
Soferim 14:8; it was customary in the thirteenth century in eastern Germany, but not
yet in the Rhine region, though little by little it penetrated there as well. An attempt
to introduce it also in Italy failed because the communities there feared prolonging the
service unnecessarily. The taking out of the Torah proper is accompanied by a few
verses of confession. Common to all rites is Ps. 34:4; however, the two verses "Hear,
Israel" and "One is Our God," mentioned in *Soferim* 9 and 10, are found only in
Romaniot and Ashkenaz, and even in Ashkenaz only on Sabbaths and festivals, but
not on weekdays. When the Torah scroll is brought to the reading table, hymnic verses
are sung.[3] Usually a procession with the Torah is held in the synagogue; the date when
this was introduced can no longer be determined.[4] The last part is the preparation of
the Torah scroll for reading, which is also accompanied by hymns. *Soferim* 14:12 cites
for this purpose על הכל, "For everything,"[5] a prayer similar to Kaddish and originating
in the geonic period, but hardly used anywhere; only the conclusion, תגלה ותראה, "May
it be revealed and may it appear," is used in Ashkenaz and Rome to begin the reading
of the Torah. According to *Soferim*, and likewise in Romaniot and Sepharad, the Torah
is elevated and shown to the congregation before the beginning of the reading, where-
upon the congregation responds with Deut. 4:44. In Ashkenaz and Rome the elevation
is done after the reading;[6] in Rome, it is done only after the scroll has been completely
closed, so that the script is not actually displayed to the congregation as desired by
Tractate *Soferim*.

Into this general framework of prayers, which was customary everywhere, each
country inserted its own prayers. Ashkenaz, for example, borrowed from the Zohar the
Aramaic passage בריך שמיה, "Blessed is the name," before the taking out of the Torah.

It first appears in Italy among private prayers;[7] after 1600 it passed into the rite books, and then into the prayer books, following the model of Isaac Luria only on Sabbaths at first, but later whenever the Torah was read. From the influence of the Kabbalists comes the custom of saying the Thirteen Attributes of God (Ex. 34:6) on certain days when the Torah is taken out of the ark. Luria's followers introduced it at first for the month of Elul; from here it was transferred to the New Year and the Day of Atonement, and finally to the three pilgrim festivals. Only Ashkenaz has retained it, and has done so on all the holidays. An even later passage is רבונו של עולם, "Lord of the world," attached to the taking out of the Torah on festivals. It first appears in *Sha'are Zion*, by R. Nathan Hannover (Prague, 1661). In the last century this and "Blessed is the name" have been widely dropped. In many congregations a prayer in the vernacular has been introduced alongside the ancient collections of verses.

A particularly solemn character is attached to the taking out of the Torah on the last day of Tabernacles, the Joy of the Torah, when the reading of the Torah is concluded. All the scrolls are removed from the ark and carried about in a solemn procession. We are no longer able to establish exactly when these processions (הקפות) came into being,[8] but by the end of the Middle Ages we find them in every country, though not always in the same service. In Ashkenaz, for example, they are held both in the evening and in the morning, while in many Sephardic communities they are held in the afternoon. Their prayers also are not uniform. The simplest is that of Ashkenaz, for while all other rites have artistic poems for this purpose, in Ashkenaz we find merely an increase in the number of biblical verses before the taking out of the Torah and the simple acrostic piyyut אנא ה' הושיעה נא, "O Lord, save," during the procession. Additional poems were needed because, under the influence of the Kabbalah, the processions were increased to seven. In the course of time, the Joy of the Torah became a popular festival in the synagogue, and the processions a kind of popular amusement for observers; in less cultivated times and places these degenerated into wild excesses and indecorous behavior.

(2)   Concerning the Returning (כניסה, הכנסה) of the Torah, we learn nothing from the ancient sources, nor does *Soferim* mention it. Only Amram speaks of it ("They return the Torah to its place"; Amram 24a and Frumkin, *Seder*, 1:398), reporting that it was accompanied by Ps. 148:13–14. These verses have actually been retained in all rites, but they have also been expanded everywhere. As with the taking out of the Torah, a procession is held when it is returned, and songs were needed for this ceremony. In Sepharad the verses from Amram are used only on weekdays, while on the Sabbath, since around 1100, the custom was to recite also a series of individual verses, Ps. 29, and Ps. 24:7ff. In the later period (after 1600), these ceremonies were disposed such that Ps. 29 is recited on the Sabbath and Ps. 24 on other days. So it has remained in Sepharad and Ashkenaz, though in Ashkenaz Ps. 138:13–14 is always recited first. For the actual returning of the Torah, all rites use Num. 10:36 and Lam. 5:21, but all use other verses besides. Ashkenaz has a group of verses between these two.[9] In the modern period, the psalm has been replaced in many places with a prayer in the vernacular.

(3)   During the reading: It has already been mentioned that in the course of time

the center of gravity shifted significantly from the reading of the Torah itself to the calling of people to the Torah and the recitation of the benedictions. Thus it came about that for everyone called to the Torah a blessing was recited beginning מי שברך, "May He Who blessed";[10] in turn, the one called to the Torah could, if he so desired, have a blessing said for anyone else, and it was the custom to give a contribution in exchange. This custom was introduced in the Middle Ages, with its roots apparently in France or Germany. Originally it was customary only on one of the days of the pilgrim festivals to give donations to the synagogue for the maintenance of the poor; this was called, after an expression from the reading (Deut. 16:17), מתנת יד, "a charitable gift."[11] (In Spain this custom was known only on the Joy of the Torah.) But before long the custom was transferred to every Sabbath: By about the thirteenth century, R. Isaac Or Zarua did not see it as an unnecessary prolongation of the service. By all appearances the congregations themselves encouraged the practice because these contributions, arising out of generosity, grew into a significant source of income. This they could not possibly forgo, since the income from direct taxation fell to the government coffers. Thus, the custom of the blessing during the Torah reading spread to all countries; and in Sepharad it even became customary for the one called to the Torah to have blessings said not only for his living family and friends, but also for the welfare of the souls of his dead relations (השכבה).[12] In the manner of such customs, the secondary eventually becomes primary, and "May He Who blessed" became for the unlettered the most important part of the Torah reading. Gradually the unfortunate situation arose that the blessings multiplied to a horrifying degree, leading to the excessive prolongation of the service, diverting attention from the reading itself, and opening the way to all kinds of abuse. The interruption of the Torah reading for the recitation of private blessings was long ago eliminated in all progressive countries.

On solemn occasions the calling of congregants up to the Torah was accompanied by special poetic introductions (רשות), which were sometimes rather lengthy. When an exilarch or a gaon was inaugurated, when a bridegroom was present in the synagogue, or on similar happy occasions for the community, the parties were called to the Torah amid such songs.[13] This became a fixed event on the Joy of the Torah, when the "bridegrooms" were called up (§25[5]).

(4)   After the reading: The Torah is not returned to the ark immediately upon the conclusion of the reading; thus prayers may be inserted between the reading and the returning.[14] Not one of these prayers is yet known to the Talmud or *Soferim*.

a.   **Weekdays.** We deal first with the short readings. In Ashkenaz, Romaniot, and Rome, the Torah is returned on weekdays immediately after the reading; only the time needed to roll and dress the scroll has to be filled. For this purpose, on Mondays, Thursdays, and fast days, a few short petitions are recited for protection for all the communities of Israel, beginning with יהי רצון, "May it be Your will." These petitions are already in Amram.[15] In Sepharad, however, the Torah is returned only after the Kedushah of the Lesson (§10[9]); thus, the rolling can be done in between, and there is no break in the service. On the intermediate days of festivals, when these petitions are not recited, a break occurs in Ashkenaz, while Rome on these days proceeds in the same way as in Sepharad.

[150]

On Sabbath afternoons there is an interruption in Ashkenaz; in Rome and Sepharad, Ps. 111 is recited. In Romaniot, "May it be Your will" is recited after all the short readings.

b. Sabbaths. The situation is completely different on the Sabbath. There is no need to insert prayers in order to fill the time, as the Torah is rolled during the reading of the Haftara; nevertheless, a great number of prayers have been added here since geonic times.

i. A blessing (מי שברך, "May He Who blessed") for all those present, as in Romaniot, or for the entire congregation, as in Sepharad, "May He Who blessed," and Ashkenaz (the second version of יקום פרקן, "May salvation arise"): To this a blessing was early added for those congregants who had distinguished themselves through charitable acts and other good deeds, and a special blessing was also added for those who had made donations to the community or the synagogue.[16] R. Judah of Barcelona[17] protested this custom, but it was so widespread that he was unable to eliminate it.

ii. A blessing for the highest Jewish authorities, the Exilarch, the heads of the academies in Babylonia, and the local sages: Since the prayer arose in Babylonia, it is in Aramaic: יקום פרקן, "May salvation arise," and דכירין לטב, "Remembered for good." These two prayers for blessing were known already in the geonic period.[18]

iii. A blessing for the ruler of the land and the civil authorities, הנותן תשועה, "He Who gives victory": This prayer is connected to Jer. 29:27 and Ezra 6:10; it, too, is very ancient, as is shown by the agreement of the Ashkenazic and Sephardic versions.[19]

iv. After the Crusades, Ashkenaz and later also Rome introduced a prayer commemorating the martyrs of the community and others who had performed outstanding service for the collectivity: אב הרחמים, "Father of Mercy." From this, the custom developed later that individuals could also request prayers for family members who had died, around the anniversary of their death: אל מלא רחמים, "God full of mercy," and השכבה. Especially on the Sabbath before Pentecost and the Sabbath before the Ninth of Av, long lists of martyrs' names were read from the memorial books.[20]

v. In Spain, on every Sabbath, a lengthy Aramaic prayer was recited for the communities in hardship: מצלין אנחנא, "We are praying";[21] in other lands this was done only when news of a specific disaster had been received.

All the prayers mentioned here, their text, and their sequence were entirely dependent on local custom, and were introduced, expanded, abridged, or omitted at will.

vi. Two other additions arose out of the need to announce to the congregation important events in the calendar, the New Moon, or a fast day, and are therefore universal. We have already described in detail the form in which the New Moon was proclaimed on the preceding Sabbath (§20[1]). The historical fasts were proclaimed with similar formulas on the Sabbath preceding them;[22] but the petition of the New Moon proclamation was replaced with a different one based on Zech. 8:19. The proclamation of the fasts fell out of use in the course of time, and only the fasts after the festivals (Monday, Thursday, and Monday, §21) are sometimes proclaimed in the form of a blessing for those who observe them, "May He Who blessed."

c. Festivals. On festivals that do not occur on the Sabbath, Ashkenaz omitted all of these additions, while the other rites would observe them as on the Sabbath. In Germany arose the custom mentioned above, of asking a blessing to be recited for relatives on the three pilgrim festivals, and of giving donations in exchange. On the Day of Atonement, prayers were recited for the souls of the dead. From this developed a special ceremony called הזכרת נשמות, "Recalling the Souls,"[23] which is still observed in western Ashkenaz only on the Day of Atonement, and in eastern Europe on the last day of the festivals (except for the New Year). On the New Year the shofar is blown in all rites before the returning of the Torah, with a blessing before the blowing of the shofar and a few verses after it. The shofar blowing in this place (תקיעות מיושב) is not original, but has been customary at least since the third century in addition to the blowing of the shofar in the course of the ʿAmida.

[152]

d.   A special kind of addition was introduced by the festival of the Joy of the Torah, when special poems were sung to glorify the Torah after the completion of its reading.[24] Even though the reference to אשר בגלל אבות, "Because of the fathers," in Amram is not an original part of the book, at least Saadia already knew of this prayer and rejected it in the form that he knew it; the text preserved in Ashkenaz is different, apparently as a result of his protest.[25] In the geonic period other "songs of praise to the Torah" were widespread.[26] As part of the glorification of the revelation there were also songs of praise for Israel, who accepted it—אשריכם ישראל, "Happy are you, Israel"— and above all for Moses, the chosen instrument of the revelation, who was deemed worthy to have direct intercourse with the hosts of heaven and with the godhead itself. The reading on the Joy of the Law describes Moses' death; Targumim and later midrashim were appended to this story, so elegant in its simplicity, lending it drama. They tell of the prophet's last hours and of his spiritual struggles, about the honor accorded him in death, and how he was buried by the hand of God. Likewise the midrash on the death of Moses (פטירת משה) was reworked for the purposes of the service, and was read in the synagogue on the Joy of the Torah.[27] This opened a wide field for the composers of sacred poetry, which they cultivated faithfully; but only a few pieces out of the old stock have survived the centuries.

In the last century, all the additions just treated have been substantially simplified. The prayers that have been preserved for the welfare of the ruler, the authorities, the congregation, and individuals present on special occasions, as well as the proclamation of the New Moon and the memorial of the dead—all have been reworked in the local language in the progressive countries [especially in the Reform communities]. They are no longer recited as they once were by the precentor, but by the rabbi, and for these *Agende* the term "liturgy" in the narrow sense has become current. [*Agenda* probably refers to a specific book: Lion Wolff, *Universal-Agende für jüdische Kultusbeamte: Handbuch für den Gebrauch in Synagoge, Schule, und Haus*, first published in 1880 by Rostock and Halberstadt (second edition, Berlin: Verlag von C. Boas Nachf., 1891). I am indebted to Professor Ismar Schorsch for making the identification.—*Engl. trans.*]

Poetic Additions

§ 31   General

(1)   The prayers discussed up to this point are called the statutory prayers;[1] they are common to all prayer books, and their text is by and large the same everywhere, apart from the changes that have been made in our time by the Reform movement. These are the prayers that were known already in the talmudic period and that were expanded and developed in the period immediately after its close. Thus, they were adopted generally and recognized as obligatory, even, to a degree, as halakha; they were the מטבע של תפלה, "formula of prayer,"[2] the prayer-content fixed by the ancient sages, which had to be followed without deviation.

But with all of the reverence for this tradition, the religious sensibilities of the Jewish people never allowed them to be enslaved to this traditional prayer; in every age they demanded the right of independent creativity, the freedom to express themselves, and to supplement the traditional forms with a personal or, more accurately, a contemporary tone. Thus alongside the stable prayers handed down by tradition, there arose a fluctuating element whose adoption and use in the liturgy was optional (רשות), left to the judgment of each individual community.[3] The religious needs, attitudes, and tastes of different lands and periods stamped its form; the culture of the surrounding world and political and social conditions increased or diminished its importance, expanding and reducing the space allotted it. Sometimes it dominated the liturgy, sometimes it was strongly suppressed. We have already observed such flexible elements of the liturgy in the prayers preceding the *Shemaʿ* (§11 and §12) and those following the *ʿAmida* (§10), but these two were sufficiently ancient to have achieved general recognition. Now we speak about prayers created in a later period. These are religious songs that expand the scope of the service and are therefore called, like the psalms, שירים, "songs," which Zunz renders "the poetry of the synagogue." For the most part other Hebrew words were used for them, names reflecting the cultural environment under whose influence the poems arose; the word *piyyut* comes from Greek, and points to the Byzantine period, while the name *ḥazzanut* is from Arabic, pointing to the Islamic age.

[154]

(2) פייטן, פייטנא, פייט, from the Greek ποιητής, is found already in the midrash, designating one who composes songs in an artistic form; as a characteristic mark of this craft, compositions with complete or incomplete alphabetical acrostics are mentioned: "When this payyetan makes an acrostic, sometimes he completes it and sometimes he does not" (*Song of Songs R.* 1:7 on Song of Songs 1:1). From the noun *payyetan* a verb, לפייט, was derived, conjugated in *pi'el* and *pu'al* as if it were a Hebrew root (יפייט, מפייט, פייט, מתחילין לפייט, תחנות מפייטות). But most common is the noun derived from it, *piyyut*. The Palestinian Targum translates the verb נגן, "to play music," in II Kgs. 3:15 with פייט.[4] Originally, piyyut denoted any kind of poetry; thus, Sabbetai Donolo (tenth century) calls the entire introduction to his commentary on Sefer Yeṣira piyyut; but predominantly the noun designates sacred poems attached to or inserted in the statutory prayers. As a synonym for piyyut, another noun is found that has not yet been satisfactorily explained, טיידי. From it, too, is derived a root, טוד or טיד, which is conjugated as if it were Hebrew. The word מפזז in II Sam. 6:16 is translated by the Palestinian Targum טדויי;[5] probably this word, like piyyut, is of Greek origin, and is to be derived from ᾄδω, ᾠδή. It always occurs together with piyyut—once in opposition to it—and it seems to mean an acrostic poem.

[For the use of the nouns *payyetan* and *piyyut*, see also J. Schirmann, "Hebrew Liturgical Poetry and Christian Hymnology," *JQR* NS 44 (1953): 130–32. There is no certainty that the term טדויי is derived from the Greek root ᾄδω.]

(3) *Ḥazzanut*, Arabic *ḥizāna*, is not as common as *piyyut*, but more ancient, and appears in the eastern countries that were the homeland of liturgical poetry. The word embraces the works of the earliest known poets; up until the thirteenth century they appear in book lists under the designation חזאנה, as collections of poems with or without commentary. An Arabic writer distinguishes explicitly between *ḥizāna* and the obligatory prayers in which these are inserted (§39).[6] The word did not remain in use as long as *piyyut*, but it has decisive significance for discerning the origins of sacred poetry.

[It appears that the term *ḥizāna* is not of Arabic origin and is merely the Arabic form of the Hebrew word *ḥazzanut*.]

(4) Another general term, though used mostly in a narrower sense, is פזמון. Derived from a verb, פזם, "to sing," this occurs in the pseudo-Palestinian Targum of Ex. 15:21 and Job 3:1 as the translation of ענה (ותען), and in the midrash in the sense of חביבות, "pleasure"; apparently, it comes from the Greek word ψαλμός.[7] Originally this word designated any rhymed hymn constructed in strophes, but later it was limited to poems with a refrain, designating either these compositions as a whole, or the refrain only. Augustine prefaces one of his songs with a line that is repeated at the end of each
stanza, and calls the poem "Hypopsalma."[8] This is a usage very similar to the one that developed in Jewish circles. In the late Middle Ages, the word *pizmon* was used to designate not the refrain, but an antistrophe that was said aloud. But even though *pizmon* usually designates compositions with a refrain,[9] it also occurs as a name for synagogue poetry in general without distinction of genre.

By its content, synagogue poetry is divided into two groups, hymnic poems and elegiac poems, which we distinguish by using Zunz's terminology *piyyut* and *seliḥa*.[10]

§ 32 *The Piyyut*

[A brief list of the types of piyyutim is included as an appendix to Ḥayim Schirmann, השירה העברית בספרד ובפרובנס, 2 vols. (Jerusalem: Bialik, 1954–56), 2:701–18. The monograph of Ezra Fleischer on Joseph Ibn Avitur (1966/7; see below, §42(2)) contains a very detailed discussion of the origin, forms, and history of the main genres of piyyut (קרובה, עבודה, סליחה, etc.). See also A.M. Habermann, *Piyyut* (Tel Aviv, 1944/5).]

(1)   Originally the word piyyut designated, as we have seen, every type of sacred poetry, but as usage developed, the term came to designate only poems of hymnic character, poems containing praise and thanksgiving, whether of general content or dealing with nature or history. Piyyut designates the genre as a whole; the individual types of poetry have particular terms, some deriving from the external form, most reflecting the poem's contents or its place in the liturgy.

(2)   The terms deriving from the external form are more general, and can apply to any composition, whatever its content or place in the service; they come from various languages, and point to the different cultural environments by which the poets were influenced. Here we list only the most important and most common names:[1]

   a. אלפביטה, plural אלפאביטין also shortened to פיביטא, serves generally for any kind of alphabetical acrostic poem.[2]

   b. רהיט, רהוטה, plural רהיטים (the meaning of the word is "bar" or "beam"): This term originally designated biblical words or verse-fragments that served as the framework for a poem; then the term was transferred to the composition itself that contained such frameworks or poems made up of variations on a biblical verse in short sentences. Instead of רהיט, we sometimes find דרמוש, Greek δρόμος, "runner"; this refers to the recurring verse, which is subject to the play of variation, but it was also extended to pieces that were recited quickly and without melody.[3] [The terms רהיט and רהוטה are in fact derived from the same root, but they do not have the same meaning. רהיט is a kind of hymn based on a verse or part of a biblical verse, and its place is before the *siluq* of the *qerova* of Yom Kippur. The noun רהוטה was used to designate a particular genre of *seliḥot* found in the rites of Sepharad and Provence. As for the word דרמוש, it seems not to come from Greek but from the Aramaic (דרמשא, דרמשוא), and it served to designate poems recited in Arabic. See A.M. Habermann, *Tefilot meʿen shemone ʿesre* (Berlin, 1932/3), 51.]

   c. מושח, a poetic form borrowed from Arabic poetry, known as the "sash poem"; the poem begins with a line stating the theme, and with which all the end-lines of the stanzas rhyme. Such poems are found only among the Spanish poets.[4] [מושח is not a genre of sacred poetry, but is the name of a strophic form of Arabic origin, used originally only for purely secular themes. From the eleventh century on, it was much used in piyyut as well, especially of the type of אהבה, גאולה, מאורה, מחרק etc.]

   d. קיקלר is apparently the Latin word *circulare*; the name was chosen because the biblical verses at the end of each stanza end with the same word, such that this word "surrounds" the entire poem. This form, too, is found only among the Spanish poets.[5]

   e. עסטריוטא, apparently derived from the Spanish word *estribot*, *estrambot*, is also a kind of refrain poem.[6] [עסטריוטא is usually a poem with two refrains that recur alternately after the stanzas of the poem. The origin of the name is unclear. See N. Aloni's article in *Tarbiz* 16 (1945/6), 231–37.]

(3)   Other names come from the place of the poem in the services. The most common name is רשות, designating an introduction to any kind of piyyut. Such a poem introduces either the prayer or the poet, who in this way presents himself before the congregation; in such a case it is more exact to speak of נטילת רשות. For רשות, sometimes פתיחה or Arabic מקדמה are used.[7] The expression מחרק seems to have a similar meaning. Just as introductory poems have special designations, so do concluding poems; the large poems that conclude a complete structure are called סילוק, and short ones are customarily referred to as כורג in Arabic or גמר in Hebrew.[8]

[In the category of introductory piyyutim belongs also the מצדר, which is found especially in geniza manuscripts. It must be emphasized that each of these nouns is used in the meaning specific to it, and they are not to be interchanged. The סילוק is not simply a long concluding poem, but a poem whose place is in the last part of the *qerova*; *khurūj*, "going out," is the name of the short concluding part of the first two poems of the *qerovot* of the Sepharadim. גמר is not a concluding poem at all, but a short *seliha* that serves as an introduction to other *selihot*.]

(4)   The liturgical function of the names that describe the poems by their content is decisive. Piyyutim are used primarily in two places in the service: in the recitation of the *Shemaʿ* with its benedictions and in the *ʿAmida*.

1. Piyyutim for the Benedictions of the Shemaʿ

A. MORNING SERVICE

For the Morning Service of Sabbath and festivals, the benedictions of the *Shemaʿ* are embellished with poetic additions, which are called by the general name יוצר (yoṣer), plural יוצרות (yoṣerot). In the earliest, times the yoṣerot were composed of the following three sections:

   a.   *Yoṣer*, named for the beginning of the first benediction, "Creator of light," to which it is attached: The oldest poem of this type is אור עולם אוצר חיים אורות מאפל אמר ויהי, "Eternal light, treasury of life; He ordered light from darkness and it was," recited in Rome on every Sabbath but in Ashkenaz only in connection with a *yoṣer*. The theme of the *yoṣer* is for the most part the story of creation; the strophes or their refrains frequently end with the word קדוש, "holy."

   b.   אופן (ofan), immediately before the word והאופנים, though this text is often replaced with והחיות ישוררו, "And the beasts sing," which is apparently of Palestinian origin: The subject of this poem, fitting its place in the liturgy, is the description of the Kedushah of the angels.

   c.   זולת (zulat), immediately before "Help of our fathers" and attached to אין אלהים זולתך, "there is no God but You": It expresses hope for better times, not infrequently treating the troubles of the present. Whenever zulat is inserted, the preceding passage, על הראשונים, "For the first," is said in the short Palestinian version.[9]

[Several payyetanim composed poems based not only on the words "There is no God but You" in the *yoser,* but also on the words "Help of our fathers"; such piyyutim are called עזרת ('*ezrat*).]

The pattern described here is the simplest one there is, but it may be expanded greatly through the addition of other piyyutim after **b** and **c:**

b1. מאורה (*me'ora*), attached to יוצר המאורות, "Who creates the luminaries." [Among the piyyutim in the geniza the name מאורות is also frequently found.];

b2. אהבה (*ahava*) before הבוחר בעמו ישראל באהבה;

c1. מי כמוך before "Who is like You" in the Song of the Sea;

c2. יי מלכנו in those rites that have these words before יי ימלוך;[10] and finally,

c3. גאולה immediately before "Who redeemed Israel," when Ashkenaz uses the Palestinian wording, "For the sake of the fathers."

These last items generally deal with God's love for Israel, or with individual religious commandments, from which they derive the hope for God's favor. Only rarely are all these additions to the *yoser,* or *yoserot,*[11] found together, and this usually happens only among the Spanish poets. Nor do they all need to come together, for it often happens that only individual items like a *me'ora* or an *ahava* were composed for a particular festival or a Sabbath.

The Spanish poets of the Golden Age sometimes began their poetic work before the *yoser,* prefacing a *reshut* both to "Bless the Lord" and to the Kaddish preceding it. Even "The breath," the prayer that concludes the Verses of Song on the Sabbath and festivals and was incorrectly considered to be part of the *yoser,* was frequently embellished with poetry.

The compositions for "The breath" include the following:

a. Introductions, known in Hebrew as רשות לנשמת, or in Arabic as *muharrak.* The form of the extant examples is that the poem is preceded by a leading verse with which the last words of each strophe rhyme. Frequently, both names, *reshut* and *muharrak,* are found together.

[158]

[The meaning of the Arabic word *muharrak* is "moved" or "having a vowel." It is not yet known why the introductory poem to "The breath" is called by this name.]

b. נשמת, plural נשמתים: poems in which each stanza begins with the word נשמת.[12] They are recited after the first passage of "The breath," before the words, אלו פינו, "If our mouths . . . ," and usually have these words at the end of the last strophe; but the authenticity of these final strophes has been challenged, and are mostly late additions.

c. אלו פינו, must mean the same as **b.** The poems begin with מודים—that is, the last word of "The breath" preceding the words "If our mouths." Perhaps they are the source of the just-mentioned inauthentic final strophes of the *nishmat* poems.

d. כל עצמותי, and

e. מי כמוך, both of them attached to Ps. 35:10 as cited in the text of "The breath," one to the beginning and the other to the end. There are also piyyutim for

f. המלך היושב, and

g. שוכן עד, but they have no particular name.

The content of all of the compositions mentioned here is hymnic. Most of them deal with the meaning of the day for which they were composed, and their form is generally the same as that of the *muharrak.*

An idea of the wealth of compositions by R. Judah Halevi for *nishmat* and *yoṣer* can be gotten from poems 88–103 in H. Brody and K. Albrecht, שער השיר: *The New Hebrew School of Poets of the Spanish-Arabian Epoch* (London: Williams and Norgate, 1906), 100 ff.

B. EVENING SERVICE

The *yoṣerot* of the Morning Service have their analogy in the poems inserted in the Evening Service on festivals and originally also on the Sabbath. The entire collection is called מערבים or מעריבות, and since about 1600, מערבות.[13] Special names for the individual parts are not known. The manner of composition is that every section of the statutory prayers has a short poem. Thus two poems precede the *Shemaʿ*, one before "Who makes the evening fall" and the other before "Who loves His people Israel." After the *Shemaʿ* there are four poems, one before "Who is like You?," one before "The Lord will reign," one before "Who redeemed Israel," and one before "Who spreads the tabernacle of peace." It must also be noted that wherever piyyutim are added, the conclusions of the Palestinian versions of these prayers are used. To these six poems, which are usually rather short, another long one is added; the short poem preceding "Who is like You?" is generally prefaced by another long poem with either a single or double alphabetical acrostic, and a refrain. Frequently, before the last part (before "Who spreads") a long prose treatment of some halakhic matter is inserted; this passage is called בכור or תוספת בכור. In Ashkenaz such an addition was adopted only for the second night of Passover. Likewise, introductory poems (רשות למעריב) to the Evening Service are also common. *Maʿaravim* were composed for all the festivals without exception, though not all have remained in use to the same extent. In the Oriental countries,[14] such poems existed even for special Sabbaths. The Spanish poets never composed for these Sabbaths, nor did this genre ever find acceptance in Spain.

[159]

2. *Piyyutim for the* ʿAmida

A. QEROVA

Qerova or *qerovot* is the generic name of all the poems that are inserted in the ʿAmida.[15] The word is derived from קרובא, which designates the precentor who passes before the ark to recite the ʿAmida; the midrash speaks of him also as ההוא חזנא דקריב.[16] Because of the usual manner of transliterating the old French plural suffix *es*, it was customary to write קרובץ, and this was falsely interpreted as an acronym of Ps. 118:15. Likewise, the word קרובץ was sometimes used for the entire festival prayer book, because it contained the *qerovot*. We have *qerovot* for special weekdays,[17] Sabbaths, and festivals. On such weekdays a poem is inserted in every benediction of the ʿAmida. The *qerovot* for weekdays generally come from the ancient period and from the Oriental countries, where the Palestinian version of the ʿAmida was in use; thus they have eighteen parts and are called שמונה עשרה, "Eighteen." Depending on the significance of the day for which the *qerova* is intended, one of the benedictions is chosen for poetic expansion, as a kind of "reference to the occasion"—for example, Benediction 14 for the Ninth of Av, Benediction 12 for the other fast days.[18] On Sabbaths and festivals the *qerova* had only seven parts, and was therefore called שבעתא, "Seven";[19] these are found only in the Additional Service. For the Morning Service the *qerova*, also called שחרית, "Morning Service," or תמיד, "Daily Service," was developed only for the first three benedictions of the ʿAmida and for the beginning of the Kedushah of the precentor; it is divided into the following parts:

a. רשות or נטילת רשות, an introduction in which the poet presents himself before the congregation. The ancient introduction begins מסוד, "From the council"; the later poets, especially in France and Germany, were no longer satisfied with this, and they composed new ones that they prefaced to their compositions.

b. מגן, "Shield," before the eulogy of Benediction 1; on the Days of Awe, before "Remember us"; composed of two parts: the piyyut itself and the concluding stanza. The first part ends with an allusion to the pericope of the day, using the expression ככתוב, "as it is written,"[20] to which several biblical verses are attached. With the last word of the last verse there then begins a short conclusion leading to the theme of the eulogy (מעין החתימה). This conclusion is called סלוק; the Spanish poets called it כרוג, and they omitted the connecting verses.

c. מחיה, "Reviver," before the eulogy of Benediction 2; on the Days of Awe, before "Who is like You?" Constructed on exactly the same pattern as "Shield."

d. משלש, before Benediction 3—that is, before the insertion of the Kedushah (קדושה משולשת) or trishagion, hence the name משלש); also concludes with biblical verses, of which the last are always Ps. 146:10 and Ps. 22:4. This poem has no concluding stanza because a large number of poems are attached to it.

Among the early poets, poems **b** through **d** are each attached to the story of one of the patriarchs, and only after **d** does the poet enter into the idea of the festival. Poem **d** is usually followed, in the works of the ancient poets, by four other poems:

e. Begins אל נא, "O God," and concludes חי וקיים נורא מרום וקדוש, "living and everlasting, awesome, high and holy."[21]

f. an aggadic-historical passage followed by אל נא לעולם תוערץ, "O God, You are ever revered," apparently a vestige of an acrostic poem by Yannai (§40) that served as a replacement when **e** was lacking.

g. A poem, all of whose stanzas conclude with קדוש, "holy," or that describe the contents of the Torah reading.

h. סלוק, a long concluding poem bearing the heading . . . ובכן לך תעלה קדושה כי אתה, "And so may our Kedushah ascend to You, for You are . . ."; it serves as a transition to the Kedushah. Usually its form is prose and its content narrative, and therefore it is sometimes also called ספירת מעשים, "Account of the event." The Spanish poets have **h** immediately after **d** and instead [of the intermediate piyyutim—*Engl. trans.*] they frequently add a special poem known as *qedusha*. Depending on the character of the Sabbath or the festival for which the piyyutim are designed, there may also be expansions, as when the Sepharadim insert a *pizmon* and *seliha*. Examples of complete compositions of this type may be found in Amram, 2:43b ff.; *Dīwān* of R. Judah Halevi, 3:240 ff.; for *qerovot* by earlier payyetanim, see Ashkenaz for the second day of each festival.

On some festivals the *qerova* is more broadly developed in connection with the Torah reading. On Pentecost, when the Ten Commandments are read, and on the

[160]

seventh day of Passover when the Song of the Sea is read, several poems are added before part **h.** These follow the Torah reading verse by verse and generally conclude with a poem on the *Shemaʿ*; they are called רהיט or רהוטה.

A particular type of *qerova* is intended for the Additional Service of the first day of Passover and the Additional Service of the Eighth Day of Assembly, when dew or rain are prayed for. These *qerovot* only go up to the middle of the second benediction—that is, to "Who makes the wind blow and the rain fall," the place at the beginning of the ʿ*Amida* where the reference to dew or rain is inserted.[22] There were several compositions of this type, but as far as we can tell, only those of Kallir were actually used in the synagogue service. These begin with two five-line poems, one before "Shield of Abraham" and the other immediately after "You are mighty"; to the second, four long alphabetical acrostic poems are added, the first of which is a kind of *reshut*; the second (in straight alphabetical order) and the third (in reverse alphabetical order) give an historical survey of all the miracles connected with dew or rain described in the Bible, and in both, the strophes end with the appropriate biblical verses, "as it is written." The fourth poem is composed of twenty-two strophes of double quatrains, each pair of strophes being devoted to the petition for rain or dew for each of the twelve months; the first strophe of each pair is based on the name of the month, and the second on its zodiac sign and the twelve tribes of Israel. The whole composition ends with a short petition for rain or for dew, the last words of which are שאתה הוא יי אלהינו משיב הרוח ומוריד . . ., "for You are the Lord our God Who makes the wind blow and brings down the rain/dew."[23] The *qerovot* for dew and rain are found only in Romaniot and Ashkenaz; they were probably also originally in Rome, though today only their very last sentences are found there. Sepharad also has poems and petitions for these two festivals (תיקון הטל והגשם), but they are recited before the Additional Service, when the Torah is returned to the Ark.

Just as the entire *yoṣer* was not always composed by a single poet and the congregations sometimes did not make use of complete structures, but only a few poems, so with the *qerova* there are isolated poems for particular benedictions. Rome, for example, has before the end of the ʿ*Amida* in the Additional Service of the three pilgrim festivals, poems called שים שלום, "Grant peace," or עושה השלום, "Maker of peace," because of their location; the Spanish poets worked these themes a great deal. The Kedushah also acquired poetic reworkings. Strictly speaking, the connecting lines between its biblical verses are already a kind of poem. But alongside these standing additions, which in view of their antiquity were already considered as an integral part of the Kedushah, longer compositions existed that interrupted the recitation of the Kedushah; they have survived only for the Days of Awe. Frequently on the festivals, and on certain Sabbaths, Ashkenaz adds after אני יי אלהיכם, "I am the Lord your God," several lines beginning with the word אלהיכם, for which they are named.

[Elbogen's description of the structure of the *qerova* is not exhaustive, because it was impossible to subsume in a single framework all of the types of *qerovot* that have come down to us. There are notable differences in their form: (a) according to their various types—that is, whether they are of the Eighteen, Seven, or *Qedushta* type (*Qedushta* is the accepted ancient name for the entire genre that Elbogen calls *shaharit* or *tamid*); (b) according to author, time, and place of composition—for example, the *qedushtaot* of Yannai and of Kallir are not identical to each other in structure, nor are the Italian-Ashkenazic *qerovot* and the Sephardic *qerovot* identical. A deep and extensive study is still needed in order to establish exactly the distinctions between these various types. For several problems in the structure of *qerovot*, see M. Zulay, *Zur Liturgie der babylonischen Juden* (Stuttgart, 1933), 4–6, 12–18, 83–84. For the structure of the *qedushtaot* of Yannai, see Israel Davidson, *Mahzor yanai* (New York, 1919), xxvi–xxxviii; M. Zulay, "Mehqere yanai," *SRIHP* 2 (1935/6), 254–65; *idem, Piyute yanai* (Berlin, 1938), xiii–xvi. For an analysis of a qedushta by Kallir, see G.H. Orman in an appendix to A. Murtonen, *Materials for a non-Masoretic Hebrew Grammar* (Helsinki, 1958; see below in the 1972 additions to §40(6)), 71–6; a comparison between it and the *qedushta* of Yannai, ibid., 76–7. An interesting source for the study of the structure of the Ashkenazi *qerova* is found in the anonymous *Sefer qerova*, apparently written in the thirteenth century. It was published by A.M. Habermann in *SRIHP* 3 (1936/7): 132–91. The Sephardic *qerova* has reached us for the most part in a very defective form. Zunz attempted to reconstruct the *ma'amadot* of the Sepharadim on the basis of vestiges that he found in various rites. See Zunz, *Ritus*, 104–16.]

B. THE OTHER ADDITIONS TO THE 'AMIDA

(A) On the New Year and the Day of Atonement (§24) the *qerovot* were expanded by many *rahitim* of various kinds. Furthermore, they do not end with the Kedushah, for lengthy poems are inserted between the verses of the latter. In the Additional Service of these two festivals, and in the Morning Service of the Day of Atonement as well, there are poems even after the Kedushah, and only after these does the 'Amida continue with "And so set Your fear." Up to this point one can still see the poems as a continuation of the *qerova*, but on both festivals the Additional Service has additions that lie outside the bounds of the *qerova* and are older than it. They even begin with a special introduction, אוֹחִילָה לָאֵל, "I hope"; Ashkenaz actually has a double introduction, for הָיָה אִם פִּיפִיוֹת, "Be with the mouths," is a second one. This introduction parallels the *reshut* in which the poet introduces himself; but in the other introductions he asked the permission of the congregation, while here he prays that God inspire him in what he is about to recite.[24]

[162]

(B) On the New Year this introduction comes before the poems of the three special benedictions, Kingship, Remembrance, and Shofar. These poems do not interrupt the body of the prayer as does the *qerova*, but they precede the introductory prayers "Therefore we hope," "You remember," and "You revealed." They deal with the contents of the three prayers, illuminating it with biblical examples. Their structure is such that each strophe ends with a word that relates to the contents of the three prayers (מלכות, שופר, זכרון). Each stanza is followed by a biblical verse, some of these being identical with the biblical verses that are then quoted in the prayer itself. These poems, like the prayers to which they are attached, are called תקיעות, תקיעתא, "Shofar-soundings."[25] They are preserved only in Ashkenaz; of the other rites only Rome knows a poetic addition, a *pizmon* for Remembrance and a *pizmon* for Shofar that interrupts the petition. Common to all rites is the short passage, הַיּוֹם הֲרַת עוֹלָם, "Today is the birthday of the world," which comes after each blowing of the shofar; Ashkenaz and Romaniot add אֲרֶשֶׁת שְׂפָתֵינוּ, "May the request of our lips," which serves as a kind of conclusion to each of the three benedictions.

(C) On the Day of Atonement we have first, in all of the ʿAmidot, the *qerova* and the *seliha* (see below, §33). Besides this, peculiar to this day is the ʿAvoda, a description of the service of the high priest in the Temple on the Day of Atonement. Today the ʿAvoda is incorporated only in the Additional Service, but originally it was included in the Morning and Afternoon services as well. These poems have no inner connection with the ʿAmida, but only the formal connection that they are said during the repetition of the ʿAmida before the conclusion of the middle benediction. Already the Talmud speaks of the recitation of the ʿAvoda by the precentor; the oldest version, discovered only recently, follows quite faithfully the text of the Mishnah, reproducing its account of the order of confessions and sacrifices. The late versions are poetic reworkings; much as they differ in detail, all are organized according to the same basic pattern, apparently going back to a rather ancient model, perhaps אַתָּה כּוֹנַנְתָּ, "You established," which is in use in Sepharad. To the Mishnah's account of the service of the Day of Atonement is attached a dramatic and vivid description of these ceremonies. The opening is an introduction beginning with the creation of the world and mentioning the chief events of the biblical story down to the election of Aaron and his sons; this leads to the service of the high priest. The ʿAvoda is followed by a prayer for blessing in the coming year, a description of the splendor of the Temple service and of the high priest, and a lament that all of this grandeur has been lost. There are poets who reworked the ʿAvoda several times; most of them prefaced it with a special introduction (רְשׁוּת לְסֵדֶר עֲבוֹדָה), and sometimes they composed introductions to the Avodot of others. Every one of the known rites adopted a different poem, thus preserving it from disappearance. But the number of ʿAvodot that have been preserved is only a small portion of what existed originally; in the geniza manuscripts many fragments have been found that give us an idea of how greatly attractive this subject was to the communities and the poets. In the modern period, ʿAvodot in the vernacular often replace the poetic ʿAvodot; only the old confession of sin has been retained in Hebrew.

[163] The Spanish poets also used to compose poems for the Morning Service describing the sacrificial ceremonies of the high priest in connection with the reading of the Torah (Lev. 16); such compositions are also called Seder ʿAvoda.[26]

(D) Nearest to the position of the ʿAvoda in the framework of the ʿAmida and to its character as a didactic poem are the *azharot*, poetic enumerations of the 613 commandments in the Torah, intended for Pentecost. In the Talmud the expression *azharot* is used to denote only prohibitions, and the extension of its meaning to all commandments, both positive and negative, derives from the opening word of the most ancient liturgical poem of this type, אַזְהָרֹת רֵאשִׁית. The number 613 goes back to a dictum of R. Simlai (ca. 200) in the Talmud (B. *Mak.* 23b), which has become generally accepted. Innumerable efforts have been made to justify it by enumerating the individual commandments, but no one has yet succeeded in drawing up a consistent and irrefutable list. Originally the *azharot* contained only general allusions to the commandments, but later they actually enumerated them, at first without distinguishing between the positive and negative commandments, and later by listing the 248 positive and the 365 negative commandments in two separate groups. R. Saadia Gaon worked all of them into the Ten Commandments, and his example was widely followed. There are *azharot* in which laws are grouped by subject, and others with no particular order, like אתה הנחלת, "You granted" in Ashkenaz, whose lack of order has always been remarked. The *azharot* may be worked into the Additional Service ʿAmida in the form of a *shivata*, as Saadia demonstrated in a difficult poem that cost him a great deal of effort. But this method is rare; generally *azharot*, like the ʿAvoda, are independent of the ʿAmida, but were intended to be inserted in the Additional Service after the verses on the sacrifices. Originally they were nothing but dry lists, but later they were embellished with poetic devices that gave them life; the introductions and transitions, especially, were artistically crafted. At the end of the *azharot* the connection with the body of the ʿAmida was effected by means of a poetic transition passage, אז שש מאות, "Then, six hundred"; this piece is so widespread in many lands, even the most remote, that it may be seen as ancient. In a few rites the *azharot* were read not in the ʿAmida of the Additional Service, but before the Afternoon Service, and in some, on the Sabbath prior to Pentecost. The distribution of the *azharot* between the two days of the festival also varies. Some poets provide the *azharot* with introductions (פתיחה, פזמון); here they had more flexibility and could express their ideas with poetic flair.[27]

The term *azharot* is used in the late Middle Ages in an extended sense also for poems that deal only with a single commandment, but in minute detail, or with all the commandments pertaining to a festival.[28] These were recited on the Sabbath prior to the festival, and they were connected with the proclamation of the festival: "Thus have our honored masters decreed. . . ." This applies particularly to the three pilgrim festivals; the Sabbath preceding all of them in the course of time acquired the name שבת הגדול, "The Great Sabbath."[29]

[The first of the Spanish poets who composed *azharot* is Isaac Ibn Giquitilla, who lived at the end of the tenth century. Large fragments of his composition were discovered and published by M. Zulay in *Tarbiz* 20 (1949/50): 161–76.]

(E) The poems peculiar to Tabernacles belong outside and immediately following the ʿAmida; they are called הושענות, "O save." This name has a long history. Solemn processions with the willow were among the rituals of Tabernacles in the Temple: "Every day they would circumambulate the altar once . . . on that day [the seventh day] they would circumambulate it seven times." (M. *Suk.* 4:5). During the procession they would sing Ps. 118:25, אנא יי הושיעה נא, "O Lord, save," or, according to other reports, its mystical variation אני והו הושיעה נא (M. *Suk.* 4:5).[30] From the recurring phrase, הושיעה נא, or more exactly from its shortened form, הושענא, the Talmud already refers to the four species or to the willow alone as הושענא (B. *Suk.* 30b ff.). In the Mishnah the seventh day of the festival of Tabernacles, the primary day for the commandment of the willow, is called "the Seventh Day of the Willow," and in the midrash and the post-talmudic literature, it is also called "The Day of 'O Save.' "[31] After the destruction of the Temple, the procession around the altar fell out of use, but the prayers connected to it were preserved in the synagogue. A substitute was found also for the procession: The Torah scroll was removed from the ark and a procession held around it, once or even three times on the first six days, and seven times on the seventh day. Only on the Sabbath was there no procession; therefore, the seventh day was fixed so as never to fall on a Sabbath, and special calendrical regulations were devised to prevent them from coinciding.[32] In the Middle Ages, a certain talmudic passage (B. *Suk.* 43a) occasioned

[164]

doubt as to whether the procession should be held with the Four Species or just the willow; though all evidence favors the willow, for several centuries now all communities have held the procession with the Four Species.[33]

The oldest reports about the processions and the prayers go back to geonic times.[34] After the conclusion of the Additional Service, the precentor began הושענא, "O save," which the congregation would repeat; then the precentor would repeat his prayer for salvation in a fuller version. On the seventh day they would vary the short cries of "O save" and repeat them seven times. Apparently these cries of "O save" soon developed into short litanies. In the geonic period it was everywhere customary to recite poems with "O save" as a refrain; Saadia says that in his time the number of such poems was extremely great. Poems were composed in alphabetical acrostic, so that one spoke of inserting "an alphabet or two"; but they are also called by the neutral expression פרקים, "sections," or פזמונים, a general term for poems. These poems must have been rather varied in content; often they were hymns, which were called שבח והודאה or דברי שבח ופיוטים; there were also petitions, called דברי בקשה or תחנונים. But in the end, all the poems that served for this purpose were given the name derived from their refrain, and all were called *hoshaʿnot*. Despite the transfer of this name to the poems themselves, the refrain itself was reduced until it was said only at the beginning and the end. Saadia, and following him Sepharad, has the alphabetical *hoshaʿnot* with the refrain "O save," two of which he uses everyday, plus a third addition beginning with אנא, "O!," with contents suited to the number of the days. The recurring refrain is תבנה ציון ברינה והעלינו לתוכה בשמחה, "Build Zion in song and bring us up to it in gladness"; on the seventh day, when three acrostics were sung, the refrain is, נהדרך בארבע מצוות ונמליכך ביום ערבה, "We shall glorify You with the four commandments, and we will make You King on the day of the willow," but this refrain, too, has been lost in the course of time, and is no longer found in Sepharad. In Ashkenaz, Rome and Romaniot, the *hoshaʿnot* of Kallir are in use. They begin with an alphabetical piece with the refrain "O save"; then comes a second passage with the refrain כהושעת . . . כן הושיעה נא, "As You saved . . . so save." The second passage is identical on all days, while the first one changes; on the seventh day all the poems are recited together, with the addition of a great number of poems. The *hoshaʿnot* of Sepharad have already diverged considerably from the litany form, as have to a lesser degree the *hoshaʿnot* of Kallir used in other rites. In Sepharad the whole structure became more complicated, owing to the fact that the festival acquired the character of the Day of Atonement, with penitential prayers attached to the *hoshaʿnot*. Despite early opposition, *hoshaʿnot* were composed also for the Sabbath, when the procession was not held. The content of the *hoshaʿnot* is above all petition for an abundant year, frequently with a petition for the messianic age attached. According to information in the *Halakhot gedolot*, *hoshaʿnot* were recited in Palestine (?) after the Afternoon Service as well. In the tenth and eleventh centuries processions apparently were customarily held in Jerusalem around the Mount of Olives, for which pilgrims came from far and wide.[35]

[The ancient anonymous *hoshaʿnot* that have reached us were certainly composed long before Kallir, who also tried his hand at this genre. According to Joseph Heinemann, these anonymous *hoshaʿnot* must be viewed as the vestiges of ancient poetic forms; see *Tarbiz* 7 (1960/1): 357–69 (also in Heinemann, *Prayer*, 88ff.)]

3. *Other Poems*

The piyyut also came into extensive use outside the *yoṣer* and the ʿAmida, especially in connection with the reading of the Torah. Special hymns, called שבחות, "Praises," were composed for the Torah, especially for the reading of particular passages such as the Ten Commandments or the Song of the Sea, as were Hebrew or Aramaic introductions to the reading or translation. Likewise, there were special blessings for the wedding feast, for circumcisions, and for similar occasions, when the people involved were present in the synagogue; there were also blessings for all those called to the Torah on festival days. On The Joy of the Torah, a large number of hymns were read at the conclusion of the reading. A special addition for this day is the story of the death of Moses (פטירת משה). The midrash of that name was embellished and rewritten in poetic form, and these poems were recited in the morning, or, in places where care was taken not to prolong the service unduly, before the Afternoon Service. "In general the piyyut came in time to entwine the whole of religious life and every spot in the liturgy; it did not merely remain in the synagogue, but entered the circle of the family, visiting at Sabbath meals, at the conclusion of the Sabbath, and at times of personal solemnities, such as mourning, births, and funerals."[36]

[The poems on the death of Moses have been the subject of a detailed study (reproduced in microfilm) by J.L. Weinberger, "The Death of Moses in the Synagogue Liturgy," Ph.D. dissertation (Brandeis University, April 1963).]

§ 33 *The* Seliḥa

[The *seliḥot* in the Ashkenazic rite were recently published in a revised edition by Daniel Goldschmidt (1965), appearing in two parallel versions, one according to the Lithuanian rite and the other according to the Polish rite. Goldschmidt has published several studies on the *seliḥot*, such as those of public fast days in the Roman rite, in *The Memorial Book for Shlomo S. Meir* (Milan, 1956), 77–89, and the rite of Cologne, in *Areshet* 1 (1958/9): 91–6).]

[166]

(1) We use the term *piyyut* for hymns of every type, but *seliḥa* is used for elegies, penitential prayers, confessions of sin, and lamentations, together with the petitions and expressions of hope attached to them. To put it in a general way, the *seliḥa* is a special prayer of fast days and days preparatory to the great fast of the Day of Atonement. The word *seliḥa* has its own history, which is also the history of the institution that it denotes. *Seliḥa* means forgiveness of sin; it is found in God, as it is said, "For Yours is forgiveness" (Ps. 130:4), and sought through His mercy (Dan. 9:9). God promised men forgiveness for their sins and showed them the way to find it. He taught them penitential prayer, which never returns unanswered; He answers the cry for help "whenever we call" (Ps. 20:10). The midrash calls such prayers for forgiveness "rites of forgiveness" (*Tana deve eliyahu ẓuta*, 42), whence the term *seliḥa* entered the realm of prayer.[1] In particular, the Thirteen Attributes revealed to Moses when he received the second set of tablets (Ex. 34:6–7) are called סדר סליחה, "rite of forgiveness"; they

belong to the ancient heritage and were very widespread, as shown by the frequency with which they are quoted in the Bible.[2] "God showed Moses the order of prayer. He said to him, 'Whenever Israel sins, let them perform this rite before Me and I shall forgive them' "; "There is a covenant that the Thirteen Attributes do not return unanswered" (B. *R.H.* 17b). This talmudic conception explains how the Thirteen Attributes became the nucleus of all prayers for atonement, so that they serve to this day as a refrain constantly repeated in all the *selihot*. And since the verse "The Lord, the Lord, merciful and compassionate God" could not be recited by itself, an introduction was provided for it explaining the talmudic thought behind the use of the Thirteen Attributes (אל הוריתנו, אל הורית לנו, "God, You instructed us").[3] At a later time, but still early enough (fifth or sixth century?) to be accepted into all rites, this introduction was expanded through the addition of the familiar אל מלך יושב, "God, the King Who sits."[4]

(2)   A prayer for forgiveness of sin has no point unless it is preceded by confession of these sins; the customary confession belonging to the liturgy of every fast day is accompanied, on the one hand, by a description of human sin and weakness, and on the other, of the holiness and graciousness of God. The fast-day liturgy provided the model. Prayers from the Bible containing confessions, especially those in Daniel and Ezra, were made the starting point; biblical verses were made into lectionaries, or penitential psalms were recited in order to plead for forgiveness.[5] All of this was called פסוקי ריצוי וסליחה,[6] which was soon shortened to *seliha*. In the *selihot* cited by Amram, especially in the manuscripts, as well as in those of Romaniot and Rome, the important role once filled by the biblical verses is still evident, as is the fact that originally it was the verses that bore the name *selihot*. The criteria according to which they are arranged are also discernible; thus, one group of verses contains the word אל, "Do not," while others have טוב, "Good," and yet others have הביטה, "Look," or other words; or the last word of one verse is the same as the first word of the second (for example, כי אתה שומע

[167]   תפילה \ שומע תפילה . . .). Zunz listed several dozens of such key words.[7] In brief, in this way the listener and the worshiper were provided with familiar points that enabled them to follow the precentor's prayer and respond to it. Where no appropriate verse was found with which to begin, simple introductory passages were compiled out of biblical phrases such as: כי על רחמיך הרבים, "For on Your great mercy," or לא בחסד ולא במעשים, "Not with kindness and not with deeds," or לך יי הצדקה, "Yours, O Lord, is righteousness," or מה נאמר לפניך, "What shall we say before You," and so on, which were then followed by biblical verses.[8]

(3)   The natural conclusion to the confession is the petition for help, for a change of the difficult present conditions. This petition was formulated in litanies of the simplest kind: אלהינו בשמים יהמו רחמיך עלינו, "Our God in heaven stir up Your mercy over us," and so forth; cries to God beginning אלהינו שבשמים, "Our God in heaven," אבינו מלכנו, "Our Father, our King," חטאנו לפניך, "We have sinned before You," רחם עלינו, "Have mercy on us," or עשה למען, "Act for the sake of . . . ," and so on.[9] The fast-day liturgy of the Mishnah already provides an example of such a litany, in which biblical personalities and the acts of salvation granted them are referred to with the formula: מי שענה הוא יענה . . . , "May He Who answered . . . answer you." Understandably, such litanies passed over to the *seliha* services; they begin with כענית, "As You answered," מי שענה,

"May He Who answered," or in Aramaic, רחמנא אדכר לן, "Merciful One, remember for us . . ." All the litanies were expanded in the course of time, and then were again shortened; the simplest means of expansion was the alphabetical acrostic (ענני אבינו, ענני בוראנו, ענני גואלנו, "Answer us, our Father . . . our Creator . . . our Redeemer"; עשה למען אמיתך, בריתך, גדלך, "Act for the sake of Your truth . . . Your covenant . . . Your greatness." To the ancient Hebrew litanies, Aramaic ones were also added: רחמנא חטאן, "Merciful One, we have sinned," and the like; fragments of these have been preserved in the *seliḥa* collections. Just as they themselves are called תחנות in the manuscripts, so we still see in the Supplications vestiges of the ancient *seliḥot*. Such were the simple elements of which ancient *seliḥot* were composed; the same *seliḥot* probably were used on all the fasts, and probably on no other occasion but fasts. In Ashkenaz we find *seliḥot* close to the ancient pattern on the fast of the eve of the New Moon, which was introduced only rather late.[10]

(4)   This ancient and simple material of the *seliḥa* prayers was not adequate for the needs and tastes of later generations. As piyyut came to enjoy growing favor and ever-wider dissemination, when all the prayers were being embellished with poems, the *seliḥot* could not remain unaffected. The poems first composed were simple and unadorned, but deeply felt; later came elaborate structures in which the artificiality of the form often suppressed the content. In external form, language, and style of expression, they are no different from the piyyutim. But they could not be as varied in their contents, for they were limited to the elegiac subjects appropriate for prayers for forgiveness: the description of sin, of the weakness of man and the transience of his life; lament over the vanished glories of the past, oppression and persecution; petition for forgiveness through God's mercy, for the downfall of the oppressor, for redemption, and for the fulfillment of messianic hopes. None of these subjects was peculiar to the *seliḥa*; they could be dealt with in piyyut. But while the piyyut was free to deal with all other religious subjects, the *seliḥa* was limited to these. The poetic *seliḥa* was simply a species of the piyyut.[11]

(5)   In order to make room for the insertion of the poetic works, the traditional stock of biblical verses and litanies was divided into groups, between which the poems were inserted. These were composed with a view toward the place at which they would be inserted, and were adapted by their contents or by their opening word to the groups of verses; thus in Romaniot we find poems for יודו ליי (Ps. 107:8) and ואני ברוב חסדך (Ps. 5:8), and so forth ("*seliḥot* ordered in accordance with a verse").[12] [168]

A famous example is the *seliḥa* of Solomon Ibn Gabirol, שופט כל הארץ, "Judge of the whole world," which is attached to verses containing the word שופט, "judge," the last of which is Gen. 18:25, that concludes "Will the Judge of the whole world not do justice?"[13]

["Judge of the whole world" is by a poet named Solomon, but it cannot be attributed to Ibn Gabirol.]

The inserted poetic compositions were originally called פזמון (*pizmon*); later they were all called *seliḥot*, and the name *pizmon* was reserved for those with a refrain. The other *seliḥot* were designated by special names derived from their location or contents, as listed below. The verses then were called, by distinction, פסוקים, "verses," or פסוקי

רחמים, "verses of mercy."[14] The material originally called *seliḥot*—that is, the verses and litanies—were the fixed, and the poetic *seliḥot*, the variable element. The adoption of the latter was not subject to any regulation, but the rule was, "*seliḥot* are recited in accordance with the need of the hour."[15] In Rome and Romaniot the poetic compositions remained apart from the ancient *seliḥot*. In Rome they were not even put into the prayer book, but were added at the discretion of the precentor ("and *seliḥot* are recited as the precentor wishes"), who probably had them in a special book.[16] In Romaniot, after the complete text of the ritual of atonement, there is a collection of poetic compositions from which each congregation selected whatever was customary there for inclusion in its service. The situation was similar in Spain, where the number of *seliḥot* inserted was not very great. But the situation was completely different in Germany and France. Here the poetic works prevailed, displacing the groups of verses, which were progressively abridged until most congregations paid no attention to them at all. In these countries the term *seliḥa* denotes only the poetic compositions, of which there were extensive compilations by the twelfth century.

(6)   Another change occurred in the *seliḥot* service. Originally it was intended only for fast days. These were of different types: commemorative days and occasional fasts. The latter were ordered for times of drought or other disaster, because every misfortune was understood as the consequence of sin, and atonement had to be made for the sin. The liturgy of these fast days, as we have it in outline in the Mishnah, survived long in the Orient,[17] though here and there enriched by poetic compositions. On the historical fasts, *qerovot* were in use in Palestine, and thus no need was felt for other poems within the *seliḥot*.[18] But in Babylonia, where *qerovot* were not in favor, the Mishnaic practice for drought-fasts of inserting *seliḥot* into Benediction 6 of the ʿAmida was followed. To the poetic insertions fell the task of describing the event on account of which the fast day had been proclaimed. This form of the fast-day ritual came to prevail.[19] The number of historical fasts increased greatly, as death dates of biblical personages and dates of other misfortunes of biblical and later times were established and made into fast days. To be sure, these days were not widely observed or long preserved, any more than were the fasts undertaken by individual ascetics and whole communities that followed their example. Alongside the biblical fasts (§21), fasts continued to be observed after Passover and Tabernacles, but were transferred to Monday and Thursday, when many already fasted. To these were added the great number of local memorial days, which multiplied as a consequence of the tragic course of Jewish history. Days of riot and expulsion were stamped on the memory of the communities as days of mourning, and the days of martyrdom were observed by later generations as fast days. Zunz was the first to compile a comprehensive list of such memorial days, which has been repeatedly supplemented with data from ancient and modern times. Wherever a fast was held, *seliḥot* were part of its liturgy; they were recited in accordance with the old custom, and the occasion for the fast provided the theme of the poetic additions. The *seliḥot* of those days have provided the source material for the history of the persecution of the Jews.

(7)   The Day of Atonement has a special position among the fast days because it is both fast and festival, and the poetic additions to the service give expression to

[169]

both aspects. According to Amram, on this day the precentor inserts into the ʿAmida a combination of *qerova* and *seliha*—that is, some poems for the first three benedictions of the ʿAmida which are optional, and the *selihot*, which are the obligatory duty of the day. Amram calls such compositions *maʿamad*, or more exactly מעמד שיש בו רצוי וסליחה, "A *maʿamad* of propitiation and forgiveness."[20] The Spanish poets used to compose such *maʿamadot* for the Day of Atonement containing both *qerova* and *seliha*, in which the *seliha* was organically integrated into the various sections of the *qerova*. Al-Ḥarizi names Joseph b. Avitur as the first of the Spanish poets to compose a *maʿamad* for the Day of Atonement.[21] The term was then transferred in Spain from this fast to the others; thus, Al-Ḥarizi calls Gabirol's compositions for fast days מעמד הצומות. To be sure, neither the name nor the organic connection between the poem and the poetic *seliha* spread to the other communities. But near the end of the ʿAmida, before אלהינו ואלהי אבותינו מחול לעוונותנו, "Our God and God of our fathers, forgive our sins," *selihot* were also introduced; at the same time, the confession was advanced to an earlier point (see above, pp. 125–126).

(8)   All the cases mentioned above refer to fast days, and on these the *selihot* always remained within their traditional framework, being recited during the course of the ʿAmida or immediately thereafter. But a new type of *seliha* emerged for the days preceding the Day of Atonement. At first these were for the Ten Days of Repentance, when many fasted. But because it was necessary to refrain from fasting on some of these days—that is, on the New Year and the Sabbath—the pious would make them up by beginning to fast four days in advance of the New Year. Over time, the number of days increased, so that some people fasted beginning on the New Moon of Elul, forty days before the Day of Atonement; this corresponds to the time that Moses spent on the mountain before receiving the second set of tablets and the revelation of the Thirteen Attributes (Deut. 10:10).[22] On all of these days fixed as fast days in any given locality, "*selihot* and supplications and petitions" were also recited; and since these days fell during a period specifically associated with the forgiveness of sin, they came to be called "The Days of *selihot*." Their number varies from country to country. To this day there are places where the recitation of *selihot* begins on the First of Elul, but in this country they begin on the Sunday before the New Year, a week earlier if the New Year falls on Monday or Tuesday. Since the Sabbaths do not count, there can be four to nine days of *selihot* before the New Year and six following it.

[For the various combinations of *selihot* for the nights of Elul in Sepharadic and Provence, see H. Schirmann, "Qoveṣ seliḥot minhag sefarad," *Areshet* 5 (1972).]

On the Days of *selihot* the services begin before dawn (משכימים לסליחות), and sometimes at midnight; hence, the services are called "vigils" (לילי אשמורות or אשמורות). Like the compositions for fast days they are also called *maʿamad*.[23] Fasting was not universally considered obligatory. On these days the *selihot* were independent of fasting, and could not be inserted into the ʿAmida, because the service was held at night, with no connection to the daily services.[24] Therefore the introduction to the *Selihot* service is different from that of other fast days; it does not begin with "Forgive us" but with Ps. 145—that is, "Happy"—followed by a longer verse-group, "Yours O Lord is the righteousness," only then coming to "God the patient." On the Days of *selihot* up to and including the Day of Atonement (in Amram there is a *selihot* service for the two

[170]

nights of the New Year, as well), the number of poetic *selihot* is very great, much greater than on other fast days.[25] All rites possess a great supply of poetic *selihot* for these days, enough that no *seliha* need be repeated. *The Rite of Tripoli* has *selihot* by a single poet, Isaac Ibn Ghiyath, for as many as twenty-three days in Elul. The first night and the eve of the New Year are particularly rich in poems, but on the eve of the Day of Atonement the number was reduced out of consideration for the extensive liturgy of the following day. The rites vary considerably in this matter from country to country and from community to community. The choice of poetic *selihot* was completely free and arbitrary, and was not bound even to the rules governing the order and the content of the poems, and therefore the variation between the rites is even greater for *selihot* collections than for piyyutim.

Like the piyyutim, the *selihot* also have groupings that derive their names from the poems' contents, external form, or position among the prayers:

a. **According to position:**

   i. פתיחה, "Opening," the poetic *seliha* that comes first; in Amram the introductory *seliha*, generally a short one, is called גמר, "End."

   ii. The final *selihot* are called מיושב in Amram, because they are connected to the Supplications, during which the precentor is seated; Rome uses the term תחינה מיושבת.[26]

b. **According to poetic form we distinguish:**

   i. פזמון, a *seliha* with a refrain, which may be either a whole strophe or a single line. In the *seliha* collections of Ashkenaz the *pizmon* is usually the last *seliha* among the poetic ones, or at least the last before the second recitation of ויאמר ה' סלחתי כדברך, "And God said, I have forgiven, according to your word." In Oriental countries, the refrain as such is called *pizmon*, in Amram generally abbreviated to פז.[27]

   ii. מסתאג׳יב. This term, which comes from Arabic, designates something that recurs—that is, the rhyme word. The poem is prefaced by a biblical quotation, either a verse or part of one (as a rule a verse from the following group), the last word of which either occurs at the ends of the strophes or is rhymed with them. This pattern is found only among the Spanish poets.[28]

   iii. שניה, and iv. שלישיה, poetic *selihot* with units of two or three lines.[29]

   v. שלמונית, "complete," a *seliha* with four-line units. Most of the *selihot* with this name are by Solomon the Babylonian of Rome, hence the attempts to derive the term from his name, Solomon; but more than a few *selihot* of this type were composed by authors who bore other names.[30]

   vi. חטאנו, a *seliha* with the recurring phrase, חטאנו צורנו, "We have sinned, our Rock"; for the most part it deals with the sufferings of the Jewish people or with particular martyrs, especially the "Ten Martyrs."[31]

c. **Based on content are the following terms:**

   i. תוכחה, a self-rebuke; in Amram's collection it is generally the first *seliha* after the introduction. Like the מסתאג׳יב, its poetic pattern is that it begins with a single verse as a kind of leitmotif, with the difference that this is not repeated. The Spanish poets inserted the *tokheha* into each *ma'amad*.[32]

ii. בקשה, "petition"; not always poetic, often a lengthy prose prayer beginning ארני, "O Lord," or אנא, "O." It belongs to the *ma'amad* more than to the *seliha*.[33]

iii. גזרות, a description of the bloody persecutions and devotion unto death of the Jewish communities. Found nearly exclusively in France and Germany.

[For various editions of the Ashkenazic *gezerot*, see in the supplementary material, §41(10). For poems on the binding of Isaac, see the study of Shalom Spiegel mentioned below, §41(11). For the confession, see G. Ohrmann, *Das Sündenbekenntniss des Versöhnungstages* (1934).]

iv. עקידה, commemoration of the binding of Isaac. The early fast-day litanies already referred to Abraham and how God heard his prayer on Mount Moriah. The composers of the *selihot* never tired of the theme of the readiness of both father and son for the sacrifice. The poems' elegiac conclusion refers to the readiness of fathers and mothers in every age to sacrifice themselves together with their children for their faith in God. The Sepharadim frequently combined the *'aqeda* with the *qerova*, usually with the *mehaye*, where it was customary to refer to the patriarch Isaac.

v. תחנה, a prayer about the relations between God and the Jewish people. The choice of name reflects the location of the *seliha*, which is always connected with Supplications, the conclusion of the fast-day liturgy. In the collection of Amram it includes Ex. 32:12, familiar from the Supplications of Monday and Thursday.

vi. מְקַדְּמָה is the name of several *selihot* for the New Year in Amram; they are opening poems distinguished by the addition לזכרונות, למלכויות, למשפטיות, and ולשופרות because each of the strophes rhymes with the word שופר, מלכות, משפט, זכרון.[34]

vii. וידוי is the name for confessions for sins, written in continuous prose; they usually begin רבונו של עולם, "Lord of the world."

(9) A special genre of elegiac poems with descriptions of persecutions and martyrdom as their content are the קינות (*qinot*) for the Ninth of Av. The name *qina* is biblical, denoting the lament for the dead. The Talmud uses the word *qinot* to refer to the Scroll of Lamentations, but later it was used for the poetic elegies recited after the reading of this scroll on the day of mourning for the destruction of Jerusalem. Among Arabic-speaking Jews, the name אלמרתיה or מרתיה was used, which was then back-translated into Hebrew as תמרור.[35] The most ancient additions to the Ninth of Av service were, as on all other fast days, *selihot*, as we are told by Amram[36] and Saadia. But even before their time, another type of elegy became current, *qerovot* with extensive expansions of Benediction 14 of the *'Amida*, the benediction with the eulogy "Builder of Jerusalem." Kallir was the first to develop this poetic form.[37] Two *qerovot* for the Ninth of Av by him are extant, one of which is in use in Rome and Romaniot, and the other in western Germany. In these a great number of *qinot* were inserted: twenty in Ashkenaz, and many more in Rome and Romaniot. But only in Rome and Romaniot have the *qinot* kept their original place within the *qerova*; in all the other rites they were separated from the *'Amida*. In Ashkenaz they are recited only after the Torah reading, and in Sepharad, immediately after the *'Amida*. Thus, in Sepharad the *qinot* occupy the same place as the *selihot*, and in fact their beginning is in every way identical to that of the *selihot*, apparently a vestige of ancient times. The separation of the *qinot* from the *'Amida* led to the introduction of some *qinot* also on the night of the Ninth of Av.

[172]

One of the causes for separating the *qinot* from the *qerova* was probably their increasing length and expanding content. The themes appropriate for the *qinot* are mourning for the destruction of the Temple, the priests, and the cult; the desecration of the sanctuary by the enemy; the destruction of the two kingdoms of Judea and Israel; and the contrast between oppression in exile and the happiness of the people in its land. But like the *seliḥa*, the *qina* reflects also on the cause of the suffering and the sins of the fathers, their disobedience to the prophets' rebukes, the mercies of God throughout the course of history, and Israel's ingratitude. These subjects are reworked in many and varied ways; and the poems turn into a crushing indictment of the people's sin and a complete justification of God's decree. Despite all the suffering, there is no doubt about God's righteousness and love. Thus, the *qinot*, like the prophetic rebukes, conclude with a call for repentance, promises of consolation, and descriptions of the future salvation. The poets of Spain, Provence and Africa almost always depict the suffering in general terms without going into detail, whereas the poems of Kallir go into great detail on all the subjects, especially the present oppression. From this, the later poets derived for themselves the freedom to immortalize in their *qinot* the sufferings that they had experienced, which they or the affected communities designated for the Ninth of Av. From the first crusade in 1096 to the time of the Black Death (1348–49), general and local pogroms directed against the Jews and catastrophes like the burning of the Talmud in Paris served the poets in Germany and France as material for *qinot* that sooner or later became part of the stock of the *qina* collections. In Spain persecutions were not as frequent, but there too the severe persecutions of 1391 were immortalized in *qinot*. Among the later *qinot*, Judah Halevi's ציון הלא תשאלי, "Zion, will you not greet," won particular favor; in it, longing for the holy sites and love for the ruined ancestral homeland found tender and deeply felt expression. It was followed by a great number of imitations addressing Zion directly and beginning with the word ציון; they were therefore called ציוני or ציון (*Zionide*), and were considered a valuable and indispensable component of the collections of all rites. The number of *qinot* became quite considerable over time; the communities often occupied the entire morning with their recitation, and only in recent times have they been reduced, with Reform communities having only one or two.

[The *qinot* for the Ninth of Av have also been published in a revised edition by D. Goldschmidt (Jerusalem: Rav Kook, 1957/8). A special collection of *qinot* according to Sepharad was published by S. Bernstein under the title *ʿAl naharot sefarad* (Tel Aviv, 1955/6). More than thirty *qinot* beginning with the word ציון are listed in Davidson, *Oṣar*, 3:321–23.]

PART TWO

The History of Jewish Liturgy

The Period of the Statutory Prayers

§ 34   The First Signs of Regular Public Worship

(1)   The history of liturgy is the product of the history of religious thought; whatever is in the foreground of religious thought aspires to make its mark on worship as well. But this aspiration was not completely realized. In religion, as in other areas, development is by steps, never by skips. Ancient institutions and prayers sanctified by tradition cannot be completely displaced. Usually the outcome of the struggle is a blend of old and new. As far as we can view the development, it was such that the original nucleus of the liturgy has always been retained, the most ancient elements being found in it today as at the beginning. But the manner in which the liturgy is performed, the influences that sought to gain control over it, the husks that came to envelop the nucleus—none of these stood still through the course of time, but varied with the environment. The three periods into which we have divided the history of the liturgy (§5) did not all take the same position with regard to changes in the prayers. The first and the third periods display greater freedom than the second. This does not mean that the second period lacked independence of judgment and will toward the traditional liturgy. Critical judgment was applied to the poetry, to the new additions to the service that were recognized as such and could therefore be easily changed or removed, but no doubt was permitted to touch the statutory prayers, which were left in their original form except for insignificant changes that were simply caused by time. By contrast, during the two other periods there was no hesitation about attacking even the statutory prayers. In the period when they were created, it was considered justifiable to treat them freely; the only reservation was that traditions that even then were considered to be of hoary antiquity were treated with extreme respect. This has not been so in the modern period, whose hallmark is criticism. Our age arrogates to itself the same unrestricted freedom with regard to the liturgy as it does in every area of human activity and thought; it is not deterred by either the significance of inherited ideas or their antiquity from applying to them its own critical powers.

[178]

(2)   It is not easy to follow the development of the liturgy in detail, for frequently the changes had occurred long before they are mentioned in the sources. Usually, the authors of the literature think to mention these changes only long after they have already come into effect. As for the most ancient period, there is an additional difficulty that we do not have direct contemporary sources. By the time we find literary sources about the liturgy, it is already a finished product, with no witness to the centuries of its emergence and the first steps of its development. The tradition is handed down from a later point of view, often describing institutions of early periods as they were then familiar, without thought to the contrast with their original form or to the intermediate stages.

Our study has to begin with the question of how the synagogue came into being, and to examine its origins. It is well established that this institution was previously unknown anywhere, and that it introduced a new manner of worship;[1] but as to the time and the circumstances that called it into being, we have no historically reliable data. Its founding marks one of the most important steps forward in the development of religion; it was the first time in human history that regular assemblies for worship were held at sites that had no other sanctity than what was bestowed upon them by the community of the faithful. It was a liturgy that freed itself from the practices theretofore customary among all peoples, relinquishing all such accessories as sacrifices and other offerings and intermediation by priests, and placing man and his spiritual life at the center of the liturgy. It is the same kind of liturgy as came to prevail in the European religions, and thus became familiar to all of civilized humanity.

As with all the peoples of antiquity the Jewish cult began with sacrificial worship, the only form of worship to which real significance was attached. Doubtless, prayers were recited already in the period of the First Temple, but we hear nothing about how they were performed, nor do we have evidence that they were held regularly every day or on particular days. How did one arrive at the communal worship and the regular religious assemblies of later times? How did it happen that the one central sanctuary [that is, the Temple—*Engl. trans.*] was replaced by the innumerable places of worship, the so-called little sanctuaries [that is, synagogues—*Engl. trans.*]?[2] This change did not occur suddenly or at once; rather, for centuries, the two institutions, Temple and Synagogue, existed side by side. But the synagogues continually spread, growing continually in power and importance to religious life. They made the Temple dispensable,[3] with the effect that its fall did not create a vacuum in religious life. We know the consequences of this movement, but not the motivating forces that were operating at its beginning. In attempting to account for the rise of the synagogue we confront insurmountable obstacles. Without direct information we cannot find a definite answer; we can only resort to conjectures, deduced from such facts of the Temple ritual and the evolution of Jewish religious history as might have been able to affect the development and early shaping of the liturgy.

[179]

(3)   Among the oldest examples of a service in which not sacrifice but prayer was in the foreground were the fast-day assemblies.[4] These were held even before the Babylonian exile, and even that early, not always at the site of the altar. They were always accompanied by prayers; sometimes no sacrifice was offered at all, the whole ceremony consisting of nothing but prayers. Fast-day assemblies with their petitionary prayers had

a great influence on the later formation of the synagogue service, but a description of their customary ceremonies has come to us only from a late period. Though the Mishnah describes them as they were in tannaitic times, most of the elements in their description, in fact the most important of them, so match the narratives in the Bible and the depictions of fasts in the Apocrypha that there can be no doubt of their antiquity.

(4)　But the fast-day liturgical assemblies were only rare and occasional phenomena, and we are seeking models for daily prayer. Scholars are unanimous that the origins of such religious assemblies are to be sought in the Babylonian exile. In Babylonia the Jews were lacking a common center. If they intended to maintain their link with the past, to preserve their national and religious identity, to revive and strengthen the consciousness of their unity, the only thing for them to do was to unite and to give expression to the ideas and feelings that throbbed in all of them. The prophets within the exile community strengthened the people's religious consciousness through scriptural readings and the instruction connected with it, consisting of a combination of rebuke and consolation, thus preparing the ground for the national rebirth. Especially on Sabbaths and national memorial days, the people would assemble to hear the words of their teachers. Here lie the roots of the regular assemblies for divine worship, the main content of which we must see in the readings and teachings from the sacred Scriptures, and the common confession of faith. Teaching and the confession of faith, the liturgy's oldest components, gave it its particular character. It must be assumed that after the return to Zion the assemblies imported from the Diaspora were continued in Palestine, and that they went on even after the Temple was rebuilt and the sacrifices restored.[5]

(5)　The new type of worship made its mark even within the walls of the Temple of Jerusalem. The first definitely attested example of daily public worship comes from the Temple itself. The priests on duty, "men of the watch," interrupted the offering of sacrifices every morning in order to go the Chamber of Hewn Stone, there to devote a short while to prayer (M. *Tam.* 5:1).[6] This ceremony was quite remote from having any priestly cultic character. In the Temple itself, with its prescribed sacrificial rites and Levitical songs, no provision was made for public prayer, and even when such was introduced it remained only loosely connected with the cult. The priests were assigned no function in this service; nor did it take their status into consideration. Nor did the language of the prayers match that of the cult, for the priests spoke Aramaic during the service,[7] while Hebrew prevailed as the language of prayer. The contents of that daily liturgy of the priests recalls the Diaspora assemblies for the profession of the faith. Biblical passages predominated: A few passages from the Torah giving expression to the central elements of the faith were recited, like the Ten Commandments, the *Shemaʿ*, and perhaps also a few core passages of national character, like the speeches of Balaam. The biblical components were framed by an introduction and a conclusion. The introduction gave thanks for the revelation, and in the conclusion the community affirmed that the revelation granted their ancestors was still the contents of their faith ("Benediction of the Torah," "True and certain"; see above, §7[7]). If a further prayer was added for the gracious acceptance of the sacrifice (עבודה, now Benediction 17) and a kind of priestly blessing ("Benediction of the Priests"), this shows a certain attention

[180]

to the status of the priests and the site of the service but does not affect our judgment as to the origin of this institution itself.

(6) The post-exilic period brought about a closer relationship between the people and the cult. The position of people and Temple had undergone a fundamental change during the exile. The old view of the value of the sacrifices per se no longer suited the new spirit, which demanded personal piety and the participation of every individual in religious life, "the service of the heart." Had this manner of thinking been pursued consistently it would have led to the elimination of the sacrifices. Though this conclusion was not reached immediately, institutions were created permitting the people a more active participation in the cult.[8] Individual pietists, whether they lived permanently in Jerusalem, or whether they only visited it, were in attendance at the Temple during the daily sacrifice and personally received the blessing that the priests, standing on the steps of the court, would bestow upon the people, prostrating themselves in prayer and sending their petitions to heaven. They listened to the songs of the Levites, which achieved considerable renown during the period of the Second Temple, as attested by Chronicles.[9] The Psalms, the hymnal of that age, were sung by the Temple singers, but the congregation participated in the song by responding with "Amen," "Hallelujah," or with longer responses ("Give thanks to the Lord, for He is good, for His mercy is everlasting": I Chron. 16:41; similar significance is attached to the doxologies concluding each of the books of Psalms).[10] Thus, the Psalms became communal songs dearly beloved by the people, and widespread among them. This explains their tremendous influence on the liturgy and on religious life in all ages.

In order to guarantee the people's participation in the sacrifices, the institution of *ma'amadot* was established—that is, representation from the rank and file of the people.[11] In order to mark the sacrifice as a communal undertaking, it had to be offered in the presence and with the participation of the community. And since it was impossible for the entire people to be in attendance in Jerusalem for the sacrifices, the "prophets in Jerusalem" divided them, as the priests and Levites were already divided, into twenty-four "courses" (משמרות). One week every half year each of these in rotation would send a mission to Jerusalem that would "stand over" (עמדה על גביו) the sacrifice, and which thus was called מעמד or עמוד. During this week of service the representatives of the people would hold four services each day (Morning, Additional, Afternoon, and Closing of the Gates), consisting of prayer and the reading of the Torah; likewise those who remained at home held daily assemblies for the same purpose (M. *Ta.* 4). The establishment of the *ma'amadot* created for the first time prayer services that were held regularly throughout the land, even on weekdays, though at widely separated times.

How did the four different services come about?[12] Of the two daily sacrifices, one was offered in the morning. In the ancient period, the other was offered just before nightfall; later it was moved to the early afternoon (two and a half hours after midday; M. *Pes.* 5:1). From observation of the sun's rising, setting, and zenith, three times of prayer were established, evening, morning, and noon, as Scripture says in Ps. 55:18. These times are mentioned as the regular practice of a pious man like Daniel (6:11). The famous aggadist, R. Samuel b. Nahmani, at the end of the third century, still saw this as the reason for the establishment of the three prayers customary in his time (Y. *Ber.* 4:1, 7a). The four hours of prayer of the *ma'amadot* are thus the product of combining these two orders. In the morning the sacrifice and the service occurred together; out of the midday service the Additional Service was created; in the afternoon the second daily sacrifice, that of late afternoon (בין הערבים), originally corresponded to the Evening Service, but after the time of the sacrifice was changed, there arose out of it two prayers, one before the sacrifice at the ninth hour (Acts 3:1), known as מנחה, and the second at evening when the Temple gates were closed, known as נעילת שערים or, for short, נעילה.

We have no information about the form of the *maʿamad* liturgy. All that we are told is that both in the morning and at the Additional Service two passages from the story of creation were read, and that in the afternoon the same passages were repeated from memory (M. *Ta.* 4). From the variation in the procedure we can deduce that the regulations do not all come from the same period, but that changes have occurred in them. At each of these services the Blessing of the Priests was also said, but this was not always possible outside the Temple because priests were not always present. We do not know for certain whether psalms were also incorporated into the liturgy of the *maʿamadot*, but since these assemblies were attached directly to the Song of the Levites, it may be assumed that originally a few psalms were included in them. In the morning, passages dealing with the confession of faith, such as the decalogue, were recited.[13] Finally, it seems probable that each service had room also for petitions. We know that in times of trouble, villagers would look to their representatives in Jerusalem to pray on their behalf (B. *Ta.* 22b). Whatever the entire community sought to achieve in times of danger through their prayers and fasts, the *maʿamad* representation was expected to seek through their prayers. The people may even have seen those men of piety and good deeds chosen to observe the sacrifice as designated representatives of the community, as intercessors, and this may have led to the introduction of petitions into the prayers of the *maʿamadot*. At first these petitions may have been the contents of the Additional Service, a service parallel to the liturgy of fasts and modeled after it, but eventually they were transferred to the other services as well. The form of these petitions may be inferred from the prayers in Ezra and Daniel, whose forms are strikingly similar to each other;[14] by analogy we may assume that these petitions began with hymns, and that the statement of the petitions was preceded by acknowledgment of sin.

(7)   All the above-mentioned institutions contributed to the material of the synagogue service: From the assemblies in the time of the Babylonian exile it drew the reading and explication of Scripture; from the liturgy of the priests it drew the confession of faith and the Priestly Blessing; from the Song of the Levites it drew the psalms; and from the *maʿamad* services, the petitions. The most important contribution was made by the *maʿamadot*, for through them prayer was first transferred to any location and was held regularly every weekday.

But a rather long time passed before this new creation was able to spread and become generally accepted. The difficulties encountered by the community in the first decades of the Second Temple, the internal strife and the external disruptions, were not favorable to the new measures. We are probably right to assume that at first they had little force and stability. This they would have achieved only when Ezra and Nehemiah brought security to civil life, and order to religious institutions. In Babylonia, the

[182]

assemblies that had begun in exilic times were continued. There is no doubt that Ezra, who made knowledge of the sacred scriptures and the observance of its laws into the cornerstone of religious life, revived the assemblies in Palestine as well and elevated them to regularly held events. Only as a consequence of his and Nehemiah's intervention can we assume that the *ma'amadot* were punctiliously held; only later was a daily service with fixed forms eventually established. The Jewish tradition derives the basic forms of prayer from the men of the Great Assembly who "established for Israel benedictions and prayers, Kiddush and Havdala" (B. *Ber.* 33a).[15] This tradition rests on a firm foundation; public worship was created and became widespread in the centuries between Ezra and the Syrian persecution, not all at once but in stages, through the development and expansion of existing institutions.

(8)   Assemblies on Sabbaths and festivals had long been customary. On weekdays they were held at first only twice a year, during the week of the *ma'amad*, but from this it was an easy transition to the regular holding of services even when it was not the turn of the particular district to serve. Independent of the times of community worship, the domestic observances held by many pious individuals morning and evening continued in place.[16] With the deepening of Jewish piety, the need for public worship increased. Not only the distance from the sites of the cult, but above all the longing for an experience of devotion and for edification called the daily synagogue service into life. In the Temple in Jerusalem, where the *ma'amad* assembled regularly, a service was held every day without exception. But outside the Temple as well, the habit established by the *ma'amad* week and the custom of home prayers led gradually to the holding of services every day without distinction. It was not possible to hold such an extensive service as was held at the *ma'amad* without crippling people's ability to earn their livelihood. Accordingly the services peculiar to the Temple—that is, the Additional and Closing services, were eliminated, and public services were held only in the morning and in the evening, before and after working hours. Besides this the ancient nighttime prayer was preserved as a domestic service, until it became a third daily service under the name ערבית, "Evening Service." The Additional Service was held only on special days, on Sabbaths, holidays, and other semi-festivals when an additional sacrifice was required.[17] The Closing Service was held only on public fast days, and later only on the Day of Atonement. The contents of the synagogue service also had to undergo changes; thus, for the sake of brevity the Torah reading was eliminated from the daily service and reserved for special days only. On weekdays the Torah reading was prescribed only for market days because on those days the villagers would come to the towns. At home they had no communal worship, and on festivals they were not able to come to the city; nevertheless, they were not excluded from the beneficial influence of the Torah reading.[18]

Once public worship became a fixed institution, the formation of a fixed liturgy of prayers was inevitable. It is hard to imagine that an individual would pray every single day without repeating himself, and without his prayer eventually acquiring a fixed pattern; but it would be impossible for a community to assemble for prayer at regular intervals without fixed patterns emerging and recurring regularly. If we bear in mind that the liturgy had to serve all the congregations in Palestine, as well as an extensive Diaspora community that was growing from year to year, only uniformity of the liturgical ceremonies could guarantee religious unity. For this purpose it was essential to create fixed patterns.[19]

(9)   As to how exactly this happened, and at whose instance, the tradition is silent. It embraces, as noted, all the authorities to whom the first formation of the synagogue service is due under the rubric "the men of the Great Assembly." It was they who added prayer, in the narrow sense of the word, to the instruction and the confession of faith, they who established the familiar forms of prayers of praise and petition. The stylization of the basic patterns of all prayers, the benediction, goes back to them. The direct address to God in the form "Blessed are You, Lord," which is not yet found even in the latest biblical books (except for two verses, Ps. 119:12 and I Chron. 29:10), is a clear expression of strongly marked religious individualism that these authorities turned into the basic foundation of all the prayers. Hymn and panegyric became and remained the form in which the congregation held dialogue with its God; even where it lays its petitions before Him, it concludes with words of blessing. The first fixed liturgy also belongs to that period.[20] It is composed of two parts: confession of faith, and prayer. The communal confession of faith was present already in the first liturgical assemblies, and took the form of the reading of certain biblical passages. That all come from the Torah shows that they were combined at a time when no other part of Scripture had yet acquired canonical status. Not all these biblical passages have been retained in the liturgy. The Ten Commandments, for example, were removed in the early days of Christianity for polemical reasons (B. *Ber* 12a; Y. *Ber.* 1:3, 3c), but that they too were originally included in the daily service is proved by the liturgy of the priests mentioned above (subsection 5), by the addition found in the Septuagint before Deut. 6:4, and by the Nash Papyrus discovered ten years ago [first published in 1903— *Hebrew trans.*]. On the other hand, not all three Torah passages contained in the Recitation of the *Shema‛* today were found in it in its original form; at least the third passage was incorporated only at a somewhat later stage. The pieces bearing on confession of faith were framed by hymnic prayers—that is, benedictions—just as described in the priestly liturgy, which itself stood under the influence of the Great Assembly. To these several communal petitions (תפלות) were added; these were a later part of the liturgy, and were always seen as such, for the *Shema‛* is considered a biblical commandment, but the *‛Amida* is not. The assemblies for the profession of faith did not yet know of petitions; there, the common service was followed by silent prayer unregulated as to form or content. This was left entirely to the desires and mood of the worshipers; it was a private devotion within the public service, in which everyone could recite his personal desires. The ancient sources call this individual prayer *Words*, but later it received the designation, derived from a biblical expression, *Supplications*. Among the public services we first find petitions in the fast-day prayers. From these they entered the *ma‛amadot*, and thence, under the name "Prayer," they entered the daily public prayers (as the *‛Amida*). The structure of the *‛Amida*—hymnic introduction, petitions, and thanksgiving—clearly goes back to biblical models, and therefore cannot have originated very long after the biblical period. The contents of the petitions were originally very general. Like the petitions in the late biblical books, they seem to have taken as a starting point the sinfulness of man; and the material things for which worshipers prayed were only such as were indispensable to everyone, and therefore equally dear

[184]

to the hearts of all members of the community. To these belonged also several wishes of the community as a whole, such as the petition for Jerusalem and the Temple, and, rather early, as we learn from the Apocrypha, for the uniting of all of Israel's scattered people. Late biblical and apocryphal prayers explain the practice of introducing the prayers by referring to the covenant between God and the ancestors. This testifies to a firm and self-assured faith in the continuing protection and favor of God, a faith that the later generations did not always share. The confession of sin also flows from a perfectly sound consciousness, and is free of the masochistic self-reproaches of the period before the destruction of the state. Further, every service had to be accompanied by the Blessing of the Priests. That this could not always be performed has already been mentioned, and it was rather early eliminated from the Afternoon Service (B. *Ta.* 26b).

The ordinances of the men of the Great Assembly had to do only with the order of the prayers and their content, but not with their texts. The text was not established and prescribed, but was left to the inspiration of the moment. To be sure, it was inevitable that in the course of time certain formulas were created for particular items (מטבע של ברכה, טופס ברכות); in Daniel one can already discern the influence of the liturgy on the formulation of religious ideas. The prayers of the ancient period were short, simple in style, and clear in diction. A primal energy of faith and feeling provided the worshiper with the ability to say much in few words, for the vocabulary seemed to flow of its own from the familiar phrases of Scripture.

The prayers were so simple, and their ideas so generally applicable, that they could be used for every day of the year without distinction. It can hardly be assumed that special formulas existed for the Sabbath and festivals; the nucleus of the service—the profession of faith with its surrounding benedictions, and the opening and concluding benedictions of the 'Amida—is identical for all days of the year to this day. The distinctiveness of the Sabbath and festival prayers lay in the reading of the Torah and its exposition, which occupied most of the time of the service. The Sabbath was also greeted when it entered and departed by the domestic observances of religious fraternities;[21] the formulas used for these purposes (Kiddush and Havdala) are also [according to tradition] the work of the men of the Great Assembly. On festivals such solemnities were not customary, but instead the pilgrimage was held; and on the Day of Atonement one would contemplate the service of the high priest.[22]

(10)   We are not told how long it took for regular public worship to become universal. It is noteworthy that the complaints in the books of Maccabees about the prohibition of religious activities and ceremonies include no reference to the prohibition of public worship. Nevertheless, a number of verses in these books allude to that fact that it was already being held in the widest circles. If it had been introduced later, our sources certainly would not have neglected a fuller discussion of the innovation. In the later quarrels of the parties, we never hear of any dispute about public worship as such or about the details of its execution. Likewise, Ben Sira and Daniel definitely contain indications presupposing the existence of organized worship. We have certain information from the Diaspora. Agatharchides of Cnidos, writing around the middle of the second century B.C.E., speaks of the public worship of the Jews, and mentions that the Jews linger in their synagogues the entire Sabbath day until a late evening hour.[23] This shows how lengthy was the explication of the Torah in those days.

[185]

(11)   The Hasmonean rebellion must have been an important turning point in the development of the synagogue worship. Prayer was already so naturalized that it had become something upon which one could reflect. It was a powerful factor in the life of the people; all the thoughts and feelings fermenting among them sought expression in it. The notion of redemption became the focus of religious imagination, and longing for freedom not only from oppression and misfortune in this world, but also for messianic salvation, became an important impulse to religious development. The exodus from Egypt was the event that people of this period brought to mind gladly and often, and the redemption from slavery in Egypt became the symbol of redemption in general; its commemoration became an important component of daily prayer. Petitions for the coming of the messianic age entered the ʿAmida, and religious life became filled with the national spirit.[24]

[Recently, various scholars have attempted to follow the stages in the development of the statutory prayers in antiquity; compare, among others, Allon, *Talmudic Age*, 1:261ff.; *idem, Meḥqarim*, 1:280, 284ff.; Baer, *Yisraʾel*, 30ff.; Liebermann, *Tosefta*, 1:53ff.; S. Talmon, "Maḥzor haberakhot shel kat midbar yehuda," *Tarbiz* 29 (1959/60): 1ff.; Heinemann, *Prayer*, 29ff., 52ff., 78ff., 138ff.; M. Lieber, "Structure and History of the Tefilla," *JQR* 40 (1949–50): 331ff.; E.J. Bickerman, "The Civic Prayer of Jerusalem," *Harvard Theological Review* 55 (1962): 163ff.]

§ 35 *Prayer in the Tannaitic Period: Before the Destruction of the Temple*

(1)   Before the tannaitic period we have no really solid ground on which to stand; only with the Mishnah do we first encounter coherent reports as to the form and content of the liturgy. Here, however, we face the difficulty that the Mishnah in its present form was completed only around 200 C.E., and that the many anonymous statements it contains cannot always be dated with exactitude.[1] Yet, often a parallel source informs us of the names of the sages who took part in establishing a particular institution, permitting us to determine when it came into existence or to fix a time by which we can be certain that it was already in existence.[2] For the history of the liturgy, the Mishnah must be seen as a late source, for even its most ancient parts show a fairly advanced stage of development, when the basic patterns and structure of public prayer were already complete, and their shape essentially the same as they are today. Yet a long and not always peaceful development must have preceded any such fixing of the institutions. At the beginning of the Common Era the service of the synagogue and its main prayers were a matter for scholastic discussion.[3] They had already lost their free and artless character, and their forms had become so entrenched that they had acquired a rote character. Their correctness of wording and usage, the possibility and permissibility of deviating from them, are all studied by theologians and examined with a casuistic eye. The prayers are known to everyone, and the synagogue service is so widespread that it is considered an ancient Mosaic institution. So it is seen by Philo[4] and Josephus,[5] and by the talmudic sages.[6] No one raises any doubts as to its legitimacy or obligatory

[186]

nature, and in this all the sects concur, whatever their other disagreements.[7] Wherever Jews live, regular public worship is held.

(2)   Originally, probably only the congregation had a fixed order and time for prayers. The individual worshiped whenever his feelings motivated him to do so, and said whatever he was inspired by his piety to say. At public services he listened silently, participating only through the responses and the silent prayer at the end, when, though surrounded by the congregation, he was again alone with himself. Now, however, the situation was different; it is testimony to how widespread and recognized communal prayer had become that, now, prayer was no longer seen as communal worship alone; the individual, too, saw himself as obligated to recite the very same prayers. The liturgy became common property; every individual Jew knew it and repeated it daily. The liturgy conquered the entire people and dominated all of life. Not only was the synagogue visited at the times of prayer, but artisans and laborers would interrupt their work to pray (M. *Ber.* 2:4);[8] people prayed while walking on the road; and some liked to stand at a street corner or in a lane and pray in public (Matthew 6:5).[9] This is not the place to describe the immeasurable value of daily devotions, of hallowing a period of time every day in order to forge a bond between the mundane and the divine, of elevating the workday to a festival, of cultivating religion and deepening one's piety.[10] Two thousand years of Jewish, Christian, and Islamic religious life are faithful witnesses.

We are no longer able to uncover the factors that brought about this development, one of the most important in the history of religions. Certainly it reflects the influence of individual pietists, distinguished masters of prayers, such as Ḥoni the Circle-Maker[11] and R. Ḥanina b. Dosa;[12] but we must not overlook the fact that the entire movement of pharisaic pietism had as its goal the spiritualizing of religious forms and the cultivation of personal religiosity. There were many circles and groups of God-fearing people (חסידים הראשונים or ותיקין), who are said to have made a principle of beginning their prayers early, praying with deep devotion, and abandoning thoughts of this world. Today we can no longer say whether they emerged from the sect of the Essenes, nor can we identify this sect's contribution to the formation of the synagogue service.[13] It does not seem especially likely that the exponents of extreme asceticism inspired imitation.

[187]

(3)   As a result of its dissemination, synagogue worship took on a different character, and instruction was displaced as its main purpose by prayer and reverence. The profession of faith, the *Shemaʿ*, was recited as before, but the original significance of these scriptural readings was progressively lost, and they were given a scholastic interpretation,[14] according to which the commandment of twice-daily prayer and the memorial commandments of phylacteries, fringes, and mezuza were derived from them. All of these commandments became equally rooted among the people, and they were often misused by people of the sort whose attention was naturally drawn to externals (Matthew 23:5); but more often they were a spur to spiritual uplifting. Thus the weekday prayers are already distinguished from those of Sabbaths and festivals, and the sages worked on clarifying and introducing further casuistic distinctions. Tractates *Berakhot*, *Rosh Hashana*, *Taʿanit*, and *Megila* give us a picture of how far individual prayers and liturgical institutions had already taken on a particular character,[15] to what extent they

had become widespread, and how they were debated in the academies. No ancient source provides a detailed and exhaustive description of the liturgy, but they presuppose that it is generally familiar and accessible to all.[16]

(4)   Let us survey the liturgy insofar as it can be educed from the Mishnah.[17] It consists of two parts: the Torah reading and prayer. The prayer itself has two main parts: the recitation of the *Shema*[18] and the *Amida*. The *Shema* is recited in the morning and the evening, and the *Amida* is said in the morning and afternoon. The *Shema* consists of the three passages from the Torah, though the third was omitted at night.[19] In the Morning Service it was prefaced by two passages of prayer and followed by one ("In the morning he recites two benedictions before it and one after it") and "In the evening, two before it and two after it."[20] Of the two benedictions preceding the *Shema*, one deals with the morning or the evening, and the other expresses gratitude for the revelation; of the benedictions after the *Shema*, the first confirms the profession of faith, and attaches it to an expression of gratitude for the redemption from Egypt. But the second benediction, which is peculiar to the evening ("Make us lie down"), serves as a replacement for the *Amida*, which is not recited, and contains the petition for God's protection at night. The text of the two passages common to both the Morning Service and the Evening Service need not originally have been different in the two services; to this day the great similarity between them permits the conclusion that they were originally identical. It is even possible that the opening "Creator of light" was used both morning and evening, for it speaks about both the creation of light and the creation of darkness together. Just as the profession of faith is identical every day of the year, so this portion of the service was the same every day.

The *Amida* was the petitionary prayer par excellence; there and only there did the congregation lay its petitions before God.[21] Today we can no longer tell definitely how many benedictions it had, and whether it had a uniform composition. We know only how it was constructed. The beginning was hymnic and the middle portion contained the petitions; the last portion is usually said to contain thanksgiving, but in fact it contains, alongside the thanksgiving, two petitions, both vestiges of the liturgy in use in the Temple during the prayer of the priests. The contents of the petitions, besides the themes that we have already found in the prayers of the *ma'amadot*, was essentially of national character; its subject was the future of the people—that is, the messianic salvation. The opening and closing benedictions already have their own names (M. R.H. 4:5), and they are retained throughout the year unchanged, while the intermediate benedictions are used only on weekdays. On the New Moon and the intermediate days of festivals there are special additions,[22] and on fast days the *Amida* is supplemented, as has been customary since ancient times, with an increased number of petitions.[23] On Sabbath and festivals the petitions of the *Amida* are reduced to a single one [more exactly, to a single *benediction*] for the proper sanctification of the day;[24] the New Year is an exception, for on it the middle benedictions of the *Amida* are expanded from one to three. On the Day of Atonement the confession of sin is added. When a festival coincides with the Sabbath the schools of Hillel and Shammai differ as to whether the petition [read "the blessing"] about the two sanctities should be combined or separated. But all are in agreement as to whether the number of benedictions should be seven or nine; the numbers are recognized by both sides, and both refer, in the course

[188]

of the dispute, to practice long sanctified by generations of usage (T. *Ber.* 3:12ff; T. *R.H.* 4:11).

On festivals, both on the full festival days and on the intermediate days, as well as on the New Moon, there is an Additional Service,[25] in which the ʿAmida is also recited. It seems that the Additional Service was not recited everywhere, but only in big towns with a community association (חבר עיר; M. *Ber.* 4:4)[26]—that is, centers of a *maʿamad*—and it may be assumed that the text of this ʿAmida was no different from that of the others. R. Joshua b. Ḥananya describes how, in his youth (ca. 60 C.E.), he used to attend Morning, Additional, and Afternoon services on Tabernacles, of which the first was recited after, the two others before the corresponding sacrifice. Here is an instructive example of the coexistence of prayer and sacrifice (T. *Suk.* 4:5).[27]

We cannot tell from the Mishnah to what extent the psalms were used in the service. We know only that the Hallel psalms were recited eighteen days in the year, immediately after the Morning Service; the recitation of these psalms was opened and concluded with a special benediction ("the benediction of the song").[28]

Except for the recitation of biblical verses, only the thought-content of the prayers was fixed, not their text. It was prohibited for a biblical verse to serve as a benediction without some addition. Some of the prayers begin with ברוך, "Blessed," and others do not; most have a concluding eulogy (חותם)[29] containing the gist of the benediction, but this was not absolutely necessary. The prayers are recited by the precentor[30] aloud from beginning to end, while the congregation says only the responses. Every service was recited separately, and for each one a different precentor came forward. The orientation during the ʿAmida was toward the east, so that the worshiper faced the Holy of Holies in the Temple.[31] No public worship took place in the evenings. The synagogue service was generally short. An exception was the service of the Day of Atonement, which was devoted entirely to prayer. Its liturgy was so greatly expanded that its length became proverbial.

[189]

(5) To the synagogue service belongs also the reading of the Torah.[32] On the two market days, Monday and Thursday, on the Sabbath in the morning and the afternoon, on festivals and on other holidays the Torah was read; on Sabbaths and festivals the prophets were read as well. On weekdays, festivals and half-festivals the reading was short; on the Sabbath it was longer but not much so. On festivals passages having to do with that particular day would be read, while on the Sabbath, already in ancient times, they began reading the Torah in order, though without being bound to a fixed cycle. The readers of the Torah were the members of the congregation themselves, who would read in turns. Wherever possible, even in the Diaspora, the reading was done in Hebrew, but in an emergency the vernacular was permitted. The reading was accompanied by the translation and the explication of the pericope. In all likelihood these were originally identical, for the translation was not a literal one, but incorporated a kind of commentary. But in the period of which we are speaking the two were already separate: The interpretation became independent, and the preachers no longer adhered to the scriptural text just read, but attached to it free and independent reflections on a theme which they deemed important. These discussions dealt with details of religious law, but more especially with religious doctrine and messianic hopes.[33]

(6)   In Hellenistic lands the reading of the Torah and its explication stood in the center, according to the description of Philo;[34] but this is limited to the Sabbath and betrays a desire to lend the picture as much a philosophical touch as possible. According to him, this study of the Torah occupied the entire Sabbath until a late evening hour, turning the synagogues into schools for education and moral training. We do not know about the character of the services that were held there but may assume that at least the professions of faith were recited. We learn that the Therapeutae[35] offered thanksgiving to the Creator every morning and every evening for the physical and spiritual light, and that on the Sabbath, especially on their great special festival, the night of the Seventh Sabbath, they sang prayers of thanksgiving, psalms, and hymns that they themselves composed. The language of the prayer in the Diaspora synagogues was Greek, and even in Palestine the Hellenists employed Greek as the language of prayer.[36] The service was performed in the Diaspora in the same manner as in Palestine: the precentor recited it aloud, while the congregation generally sat quietly, joining in only with the responses.

§ 36   *Prayer in the Tannaitic Period: After the Destruction of the Temple*

(1)   The fall of the Jewish state did not influence the development of the synagogue service more than did any other great event in the people's history. The destruction of the Temple and the cessation of sacrifices did not result in any tremendous upheaval in the manner of worship; the status of the synagogue in religious life was already so firmly established that no noteworthy shift occurred. But it is clear that from this point on, the synagogue service became the focal point of the liturgy, acquiring a dominant position not only in practice, but also particularly in religious thought and theology. For until then one prayed not only in the synagogue but also in the Temple, where many would go in order to participate in the service; whereas from this point on, the synagogue was the only place where the community could hold its prayers. The theory that prayers are a replacement for sacrifices belongs to the thinking of a later age;[1] it was a less than literal interpretation of the prophet's words, "We will replace bulls with our lips" (Hos. 14:3). Such an idea never occurred to the generation of the Destruction. R. Yoḥanan b. Zakkai, as is well known, declared acts of charity a replacement for sacrifice,[2] and not one of the tannaim viewed prayer as a replacement for sacrifice. They adopted the times of sacrifice as the times of prayer,[3] but otherwise lived with the conviction that the institution of prayer, like that of sacrifice, originated in hoary antiquity. For public worship had existed even before alongside the sacrifices, and when the latter lapsed, the former continued in full force just as they had been. The order of the prayers per se could remain unchanged, and only in the details was some revision needed to allow for the new circumstances. This was done not by eliminating the sentences that no longer suited reality, but by changing their import; to the extent possible their traditional language was retained, but little additions were made that adjusted their sense to reflect the new conditions. This is what was always done, both then and

[190]

later, whenever extensive alterations proved necessary; in that ancient period when prayers recorded in writing were unknown, it may have been the only possible way to guarantee the tradition without throwing the worshiper into confusion. In addition, everyone hoped that the Temple service would soon be restored (מהרה יבנה בית המקדש),[4] and that it would be possible to restore the text of the prayers [to the extent that a single fixed text existed at all] to its original state.

The petitions for the acceptance of sacrifices could not be retained in their exact wording, and instead of the petition for the preservation of Jerusalem, there were now petitions for its rebuilding. The coming of the Messiah and the renewal of the world became even more urgent than before. With the Song of the Levites silenced, the psalms found a new home in the synagogue, and many of the pious made them a regular part of their daily prayers. The Priestly Blessing also was retained and, by means of a few new regulations necessitated by the new situation, was incorporated into the 'Amida. Where no priests were available, a special prayer replaced Blessing, in which the precentor recited the Blessing's verses. Likewise, it was necessary to reorganize certain rites that until then had been connected with the Temple, such as the blowing of the shofar[5] on the New Year [when it occurred on the Sabbath] and the use of the four species on the second through the seventh day of Tabernacles [for on the first day it was customary everywhere even before the Destruction];[6] whatever could be transferred to the synagogue in any manner at all was saved and incorporated into the liturgy.

(2)   Other innovations were products of the religious ferment of that period. There was no longer any possibility of avoiding a confrontation with nascent Christianity, for the Jewish Christians continued to attend the synagogue, and introduced practices that led the worshipers astray (M. *Meg.*, end).[7] [It is very doubtful that this Mishnah refers to Christian practices.] In accordance with their faith in the resurrected Christ, who acquired more and more divine attributes as the movement developed,[8] they expanded the simple benediction formula, giving it a form of the kind frequently encountered in the extant remains of ancient Christian prayers, which are but one step removed from paganism. Finally, as demonstrated by the example of the Apostles and as confirmed by later reports, they exploited the synagogue as a convenient base for spreading propaganda, for by serving, like all the other congregants, as precentors and preachers, they succeeded in giving expression to and widespread distribution of their ideas. Around the year 100 this ended in a complete break and the expulsion of the Jewish Christians from the synagogue [see §8(10)—Engl. *trans.*]. One means of defense against them was the introduction of the Benediction against the Sectarians, which R. Gamaliel II at Jamnia ordered Samuel the Lesser to compose ("Is there anyone who knows how to establish the text of the benediction against the heretics? Samuel the Lesser got up and composed it"; B. *Ber.* 28b).[9] The express purpose of this prayer was to spoil synagogue attendance for the Jewish Christians or to render it impossible for them to attend. Only with this prayer was close attention paid that it be recited in its exact wording, and that the condemnation of the sectarians not be suppressed; thus, it was no longer possible for a Christian either to serve as a precentor or to stand in the ranks of the worshipers listening quietly while his community was cursed and the congregation responded "Amen." There is another regulation that can

[191]

be fully explained only by the history of the period. It dictates that if a "Cuthean" recites a benediction one may answer "Amen" only if he has heard the entire benediction (M. *Ber.* 8, end). If this refers to the Samaritans,[10] such severity would be inexplicable; for if the consideration is that they pronounced the name of God improperly, it would be enough to hear the eulogy in order to make a judgment, and it would not be necessary to hear the rest of the benediction. Otherwise, answering "Amen" is not prohibited even when the benediction one has heard was recited by a heathen. Why, then, this particular stringency with respect to "Cutheans"? If we examine the ancient benediction formulas of the Christians, such as Εὐχαριστοῦμέν σοι, πάτερ ἡμῶν, ὑπὲρ ... ἧς ἐγνώρισας ἡμῖν διὰ Ἰησοῦ τοῦ παιδός σου· σοὶ ἡ δόξα εἰς τοὺς αἰῶνας, "We give thanks to You, our Father ... Who proclaimed to us through Jesus, Your son; glory is Yours forever" (*Didache* 9:2), and especially Ὁ θεὸς ὁ παντοκράτωρ, ὁ ἀγέννητος καὶ ἀπρόσιτος, ... ὁ θεὸς καὶ πατὴρ τοῦ Χριστοῦ σου τοῦ μονογενοῦς υἱοῦ σου, "The God, Lord of the world, Who was not born, to Whom no one is related ... The God, the Father of your Messiah, Your only son," and the other prayers of the *Apostolic Constitutions*,[11] we find that the beginnings and endings are perfectly correct from a Jewish point of view. Only in the middle do the objectionable sentences occur; that is the reason for the ruling that only one who hears the entire benediction may answer "Amen," thus identifying himself with it. And since we know how commonly the word מין, "sectarian," was altered in the manuscripts to כותי, "Cuthean," and the like, we may infer that in this text, too, such an alteration may have occurred,[12] obscuring the meaning of the regulation to the point of unintelligibility.

Relations to the heretical Gnostics[13] also had to be clarified. Among them there [192] were various trends, each of which cultivated its own particular deviation from the community norm. Particularly singled out for denunciation were the dualists, who believed in two divinities, [and perhaps] therefore would repeat certain words in their prayers: מודים מודים, "We give thanks, we give thanks"; שמע שמע, "Hear Israel, Hear Israel."[14] Others may have attached magical concepts to the prayers, and for this purpose rearranged and even reversed the order of the words (למפרע).[15] Finally there were those who predicated only certain attributes to God, stressing His goodness as opposed to His omnipotence, and who even sought to limit the pure worship of God to good people, who were seen as a kind of special order.[16] The sages rejected all these deviations more or less decisively, but naturally they attacked with particular vehemence those that in any way offended against the doctrine of monotheism. They did not immediately achieve complete success, for many deviations denounced as early as the second century were still encountered here and there in the fourth century.[17]

(3) The troubles of the times, the political upheavals and the inner ferment led R. Gamaliel II to institute fixed regulations in the area of public worship, as he did in many other areas, and to give an official stamp of authority to what until then had been merely customary. The passages belonging to the recitation of the *Shemaʿ* were already well established, and there was not much to change in them except that the reference to the exodus from Egypt, formerly omitted from the Evening Service, was now prescribed.[18] In connection with the ʿAmida, freedom and arbitrariness had been prevalent until that time. Therefore, at the initiative of R. Gamaliel, the ʿAmida was edited; this was done by a certain Simon, otherwise unknown, whose profession was flax-working:

"Simon the Flaxworker[19] edited (הסדיר) the Eighteen Benedictions in the presence of R. Gamaliel in order in Yavneh" (B. *Ber.* 28b). This editing must not be understood as the fixing of the whole prayer from beginning to end; this was actually impossible, as the recitation of the prayer was permitted in any language at all (*Soṭa* 7:1). Variations in the text occurred even afterward, and never ceased; in fact, about a century after R. Gamaliel, the demand was still being heard that the text should not be frozen, but should always contain something new—"One must say something new in it" (B. *Ber.* 29b). The editing had to do primarily with the benedictions and their order; but even the latter was, at least in theory, not taken as final, for it could be altered at will—"The middle benedictions have no order" (B. *Ber.* 34a). The main point was that the number of benedictions be fixed; this number came to eighteen, and from it the prayer got its name, שמונה עשרה ברכות, "Eighteen Benedictions." This limitation could be attained only by recommending that some benedictions, previously separate, should now be combined. But the possibility of keeping them separate was not completely excluded, and in one case use was made of this option in Babylonia when the prayer acquired a special petition, the nineteenth, for the Messiah of the House of David.

Long before the ʿAmida was edited, it was certainly already customary to recite it not only in public but also at home, by the individual. Earlier the greatest freedom was possible as to this, but the prayer had now become so long that the question arose as to whether every individual was to be obliged to recite such a lengthy prayer. Most of R. Gamaliel's contemporaries, unlike the rabbi himself, were not so inclined; some sought to shorten the prayers, and others wished to leave the traditional freedom of formulation unrestricted (B. *Ber.* 29a). A short epitome of the entire ʿAmida, or at least of its middle benedictions, was actually in use: הביננו, מעין שמונה עשרה (B. *Ber.* 29a). But what about public worship? Until then the precentor would recite the ʿAmida aloud, and he, too, enjoyed the extensive freedom of formulation; but once he was obliged to observe a particular order and had to adhere to the prescribed eulogies, he was given some time for reflection before beginning his prayer ("The precentor prepares himself"). Thus, an interruption was created in the order of the service, in which the precentor got his prayer in order. Should the members of the congregation who were present be obliged to recite the prayer silently during this time, to the extent that they were capable of doing so, or should they not? R. Gamaliel saw no need for this,[20] apparently because he laid the emphasis on communal prayer; but in this matter the final decision was in favor of individual prayer. From then on, the ʿAmida was first recited silently by the congregation, and afterward aloud by the precentor. Disregarding transient and isolated deviations, this custom has stood unchanged until the modern period.

[193]

The ʿAmida became part of every service. It was declared obligatory even for the Evening Service, when no public service was held. Over this question arose a great dispute that threatened to cause a split in the circle of the sages of Yavneh, and temporarily cost R. Gamaliel his office. The deeper meaning of the dispute was actually whether the Evening Service should have official status or not. In theory the opinion prevailed that the ʿAmida in the Evening Service was optional, but for practical purposes it was incorporated into the service and was distinguished from the other ʿAmidot only in that it was not repeated aloud.

The language of the ʿAmida was simple, and the text of the benedictions was mostly short, based as much as possible on biblical texts, even incorporating whole verses verbatim. Through extensive usage it became disseminated and very familiar (שגורה בפה),[21] so that many knew how to recite it without the help of the precentor. We should not entertain any exaggerated notion of the extent of synagogue attendance, especially on weekdays. Because of the difficulty of earning a livelihood, not many were able to attend the synagogue regularly, and even the sages were not always prepared to interrupt their lessons to come to services.[22] Out of consideration for these difficulties the service could not be very long. An individual worshiper was free to make his prayer as long as he wished, but in public it was necessary to take care to avoid unduly burdening the congregation.[23] The *'Amida* became completely rooted even in the life of the individual. Here something was achieved that no other religion until then had achieved: Religious individualism attained a complete victory, and personal piety became so widespread that later it was frequently in a position to influence even public worship. The individual prayer of antiquity, the "words" and "supplications" continued to exist, following the *'Amida* as the part of the liturgy that remained untouched by regulations from above. The more the liturgy came to be governed by strict rules, the greater the benefit that was seen in a prayer that remained a private matter, where each individual could express his feelings freely and pour out his heart as the spirit moved him.

(4)   In this period further progress was made in differentiating the prayers for different occasions,[24] especially for distinguished weekdays. The distinction between weekday prayers and the prayers of Sabbaths and festivals was long established, but now this distinction was extended to weekdays of a somewhat solemn character. This refers to the New Moon, Hannukah, and Purim. The sages of the period under discussion are the ones who participated in the debates about the regulation of the additions for these days; whenever the discussion is about special prayers for the rainy season or the place of Havdala on Saturday night, the same names keep recurring. To what extent the festival liturgy was developed we do not know; but it does not seem to be an accident that R. Akiva is the first who is reported to have held the service of the Day of Atonement over the entire day;[25] perhaps the first traces of the *'Avoda* for the Day of Atonement go back to this early period.

[194]

(5)   As for the Torah reading, the rule was already established that the entire Pentateuch is read in order, but the reading was not yet attached to a particular season, and there was no definite cycle.[26] Opinions were still divided as to the number of persons called up to the Torah on different days.[27] The exposition of the Torah continued to be an important part of the Sabbath and festival service. Little by little it freed itself from its subjugation to the text, and took on the form of free sermons. To some extent it had to compete with the lectures of sages, which did not always take place in the synagogue and were not bound to the weekly reading.[28] No new religious ideas emerged in this period. If we think about what that generation experienced, we can only marvel at the strength of their faith. Despite all of the sufferings that they endured, despite all the hardship and oppression, they held fast to their trust in God. They had not lost their confidence in God's mercy, inherited from their ancestors, nor was their religious spirit dampened or dimmed. The worshiper believed with unshaken faith that his prayer was heard.

(6)   The Bar Kokhba rebellion and the Hadrianic persecutions brought about the total collapse of Jewish public life and the dissolution of all of its organizations and institutions, and resulted in the transfer of the center of Jewish life from the south of the land to the north.[29] In the period of the restoration (after 140) the first task was to reassemble the scattered folk and to restore the earlier order. All who had witnessed the old order had died. The tradition had been weakened by the great shock; part had become unclear, and part was completely forgotten. In every society, numerous institutions are conducted routinely, without anyone making special note of their procedures; only when some interruption in their routine occurs do people begin to reflect on the details, which by then have often vanished from memory or turn out never to have been fully clarified. After the assemblies for prayer had been long proscribed and the customary practices of the land of Judea mostly disrupted, it was necessary first of all to restore the service of the synagogue. Doubtless at that time it sometimes happened that individuals with authority took only their own personal traditions or views as their criterion and unilaterally suppressed customs different from their own that had formerly enjoyed full recognition. But as a rule, tradition was respected, because it was believed that only in this way could the liturgy be properly performed.

In many questions touching the liturgy, we find the leading figures of the age occupied in discussions that afford insight into the new tendency and the new problems.[30] In studying the New Year liturgy, for example, we constantly encounter the names of the same sages, who were trying to restore the old traditions as much as possible. The order of the prayers, how to make up the number of nine benedictions, the biblical verses, the eulogies—everything suddenly seems unclear. The reality is that that formerly a variety of customs existed side by side,[31] while now people sought a single fixed order. Such difficulties, sometimes due to the influence of outstanding personalities and sometimes due to variations in local practices, had to be overcome, and opposing opinions had to be harmonized. It must be noted that even in those years of cruel persecution the old spirit still reigned. One does not observe any signs of resignation and despair or morbid obsession with sin and self-reproach; the hopefulness of old abides in its full strength.

[195]

(7)   Hardly any new prayers were introduced in this period; at most the old ones were expanded.[32] It seems that the age no longer felt itself strong enough to take initiatives, but was content to possess the past. Accordingly, casuistic debates about prayer were accorded the most detailed attention.[33] The times of prayer, for example, were already established by this period and, following ancient practice, people would assemble in the synagogue at accustomed times. But then this became the subject of reflection and discussion, and the times for the beginning and ending of every prayer had to be exactly defined.[34] The earlier generations permitted greater freedom in these matters, but the later ones sought to regulate everything with precision. The general rule was that the tradition of the past must be maintained. But since conditions of life had changed, and it was not always clear just how the ancient tradition was to be applied, frequent misunderstandings occurred and incorrect legal decisions were made. The fundamental error was that every detail of the liturgy was thought to rest on ancient laws, whereas most of the rules had actually developed freely. Even disturbances that were likely to occur during prayer were the occasion for numerous discussions.[35] But the goal

that apparently was always before the eyes of the sages—to account for every possible situation—could not possibly be attained. Even the amount of intention (כונה) required for prayer was the subject of discussion.[36] But it must never be forgotten that the rules laid down by halakha pertain only to the correct external performance; they are comparable to the rules of prayer and *Agende* of our time. But the internal pious intention was a matter for the individual, and was treated in aggadic contexts.[37] The very sages who took a dialectical approach in halakha and bound prayer in chains expressed completely different views about this very matter in their homilies and sermons. Their words breathe a spirit of deep piety and vibrant religiosity.

In accordance with the spirit of the time, the details peculiar to the special days were discussed: the changes, additions, and even possible errors.[38] The jurists took control of these problems, regulating them in their fashion by making rules. Since nothing pertaining to liturgy could be reduced to writing, no *Agende* could be drawn up, and thus all these details had to be subjected to casuistic argument. The disputes of the sages did not yet touch life and true piety; the liturgy retained a great deal of freedom. But in later times these discussions were taken up, viewed as authoritative, and codified.

§ 37 *Prayer in the Amoraic Period* [196]

(1)   The amoraic period brought with it important advances in the history of prayer. Here, too, we face the difficulty mentioned above, that reports about matters that developed over a long period of time appear together in the sources, for the Talmud reports the products of three centuries' work all at once, and it is not always easy to distinguish what belongs to an earlier period and what belongs to a later period. The amoraim found a complete system of prayer ready-made; public worship had already been long customary everywhere, and individuals were already in the habit of regularly holding their own services. Openings for further development were made on the ground of what already existed. This occurred simultaneously, but differently, in Palestine and Babylonia. As in many other areas, definite differences arose, and the Palestinian rite differed from that of Babylonia.

(2)   The amoraim essayed first and foremost to create fixed patterns for the liturgy, and to introduce regulations of universal applicability from which one might not deviate. This could most easily be accomplished if all members of the community would participate in communal prayer in the synagogue. The contrast with the silence of the earlier generations on this matter demonstrates strikingly the great value attached by the amoraim to community worship. Out of a very large number of rabbinic dicta that express this idea, only a few can be cited here; at the beginning of Tractate *Berakhot* we meet them on every page. For example: "Where ten worship, the Divine Presence is among them"; "The Holy One, Blessed be He, is found in the synagogue"; even "Prayer is heard only in the synagogue" (B. *Ber.* 6a). Therefore, it is considered very meritorious to attend the synagogue, and blameworthy to neglect to do so. The Babylonians are praised and esteemed because they come to the synagogue early in the morn-

ing and late in the evening (B. *Ber.* 8a).[1] To be sure, reservations with regard to this esteem can also be heard. The sages were not always happy to have to interrupt their lectures in order to attend the synagogue. In conscious opposition to that one-sided point of view they declared that the four walls of the house of study are dearer to the Lord than all synagogues (R. Ḥisda, B. *Ber.* 8a), and some recited their prayers in the house of study where they lectured. Some sages even carried on with their studies during the synagogue service itself, during the reading of the Torah, for example (B. *Ber.* 8a).

But according to the view of that period, one who did not pray in the synagogue had at least to say his prayers at the same time as the congregation, for that moment is "the time of acceptance" of which Ps. 69:14 speaks. One story may be quoted that illuminates clearly the interests that were at work here. In B. *Ber.* 7b, we read:

> R. Isaac[2] said to R. Naḥman, "What is the reason that the master does not come to the synagogue to pray?" He said to him, "I am not able."
> He said to him, "Let the master assemble ten and pray."
> He said, "It is too hard for me."
> "Then let the master say to the precentor that when the congregation is reciting the ʿAmida he should come and notify the master."
> He said to him, "Why all this?"
> He said to him, "For R. Yoḥanan said in the name of R. Simon b. Yoḥai, 'Why is it written "And as for me, may my prayer be at a time of acceptance, O Lord?" ' This refers to the time when the congregation is praying."

[197]

This discussion between two sages is most instructive, for the zeal of the one and the astonishment of the other are equally typical. It seems that R. Naḥman has no conception of the purposes so dear to the heart of his importunate colleague.

Like the congregation, the individual ought to worship always in a fixed place. The synagogue is a "little sanctuary," and as we shall see below, several regulations pertaining to its location and construction are intended to make it resemble the Temple. But some of these conditions are applicable even to the room used for prayer in a private house. In conformity with the importance of prayer, it should be the first thing with which a person begins his day; one should not do his work or taste anything before praying. The early amoraim used to begin their day with a lecture, but the later ones thought this improper (B. *Ber.* 24b). There is one service whose obligatory nature is repeatedly emphasized. The Afternoon Service occurs at a rather inconvenient time, making it hard to perform outside the Temple. Held in the middle of the day, it interrupts work, and in the evening it is likely to conflict with the Evening Service. Without doubt it was often neglected, and therefore it was necessary to stress firmly that "a person must always be punctilious about the Afternoon Service" (B. *Ber.* 6b, and compare 28b). The Evening Service too was elevated to the status of a public service, and was recited immediately upon nightfall. Consequently, a second recitation of the *Shemaʿ* just before bedtime was prescribed, and in this way a new nighttime prayer was introduced: קריאת שמע על המטה, "the bedtime recitation of the *Shemaʿ*."

Thanks to the increased importance attributed to prayer in general, long prayers were no longer considered improper, but rather were thought more certain to be heard.

Particularly in time of trouble or danger, additions were permitted, and even their insertion into the 'Amida itself was not proscribed. The traditional Supplication continued to exist as an individual prayer, but the art of individual prayer and confidence in it vanished. Accordingly, recourse was made to models provided by famous men, whose private prayers were handed over to the public and imitated by them.

(3) The age's attitude toward prayer was expressed in the further development of existing models; simple formulas were filled out, and the frequent repetition of prayers was replaced by variety. A great variety of liturgical patterns and formulas emerged particularly in Babylonia. Here the intensive cultivation of religious life and the attraction of the broad masses to participation in religious activity from the beginning of the amoraic period on are expressed especially clearly in the field of prayer. Mar Samuel and his colleague Aba Arika, known simply as Rav, the two founders of Talmud study in Babylonia, contributed greatly to the development of the liturgy, and we find the marks of their activity in nearly every service.[3] We find Rav taking part in the formulation of the benediction (B. *Ber.* 12a). The benedictions of the *Shema'*, originally identical for the Morning Service and Evening Service, are now varied: "With great love" in the Morning Service is by Samuel (B. *Ber.* 11b). From Rav comes the distinction between "True and Certain" and "True and Faithful" (B. *Ber.* 12a). Both dealt with the abbreviated 'Amida: Samuel transmits the telescoped formula "Give us understanding" (B. *Ber.* 29a), while Rav has a part in introducing the petition for the Davidic messiah (B. *Sanh.* 107a) [?], composed out of esteem for the dynasty of the Exilarch (B. *Pes.* 117b) [?]. In the area of the Sabbath and festival prayers, the influence of these two sages is even more abundant, for much of what we have today seems to have been created new in their time. Thus, the Evening Service at the beginning of Sabbaths and festivals was introduced in Babylonia, as was a special form of the repetition of the 'Amida on Friday night in order to lengthen the service ("One Benediction Replacing Seven"; see above, §15[1]). Likewise, the insertion of biblical verses in the Friday night 'Amida is attributed to Rav (B. *Shab.* 119b), and from here they seem to have entered the other Sabbath 'Amidot as well. The Additional Service, befitting its origin in the *ma'amad* assemblies, was held only as a public service; as such it was known to and regulated by Mar Samuel. But already in his time some had begun to recite it privately. In its text it was identical with the other 'Amidot (compare "One prays and prays again"; B. *Ber.* 30b), but Rav associated it with the Additional Sacrifice, and accordingly he demanded a change in its text, insisting that it include a reference to the sacrifices (Y. *Ber.* 4:6, 8c).[4] This requirement was not particularly logical, for if the prayers were to be seen as a replacement for sacrifices, it would have been appropriate also for the weekday 'Amida and the 'Amidot of the Sabbaths and festivals to refer to them as a replacement for sacrifices. But the requirement was adopted as suiting the conception current among the public at that time, and the Additional Service acquired such an addition. The consequence was that the Additional Service of festivals also acquired a reference to the pilgrimage of antiquity. Later a new introductory formula was composed, ומפני חטאינו, "And because of our sins," so that this 'Amida has quite a different appearance from the others. Also for the festivals we have from Rav and Samuel the passage for insertion at the end of the Sabbath, called "The Pearl," which begins with ותודיענו, "You proclaimed to us," to which very likely "You chose us" and "And You gave us" also

[198]

belong. They also had a part in the prayers accompanying the confession of sin for the Day of Atonement. For the ʿAmida of the Ten Days of Repentance it was Rav who introduced the formulas, "King of judgment" and "Holy King" (B. *Ber.* 12b). His activity in the reworking of the New Year services is clearly to be seen. The introduction to the Remembrance verses is called explicitly תקיעתא דבי רב in the sources, and in all likelihood the introductions to the two other benedictions are also by him. Formerly these three benedictions consisted of biblical verses loosely connected to each other and concluding with a eulogy, but Rav formed them into prayers, prefacing the groups of biblical verses with introductions that summarize the religious ideas of these characteristic New Year prayers and ending them with a petition suitable to their content. The pattern of all three benedictions is so similar that there is no reason to doubt their common origin; their contents are so elevated and their language so noble that we can only view Rav as a prayer-writer of considerable stature.

[Rav and Samuel did not introduce all the prayers mentioned above, and they certainly did not compose all of them. We have already noted (above, §24(5)) that it is doubtful that Rav was the composer of the Kingship, Remembrance, and Shofar prayers as we have them. It is probable that Rav and Samuel did not compose some of these prayers, but merely transmitted traditions that they had received. There is, for example, no foundation for the assumption that Samuel composed "Give us understanding," for we also know of a Palestinian version of this prayer (Y. *Ber.* 4:3, 8a) that is only slightly different from Samuel's version. It is not even likely that Samuel "edited the text of this prayer in accordance

[199] with the Babylonian custom," as is the opinion of Louis Ginzberg (*Perushim* 3:321, where the Yerushalmi's version of "the Eighteen Benedictions of Samuel" are also discussed). There are also variant readings with regard to the names of the sages in some of the above-mentioned sources (such as B. *Shab.* 119b). There is no hint that Rav introduced the petition for the Davidic messiah, and certainly no evidence that this benediction was composed out of respect for the dynasty of the Exilarch (see above, §8, end). Despite the uncertainty touching many of the details mentioned above, there is no denying that Rav and Samuel gave attention to matters of prayer and contributed to its formation. On this subject, compare now J. Neusner, *A History of the Jews in Babylonia* (Leiden: E.J. Brill, 1966), 2:159ff., and the literature cited there.]

Many other details that go back to Rav and Mar Samuel may be mentioned (compare, for example B. *Ber.* 60b; Y. *Ber.* 1:8–9, 3d for "We give thanks"; Y. *Suk.* 3:4); they all reflect the same desire to provide the liturgy with a uniform shape, to fill out the existing prayers, and to fill in lacunae through the introduction of new prayers.

In Palestine their contemporary, R. Yoḥanan, worked in the same direction.[5] About him, too, a great number of details show that he was involved in liturgical development. We have no knowledge that he also composed new prayers, nor is it likely that he did so, for the Palestinian sages had no reason to abandon their ancient tradition and to replace it with new texts.

As for the late amoraim, the names of Abaye and Rava are frequently mentioned in connection with questions about the order of prayers (compare, for example, B. *Ber.* 27b, 29a; B. *Pes.* 117b; B. *Yoma* 87b; B. *Soṭa* 40a; and so on). Their disciple, R. Papa, took an equally active part in the development of prayers, mostly in accordance with his rule of combining texts when different traditions of prayers or eulogies exist, and in this way avoiding the difficulty of making a choice.[6]

(4)   The details transmitted to us by the sources about the shaping of the prayers in the amoraic period, especially the datable details, are exceedingly few relative to the length of the period. Nevertheless, it is worth our while to survey in a general way the extent of the development of public worship at that time. The following picture emerges: The ritual order, as far as it relates to times of prayer and liturgical structure, is by and large fixed,[7] and is little different from the ritual customary today. But as to the text of the prayers, we may say that nearly everything is still in flux.[8] Even at the end of our period, surprisingly few passages of prayer have a settled text. Hardly a single liturgical passage is mentioned in the Talmud without differences in wording being cited; given the Talmud's unsystematic manner, these texts probably would not even be mentioned but for these differences. Even the basic pattern of the benediction is still under discussion; Abaye, in the middle of the amoraic period, is still inclined to accept the opinion of Rav, but the formula eventually adopted follows that of R. Yoḥanan, his opponent (B. *Ber.* 40b). Of the benedictions before and after the recitation of the *Shemaʿ*, not one, whether in the Morning or the Evening service, can have had a fixed text. There was no unanimity with regard to the third passage of the *Shemaʿ* in the evening. As for the ʿAmida, we have reports of a variety of deviations, and some precentors permitted themselves to recite texts not known to or expected by anyone. Yet, what is reported to us is only a small part of the variations that actually existed;[9] how numerous these variations were may be judged from the long list that we had to cite in the detailed discussion of the ʿAmida (§9). The additions for distinguished days were particularly subject to dispute,[10] as was the abbreviated text, "Give us understanding." Everything following the ʿAmida is completely unfixed; one person would recite Supplications and another would not, each individual at his own discretion ("One who is in the habit of reciting Supplications after his ʿAmida"; B. *Ber.* 29b). No text is fixed for this purpose; personal prayers by individual sages are handed down in which each person followed his own inclination. We hear also about variations in connection with the festival prayers,[11] both of the pilgrim festivals and of the Days of Awe. When one reads, for example, the discussions of the Remembrance verses and so forth, of the New Year, or of the confession of the Day of Atonement, one can see that no firmly fixed text yet existed at all, and that until that time everything was left to individual discretion. Similarly many details concerning the reading of the Torah are unsettled,[12] and the discussion does not always lead to a decision; not surprisingly, these questions are debated for several generations in succession. We frequently find in the Talmud praise or blame for a precentor who does or does not do something. This fact deserves particular attention;[13] such expressions of approval or disapproval are in order only if the precentor is not bound to a fixed text, but is given a certain freedom of activity. In the amoraic age, people still saw themselves as properly qualified to compose their own prayers independently; the few prayers from that period whose text has been transmitted show forcefulness, a healthy religious outlook, and much talent to express religious ideas and feelings. The people of such an age could not tolerate being limited to a particular prayer text, and so many texts existed side by side. Up to a point, the force of tradition probably created unity in the main centers, but divergences came into being that remained long-standing, without anyone taking an interest in or having the intention of disturbing them.

[200]

(5)   The most important differences were those between Palestine and Babylonia. Those that were later collected (*Hiluf minhagim ben bene bavel livene eres yisraʾel*) have mostly to do only with external conduct of the liturgy; the differences in the prayers with which we are dealing were never collected. We hear about them only incidentally, particularly because of the new manuscript discoveries, which mostly reflect the Palestinian tradition. A few examples illustrate what is meant. The concluding formula of Redemption [after the Recitation of the *Shemaʿ*] in Palestine, according to the ancient sources, is (מלך) צור ישראל וגואלו, "King, rock of Israel, and its redeemer";[14] while the Babylonian Rava introduced גאל ישראל, "Who redeemed Israel" (B. *Pes.* 117b); on festivals when the piyyut, which originated in Palestine, is added, Ashkenaz still has the Palestinian eulogy. On the same occasion Ashkenaz has in the Morning Service the concluding formula from the same source—בגלל אבות תושיע בנים, "For the sake of the fathers save the sons"—which in Rome is constant throughout the year. For the preceding passage, "True and certain . . . for the first ones," Ashkenaz knows a short, compressed version, which also is used in connection with piyyut.[15] All these texts are found also in manuscripts from the Cairo Geniza, showing that they are elements from the Palestinian rite that were transferred to Ashkenaz together with the piyyut. In the Palestinian daily Evening Service, the final benediction of the recitation of the *Shemaʿ* has the eulogy "Who spreads the tabernacle of peace . . . ," while in Babylonia a distinction is made in this benediction between weekdays on the one hand, and Sabbaths and festivals on the other.

[201]

The *ʿAmida*, in its Babylonian recension, was composed of nineteen benedictions, while the Palestinian recension has eighteen; this distinction survived for centuries, and is still present in Rome and Ashkenaz whenever *qerovot* are inserted in the *ʿAmida* (§32). The text of Benediction 3 in the Palestinian version, "Holy are You and awesome is Your name," is preserved in the prayer book only on the Days of Awe; while the eulogy "the holy King," introduced by Rav for the Days of Repentance, is not known in Palestine. The Palestinian version of the *ʿAvoda* was preserved in southern France, and its eulogy is found also in Ashkenaz whenever the blessing of the priests is recited [outside of the land of Israel]. The eulogy עושה השלום, "Maker of peace," is found in the prayer books only on the Ten Days of Repentance, but it is shown in the ancient sources formerly to have been the conclusion for every day. There were differences in the insertions as well. The Kedushah was recited in Palestine only on Sabbaths and festivals, while in Babylonia it was recited every day. In Babylonia, when no priest was present, the biblical verses of the Priestly Blessing were recited by the precentor, while in Palestine this was not permitted, and only the concluding verse, "And they will place My Name upon the children of Israel, and I will bless them" was permitted to be said. On fast days the Palestinians followed the ancient custom that the Priestly Blessing is recited several times a day, while in Babylonia it was recited only once. Of the seasonal insertions the Palestinians recited in the summer "Who makes the dew fall," which was unknown in Babylonia but which, surprisingly, was adopted even by rites that are otherwise dependent on Babylonia.

In the Sabbath prayers Palestine had different additions to the *ʿAmida* from those in Babylonia. The introduction of the Additional Service in Sepharad, "You bade Moses," goes back to a Palestinian source. The *ʿAmida* for festivals developed in the two lands in totally different forms; not only was the deviation of the *ʿAmida* of the

Additional Service from other ʿAmidot very slight in Palestine, being limited almost exclusively to the biblical verses, but even the train of thought and the structure of the Palestinian ʿAmida differed considerably from those customary in Babylonia. In addition, the Babylonians observed the second day of festivals, and they imposed certain modifications in the calendar.

For the Torah reading the Babylonians introduced the annual cycle instead of the triennial one, and this naturally involved a change in the Haftara. Furthermore, they had to alter the festival readings out of consideration for the two days of each festival. They also had the custom of reading an additional pericope on days that have an Additional Service and on the four special Sabbaths, so that on these days they read not from one scroll but two. In Palestine it was long the practice for the one called to the Torah to read his own passage, while in Babylonia from early times the precentor would help him. In Palestine they knew, as in ancient times, only one benediction before the entire reading of the Torah and one after it, while in Babylonia each person called to the Torah recited a benediction over his short passage at the beginning and the end. The benedictions of the Haftara were more developed in Babylonia than in Palestine; the middle benediction, in particular, underwent a similar development to that of the analogous benediction of the ʿAmida.

It seems that in Babylonia itself the different districts had different rites,[16] and quite probably these differences increased with time through the fluctuating influences of the leading sages of each period. It is related that Rav was astonished at hearing one congregation reciting the Hallel psalms on the New Moon, but from the manner in which this was done he soon realized that it was an ancient custom (B. *Ta.* 28b). He had the same experience on other occasions when he observed practices that were strange to him (compare, for example, B. *Meg.* 22a). But most important is that, despite all the motion in the direction of fixed norms, a great number of individual elements were preserved. In any case, Babylonia had, since antiquity, an independent tradition, which could be influenced by Palestine in many important details, but not in all.

[202]

(6)   The amoraim strived to achieve two things: to bring everything into fixed forms, and to imitate the exemplary behavior of famous men. The private prayers that we have frequently mentioned[17] can only have become publicly known by disciples asking their masters for them and then handing them on. They would study and follow the example of the master down to the tiniest and seemingly most insignificant detail ("This is Torah and I have to learn it");[18] thus, it is hardly astonishing that in such an important realm as prayer they observed the behavior of the great men of the age very closely, and recommended that it be imitated. This could also have a deleterious effect, when observances undertaken by an individual as stringencies meant for himself, with no thought of making them binding on others, later were turned into generally valid norms. In the amoraic period this did not yet happen, or it happened only seldom, but in later centuries it was a common phenomenon, one that was not always beneficial to religious institutions. Another goal, or at least a common tendency, was to increase the amount of praying. Unlike the preceding centuries in which short prayers were considered the best, this generation found no harm in lengthy prayers; on the contrary, these were even thought desirable, though the principle that the congregation should

not be unduly burdened was never rescinded. We have mentioned the dictum of R. Pappa: "Therefore we should recite both of them"; he was not alone in his views, for others, too, favored heaping up of prayers and prayer formulas.

(7)   Besides the above-mentioned goals, there was a desire to cast as much as possible into fixed and established molds. This goal occasioned a great many halakhic discussions,[19] giving the impression that the amoraim viewed the entire realm of liturgy from a purely legalistic point of view and forced everything into a rigid framework of regulations. But no faithful picture can be gained solely from the halakhic discussions. Wherever we are able to look into the minds of the amoraim, we become aware of them not merely as desiccated legists, but as men of delicate religious sensibilities. With all their talk of prayer as a duty, with all their debates as to the details of how this duty is fulfilled, when we inquire about their personal opinions all casuistry and argumentation fall away, and reverence is left as the sole requirement that they impose: If one is unable to pray with reverence he is advised not to pray at all. How sharp is the sarcasm directed against the precentor who heaped up attributes of God beyond a reasonable limit, or the dictum of Rava that one not relate to God as to an equal![20] These dicta are found right in the middle of halakhic material; but the true ideas about prayers must be sought in the aggada, which sets aside the legalistic point of view and is concerned only with the religious spirit and personal piety.

[203]

(8)   An important point in the development of the liturgy was the change in certain religious attitudes that occurred in that period, especially in Babylonia. Unfortunately Jewish religious history—that is, the changes undergone by individual concepts in the course of time—has not yet been fully studied, and therefore it is not easy to be very specific about it. We shall content ourselves with one point: It is likely that at that time a new conception of the messianic era arose.[21] In the current text of the ʿAmida the petition in Benediction 14 is, "And to Jerusalem Your city, return in mercy," and the eulogy of Benediction 17 is, "Who restores His presence to Zion." This conception localizes the presence of God in Zion, and therefore declares it necessary for Him to return to it at the end of time. But this cannot always have been the prevalent view. The corresponding passages in the Palestinian version do not yet allude to it, and therefore it must have had its origin in Babylonia and in the amoraic period.

[The idea of the restoration of God's presence to Zion is expressed also in texts of Palestinian origin, like the text of the ʿAvoda benediction: אנא . . . השב שכינתך לציון וסדר העבודה לירושלים, "Oh God . . . restore Your presence to Zion, and the order of the Temple service to Jerusalem," recited in Ashkenaz (outside of Palestine) in the Additional Service of festivals and quoted in *Midrash tehilim* to Ps. 17. Compare Heinemann, *Blessing*.]

Likewise, there is no overlooking the fact that Babylonia is the source of every superstition in the world. Some of the amoraim were affected by these errors of their native land, and were subject to fear of demons, nightmares, and witchcraft.[22] The text of the prayers was only rarely affected by these, and remained simple and natural; but the synagogue service was not infrequently touched by them. Especially in later centuries, when every word in the Talmud was seen as binding, and when people lived in fear of witches and demons, these errors led to sorry consequences.

§ 38 *The Expansions and Embellishments of the Statutory Prayers*

(1)   The amoraic period was still a creative one in which people dared to compose new prayers; and though these prayers remained within a framework established in the past, they still raised new ideas of their own. But this power failed at the end of the talmudic period, and was followed by a slack time, when further development was hindered by severe persecution. In Palestine oppression put an end to assemblies in the houses of study;[1] no authoritative academies existed for centuries, and, what makes our work difficult, no coherent data about the further development of religious life can be found from that period. In Babylonia, too, the situation of the Jews deteriorated;[2] there, too, the almost uninterrupted hostility limited intellectual creativity and productive activity. The later generations of the amoraim and the saboraim who followed them[3] were content with collecting and securing the treasures that they had inherited from their predecessors. In liturgy, their contribution was inestimable, for they were the first to commit the prayers to writing, thereby guaranteeing the continuity of their transmission. But in the area of independent creativity, their powers were inadequate, and they could only content themselves with taking over ready-made thoughts and themes, developing them and filling them out. Even in that age the need for new creativity did not vanish, for every age is moved by the desire to render its contribution to the enhancement of public worship and to expand the traditional prayers in accordance with contemporary taste. But this need was no longer satisfied in the same way as before, and it found its outlet in a different direction. The age of free additions, of independent work on the liturgy, was past, and the existing foundation was considered binding and immutable. But even this age was not completely without its own creations, for in it we find much that is not yet mentioned in the Talmud. *Soferim*, which stands at the end of this period, cites or presupposes prayers not known to the amoraim. These prayers are mainly expansions or elaborations of previously existing ones, together with which they form the great corpus of the statutory prayers. Other creations of that period are the first beginnings of the supplementary prayers for festivals, and especially those of public fast days.

[According to the information available today, and in accordance with the different chronological picture that follows from them, the "end of the talmudic period" cannot be viewed as a period in which creativity in the area of prayer came to an end; on the contrary, important liturgical poets were active in Palestine in the fourth and fifth centuries, among whom, besides poets whose names are unknown to us, were Yose b. Yose and Yannai, who mark the high point of ancient religious poetry. These poets were not content to embellish the statutory prayers, but composed a multitude of poems intended to replace the routine text of the statutory prayers on festivals and even on Sabbaths. Since the piyyut was already very highly developed by the end of the amoraic period, a considerably earlier date may be assumed for the composition of several of the quasi-poetic prayers mentioned below, such as "Blessed God, great in knowledge," "You instituted the Sabbath," and so on, as well as the compositions mentioned below in §38(8); compare, further, below, pp. 220 and 238.]

[204]

(2) Typically for the age, the prayers were developed by the simplest possible means: by use of biblical material, by varying existing patterns, or by wordier development of existing prayers and themes. A very common method was the use of passages from the Bible;[4] whole chapters or individual verses from Scripture were added to the existing prayers. Thus, for example, arose the great collection of the Verses of Song for the daily Morning Service (§11). At first, psalms customarily recited by individual pietists were brought into the service, and then other passages were added, like the prayer of David (I Chron. 29:10ff.), the Song of the Sea, and so on, and to the poem's last verse, Ex. 15:18 a few other verses containing the word מלך, "King," were added.[5] This example also shows how easily such expansions could be made. Another example is "Praise the Lord, call upon His name" (I Chron. 16:8–35), an ancient levitical hymn to which a significant number of biblical passages has been appended; today these appear to be somewhat random, but doubtless they were originally arranged according to some plan or pattern. Before Ps. 145 stand two verses beginning with אשרי, "Happy," but originally there were many more. We have other such groups of biblical verses in the daily Supplication beginning ואנחנו לא נדע, "But we do not know," and in the same way the prayer "And a redeemer will come to Zion" was composed. A similar composition is "Blessed is the Lord forever," in the Evening Service; its composition is explicitly attributed by the sources to the "rabbis after the age of instruction"—that is, the generation with which we are dealing. Here the tetragrammaton is the unifying principle, as it is in "May the glory" in the Morning Service. On the Sabbaths we find "And the Israelites shall keep" before the ʿAmida, and other biblical verses within it. Palestine had collections of biblical verses from all three sections of the Bible in the festival ʿAmida, similar to those that had been customary in the ancient period on the New Year. Common to all these biblical lectionaries is that the verses are compiled loosely one after the other, without any thematic connection or transition, the connection being made mostly by external features like common words. Sometimes verse groups were instituted in fulfillment of instructions from an earlier period; thus "And the heavens and the earth were finished" is connected with an instruction in the Talmud. A somewhat more advanced stage is displayed by prayers like "And He, being merciful" (above, §10), which contains many passages taken from the Bible verbatim, alongside others that derive from the language and style of Scripture, but show a rather simple reworking of their themes.

(3) Another easy way to expand the existing material was to vary the prayers. An example is the middle benediction of the Sabbath ʿAmida. Unlike the festivals, which have a single version for all four services, here every service has its own version. To have four identical texts for the Sabbath, which recurs every single week, would have been too monotonous, but it was tolerable on the festivals, which occur far less frequently. The "Creator" was provided with insertions that embellished it; some of these relate to the events of the creation story and therefore change daily. For the Sabbath it was greatly changed and considerably expanded. For the beginning and end of the Sabbath some rites provided the appropriate benedictions with special additions relating to the special character of the day. A rich selection of opening formulas and transition formulas was given to the Kedushah; all are products of the post-talmudic period, before which no trace of them can be found. They all deal with the same subject in different words.

(4)   Sometimes prayers were worked out in accordance with talmudic dicta. The whole area of the Morning Benedictions arose out of B. *Ber.* 60b, in that the suggestions given there were formulated as benedictions. Benedictions were needed at the beginning and end of the recitation of the Verses of Song; these were created by developing the Talmud's few references to "The Benediction of the Song." The use of synonyms, already permitted by the Mishnah for similar prayers, was imitated here also (compare במקהלות, "Among the congregations" and "May Your name be praised," with M. *Pes.* 10:5). This also led to the enrichment of Kaddish and is especially noticeable in "May the name of the King be blessed," doubtless a late addition to "Bless the Lord," and in the hymn "For everything," which is similar to Kaddish and which is recited before the reading of the Torah. The prayers after the reading of the Torah— such as "May He Who blessed" for the congregation and those who contribute to its welfare, the prayer for the government, the petitions for persecuted Jews, the proclamations of the New Moon and of public fasts—were a working-out of older ideas. Such accretions could be easily attached to an institution like the reading of the Torah, which existed independently and had but a loose connection with the other elements of the liturgy. The prayers mentioned here certainly did not all arise simultaneously, and even more certainly were not accepted at once, but they must have spread very quickly, for they are common to all prayer books in all lands.

[206]

(5)   For the embellishment of the service certain artistic forms were employed that were easy to manage and therefore in wide use. A very simple and common system at that time was the use of alphabetical order for the words or sentences. This system could call upon biblical models in which the alphabet is used in various ways,[6] though always with whole sentences. The most famous example of a prayer arranged alphabetically is the confession "We have sinned," where the beginnings of the words follow the alphabet; in the other confession "For the sin," it is the characteristic words at the end of each line that are arranged alphabetically (. . . באונס, בבלי דעת, "Under compulsion, in ignorance . . ."). No less familiar is the passage in "Creator"—"Blessed God, great in knowledge"—which today seems like a fixed part of the prayer, but which originally stood independently as an addition intended to embellish the text. It was one composition among many serving the same purpose, which had the good fortune to be accepted in the prayer books while the others vanished or are only now turning up in manuscripts after a millennium of oblivion. The alphabet—and this was no innovation—did not always have to be complete, but could be interrupted and taken up again at the poet's whim. For this too we have an example in "Creator" in the words כולם אהובים ברורים . . ., גבורים . . . עושים . . פותחים, "All are beloved . . ." Another innovation was that the alphabet could be used in reverse order, as we have it, for example, in the insertion for the Additional Service of the Sabbath, תקנת שבת רצית קרבנותיה, "You instituted the Sabbath." The combination of the two alphabetical systems is displayed in the additions to the benedictions of the *Shemaʿ* at the beginning and the end of the Sabbath. Likewise, in the Morning Service of the Sabbath,[7] the manuscripts give the benedictions in an alphabetical version not known from any other source. Once the acrostics were in existence they could then be reworked, with the alphabetical words expanded into alphabetical sentences. Thus the poem "God the Lord" is simply an alphabetical expansion of "Blessed God, great in knowledge" just mentioned.

(6) Another way to rework the texts was to develop individual sentences further in the style of the Targum or the midrash.[8] Thus in "Creator" of the Sabbath, the four clauses of the sentence אין כערכך ואין זולתך, אפס בלתך ומי דומה לך, "There is none to compare to You," are each followed by a commentary in midrashic style. A similar procedure was followed in the description of the Sabbath rest in the Afternoon Service of the Sabbath (מנוחת אהבה ונדבה, מנוחת אמת ואמונה, "Rest of love and free will, rest of truth and faithfulness.") Or rhyme was used to join sentences with similar sounds, as is found again in "Creator": רחם עלינו אדון עוזנו צור משגבנו מגן ישענו משגב בעדנו, "Have mercy upon us, Lord of our strength," and so forth). But the devices described here do not entail any real expansion of the thought-content of the revised prayers.

[207]

Sometimes the last word of a passage was taken as the starting point of a new piece, which began with a variation on this word. Thus, after יוצר אור . . . עושה שלום ובורא את הכל, "Creator of light . . . Who makes peace and creates all," there comes on the Sabbath הכל יודוך והכל ישבחוך והכל יאמרו, "All will acknowledge You. . . ." Similarly, "God the patient" ends with the same word, אל, "God," with which it began. These are the first signs of rhythm that began to spring up in this period; but their influence is felt more in the additions for special occasions than in the statutory prayers.

(7) Hand in hand with the expansion of the statutory prayers came the development of the synagogue service for special days; particular attention was paid to the ritual for days of *seliḥot* and fasts. The *seliḥa*-prayers, which are peculiar to fast days, consisted of groups of biblical verses or psalms that, as noted above in connection with some of the statutory prayers, stood together but had only the loosest connection with one another; the introductions were in the simplest form, using biblical vocabulary. The introduction to the Thirteen Attributes, "God, the King Who sits," "God, You instructed us," also preserves this style. But the main material composed at that time for fast days was the litanies—prayers in short sentences of uniform pattern, intended for recitation alternating between precentor and congregation.[9] Because of their structure they may be compared to the collections of biblical verses mentioned above. Some are made in the order of the alphabet, others are built around individuals and historical events. The method was not entirely new, for an example of this type of litany is already found in the liturgy for fast days in the Mishnah—"May He Who answered" (M. *Ta.* 2)—and one of the most familiar, "Our Father, our King," goes back to R. Akiva. They grew considerably in the liturgy, with a few individual lines expanding into extensive prayers; it was no harder to expand them than to invent new, similar ones. In this way the tremendous number of litanies found in our prayer books came into being. Their variety is even more striking if we take into consideration the rarer rites and the liturgies in manuscript. Much of the litany material passed over into the Supplications. Many were composed in Aramaic, the language of the Babylonian Jews. The Aramaic litanies have just about disappeared from the Ashkenazic liturgy, but their existence is well attested elsewhere. Zunz, *Literaturgeschichte*, 17f., cited a considerable number of such compositions and attributed them to the period with which we are dealing.

(8) To the other fast days belong also passages that, with all of their simplicity of structure and content, display the beginnings of artistic form. They have neither rhyme nor meter, but they do have a certain rhythm, being divided into little clauses

with about the same number of syllables in each; for the most part their sentences are alphabetical, but this condition is not absolute.[10] Examples are אנשי אמנה אבדו, באים בכח מעשיהם, גבורים לעמוד בפרץ, דוחׅ֯ם את הגזירות, "Trustworthy men have perished,/ who could come forward by force of their deeds;/ mighty ones to stand in defense,/ warding off calamities") or תמהנו מרעות, תשש כוחנו מצרות, שחנו עד למאד, שפלנו עד עפר, "We are horrified at the evils;/ our strength is gone because of troubles;/ we are very humbled;/ we are low down to the dust"; or אל תעש עמנו כלה, תאחוז ידך במשפט, בבוא תוכחה נגדך, שמנו מספרך אל תמח, "Do not destroy us;/ may Your hand seize justice;/ when [our] reproach comes before You,/ do not wipe our name from Your book."[11] These passages recall the poems of the Syriac church and are built in the same pattern. Powerful reciprocal influences must have been operating at that time between Judaism and the church, though we are not able to identify here who influenced whom.[12]

(9) The additions for festivals are somewhat more involved in form and more complex in their structure than the additions for fast days. Even in early times the service of the Day of Atonement was very long: "The service of the Day of Atonement is long" (B. *Meg.* 23a). Its hallmark is the confession, for which the Talmud, as noted above, did not fix any special wording, and which only later acquired the familiar alphabetical text found in the prayer books. To this was added at an early time the custom of recalling in the service the sacrifices offered on that day by the high priest in the Temple, by inserting the ʿAvoda in the ʿAmida.[13] The oldest preserved ʿAvoda is extremely simple in its style. It follows the description of the Mishnah, mostly using its very language; in all probability it dates from the talmudic period. But the very next ʿAvoda, "You established,"[14] in Sepharad, is of a completely different type. The close connection with the Mishnah has been broken, and even though the subject was prescribed and the traditional order obligatory, nevertheless the description was as freely handled as permitted by the given framework; the language is absolutely independent and the acrostic is used as an artistic device. A new element in "You established" is the introduction, which sketches in broad strokes the history of the world down to the rise of the priesthood. From the moment when it was introduced, this theme became the one controlled by the poets, and a model for all successors. The introduction was the part in which the poet could freely display his skill; accordingly, the later poets devoted more space and attention to it than they did to the body of the ʿAvoda. Here, at its first occurrence, it is thoroughly and skillfully developed, but it is not artificial. The description of the sacrificial service is followed by a series of passages that are also new, and that recur thereafter in all rites, either in the same form or in forms that developed out of it. In them, the prayer of the high priest in the Holy of Holies is spun out alphabetically and, based on a passage in Ben Sira, the glorious radiance of the high priest and the splendor of the rite he performs are exuberantly described. The olden times and their splendor are praised beyond all bounds; their disappearance because of the people's sins and their replacement by the misery of exile are lamented with words of woe. The stylistic devices used to express these ideas are the same as those used in the prayers described above: simple or double acrostics, and a rhythm of stichs, the same simple elements with which we are familiar from the development of the liturgy of fast days and *seliḥot*.

{208}

(10)   The *azharot* of Pentecost were also simply embellished. In their most ancient form they were dry lists of positive and negative commandments without any connecting links, but they were soon developed so as to include comprehensive surveys, division into classifications, and evaluations of each separate class, with rhythmical poems to conclude the whole.

(11)   To the same category and the same period belong the earliest *hoshaʿnot* for Tabernacles. They are all simple litanies, adorned only by acrostic.[15] The introductions for the precentor, like אוחילה לאל, "I hope in God," and היה עם פיפיות, "Be with the mouths," also testify to the nonartificial form characteristic of the period, as do the simple language derived from the Bible, the simple structure of the ideas, and the short rhythm based solely on stress. The precentors apparently also composed the formulas of address that precede certain prayers, short sentences with simple ideas that later served as models for many similar sentences, and above all as starting points for long and complex piyyutim (ובכן נמליכך מלך, ובכן לך תעלה קדושה, "And so may the Kedushah ascend to You," "And so we enthrone You as King").[16]

[209]   (12)   Most of the expansions of the basic prayers with which we deal here are common to all the rites, and accordingly they arose in a period when an equal degree of influence on all Jewish communities was still possible. They also had in common simplicity of form and language. No rhyme, difficult neologisms, or obscure allusions to midrashic exegesis are to be found in them.[17] Many texts of this ancient period underwent further development or expansion;[18] a comparison with the later forms brings out the characteristic qualities of the original versions—and their preferability. These prayers also are merely appended to the existing prayers, without breaking their traditional order. Finally, all of them are anonymous; the authors did not indicate their names, nor did tradition preserve their identities.[19] The homeland of the earliest additions to the basic prayers was overwhelmingly Palestine or its neighbor Syria. Only there was the Hebrew language sufficiently cultivated that it could be managed with stylistic correctness, and only there could it be made to speak so expressively. The Babylonian compositions that we have were composed in Aramaic and follow completely different trains of thought. It is true that tradition attributes the ancient *azharot* to the Babylonian academies, and in fact their contents are limited to such dry lists that objection to this tradition is unnecessary; but one factor speaks against it, namely, the fact that the Babylonian attitude to such additions was not particularly friendly. In Babylonia, the tendency was to bring the entire field of liturgy into fixed and immutable forms. In Palestine, the opposite approach prevailed; there, variety in the service was sought and the desire was to have as many prayers as possible so that the same ones did not always have to be used. They also had self-confidence that they could enrich the liturgy; and Palestine still had sufficient authority, particularly in questions of this type, to impose its will even in the face of Babylonian opposition.

The Period of the Piyyut

§ 39   Piyyut

(1)   By ca. 550 the statutory prayers may be seen as completed and their first expansions as already existing and well known. No new prayers would come into being that would be universally disseminated and considered obligatory among all Jews. But the liturgy was not frozen, nor was the stock of prayers fixed once and for all so that it was no longer subject to change. All the events that had a decisive effect on Jewish life and opinion left a noticeable mark on the synagogue service as well. But from this point on, the enrichment of the liturgy took the form of the addition to the statutory prayers of artistic poems, hymns, elegies, or petitions. They remained independent of the prayers, following their own train of thought, attached to the statutory prayers by completely formal means and not merging with them. The piyyut opens a new period in the development of the liturgy. For more than a thousand years the prevailing opinion was that this embellishment of the service was pleasurable. Its activity was not the same in all periods; but, however varied were the ways in which this spirit found expression, the constant was that the statutory prayers were untouchable, and that the liturgy could be embellished by means of external additions that evolved in various styles in accordance with the changing places and times.

Two new phenomena in the history of Judaism are connected with the closing of the Talmud: The teachings that until then had been transmitted orally were now set down in writing, and the formerly unitary tradition was split into many branches. Both innovations had their effect on the liturgy. Written prayer books came into being, a rich literature, till then unknown, which was to be of great consequence for future development. And as a literature arose *for* public worship, so a literature arose *about* worship. In the various countries, different customs sprang up, and the liturgy was affected by the process of defining, comparing, and discussing those customs. On the one hand, the external order of the synagogue worship was discussed; on the other, the inner content and the religious value of the liturgy was emphasized. Mysticism, too, came to claim a place in the service; at first it intended merely to influence the liturgy through the cultivation of pious devotion, but later it contributed to the traditional service its

[211]

219

own additions, which have some similarity to the piyyut. In the course of this long period the piyyut remained the outstanding element that stamps the liturgy.

[From Elbogen's exposition it might appear that the first blossoming of the piyyut occurred in about the sixth century, but in the light of recent scholarship we have to push this date back at least three centuries. Likewise we can no longer distinguish between a period of the statutory prayers and a period of piyyut that followed it. The truth of the matter is that the wellspring of Hebrew poetry was never stopped, even at the close of the biblical period—that is, about the second century B.C.E. Just when the statutory prayers were being edited and fixed, poems of a different type were being composed in Palestine, as a continuation of the biblical tradition, and as a transition stage to the art of the piyyut. In fact, it is possible to find some traces of piyyut style in the statutory prayers themselves. Furthermore some of these latter are formally indistinguishable from the ancient piyyutim. In the course of time a peculiarly rich and elaborate style developed within the framework of the piyyut, as well as complex forms of rhyme, alliteration, acrostic, and so forth; but all of these belong to a later period in the development of the genre. Literary scholars can, of course, not overlook the early stages, and these have not yet been sufficiently researched. The following are the texts that are currently available:

a. Poetic compositions that have come down to us from the Apocrypha (in the original Hebrew or in Greek translation) and vestiges of poems and prayers that have come down to us from rabbinic literature (Mishnah, Talmud, midrashim). The close conection that doubtless exists between the midrashic literature and the early piyyut is of particular importance. According to Zunz and the scholars who followed him, the origin of piyyut belongs to the seventh and eighth centuries (the geonic period); therefore they asserted that the poets drew the material for their poems from the main midrashim, which had been edited as independent compositions by that time. This opinion may be correct with respect to Eleazar b. Kallir and the poets who followed him, but it is difficult to accept it in connection with his predecessors. Z. M. Rabinowitz has collected in a special study, *Midreshe halakha umidreshe agada befiyute yanai* (Jerusalem: The Hebrew University, 1961), a large number of quotations from talmudic and midrashic literature that, in his opinion, served the poet as direct sources. But the study of these quotations shows that they contain at most ideas that are similar to those of the poet but not identical in language; by the same token, verbal influence is evident whenever Yannai quotes from the Bible or the Mishnah. On the other hand, A. Mirsky has demonstrated in his study, *Maḥṣavtan shel ṣurot hapiyut* (Jerusalem: Schocken, 1968), that embedded among the ancient midrashim are what may be called primitive piyyutim, and to the extent that their authors' names can be established today, these authors are mostly amoraim of the third and the fourth centuries. Likewise, A. Mirsky has demonstrated that one of the characteristic features of the ancient piyyut is the use of the "exegetical principles" in the manner of the rabbis. Thus, there is a reciprocal relationship between midrash and piyyut in its origins; these were two parallel forms in which similar ideas and themes found different means of literary expression. When we deal with the poets who preceded Kallir, it becomes difficult to decide whether the formulation as midrash was prior to the formulation as piyyut or the reverse.

b. The ancient Jewish mystical literature commonly known as *hekhalot* literature preserves a large number of ecstatic hymns. Though the differences between them and the piyyutim are not negligible, there is room for a detailed comparative study between them and the other ancient texts, especially since G. Scholem believes that it is possible to attribute the hymns in the *hekhalot* literature to the third or fourth century C.E. See G. Scholem, *Jewish Gnosticism, Merkabah Mysticism, and Talmudic Tradition* (New York: The Jewish Theological Seminary of America, 1960), 196 and compare also A. Altmann, "Shire qedusha besifrut hahekhalot haqeduma," *Melila* 2 (1945/6): 1–24.

[212]

c.　We have a few copies of piyyutim whose antiquity cannot be doubted. Two were apparently copied no later than the third century; and though these vestiges are rather limited in extent, they do testify to the antiquity of the poetic craft. See J. Schirmann, *JQR* NS 44 (1953): 132–33, and compare also M. Bet Arye, "Palimpsest München: Seride megila milifne hame'a hasheminit," *Qiryat Sefer* 43 (1967/8): 411–28.

d.　Important material for comparison is contained also in non-Jewish sacred poetry composed in Palestine and Syria in the first centuries of the Christian era. It is difficult for us today to explain how they came into being unless we assume that they were influenced by Jewish models—that is, piyyutim no later than the fourth century, for in this century lived St. Ephrem the Christian, author of a great number of poems in Syriac, and Marqa, the most productive of the Samaritan poets. See J. Schirmann, *JQR* NS 44 (1953): 144, 146–55. The poems of Marqa appeared recently, together with a Hebrew translation, in Z. Ben-Hayyim, *'Ivrit va'aramit nusaḥ shomron*, vol. 3 (Jerusalem, 1967).

e.　The discovery of the scrolls from the Judean desert has likewise expanded the horizons of piyyut scholars. It is true that the original compositions contained in these scrolls are the work of an isolated sect and did not become part of the common literature of the Jewish people. Nevertheless, they contain most interesting material for comparative study in the field of prayer and poetry. The largest collection of sacred poems has been preserved in the sect's Thanksgiving Scroll, which has appeared in several editions (among others, that of J. Licht [Jerusalem, 1956/7]); to this group should be added a long list of other poetic compositions of various types. The scrolls have not been completely published and therefore it is too early to summarize the results of scholarship on them. Of the texts that have been preserved in the kingdom of Jordan, five volumes have so far (1968) been published, under the general name *Discoveries in the Judean Desert of Jordan* (Oxford).]

(2)　The first attempt to embellish the liturgy of festivals and fast days, which was discussed above, already involved additions of the type that may be called piyyut: The alphabetical acrostic found in a large part of them is considered one of the hallmarks of the liturgical poets.[1] Nevertheless these compositions were of a very different type from piyyut in the narrow sense of the term. First, they always remained separate from the statutory prayers, never penetrating them as did the piyyut, which interrupted the traditional sequence of the service. Second, they are distinguished from the piyyut— and this must be stressed as strongly as possible—in the simplicity of their form, the modesty of their language, and the intelligibility and clarity of their expresssion. But the piyyut is artistic poetry in every way, distinguished by its strophic structure, its use of rhyme, its artificial language, its close connection to the midrash, and the learned form of expression that follows from all the above. A tremendous difference exists between the primitive additions of the fifth and sixth centuries and the developed piy-yut of the Kallirian type. There must have been a transition period when the tradition was formed as to which places in the structure of the service could appropriately be expanded by poetry, a period when the stylistic form of the piyyut became progressively more crystallized and when everything that later appears before us as something com-plete and universally accepted was prepared and cultivated. The compositions of this transition period have been displaced by better poems that came later, so that the thought patterns of that period and even the names of its leading men have been com-pletely forgotten except for a few faint traces. But there can be no doubt that these efforts occasioned great ferment, great conflict of opinions, and perhaps bitter disputes. The piyyut did not receive a positive response everywhere from the first moment. It was oppression that tipped the scales in favor of its dissemination and its favorable accep-tance. For religious persecution put a sudden end to the sermons that had long been customary in the synagogue, making a new form of religious instruction a necessity.[2]

[213]

(3) R. Judah b. Barzilai of Barcelona, in his *Sefer ha'itim*,[3] reports on the basis of earlier authorities—רבוותא, "the masters"—that the piyyut was "only introduced at a time of persecution because they were not able to speak of the words of the Torah, for the enemy decreed that Israel might not study the Torah. Therefore the sages among them introduced as part of the prayer service the practice of reciting and teaching to the ignorant the laws of each festival in its time and the laws of the holy days and the Sabbaths and the details of the commandments in the form of songs of praise and thanksgiving and rhymes and piyyut." This is all said in passing; the chapter of his book (*Hilkhot berakhot*) in which he probably dealt fully with this matter has not been pre-served. It is not easy to decide to what persecution he is referring. One thinks first of Justinian's novella of 553 that, in arranging for the settling of syngagogue disputes (see above, §28[5]), completely prohibits the use of "the so-called Deuterosis,[4] as an inven-tion of human beings, and derived from outside the Bible; unwritten, heretical non-sense." The church fathers, too, make use of the word δευτέρωσις as a term for the oral law, especially the Mishnah. Here, where the word is used in connection with the Torah reading, it can only refer to the targumic paraphrases, or, since it is very doubtful that besides the Greek translation that caused the dispute an Aramaic translation was also read, to sermons of halakhic and aggadic content. And according to the report of R. Judah b. Barzilai, it was these sermons that were prohibited and replaced by the piyyu-tim. We would thus be dealing with a report that seeks to explain the elimination of the sermon in Palestine, then part of the Byzantine empire.

But reasonable as this assumption is, it must not be overlooked that Barceloni's source[5] was probably a Babylonian one, and would have had in view religious restric-tions on the Jews of Babylonia. Such limitations are discussed explicitly by another wit-ness; he, too, touches on the matter only in passing and must therefore be taken seriously in this case, though he is not always reliable in other matters. Samuel b. Judah Ibn Abun of Fez,[6] who converted to Islam in the twelfth century and became known as a writer under the name Samau'al Ibn Yahyā al-Maghribī, wrote an extensive critique called *Ifhām al-Yahūd* (*The Silencing of the Jews*), the subject of which is the thorough refutation of the Jewish religion. In the course of the discussion he refers to the fate of the Jews and the many severe persecutions that they underwent, commenting as follows:

> Islam found the Jews under the rule of the Persians . . . ; the latter frequently prohibited them from holding their prayer services . . . When the Jews saw that the Persians persisted in obstructing their prayer, they invented invocations into which they admixed passages from their prayers, and they called these *ḥizāna*. They set numerous tunes to them. They would assemble at prayer time in order to read and chant the *ḥizāna*. The difference between the *ḥizāna* and prayer (*ṣalāt*) is that the prayer is without melody and is read only by the person conducting the service; no other person recites along with him. The *ḥazan*, however, is assisted by the public in reciting the *ḥizāna* and in chanting melodies. When the Persians rebuked them for this, the Jews sometimes asserted that they were singing, and sometimes that they were bewailing their lot. Strangely enough, by the time the dominion of Islam arose and granted recognition to the various denominations of "protected peoples" and prayer became permissible unto the Jews, the *ḥizāna* had become a commendable tradition among them for holidays, festivities, and joyful occasions. Although no longer compelled to do so, the Jews were content to substitute *ḥizāna* for prayer.

[214]

This interesting report is not free of contradiction and unclarity; it deals mainly with the manner of the performance of the *ḥizāna* and its relationship to the statutory prayers. But one may correctly infer from it that Samau'al also knew that the custom of *ḥizāna* originated in a period of restrictions on the synagogue service, and he reproaches the Jews for retaining it even after tranquility was restored. According to him, it was the Persians who instituted the persecutions. This fits very well with the reports of Jewish sources about the period between 450 and 589.[7] Especially when he says (immediately before the passage on liturgy) that "The (Jewish) teachers were murdered, their books were burned, and they were prevented from fulfilling their religious laws," we think of the unfortunate events that, according to the Epistle of R. Sherira Gaon,[8] rendered impossible the dissemination of the Torah at the end of the amoraic and during the saboraic period, led to the closing of the houses of study, and brought exile or death to many of the leading sages. During those miserable times, which lasted, with brief interruptions, for about a century, the *ḥizāna* took root, according to Samau'al. The reason would very likely be the one cited by R. Judah b. Barzilai—the elimination of the sermons and their replacement with religious songs of edifying or didactic content; for it is hard to accept the idea that liturgical assemblies were prohibited, yet were permitted when held for the purpose of singing such songs instead of reciting the statutory prayers. Thus the persecution that occasioned the introduction of the piyyut was not that of Justinian, but rather the great persecutions of the Jews in Mesopotamia that occurred with the decline of the Sassanid empire.

[Already at the end of the eighth century, Pirqoi b. Baboi, the disciple of R. Yehudai Gaon, informs us that the rulers of Palestine decreed that the Jews could not recite the *Shemaʿ* or the *ʿAmida*; in place of these prohibited prayers the Jews began reciting *maʿamadot*, which probably refers to piyyut (Ginzberg, *Ginze*, 2:551.) Ben Baboi notes explicitly that this decree was imposed upon the Jews by the Byzantine Empire, before the Arabs came to Palestine. There are scholars who connect this persecution, because of its content, to Justinian's decree of 553, according to which the Jews were prohibited from reading the δευτέρωσις (the meaning of the term is uncertain) in their synagogues. Even if we assume that this is a reliable historical fact, we cannot deduce anything from it about the history of piyyut. The meaning is not that as a result of the persecution the Jews began to compose piyyutim and that in this way a new literary genre was created, but that instead of the prohibited prayers (and according to another source, instead of the sermons), poems containing, among other things, the prohibited subjects were inserted without the gentiles' knowledge. The art of the piyyut could, of course, have developed during the previous centuries without any connection to persecutions. See R. Edelmann, "Bestimmung, Heimat und Alter der synagogalen Poesie," *Oriens Christianus* 7, 3 (1932) and the bibliography listed in *JQR* NS 44 (1953): 141 n. 37.]

[215]

On the relationship between the word *ḥizāna* and the sermon we are also informed by the Arabic writer al-Qalqashandi[9] at the end of the fourteenth century, who in describing the Jewish community of Cairo includes in the second place among its officials the *ḥazzan*—the word is given in its exact spelling—who is "an excellent preacher (*khaṭīb*) and who reproaches the people from his pulpit (*minbar*)." Likewise, another document from Fustat[10] distinguishes between *ḥazzan* and *shaliaḥ*, according higher status to the former. On the other hand, in Jewish circles the word *ḥizāna* is used in the sense normally borne by piyyut. In particular, the poems of Yannai, one of the first of the payyetanim, are called by this term. Qirqisani repeatedly mentions *ḥizānat yanai*[11] as one of the sources of Anan, the founder of the Karaite sect. Also in the medieval book lists that have lately been published, this term occurs often in connection with the prayers of nearly all the festivals.

(4)   The piyyut did not come into being merely as a result of the above-mentioned persecutions, nor was Babylonia its homeland; it was never accepted there as a native product and a full-fledged component of the liturgy equal in status to the statutory prayers. The land of its origin was Palestine, and it arose out of a need to disseminate in a new form the religious outlook engendered by the aggadah, to adorn and enhance the festival prayers with the splendor of religious thought. "The festival poetry was the surrogate for the institution of public instruction, and little by little it came virtually to embody the standing character of the festival, its meaning and interpretation, the voice of the people's history and its spirit clothed in words" (Sachs, *Poesie*, 180). External pressure to suppress the public sermon contributed greatly to the dissemination of the piyyutim and opened the gates to them even in Babylonia, thus guaranteeing the sanction of the most recognized authorities.

The favorable climate for liturgical poetry, originally a consequence of the wretched conditions of the times, was strengthened immeasurably through contact with the culture and poetry of the Arabs (after 635). From the Arabs came the new artistic structures that lent liturgical poetry its beauty and vitality. From the Arabs the Hebrew poets learned about rhyme and later also meter; from them they acquired the custom of the acrostic;[12] and their manner of inserting quotations from the ancients inspired the Hebrew poets to develop the mosaic style. Synagogue poetry had existed before the Jews became acquainted with the works of the Arabs, but it was developed and refined, disseminated and enthusiastically adopted only thanks to the great interest aroused by Arabic poetry; without this, poetry would never have enjoyed the recognition of the authoritative circles or found the variety of its artistic forms. The domination of the piyyut may be dated from the time of the conquest of Palestine and Babylonia by Islam. By the time a century had passed (that is, before 750),[13] it controlled the main parts of the service; the places where it was inserted were fixed; and the pattern according to which it was divided among the various sections of the service was already generally accepted. There must necessarily have been a lengthy period of preparation and development prior to the establishment of the final form.

[216]

[Rhyme in Hebrew poetry is considerably older than Arabic rhyme of the *jāhilīya* period (the period before Muhammad). See *JQR* NS 44 (1953): 136–38. Arabic influence on the early Hebrew piyyut—that is, before 635—is absolutely ruled out. The ancient Arabic poets never used acrostics; for this "embellishment" see *JQR* NS 44 (1953): 145, 153, 159. On the other hand, Hebrew poets used quotations based on biblical verses long before the Arabs inserted Koran verses into their poetry.]

(5)   The most important step in this development was the penetration of the poetry into the *'Amida*, the innovation that poetry was no longer recited as something attached to the traditional prayer but *as an interruption within the prescribed rite*— "Included in the prayer" (*'Itim*). The piyyut thus had achieved full rights, and no further impediment stood in the way of its spread.[14] Initially, it entered only the first benedictions of the *'Amida* as *qerova*, but it soon conquered the entire *'Amida* for itself. From there it proceeded to "Creator"; here too it first took possession only of the main positions, but gradually it won new positions among the various prayers. Nor did the spread of liturgical poetry end with "Creator," for ultimately even the passages that begin and end the Verses of Song were provided with piyyutim. Like the Morning Service, so the Additional and Evening services and, to a lesser extent, the Afternoon Service,[15] came under the sway of the piyyut. Alongside the prayers, the Torah reading and Haftara afforded the poets[16] places to attach poems, and even the biblical passages and litanies in the *seliḥot* were interrupted by poetic pieces. In short, the poets did not leave poetry out of any place in the service, any ceremony, or any other occasion that offered the possibility for adding it. And opportunities continued to increase. Originally, the piyyut was intended for festivals and special Sabbaths, but it also took control of the minor festivals and the fast days; and just as collections of midrash existed for the entire year, so poetry was composed for every Sabbath in connection with the pericopes of the triennial cycle. It is not even ruled out that poems based on the Sabbath pericope were composed for weekdays. But poetry did not limit itself to the needs and experiences of the community; the events of the life of the individual also became its subject—births, marriages, and the deaths of members of the community all made their contribution to the development of the liturgy. This does not mean that in every community at every time all the genres of piyyut were equally developed or recognized, for in this matter there was great local variation. Not all the communities were equally devoted to piyyut. Those who appreciated it were often surprised by a poet, not knowing in advance whether or at what point in the service they would hear poetry. This was the advantage of the piyyut over the statutory prayers: Neither the wording nor the number nor the order of the poems was subject to any regulation or limitation.[17] Except for the rule that it had to be appropriate for the contents of the prayer to which it was attached, it could be recited, eliminated, or exchanged for other compositions, all in accordance with the taste of the community and its mood at the time. The poetry's

[217]

main power resided in its flexibility; one of the chief reasons for its popularity was that it could be continually renewed. The community never tired of it because it could always eliminate works it did not like and replace them with new and better ones; or, whenever the taste of the community changed, it could replace poems whose time had passed with poems more in accord with the taste of the times. The piyyut lent the entire service great flexibility, introducing a desirable interruption in the constantly recurring, never-changing statutory prayers. Its first great successes came largely from the desire for change, though it must also be admitted that its content and artistic form suited the needs of the times. Poetry became an important factor in the liturgy, blazing its path and asserting itself in the face of mighty opposition from many quarters. Production grew continually, and the number of poems increased immeasurably. Printed prayer books afford only an inadequate impression of the rich stores of poetry formerly available to the synagogue and of their importance in religious life. In the prayer books, the piyyut appears as a fixed and immutable element in the order of the service, available to every individual, and capable of being read by the entire congregation. This is deceptive because originally it belonged solely to the composer, who recited it and used it as he wished. But above all, it must be remembered that only the smallest part of the great stock of the manuscript collections could be incorporated into the printed editions. Zunz, in his *Literaturgeschichte der synagogalen Poesie*,[18] deals with more than four hundred poets, mentioning 1,816 *selihot*, 40 *qedushot* for the Additional Service, 57 *Ma'arivot*, 70 piyyutim for "The breath," 70 metrical *baqashot*, 100 *qerovot*, 120 *reshuyot*, 120 *tokhehot*, 150 *mustajāb*, 150 compositions in Aramaic, 180 Supplications, 200 *hosha'not*, about 600 poems and piyyutim in the narrower sense, 600 *qinot*, 600 *yoserot*, and fragments of *yoserot* (*ofanim*, and so on). In the half-century since then the number has increased greatly, and unknown poems salvaged from the Cairo geniza alone are now counted in the thousands.[19]

(6) The piyyut is not a uniform construct; from its beginnings in the sixth or seventh century down to this day—for in some Oriental countries the age of the piyyut is not over—it has undergone many changes. Its forms and content, language and style of expression all changed with the lands and times in which it arose; it kept step with the general culture of the Jews, having the same high points and low points. With changes of taste and intellectual tendencies, the use of piyyut changed, as did its appeal.

(7) The content of the poetry was determined by its function, for the poem's purpose was to make up for the sermon and to serve the community as a replacement for the instruction and edification that formerly was provided by the latter (§29). The poet came to replace the preacher, and like him, he had to deal with the total field of religious doctrine, institutions, and ceremonies, the ancestral history and hopes for redemption. One of the earliest tasks of exegesis was to explain the meaning of the festivals and their customs; this was taken over by the poets, who first devoted their efforts to explaining the ideas and symbols of the festivals. But they soon expanded the area of their activity. "The inexhaustible riches of the aggadah were poured into the religious poetry, which now wove into the framework of the liturgy the national literature, national history, the principles of the faith, and often even the details of religious law,

[218]

and which itself became the expression of all the activities and sufferings of Israel."[20] These sufferings formed a sorry chain that continued unbroken down to the time of the poet. The poets themselves had sipped its bitter goblet, had witnessed the pogroms and persecutions of their communities, had heard the wailing and cries of their relatives and friends as they were harried to death; the sighs that burst from their unhappy hearts became the entire community's lament. Humbly they turned their eyes toward the Director of men's fate with the passionate prayer that He speedily bring the time of redemption that He had so surely promised. In this age of constantly raging destruction, the *seliha*, which until now had mainly given expression to the general religious themes of exile and redemption, sin and atonement, man's weakness and God's mercy, acquired a personal and contemporary tone. It reflected the mood of the innocent victims of religious hatred, their unshakable loyalty to the faith of their fathers, and their indestructible confidence in the appearance of the messianic redemption.[21]

The style of the piyyut was also influenced strongly by the style of the aggadah. In the earliest period the exposition of the poets followed closely the model of the midrash, repeating its thoughts and often its very language. Where the curriculum of the Jews remained limited to the Talmud and midrash, Hebrew poetry continued to draw its material from these sources, but in places like Spain, scientific studies broadened their knowledge and intellectual horizons; where philosophy guided religious thought into a different direction, there poetry too acquired new forms. The new cultural elements enriched its material, and the new ways of thinking influenced its content.[22] Poetry was open to all influences; it reflects its authors' educational levels and the dominant tendencies of their periods, and was affected by philosophical and scientific, mystical and kabbalistic concepts. All these became amalgamated with the biblical and aggadic elements that it possessed as a result of its own tradition. The didactic content is both the strength and the weakness of the piyyut. It performed an extraordinarily valuable service as the medium for dissemination of religious ideas, edifying stories, and the consolatory promises of the aggadah among the widest possible circles of the community. How great was the religious feeling excited by the piyyut! What courage it offered the downcast! What consolation it instilled in the despairing! But the convenient accessibility of the material could easily become an inducement to facile rhyming, encouraging many who were not poets to try their hand at writing piyyutim. Fixed forms were established that were too easy to use; the same places in the service and the same occasions attracted the same ideas: Certain themes like the suffering of the Ten Martyrs,[23] the binding of Isaac, and the recitation of the Kedushah by the Hosts of Heaven[24] came to be constantly repeated and treated in routine clichés. It was intrinsically hard to invent original and telling ways of expressing all these things; only few succeeded, but many became longwinded and indulged in monotonous repetition. The poets of the Golden Age[25] did know how to free themselves completely from all external influences and to follow only the feelings of their hearts. But in the periods of decadence, the reliance on the old forms again preponderated, now, however, with the addition of the model of the classical poetry. Because of the ease with which it could be adopted, the piyyut became a source of instruction as well as the spokesman for faith [219] in God and His mercy, trust in the power of prayer, and confidence in the fulfillment of the promises for the end of time. From this point of view, it fulfilled its important mission and continues to do so wherever its content and manner of expression are still in harmony with the feelings of the faithful.

(8)   No less important than the content of the piyyut was its external form. It was an artistic poetry, and was therefore subject to the laws of taste of its time and place. These requirements changed, and the poetry continually changed forms in conformity with them, becoming ever more varied and complex. It advanced with all the new developments and appeared in the most varied forms. At first the only thing uniting the lines was the alphabetical acrostic, but later this was joined by rhyme. Changing rhymes lead to division into strophes, and where a single rhyme runs through the entire poem, refrains or biblical quotations frequently take over the function of dividing it into strophes. The alphabetical acrostics alternate with others indicating personal names or biblical verses; these may occur together with or in exchange for the alphabet. The structure of the lines was at first determined by a particular rhythm, but eventually this was replaced by meters of a highly crafted type. Each of the forms listed here becomes, with time, more and more artistic, even artificial.

(9)   We first treat the acrostic (סימן, later חתימה).[26]

a.   **Alphabetical.** Various forms of alphabetical word- or sentence-order are found from the very beginnings of sacred poetry. The piyyut was able to make use only of alphabetical lines,[27] and this it does in a great many ways. Like the psalms, the piyyut may have a different number of lines beginning with the same letter of the alphabet, so that there may be strophes of one line, two lines, three, four, up to ten and even eighteen and twenty-four lines. Even within a single poem not all the strophes are of the same length, and the individual lines occur in greatly varying combinations. The poet does not limit himself to simple alphabetical acrostics, but he may equally well use reverse alphabetical acrostic (תשר"ק), and also, though not so frequently, other arrangements of letters known from the Talmud such as אח"ס בט"ע, אלב"ם, אתב"ש, and even אי"ק בכ"ר.[28] In one poem several different acrostics may occur together.

The acrostic may also consist of:

b.   **Biblical verses.** The poets from the time of Kallir on frequently use biblical verses as acrostics.[29] Thus, on Passover, the *yoṣer* uses the beginnings of the verses of the Song of Songs; on Pentecost, the beginnings of the verses of the Ten Commandments are used, and on The Eighth Day of Assembly, the beginnings of the blessing of Moses and the story of his death are used. These are used as the beginnings of the lines, as the beginnings of stanzas, or even in the middle of the stanzas. The biblical verses may be combined with alphabetical acrostics, with the alphabetically ordered words occurring after the words from the verse. Like the letters of the alphabet, biblical verses may be used in the most varied combinations. One of the most artificial combinations, fortunately an uncommon one, is the *qerova* for the Ninth of Av by Kallir in Rome.[30] The first line of each stanza begins with the first word of the successive verses of Lamentations, chapter 5, which does not have the alphabetical acrostic, and with the first word of a verse from chapter 4; the three following lines begin with the opening word of the verses of chapter 3 in reverse order (3, 2, 1, 6, 5, 4), and the fifth and sixth lines begin with the opening word of a verse from chapters 2 and 1. The sixth line ends with the last two words of the verses of chapter 5 with which the stanza began. But even this does not exhaust the complexity of this piyyut, which is considerably increased by the rhyme.

Much more common and more important for the student of the history of literature are:

c. **Name acrostics.**[31] There is biblical precedent for the poet indicating his name on his composition, but the acrostic form in which this was done is borrowed from the Arabs, and in any case is not attested before the period of Arabic influence. The name may appear toward the end of the poem, after all the letters of the alphabetical acrostic, or the name acrostic may occupy all the line or stanza beginnings. Sometimes the poets sign only their own name, but usually they add the name of their father, in the early period often using the Palestinian form בירבי, "son of." Since the tenth century one finds also cognomens and family names such as טוב עלם, "Bonfils," האָרוך, "Del Lungo," דג קטן, "Fischlin." The homeland of the poet or of his family may be given, as in ירחי, "of Lunel"; האזובי, "of Orange"; or גראנטי, "of Granada"; and so forth. From the middle of the twelfth century on, we find honorific titles or professional designations such as רופא, "doctor"; פרנס, "Parnas"; חזן, "Cantor"; חבר, "Rabbi." The Spanish poets preface their name with the word אני, "I," and add after it הקטן, "the little," or toward the end of the eleventh century, הצעיר, "the little"; others, especially in periods of persecution, write in this position העלוב, "the wretched," or הנדכה, "the oppressed." Sometimes formulas of blessing are added to the names. At first these were simple and short, like חזק, "Be strong"; יחיה, "May he live"; יגדל, "May he be great"; but they became longer and longer until we find formulas like יגדל בתורה ובמעשים טובים אמן חזק ואמץ, "May he grow in Torah and good deeds, amen, be strong, and valiant"; יגדל ויחי לנצח חיי עד סלה אמן נצח; "May he grow and live forever for eternal life, forever, amen, and ever." To this were added other types of blessing formulas or biblical verses containing prayers such as Neh. 13:22. There are also additions that relate to the contents of the poem, like a famous poem by Judah Halevi for the Day of Atonement in which the acrostic reads יהודה הלוי בר שמואל המודה לאדוניו המתודה על עווניו ביום הכפורים, "Judah Halevi, the son of Samuel, who confesses to his Lord and acknowedges his sin on the Day of Atonement."[32] Nor were the poets satisfied with signing their own names and the names of their fathers, but sometimes they added the name of a brother or of a son together with long blessing formulas.[33] R. Simon b. Isaac signed his *yoṣer* for the second day of the New Year, אלחנן בני יפול חבלו לחיי עולם, "Elhanan my son, may his portion fall in eternal life." Solomon the Babylonian, in the *yoṣer* for the second day of Passover, signed מרדכי הקטן יגדל בתורה כהוגן וכשורה, "Mordecai the little, may he grow in Torah as he should and ought." Some also gave their complete pedigrees; R. Yeḥiel b. Joseph (ca. 1340) counts so many ancestors that the acrostic requires no fewer than 114 letters.[34] Names and epithets of God may also be found as acrostics, as can by-names of the festival for which the poem was intended, or passages from the prayers peculiar to them. In short, the greatest variety, even an excess of poetic devices, is intended to embellish the poetry.

(10) Corresponding to the acrostics at the beginning of the line is the rhyme at its end. Some have sought the source for this in the Bible, but wherever similarity of sound occurs in the Bible it is merely a coincidence.[35] Conscious use of rhyme can only be explained by Arabic influence; before Kallir's time, as noted by the medieval grammarians, no rhyme is found in the Hebrew language. These rhymes may alternate from stanza to stanza or they may run through the entire poem, such that a single syllable

or a whole word concludes every line or occurs only at the ends of the stanzas. In the latter case, the other lines may remain without rhyme, or they may be united by a new rhyme or several changing rhymes. It was considered a special refinement to arrange the verse-endings such that the last word of the first line is the first word of the second line, and so on. These chain words are already found in unrhymed poems. In acrostic poems the rhyme and the acrostic are joined in such cases, for the words determined each other. The craft may be extended to the use of rhyme or chain words at the half-line.[36]

The rhymes are often connected with the poem's contents. Thus in the poems for Kingship, Remembrance, and Shofar, the stanzas conclude with מלוכה, "kingship," זכרון, "remembrance," and שופר "shofar"; in the poems for dew and rain, they conclude with the words טל, "dew," and מטר, "rain"; the same is true for other poems.[37] But above all the rhymes are influenced by refrains and biblical verses. Frequently the refrain determined all the line-endings, which all had to rhyme with it. In the *mustajāb*, the recurring verse preceding the entire poem determines the end of each stanza; it is usually a biblical quotation.[38] Biblical verses frequently conclude the stanzas. The grammarian Ephodi[39] sees as a great virtue of Hebrew liturgical poetry its ability to incorporate biblical verses verbatim; this remark seems to be directed against the hymns of the Christian church, which follow the same practice, but necessarily quote the Bible in translation. In the *qerova* for the Ninth of Av by Kallir, mentioned above, each stanza ends with a biblical verse beginning with למה, "Why," the last word of which establishes the rhyme of the entire stanza. We can learn how early acrostic and rhyme were used among the Jews and viewed as indispensable by the poets from the activity of R. Saadia Gaon, who as a young man (in 920) drew up two alphabetical lists of Hebrew roots, one arranged according to the first letter and one according to the last letter, to enable poets to use them for acrostics and rhymes. This activity occupied him for some time, and he frequently returned to augment it. The extant fragments of his *Agron* give a picture of the aspirations and needs in this area at that time.

(11) As the beginning and the end of the line were connected by acrostic and rhyme, so the line itself was subject to rhythm and meter. The question as to the extent of rhythm and meter in biblical poetry has recently been often raised and much disputed.[40] The Jewish poets and linguists of the Middle Ages knew nothing of it, and they never thought to look to the Bible as a model for meter and rhythm. The statutory prayers observe the biblical rule of parallelism, the only stylistic rule to which they are subject. The first simple expansions of the statutory prayers and the ancient piyyutim make use of a rhythm that matches the word stress, as noted above. This long remained the practice of liturgical poetry. The rules of rhythm were not always observed with great care, and especially among the poets living in Christian lands, who paid but little attention to keeping the lines equal in length. This was not so for the poets in Islamic countries, who had learned from the Arabs to take into account the quantity of the syllables in verse (שירים שקולים, "metrical poems"). Thus, meter was introduced into Hebrew poetry, first for secular, later for sacred poetry.[41] R. Saadia Gaon still knows nothing of metrical verse in the Hebrew language; but his disciple Dunash was the first to make use of meter. He was therefore accused of introducing foreign elements into the craft of poetry, to the detriment of the Hebrew language.[42] This accusation was never

silenced; frequent complaints were raised that meter was a foreign bondage not suited to the Hebrew language. Strangely enough, even poets like R. Judah Halevi[43] and R. Judah al-Ḥarizi[44] proclaim their dissatisfaction with this intruder, but that did not prevent them from following strictly the Arabic models. No poet of the Golden Age in Spain had any compunctions about composing metrical poems, and sometimes even critics raised their voices in praise of meter. The adaptation of the Arabic meters to Hebrew was not a simple matter, for it was necessary first to establish a method for evaluating syllable quantity.[45] Several important meters necessarily had to be eliminated, but to the extent possible all the Arabic meters were taken over. Conflicting reckonings exist as to the number of these.[46] According to Hartmann, "In the rhymed poems, that is, poems with lines of equal length concluding with the same rhyme, [there are—*Engl. trans.*] forty-seven meters; and in the strophic poems, that is, poems composed in groups of several lines with a common rhyme in the last line and a separate rhyme in the other lines, [there are—*Engl. trans.*] sixty-four different meters, so that the total is one hundred eleven meters."[47]

The acceptance of rhythm and meter was eased by the fact that it was customary to sing the piyyutim according to particular tunes.[48] Samauʾal al-Maghribi mentions explicitly as a distinguishing feature of *ḥizāna* that it is sung by the precentor, while the congregation accompanies him with exclamations and singing, helping him with the melody. Prayer books—manuscript editions rather more than printed editions—actually designate the tune according to which a particular poem is to be sung. Beautiful tunes are required, and they should be sung with a beautiful voice (מדות נחמדות בקול ערב). The term for "melody" is נועם, and also נגון or טעם; among Arabic-speaking Jews the most common word is *laḥn*. The melodies were adopted from everywhere: Folk tunes and songs from every cultural level provided the material.

[Al-Ḥarizi does not speak against Arabic meters in the eighteenth chapter of the *Taḥkemoni* or anywhere else. No complete list of all the forms of the meters used in the Spanish period has yet been drawn up, but their number is considerably greater than the estimate of M. Hartmann. David Yellin counts in the nonstrophic poems of Samuel the Nagid fifty-seven different forms (David Yellin, *Ketavim Nivḥarim* [Jerusalem, 1935–39], 2:190–215), and other poets employ forms that are lacking in this list.]

(12)   The poets created their own language. They attempted to follow biblical language as much as possible, for "The synagogue poets took the gems for their pearl necklace from the midrash and the string from the Bible" (Zunz, *Poesie*, 126). But the biblical vocabulary was hardly adequate, for they had thoughts and concepts to express that were not current earlier; and those indispensable artistic forms, acrostic and rhyme, severely limited the choice of words and greatly increased the difficulty of expression. Thus, the poets were forced to reach beyond the inherited linguistic material and take recourse in linguistic innovations. This was not a new procedure, for the Mishnah and the Talmud in their time had also followed this practice, and had contributed to the development of the Hebrew language by their innovations of grammatical forms and new words. Even the statutory prayers were not always limited to biblical vocabulary, but here and there late Hebrew vocabulary was used. But all these deviations from classical style were nothing compared to the innovations of the synagogue poets, who permitted themselves to develop a linguistic style and form of expression peculiar to themselves alone.

[223]

The characteristics of the language and style of synagogue poetry have been collected and classified by Zunz with remarkable patience and care.[49] He summarizes them under the following three headings: The poets make use of "a. words and expressions from the Talmud, midrash, and targumim; b. exceptional inflections [of the noun and the verb], unusual syntax, and neologisms; c. stylistic peculiarities and characteristic expressions."

a. The poets certainly had the right not to limit themselves to biblical vocabulary, and to exploit also the Hebrew words that first occur in talmudic literature. This was in accordance with the natural development of the language. Their error was in using indiscriminately the entire vocabulary of the available literature as if it were all classical, in borrowing words from Aramaic,[50] even Latin and Greek,[51] and treating them as if they were pure Hebrew. It was through them that foreign words like לבלר (*libellarius*), תרף (θεραπεία), קטגור (κατήγορος), and סניגור (συνήγορος) entered the language; some, like טכס from τάξις, they conjugated as if from Hebrew roots. We encounter this phenomenon to a limited degree already in the Mishnah and the Talmud, and the early poets did not go much further; but the later poets did, especially those of France and Germany, who lacked the restraint of sound grammatical studies and linguistic knowledge.[52] With their strong preference for little-known and unusual expressions, and with their view that artificiality is art, they accepted into their poems many Aramaic words and even whole Aramaic sentences; for certain purposes such as introducing the Torah readings, Aramaic seemed to them altogether more appropriate than Hebrew.

b. The synagogue poets did not consider themselves bound by the laws of the language, but even in this regard they followed the path already laid out by the Talmud. They constructed plurals for words that have none,[53] like proper nouns and particles, and they did not hesitate to employ irregular suffixes with the plural. They used the absolute and construct forms of the noun[54] indiscriminately. They used the inflectional suffixes of the noun and the verb indiscriminately, as well, while on the other hand they attached particles to the verb that can be used only with nouns. They treated all weak verb stems as if they had the same irregularity, in this way arriving at identical forms for verbs of different patterns. It was their regular practice to use verbs in conjugations in which they do not occur in the classical language. They had a particular fondness for the passive conjugations, especially for passive participles, which serve as regular epithets for the heroes of the poetry. For this purpose participial forms not found in the ancient language are used, and there is no hesitation in forming passives out of intransitive verbs.[55] Particularly characteristic of the synagogue poets was their penchant for inventing new words; they used nouns unknown from any other source, introducing for this purpose no fewer than forty noun patterns not formerly in use. Some are created by disregarding the suffixes required by the root or by the usual patterns of noun formation, others by false analogy. In most cases it was the bondage of rhyme that forced them to impose these innovations upon the language.

[224]

c. With a certain amount of practice it would be possible to find one's way through the unusual and incorrect word formations, but what makes the synagogue poetry particularly difficult, and often impossible to enjoy is the obscurity of the poets' manner of expression. They loved to use rare words, presupposing extensive familiarity with the Bible, Talmud, and midrash. But above all they loved to embellish their style with figurative usages deriving from the Bible or Talmud. In describing Israel's history, for example, they borrowed epithets for the people and its leaders from the most out-of-the-way names, similes, or events, and often the allusion is contained in a single word, so that the reader is confronted with an actual riddle. Likewise the enemies of Israel are designated by the names of every nation mentioned in the Bible, by the characteristics attributed to them, and by the imagery that describes them. For this, too, the poets had precedent in the language of the apocalypse and midrash; but as the productions of the poets exceed those of the ancients in quantity, so they surpass them in difficulty and in the abundant riddles that they pose.[56]

[The studies of Zunz remain to this day the main source for knowledge of the language of the poets. Additional material from this field is scattered in many places, especially in articles published in *Leshonenu*. Preeminent among the modern linguists are M. Zulay ("'Iyune lashon befiyute yanai," *SRIHP* 6 [1945/6]: 161–248, etc.), H. Yalon, and S. Abramson.]

(13)   The piyyut's manner of expression has been much criticized, and it does provide purists with plenty of opportunity for finding fault. Best known is the accusation of R. Abraham Ibn Ezra,[57] who enumerates four flaws in poems of the Kallirian style that disqualify them for use in prayer: the obscure language with its abundant allusions, the mosaic use of passages from the aggadah, the use of talmudic vocabulary, and incorrect use of the Hebrew language. But Kallir has found enthusiastic proponents in Zunz and especially in Heidenheim.[58] Doubtless from his point of view R. Abraham Ibn Ezra was correct, for the flaws that he enumerates, particularly obscurity of expression and the breaches of the laws of the language, are indisputedly present. But it is historically unfair to overlook the difficulties that the poets had to overcome. The task had fallen to them of composing their poems in a language that had ceased to be a living one centuries earlier and that was no longer in use anywhere but in the House of Study; and even there it was used only for the formulation of rules and laws. That they were not daunted by the attempt to revive this language, and to tease new sounds out of it, to lend it flexibility and power of expression, is a testimony to their courage and self-confidence. They went about their work with admirable daring, and the greatness of their achievement cannot be denied. They succeeded in providing the religious consciousness with new expression and new style, one in which many generations could find uplift, improvement, and instruction. The poets brought about the advancement of the Hebrew language and guaranteed that it would continue to be used as a written and literary language. True, this was not achieved without a certain amount of forcing, for "the poet struggled with a language that resisted in matters of form and content, and sometimes he wrested from it successful innovations" (Zunz, *Poesie*, 117). The linguistic innovation of the early synagogue poets astonishes with its daring, without repelling with its difficulty. For the excesses only the later generations are to be blamed. At first the rules of the language were broken out of ignorance rather than scorn; the younger poets may be blamed for not making use of the new linguistic knowledge despite the great progress that was made in their time. There was a kind of seduction in the artistic form with its severe restrictions: "Linguistically correct expression

[225]

had to yield to technical compulsion, and beauty was scorned by enthusiasm" (Zunz, *Poesie*, 123). But the obscurity of expression, the use of difficult words and enigmatic allusions, were concessions to the taste of the age; by using them the poets gave pleasure to the congregation, which loved this kind of embellishment and elaboration. It must be said that the congregations in those days must have been extremely well versed in the traditional literature if they were able to follow this difficult form of exposition. Kallir did not choose this style out of an arbitrary spirit, but rather because that was the only way in which a poet at that time could achieve renown. The Jews were influenced in this matter by the example of the other nations. Saadia, whom Abraham Ibn Ezra extolled as a composer of prayers, as opposed to Kallir, did no better; if Kallir's poems must be called obscure, Saadia's are books with seven seals. But all of world literature offers examples of poets whose works are so full of obscurities that even their contemporaries could hardly understand two lines thoroughly without recourse to dictionaries and encyclopedias; yet, this did not prevent some of them from becoming recognized as classic.[59] The classic poets of the liturgy overcame successfully the difficulties that had impeded the early poets. The champions among the poets did not bow to the rigidity of the literary form, but easily threw off the chains; "as a flaxen wick is burnt when it smells the fire" [Judges 16:9—*Engl. trans.*], so their poetic gift and genius freed itself from these bonds. They did not reject the inherited form, and often made the structure of their poems even more artistic; yet they understood how to elevate their compositions to the level of classic poetry. With their depth of feeling, the loftiness of their ideas, and the purity of their language, they came near the biblical psalms, for these were the true poets who undertook to speak, while the great majority of the synagogue poets had no poetic talent. The didactic contents of the piyyut, the display of external form, and the invention of word forms were easy to imitate, and the congregations' demand for this new adornment of the liturgy was intense. Thus, the custom of composing liturgical poetry spread like a contagious disease. The form was ready-made; precentors and scholars, both talented and untalented, used them to please the congregations with their work. The error was not in the act of composing piyyutim, but in unrestrained versifying, by the compulsion felt by people lacking any poetic feeling or linguistic understanding to compose piyyutim and *selihot*. But even if we see this as an error, it was still not completely without value. For the times and for the cultural circles for which they were intended, the liturgical poetry fulfilled its function perfectly. It merely ought not to have been made into an absolute value, as happened later. The poems spoke to each age in its language and according to its views. They were the spokesmen of the feelings and thoughts of the present; thus, they served as a counterbalance to the fixed mass of the statutory prayers.

[226]

(14)   The piyyut spread with tremendous speed and enjoyed such popularity that its status sometimes overshadowed that of the statutory prayers. One might thus assume that it was always in favor, and that it enjoyed from the very beginning the support of the chief religious authorities. This was not the case. Synagogue poetry had to withstand a thousand opponents, and in nearly every generation it was particularly the most authoritative voices that were raised against it in hostility. But they could not prevail, for the masses supported it. The great innovation in the piyyut was that it interrupted the traditional order of the statutory prayers. In Palestine, its homeland, people

were accustomed to the prayers changing frequently; they took care only to preserve the traditional order of the fixed benedictions. They were accustomed to, even viewed with favor, deviations from the accepted wording and the ordinary linguistic dress. But in Babylonia, the new prayers came up against lively protest. The Babylonian geonim absolutely opposed them because they interrupted the traditional order of the service, expanded the *ʿAmida*, and sometimes introduced ideas into places where they were foreign and inappropriate.[60] This was the same attitude that was opposed to every kind of addition, even the short prose ones that had become attached to the ancient text and that hardly appeared as innovations, such as "Remember us," and the like. Thus, we find that R. Yehudai Gaon[61] opposed in principle every addition to the traditional *ʿAmida*, including the Kedushah. And as few as are the sources from that period, they at least give us a glimpse into the course of events and show us that only little by little did all the additions take root; in every generation there was opposition to what seemed at that time to be an innovation, but by the time a generation or two had passed, that element already seemed to have full legitimacy. The gaon Kohen-Zedek[62] was still obliged to deal with the question of the permissibility even of the additions for the Ten Days of Repentance mentioned above, but his successor, Natronai,[63] had no further hesitation in permitting *qerovot* for all the festivals, Hanukkah, Purim, and the Ninth of Av, as long as the contents of every single line corresponded to the section of the service in which it was inserted. But even after this permissive ruling the opposition did not entirely cease, and as late as 150 years afterwards, R. Hai Gaon[64] had to take a position on the same questions. He boldly declared once again his opposition to this innovation, and in fact his academy, Pumbedita, held out longer than Sura in opposition to the piyyut . R. Judah b. Barzilai, in his own time, expressed the strongest possible opposition to liturgical poetry,[65] calling it an error for which people are to be rebuked and which must be prohibited to them. In his opinion, any expansion of the text of the prayers beyond the framework laid down in the Talmud was illegal, and the less added the better. He rejected even the expansions of the statutory prayers that had received general recognition by his time, such as "All give thanks to You" or "Remember us," and saw it as desirable to do battle for their elimination. But against the piyyut, that foreign element appended to the statutory prayers, he poured out all his rage. Long ago, in times of persecution, it was admitted as a replacement for the statutory prayers, but when permission to recite the prayers in the traditional manner was again granted, the statutory prayers ought to have been restored to their exclusive status and not have been displaced by arbitrary additions. The poetry disturbed the service because its content was specious; its heaping up of epithets for God sometimes bordered on blasphemy; it was unworthy for a pious man "to set aside the prayers of the prophets" in favor of "all these other piyyutim, which are merely vanity and ignorance, and which were unknown to our ancestors."

[227]

This is a most unfair criticism, arising from a love of tradition so extreme as to suppress any understanding of the needs of the times. Judah b. Barzilai never grasped that liturgical poetry introduced a new type of piety and prayer, that it served, as one of his younger contemporaries put it,[66] to supplement the statutory prayers, and that its purpose was to extol God's glory in poetic language. But his opposition failed not because of its unfairness, but because meanwhile poetry had received the sanction of time and of the example of distinguished individuals. If a luminary like R. Saadia Gaon was counted among the poets, poetry could not be declared prohibited. R. Gershom[67] already thought Yannai sufficiently distant in time to be deemed an authority and support for piyyut, though he probably knew no more about him than his name. Since he knew the names of a whole series of distinguished synagogue poets, and regarded them as authoritative, R. Gershom permitted the unrestricted recitation of piyyut. It was only natural that his venerable voice was heard throughout France and Germany, and that poetry was gladly admitted there as a hymnic enrichment of the service. R. Tam[68] was then the first to count Kallir among the tannaim, finding in this the strongest justification for the piyyut.

But the mere fact that liturgical poetry was so often in need of such vigorous defense shows how often and how vigorously it was attacked. The most famous people were among its opponents. Abraham Ibn Ezra,[69] for example, warned against the use of foolish and unintelligible poems. Maimonides, too,[70] condemned vigorously the manner of the poets who love to compose poems with long compilations of epithets of God in the belief that this brings them near to Him; but actually, they ". . . speak unintelligibly, and, in their zeal, they came near to blasphemy." Very typical was the approach of al-Ḥarizi.[71] In the *maqāma* about the cantor of Mosul, he ridicules the folly of exaggerating the value of liturgical poetry. In Mosul he hears people singing the praises of the community's admired cantor, and he is eager to observe him in a service. But his hopes are disappointed, for the man makes the grossest mistakes even in the simplest statutory prayers, and then he afflicts his ignorant and foolish congregation "with piyyutim without form or content, with blind and lame verses, no taste or force" until some of the people fall asleep for sheer exhaustion and others flee in disgust. One intelligent man in the congregation, al-Ḥarizi himself, criticizes the neglect of the statutory prayers in favor of the poems, but he encounters a number of opponents who declare that the poetry is the essential thing and that the other prayers ought to be displaced in favor of it. They compare the singing of the piyyut to the songs of the Levites in the Temple, and claim that it is commanded in the Bible, which does not even mention the statutory prayers. Finally they point to the fact that liturgical poetry is accepted and beloved in all communities without exception, and that they could not lag behind the others. To this al-Ḥarizi replies that the piyyut is perfectly in order where it is understood, but in a congregation of ignoramuses like this one it is actually a danger to religion. It is impossible to reproduce al-Ḥarizi's sharp wit in a foreign language, for translation blunts the arrows of his scorn. But his meaning is clear: He is not a blind enemy of the liturgical poetry, but he demands that a proper balance be maintained and the congregation's powers of comprehension not be overestimated.

Similar claims were made against the piyyut in all the centuries that followed.[72] The complaints are that it interrupts the sequence of prayer, that it lengthens the service unduly, and that it is not understood by the congregation. This last complaint is heard more frequently as time goes by, and even the many commentaries on the piyyutim that were composed over the ages could not eliminate this problem. The poetry remained enigmatic even to scholars, let alone to the masses of worshipers. The consequence was that the congregation would disturb the service by talking or in other ways. Scholars would avoid as much as possible participating in the lengthy public service or they would salvage the time used for reciting the poetry by studying Torah, setting in turn a bad example for the congregation. Many who wished to avoid giving this offense did

[228]

not participate in the recitation of the poetry but also did nothing else during this period. But the opposition was too late; by al-Ḥarizi's time, the day of the piyyut had passed and understanding for this particular means of spiritual elevation was dying out. At the same time, a certain number of liturgical poems had acquired a secure place in the various congregations. As manuscripts decreased and printed books proliferated, as understanding for historical and local character decreased, as meaningless customs came to be adhered to more stubbornly, the more entrenched did the piyyut become, and the less could its position be shaken by even the chief authorities of religious law such as R. Joseph Caro[73] or R. Elijah of Vilna.[74] They were heard among the learned, but the masses could not be influenced away from their old habit until a new time and a new culture broke their resistance. The modern period has mercilessly eliminated the great mass of unintelligible and worthless poems; but at the same time it has known how to appreciate properly the historical significance of these poems, and has had no compunctions about retaining in the prayer book piyyutim of true poetic value.

§ 40 *The Main Liturgical Poets: Up to and Including Kallir*

[229]

(1) We now come to survey the activity of the synagogue poets. It is clearly impossible to enumerate all the poets who ever contributed to the enrichment of the liturgy; this would mean repeating Zunz's comprehensive book on the history of the liturgical poetry and supplementing it with the many discoveries made since its appearance.[1] Even then the literature would not be completely catalogued, because the great abundance of anonymous poetry would still not be accounted for. Such a full literary-historical list would go far beyond the framework of this book, and would not even be useful, because most of the literature with which Zunz dealt is not accessible, but is preserved only in manuscript. We intend to treat only those synagogue poets who actually made an impact on the history of the liturgy. The ancient sources in which the names of the poets are collected are but few.[2] Little was known about the poets as individuals, and that little was mostly of a legendary nature. The earliest poets, particularly, have vanished into the mass of legends that were told about them, and it was their fate that their names were forgotten though their compositions were preserved.

(2) The history of liturgical poetry is not uniform, but must be divided into various periods. The earliest period, when the poets still had to find the forms and rules of poetry, lasted until ca. 750, reaching its peak in the work of Kallir. This period was followed by one in which the poets' whole effort was directed at imitating the model of the ancients, and composing in their spirit, style and form. To this period belong first the earliest eastern poets, and then also the poets who wrote liturgical poetry in Christian Europe. These are the payyetanim in the true sense of the word; their period lasts to ca. 1250, but with occasional offshoots in later centuries, and continuing along the same lines in the Orient to this day. The Spanish poets from ca. 1050 to 1200 form a third group; thanks to the influence of the Arabic art of poetry, they freed themselves

[230]

from the forms and language of the piyyut, and they mark the golden age of sacred poetry in the Middle Ages.

[The discovery of the vast poetic material buried among the fragments of the Cairo geniza has considerably changed our opinions about the history of the ancient liturgical poetry. For the importance of the geniza see P.E. Kahle, *The Cairo Geniza*, 2nd edition (Oxford, 1959), 3–13, 34–48; S.D. Goitein, *A Mediterranean Society* (Berkeley and Los Angeles: University of California Press, 1967), 1:1–28. There is no doubt that the ancient period in the history of liturgical poetry ends with the conquest of Palestine by the Arabs (ca. 635), not in 750 as Elbogen says. It appears that there were several generations between Yose b. Yose and Yannai, and at least one between Yannai and Kallir, but we cannot yet determine their dates exactly. Yose b. Yose apparently lived in the fourth or fifth century, Yannai in the fifth or sixth, and Kallir in the sixth or the beginning of the seventh.]

(3)   Liturgical poetry began with a number of anonymous compositions,[3] which were eventually suppressed by the better and more valuable liturgical poems of a later period. At first the custom of indicating the author's name in an acrostic was unknown, so that there was no tradition reflective of the liturgical poetry's earliest representatives, and their names were forgotten. From the earliest period, only a single name of a liturgical poet has been preserved, that of Yose b. Yose.[4] Of his life we know nothing. He is called "The Orphan," apparently for no other reason than that his name was the same as his father's. That he was a high priest is also merely a blind conjecture. In general, many erroneous beliefs about him were current in the Middle Ages, since nothing was actually known about him. There can be no doubt that his homeland was Palestine, for in no other land can the existence of Hebrew poets in that period be demonstrated. When he lived is unknown, but to judge from the style of his poetry it must have been fairly early, no later than 600–650. His poems have all the marks of the earliest insertions in the liturgy. He does not yet know the name-acrostic, nor does he use rhyme, but his liturgical poems are distinguished by the simplicity of their language, the nobility of their expression, and their lack of difficult midrash. In the Middle Ages it was not even counted as true poetry, but was referred to as *khutab*—that is, something close to prose. Furthermore, Yose never composed a liturgical poem for inclusion within the ʿAmida, but only poems intended as appendages to it. Finally, as far as we know, he composed liturgical poetry only for the Days of Awe. Saadia and other ancient writers speak of him with great respect, and, though he was not a Babylonian, his works spread early also to Babylonia. All this speaks for a very early period.

Of his compositions, the following should be mentioned: אהללה אלהי, "I will praise my God"; אפחד, "I will fear"; and אנוסה לעזרה, "I will flee for help," for the New Year. These poems are called תקיעתא, "Shofar blast"; each is a variation on one of the three groups of ten biblical verses on Kingship, Remembrance, and Shofar prayers, the verses being cited toward the end. To judge from their overall character and name, it is not impossible that they were intended as a replacement for the usual introductions to the three prayers in Palestine. Later, Ashkenaz no longer knew what to do with the verses, of which there were now two sets; after long disputes over where to insert them, it was finally decided to eliminate them altogether.[5] The text of the poems was emended in other ways as well, apparently because they seemed to attack Christianity. Yose also composed ʿAvodot for the Day of Atonement,[6] and today it is certain that he dealt with this genre no fewer than three times. Originally these three *'Avodot* were probably recited in the same community at three different services of the Day of Atonement. But later, when this ancient custom fell into desuetude and only the *'Avoda* in the Additional Service remained, his *'Avodot* became separated from each other and were preserved in the prayer books of different, distant lands. The first, אתה כוננת עולם ברב חסד, "You established the world in abundant mercy,"[7] was used in the Middle Ages in Burgundy and Savoy, and has been preserved until today in the rite of the three northern Italian towns of Asti, Fossano, and Moncalvo (אפם). France knew also of a poetic introduction to it beginning אתן תהלה, "I will give praise,"[8] which was attributed to no less a figure than the apostle Peter. A second composition, אזכיר גבורות אלוה נאדרי בכח, "I will recite the mighty acts of God, majestic in power,"[9] was included by Saadia in his prayer book for the Morning Service, and has recently been published from this source. Finally, there was a third *'Avoda*—אספר גדולות לעושה גדולות, "I will recite the great deeds of the One Who does great deeds,"[10] which, according to explicit testimony, was recited in the Afternoon Service. At the moment only a few lines are known, but by its form it is possible that the line חזה בתעצומות מפענח צפונות, "Behold the mighty acts of the One Who interprets the hidden,"[11] which is frequently cited in Yose's name, comes from this poem. Likewise, the poem אמנם אשמינו, "Indeed our sins,"[12] was intended for the Day of Atonement; in Ashkenaz it is found among the prayers for the Evening Service. It is a confession, intended also as a supplement to the *'Amida*. In most prayer books it has been very much abridged, with longer or shorter sections deleted, and frequently only the refrain lines preserved: דרכך אלהינו, "Your way, O our God," and למענך אלהינו, "For Your sake, O our God." A *yoser* is also attributed to this poet, of which only the first line has been preserved: אור עולם אוצר חיים, "Eternal Light, Treasury of life"; but no certain proof exists for this attribution, and it is in fact not particularly likely.

[We have as yet no scientific edition of the poems of Yose b. Yose. A new *seliha* by him was published by J. Marcus in *Horev* 2 (1935/6): 201–207. It must be mentioned that among the geniza fragments a number of unknown texts have been preserved that recall his known compositions in form and style. His name is not mentioned on them, but they could possibly be by him. Ibn Janah cites two rhymed lines from an unknown poem of Yose (*Sefer hashorashim*, 305), and M. Zulay discovered this poem in the geniza. Recently, Ezra Fleischer published a large group of poems that includes this quotation ("Mahzore piyut mitokh qedushta leyom kipur hameyuheset leyose ben yose," in *Qoves 'al yad* NS 7 [1967/8]: 1–79). All these poems seem to be by one poet, but it cannot be said with absolute certainty that it is Yose b. Yose.]

(4) In his youthful work *Agron*,[13] Saadia names as the "ancient poets"—alongside Yose—Yannai, Eleazar, Joshua, and Phineas. Of the last two, we know no more than the name. While a few liturgical poems bear the acrostic Joshua, none gives the impression of coming from such an early period. About Phineas, it is worth noting that in the chain of tradition of the Tiberian masoretes, ca. 700, an otherwise unknown academy head named R. Phineas is mentioned. There is no denying a certain connection between the flourishing of masoretic studies and the spread of poetry, for a revival of poetry would presuppose the study of the Bible and preoccupation with the Hebrew language. As little as we know about Phineas, the one certain thing is that at one time

[232]

his poems were widely disseminated, for people referred often to them. None of the known prayer books adopted his compositions, but in the Cairo geniza there are poems attributed to a certain R. Phineas that fit his supposed period admirably.

[For Joshua, see M. Zulay, *SRIHP* 5 (1938/9): 155–57. For Phineas, see the supplementary material below, §41(1). It seems likely that the poets Haduta (b. Abraham), Joseph b. R. Nisan of Shave-qiryatayim (equivalent to Naveh in the Transjordan), and Simon Hacohen b. R. Megas also lived during the period of Byzantine rule in Palestine. The poems of the first of this list were published by P. Kahle, Elbogen, Zulay, and Schirmann; a bibliography can be found in Schirmann, *Shirim hadashim*, 13–15; for a bibliography on Joseph b. R. Nisan, see Schirmann, *Shirim hadashim*, 9–10; on Simon Hacohen, see pages 3–4 in the same].

(5)   Yannai[14] was the first poet of whose works something has been preserved till our time, and one of his poems is even very widely known, namely אז רוב נסים הפלאת בלילה, "Then You performed great miracles in the night," in the Passover Haggadah. Yannai is the first known poet to make use of name acrostic and rhyme; in an ancient treatise on poetics,[15] his poems are not yet considered to be true piyyut, but rather more like biblical verses, and it is noted that his lines are not uniform, but that some are long and others short. He is also the first poet known as a composer of *qerovot* for insertion in the *ʿAmida*. He must have lived very early, for Anan, the founder of the Karaite sect, already made use of his poems, according to a reliable tradition of his adherents.[16] And if as early as ca. 770, when Anan wrote his *Sefer hamiṣvot*, the poems of Yannai were so widely circulated and well known in Babylonia that they could be relied upon as an authoritative source, we will not be going too far if we set the period of his life at least two generations earlier, and assume that he flourished at the latest around the year 700. To Saadia and R. Gershom he already belonged to the distant past. His homeland was not Babylonia, but Palestine; this is attested by the rare name Yannai and the peculiar spelling of this name that he customarily uses, יניי, which is only found in the Palestinian dialect. Furthermore, the composition of *qerovot* was permitted at that time only in Palestine. Yannai must have been very famous as a poet in the East in the early Middle Ages, for in the treatise on poetics mentioned above he is referred to as Yannai *al-maʿrūf*—the well-known Yannai. His poems filled whole volumes; *hizānat yanai*—or, as it is known in Hebrew, מחזור יניי, "Yannai's Cycle"—was a widely disseminated literary work often encountered in medieval book lists.[17] Only one poem from it has been preserved, the *qerova* אוני פטרי רחמתים, "The firstborn who opened each womb." It was intended for the Sabbath before Passover if that occurs on the Fourteenth of Nisan, or even for the first day of Passover itself; from it comes "Then You performed many miracles in the night," mentioned above. The beginning of the *qerova* was adopted in Ashkenaz. But R. Gershom relates: "R. Yannai was one of the early sages; he composed *qerovot* for every pericope of the year." [Elbogen cites the Hebrew text correctly, but translates: "for every festival"—*Engl. trans.*]. And, in fact, a fragmentary list of poems was found recently in which the beginnings of three poems and one rather long fragment from a *rahit* by Yannai are mentioned; all of the incipits are quoted in such a way that they may be assumed to have been well known, and all seem to come from a poetic version of the death of Moses. The geniza manuscripts actually contain numerous poems by Yannai that are not yet published. In Italy, and perhaps also in France and

Germany, many more poems of Yannai must have been current during the high Middle Ages than are known to us. They were not used in the synagogue because of an ugly story then current that hurt Yannai's reputation.[18] It was said that out of envy of his disciple Kallir, who had overshadowed him, he put a scorpion in the latter's shoe, thereby murdering him. Naturally, the grain of truth in the story is simply that the poems of Kallir displaced those of Yannai. But interestingly enough, similar stories circulated in Italy about famous local poets.

[After the publication of *Maḥzor yannai* (New York: Jewish Theological Seminary of America, 1919) and *Ginze Schechter*, vol. 3 (New York: Jewish Theological Seminary of America, 1928) by I. Davidson, hundreds of poems by Yannai were discovered in geniza manuscripts. It may be assumed that most of the extant poems of Yannai have already been published; but there is no doubt that significant further material is still hidden in fragments not yet studied. M. Zulay has contributed especially to the discovery, editing, and study of Yannai's works. See the following by M. Zulay, "Meḥqere yanai," *SRIHP* 2 (1935/6): 231–391; *idem, Piyute yanai* (Berlin, 1937/8); *idem,* "ʿIyune lashon befiyute yanai," *SRIHP* 6 (1945/6): 161–248; *idem,* "Rabam shel hapayetanim," *Hatequfa* 28 (1935/6): 378–87; *idem,* "Nosafot lefiyute yanai," in *Mazkeret ʿimanuel,* Löw Festschrift (Budapest, 1946/7), 147–57; N. Wieder, *Piyute yanai,* D. Heller Festschrift (Budapest, 1940/1), 32–60; J. Sonne, "An Unknown Keroba of Yannai," *HUCA* 18 (1944): 199–200; S. Lieberman, "Ḥazanut yanai," *Sinai* 2 (1938/9): 221–50; A. Diez Macho and S. Spiegel in *Sefarad* 15 (1955): 288–340; S. Spiegel, "Qerovot yanai beniqud bene bavel," *SRIHP* 7 (1957/8): 137–43; Z. M. Rabinovitz, *Tarbiz* 25 (1955/6): 290–300; 27 (1917/8): 39–60; 28 (1958/9): 279–307; *idem, Jubilee Vol.* (1962/3): 1–8; *idem, Sura* 4 (1963/4): 447–66; all the above articles contain commentaries on Yannai's *qerovot.* See, also, Z. M. Rabinovitz, *Halakha vaʾagada befiyute yanai* (Tel Aviv, 1961/2); H. Schirmann, "Yanai hapayetan: shirato vehashqafat ʿolamo," *Qeshet* 6 (1963/4): 45–66; Y. Heinemann, "Hamaḥzor hatelat shenati veluaḥ hashana," *Tarbiz* 33 (1963/4): 362–68; Y. Yahalom, "Nosafot lemaḥzor yanai," *Leshonenu* 35 (1966/7): 211–16; N. Fried, "Haftarot alternativiot befiyute yanai," *Sinai* 61 (1966/7): 277–90; 62 (1967/8): 50–66.]

(6) The best-known name among those of the early poets was the fourth, Eleazar, known for short as Kallir,[19] whom we have already mentioned frequently. No other poet was blessed with such productivity as Kallir; his poems covered all the distinguished days of the year, and were widely disseminated and highly regarded. Not for nothing was he called the prince and law-giver of the piyyut. But though we have many of his compositions, we know little of his life; the circumstances of his biography are completely obscure, and the learned studies intended to clarify them have often gone wrong. "The name of Kallir should be engraved as if on stone as a warning that even the masters of scholarship are subject to error."[20]

[234]

The only thing that we know about him for certain is his name, Eleazar, which he signed on most of his compositions in the form of an acrostic. But when we try to get beyond this, we stumble on the most contradictory assumptions. The full style of the acrostics is אלעזר בירבי קליר מקרית ספר, "Eleazar b. R. Kallir of Qiryat Sefer," with קיליר sometimes standing for קליר. If we ask for the meaning of the name Kallir, which does not occur anywhere else, we find two explanations: Some say that it is actually the name of the poet's father, and others say it is a by-name. There is an ancient explanation that derives the name from the Syriac *qalora*,[21] meaning "cake." This recalls the old custom of making children's first study of the Torah pleasurable for them by teaching them the shapes of the letters from little cakes, which were then given them to eat.[22] Our poet's parents are supposed to have given their child such dainties to eat because they saw this as an auspicious way of awakening his talent, and out of gratitude he retained the name "Cake Man." Others, dissatisfied with this daring explanation, see Kallir as an epithet derived from the place where the poet lived; this would be Cagliari[23] in Sardinia, from which he would have been called "the man of Cagliari" or Kallir. The assumption that Kallir is an epithet is supported by the fact that a poem supposedly has the acrostic אני אלעזר ברבי יעקב הקליר, "I, Eleazar b. R. Jacob the Qalir"; from this it would seem that the father's name was Jacob,[24] and Kallir an epithet. But although this tradition is offered as a reliable one, it has no foundation, and is certainly wrong. And if the style of the acrostic אלעזר בירבי קליר is examined closely, there can be no doubt that the last word is the name of the father. However, we are so accustomed to an abundance of figurative language and symbolic words in Kallir that it would not be surprising if he chose an enigmatic word for his name.[25] Until we have better information, we have no choice but to see the word Kallir as a proper name. The name Κέλερ—equivalent to *Celer*—is actually found in Jewish gravestones from Italy.[26] And even though the identification of the word with this name was made, as we shall soon see, out of a false conjecture about the place of Kallir's origin, the possibility cannot be ruled out that his father was actually called by this name, which is derived from Greek. Nor is another conjecture to be absolutely rejected, that the poet, whose works show such clear signs of the influence of Byzantine poetry, is the son of a man who bore a name very common in the eastern Roman Empire, and that the name Kallir is derived by metathesis from קיריל (Κύριλλος or *Cyrill*).[27]

Kallir's homeland, too, has been sought all over the globe. He himself calls his home town Qiryat Sefer; this is a biblical name mentioned in Josh. 15:15, but we can almost certainly assume that it is merely a symbolic epithet, for even in biblical times the name had gone out of use. Attempts to identify another place behind this name, even outside the borders of Palestine, are therefore justified. On the basis of false

assumptions about his date, and of the discovery that in the tenth century world-famous Jewish academies were flourishing in southern Italy, Kallir's homeland was located there. It was explained that the name was to be pronounced not as in the Bible, but rather as *qiryat sefar*, meaning "a coastal city"; thus, he was located in Bari or even in Cagliari, which suited the name Kallir perfectly. Then the ancient Jewish burial places were found in Porto,[28] the former port city of Rome, with the above-mentioned inscription of Celer, and it was soon agreed that Kallir's birthplace was Civitas Portus, or even Rome itself. Yet others emphasized the observation that in the writing of his name and in his use of impure rhymes, he displays much similarity with the poets of Germany, and therefore for a time it was held to be nearly certain that Kallir lived there.[29] His homeland was also sought in other countries[30] where it could be demonstrated that the study of Torah had flourished to a certain level in the period to which Kallir was assigned. Several scholars have changed their opinion about this matter repeatedly over the course of a few years, and new conjectures are constantly being raised. Progress has at least been made in the decisive refusal to seek the homeland of such an influential and universally recognized figure as Kallir outside the lands that were home to the centers of Jewish life and learning. But two countries still come into consideration, and for many years the balance wavered between Babylonia and Palestine. Through a forced interpretation some wanted to demonstrate that Qiryat Sefer referred to Pumbedita, so famous for its academy, and when unfortunately a place called Siparra was discovered nearby, the assumption seemed confirmed because the sound of the name could be easily identified with Qiryat Sefer.[31]

But Babylonia is out of the question as Kallir's homeland, for his poems unambiguously presuppose a Christian environment. Further, his approach was never recognized in Babylonia, where efforts were long made to deny acceptance of such poetry as he composed. In addition, positive evidence exists that forces us to conclude that Kallir lived in Palestine. The Holy Land was the homeland of liturgical poetry, and only there could a poet dare to accompany the entire cycle of festival prayers with poems as did Kallir. Furthermore, it was already noted centuries ago that his festival poems always presuppose only one day of the festival,[32] which was the case only in Palestine. Against this, it was argued that, in fact, poems by Kallir for the second day of festivals do exist. This is rebutted with the argument that the communities often made use of the poems on the second day quite arbitrarily, but the poems themselves were actually based on the Torah readings for the first day of the festival. The reply to this was that for some festivals we have several poems of the same type by Kallir, showing that he took the second day into account. But recently double poems by Kallir have been discovered for festivals that are nowhere celebrated on two days, such as Purim and the Ninth of Av. It is therefore definitely established that he had no hesitation in elaborating the service for the same festival more than once, reciting different poem cycles for the festivals in different years. It has also long been recognized that Kallir gives priority in his poems to Palestinian sources, and that he shows a special familiarity with Palestinian matters.[33] Most important for our purposes is the fact that he always bases his poems on the Palestinian version of the 'Amida;[34] until recently his poems were the most important evidence for the text of the Palestinian 'Amida, and now that we actually have this text we can see how closely he follows it. Thus, today it may be considered an incontrovertible fact that Kallir lived in Palestine[35] or at the least in a nearby part of Syria. The question may now be asked whether we can also identify the place where he lived and to associate the epithet Qiryat Sefer with a known city. Two recent attempts must be mentioned. The first starts from the fact that in one manuscript the acrostic appears once in the form קליר and sees this as a reference to Καλλιρρόη,[36] the usual designation of the Syrian city of Edessa in the Byzantine period. This city, a center of learning in its heyday, does deserve to be called *Qiryat Sefer*, "the city of the book." But against this at first very attractive conjecture is the fact that nothing at all is known of any important Jewish settlement in Edessa, and we have no right to assume that the attitude toward the Jews was sufficiently tolerant to encourage the advanced study of Torah. Besides, this would mean that when Kallir presents himself as a man of Kalliroa who comes from Qiryat Sefer, he is alluding to his home town with two different epithets that mean the same thing. If we are to conjecture that Kallir's home town was a city of books, the assumption would most likely lead to Tiberias,[37] which for centuries was one of the most important centers of Jewish scholarship in Palestine, and which in Kallir's time was actually the center of biblical studies, as well as the home of Phineas, who is mentioned together with Kallir as an ancient poet. We do not at

[236]

the moment have explicit evidence that Qiryat Sefer is Tiberias. In view of the many shifts already undergone by Kallir scholarship, it is best for us to refrain from fixing the place where he lived and to content ourselves with the conclusion that his homeland was Palestine.

Similarly, Kallir's period has been sought in various centuries from the second to the tenth and even the eleventh. The theories are so interdependent that false assumptions in one area result in errors concerning other aspects of his life. It was an important discovery [sic!] when, in the twelfth century, R. Jacob Tam fixed Kallir's time as that of the tannaim,[38] and identified him with R. Eleazar b. Simon, who is praised by the midrash as a poet. Until the threshold of the modern period, it was assumed that Kallir was a tanna. He was sometimes not identified with R. Eleazar b. Simon but with the even more famous R. Eleazar b. Arakh, and thus he would have lived in the first century; but that he was a tanna was hardly ever contested. It is no longer at all necessary to waste a word on this conjecture, which did so much to advance the name of Kallir and enhance the esteem for his poems, for no thoughtful person can any longer maintain that the author of such complex poems lived as early as the talmudic period. Since scientific scholarship has taken charge of the problem it has been seeking, alongside general criteria, evidence from Kallir himself about his period. His poems actually have a few indications of the time that had passed since the destruction of the Second Temple. But today we know that the copyists did not always transmit the original numbers faithfully, but took the liberty of changing dates that no longer were appropriate for their time, so that the numbers became higher as time passed. Nevertheless, there are two numbers in Kallir's poems for the Ninth of Av,[39] in which he says unambiguously that God's anger against Israel has now lasted nine hundred years. What would be more natural than to see this as an allusion to his own period, and as evidence that Kallir was writing approximately nine hundred years after the Destruction—that is, no earlier than 950? But the assumption is based on an erroneous interpretation of the verses in question. If Kallir writes אאבין תשע מאות ועוד כי לא דש בן גרני, "I contemplate that nine hundred years have passed and the Messiah [lit.: child of my threshing floor—*Engl. trans.*] has not yet appeared [lit.: threshed—*Engl. trans.*]" or לך ה' הצדקה בתשע מאות שנה שהיתה שנאה כבושה מלהשמע, "Yours, O Lord, is the righteousness for the nine hundred years when anger was repressed and not heard," he is clearly alluding to the language of the midrash (Lev. r. 7:1): "Nearly nine hundred years was the anger between Israel and their Father in heaven repressed," etc.—that is, God repressed His anger and did not translate it into action for nine centuries. The nine hundred years refer to the time from the Exodus to the destruction of the First Temple, and have no relationship to the period of Kallir. Today, knowing as we do that writers like Saadia, who died in 942, praised Kallir as a scholar and poet who lived long before their own time, there can no longer be any point in seeking Kallir's period in the tenth century. We must keep constantly before our eyes the fact that Kallir's poems had their influence on the formation of the festival prayers already in the eighth and ninth centuries. To this must be added the fact that Kallir is called the disciple of Yannai, and the latter lived, as has been shown above, around 700. Thus we can conclude that Kallir's lifetime cannot be later than 750. This assumption is in accord with the entire development of liturgical poetry as we view it today.

We have treated Kallir's personal data at such length because his name is a milestone in the history of liturgical poetry. He was the poet who gave the festival prayers the form that was to become common and generally recognized throughout the Jewish Diaspora. Kallir provided all the special occasions of the Jewish year with poems. Fifty years ago Zunz attributed to him more than two hundred poems;[40] to take account of new data from the manuscripts of the Cairo geniza,[41] we would have to double this number, and might even have to go beyond it. Kallir's poems are, for the most part, *qerovot*;[42] he composed only a few *yoṣerot* and *hoshaʿnot*, and by far the greatest part of his work is devoted to the elaboration of the *ʿAmida*. For lack of space, we do not list all his poems, but content ourselves with a brief overview. There is no great festival whose prayers Kallir did not embellish with poems, and for some, as mentioned, he composed several cycles of poems. Older evidence seemed to show that he paid less attention to the festival of Passover than to the others, but it is now clear that this impression is due only to the practice of the European communities, which had compositions by local poets and which therefore did not make use of Kallir's poems. In general, it must be kept in mind that the printed prayer books, and even the manuscripts, do not always give an exact picture of Kallir's poetic activity. Frequently such matters were treated arbitrarily: The communities deleted and added poems at will, sometimes inserting pieces by another poet more to their liking in the middle of Kallir's compositions, or eliminating pieces from his *qerovot* in order to exchange them for others.[43] Besides the great festivals, Kallir composed poems also for the four special Sabbaths,[44] in most cases not only for the Morning Service, but also for the Additional Service. He also composed poems for weekdays of solemn character: he composed *qerovot* for Purim, Hanukkah, and all the fasts accompanying all eighteen benedictions of the *ʿAmida*. We have already noted that for some of these days even these difficult compositions exist in several different versions. His poems for the Ninth of Av are particularly extensive;[45] here, he composed not merely short poems to accompany each benediction of the *ʿAmida*, but he took the occasion of the *qerova*'s fourteenth benediction to write variations on the theme of the destruction of the Temple and the sufferings of the Jews in an extended series of long poems. Even though it accepted about twenty *qinot* by Kallir, the rite of Ashkenaz still does not provide a complete picture of the poet's huge output on this subject; only from the series in Romaniot and Rome, which are double the length, do we perceive how easily Kallir could find new ways to treat the same theme.

[238]

The historical importance of Kallir's poetry lies, above all, in the fact that he created the framework for the poetic treatment of the liturgy. He was the lawgiver of the piyyut for subsequent generations and served as a model for later poets. His authority determined the points in the service to be adorned with poems. "Kallirian" came to be a descriptive term for liturgical poems.[46] But his style was also imitated, and this is the second way in which he was a pioneer: through him the aggadah became the main content of the poetic exposition.[47] Kallir's poems are intimately attached to the conception and language of the midrash; there is no ancient midrash with which he was not intimately familiar—sometimes he follows the language of the midrash verbatim. Particularly striking is the congruity of his poems with the language of the *pesiqtot*, though that is hardly astonishing, considering that his poems were intended for the very days for which *pesiqtot* were composed. Likewise, he knew and frequently used all the messianic and apocalyptic writings available in his time.[48] But Kallir is distinguished for the better from his later imitators in his manner of using the midrash. He is never enslaved to the text that he follows, but always knows how to free himself from it; he draws the matter from it, but in shaping it he is the master. This is particularly true of his way of working with language.[49] Kallir's language is shot through with obscurities, which have been discussed above at length. It could not have been otherwise, for he had decided to exploit in his poems as completely as possible the extensive aggadic material available; but he himself chose the linguistic usage. Here he was not subject to pressure from his source, but drew his language from the Bible. He is uncommonly fertile in neologisms and surprising forms, surpassing all other payyetanim in the richness of his diction and the creative force of his language, but his entire vocabulary can be easily followed back to its biblical source. Of course, his works do not lack for difficult and ungrammatical word formations, forms, and usages; but he could hardly have dispensed with these, considering the heavy armor of the artistic form into which he forced his poems. The acrostics of alphabet, names, and biblical passages and the merging of these types of acrostic, the demands of the rhyme, frequently further complicated by chain words and biblical quotations, forced him to invent new words and not to be afraid to deviate from accepted morphology and normal patterns. But we can see in his works again and again the mastery with which he could bend and flex the relatively limited biblical vocabulary to serve his purposes. It must be borne in mind that Kallir often returned to the same subject and expressed the same ideas, but it cannot be denied that each time he found a new cloak for them, and that he knew how to deck them out with ever new ornaments. Brilliant flair and profound thoughts are not found in Kallir's poems. Tied as they were to the character of the festival, and dependent upon the midrash, they moved in a predetermined orbit. Nevertheless, within the limits imposed upon him, the poet knew how to create a store of changing elements around the fixed themes and recurring images.

[239]

Kallir's poems spread in a very wide circle—to the Oriental countries, the Balkans, Italy, France, and Germany.[50] They retained their dominant position in liturgical poetry even after local poets reworked the festival prayers. They were not adopted in the lands that stood under the influence of Arabic culture; thus, they are not found in Spain or in the prayer books dependent upon it in North Africa or Asia. We cannot determine whether they were once included in them, but were displaced by the better compositions of the later period. The poems of Kallir were not only recited in the synagogue, but were also studied diligently. They are cited as authority both for substantive matters and for linguistic formations. It goes without saying that commentaries were written on them; such commentaries were vital in view of the obscurity in most of the poems.[51]

[S. Spiegel has prepared a critical edition of all of Kallir's poems, but it is not yet ready for publication. A detailed bibliography of studies on the poet down to 1931 is appended to Spiegel's article in the German *Encyclopaedia Judaica* (Berlin: Eshkol, 1928–34), 9:816–20. Of the editions of his poems and studies that have appeared afterwards, the following must be mentioned: J. Marcus, *Ginze shira ufiyut* (New York, 1932/3); *idem*, "R. Eleʿazar qalir ufiyutav," *Horev* 1 (1933/4): 21–31, 151–66; 2 (1934/5): 6–16; R. Edelmann, *Zur Frühgeschichte des Maḥzor* (Stuttgart, 1934); I. Elbogen, *Kohut Festschrift* (New York, 1935), 157–59; *idem*, *S. Krauss Festschrift* (Jerusalem, 1936/7), 307–10; S. Spiegel, "Eleʿazar berabi abun ben piyute haqiliri," *SRIHP* 5 (1938/9): 267–91; A. Scheiber, "Piyut qaliri hamuva ʿal yede qirqisani," in *Ginze Kaufmann*, vol. 1 (Budapest, 1948/9), 4–36; G. J. Orman, in A. Murtonen, *Materials for a non-Masoretic Hebrew Grammar*, Hebrew Parts 1–23 (Helsinki, 1958), 68–83; A. Mirsky, "Muqdam umeʾuḥar befiyute r. eleʿazar haqiliri," *Qiryat Sefer* 35 (1959/60): 237–39; E. Fleischer, "Parashat ʿaser teʿaser," *Tarbiz* 36 (1966/7), 122–28; idem, "Leʿinyan hamishmarot bapiyutim," *Sinai* 62 (1967/8): 13–40; idem, "Qerova ḥamishit letishʿa beʾav meʾet r. eleʿazar berabi qalir," *Sinai* 63 (1967/8): 32–49; Ḥ. Schirmann, "Haqerav ben behemot velivyatan," *Divre haʾaqademia haleʾumit* 3, 3 (1967/8).]

§ 41   *The Main Liturgical Poets: Kallir's Imitators*

(1)   Not only was Kallir's example decisive for the status of liturgical poetry and its acceptance into the liturgy, but its effects were felt for centuries, for the forms that he had cast were accepted by everyone who was later called into the field to contribute to the shaping of the synagogue service. With the exception of the Spanish Jews, all the poets of the post-Kallirian period adhered more or less closely to his style of work; composers of *qerovot* followed him in every respect. The first heirs of Kallir still saw themselves as having major responsibilities, for they felt it their duty to fill the gaps they found in Kallir's festival cycle. As we have seen, a number of Kallir's poems vanished in the course of time because of insufficient care in the transmission of his work. Furthermore, because Kallir composed poetry only for the first day of the festival, the later poets saw the need to compose poems for the festival days for which he had not provided poems. This process continued until around 1050. By then the festival cycle may be seen as completely finished, and liturgical poetry had achieved unquestioned status in all communities; occasional protests raised by sages were fruitless in the face of the approval of the masses. Because of the popularity of the liturgical poetry and its wide dissemination, the craft of poetry increased in prestige, and the leading men of each generation aspired to try their hand at it. Thus after 1050 the number of poets increased greatly. Scholarship was now widespread among the Jews of Europe, and knowledge of the Talmud and midrash and familiarity with the Bible and the Hebrew language had increased. "In the Roman and German lands, which already stood under the influence of the achievements in grammar, biblical exegesis and poetry, no district at that time lacked a rabbi or a cantor to embellish the public and private worship with homilies or poetry."[1] As the number of poets grew, so did the opportunities for the use of liturgical poetry. Kallir had composed a great many *qerovot*, but only a few *yoṣerot*, and as his followers had not filled all the lacunae, the later poets had plenty of room for activity. Besides, originally only the great festivals and the most important Sabbaths were accorded poetry, but now the number of such Sabbaths increased greatly; whenever the character of a Sabbath or its Torah reading afforded any reason at all for poetic expansion, it was taken advantage of. Especially popular was the *yoṣer*. Complete ones were not always composed, but frequently only a few parts; at the same time, the structure of the *yoṣer* was expanded and provided with poems in places that formerly were devoid

of poetry. Further, significant personal events were taken into account; *yoṣer, qerova* and introductions to the Torah reading dealt with weddings, circumcisions and other occasions that brought the participants to the synagogue. Finally, the continually worsening persecutions provided many opportunities for the poets to compose *qinot*, and martyrdom, which the Jews had to endure without let-up after 1096, found its echo in the synagogue. The poets immortalized the witnesses to the faith in their poems, thereby providing the halo to their heroic deaths. The fathers' loyalty to their faith was an admonition and an encouragement to following generations, who honored their memory with their tears and, when necessary, by following their example.

[241]

[In the course of the last forty years, our knowledge of the development of liturgical poetry between the seventh and the eleventh centuries has expanded greatly, and it is difficult for us to maintain some of the opinions of Zunz and Elbogen. The years around 1050 cannot be seen as a turning point, and it cannot be said that only thereafter did the number of poets increase noticeably or that most of them have followed Kallir. In the manuscripts, the works of dozens of authors belonging to this period have been discovered, and study of them is only at its beginnings. We have to content ourselves here with a few references to the rich literature that is almost entirely found in geniza manuscripts. For now, see: M. Zulay, "Letoledot hapiyut beʾereṣ yisraʾel," *SRIHP* 5 (1939): 107–108; *idem*, "Ben qotle hamakhon leḥeqer hashira haʿivrit," in ʿ*Ale* ʿ*Ayin* (Jerusalem, 1951), 83–124; H. Schirmann, *Shirim ḥadashim min hageniza* (Jerusalem, 1966). Among the most prominent poets we should mention Phineas the Priest, who lived apparently in the eighth century in Kafra near Tiberias (on his dates, see M. Margulies in *Tarbiz* 29 [1959/60]: 339–44; several of his poems were published by A. Marmorstein, M. Zulay, and E. Fleischer. Marmorstein—see above, §20(1); Zulay—*SRIHP* 1 [1935]: 139–74; 5 [1939]: 121–46; "Ereṣ yisraʾel vaʿaliyat regalim befiyute r. pinhas," *Yerushalayim* 4 [1952]: 51–81; Fleischer—*Sinai* 60 [1966/7]: 209–27; 61 [1967] 30–56). The craft of liturgical poetry spread in that period also to the lands adjacent to Palestine and to North Africa. One of the most productive poets who ever lived among the Jews was Solomon Sulaiman al-Sinjari, who seems to have lived in Iraq in the tenth century (on him, see Schirmann, *Shirim ḥadashim*, 46–48). Around 1000 Joseph al-Bardani lived in Baghdad; his contemporary was Samuel bar Hoshaʿna Heḥaver, known as Samuel the Third, who moved from Palestine to Egypt and died there (on him see Schirmann, *Shirim ḥadashim*, 63–65; M. Wallenstein, *Some Unpublished Piyyutim from the Cairo Geniza* (Manchester, 1956). Some of the poems of R. Hai Gaon (939–1038) must be singled out for their literary merit; see H. Brody, "Piyutim veshire tehila merav haya gaʾon," *SRIHP* 3 (1937): 3–63.]

(2)   Few of Kallir's immediate successors are known to us by name.[2] This was the period when the center of gravity of Jewish life and learning shifted gradually to Europe. Not all the compositions of the eastern writers were accepted there; for the most part only works of particular importance or works whose immortality was guaranteed by the fame of their author were accepted. Thus the name of only one eastern synagogue poet has come down to us from the centuries immediately following Kallir's time, and only thanks to its bearer's great celebrity as a scholar. This was Saadia b. Joseph (892–942),[3] "the most famous of the geonim, who in his liturgical poetry speaks in a language most fluent and difficult, sometimes as a worshiper and sometimes as a payyetan, but never as a true poet." Saadia's poems were not adopted by any known prayer book, but they

were preserved thanks to his great collection of "prayers and praises"—that is, his own prayer book, which is discussed in a different connection. Here we speak only of his poems. Three great compositions of his are dedicated to Pentecost and deal with the 613 commandments. One of them, in Arabic, begins with *hāʾulāʾi 'l-kalimāt*, "These are the words"; it was intended for the Pentecost *ʿAmida*, and may perhaps still be recited in some of the communities of North Africa. Its contents were outlined by Zunz in *Literaturgeschichte*, 96. A second treatment of the same theme is found in a liturgical poem beginning with the words, את ה' אלהיך תירא, "Fear the Lord your God."[4] In six sections arranged alternately in forward and reverse alphabetical acrostic, each composed of eleven rhymed stanzas of four lines each with chain words, the 613 positive and negative commandments are enumerated. It is not merely a dry listing, for the composer has sorted the laws into categories, and has carefully noted at the end of each category the number of commandments included in it. The work has no [name-] acrostic, and thus there is no internal evidence as to the author; doubts have actually been expressed about its authenticity, but without justification, as the enumeration of the commandments and the style accord completely with Saadia's other similar compositions. He treated the theme of the commandments for a third time in *qerova*, beginning אלהים אצל יום הלזה מימים ימימה, "God set aside this day long ago." Among the liturgical poems known to us today, hardly another compares with this one for artificial structure and difficult style. Saadia not only worked into it the 613 commandments, but he subsumed them under the Ten Commandments, and he imposed upon the whole a ponderous external structure that forced him to resort to the strangest neologisms and most incomprehensible phrases. Saadia's *azharot* are divided into three parts. The beginning and the end form a completely regular *shivʿata* accompanying the seven benedictions of the *ʿAmida*, while the middle, beginning אנכי אש אוכלת וניחרת מכל הנהרות, "I am a consuming fire, brighter than anything that blazes," is devoted to the commandments. Saadia founded this monstrous structure on various types of biblical verses. He begins each of the strophes in sequence with one word from Ps. 68:8–9; the middle of each strophe begins with the words of Song of Songs 1:1–14; and, in the *azharot* proper, he adds to the beginning the words that begin each of the Ten Commandments. Just as he decorates the beginnings of the lines with quotations from the Bible, so he decorates their ends: The fourth line of each stanza is always a biblical verse, and all the preceding lines have to rhyme with it. In enumerating the commandments, he concludes each section (that is, each of the ten groupings corresponding to the Ten Commandments) with the same conclusion as in the corresponding biblical verse. It goes without saying that such a framework allows no room for real poetry. Saadia labored at following in Kallir's footsteps, but failed, surpassing him in artificiality but falling short in that which constituted Kallir's art.

Saadia liked to go back to the subject of his great works in several different ways. For the *ʿAvoda* of the Day of Atonement,[5] we have two different versions. One begins באדני יצדקו ויודוהו, "In God they will be vindicated"; like the *azharot*, it is constructed in a most artificial pattern. It has an alphabetical acrostic by strophes, each strophe being composed of eight lines all beginning with the same letter of the alphabet. As an additional difficulty, the odd lines begin with the preposition ב before the acrostic letter, and the second half of each line must end with a biblical quotation, the last word of which is the same as the first word of the preceding odd-numbered line. The odd

[242]

and even lines are further paired by end-rhyme. The lines are divided into half-lines by a caesura, and the first half-lines of the strophe are linked by monorhyme. The contents of the ʿAvoda do not go beyond the ordinary, with Saadia unmistakably following in the footsteps of Yose b. Yose. Like him, he devotes by far the larger part of the poem to the introduction, and describes the Day of Atonement ritual only in the second half. In justice to him it must be said that he did his best to lend life and drama to this description, but the great effort he was forced to expend in preserving the external form could only be deleterious to the content. According to Saadia's own testimony, he composed other Avodot (פואסיק), one of which has recently been found nearly complete. It begins אלהים יה מקדם, "God, Lord from of old." It, too, has twenty-two stanzas, each with four double lines in alphabetical order. Its structure is much simpler than that of the above-mentioned ʿAvoda. The odd and even verses of this poem are monorhymed separately, the even ones in *im* and the odd ones in *na*. The poem is rendered a bit more complicated by the chain words, for the even lines end with the same word as the one with which the following odd line begins, so that the same word occurs twice in succession. The language of this poem is much simpler than that of the preceding one, but the content is identical, so much so that the stanzas correspond, though the second poem is rendered on a much smaller scale. Neither has an acrostic attesting that Saadia was its author, but both are attributed to him, and there is no reason to doubt the attribution. Of his great compositions, Saadia's cycle of *hoshaʿnot* must also be mentioned.[6] The *hoshaʿnot* for the individual days are divided into three parts, the first beginning always with למען, "For the sake of"; the second, with ענה בהושענא, "Answer [when they cry] 'save us' "; and the third, with the refrain, mentioned above, תבנה ציון ברנה והעלנו לתוכה בשמחה, "Build Zion in song and bring us up to its midst in joy." For the seventh day Saadia did not add to the number of *hoshaʿnot*. Most of the poems of this cycle are identical with those in Sepharad. Their language is much simpler than that to which we are accustomed in Saadia; therefore, it is very questionable how many he actually composed and how many he may have taken over from others. His lesser works are a number of *seliḥot* for fast days or for the days of repentance.[7] Their style is rather ponderous, as is typical for Saadia, and they are mostly attached to specific themes such as the twelve tribes of Israel, the twelve stones in the breastplate of the high priest, the destruction of the seven sanctuaries, and so forth. The authenticity of the attribution of these poems to Saadia can also not be taken for granted, but some have recently been found in geniza fragments where they are designated as his works.

The best compositions with which Saadia enriched the prayer book are the two "Petitions," one of which begins אדני שפתי תפתח, "Lord, open my lips," and the other, אתה הוא ה' לבדך, "You are the Lord alone." These are his two works praised by Abraham Ibn Ezra because of their powerful feeling and simple style, and in fact they are Saadia's only compositions to be accepted into the prayer book. The text that we have before us certainly justifies the praise that has been lavished on them. They are based mainly on biblical verses, being composed partly of actual verses and partly of sentences in biblical style. They express a simple and deep faith. In the form in which they have come down to us, they are not completely authentic, for later additions have been inserted in them and compositions by later authors have been appended to them. A complete analysis can be found in Landshuth, ʿAmude, 239ff.

Saadia's style represents the uppermost limit of ponderousness and difficulty of which the liturgical poetry is capable, and for that reason the author of the treatise on poetics, mentioned several times above, sees his poems as the last aftergrowths of the form. Because of their difficulty, Saadia's works were not suitable for use in the synagogue; but because of the high respect enjoyed by his name they were often studied and cited. Saadia's poetic efforts were important in that not only did he try his own hand as a poet, but he dealt with the theory of poetry as well. The many worthless poems circulating in his time caught his attention and induced him to compose a kind of textbook for the improvement of the language and style of the poets. Today we have fragments of his *Agron*,[8] which he originally planned as a kind of rhyming dictionary, and in which he collected the roots of the Hebrew language in alphabetical order by first and last letter. In his later years Saadia expanded this early composition; he turned his attention also to the contents, the "soul of poetry," and added a treatise on poetics, in which he dealt with the style of poetry and its imagery.

[After the appearance of this book, a great part of Saadia's poems were collected in two books, *Sidur rav saʿadia gaʾon,* with a special appendix by M. Zulay (377–425); and M. Zulay, *Haʾaskola hapayetanit shel rav saʿadia gaʾon* (Jerusalem, 1964). Bibliography in Schirmann, *Shirim ḥadashim,* 34; see also S. Abramson, "Lapiyutim besidur rav saʿadia gaʾon," *Sinai* 29 (1965/6): 133–45. *Sefer Haʾagron* appeared in a new edition by N. Aloni (1968/9). Incidentally, Saadia was born in 882.]

(3)   In the period after Saadia, important poets follow each other almost in succession, and the names of the first European poets appear. At first they are all from Italy, the land that served as a bridge for Jewish scholarship between Europe and the East. The spread of liturgical poetry is a sign of the growth of scholarship and the increasing stability of community institutions. The first name of a poet from Europe is that of Solomon b. Judah the Babylonian, ca. 950–980.[9] His by-name refers to his native city, Rome, which had been called metaphorically Babylon since the time of the apocalypse. At one time, Solomon was a poet widely read and respected. He is often named together with Kallir, whom he imitates in most of his poems, successfully for the most part, though his sentence structure is frequently even more cumbersome, his exposition more obscure, and his language more difficult. A great part of his works are preserved only in manuscript, and only a few were accepted into the prayer book. Among the latter, אור ישע מאשרים, "Light, salvation of the gladdened ones," is particularly famous. It is a *yoṣer* for the first day of Passover; in it the author signed his own name four times and the name Mordecai, apparently that of his brother, appears three times. Already Rashi wrote a commentary on this poem, which was adopted in Ashkenaz, Romaniot and Rome. Solomon also composed a number of *seliḥot,*[10] a few of which were disseminated via the prayer books. Through all his poetry runs a tone of mourning "like a silent groan, barely repressed, seizing hold of every reader." We do not know whether he witnessed persecution, but from the tone of his laments we must assume that he did. In the area of the *seliḥa* he was seen as the model, and the *seliḥot* that are patterned after his are called שלמונית.[11] Of his great compositions, his ʿAvoda אדרת תלבושת, "The splendid garment,"[12] one of the lengthiest and most complex poems of its kind, must be mentioned. It shows fine poetic delicacy in that it dwells at length on the stories of creation and of the patriarchs; but the poet's strengths were not adequate to the task. It is still in use in Romaniot.

[Solomon the Babylonian was not the first Hebrew poet who lived in Europe. He was preceded by several colleagues in southern Italy belonging to the ninth and tenth centuries, the most important of whom is Amitai b. Shefatia of Oria. The poems of this early school have been nearly completely assembled in the appendix to *Megilat ahima'aṣ* in the edition of Benjamin Klar (Jerusalem, 1943/4), 65–120. On the early Hebrew poem in Italy, see Luzzatto, *Mavo*; J. Schirmann, "The Beginning of Hebrew Poetry in Italy," in *The World History of the Jewish People: The Dark Ages* (Tel Aviv, 1966), 249–60; 429–32, with detailed bibliography. Many examples from the works of the Italian poets are included in H. Schirmann, *Mivḥar hashira ha'ivrit be'italia* (Berlin, 1933/4). A critical edition of all the poems of Solomon the Babylonian has been prepared by E. Fleischer; it is to be published together with a detailed study of the poet and his works.]

(4)   The next poets belong to the Kalonymus family, famed for the numerous leaders that they gave the Jewish people.[13] The family originated in Lucca in Italy. After one of its members helped to save the life of the emperor Otto II in 982, the family, furnished with a valuable privilege, moved to Mainz, where they filled an important function. Since the members of the Kalonymus family who immigrated to Germany continued to bear the by-name "of Lucca," it is often hard to determine whether the bearer of the name lived in Italy or in Germany. In addition, there is the problem that the same names were passed on in the family from generation to generation and keep recurring, so that it is often difficult to distinguish between grandfathers and grandsons who bear the same name. In all probability this family had great influence in the formation of the Ashkenazic liturgy, for they brought with them the traditions current in Italy. In later centuries, their immigration was connected with the transmission of the "mysteries of prayer"; it is certain that they brought with them many elements of the Italian and Palestinian rites and planted them on German soil. Among these, apparently, was liturgical poetry. The first poet of this family was Moses b. Kalonymus, known as Moses the Elder.[14] He dates himself when he says in one of his verses, זוללתי עתה ללאת יותר מתשע מאות, "I am consumed to exhaustion now more than nine hundred years," according to which he must have lived about nine hundred years after the destruction of the Temple—that is, ca. 980. His main work is a *qerova* for the seventh day of Passover, אימת נוראותיך, "The terror of Your awesome deeds," which entered several prayer books. It is studded with midrash and is in the Kallirian style, but is one of the best imitations of its kind, with power and musicality. Another poet of the same family is Kalonymus of Lucca,[15] who may have flourished earlier. R. Gershom praises him as a sage, saying that he composed *qerovot* abounding in aggadah for all the festivals. But hardly any of all these poems is extant; Zunz attributes to him the *rahitim* for the Day of Atonement based on Jer. 10:7. They, too, show great ability. Better known is his son, Meshulam b. Kalonymus,[16] who is also sometimes said to have been Italian and who may have been born in Italy, but who certainly died in Mainz,[17] where his gravestone has even recently been rediscovered. He, too, is praised by R. Gershom as a celebrated sage, and we know that he was in contact with the leading men of his time. He was also a prolific poet. Of his compositions, particularly famous is his *qerova* for the Day of Atonement—אמצת עשור, "You adopted the tenth day," used to this day in Ashkenaz for the Morning Service. It contains the acrostic משלם בירבי קלונימוס several times, attesting to his authorship. The *qerova* as we have it today consists of more than

thirty pieces, but not all are by him, for much extraneous material has intruded, including the above-mentioned poems of his father. For the Additional Service he composed two versions of the ʿAvoda,[18] including אמיץ כח, "Mighty in strength," used in Ashkenaz. Among known ʿAvodot, this work is the least regular in its poetic structure; it is typical of the later Ashkenazic poets as well, in that they often neglect the fundamental principle of poetry—uniformity of pattern. Surprisingly, we find that the poem lacks rhyme. It has been shown that the author's intention was to abridge the ʿAvoda of Yose and to put it into a form more in accordance with the taste of his contemporaries, full of hard words and complicated expressions. Besides the alphabetical acrostic, he also had to devise a relatively lengthy acrostic for his own name. Because he was not able to extricate himself from all these difficulties, his ʿAvoda came out very irregularly—sometimes they were very condensed, jumping from idea to idea, and at other times they went into great detail. The ʿAvoda also has an introduction, אטיף ארש מלולי, "I will speak the prayer of my speech," which was omitted by the congregations and remained buried in manuscripts until quite recently. The same happened to his second ʿAvoda, אשוחח צור נפלואותיך, "I shall speak, O Rock, of Your wonders," which seems to have been customary in medieval Saxony and Bohemia, and which is usually found in Ashkenazic manuscripts in the margin of "Mighty in strength." Its structure is much more regular. The whole poem consists of four-line stanzas with rhyme. Its contents match those of "Mighty in strength," and it follows Yose even more closely. Besides the Day of Atonement, the poet also composed for Passover; Ashkenaz has several of his pieces among the poems for the second day. But his poems met the same fate as did many others: Scribes and the congregations found them too long and shortened them in one way or another, removing especially the biblical verses intended to adorn the stanzas.

[The poems of Moses the Elder were printed as an appendix to the poems of Simon b. Isaac in pages 191–218 of the edition by Habermann; see below, §41(5). Critical editions of the poems of Kalonymus the Elder and Meshulam his son do not yet exist. For the early Kalonymid poets, see the English article by H. Schirmann mentioned above in §41(3).]

(5)   All the poets just mentioned sought their main field of activity where they found lacunae in Kallir's festival cycle; they enabled the congregations to complete the cycle of poems wherever Kallirian material was lacking. The most important of the poets who were active in this way in Germany was Simon b. Isaac b. Abun of Mainz, ca. 1000.[19] He is sometimes called "The Great," was generally revered as one of the great men of his age, and was even widely thought to be a proven miracle worker. He seems to have earned particular gratitude for preventing or halting a persecution of the Jews in Mainz in 1012;[20] his efforts to save the communities earned him the inclusion of a prayer for his soul in the service. His name is mentioned favorably in every connection, especially in the area of liturgical poetry. His compositions were accepted nearly everywhere in Germany and France, and they are the best and finest complement to the poems of Kallir. It may be said with assurance that wherever poems by Kallir were lacking (except for those few cases where the above-mentioned poets supplied the community's needs) Simon b. Isaac came to the rescue and filled in the lacunae. Thus, in Ashkenaz we have the *yoṣer* and complete *qerova* for the second day of the New Year, for the seventh day of Passover, and the second day of Pentecost. He also composed a *yoṣer* for the intermediate Sabbath of Passover. He, too, followed in Kallir's footsteps

[247]

and those of the later poets as well, but he was not gifted with their force of exposition, and he particularly lacked their talent for conciseness. The formal devices of his poems are the same as those of the other poets: alphabetical acrostic, name-acrostic, and sometimes even rhymes and refrains of unusual length. He was unlucky as to the latter, because they were frequently eliminated in the course of time. In general the desire for brevity took a toll on his poems.[21] Thus, half of the *rahit* beginning מלך עליון, "Highest King," has disappeared, for originally every stanza beginning "Highest King" was accompanied by a stanza beginning מלך אביון, "Wretched King," juxtaposing the greatness and might of the King of Kings against the impotence of the flesh and blood king.

Simon seems to have been the first Ashkenazic poet to compose poetic introductions, and to introduce this genre; later poets imitated him, shamelessly composing introductions to the compositions of others. Many items in the festival prayer book were falsely attributed to Simon, like the *azharot* אתה הנחלת, "You granted," in Ashkenaz, which is already quoted by earlier authors, and which also differs from all of Simon's other compositions in lacking rhyme. Simon probably never composed *azharot* at all, for Ashkenaz already had enough versions of this genre; nevertheless, it is not impossible that a composition of this type by him has been lost. He composed a great many poems for the Sabbath, for at that time the number of Sabbaths that had to be honored with a special poem began to expand considerably; here, too, Simon served as a model for many followers. Finally, his activity in the area of the *seliha* must be mentioned.[22] Here, too, a change occurred in the tenth and eleventh centuries; poetic *selihot* became more and more entrenched, displacing the earlier simple, nonrhyming compositions, which were often superior to all the artificial productions of later times in poetic spirit and, above all, in depth of religious feeling. We have a great number of *selihot* by Simon, as well as Supplications and introductions to the *selihot* of the Day of Atonement and the weeks of *selihot*. The poet appears as precentor and speaks on behalf of the community. Besides his pervasive consciousness of sin, he laments the suffering of the age, and the cruel persecutions, in which Jews were prohibited from acknowledging their faith, many were forced into apostasy, and many preferred suicide; the women particularly stood out for their courageous self-sacrifice, throwing themselves into the flood in contempt of death, rather than falling alive into the hands of their persecutors.

[248]   [The poems of Simon b. Isaac were published by A. M. Habermann, *Piyute rabi sh'imon berabi yishaq* (Berlin and Jerusalem, 1937/8). In this edition all his piyyutim and *selihot* were assembled from manuscripts and old printed editions.]

(6)   The same depressed spirit as in Simon's *selihot* recurs in those of his slightly younger contemporary, R. Gershom b. Judah, known as the "Light of the Diaspora."[23] His historical importance is not in the area of liturgy, but he did compose *selihot* and bewailed the persecutions that he suffered, in the course of which his son, as is well known, was forced into apostasy.[24] One of Gershom's poems is particularly famous, the refrain poem אבדנו מארץ טובה בחפזון, "We have quickly perished from the good land," with its introduction, זכר ברית אברהם, "Remember the covenant of Abraham," for which the entire *selihot* service of the eve of the New Year is named. Neither the author's prestige nor the poem's popularity saved it from being considerably abridged, a fate that befell many of this master's other compositions. Benjamin b. Zerah[25] is known mainly as the

author of *selihot*. He was given the epithet "The Great," and is sometimes called "Master of the Name," not because he was a miracle worker, but because one of his *selihot*, אנא ה' האל הגדול, "O Lord, the great God," is built around the beginnings of the divine name of forty-two letters. In his *ofanim* he also frequently employs divine names. As to his dating, he himself mentions 990 years after the destruction of the Temple, (ca. 1060); his homeland is probably to be sought in the Balkans. He composed a great number of *selihot*, some of which were taken also into Ashkenaz and are recited with great solemnity, like the ʿaqedot אמונים בני מאמינים, "The faith of the children of the faithful," and אהבת עזוז, "Love of the mighty God." They are mostly in a simple style, and full of deep, sincere feeling; their content is mainly lamentation, for this author too probably witnessed persecutions in his land. Besides *selihot*, he also composed *yoserot*; Ashkenaz preserves his poems for the Sabbath before Passover: אתי מלבנון כלה, "With me from Lebanon, O bride." His *ofan* is lively and dramatic, for its stanzas are devoted alternately to the song of the angels and the response of the Jewish people.

From the same period two other poets may be mentioned who were especially respected because of the unusually artistic form of their work. First, there was Joseph b. Solomon, of Carcassonne,[26] who must have written before Rashi. His *yoser* for the Sabbath of Hanukkah beginning אודך כי אנפת בי, "I give thanks to You because You chastised me," is used in Ashkenaz and Rome; it is built of strophes with a ninefold alphabetical acrostic. Such extensive use of acrostic is found only rarely even among the ancient poets, and then only in the ʿAvoda. Naturally, it made the language particularly difficult, and therefore the poem was early provided with commentaries. Joseph's contemporary, Ṣahlal b. Nathaniel,[27] took an even more original tack; he is known as the author of one single poem that achieved renown for its structure. His hymn לצור יעקב, "To the Rock of Jacob," consists of 248 lines with the constant rhyme *rim*, of which the poet was exceedingly proud. The poem is remarkable for its contents in that it is the first description derived entirely from *Sefer yesira* of the unity of the Creator and of His act of creation. In accordance with the outlook of this ancient work, all of creation, including man, is derived from the combination of the letters of the alphabet. At the end the poet goes on to expound God's goodness and His benefactions to Israel; and since he refers specifically to the victories of the Hasmoneans, it must have been composed for Hanukkah. Ṣahlal's birthplace must be sought in France or the Balkans. His poetry exemplifies some of the strange fruit that the liturgical poetry bore; though completely artificial, pedantic, and remote from both the content and tone of true prayer, it nevertheless enjoyed great esteem in the Middle Ages.   [249]

[Only ten liturgical poems by R. Gershom remain. They were collected and published in a pamphlet, *Rabenu gershom meʾor hagola: selihot ufizmonim*, by A.M. Habermann (Jerusalem, 1943/4). The many poems of Benjamin b. Zerah have not yet been collected, and in part have not even been printed. According to Zunz's conjecture, Benjamin lived in southeastern Europe, that is, in the territory of the Byzantine Empire. The *yoser* of Joseph b. Solomon tells the story of Judith and Holofernes, an unusual subject among our liturgical poets. Ṣahlal b. Nathaniel apparently lived in one of the Arabic countries, but outside of Islamic Spain.]

(7)   Around 1050 a new period opened up in the history of liturgical poetry. From this point on hardly any room remained for simple compositions, and the poets now

applied themselves to fleshing out the existing framework, in that they cultivated the poetic *seliha* even more than had the previous generations. From the point of view of language, the period showed some progress; linguistic studies gradually began to flourish, and thus more attention was paid to stylistic accuracy. Some freedom from the patterns of the early poets appeared. The new poets were no longer so tightly bound to midrash, and preferred the Bible, though they did like to clothe its content in talmudic and midrashic language.

There is no doubt that they were influenced by the flourishing poetry of contemporary Spain, but it is not easy to establish exactly the extent of this influence. At the beginning of the new period stand two poets of northern France, both highly respected as talmudists. They were the last sages who had to give a serious opinion about the propriety of liturgical poetry within the liturgy; of course both gave it their sanction. The first was Elia b. Menahem the Elder of Le Mans.[28] He was the author of large-scale compositions, especially אמת יהגה חכי, "My mouth speaks the truth,"[29] *azharot* in rhymed quatrains with alphabetical and name-acrostic. The poem is executed with great skill, listing both the biblical and rabbinic laws one after the other; in the case of the prohibitions, those with a severe punishment are cited first, followed by those whose punishment is lighter. Elia's *azharot* were much admired, often cited as authoritative commentaries on the biblical and rabbinic commandments, and vigorously discussed among the learned. Another great composition of his is called *Seder*, or, more fully, סדר המערכה, "The ritual of the [sacrificial] order." It is a collection of all biblical passages that must be recited daily in the Morning Service, and contains two long prayers, אתן תהלה לאל, "I give praise to God," and אתה מבין תעלומות לב, "You know the secrets of the heart," that have been accepted into the prayers of the Day of Atonement; Rome, in its older editions, contains the entire piece. Elia was also known as the composer of *selihot*,[30] but most have been lost, together with the French rite that contained them. His contemporary was Joseph b. Samuel Bonfils (טוב עלם),[31] who originated in Narbonne, a site of ancient Jewish tradition, and taught in Limoges. He was highly respected as a collector and disseminator of halakhic literature, and he had outstanding status as a liturgical poet; his work shows daring flight of imagination and lovely images. Not many of his compositions were accepted into the prayer book, though he composed complete cycles of poems for nearly all festival days. His poems have mostly been lost, together with the old French rite, and only a few have been preserved in other prayer books. Among them are the *ma'arivot* for the first evening of Pentecost, וירד אביר יעקב, "The mighty one of Jacob descended," and for the first evening of Tabernacles, אוחזי בידם ארבעה, "Those who hold the four in their hand," both of which have the acrostic of his name. We also have his *yoser* and *qerova* for the Sabbath before Passover, eleven poems all told, including an extensive halakhic treatise אל אלהי הרוחות, "God, the god of spirits," the conclusion of which, חסל סדור פסח, "The Passover rite is finished," has been incorporated into the Haggadah. This composition of Joseph also won great respect and was provided with several commentaries. He also composed several *yoserot* for the Sabbaths following Passover, and may have been the first to compose poems for these Sabbaths. Besides the old French and the old Ashkenazic rite, the Greek rite has also taken in some of his compositions.

[The poems of Elia the Elder and Joseph Bonfils have not yet been collected; Joseph was the most productive of the medieval French poets.]

[250]

(8)   The greatest poet in that generation was Elia b. Shemaʿiah. According to a tradition of unknown origin, he was born in Bari in southern Italy, where there was at that time a famous Jewish academy that was proverbial as far away as France and Germany; otherwise we know nothing of his life. He is one of the best of the *seliha* writers, one who often neglects accepted artistic forms in order to devote more attention to content and language. He maintains rigorously the tripartite structure of the *seliha*—complaint, petition, and hope; his themes are not numerous, and they always revolve around the same point, but in each of his poems one marks that the words come from the heart of a deeply sensitive man. The content is mostly elegiac; the poet strives for words that will give expression to his sorrow for his people's suffering. He attributes this suffering to the sins of the age, but does not grovel beneath the weight of sin; he is always able to press forward toward confidence that God will eliminate the sins and the enemy together. Hardly any other *seliha* composer found such intense, heartfelt expression for the insignificance and helplessness of man as against the greatness and might of God. The number of Elia's *selihot* exceeded thirty, some being the most beautiful and best in the Ashkenazic rite, including אדון בשפטך אנוש רמה, "Lord, when You judge the worm, man"; אויתיך קויתיך מארץ מרחקים, "I longed and hoped for You in a distant land"; אריה ביער דמיתי, "I am like a lion in the forest"; אקרא בשמך להחזיק בך אתעורר, "I call on Your name and arouse myself to cling to You"; אתה חלקי וצור לבבי, "You are my portion and the Rock of my heart."[32]

[The *selihot* of Elia b. Shemaiah have mostly been printed in collections of *selihot* and prayer books of the Ashkenazic rite.]

(9)   Highly celebrated in medieval Germany was Meir b. Isaac,[33] who served as precentor in Worms during the period when Rashi lived there, and who is usually called by the epithet "The Precentor." He was regarded as one of the best connoisseurs of prayer rites and liturgical customs; his way of organizing and performing the service was thought the last word, and he was considered the authority on the text of prayers and liturgical poetry. He allowed himself many innovations that then came to be accepted on his word. As a poet he was very popular, and was praised as unique for his ability to compose *selihot* on themes of aggadah, halakha, and the commandments; later the communities included his name in their prayers for the dead because he "enlightened the eyes of Israel with his poems." He contributed greatly to the embellishment of the liturgy, but only a few of his compositions proved long-lived. His compositions were used in his native city, Worms, where some are still in use; others were customary in central Germany, but later, with the unification of the rite, they disappeared, and only a very few found wider dissemination. Meir's style is not uniform in quality; in his wedding poems, of which he composed not a few, he is very simple; he is obscure in the *yoṣerot*, of which only one is still in use outside of his own city of Worms; and he is fluent and touching in his *selihot*. Some poetic types are characteristic of him, and were first introduced in his time, for example, the lengthy halakhic excurses (בכור) in the *maʿarivot*. One of these, אור יום הנף, "The night preceding the day of the waving," for the second night of Passover, has been preserved throughout Ashkenaz, while the other, אזכרה שנות עולם, "I recall the ancient years," for the first night, remains only in western Ashkenaz.

Another type of poem introduced by him is the Aramaic introduction to the Tar-

[251]

gum of the Torah reading and the Haftara on those festivals when the Aramaic Targum was read in Ashkenaz. One of these, אקדמות מלין, "The beginning of words," for the first day of Pentecost, has been preserved. This poem praises the creator-lawgiver as the friend of Israel; to them earthly and heavenly joys are promised for the time of redemption. This poem became a particular favorite for its passionate and colorful description of the future salvation promised the righteous in the messianic age, and therefore it alone, of all the poems of its kind, survived the vicissitudes of time. Meir's *selihot* are devoted mostly to the binding of Isaac, or Supplication, which comes thematically to the same thing. Perhaps this characteristic is one of the first signs of the dark spirit that overtook German Jews toward the end of Meir's life because of the bloody persecutions of 1096. Of his younger contemporaries we mention briefly also Rashi (1040–1105).[34] Rashi's fame rests mainly on his unexcelled commentaries, but naturally every activity of a person of such stature was the object of full attention. Thus, as the editor of a prayer book, as the main authority of the *Mahzor Vitry*, and as a commentator on liturgical poetry, Rashi had great influence on the formation of the synagogue service. He tried his skill also as a poet, but he composed only *selihot* suffused with dark misery and bitter lament. His two *selihot*, ה' אלהי הצבאות נורא בעליונים, "Lord, God of hosts, awesome among the celestials," and אז טרם נמתחו, "Of old, before the heavens," are still used throughout the Ashkenazic world. Another introduction, תפלה לקדמך, "To come before You with prayer," is used only in the Altneuschul in Prague. The content of the *selihot* is borrowed from targum and midrash; the style is simple and clear. Rashi was not a poet of particular force, but his healthy spirit saved him from artificiality and breaches of good taste. In his whole circle, in the academy that he founded, it was customary for the distinguished talmudists to try to enrich the synagogue poetry, and nearly all outstanding tosafists tried their hands as poets, without in this way winning special fame. The most famous in this field was Rashi's grandson, Jacob Tam,[35] whose Aramaic Haftara introduction, יציב פתגם, "A true word," is still used today in many places in Ashkenaz.

[252]   [There does not yet exist a reliable edition of all the poems of Meir b. Isaac (נהוראי), but his Aramaic poem "The beginning of words" has many editions, commentaries, and translations. See Davidson, *Osar*, 1:7314 (and compare also 4:274–75). The poems that are definitely attributable to Rashi (seven altogether) have been collected and edited by A. M. Habermann, *Piyute Rashi* (Jerusalem, 1940/1).]

(10)   A very large number of Ashkenazic poets were inspired by the terrible persecutions that preceded the First Crusade; they expressed the depression and despair that overcame the Jews of the Rhineland at the sudden, unexpected outbursts of popular hatred against them.[36] The first author of elegies who laments the atrocities of the First Crusade is Menahem b. Makhir of Regensburg,[37] friend and correspondent of Rashi. He composed the *qina* אבל אעורר, "I call for lament," recited in Ashkenaz on the Ninth of Av, which describes in a general way the sufferings of 1096. This *qina* has the acrostic אנכי מנחם העלוב ברבי מכיר, "I, wretched Menahem b. R. Makhir"; the epithet "wretched" is intended to denote his depressed spirit. Menahem is also the author of *selihot* for the Seventeenth of Tammuz and the Thirteenth of Adar. He also composed *yoser* pieces for Sabbaths, some of them for Sabbaths that did not yet have poetry. He was also the first poet in Germany to write a poetic *nishmat*, perhaps reflecting already the

influence of the Spanish poets. He was also the author of the *hosha‘na* כהושעת אדם יציר כפיך לגוננה, "As You saved the man You created, protecting him," customarily recited in Ashkenaz on the Sabbath of the Intermediate Days.

Another poet who describes the hardships of 1096 is David b. Meshulam;[38] he was one of the ambassadors of the community of Speyer who in 1090 returned from the Emperor Henry IV with the most favorable writ of privilege. The sudden reversal in the status of his community rings through his poetry. He is the composer of the *seliha* אלהים אל דמי לדמי, "God, do not be silent over my blood," which describes the cruelty of the crusaders; its text has been variously corrupted. The same subject was treated by Kalonymus b. Judah of Mainz,[39] apparently a son of the Judah b. Kalonymus who also participated in the embassy to Emperor Henry. He composed two *qinot*, מי יתן ראשי מים, "If only my head were water," and אמרתי שעו מני, "I said turn away from me," and several *selihot* including את הקול קול יעקב נוהם, "The voice, the voice of Jacob roaring," and אפפוני מצוקות, "Hardships have surrounded me," which are all devoted to lament over the destruction of the once flourishing and famous communities on the Rhine. Kalonymus also acquired a reputation as the composer of other synagogue poems, including many *yoṣer*, *ofan*, and *zulat* poems for the Sabbaths. He used the last genre particularly to express his lament over the sorrowful events of his time; from then on the *zulat* was frequently employed to recount persecutions, and was composed for all the Sabbaths between Passover and Pentecost. Kalonymus also composed poems for the Sabbaths of special occasions, like the seven days of the wedding feast, circumcisions, and the like.

Finally, among the composers of lamentations on 1096, Eliezer b. Natan of Mainz must be named.[40] His are the two *zulatot* אלהים באזנינו שמענו, "God, we have heard with our ears," and אוי לי על שברי, "Woe to me for my destruction," as are the *selihot* אלהים זדים קמו, "God, the wicked have arisen," and אך טוב לישראל, "But it is good for Israel," which lament forced conversion and the communities' self-sacrifice. Eliezer, who lived to an advanced age, witnessed the incitements preceding the second crusade in 1147, toward the end of his life; on them he composed a bitter lament, the *seliha* את הברית ואת השבועה, "The covenant and the oath." Nor were these his only contributions to liturgical poetry, for he composed several *yoṣerot* for the Sabbath of the Ten Days of Repentance and for family celebrations. But more important, he studied and wrote learned commentaries on the ancient poems.

[The poems of Menaḥem b. Makhir, Kalonymus b. Judah, and Eliezer b. Natan (ראב"ן) are scattered in many printed books and manuscripts. But their *qinot* (גזירות, "[poems about] persecutions") were published together with similar poems by other poets in special collections that are devoted to the medieval persecutions, such as Salfeld, *Martyrologium*; S. Bernfeld, *Sefer hadema‘ot*, 3 vols. (Berlin 1923/4–1925/6); A. M. Habermann, *Sefer gezerot ashkenaz veṣarefat* (Jerusalem, 1945/6). The *qina* of David b. Meshulam is published in Bernfeld, Habermann, and elsewhere.]

(11)   Bloody events like the one of 1096, though not always to the same horrifying extent, recurred frequently. At that period of religious excitement, when the masses saw the Jews as the cause of every trouble and every hardship, hardly a decade passed when some community did not fall victim to popular rage or to passion violently unleashed. In the liturgical poetry, a monument was raised to the Jewish communities'

[253]

steadfastness in faith, to their sacrifice of material goods, and to their devotion unto death. The many poems were frequently the only remaining witnesses to the heroic spirit displayed by the Jewish communities when put to the test; most of them were recited only in those communities whose troubles they related, and therefore have until recent times existed only in manuscript. This period called forth a great many poets who were not particularly important to the nation or its history, and whose names can therefore be passed over. Their only merit is that they immortalized the deeds of the community members who gave their lives for the sanctification of God's name. Of these we mention only a few that have some claim to general interest. Joel b. Isaac Halevi of Bonn[41] tells of the events of the Second Crusade in his poem יבכיון מר, "They weep bitterly"; so does his compatriot Ephraim b. Jacob,[42] who personally lived through this age of horrors. The striking feature of his poems is that they make frequent mention of persecution and its victims, so that the reader feels that they come from a world soaked in blood. Incidentally, he was the last poet in Germany to compose in Aramaic. His most important contribution to the synagogue service is his extensive commentary on the *Maḥzor*, which, to judge from the part that has been published, was a very important work, citing sources from ancient literature. Frequently confused with him is his contemporary, R. Ephraim b. Isaac of Regensburg,[43] who is famous for his halakhic writings. His poems excel among those of the French and German poets in being "short but clear; delicate but pointed. He uses a clear and fluent language adorned with biblical and talmudic allusions." Of his poems, only the *seliḥot* became widely known, such as אבותי כי בטחו, "Because my ancestors trusted," for the Tenth of Tevet, and a few, like אם אפס רובע הקן, "Though even the sacrifice of a quarter-shekel dove is no more," and אם יוספים אנחנו, "If we continue," for the Day of Atonement and for the days of *seliḥot*. A later poet was Menaḥem b. Jacob,[44] who died in 1203 in Worms. He composed many *yoṣerot*, *qinot*, and *seliḥot*, all with the same sad content peculiar to the age. Next to Ephraim, he was the last to treat the theme of the Ten Martyrs. Finally, from among the circle of the tosafists we mention Meir b. Barukh of Rothenburg[45] (d. 1293), the most famous of all the rabbis of Germany, whose enactments and customs had decisive influence on the formation of the synagogue rite of Germany. He was a prolific liturgical poet, especially of fast-day poems. Of them we mention only the *qina* on the public burning of holy books in Paris in 1244, שאלי שרופה באש, "Greet, O you who are burnt in fire," which was accepted into all prayer books of Ashkenaz, including even the Reform prayer book, for the Ninth of Av.

[The *qinot* about the persecutions of the twelfth and thirteenth centuries were also published in the collections mentioned in the preceding paragraph. The poems of Ephraim b. Jacob of Bonn were published by A. M. Habermann in *SRIHP* 7 (1957/8): 215–96. His poem on the binding of Isaac was published with an extensive introduction by S. Spiegel, in the *Alexander Marx Festschrift*, Hebrew part (New York, 1950), 471–547. On his commentary on the *maḥzor*, see A. A. Urbach, *Sefer ʿarugat habosem* (1962/3), 4:39–70. The poems of Ephraim of Regensburg were published by A. M. Habermann in *SRIHP* 4 (1937/8): 119–96. The poems of Menaḥem b. Jacob and Meir of Rothenburg have not appeared in individual editions.]

[254]   (12)   With time the number of poets and of their compositions decreased. The liturgy in its main branches was richly provided with poems, and the communities had

already chosen their poems from the stock that stood at their disposal, and were not interested in exchanging them or in replacing the old with new. But even now, the well-springs of sacred poetry had not dried up completely. Individual poets continued to appear in every age and they always found an opportunity, whether sad or happy, that inspired them to compose poetry.[46] Sacred poetry had a new period of efflorescence in some of the Oriental countries beginning in the sixteenth century. The Sephardic rite, which had been brought to these countries by the Spanish and Portuguese refugees, was almost entirely lacking in poems. Thus there arose in the Jewish communities of the Balkans, Yemen and Persia a significant number of poets who adorned the liturgy worship with their compositions. They did not always limit themselves to Hebrew, but sometimes wrote in their vernacular. Hardly any had particular artistic significance, for in general they follow the model of the ancient religious poetry; but occasionally the imitations have real value of their own.

[It is not true that the prayer books brought by the exiles from Spain and Portugal were nearly devoid of poems. On the contrary, wherever these Jewish exiles established communities, the liturgical poetry of their ancestors was accepted, not only that of the eleventh- and twelfth-century Golden Age, but also that of the thirteenth and fourteenth centuries. Besides, the descendants of the exiles composed new poems, and in the first generations after the arrival in their Diaspora countries, talented poets arose among them, like R. Israel Najara in Palestine and Mandil Ibn abi Zimra in Algeria (sixteenth century). The influence of the Sepharadim was felt in the poems that were composed all over North Africa, Italy, Turkey, Syria, Palestine, Persia, and India. The Jews of Yemen were, to be sure, very far from western Europe; nevertheless, they were influenced by their Spanish brethren long before the period of the exile, and in Yemen the craft of liturgical poetry reached its height in the sixteenth and seventeenth centuries.]

§ 42 *The Main Poets: The Poets of Spain*

(1) In Spain sacred poetry attained its fullest flowering and its most perfect expression; never again did there appear so many religious poems that were perfect in form and content. The golden age of Hebrew poetry in Spain began after the passing of the great sages of the East, and it carried on what was begun there. [255]

> When easterners hid from the battle of song,
> The Spanish poets trooped right along.
> When visions to easterners were denied,
> The western poets prophesied.
> Judah al-Ḥarizi, *Taḥkemoni*, chapter 18

The poets active in Spain between 1000 and 1150 mark the high point of Hebrew poetry in the Middle Ages. These Spanish poets also based their work on the poetry of the East. They, too, drew on the model handed down by Kallir and his followers, but they were the only ones who freed themselves completely from their predecessors. They blazed trails of their own, replacing the pedantic style of the piyyut with the lilt of poetry, and the learning of the midrash with the flash of their imagination and emotional life. The prayer books of the Jews of Spain are the only ones that remain free of the old type of piyyut, or that suppressed it in favor of the far superior compositions of local poets. Thanks to the influence of Arabic culture, scholarship and poetry flourished among the Jews; from it they derived their aspirations to learning and science, to the beauty and harmony of forms. Most of the poets were men of general education, schooled in the sciences, and thoroughly versed in all the literature of their time, above all in the abundant products of the Arabic poets. But beyond formal learning was the contribution of their own talent, for all were secular as well as sacred poets, and sacred poetry was only one of the fields to which they applied themselves, only one aspect of the art that they cultivated. Precisely here lay their superiority to the poets of the other lands, that they were true poets, artists of authentic poetic genius. Also common to all the sacred poets of Spain is the fact that they composed in great quantity; every one of them wrote nearly as many poems as Kallir, who elsewhere was unrivaled for quantity. History did not treat their poems as kindly as their quality merited, for the great catastrophe that overtook the Jews of Spain destroyed the communities and their poetic treasures with them. For a long time, the compositions of the Spanish masters did not attract much attention; only in our time has attention again been drawn to them, and they have again become the object of scholarly study. Most of them had to be rediscovered from manuscripts, others from rare prayer books preserved in isolated communities of Provence, North Africa, and Turkey. Only in very rare cases have the poems reached us undamaged, as the poets wrote them. It was typical of the Sepharadim to compose extensive compositions rather than small, isolated pieces. But the communities lacked a sense for literary history and did not mind breaking up a structure, omitting some pieces or inserting poems by other poets that, for whatever reason, seemed to them to be appropriate.

[256]   The Sepharadim did not come by their craft automatically, but strove for it and labored honorably to perfect it. Their high point was preceded by *Sturm und Drang*, a period of groping and feeling their way. The Spanish poets, too, had first to learn to delimit their field, to find their form, and to master the language. Progress in poetry went hand in hand with scientific research. The results of biblical scholarship, the achievements in linguistic studies, the refinement of religious-philosophical views blazed new paths for poetry and provided it with new means of expression. The two great patrons of Spanish Jewry mark turning points in religious poetry as well: "In the days of Hasdai the Nasi they began to chirp, and in the days of Samuel the Nagid they sang aloud."* The poets of Spain may be divided into two groups: Joseph Ibn Avitur and Isaac Ibn Ghiyath are the best-known representatives of the first, preparatory period; Solomon Ibn Gabirol represents the transition to the high period, with the two Ibn Ezras and Judah Halevi representing the pinnacle.[1]

(2)   Joseph b. Isaac Ibn Avitur,[2] known also as Ibn Santas or Satanas of Merida, ca. 970, was the first sacred poet of Spain. He was a master in all the branches of rabbinic literature and had complete control of the Arabic language and a thorough knowledge of Arabic culture. As a synagogue poet, it was he who created in Spain the patterns and the rules observed by those who followed. He was the first to compose a *ma'amad*[3] for the Day of Atonement—that is, the complex of piyyutim and *seliḥot*

that became permanently standard in Sepharad. It is very likely that he composed the *ma'amad* for all the services of the Day of Atonement; at least it is certain that one by him for the Additional Service was widely used. To this *ma'amad* belonged the *'Avoda* אלהים אל בך יצדקו, "Lord God, to You . . .,"[4] of which only the introduction, אבואה ברשיון מחוללי, "I come with the permission of my Creator," has been preserved in Sepharad. Likewise, we have *qerovot* by him for the Afternoon and Closing services. His Kedushah was highly celebrated.[5] It is based on the midrashic conception that Israel sings the Kedushah on earth at the same time that the angels are singing it in heaven, and describes in poetic language the antiphonal song of Israel and the hosts of heaven. "Its striking, pregnant brevity reveals a deep national spirit and a powerful, clear historical consciousness." Ibn Avitur was a very productive poet; more than one hundred of his poems are still known. Among them are *qerovot* for all the festivals, and *yoserot* for many of the special Sabbaths, and even for private festivities such as the seven days of the wedding feast. His well-known cycle of *hosha'not*[6] is very rich in interesting and new expressions for the same idea; most of it has been preserved to this day in Sepharad. Avitur's language is not by any means perfect, but is occasionally difficult and ponderous. It recalls the early liturgical poets but betrays poetic power, justifying al-Harizi's judgment that Ibn Avitur's poetry is attractive and valuable. He still shows the influence of the style of the old piyyut, in that he goes in for pedantic disquisitions. He makes much use of midrash, but even in this he may be seen to be going his own way. He devotes special attention to natural science, showing a deep interest in the world and everything in it, and he enjoys depicting whatever the midrash relates about natural phenomena and about the various creatures with which the world abounds. Thus his style is more plastic, and his descriptions more lively and exciting than those of Kallir.

[257]

[Of Joseph Ibn Avitur no fewer than three hundred sacred poems are known today. Ezra Fleischer has collected them all and prepared them for publication; he has also written a most detailed study about them, which was offered as a dissertation to the Hebrew University of Jerusalem (1968, in mimeograph form). See also the texts and bibliography in Schirmann, *Shirim hadashim*, 138–47.]

(3)   Similar to Ibn Avitur's poetry is that of Isaac b. Judah Ibn Ghiyath,[7] known also as Isaac b. Moshia, who served as rabbi of the famous community of Lucena and died in 1089. He acquired great fame as a rabbi and talmudic scholar. His treatise on the festival laws is full of important details about the liturgy; it is used extensively below as an important source for our knowledge of the prayers and the institutions of that early period. Ibn Ghiyath came from a family of gifted poets and made outstanding contributions to the poetry of the synagogue. Moses Ibn Ezra extols him as having surpassed all his predecessors in several fields. Among all the poets of Spain he is the one who shows the greatest wealth of individual characteristics and novel expressions. Even in his works the external form is not particularly attractive and the language is not yet free of difficulties and obscurities. The rhyme, which he knows how to insert with great skill, often forces him to employ difficult linguistic forms, in which he frequently recalls Kallir. But his style as a whole shows marked progress compared with that of the prince of ancient liturgical poets, especially in the lovely sound of his verse. He often recalls Kallir also in the enigmatic quality of much of his poetry, due to the compression of

its many themes. But here too the new direction is immediately recognizable, for the aggadah has been replaced by scientific material, from which a good part of his poems' content is borrowed. In Ibn Ghiyath's poetry we find a mass of information from the areas of anatomy and physiology, psychology and astronomy; in his works the cosmogony of *Sefer yeṣira* and the philosophy of the Greeks are frequently shaped into alphabetical hymns and prayers. Thus, when he composes an *ʿAvoda*,[8] he lingers long and lovingly on the miracles of creation, which afford him the opportunity to weave in scientific remarks and data; he treats exhaustively the history of early humanity down to the Tower of Babel because here, too, he is able to employ both his imagination and his learning. But to the main subject of his description, whose subject matter and organization were prescribed and on which he could not set his own personal stamp, he devotes only the last third of his poem. His poetic compositions, of which today more than 120 are known, may be divided into four groups: *maʿamad* for the Day of Atonement, of which the above-mentioned *ʿAvoda* is a part; *seliḥot* for the penitential days; piyyutim for festivals; and poems for the early Morning Service. The delight he takes in displays of erudition as described above is not found in all of his poems but mainly in the *maʿamad*. But even this *maʿamad* ends with a prayer "of which not one of the prophets of Israel would have been ashamed, either as to style or content."[9] A distinction must be drawn between Ibn Ghiyath the flawed poet, and Ibn Ghiyath the incomparable composer of prayers. His penitential prayers for the entire month of Elul constitute a unique creation, of a kind of which no other poet can boast. He returned to the subject of his community's dawn services no fewer than twenty times, yet each time he knew how to find new means of expression for deep religious content. Prayers for atonement, calls for return to God, petitions for the restoration of the oppressed people and its Temple—all of these recur in all his *seliḥot*, but always in a pure and emotional form. Ibn Ghiyath's poems are widely used, mainly among the communities of North Africa, especially in Tripoli, where they fill the greater part of the prayer book.[10]

[258]

[Isaac Ibn Ghiyath composed several hundred piyyutim and *seliḥot* that have not yet been completely collected. Recently, more than one hundred poems were published by S. Bernstein, J. Marcus and others. See the list in Schirmann, *Shirim ḥadashim*, 187–89.]

(4)   As against the tremendous abundance of poetic compositions of the two poets just discussed, the work of their contemporaries, Bahya Ibn Paquda[11] of Saragossa and Isaac b. Reuben[12] of Barcelona seems insubstantial. Nevertheless, they must be mentioned here briefly—the one for the deep and true piety that came to expression in his two prayers, the בקשה, "Petition," and the תוכחה, "Rebuke," and the other for his skillful use of biblical verses at the ends of strophes, which he displays in his formerly much-cited איזה מקום בינה, "Where is the site of wisdom?"

[For the poems of Baḥya Ibn Paquda, see Schirmann, *Shirim ḥadashim*, 203–204, 205–208 (new poem); incidentally, it does not seem likely that he belongs to the generation of Ibn Ghiyath but to that of Moses Ibn Ezra. On Isaac of Barcelona (b. 1043), see Schirmann, *Shirim ḥadashim*, 196–99 and (new *tokheḥa*), *Areshet* 4 (1966).]

(5)   Greater than all those discussed until now is Solomon b. Judah Ibn Gabirol of Cordova,[13] "a poet whose poems are consecrated by the intellect, a thinker whose thoughts are transfigured by poetry."[14] He was filled with enthusiasm for the Hebrew

language; from earliest childhood he made it his goal to restore its original charm and freshness, and he strove to make it possible for the song of the pious singers of old to be heard in it again. Faithful to his goal, he did more than anyone else for the dissemination of Hebrew poetry. Tried by hardships and pursued by fate, and therefore often filled with dark thoughts, he made religious poetry his refuge. Here he could restore his soul's balance, and elevate himself to the pure harmony of a faithful heart. Here the proud thinker and the daring doubter is transformed into a humble worshiper. Ibn Gabirol was active in all the fields of religious lyric. We have from his hand hymns and meditations, *seliḥot* and prayers, *qinot* and hopeful, longing visions of the future in the most varied forms and styles:

> The dominant character of nearly all of them is a dark seriousness, a harshness that mercilessly strips life bare of all its radiance and dazzling color, as well as humble devotion to God rising from the depths of consciousness of the human soul. Gabirol's condemnation of the insignificance and vanity of the mundane is severe; unwearyingly he warns of the helplessness and fragility of all earthly things; untiring are his efforts to show in inexhaustibly varied imagery the uncertainty and fickleness of fate. But just as noble and elevated is his pure, light-filled soul whenever he speaks from a heart filled with the greatness and splendor of the Lord, with the exaltedness and holiness of this greatest object of human thought and conception, whenever he brings like a sacrifice of thanksgiving the noble gift of poetry so bountifully bestowed upon him, ennobling God's most beautiful and splendid gift through the lofty use to which he puts it.

[259]

Ibn Gabirol's poems, which number a few hundred, encompass the entire cycle of prayers of the Jewish year. Besides the *ma'amad* for the Day of Atonement and its poems of rebuke and atonement, we have his compositions for the three pilgrim festivals, Purim, Hanukkah, the Ninth of Av and the other fast days. He enriches the prayers with additions to all the parts of the *yoṣer* and with charming little poems to begin and end the Morning Service. No other Hebrew poet knows how to strike so exactly the tone of prayer.

The most valuable poetic achievement, in which religious, national, and philosophical writing are combined into a harmonious whole, is his great didactic poem כתר מלכות, "The Kingly Crown,"[15] which unites in poetic form the picture of the world as it was then conceived with the fundamental principles of Judaism. The work begins with the believer lifting his eyes to God, whose wondrous revelation is shown in the cosmos, sphere by sphere "as it proceeds in its various parts from the Almighty." From this height, the poet descends to man, praising his soul as a ray of light ignited by the power of divine wisdom. And just as he had earlier sought to apply his poetic powers to praising the greatness and might of the Creator, so he now cannot find enough traits of humility with which to express the degree to which man falls short of this highest perfection. This remarkable poem, one of the most marvelous products of philosophical poetry in world literature, concludes with a prayer and a confession of sin.

It is very doubtful that "The Kingly Crown" was originally meant for the synagogue, but its deeply religious content lent it such value in the eyes of the communities that it was adopted in all rites as a supplement to the Day of Atonement liturgy. The same happened also to many of Ibn Gabirol's shorter poems, which he did not compose for use in the synagogue, but which were adopted in most prayer books as the supreme expression of the religious spirit and trust in God. There is no rite that does not contain a large number of Gabirol's prayers and poems. Therefore, his large compositions were often broken up, and only certain sections taken up by the communities. But his spirit lives on, and the influence of his lofty piety is felt even today; throughout the Jewish world the memory survives of the one of whom Heine said:[16]

> Yes, Gabirol, that truehearted
> God-enraptured minnesinger,
> Pious nightingale who warbled
> To the God Who was his rose—
>
> That sweet nightingale, who caroled
> Tenderly his lilting love songs
> In the rayless darkness of the
> Gothic medieval night!

[260]   Ibn Gabirol's historical importance is that he brought the sacred poetry of the Jews of Spain toward its perfection. In no other poet's work is the transition from piyyut to lyrical poetry so clear. In his youth he still wrote in the manner of the ancient poets, and in his piyyutim as in theirs one encounters the difficult expressions and harsh and unusual linguistic forms that are the hallmarks of the ancient poetry. But as he developed he moved more and more toward a classical style and a nearly perfect form of expression, and his poetry often recalls the beauty and charm of biblical verse. He was the first to introduce meter, the artistic device of Arabic poetry, into religious poetry. He did not employ it in all his poems, and he never allowed it to control him, but he treated it with total freedom, preferring to revert to the old kind of simple rhythm rather than to force the content or diction for the meter's sake. The impression made by Ibn Gabirol's poetry on his contemporaries was already a very great one. Moses Ibn Ezra, who lived only a generation later, characterizes his poetry as follows:

> Gabirol was a perfect and articulate writer, who reached the highest perfection in the craft of poetry. He knew how to use the most delicate language, and therefore he was seen by everyone as the master of the word, craftsman of rhyme; his style is polished, his expressions are fluid, and his treatment of the subject matter is charming. All eyes are lifted to him in admiration, and all of the later poets made use of the stamp that he impressed upon the language.[17]

Al-Harizi, who was born a century after, and who already was very familiar with works of the great poets of Spain, is still full of praise for Gabirol's incomparable poetry:

> He alone ascended to the highest rank in poetry, and metaphor gave birth to him on the knees of intelligence . . . For the poetry of all the poets who were before him was as vapor and void, and after him no one rose up like him. And all who came after him learned from his literary sense and received the spirit of poetry from him and God anointed him as King of poetry over all the children of his people, "The Song of Songs which is Solomon's."[18]

[The first to compose metrical sacred poetry in meter was Dunash b. Labrat (960). Ibn Gabirol's sacred poetry has not yet appeared in a full critical edition. A list of his poems that appeared after the edition of Bialik and Rawnitzki is given in Schirmann, *Shirim hadashim*, 167–68. Among the studies that deal especially with Ibn Gabirol's sacred poetry, we mention K. Dreyer, *Die religiöse Gedankenwelt des Salomo ibn Gabirol* (Leipzig, 1930).]

(6)   The poetry of the Jews of Spain reached the highest point of its achievement in the generation after Ibn Gabirol;[19] Moses and Abraham Ibn Ezra and Judah Halevi are the three stars in the shining constellation of Hebrew poetry. Their predecessors had prepared the ground, struggled with the innovations in language and form, and, especially Ibn Gabirol, created models for those who followed. And on this newly won soil, cultivation could now be carried out and brought to perfection. Flexibility of expression, beauty of form, and loveliness of sound are now the adornment of poetry. Poets represent the highest culture of their age; because they are deeply rooted in the sciences, they use talmudic and midrashic elements to a considerably diminished extent, though they do not eliminate them completely. These three artists represent Hebrew poetry for the first time since the period of the psalms in its natural beauty and supreme charm. The oldest of the three was Moses Ibn Ezra of Granada,[20] who was still alive in 1138. He was famed as a poet who controlled all spheres of poetry, and was celebrated by al-Harizi as one of the brilliant masters. He had unusual, rarely matched versatility in liturgical poetry:

[261]

> The purity of his language, the ease with which he can discover new aspects and new details in subjects that had been so often treated before him and by him; the refinement of the forms that nearly always take surprisingly successful shape even in the most complex meters and the most elaborate rhythmical structures; the lovely sound of his rhymes—all testify to a richly talented spirit who manages his artistic tools with practiced mastery and multiplies them through use.

In no author does the influence of the Arabic poets stand out so strongly as in Moses Ibn Ezra, a poet who makes use of the artistic forms of Hebrew poetry in the most varied ways. But here also lies a certain flaw, for it often seems as if the external form was everything to him: polished, embellished language, sharp and witty expression, and the perfect biblical verse often seem to be the main point of the poetry, while truth and depth of feeling are given second place. Moses Ibn Ezra is the poet who achieved the highest mastery of artistic form. He expresses his ideas in very individual ways; no other poet uses so many images and figures of speech. He displays his highest artistry in the realm of the *seliha*, apparently the genre best suited to his temperament and spirit. He composed a great number of *selihot*, thereby acquiring the epithet הסלח, "The *seliha* poet."[21] The call to repentance and humility, the thought of the Day of the Lord, of the perishability of all material things, the picture of the day of death and the last judgment all echo in his *selihot*. He did not limit these merely to general meditations and admonishment for the community, but always kept the "I" at the focal point of his poetry. For these are personal confessions, reflecting both what he saw as life's emptiness and vanity, as well as the efforts of self to rise and break through to the divine omnipotence. A new element in the work of Moses Ibn Ezra is the appearance of the numerous observations on nature, not merely the few facts in the aggadah, as in the earlier poets, but emerging from the depths of the poet's heart. They herald a new age when poetry no longer is derived from ancient models, but from the confession of a great poet's spirit.

The poems of Moses Ibn Ezra, of which more than two hundred are known,[22] spread to distant lands. His *dīwān* has not yet been published, and though most rites accepted only a few poems, hardly any rite exists that did not adopt something of his. Many are in the prayer books of Provence and North Africa.

[The secular poetry of Moses Ibn Ezra was published in a scientific edition by H. Brody (Berlin and Jerusalem, 1934/5–41/2), and will soon reappear in a new and revised edition. It received a thorough literary analysis by D. Pagis (see n. 22). His liturgical poetry still awaits complete publication. For the time being, see the selections by H. Brody, *Maḥberet mishire moshe ben yaʿakov ibn ʿezra* (Philadelphia, 1933/4), with an English translation, and S. Bernstein, *Moshe ibn ʿezra: shire qodesh* (Tel Aviv, 1956/7). Bernstein's collection assembles nearly 240 poems, and the total is probably more than three hundred. A list of his new works published after 1937 is found in Schirmann, *Shirim ḥadashim*, 220–22.]

[262]   (7)   All the qualities of his predecessors are united in Judah b. Samuel Halevi of Castile (1085–1145),[23] the most famous of all the poets of Spain in the Golden Age, of whom Heine says,[24]

> It's through thought Gabirol sparkles,
> And it's thinkers that he pleases,
> Whereas Ibn Ezra sparkles
> In his art, and suits the artist—
>
> But Jehuda ben Halevi
> Has both qualities together,
> And he is a mighty poet
> And a favorite of all.

Behind each of his poems stands not only great poetic talent but also a pure soul, a visionary nature of passionate enthusiasm, and a noble sensibility.

> Pure and truthful, without blemish
> Was his song—his soul was also.

Judah Halevi can only be called an embodiment of the religious genius and the most splendid flowering of the Jewish spirit. The crowning glory of his lyric is his religious poetry. All the passionate faith of Jewish worship, of the prophets, and of the psalms were revealed in him. He sang of God, Whom he felt inside himself, Whose message he bore within his soul, Whose existence he sees attested in the history of his people, and Whose might is proclaimed by the cosmos and everything within it. He is as aware of the vanity of earthly existence as anyone; he calls for humility and submission to the will of the Almighty, and for repentance, which points the way to nearness to

God, man's highest goal. His prayers are more passionate and more deeply felt than those of his predecessors. But this is not what makes Halevi's poetry unique. Where he outdoes the other poets is in his unsurpassed devotion to his people, his love for whatever is holy to them, his immersion in their past greatness. For him, Israel's past lives on. He holds converse with the great men of old, he sees the mightily pulsing life of his tribe, shares in its struggles, suffers with its martyrdom, and rejoices with its hopes. Before him,

> the gates of ruined Zion are opened, the Temple's golden halls lie wide before his eyes, frequented by righteous priests and colorful masses of faithful God-fearers; he smells the fragrant incense, hears the songs of the Levites, and sees the streets of Jerusalem thronging with people, when God restores the exiled communities of his people like dreamers to their homeland.

No poet like Judah Halevi knows how "to feel the splendor of the past and to describe it within the narrow framework of a little poem; he holds together past and present in a firm hand, and he knows how to spread the bright shimmer of a joyous future over the night of a dismal present."[25]

All the longings that his heart felt for the sites of the glorious Jewish past Halevi expressed in his Zion poem ציון הלא תשאלי, "Zion, will you not greet," the most famous of all of his sacred poems, "which still sounds solemnly in all of Israel's synagogues on the day of mourning for the destruction of Jerusalem and imbues the hearts of all the faithful with great uplifting of the spirit." Of it a distinguished Christian critic has said,

[263]

> There is nothing in all of religious poetry, including Milton and Klopstock, that could be placed higher than this lament, in which the language has opened generously all of its treasures and charms before a man who sought to express and to employ not the vanity of his artistic mastery, but his pious devotion and self-abnegating humility.[26]

We cannot determine whether Halevi composed large cycles of poems, but the number of his poems was extraordinarily great. Even in his lifetime, collections of more than three hundred of his sacred poems were compiled, and many of his poems were accepted into prayer books.[27] There is no rite without some poem by him, and even the Karaites did not shrink from embellishing their prayers with his works. He cultivated all genres of sacred poetry, writing poems for all the festivals and distinguished Sabbaths and other great occasions. He wrote for every part of the service that seemed suitable for poetry, for most of them more than once. He also made use of purely scholarly material, and was not afraid to dress up legal precepts in rhyme, but every one of his poems has some unmistakable feature that betrays the author. What distinguishes him is the sincerity and intensity of his feelings. Throughout his poetry we find harmonious balance and reasonable limits, never unnatural distortion or forced pathos. He never loses his power or beauty of expression, even at moments of highest enthusiasm and deepest lament. Never does one encounter in him anything forced or coarse, or anything said merely for the sake of the form. It is as if the linguistic material, ordinarily so resistant and inflexible, sought to spare the poet every struggle and came to him on its own, so that he had only to express the feelings that throbbed deep in his soul. The appropriate word or the expressive biblical verse always comes to him without effort, and everything that customarily impedes the understanding of poetry—meter and rhyme, acrostic and refrain—is formed under his masterly hand into the noblest and most delightful loveliness. He breathes the spirit of poetry even into things formalistic, and as with every true artistic creation—as with nature itself—the pleasure is not disturbed by anything external or eccentric. Thus in Judah Halevi, ancient Hebrew poetry was revived in its full glory, and from him the sounds were again heard that once flowed from the psalmists. Judah al-Ḥarizi wrote:

> But the songs of the Levite, R. Judah, are a wreath of grace for the head of testimony and a line-circlet of carnelian and topaz on its neck. He is the right-hand pillar for the edifice of poetry. He brandishes his spear against the giants and leaves all the heroes of poetry slain. All his poems break the hearts of the scholars. Before him Asaph almost dies and Jeduthun's hand grows slack, and the song of the sons of Korah becomes wearisome. He came into the treasury of poetry and despoiled the treasure-house. He took all its delightful vessels and then he departed and locked the gate after he had gone out . . . For his tongue is a polished and sharpened arrow in the art of the piyyut. In the poems of prayers, he draws and subdues every heart . . . In his elegies he causes a cloud of weeping to flow and he breaks it asunder [Judah al-Ḥarizi, *Taḥkemoni*, 1:80–81].

[264]   [Judah Halevi was born no later than 1075 and died, as demonstrated by S. D. Goitein in *Tarbiz* 24 (1954/5): 34, in 1141. In the poet's *dīwān*, ed. Brody, volumes 3 and 4 are devoted to liturgical poetry. They contain 316 poems without commentary, sources, or variants. But tens of other poems have been published outside that edition; see Schirmann, *Shirim ḥadashim*, 235–36, 239. On Halevi's sacred poetry, see, among others, I. Heinemann in *Keneset* 9 (1944/5): 163–200.]

(8)   Not of Halevi's distinction, but a poet of significance and of great influence on the liturgy, was Abraham b. Meir Ibn Ezra of Toledo (1093–1168).[28] He could not devote himself exclusively to poetry like his contemporaries discussed above, because a contrary fate forced him to wander from place to place about the world, struggling and scrambling to eke out a wretched living by teaching and writing learned books. The restless wanderer did not have the peace and quiet for poetic creativity, and was anyway more inclined by nature to the exact sciences than to the life of imagination. But the definite talent dormant within him made him capable of noteworthy achievement. His particular contribution was to disseminate among the Jews of Christendom the achievements of their coreligionists in the realm of Islam. No other poet recognized and expressed so clearly the gap between the piyyut and classical poetry. By cultivating and disseminating classical poetry he became its herald and teacher in the lands of Roman Christianity. He himself lacked the emotional intensity and warmth of the true poet. He was dominated by intellectual wit, and in his verses he clearly lays the greatest weight on the clever remark, the surprising turn of phrase, the brilliant witticism. "The soaring outburst of feelings of a great spirit finding expression in passionate hymns, the lofty nobility of a poetry that leaps upward and therefore flies upward—all of these we find but little in the liturgical poetry of Abraham Ibn Ezra" (Sachs, *Poesie*). On the other hand, he is very punctilious about order and clarity of thought, and about purity

of form. He made up for the deficiencies of his poetic talent by never daring to compose large-scale compositions, and except for an ʿAvoda, we do not know of any large work by him. His 150 extant liturgical poems are mostly short ones for individual sections of the prayers, particularly *nishmat, ahava,* and *geʾula.* In these short poems he could always treat an idea complete in itself, a religious or philosophical thought, a moral doctrine, or an event from national history. Even though his poems usually contain a reflection, wise maxim, or admonition, they are effective because of their polished form, their elegant, intelligible rhetoric, and their valuable content. Thus, the short poems of Abraham Ibn Ezra met with considerable appreciation and distribution; most of them are found in Provence and North Africa, like the works of the other Spanish writers, but they made their way to even more distant lands.

Many other poets lived during the golden age of classical poetry besides the few leading ones that we have mentioned. Though they did not reach the same level, they nevertheless did important work, some of which was incorporated into the prayer books. The great Hebrew poets in Spain brought liturgical poetry to the highest possible level of perfection, but in so doing, they also brought about the end of this literature. For the liturgy was now provided with a wealth of poetic material, and it was impossible to produce anything new that was sufficiently valuable to compete with what already existed. From this point on, the religious feelings of the faithful would have to find other forms of expression and areas of activity.

[265]

[From Abraham Ibn Ezra we have not 150 but more than four hundred liturgical poems, which have been prepared for publication with commentaries and variants by Israel Levine (see the sample in *Oṣar yehude sefarad* 6 [1963]: 47–66). Great collections of sacred poetry by this poet were published by S. Bernstein, H. Brody, N. Ben Menahem and others. See Schirmann, *Shirim ḥadashim,* 269–71. Incidentally, he was born in Tudela, not Toledo.]

§ 43 *Prayer Books and Orders of Prayer*

(1)   In order to gain a clear view of the history of the liturgy from the time of the fixing of the statutory prayers, we have to clarify the origin and development of prayer books and rites of prayer and to examine more closely the tools of the tradition. In the ancient period there was a strict prohibition against writing down the prayers.[1] As long as the transmission of the whole tradition was exclusively oral, prayers, too, had no written texts. This had the disadvantage that the textual tradition was uncertain and unstable. It is noteworthy that, nevertheless, it took a fairly uniform shape. Especially when we consider the wide dispersion of the Jews, it is astonishing that they were able to make their way for centuries without committing the prayers to writing. This can only mean that careful and persistent efforts were invested in teaching,[2] and that a tight connection was continuously maintained between the congregations and the central authorities through the institution of emissaries.[3] The possibility, however, cannot be entirely excluded that, since communication by letter was unavoidable, prayers were sometimes transmitted in writing.[4] The prohibition of writing was not always strictly observed with respect to the aggadah, for we know that in ancient times books of aggadah existed and

were in use.[5] Thus, it is also possible that precentors permitted themselves to prepare written texts for their own use. But it must also be noted that nowhere does the Talmud or midrash mention a prayer book or the writing down of prayers. We hear much about the errors of precentors, but never of the unauthorized recitation of a prayer from a written book, and never is a prayer text declared invalid because it was not recited from memory. But it must also be noted that the need for a written text was not as great then as later, because the prayers were shorter and simpler and their text was not fixed word for word. It was sufficient to observe the correct order and train of thought expressed by the benedictions. Only the biblical quotations had a fixed text, and these

[266]

did exist in writing; but the rest of the prayers could be worded in any way desired, and for this purpose it was customary to use brief and simple language drawn to the extent possible from the language of the Bible. The advantage of the oral tradition was that the prayers were not frozen into fixed and immutable formulas, but always remained in flux, and the congregation or the precentor could put as much feeling and religious emotion into them as they wished. The formulation evolved of its own accord, with time. Even taking into account that the art of poetry and improvisation were much more widespread in Eastern countries than among us, we still have to ask what was the source of the prophetic power that in every place and in every age bestowed the inspiration to find new means of expression for prayer. Only with great difficulty did the Palestinians become accustomed to having to use a permanently fixed text for all their prayers. Apparently, the many recently discovered shorter and longer poetic reworkings of the statutory prayers that appear so strange to us were devised only in order to bring variation to the service and to preserve it from monotonous repetition.

(2)   Finally there must have come the stage of writing down the prayers, and of editing collections and orders of prayer. These two must be distinguished, for at that time they were not connected to each other. The prayer rites to which we have referred were not prayer books in our sense; for the most part they indicated only the rules for the order of the prayers and proper conduct during their recitation. They did not contain the prayers in written form, for these were found in separate copies. The oldest thorough and systematic work devoted to prayers is Tractate *Soferim*, written about the sixth century, though in its present form it contains several late additions. What we learn in this source about prayer is mentioned only in passing, to the extent needed to fill out the rules for the Torah reading.[6] Therefore, except for a single insignificant comment,[7] it does not deal with weekday or Sabbath services, but only with festival prayers. Even for these the service as a whole is not described; only the psalms, the special insertions, and alterations to the eulogies are mentioned, along with several rules pertaining to the manner of the synagogue service. Thus, *Soferim* is not a treatise about the entire liturgy, but about the Torah reading; this, however, it treats in complete detail. It begins with the rules for writing a valid copy of the Torah; it then takes up the manner in which the Torah is read. The prayers connected to the Torah reading are the only ones for which the text is given verbatim; the others are mentioned only in passing. As is well known, *Soferim* is mostly based exclusively on Palestinian customs and prayer texts, though here and there Babylonian influences may be detected. It is also noteworthy that in Babylonia, too, the first written reports about the synagogue service are the regulations for the reading of the Torah drawn up by Yehudai. This gaon

saw the use of written texts for the *seliḥot* and *qerovot* of the Day of Atonement as an innovation of dubious value, which he was not at all inclined to permit on other festivals; he would certainly not have permitted the use of books for the statutory prayers.

(3) But in the meantime a new force arose, with ever-growing power and influence over the tradition and the statutory prayers, one that was largely responsible for the editing of the first prayer books: the local customary prayer rite.[8] An institution that developed rather freely in far-flung lands over the course of centuries would naturally be subject to great variation in actual practice. That the congregations organized their own distinctive prayer rites shows the extent of individual participation in the liturgy and the lively interest that it enjoyed. At first prayer was governed by only the few fixed rules and binding institutions (*halakha*) in the Mishnah and Talmud. These concerned the order and sequence of the prayers, the text of most of the eulogies, and the Torah reading. The early sages were very far from editing a manual with detailed, binding rules for the synagogue service, the manner of recitation of the prayers, and the conduct of the congregation. Ancient traditions were handed down from generation to generation, but they did not at all have the force of law. The Mishnah knows of local variations in practice (מקום שנהגו),[9] which have the right to exist side by side; in the Talmud, which deals more fully with worship and prayer, the extent of these is much greater. In some cases the tradition about such customs became uncertain with the passage of time, but they were honored as handed down in each congregation and were allowed to stand if any justification at all could be found. Such customs involved the form of the liturgy, the use of certain prayers or ceremonies, and the addition of new materials. But in the course of time it developed that practices long considered customary had acquired a fixed form and binding character. Thus, something that was customary in one place on the basis of an ancient tradition could come into conflict with a custom that had acquired legal status somewhere else, and it even occurred that customs supplanted institutions that had been fixed as law (מנהג מבטל הלכה).[10] The origins of the customs could be quite various;[11] sometimes a custom could be a bad one, from which the religion had to be protected. Therefore, only the practice of individuals of recognized piety (מנהג ותיקין) was accepted as binding, and in fact the customs and practices of respected men, especially of beloved teachers, were carefully studied, followed, and recommended for imitation. Only the prayers fixed in the Talmud and, of these, only the parts actually mentioned there—something that sometimes was merely a matter of chance—were considered as binding institutions; all other parts of the liturgy were considered merely customary. Thus, only the reciting of the *Shemaʿ* and its benedictions, the ʿAmida, and the reading of the Torah were bound by rules, while in the other parts the custom was allowed to develop without restriction; the noticeable differences that we have observed (§§10–12) in the Supplications, Psalms, and Morning Benedictions show how much these diverged. In the individual lands, varying practices and even variant forms of the statutory prayers emerged; and even in different districts and communities within the same land there could sometimes be great differences as to opinions and institutions. The widening dispersal of the Jews encouraged the formation of deviant forms. Sometimes influences of diverse origin would come together in a single community, leading to the conflation of rites, so that to the eyes of a later observer there seems to be no consistency in the practice. The history of the congregation was what fixed the shape

[267]

of its liturgy. Likewise the educational level and the style of life, the atmosphere and culture, the customs and language, the outlook and behavior of the surrounding population all had their own influence on the liturgical institutions and the customs of the Jews. Life does not allow people to seal themselves off hermetically from each other; wherever different strata of society live side by side they influence each other's customs and practices. The give-and-take is constant, and only external circumstances determine whether the natives or the strangers will dominate. It was the same with the liturgy, which was never completely free of foreign infiltration.

> The doctrine of emanation, astrology, godfathers, rhyme, and prayers for the dead the Jews received from the outside; ecclesiastical terminology, ritual customs such as hopping during the prayer service, others got from the Jews. For a thousand years there have been constant complaints about foreign elements that have become rooted among the Jews.

In a few places, the customs struck deep roots, and could no longer be dislodged. Especially when beloved teachers or cantors stood behind these innovations, even the great leaders of the age failed in all their efforts to eliminate them.

Thus local variations emerged at an early time, and prayers and synagogue customs could diverge even in adjacent places. Contact between localities and scholars' travels frequently made congregations aware that their practice differed from what was generally accepted. If they were thereby thrown into doubt, they would turn to the authorities for explanation and guidance. From the time the gaonate came into being, the geonim were besieged with inquiries about liturgical matters.[11]* Often they had to decide between differences in the text of the prayers or the forms of the synagogue service. In the meantime numerous congregations arose in North Africa and Europe, as far as the extreme West, which were not always certain exactly what was required by law or tradition. Furthermore, sects arose that did not spare the traditional liturgy their attacks; in order to win adherents they would create disturbances among the congregants by casting doubt on the authority of their traditions. With the spread of the Karaite sect, questions to the geonim on liturgical matters became more numerous and lengthier, as did their answers. The geonim insisted on strict observance of the tradition, and rejected any "deviation from the words of the sages," not merely as error, but actually as sin. But the geonim did not achieve more than a limited success, and only in a few rare cases did the congregations agree to abandon their customs. Not infrequently the proclamations and efforts of the academies to whom the questions had been directed simply increased the number of variations and added to the confusion.

(4) The lack of uniformity in the liturgy and the resulting difficulties for anyone who wanted to find his way in this matter led to the composition of the first known prayer orders.[12] Typically these were written for the sake of distant communities. It was the congregation of Lucena in Spain whose request induced Natronai b. Hilai of Sura to compose his prayer book.[13] The principle that the daily service is derived from the dictum of R. Meir, "A person must recite one hundred benedictions every day," was known in Spain as well; the community wanted to know just what are the one hundred benedictions. The gaon organized his response in accordance with the wording of the

question. He enumerates one by one the benedictions that one has occasion to recite in the course of a day, from morning to evening; in his reckoning he includes also benedictions that are not part of public worship, like the Morning Benedictions and Grace after Meals. In accordance with the question and the form of the answer, he enumerates only the eulogies, and even that he does only for the less familiar benedictions, but not for such familiar ones as the eighteen benedictions of the ʿAmida. Natronai is content to produce a guide of the most narrowly conceived form and text, without entering at all into the details of the execution, so that his entire prayer book is just a skeleton of a mere four printed pages. But this does not exhaust Natronai's contribution to the liturgy, for in innumerable responsa he took occasion to express his opinion about specific questions. He was one of the sages who polemicized most violently against the deviations of the Karaites, evidence that this sect's propaganda at that time was vigorous and apparently successful. It is not easy to know the state of prayer books in Natronai's time, but it may be inferred that by then precentors were generally using them without arousing opposition.[14]

[269]

Far more detailed is the prayer order for the entire year (סדר תפלות וברכות של שנה כלה), which Natronai's successor, Amram b. Sheshna, also sent to Spain, apparently to Barcelona. This prayer book contains long disquisitions on prayer and lists all the customs connected to conduct in prayer, but it also gives the text of the prayers. There can be no disagreement that Amram's order as we have it is not the original book. That the texts of the prayers cannot have come from him in exactly the form that they are before us in print is proved by comparison with his other reliably transmitted statements. The recently discovered manuscripts of the book deviate in many points from the printed edition, lacking several texts that in fact do not belong to public worship, and including long passages whose absence in the printed edition has quite rightly aroused comment. Even in the text of the prayers, many variations occur among the traditions. What emerges clearly is that over time copyists added to Amram's prayer order texts that were customary in their own lands. In one manuscript the influence of the Spanish communities predominates; in another, that of Provence; in a third, the false practices of the Kabbalah. It may now be asked whether originally the order of Amram contained the texts at all, or whether it consisted only of halakhic instructions and information about customs, interspersed with brief data about the eulogies, after the manner of Natronai. The many early medieval quotations from this prayer book never include the text of the prayers; thus, the conjecture cannot be disproved that originally it did not include the text.[15] Nor has the halakhic part reached us undamaged. Besides the easily recognizable later additions, other changes must have been made to the text; it frequently contradicts Amram's well-attested statements in other sources, while omitting opinions of his that are elsewhere widely transmitted. Frequently, Amram's opinions are based upon the views of his predecessors and the custom of the two Babylonian academies, as well as on the liturgy of the house of the Exilarch, in which apparently the tradition was preserved with particular care.

Throughout the Middle Ages, Amram's prayer order was one of the most important and most widely used sources for the liturgy. Known as סדר רב עמרם or יסוד העמרמי, it was cited frequently by nearly all the important medieval sages wherever they lived or taught. But beyond this, the most important prayer books and halakhic writings about liturgy are actually based on it. Wherever possible they copy long passages from

[270]

it verbatim. Amram is the foundation of their discussions, and the later or divergent material is cited merely as a supplement to his work. Untroubled by the fact that the liturgy in their own countries had taken a completely different form, and that the prayers had acquired a new wording, they inserted the texts, as stated above, right between Amram's regulations. Thus new and different editions of this important book came into existence. If Amram did actually transmit the text of the prayers, it could only have been the statutory prayers, while the many poems that in his time were already widely disseminated and everywhere accepted he mentions only by name, without giving the text. On the other hand, he did provide places in his composition for the *selihot*, mainly the original stock of biblical texts and litanies.[16]

The first proper prayer book in the modern sense is the *Collection of Prayers and Praises* (*Jāmiʿ al-ṣalawāt wa 'l-tasābīh*), by the gaon Saadia b. Joseph.[17] It is not preserved in its entirety, but has come to us in fragments. These can, however, be filled out with various smaller fragments, so that, but for the beginning and the end, very little is missing. Not yet published, the work is known to us only from quotations in medieval authors and brief reports in recent studies; but on the basis of these, all agree that it is a most important work and a source of primary importance for the history of the synagogue service. [The prayer book has been published; see Saadia, *Siddur*.] Saadia was led to compose his prayer book by his observation that prayers had been so often added to, deleted, and abridged that some had disappeared from the liturgy, others were preserved only in the devotions of individuals, and some had been altered beyond recognition. Already he laments the fact that scholars were arrogating to themselves the freedom to introduce innovations not grounded in tradition, that the mass of new materials had displaced the ancient customs, and that, as a result, the local rites had come to differ greatly from each other even in neighboring communities. Saadia's prayer book contains the statutory prayers and many poetic additions. The entire work is divided into two sections, the first dealing with the prayers of ordinary days, and the second with the festival prayers. He also adds in Arabic the laws pertaining to prayer, sometimes amounting to substantial treatises that explain the individual prayers, going into their purposes and sources. But Saadia was not simply a collector and a halakhist, but also a systematic theologian; therefore, he attaches to the text of the prayers essays of varying length on the significance, content, and importance of the liturgy, the prayers, and the ceremonies connected to them. Saadia may have composed his prayer book only after transferring his residence to Babylonia, but the text of the prayers and the rituals that he transmits show clearly the influence of his native Egypt, in the traces they contain of the Palestinian rite that was there in use. Accordingly his instructions and several of the prayers that he recommends met with vigorous opposition from the Babylonian geonim.[18] At one time Saadia's prayer book was widely circulated, especially in Egypt, the land for which it was intended; but the book was also taken seriously in Spain, where it is frequently cited as an authority. Later it became known also in Yemen, apparently through Maimonides, and much was adopted from it verbatim by the communities there.

[271]

In the East it seems to have long continued customary for distinguished sages to compose prayer books.[19] Most such works give only general information about the conduct of the service, the customs considered correct by the author, and, frequently, explanations for them. Sometimes in the course of these discussions individual passages from the prayers themselves are also cited, especially such as may have been in dispute, but not extended prayer texts. After all, the prayers were not the authors' compositions, and the sages would not have published them under their names; furthermore, the texts were already in the hands of the communities at whose request the books were being written, and thus it would have been superfluous to send them. All of these compositions are lost; what we know of them we learn for the most part from the systematic ritual books of the eleventh and twelfth centuries, such as the *Halakhot* of Isaac Ibn Ghiyath,[20] *Sefer haʿitim* of Judah of Barcelona,[21] or the *Eshkol* of Abraham b. Isaac of Narbonne.[22] Their lengthy extracts from the ancient literature influenced the communities and induced them to adopt new customs and prayer texts. Only with Maimonides' *Mishne tora* do we again encounter the combination of prayer texts with discussion of the synagogue service.[23] It contains first, in model arrangement, all the laws and customs connected with prayer, and as an appendix, the texts of the prayers for the entire year (סדר תפלות כל השנה). This was later abridged by copyists, and has therefore reached us in very fragmentary form. [It was published in a critical edition based on a manuscript by Daniel Goldschmidt in *SRIHP 7* (1957/8).] In Egypt, and perhaps in Palestine, services were long held in accordance with the order of Maimonides, and in Yemen it is the basis of the prayer book to this day.

In Germany and northern France, the development was similar. The example of Isaac Halevi of Worms, whose innovations have been described in several places above, shows us the extent to which famous scholars had the power to change the prayers and customs. In all likelihood he knew of new sources on the liturgy that led him to intervene in it. The first order of prayer for these two lands was composed by Rashi or his school.[24] Rashi's prayer book resembles that of its predecessors in giving only a description of the synagogue service and an explanation of the customs observed there, but it does not contain the texts. It seems to have been intended as a guide to religious life, especially for the festival seasons; therefore, it dwells at length on the laws connected with the Sabbath and festivals. Very different in character is *Mahzor Vitry*, which comes from the same circle, and whose author was Simha b. Samuel of Vitry. Here we have again, after a long interval, a work that combines instructions about the order of prayer with the texts themselves. Alongside rules that are often copied verbatim from Amram, we find the prayers with an explanation of their texts, the scriptural readings with Aramaic paraphrases for the festivals, and long appendices such as *Pirqe avot*, a digest of the laws of the calendar, laws for the preparation of ritual objects, and so forth. At the end we find a great collection of poems arranged into several divisions. This shows that in those days manuscripts were still being provided with rich stores of poems; that such appendices were arranged in the order of the liturgy; and that the precentor was free to decide at a given moment which poems he would perform. In the appendix that has been preserved under the name *Quntres hapiyutim*, we find poems only for the Evening Service, *yoṣer* and *nishmat*, but there is no doubt that the genres now lacking were originally also present, especially the *seliḥot* and the *qerovot*.

[272]

(5)   No such extensive prayer books were composed afterward. Poems in such quantity were brought together only in special collections of piyyutim; otherwise, only those prayers were copied down that the individual communities actually used in their own local rites (מנהג).[25] Thus, two types of prayer book came into being: those in which

the statutory prayers alone were copied, mostly for private use, in which case they would sometimes be provided with translation; and more comprehensive collections of the statutory prayers and the poetry, which came to be called *maḥzor*. The great abundance of poems made the differentiation of the rites especially clear. Already in the tenth century the grouping of the festival prayers was not identical everywhere; later the local rites diverged more and more from each other because taste developed differently and because domination by local poets and local customs had a decisive influence on the liturgy.[26]

No rite has been uniformly preserved anywhere in its purity. Conflation began as soon as regulations and prayer books originating in Babylonia began to encounter and merge with Palestinian traditions. Furthermore, the many wanderings had the effect of bringing together and keeping in contact the most varied traditions. The prayer orders of the different countries acquired a different character depending on which element predominated. The Palestinian rite is preserved to the greatest extent in the prayer orders of the Balkans,[27] where nearly all the psalms and many texts of the statutory prayers are still found. Considerably fewer vestiges are preserved in the rite customary in Italy,[28] while relatively few of the prayers of the Palestinian rite could be salvaged in Germany[29] and France. Babylonian influence predominates almost exclusively in the Sephardic prayer book,[30] but there, too, not all prayers were customary everywhere; in Toledo, for example, many texts were used in their Palestinian form, a phenomenon that probably goes back to Saadia's prayer book. In general, it must be remembered that the local rites were not compiled with scientific exactitude, or on the basis of research into sources. They grew at random, developing according to whatever influence prevailed at the particular time. Boundaries could not always be exactly observed, and the spread of wild growth could not always be prevented. The shape taken by the local rites was frequently determined by place of origin of the founders or that of individual sages of repute, and by the traditions that they brought with them and wanted to impose.

[273]

The differences in the liturgy did not stand out in the statutory prayers, for these were identical in their order and for the most part in their text, and the variants in them were rare and not blatant; the real difference came in only through the use of poetry.[31] The piyyut had its own fate; ancient poems, especially those of Kallir, were carried to all countries, but later were joined by works of local poets that displaced them to a greater or lesser extent. But even with regard to the piyyut the tradition hardly ever remained uniform. Extensive compositions were not always preserved in their entirety, but large parts were deleted or interrupted by works of other poets. When congregations came to know and like new poems, they adopted them without asking where they originated; thus, poems of the Spanish poets found their way into every rite. In this way, a mixture of poems came into being, but the overall type remained uniform. Like the statutory prayers, liturgical poetry falls into two groups.

Countries that are related in their statutory prayers—the Balkans, Italy, France, and Germany—are also similar in their piyyut. First, they have the same manner of embellishing the festivals and many of the special Sabbaths with *yoser* and *qerova*. The names of the poets that are encountered in these countries are frequently the same ones; individual parts have been variously adorned with poems by local poets, but the name of Kallir remains dominant and characteristic. The similarity of this development stands out most clearly when one studies the poetic material of certain special days.

On the Ninth of Av, for example, the above prayer books all employ his *qinot*.[32] Among the different countries, even among the different congregations, there are great differences between the rites, but the tendency is identical in all. Kallir's cycle of *qinot* was preserved in its purest form in the Roman rite, where we find his *qerova* and the *qinot* composed to expand it in nearly their original form. Romaniot has adopted many more foreign additions. Ashkenaz, in its western portion, has a different *qerova* by Kallir; in its eastern portion this is lacking and the *qinot* have been separated from the *qerova*. But even in Ashkenaz the first, and the largest consecutive series of *qinot*, are taken from Kallir's *qina* cycle. It is the same with the *hoshaʿnot*.[33] All these countries built their cycles exclusively or mostly on Kallir's poems. On the Day of Atonement,[34] only the *selihot* and confessions were originally considered obligatory, for the use of *qerova* was considered optional. In the period of the dominance of the piyyut a change occurred, in that the *qerova* and the hymn were placed side by side with the *seliha*, and the latter was developed in a poetic form; piyyut material was dressed in the form of a *seliha*, and a special *qerova* was composed for the entire ʿAmida. The countries that we have mentioned fitted out the ʿAmida of the Day of Atonement in exactly the same way. They have a common *yoser* and *ofan*; of the *qerovot*, two were used by all of them, though one occurs in different services. Again, the congruence of Italy and the Balkans is greater than it is with Ashkenaz, but for all the deviations, the general tendency is the same, and the differences are due only to the work of local poets. We may not base our judgment only on the present situation; when we examine the old manuscripts, the overlap among the poems is even clearer. Common to all of these countries are also several pieces in the Additional Service like the famous ונתנה תקף, "We relate the might" [which is also found in a manuscript in the Cairo geniza].[35] The ʿAvoda poems were different. It was customary for each country to have its own ʿAvoda, but the passages appended to it, and especially the *selihot* following it, show the closest connection.

[274]

The services of these three days developed quite differently in Sepharad,[36] but even here the practice was not uniform. One must at least distinguish between Catalonia and Castile, but the basic features and general structure are the same. For the Ninth of Av, Sepharad typically has a large number of psalms and *qinot* of general contents; of the rich and detailed *qinot* of Kallir it knows nothing. On the other hand, the three Sabbaths preceding the fast have extensive *yoser* compositions. Likewise the order of the *hoshaʿnot* is different; the structure and poetic development are completely different from those of Kallir. But the difference stands out particularly in the service for the Day of Atonement. In the many prayer collections of Spanish origin there is hardly any ancient matter, except for the ʿAvoda. The poetic elaboration of the service is the work of the famous local poets. Typical of them is the *maʿamad*. The poetic *seliha* became part of the poetry belonging to the *qerova*, while the *selihot* in the ancient sense of the word, including the simple traditional litanies, come after the ʿAmida. For part of the Sephardic order of prayer it is characteristic that it does not know the poetic *maʿariv*, that it does not have *yoser* or *qerova* for the pilgrim festivals or the special Sabbaths, and that it does not have Aramaic paraphrases of the Torah reading in the Haftara, while a different branch of Sepharad does have such piyyutim. The Sephardic order of prayer came to have great influence and spread throughout many countries, especially North Africa, where most communities followed its pattern in embellishing the festival prayers. But in its eastern parts, like Tripoli and Egypt, the tradition of Saadia [may have] had a determining influence on the statutory prayers. Southern France was a transition area between these two groups. Provence[37] was in contact both with Spain and with northern France, and therefore in its communities one finds many borrowings from both groups, in the statutory prayers as well as in the poetry. The places in the service where poetry is inserted conform to the pattern of northern France, while the poems themselves are often taken from the works of the great Spanish writers.

The geographical limits of the prayer rites were never rigidly and immutably fixed; even within the territory of a single rite there was a greater or lesser degree of freedom. The composition of the communities was not always stable, and taste kept changing. Furthermore, until 1150 the poets were very productive, so that new material was constantly being produced. The number and contents of the poems were not entirely fixed, but could be changed from time to time. It seems that, except on the Days of Awe, only the precentor had a collection of piyyutim at hand, and it was entirely up to him to determine how they were to be used. Particularly arbitrary was the selection and order

[275]

of *selihot*.[38] Each place went its own way as to the number of biblical verses, their distribution, and the insertion of poetic material; on only a few of the fast days were the *selihot* to be recited definitely fixed; most came into being because of local events and memorial services of the particular community, and their number and status varied rather frequently. Nor was there any uniform practice with respect to the days of *selihot* preceding the Days of Awe; in some regions only a few days were used for this purpose, while a whole month was used in others. Sepharad was content to repeat the ancient litanies every day. Other countries had different poetic pieces for each day, but neither number nor content were subject to fixed rules; they could be accepted in various ways, and their influence on the rite was varied. On such details did the formation of the prayer rites depend; so it came about that every large rite was divided into subdivisions.[39]

(6) Awareness of the many differences between neighboring congregations in those parts of the service not stipulated by the tradition led to their being collected and committed to writing. A new literature thus arose,[40] permitting us a glimpse of the flexibility of certain elements in the liturgy, but also contributing to the fixing of the parts of the service that until then had been free. The mere description of the deviant practices did not necessarily compel their introduction or observance anywhere, but the fact that so many details are reported indicates that great importance was attached to them. Later generations, which regarded all the literary documents of the past as having deep significance and binding force, drew their own conclusions from this, and *custom* actually became a *force*. The behavior of the ancestors was studied in all detail and with all piety; to the extent possible they were recommended as a model for imitation. The rules "custom displaces law" and "do not abandon the custom of one's father and do not turn one's back on the usage of one's mother" were often repeated and much insisted upon; the "customs and orders" or the "right customs" are not merely frequently repeated turns of phrase, but in time became the most influential element in the liturgy. Collections of customs worthy of emulation were therefore compiled already at an ancient period. Whether they go back to outstanding respected individuals like R. Meir the Precentor of Worms[41] or whether they are the customs of famous ancient communities like Cologne, Mainz, and Speyer, they are carefully recorded, col-

lected, and recommended as a criterion for posterity. This literary genre was particularly cultivated in Germany and France. The collection edited by Abraham b. Nathan of Lunel[42] became particularly important. He was born in Provence, spent his youth in the important community of Lunel, and afterwards migrated to northern France and finally to Spain. He observed attentively the customs followed in the synagogues everywhere. In the centers of scholarship that he attended he probably met colleagues from other countries and made inquiries of them; thus, in his book מנהיג עולם, "Universal Guide," ordinarily known simply as the *Manhig*, composed in Toledo in 1205, he could report what he had seen or heard of the customs of northern France, western Germany, Burgundy, Champagne, Provence, England and Spain. He also incorporated many citations from the literature; he seems to have copied and glossed great liturgical collections like the *Maḥzor Vitry*. His work, one of the most valuable for the historian in this area, did not get sufficient attention, and was transmitted defectively; it was often abridged or altered by the insertion of passages from works by others. Meir of Rothenburg's work is particularly important for Germany. His customs were diligently followed, noted down by his disciples, and transmitted to future generations. He himself compiled an order of benedictions, but most of the material was reworked by his disciples into other books: Samson b. Zadok wrote the *Tashbeṣ* in 1292, but the original extent of this work cannot be completely determined because of the complicated history of its transmission. Meir ha-Kohen, collector of the הגהות מיימוניות (*Hagahot maimoniyot*), "Maimonidean glosses," accompanied the text of the prayers in Maimonides with information about the varying customs in Germany. Meir of Rothenburg served as a model also for the later law codes down to and including the *Ṭur*. In Italy, Zedekiah b. Abraham,[43] Meir's younger contemporary, composed his ritual compendium שבלי הלקט (*Shibole haleqet*), "Gleaned ears." This is actually a complete code of ritual law, but its starting point is public liturgy, and it deals mainly with subjects connected with it. The author does not often give his own opinion, offering instead lengthy citations from earlier works to which he had access; he also collects whatever customs he was able to observe, thus making his book a most useful and instructive one. Similar work was done at the beginning of the fourteenth century by Aaron ha-Kohen b. Jacob of Narbonne.[44] Expelled from his homeland, he composed in Majorca his comprehensive ארחות חיים (*Orḥot hayim*), "Paths of life," the first part of which deals solely with matters of liturgy. He says explicitly that his book was intended for people like him, who have been driven away from their homelands and are therefore without books or tradition. His book excels for its method, its rich contents, and its verbatim citations from sources, the most important of which come from the lost parts of the *Sefer haʿitim*. The book was later abridged, altered, and partially rearranged for Ashkenazic use by Shemaria b. Simha; under the title כל בו (*Kol bo*), "The Comprehensive," it enjoyed wide distribution from the sixteenth century on. For Spanish Jews the leading figure is David Abudarham. In 1340 he composed in Seville a commentary on the prayer book that soon became very popular because of its clarity and simplicity;[45] in his commentary he included information about synagogue customs, which in this way also gained wide circulation.

The authors mentioned up to now described mainly the customs known to them from personal observation or from ancient literary works. With the decline of independent spiritual activity among the Jews and curtailment of thought because of political

[276]

and social pressure, ever more importance was attached to collecting the traditions of the past. Lacking the courage and tranquility to write bigger and better books, they concentrated on editing such collections, in the process studying and fixing every little detail of prayer and synagogue custom. Ancestral custom acquired exaggerated importance. Already in 1313 Menahem b. Joseph of Troyes wrote his סדר טרוייש, "Rite of Troyes,"[46] for the explicit purpose of instructing the precentors on how to conduct the service in accordance with the true custom of the Troyes community, so that they neither stand there like ignorant emptyheads nor appear before God like fools or dreamers and commit serious errors in their important office. The contents of the ten chapters that follow bear no relationship to the importance claimed for the book in its introduction. They deal with prayers whose text had never been fixed, and the reciting of which had formerly been up to the judgment of the congregation—for example, the use and placement of the psalms, the Supplications, the prayers during the Torah reading, the exact fixing of the pericope in the Torah and Haftara, and, finally, the selection of piyyut and *seliha*. Especially after the period of the Black Plague (1348–49), what has rightly been called the "plague of rites" became an epidemic in Germany and Austria.[47] Because of the shock that had befallen the communities, older institutions, regulations, and practices were forgotten; therefore, these were studied with a thoroughness more than sufficient to astonish a modern-day reader. These studies had some justification to the extent that their purpose was the reestablishment of the continuity of tradition and to the extent that they served to overcome the disorder and confusion that had spread to many places. But they went much further, and bestowed such exaggerated attention on such minuscule matters and unimportant habits that we can only view it as morbidity, the pathetic sign of a period of decadence. The best-known record of ritual practices is the one disseminated under the name of the *Maharil*—that is, R. Jacob b. Moses Möllin of Cologne (1356–1427).[48] This collection, put together by Zalman of St. Goar, includes also the customs of R. Shalom of Vienna and of R. Abraham Klausner. Noteworthy is the degree of importance ascribed by the collector to his work and research:

> I have taken pains to observe precisely the customs and usages of that man of God, Jacob Möllin; I did not hesitate to report matters that appear simple and generally familiar, so that it may be known how he observed them. For he is worthy that his practice should be followed, inasmuch as he had the traditions of our great masters and was very punctilious in following their practice.

The writer sees himself as unworthy to compose such an important book; but his notations had been much used by others, disseminated, and made known against his will, so that finally he found himself prepared to publish them, thereby filling a generally felt need. The result of this detailed study of ritual practice was that, now, whatever could possibly be fixed was fixed, every word carefully attended to, and thorough research instituted about any point where doubt could obtain: every *yoser*, even every melody in use in one of the then great communities of the Rhineland or Austria, or in the circle of one of the famous sages, every hand gesture and every prostration of every authority was thoroughly and carefully reported. The effort and care that were expended on these minutiae arose out of an exaggerated esteem for custom; "custom is the main thing" or "the custom of our ancestors is equivalent to the revelation"—such slogans were constantly repeated in those days. As a consequence the last vestige of freedom vanished from the synagogue service, and all the prayers, customs, and usages were fixed in writing. The importance and the esteem accorded such traditions only increased with time. Rite books formed an important source for codification of the rite already in the *Shulhan 'arukh*, and the more time passed the stronger became the force of custom. Finally, it reached the point that any change in ancestral custom was strictly prohibited. Thus care for customary practice became a morbid obsession, confirming the harsh observation of a medieval sage that excessive concentration on the custom could lead the communities to perdition.[49]

(7) The fixing of the custom in such detail was particularly destructive because the tradition of the prayers, especially of the poetry, was not at all reliable. This is not surprising, for the communities' life was so unstable. The frequent expulsions, the annihilation of great communities, the hasty flights in which one might barely escape with one's life, rarely with his literary property, the eradication and burning of Jewish books—all these frequently brought about the destruction of prayer books and the poetic treasures they contained.[50] The example of Worms[51] was probably repeated often: Here, a single and incomplete copy of the prayer book was saved from a fire, so that, of a certain poem, only half remained, and from then on only that half could be recited. Such unintentional destruction of poems was not particularly rare. To this must be added other causes of confusion inherent in the transmission of manuscripts. The least of these are scribal errors. Also, the congregations frequently inserted poems in places other than the ones intended by the authors. But even worse was that they arbitrarily shortened poems that seemed to them too long. Whole sections of piyyutim were skipped; hence the copyists did not bother to vocalize them completely or even to copy them, so that they fell out of the manuscripts altogether. The biblical verses inserted in the poems nearly always suffered the same fate. Over-long stanzas were eliminated at the whim of the copyist and banished from the prayer books. In the manuscripts of the Sepharad, the concluding strophes (כרוג) and frequently the *yoser* and the *qerova* were often skipped. In Ashkenaz they would frequently skip half of a poem, for example, the strophes beginning "Wretched King" in the New Year hymn "Highest King," and the strophes beginning "The works of man" in the hymn "The Works of our God." Only rarely were such pieces retained unabridged. The peculiar fate of Provençal prayer books was to contain compilations of fragmentary piyyutim; they are particularly rich in bits and pieces of whole and half strophes. The omissions in manuscripts are innumerable, especially in alphabetical poems or litanies, where lines representing whole letters were dropped; hardly any rite preserves all the lines, but the ones that are omitted vary completely from one rite to another. On the other hand, the litanies are sometimes lengthened, as in "Our Father, our King," which has twenty-two lines in one version and forty-four in another.[52] Already in the twelfth century we hear complaints about the abbreviation of *selihot*; it was even easier for them to divide the poems into parts and to connect fragments by different writers, as was often done.[53] They also did not hesitate to compose additions to the prayers and piyyutim of others; sometimes a few lines would be eliminated from a poem and, with total lack of critical sensibility, extraneous fragments would be stuck into the middle. With all the ahistori-

[278]

cal tampering and fragmenting in the manuscripts, we can console ourselves with the fact that only extremely rarely do we find noticeable and intentional changes in the fixed prayers.

[279]   (8)   Very important changes in the shape of the prayer books occurred on the threshold of the modern period. The primary reason for this was the expulsions and wanderings of the Jews, in which, as a matter of course, they usually lost their books. As a result of the sudden expulsion of the Jews from Spain, members of various communities had to unite into a single congregation. It was impossible to hold separate services in the new settlements according to the rites of Saragossa, Seville, Toledo, Barcelona, and so on. Even in the great communities like Constantinople or Salonica,[54] where at first the exiles from a single town formed a congregation following their native practices, this segregation could not be maintained, and with time the service became more and more uniform. The short and simple prayer rite of Catalonia was introduced among nearly all Jews from Spain and Portugal, and it came to dominate in all the eastern lands to which Sephardic exiles wandered. The development was similar in Germany. The Jews who were forced eastward were not able to maintain for long the ancient customs of Saxony and Swabia, Bohemia and Austria, and all the other varied rites and subrites. Their practice too became uniform, and only a handful of great communities such as Prague and Posen, Worms and Frankfurt maintained in some matters the peculiarities of their tradition.

The invention of printing[55] stamped the prayer book no less than the breakdown of the communities. Understandably, prayer books were among the first printed products in the Hebrew language, and it was not long before printed prayer books were produced for all rites. Printing brought about a revolution in this area, for now it was the printer who determined what would be included in the collections of prayers and what would not. These printers were not scholars, and did not go to any trouble to find the most accurate texts for their editions; what was printed was determined by chance, and in most cases by the balance sheet as well. For the printers the wealth of manuscripts was an unnecessary impediment; the important thing to them was that the books be easy to use and not too expensive. Therefore they reduced the material to be taken from manuscripts as much as seemed possible. The variety of rites also had to be reduced, for it did not pay to publish prayer books of particular traditions for every tiny group.

But the new craft had important consequences for the development of the liturgy even apart from the arbitrary procedures of the printers. The first was a positive one, for from now on the tradition became much more reliable and certain. It became easier to cultivate knowledge of the Hebrew language, teaching was simplified, and reading easier to learn. Now every congregant could have a copy of the prayer book in his hand. Manuscripts had been rare and expensive and not available to the average person; worshipers had prayer books only on the Days of Awe, and after the great persecutions even these copies generally disappeared. But now it was much easier to acquire a prayer book and they became so common that hardly a Jew was without one.

A negative consequence of the new manner of reproduction was that church censorship of books was intensified. Already in the Middle Ages accusations were repeatedly brought concerning certain passages in the prayer book, such as "It is our duty" and "And to the informers," and these texts were altered as a consequence of these accusations.[56] But now the supervision of Hebrew books was intensified; denunciations by apostates became more frequent and the Inquisition became the "supervisor of the Jewish curses and groans." Even their complaint about the oppression and persecution "came under supervision, though this had been the only freedom that the Jews had preserved in their consciousness until now." In the *seliḥot*, overly harsh phrases had to be changed and sometimes whole passages deleted. At first such deletions were marked by leaving a space, but eventually these spaces too vanished, a kind of "silent death sentence." The alterations due to censorship sometimes led to ridiculous distortions about which it is difficult to write without waxing satirical. In the end, the Jews often changed the text themselves, so as not to incur the church's hostility and punishment.

Another source of error was the negligence and ignorance of printers and typesetters, through which the text of the prayers became very garbled.[57] It may seem almost unbelievable that the rabbis allowed such mistakes to spread, but they too had little understanding about the importance of careful printing and exact language, and thus probably could do little to correct the situation. Cantors and elementary teachers, who dominated the field, themselves spoke with unclear and inexact pronunciation; this they disseminated, and the printers perpetuated their errors. Of what use were the complaints of scholars and conscientious prayer book printers like Sabbetai Sofer of Lublin (1611), of what value the daring emendations of linguists like Solomon Hanau (ca. 1710)? The congregations did not listen, and the old errors stood. Tradition sanctified every error and every flaw; it took the revolution of a new age to improve the situation.

The worst consequence of this development was the deification of the letter. It arose out of piety and the desire to fulfill the law faithfully, but it amounted to an intensification of the old "plague of rites," with even more severe consequences. Scholars who did not deem such matters beneath their dignity knew very well how much real value could be attributed to this new authority; nor were they ignorant of the many accidental circumstances that led to the rise of the printed prayer book. But most scholars believed that what was was right; and to the ignorant masses the prayer book in their hand appeared binding as the Torah given on Sinai, as if to change it were mortal sin. No one could harbor strong feelings for such a liturgy in which custom and prescript were the be-all and end-all, and in which the feelings of the heart had no status. The deadly force of reverence for the letter caused great harm to the liturgy, for the spirit that had the power to revive it was moribund. In the absolute absence of general education, discipline, and order, the effort to dislodge the rigid faith in the written letter led to such disruptions that, on the threshold of the modern age, the form of the liturgy had become absolutely untenable.

§ 44 *The Influence of Mysticism on the Synagogue Service*

(1) "A prayer without inner devotion is like a body without a soul." This maxim locates the source of prayer's vitality in devotion of the heart;[1] where this devotion is

absent, prayer loses its point and can deteriorate into sacrilege. Public worship was originally instituted because of the believer's need to lift his heart up to his Creator, and every conscious innovation and change in the liturgy that occurred in later times flowed from the desire to intensify and deepen the service of the heart. Thus at the early stages of prayer or of a particular liturgical form, matters of inward piety are not dwelt upon, but taken for granted. Only when prayer becomes routine, when prescribed prayers are instituted to be recited at specified times, does the possibility arise that they will become a formality. Because no religious community can dispense with such canonization, every religious community is periodically threatened by the danger that its prayers will turn into a pedantic ritual of mere lip service. It was the task of religious instruction to fight the formalization of the liturgy with every possible means. And in fact, alongside the rich literature dealing with the origin of the external form, there is a no less ramified literature on the mental attitude and reverence requisite for prayer. The same two demands are nearly always found side by side in the same texts, but the doctrine of the service of the heart is not usually codified and was not the subject of study in the academies. Instead it was emphasized in a thousand popular books that circulated among the masses and became their common property. The admonitions of the prophets and the psalmists against the formalization of the liturgy echoes throughout the rabbinic literature; everywhere the first demand made of the worshiper is for כונה, "devotion in prayer." "Devotion in prayer means that one should clear his heart of every thought and see himself as if he were standing in the presence of God."

(2)   Alongside the demand for devotion, obvious even to sober, rationalistic teachers of religion, there are also aspirations toward religious ecstasy that seek to achieve their highest effect by means of worship. All the schools influenced by mysticism see prayer as one of the most powerful and effective means to bring about the desired state of unmediated mystical union between man's soul and the divinity. Judaism never lacked for sects of a more or less definitely mystical character, and each had its influence on the liturgy: some by devising special techniques to enhance devotion, and others, the majority, by introducing new prayers or even new types of prayers that were filled with their enthusiastic ideas. These mystical sects were not always successful to the same degree; at times mysticism achieved but slight recognition from official circles or none at all, while at other times it received their enthusiastic approbation. But always it won the hearts of the masses, in whom man's natural longing for the divine was not neutralized by intellectual cultivation. For this reason, the synagogue could never long deny mystical ideas access to itself.

[282]

(3)   The oldest example of mystically inclined pietists in the post-biblical period are the Essenes and the Therapeutai,[2] who embodied a powerful spirit of inner devotion and religious contemplation. Modern scholars have often asserted that the basic structures of the Jewish liturgy were created by the Essenes. We have no reliable data on this subject, and the hypothesis is unlikely. A significant argument against Essene origin is the tranquil joy of the Jewish prayers and the complete absence of ecstasy in them. But not all pietists were untouched by this spirit, and even among the Pharisees and the later rabbis there was no lack of worshipers who strove in all their devotions toward the inner experience of the godhead. Among them were the חסידים הראשונים, "early

pietists,"[3] or the וָתִיקִין, "pious,"[4] who watched for the moment of sunrise so that they could immediately recite the proclamation of faith in the one and unique God, who would spend an hour in reverent preparation and pious withdrawal before praying. We meet with individual visionaries and ecstatics throughout the talmudic period. The talmudic sages are not always the dry formalists so well known to us; among them were numerous adherents of the doctrine according to which prayer depends upon special preparations and accompanying gestures in order to bring the worshiper near to God. They saw to it that the debates and laws applying to the external order and formalities of prayer did not gain the upper hand.

(4)   Only in the post-talmudic period do we encounter the mystics as a unified group with uniform goals. Reacting against the one-sided preoccupation with religious law and against the excessive esteem accorded studies that leave the heart cold, the movement of the Merkava (chariot) mystics arose. These were mystics who observed fasts on consecutive days and hung their faces to the ground as they murmured all sorts of hymns in order to become filled with the divine. They called this "descending to the merkava"; and in the tannaitic period *merkava* was the generic term for all esoteric speculation. "The events in heaven, particularly those that occur in the immediate vicinity of God, the court of heaven with its troops and ranks, and especially the varied panegyrics with which the angels praise the hidden Creator—all these are the subject of the Merkava."[5] The thoughts and goals of these mystics are set forth in the *hekhalot* literature, in the description of the seven chambers of heaven filled with angels, which the mystic believed he could see and among whom he could walk. The oldest *hekhalot* book that has reached us, *Hekhalot rabati*, is composed for the most part of Kedushah hymns,[6] "strange fantasy-pieces of varying length, each ending with the trishagion. The hymns lack any real thought-content, but occasionally they are suffused with a passionate fantasy carried on top of a surging wave of words." The main subject of these books is the angels, their song, and their praise of God. To designate God, a rare and mysterious name is used. At the book's end are hymns intended for the highest level of ecstasy, including הָאַדֶרֶת וְהָאֱמוּנָה, "The splendor and the faithfulness,"[7] which has entered nearly all prayer books and is composed of that abundance of half-intelligible words typical of the prayers of these mystics. The intense veneration of God is expressed through the heaping-up of words that are equivalent in meaning and similar in sound, but that say little and do not advance the train of thought. These hyperbolic hymns are by preference placed in the mouths of the angels, who are introduced and brought forward in troops and camps. In all this they differ considerably from the sober piety of the Bible, the Talmud, and the ancient prayers, which were oriented rather toward the psalmists' proverbial words, "to You silence is praise." In the mystics' zeal to disseminate their ideas, it is not surprising that they had great influence on the liturgy. Even in the statutory prayers there are passages where the abundance of the vocabulary bears no relationship to the content, and where, by contrast to other passages, the angels play a significant role. This is clearest in the Kedushah, the favorite prayer of the members of these circles, who saw themselves as divinely charged to cultivate and disseminate it, and who expected God's grateful recognition in return. The Kedushah of "Creator" has all the earmarks of this group, to which it owes its acceptance into the weekday Morning Service. Likewise, the variety of formulas introducing the Kedushah of the

'Amida and connecting its biblical verses arose only thanks to their activity. Above all the idea of the "crown" placed on the head of God simultaneously by the heavenly hosts and by Israel is authentically mystical. Besides the Kedushah, the Kaddish is also one of the prayers favored by the ecstatics. The passage יתברך וישתבח, "May it be blessed and praised . . . ," which follows the core-line "May His Great Name be blessed," contrasts with the rest of the prayer by being in Hebrew and does not advance the theme. It probably originates from the same source. Similar heaping-up of synonyms is found in such prayers as "True and Certain" and "May Your name be praised"; it is noteworthy that the number of words is identical in both cases. Nor did the liturgical poetry remain untouched by these mystics' influence. The Kedushot of Kallir, with their detailed descriptions of angels, so reminiscent of the *hekhalot*, are clear evidence. The dissemination of the piyyut itself may have occurred as a consequence of the demand for hymns aroused by the mystics; certain fixed formulas that frequently recur in them (like ובכן נעריצך, "And so, we revere You," and ובכן נקדישך, "And so, we sanctify You") make this likely.[8]

(5)　We do not know how long the Merkava mystics remained in the foreground, but it is certain that mystical ideas won over broad circles of the people and had great influence for centuries. A direct line connects the mysticism of the geonic age to similar tendencies that won significance in Germany from the middle of the twelfth century. The "mysteries of prayer" (סודות התפלה) that began at that period to fulfill a function of immense importance are attributed to a certain Aaron b. Samuel.[9] Formerly thought to be a "figment of the traditionalists' imagination," this person is now known to have been born in Baghdad and to have come to Italy around 850, where, after traveling the length and breadth of the land, he eventually vanished as mysteriously as he had appeared. The story of his life was so embellished with legends that we can no longer distinguish its true features, but all the data in our hands describe him as an unusual person who performed many miracles using the mysterious name of God. Not surprisingly, he was revered as "the father of all mysteries." Among the pietists of Germany, there was in circulation a genealogy of teachers of mystical doctrines.[10] The individual names it contains are doubtless spurious; all that we can safely conclude from it is that the tradition saw the mysteries as having originated in Italy, and ultimately in Aaron's sojourn there. Probably when the Kalonymides emigrated they brought the "mysteries of prayer" with them and continued to cultivate them within the family until Samuel the Pious and Judah the Pious made them into a very influential force.

[284]

Samuel the Pious b. Kalonymus the Elder, born in Speyer in 1115, and his son Judah the Pious b. Samuel the Holy,[11] who died in Regensburg in 1217, were the founders of mysticism among the German Jews. This movement was a reaction to the dominance of the study of Talmud as it was developed at that time by the casuistic system of the tosafists. But these two "pietists" are not to be seen as opponents of the Talmud, for both were authorities on religious law; they simply desired to give the longings of the heart their due and to bring to realization a profound ideal of piety and morality. Both went their own ways, consciously and decidedly deviating from the tendency of their times. What concerns us here is their opinion about prayer and the synagogue service. The talmudists held that piety must be expressed first and foremost in the study of Torah; accordingly, they reduced as much as possible the amount of time to be devoted to prayer. But the mystics emphasized that prayer is the highest expression of piety: Not satisfied merely with the received form of public worship, they demanded ecstatic intensity in relation to God, which the soul can attain only through contemplation and abnegation of the things of the world. Since true prayer is the ascent of the soul to God, one can only pray properly in a state of ecstasy. With this attitude as their starting point, these two pietists revealed to their contemporaries the hidden meanings of prayer, till then the secret heritage of their family. Samuel's father, who died while Samuel was still young, transmitted the "order of prayers and their secret meaning" to Eleazar the Precentor in Speyer, so that he could transmit them to Samuel when the latter would be old enough. Samuel then cultivated these doctrines with all the strength of his rich imagination and deep spiritual life, and transmitted them through his own son. The contents of these mysteries can be learned from the commentaries on the prayer book that these two composed, though these have been distorted by reworking and later additions, and by their opinions on the meaning of prayer found in *Sefer ḥasidim*[12] and in the writings of their disciple, Eleazar of Worms. They demand full spiritual concentration in prayer, and the direction of all of the thoughts of the heart to heaven. Conduct in the synagogue must be appropriate to the sanctity of the place where we approach the Lord of the world; strong words and harsh rebukes are addressed to the people of the age for neglecting to apply themselves to the cultivation of such conduct. One should pray only in a language that he understands, for prayer requires proper intention, which is impossible unless the contents are understood. The highest moral demands are made of the precentor: moral purity, humility, and unselfishness; he must be generally liked and not at odds with the community. He must understand his prayers, and must not seek to display his beautiful voice, but rather to awaken the heart of the congregation with his prayer. His prayer must be grounded in sincerity and emotion. One who is not actually suffering hardship or one who has a personal interest in the inflation in food prices may not serve as precentor on a fast day on account of drought. One who is not moved to tears should not recite *seliḥot* before the congregation that depict the worshiper as weeping. Artistic poetry in which the author has laid stress on externals, like "non-Jewish" rhyme, is rejected. The pietists do not oppose liturgical poetry on principle, but they find a large number of poems objectionable. They themselves composed religious poetry. Samuel the Pious wrote the *hoshaʿna* כהושעת אב המון צבאות, "As You saved the father of the multitude of troops," of which only two lines together with the biblical verses appended to it have been preserved in the prayer books. Several prayers are also attributed to Judah, but we cannot speak definitely about them. Like all mystics, they were fond of hymns; thus one of the longest and noblest hymns in the prayer book, שיר היחוד, "The Song of Unity," is attributed to the father,[13] while its conclusion, שיר הכבוד, "The Song of Glory," is attributed to the son. Since the doctrine of the Divine Glory is at the center of Judah's theosophy, there is no reason to cast doubt on this tradition; at the very least the poem may have emanated from the circle of his disciples. Other hymns must have been lost, for *Sefer ḥasidim* speaks explicitly of newly composed prayers. But the main point continued to be to achieve devotion in the recitation of the traditional prayers. All of mysticism is colored by a conservative spirit; its intention is not to set aside the tradition but to fill it with the spirit of piety that it demands in prayer. The means for elevating the soul to the state of ecstasy is addressing the angels, who populate the entire world and with

[285]

whom the worshiper is in constant contact; the use of the mysterious names of God; and the use of artificial alphabetical acrostics. The letters have profound significance, for there is not a single unnecessary letter in the prayers, nor is a letter lacking; their number and order have mystical meaning. Therefore, the Ashkenazic pietists used to count the words and letters in each of the benedictions of the ʿAmida; they asserted repeatedly that one may not add or drop a single one,[14] for the whole structure was erected for a particular purpose, and whoever changes a word in the "most holy" prayers will have to render account to God. What the earliest pietists only hinted, their disciple Eleazar b. Judah stated plainly and in great detail in his book *Roqeah*.[15] He turned Ashkenazic pietism into a popular movement, and made the art of "removing the wall from before the eyes of the soul in order to behold the godhead" widely known. The hosts of visionaries and the longing for visions increased. On the other hand, there were plenty of sober thinkers who denounced the forcible inducing of ecstasy, not only because this state is not always attained, but because even when it is, the soul afterwards sinks back into a state of confusion. In fact this whole movement was one of unhealthy extremes; the period was deficient in clear and prudent thinking, and a great deal of superstition became part of the mixture. Nevertheless, it cannot be denied that what was being taught here was an ideal of uncommonly pure and profound piety. This ideal long dominated the Jews of Germany, affording them spiritual uplift even in times of the greatest hardship. In prayer they could forget themselves and their troubles, and could feel themselves completely at one with their Father in heaven.

(6)   The Kabbalah, which originated in Provence and was cultivated mainly in Spain, went a different way from that of the German pietists.[16] It was a reaction against the rationalism of Aristotelian philosophy, which had been disseminated particularly by the writings of Maimonides, and against the evaporation of Judaism in theoretical speculation. Thus from the beginning its concern was primarily theoretical, with the doctrines of God's incomparability and of the emanations of the spheres in the foreground. But the Maimonists had also given offense through their allegorical exegesis of Jewish ritual law; it was therefore only natural for their opponents to accord the ritual law strong affirmation. Magical power was attributed to the performance of ritual acts; these ensure the continued existence of the world and draw down to the lower world the blessing from the world of the spheres. For this purpose prayer was considered to be particularly important; but it had to be understood in its most profound signification and recited precisely according to precept, because the prayer draws down the fullness of grace that proceeds from God. This bounty does not come from Him directly, but through the mediation of the spheres. The tradition must be followed exactly, for only in this way can one exercise the necessary influence on the upper world. It was not long before practical mysticism became known in Spain and became amalgamated with the theoretical. In the Zohar, composed ca. 1300, the union of the two is already complete. Now every means of achieving ecstasy known to us from the Ashkenazic pietists is encouraged: invoking angels, manipulating the letters of the alphabet, hypnotic gestures, and all sorts of techniques that permit man's soul to be translated to the celestial realm, where it can view the supernal splendor. Naturally, prayer again takes first place among the means that serve to unite the upper and lower worlds. "What the burning flame does to the coal, that is what prayer accomplishes for the elevation of man to

[286]

the world of light." The angels, who are the masters of the spheres, stand ready to receive the true prayers; Sandalfon weaves them into a crown for the infinite God, and Metatron attends to the worshiper's reward by directing the heavenly blessing toward him. The Zohar's view of the meaning of prayer enhanced its status tremendously. In an age when traditional prayer was viewed with apathy by the enlightened and incomprehension by the masses, the Zohar lent prayer new value, and created for it a kind of apotheosis. The Zohar's fantastic ideas freed many downtrodden people from the burdens of their lives; the spiritual uplift that they experienced in traditional prayer and in the recitation of the kabbalistic hymns gave them a taste of the world to come in the midst of the hell of their everyday lives. But at the same time we must not close our eyes to the severe harm done to Jewish piety by kabbalistic theory. It turned prayer into a tool for forcibly bringing about magical effects. By introducing intermediaries between God and man, it spelled a fateful regression in the history of the Jewish religion. Finally, the new doctrine gave a boost to all kinds of superstition.

(7)   Under the influence of both mystical movements, the efforts to fix the traditions of prayer were understandably intensified. If every word and every letter, every motion and every gesture produces an infinite number of effects, then the tradition must be explored and taught in the most exact and detailed way. In a period of intellectual health and sound spiritual life the fact that the customs are so varied would have undermined these doctrines; but this was a period of decline, one less able than any other period to accept such considerations. In the face of the insecurity of life and the fear of the troubles and dangers threatened by tomorrow, the spiritual exaltation provided by the pietistic exercises of the Kabbalists was very desirable. With the deterioration of spiritual life and the establishment of Zohar as a "holy book," the influence of its doctrines increased.[17] After the expulsion of the Jews from Spain, the Zohar found fertile ground in the Holy Land, in the new Jewish community of Safed.[18] Only rarely has history brought together in one place such a large number of enthusiastic and gifted adherents to a single doctrine as it did at that time in the circle of the kabbalists of Safed. The whole atmosphere was suffused with mystical ideas, and a great community was prepared to fulfill the practical demands that followed from them. It was a city of "saints and men of deeds" headed by distinguished talmudists like David Ibn Zimra and Joseph Caro, popular preachers like Moses Alshekh "the Saint" and Abraham Halevi Berukhim, and poets and visionaries like Solomon Alkabetz and Moses Cordovero. But they were all overshadowed by Isaac Luria,[19] whose short life of thirty-eight years and whose sojourn of only two years (1570–72) in Safed were enough to earn him nearly the adulation due a deity. Isaac Luria was the sun in whose rays the light of all the other stars seemed to pale. The new Kabbalah, which spread to wherever Jews lived, was attached to his name. The institutions of the "Holy Ari," as Luria was called by his followers, still enjoy unparalleled respect among all the Jews who have not been touched by the spirit of the religious movements of the modern period. Isaac Luria built a new system founded on the Zohar, but the actual goal of his doctrine and that of the circle of the Safed kabbalists was the absolutely practical one of preparing the age for salvation, when the order of the cosmos will reach its perfection (עולם התקון). In pursuit of this exalted moral goal, a kind of religious order came into being in Safed,[20] demanding of its members human virtues at the highest, almost superhuman level, a spirit of

[287]

repentance that takes hold of the whole man and transforms him from within. Among the pietistic practices of the Safed kabbalists, liturgical assemblies and prayer again played an outstanding part, and new liturgical institutions were devised that spread to all countries. For Luria, prayer is one of the most important functions of life; through his intense attachment to God, man becomes a receptacle for new reflection of the divine light and a new emanation of His grace. Every utterance in prayer has, besides its literal meaning, a profound mystical meaning; one who recites a prayer without devotion, or who desecrates it with impure thoughts, delays the time of redemption. Therefore, special preparations—כונות, "prayers of intention"—were devised, that is, words designed to focus the worshiper's thoughts in prayer toward one of the holy names, and יחודים, "unifications"—that is, the manner in which a particular occurrence of the divine name in the context of a prayer should be emphasized and pronounced.[21] The members of the mystical circle of Safed were required to meet with a fellow member every day to discuss the true way of service to God. Not content with the three daily services, which they were urged to attend regularly, they introduced a Midnight Service (תקון חצות): On every weekday they would assemble in the synagogue at midnight in mourning clothes, sit on the ground, recite lamentations for the destruction of the Temple and the dispersal of Israel, and conclude with a confession of their sins, the great burden of which continually impedes the final salvation. On the Sabbath eve, every member was obliged to make a reckoning of his deeds of the preceding week; afterwards, they went out to the fields or to the court of the synagogue in their Sabbath clothing to recite the Song of Songs, some psalms, and the song לכה דודי, "Go, my friend," in order to welcome the "Sabbath Queen" with due honor.[22] They saw all of life as one continuous liturgy. The kabbalistic masters would wander about the region with their disciples singing hymns, and teachers were sent everywhere to teach the women and children the prayers and hymns. On the eve of the New Moon, they would hold a fast day, with prayers and *seliḥot* like those of the biblical fast days, and with mortifications that had been customary only on the Day of Atonement. Of course, the fast days commemorating the destruction of the Temple were made even more stringent; on the Seventeenth of Tammuz they would sit in the synagogue from noon on, and on the Ninth of Av they would not leave the synagogue at all, but would spend the whole day in lamentation. On the night of the seventh day of Passover, of the first day of Pentecost, and Hoshana Rabba, they did not sleep at all, but spent the night singing hymns or reading passages from the Bible and the Zohar. They connected the forty-nine days of the Omer with the forty-nine words in Ps. 67, each day corresponding to a word; this word had to be emphasized, so that it could fulfill its function. The symbolic lamp fashioned out of the words of the psalm even acquired magic significance as an amulet and a reminder of piety. It was provided with all sorts of unintelligible, superstitious symbols and affixed to prayer books and the synagogue walls. On the night of the Day of Atonement they also did not sleep, but devoted the night to studying the laws of the day and to reciting various types of hymns.

[288]

Such a life of constant ascetic practices, mourning rites, and confessions may seem rather dismal, but it was not so. The aspirations of the Safed kabbalists pointed in the opposite direction, for they were imbued with the joy of men who feel themselves close to their God. Sabbaths, New Moons, and festivals were especially times of the purest joy and the most exalted spirits. The communal meals[23] and the songs sung at them gladdened the participants and aroused in them ecstasies like those of spirits participating in the pleasures of Paradise. Israel Najara,[24] the most talented poet of the age, "who knew how to charm even the angels with his songs," would dazzle his comrades with melodies that made them feel themselves transported to heaven.

Lurianic mysticism, with its liturgical innovations, spread in every direction as swiftly as an infectious disease. No other movement was to have such a powerful effect so quickly on the liturgy and the prayer book. Luria's apostle, Ḥayim Vital Calabrese (d. ca. 1620),[25] propagated the new doctrine so that its adherents spread into all the lands and conquered all the communities. Luria's mystical approach to prayer was disseminated by the printing press, which brought the new prayers, unintelligible meditations (כונות), fasts, and penances everywhere. Zunz writes:

> No rite was spared, as attested by daily and festival prayer books from Tlemcen to the Crimea. Innumerable prayers beginning "May it be Your will," names of angels, and sefirotic bombast immortalized superstition and spirit worship. What was significant in public worship was pushed to the background, and in its place came charms and talismans filling the prayer books and the heads of the masses.[26]

From Palestine, Lurianic fanaticism passed first to Italy, where Menahem Azaria Da Fano[27] won converts to it. There the first Minor Day of Atonement ceremony was held; there fraternities were established that fasted and prayed every Monday and Thursday; and there the early Morning Devotions (שומרים לבקר) and Midnight Services of lamentation (תקון חצות) were introduced. "Selections were chosen from Ashkenaz, Sepharad, and Rome, and new pieces were fashioned to be added to them, partially kabbalistic in content, and this new prayer was declared to be the more important and more certain to effect the redemption than public worship." All collections of this type were called *tikun*.[28] The texts of the Sephardic rite published from that time on are full of instructions in the kabbalistic spirit of Luria.

[289]

What did the most for the dissemination of Lurianic mysticism was its taking root also in Poland, home of the greatest concentration of Jews. Since the thirteenth century the "mysteries of prayer" had never retreated from the foreground, and were brought to Poland during the migration there by the sages. At first they remained a kind of secret doctrine whose content was entrusted to only a few select disciples. Only around 1600, when the condition of the Jews deteriorated in Poland, too, did people reach for the kinds of consolation that flowed abundantly from the Lurianic Kabbalah. Nathan Spira,[29] who died in 1633 in Cracow, won many adherents for it through his popular and widely distributed collection of sermons, *Megale ʿamuqot*. But it owed its greatest success to the propaganda of Isaiah Horwitz.[30] Filled with reverence for the masters of Kabbalah, he rejected the most prestigious rabbinical posts that were offered him in Germany and made pilgrimage to Palestine, where he died in Safed in 1630. He acquired the reputation of a saint, and his book, *Shene luḥot haberit*, made a decisive contribution to the dissemination and general acceptance of the ideas of Luria and the adoption of the new prayers in the synagogue service. Though his prayer book *Shaʿar hashamayim*, in which Horwitz assembled his whole kabbalistic arsenal, appeared only in 1717, the ground was already prepared for this new seed by the publication of the prayer book *Shaʿare ṣion* in 1662 by Nathan Hanover,[31] the historian of the cossack persecutions. These were the main sources from which the new revelation flowed in every direction; from this point on not a single prayer book was given to the printer without these additions. The visionary spirit did not stay limited to Poland, for the swarms of refugees wandering about the communities of western Europe after the pogroms of 1648 and 1649 brought it with them to Germany, Holland, and England. A great number of additions from this period became permanent in the prayer book,[32] such as the poems "The Living God be exalted" and "Eternal Lord" at the beginning of the Morning Service; the verses Num. 10:35 and so on, the hymn "Blessed is the Name," and the various other prayers recited when the Torah is taken out of the ark; the Sabbath song "Go, my friend," several petitions to angels, such as those between the sections of the shofar-blowing; the Song of Unity; and "The Kingly Crown" by Ibn Gabirol. Among these pieces are some of a very high level, for the kabbalists undeniably knew how to choose materials that uplifted the heart and encouraged a spirit of piety. But there are also many passages attesting to the crassest superstition. There is no doubt that these peculiarly Lurianic innovations, such as the *tikunim, kavanot,* and *yihudim,* which have long vanished from western European prayer books, imposed a heavy burden on religious life and were actually a mockery of true prayer.

[290]   (8)   The Sabbatean upheaval proclaimed the bankruptcy of the Kabbalah, and the humiliating decline that came in its wake was sufficient to awaken the hearts from their drunken stupor to complete sobriety. But the Kabbalah experienced a kind of renaissance through Hasidism.[33] This movement was a reaction against the extreme pedantry of talmudism and the wild growth of ritual formalism. It arose among the ignorant and oppressed, who found no satisfaction in the prevailing religious life of the community, and who sought warmth of feeling instead of rigid formalism, and enthusiasm in place of dry casuistry. Israel Baal Shem, the sect's founder (d. 1761), was not a scholar, but a child of nature filled with passionate faith and consumed with longing for the divine—not a pedant, but a man of near-raving enthusiasm, graced with the joy of the constant stream of revelation that flowed to him. What made Hasidism so popular was that it demanded nothing more than an open heart, a human soul ready to abandon itself in order to restore itself to a clarified state. Israel Baal Shem renewed Luria's ecstatic system. The core of religion in his thinking is true love for God, together with intense faith and unshakable trust in the power of prayer. Thus, he could never have enough of prayers and hymns of praise. In his opinion, every true prayer has the power to influence the upper realms; it must not remain subjugated to the petitions and requests of the individual, but it must bring him closer to the Creator. One must eliminate his own individuality in his prayer; his soul has to tear itself free from its mundane abode and lift itself above the world of the tangible to the realm of divine grace. Thus prayer was for Hasidism the be-all and end-all; by engaging all of their coarse and natural strength, they sought to bring themselves to ecstasy, not scorning even the drinking of spirits as a means of achieving a trance-like state. Since they thought that ecstasy was indispensable to prayer, they were not particular about the traditional times of prayer or about holding communal services; they would assemble in special conventicles, and even in these they would pray individually when the moment of ecstasy arrived. They abandoned the prayer books of the Polish rite and introduced the prayers of Isaac Luria (*tikun haʾari*), in a kind of break with their local liturgical tradition.[34]

It cannot be said that this movement was a blessing for religious life, for the price of their striving for intensity was the perversity of their superstitious beliefs and their uncivilized conduct. "It was amusing to see how they would interrupt their own prayer with weird sounds and ridiculous gestures (which must be seen as threats and insults against their enemy Satan, who sallies forth to interfere with their concentration and prayer), and how they so wore themselves out that at the service's end they would collapse as in a swoon."[35]

(9)   According to its principles, Hasidism represents an absolute rebellion against the synagogue service, and no more convincing proof exists of the intolerable condition of the synagogue service than the fact that so many turned their backs on it—not out of lack of faith or out of skepticism, but out of a true longing for piety. This should have been taken as a serious warning that the liturgy was in need of revision. But no change occurred because Hasidism did not keep to the oppositional position of its founders, but instead sought compromise with rabbinic Judaism. Thus, its effect on the synagogue service was more deleterious than it was an improvement. It strengthened the conservative tendency and faith in the written word, the ascetic spirit of renunciation, and the striving to compel the advent of the messianic age; it brought with it new plagues in the form of commotion and unrestrained wild gestures. Thus, the second period in the history of prayer ended in a state of extreme decadence. It began with a small number of prayers and a wide range of freedom, with rites that were suited to the needs of the community, and with an appropriate manner of prayer and instruction. All of this was now reversed. The prayers became long and predetermined from beginning to end; rituals intended for different periods and different circumstances were observed with strict exactitude as if stringently prescribed;[36] instruction was eliminated and Torah reading degenerated because of the many bad practices that had accrued to it; liturgical poetry, originally intended to teach, had taken over the synagogue service, but was no longer intelligible. The service was led by unschooled precentors who chose melodies tastelessly and at random, and who thus lengthened the service even more. It is hardly surprising that in such an age complaints were raised about lack of devotion and attentiveness, about disruptions and disorder. If the synagogue service was to survive, it would need thorough renewal and revivification. Both were brought about by the modern period.

[291]

The Modern Period

§ 45 *The First Reforms in the Synagogue Service*

(1)   The modern period opens with Moses Mendelssohn, the "reformer of German Jewry." His appearance marks the start of the aspirations that have dominated the internal history of the Jewish people for more than a century. This is not the place for an exhaustive treatment of the Reform movement; only its attempts to improve the liturgy are our theme.

The Jews awoke from a dream of centuries; the longing for the messianic redemption retreated in the face of the desire to live in comfort in this world. The Jews sought to find their way once again among men, abandoning their separateness and seeking to be like everyone else. They demanded civil rights and sought to improve their status within the political system; the improvement of their civil status and the attainment of full equality became the slogans that guided their thinking and activities for several generations. With the improvement of their educational system their sensitivity to order and discipline increased and their appreciation for beauty of form and sound became more refined. They took pains to acquire general education and were swept away by the current intellectual trends. The critical thinking that had taken hold of all Europe came to dominate their religion as well. Pious exercises were no longer their sole or even their main concern; the hegemony of dogmatism over the Jewish religion, which had lasted throughout the Middle Ages, was overcome. In the approach to all problems there arose a new and fresh spirit.

The liturgy could not go completely untouched by this mighty upheaval in the lives and thinking of the Jews. Its forms no longer suited the demands of the new age. They repelled both eye and ear, and could neither satisfy the mind nor warm the heart. Many educated people, unable to find the precious core within the unattractive husk, were lost to the synagogue, even if they did not give up the faith. Against them stood the overwhelming majority, who saw every intentional change as treason against Judaism. A tiny group of intelligent people sought reforms that would not harm the essence of the liturgy, such as the simplification of the prayers, the elimination of the bad customs that had infected the liturgy, and the introduction of aesthetic forms and conduct appropriate to the house of God.[1] But before these things came to be, a new age arose, bringing with it new political ideals and creating a new concept of humanity; doubts arose as to whether the wording and thoughts of the traditional prayers suited these concepts; demands were made to change that which no longer seemed to fit the spirit of the times. Finally, scientific thought brought about a critical examination of the entire tradition. The upshot was the demand for the complete revamping of the institution of the synagogue.

[293]

The Reform movement aroused great agitation; it often seemed that no possibility existed of healing the rift between the adherents to the tradition and the supporters of innovation. It led to intense struggles and splits in the communities. Not all Jews were equally affected by the new trends. The "Portuguese" communities were not touched at all, for the Kabbalah had choked their life away. They were never again able to return to vigorous spiritual activity. Their prayers and their prayer books were never freed from the appendages with which mysticism had burdened them. The masses of Jews in Eastern Europe labored under severe political and economic repression that kept them from taking part in the new progressive movement. Hundreds of thousands remained captives of Hasidism, and wide circles sank into total apathy. Only in western Europe, where the Jews registered undreamed-of successes in every area did the problem of prayer move people's spirits deeply. Germany was in the center of this struggle; from it Reform tendencies eventually spread to England and America, and finally returned to influence the land of their origin.

(2) Although a new generation with better education and more refined taste had arisen, the liturgy continued along in its old way, and tradition, with all its ugly excrescences, continued to dominate it unchanged. As time went on, this situation became intolerable, and something had to be done to meet the new demands. The disciples of Mendelssohn, in whom sensitivity for the Hebrew language and its poetry had awakened, were the first to complain about the ugly and slovenly manner in which the prayers were recited in the synagogue. Schooled in the philosophy of the Enlightenment, their minds could not be satisfied with mystical ideas. Their first efforts were directed at disseminating carefully edited versions of the prayer book, purified of the errors it had suffered under Kabbalistic influence. Among those who performed particular service along these lines, it suffices to mention Wolf Heidenheim (1757–1832),[2] who has been correctly called "the Mendelssohn of the prayer book." To him belongs the credit for opening a new age in the history of the prayer book. His editions of the *siddur* and the *maḥzor* excel both in accuracy and appearance; the accompanying translation was the best possible for its time, and the commentary was a pioneering work in the study of liturgical poetry. Heidenheim dropped all the additions to the prayers that had been introduced in the wake of Lurianic mysticism, except for a very few vestiges. His texts, together with the translations by Michael Sachs,[3] were accepted as authoritative even in circles not sympathetic to reform. This purging of kabbalistic accretions was a decisive step, a farewell to views and traditions that had dominated in the preceding period. It was one of those quiet revolutions that, without attracting much attention, actually have epoch-making significance. The prayer book edited by

Seligmann Baer,[4] following Heidenheim's method, represents, for all practical purposes, perfection as regards accuracy of text and correctness of vocalization. At the same time, it represents a retrograde step, since it took up again many of the old, distorting accretions. Thus, it subscribed to the romantic reaction that was ushered in with the nineteenth century.

Translations of the traditional prayers also gradually became more widespread, making an understandable liturgy accessible to those who did not know Hebrew. Among the Portuguese and Italian Jews, translations of the prayers had been common for centuries, with no one objecting to this practice.[5] In the realm of the Ashkenazic-Polish rite, a Yiddish translation had long been available, but translation into the vernacular was prohibited wherever the Polish rabbis were in authority. When Isaac Pinto[6] attempted to publish an English translation of the prayers in London, he came up against such bitter opposition that he was forced to print his book in New York. The lot of the first German translation was no better. In 1786 David Friedländer published a translation of the prayers and the Sayings of the Fathers with a commentary, printed still in Hebrew letters. While this book was not put under the ban, as Mendelssohn's translation of the Bible had been in its day, it was publicly attacked by the preacher Eleazar Feckeles in Prague, and Friedländer felt the need to defend himself in an "Epistle to the Jews of Germany." Nevertheless, in 1788, Isaac Euchel published a new translation in German letters; this was followed by translations into Dutch, Danish, and Hungarian, and eventually into all the languages spoken by the Jews, without the need to fight great battles over the permissibility of translation. Except for the most extreme circles of Hasidim, who to this day maintain that Yiddish is the only permitted and legitimate language of the Jews, no one has again come out in opposition to translation into the vernacular.

[294]

(3)   While these were deviations from tradition, they did not alter the liturgy as such. The much-lamented abuses, the length of the services, the burden of unintelligible liturgical poetry, the disruptive commotion, especially accompanying the reading of the Torah—none of these was thereby eliminated. No one dared to interfere with the well-established order of the synagogue, until, through the French Revolution, the peoples' right to self-determination claimed victory over the unbridled control of authority. In 1795 there arose in Amsterdam a society called *Felix Libertate*, the main goal of which was the struggle for emancipation; at the same time its members demanded reforms in the liturgy, removal of the liturgical poetry, and the alteration of prayers that assumed a political or social disparity between Jews and non-Jews. Since the community leadership and the rabbis opposed them, they founded their own congregation, Adath Jeshurun.[7] In numerous polemical writings published by both sides, the question of the justification of the demanded reforms was discussed. When, later, Napoleon convened the Great Sanhedrin, many hoped that a comprehensive liturgical reform would proceed from this group. But everything remained as before; the only effect this assembly had on the liturgy was a consistorial order of 1807,[8] in which the rabbis were given the responsibility of seeing to order in the synagogue and of giving a sermon every Sabbath in the language of the land. This was an innovation in every country, for although sermons were not unusual outside Germany, they were not a regular institution. In Germany sermons in pure German were an isolated phenomenon,

which were tolerated on special occasions. Since the government had now made them obligatory, they had perforce to be permitted; but there was at first a dearth of qualified speakers who were sufficiently in control of the language.

[295]   The requirements of the consistorial order acquired real meaning when they were transferred to the kingdom of Westphalia and were applied strictly by Israel Jacobsohn.[9] Jacobsohn was not a reformer in the true sense, for he lacked theological knowledge and scientific depth; but he was a man with a grasp of practical things, quick, decisive, and energetic. His greatest wish was to give Jewish institutions a contemporary, appealing appearance that would be attractive even to outsiders. He therefore laid great stress on eliminating all the formal defects of the liturgy and on the beautification of its forms. As far as his authority went, he insisted on the introduction of the German sermon and organized singing. In the synagogues of the consistorial territory, liturgical poetry was eliminated and a few prayers containing laments about oppression and persecution were changed as not being in harmony with actual political circumstances. This all was accepted, though with some resistance. But unfavorable notice was taken of Jacobsohn's introduction of German prayers and hymns into the services of the consistorial school of Kassel, and he aroused general outrage for having an organ played in the synagogue which he built in Seesen. The liturgy consisted mainly of the traditional Hebrew prayers unaltered, but the German part encountered many objections. Jacobsohn based his decisions on the fact that the knowledge of the Hebrew language was in decline; but his opponents countered that suppressing Hebrew from the synagogue service would lead to even greater neglect of the ancestral language, which was at once the language of sacred scriptures and the only tie binding together the entire community of the faithful.[10] Thus, already at the movement's very first beginnings, the same arguments were being leveled against each other as those with which the battle is still being fought a century later. As was done in Seesen, an hour for prayer assembly was also held in the Philanthropin school in Frankfurt am Main every Sunday,[11] and later, on the initiative of Johlsohn, who also composed a song book for this purpose, every Sabbath. The form of the new liturgy, especially the German songs, was in many portions an imitation of Christian models, which of course gave considerable offense, but after a short time it was recognized as correct and accepted without objection. With the help of school discipline, the services held in the Jewish educational institutions accustomed the pupils to orderly and dignified behavior in the synagogue, to the sermon, and to choral singing. Even more important was the fact that these arrangements also pleased the parents of the students, and they too participated in them. In this way sermon and singing, order and reverence became a spiritual need for large circles of people, and the regular German sermon became widespread, so that very soon it was no longer regarded as something strange.

Jacobsohn also attempted to make the confirmation of boys and girls a regular institution.[12] But a required catechism lacked any roots in the past, and could not become permanent. It became part of the synagogue service only in Reform communities in Berlin and the United States. Confirmation was included in the Reform program of several governments that were favorably disposed toward the Jews, for they thought that it would guarantee that Jewish youth would be given instruction in the language of the country. In Denmark it was given legal status.[13] In the few congregations in that country a rather free spirit prevailed, so that the sermon in Danish and various other

reforms in Jacobsohn's spirit found enthusiastic supporters. In every country where the   [296]
acculturation of the Jews in the local language and the local way of life were a new phenomenon, the desire to give this development some degree of clear expression in the
synagogue service was repeated.

(4)   Jacobsohn's move to Berlin, in 1815, was an event of great significance. Here
the indifference of the enlightened circles toward traditional Jewish institutions had
reached a shocking level. Here Mendelssohn's disciples had attempted to shape the
intellectual content of the Jewish religion anew in the spirit of the Enlightenment, but
the community had remained completely stagnant. Immediately after the promulgation
of the edict of March 11, 1812, David Friedländer wrote his pamphlet "On the
Changes in the Synagogue Service Rendered Necessary by the New Organization of
the Jewish Community in the Prussian States," and tried to gain the support of the
government for thorough change.[14] Besides "creating an appropriate external form,"
he demanded "the complete and unrestricted introduction of the German language in
the service." More decisively, he wanted to eliminate all prayers with messianic content
and to expunge references to the hopes for the future since they had supposedly lost
their point once emancipation had been granted. Thus he was carried away by one of
the most dangerous errors of the Jewish enlightenment, which stripped the messianic
ideal completely of its spiritual content and interpreted it as the attainment of worldly
success and political equality. Not surprisingly, Friedländer's pamphlet aroused great
attention, but it had no consequences outside of a few polemics that were written
against it.[15] When Jacobsohn established his residence in Berlin, he held services in
his own house on Sabbaths and festivals with organ accompaniment, German choral
singing, and a regular sermon.[16] The order of prayers was more or less the traditional
one, but the opening portions were much abridged or translated into German; the main
innovation was that the 'Amida was not repeated and the Additional Service was completely eliminated. Hebrew prayers and the reading of the Torah were done in the Portuguese pronunciation, which was held to be more accurate. Jacobsohn's services met
with strong approval among the many cultured people of the community, and a larger
hall was soon needed for them. But the new institution was not long-lived; as early as
December 1815, it was prohibited by the government, because the old Jewish regulation
of 1750 forbade holding public services outside the community synagogue. These
prayer assemblies were thus interrupted for a time. But since the most influential members of the community were very desirous of continuing the service in a form that
appealed to them, they made use of the need that had arisen to renovate the synagogue
as an excuse to revive services of the type established by Jacobsohn. For this purpose
they published a hymnal and a prayer book of their own for Sabbaths and festivals.
Once again the changes had to do more with the form of the prayers than with their
contents; they consisted essentially of more extensive use of German in the Morning
Benedictions and the Verses of Prayer, and a few variant readings from the Sephardic
rite; the Additional Service was also restored. Likewise, on the festivals most of the
Hebrew service retained its traditional form, except that the liturgical poetry was greatly
abridged. (On the Day of Atonement much of it was, however, retained.) Though the
deviations from the traditional liturgy were not extensive, many saw the German sermon, the prayers and German hymns, and the organ accompaniment as religious com-

[297] pulsion. They complained to the government, demanding the expeditious restoration of the community synagogue.[17] But the supporters of the changes did not want to complete the building until they could come to an agreement about the reforms; they wanted to expand the synagogue so that two prayer services could be held in it simultaneously. This is what actually happened when the opponents had the synagogue, with difficulty, fixed up for traditional services. The extended conflict between the parties and the government investigation eventually led to the unfortunate consequence that, by a royal decree of December 9, 1823, any change in the Jewish service, including the sermon and the hymns in German, was prohibited in principle. Likewise, in other Prussian communities such as Breslau and Königsberg, the German sermons that by now had been in use for quite some time were eliminated.[18] Thus for several decades all progress in the synagogue service in the territory of the Prussian kingdom was blocked.

(5)   At that time the need was felt everywhere to change the synagogue service and to give it a form that would better suit modern sensibilities. Particular attention was aroused by the establishment of the Neue Israelitische Tempelverein in Hamburg.[19] There, in 1817, a great number of community members formed a union, with the purpose of

> producing a dignified and well-organized prayer rite in accordance with which the service should be conducted on Sabbaths and festivals as well as on other solemn occasions, in a special Temple to be established for this purpose. In particular there should be introduced into this prayer ceremony a sermon in German and choral singing accompanied by organ.

This, for the first time, was a congregation formed for the purpose of holding a Reform service. The prayer book published on the occasion of the opening of the Temple in the fall of 1818 deviated substantially from all the prayer books known till then.

Services were held only on Sabbaths and festivals; therefore the prayer book contained only the prayers for these days. Later an appendix appeared with prayers for Purim and the Ninth of Av. The external characteristics of the Temple service were mixed choral singing, the playing of the organ, a regular sermon in German, and German songs, for which the preacher Kley published a special hymnal. The prayer book was based on the tradition of the Portuguese rite, and the Hebrew was pronounced according to that tradition. The selection of prayers was based on the distinction between "typical" and "accessory" prayers. The typical ones—"that is, those that have at all times been considered substantial components of Jewish worship"—were "rigorously retained, and only the accessory prayers have been treated with freedom." The use of the Sephardic prayer book brought about many deviations from the text of the prayers that was familiar to most of the Jews of Hamburg, but within the prayer book that came to be used, the text was retained almost without change. The most noticeable innovation was that even many of the fixed prayers were not recited in Hebrew but in German translation. In the Friday night service, the Welcoming of the Sabbath was omitted, on the grounds that it had not been known in ancient times. The service began with Ps. 92, then continued with the Evening Service in its traditional text; but only the *Shemaᶜ* and the passages after the ᶜ*Amida* were recited in Hebrew, while all the rest was recited in German. In the Sabbath Morning Service, the Morning Benedictions and the Verses of Song were considerably shortened (§§11, 12), and were given in German; the *Shema*ʿ and its benedictions were done in the same manner as in the evening. The ʿ*Amida* was recited aloud immediately and in Hebrew, with the insertion of the Kedushah. For the reading of the Torah, the triennial cycle was introduced. The reading was done in the Portuguese pronunciation and without cantillation, and the Haftara was omitted. German hymns were sung when the Torah was taken out and replaced, and before and after the sermon. The ʿ*Amida* of the Additional Service was also recited aloud immediately. On the festivals the stucture of the prayers was the same as on the Sabbath. On the pilgrim festivals liturgical poetry was not recited, as consistent with the Portuguese rite; but on the Days of Awe a great number of poems was retained, all of them in accordance with the Portuguese tradition. The Day of Atonement service lasted, as was traditional, the entire day. When the prayer book for Purim appeared, it included the innovation of replacing the intermediate benediction of the ʿ*Amida* with the summary text "Give us understanding."

[298]

The changes in the prayer texts were not very significant, and did not touch on the main points, but only on details of style. The purpose of the innovations was above all to shorten and simplify the service, to make the prayers more intelligible than before, and to have them speak to the hearts of the worshipers. Only two innovations had fundamental importance. In the Additional Service the petition for the building of the Temple and the restoration of the sacrifices was replaced with a petition that the prayer be accepted in place of the sacrifice. Further, there was a revision in the text of the petition for the bringing of the messianic age. Nevertheless the expression of hope for the future was not completely eliminated, but was retained more or less in its traditional form. Wherever the text dealt with the historical importance of the Jewish people or wherever it was possible to interpret the messianic ideal in a symbolic or purely religious way, the text was left untouched; but where the nationalistic side of the hope for the future was stressed and the prayer dealt with the general restoration of the Holy Land and the assembling in it of the exiled communities, the sentences were given a more general and symbolic meaning.

Except for the mixture of German and Hebrew passages in the same prayer and the changes in the Torah reading, this prayer book's deviations from tradition must be described as very moderate. It was not revolutionary, for the founders were far from intending to break with the Jewish community as a whole. Their only goal was to "give the entire ritual dignity and effectiveness." In no respect did they seek to cut themselves off from the religious observances of the Jews. Educated laymen, not theologians, edited the prayer book for the needs of the moment. They did not see it as finished work, final and immutable. It had come into being under the sign of progress and development, and would need to be reappraised and altered from time to time. The prayer book was not a masterpiece; its authors anxiously avoided taking positions of principle, and they adopted a variety of compromises in order to satisfy as many different groups as possible. Thus, Abraham Geiger criticized it severely and rejected it as reactionary because it was lacking "in almost every point a clear and purposeful application of the principle of progressive religion."[20] Others criticized it because it seemed to them too extreme,[21] did not pay sufficient attention to the views of the community, and moved too rapidly away from the dominant religious outlooks. Even adherents of progress, people who in general did not deny their esteem for the liturgy of the Temple as a whole, attacked it, especially on account of the deviations in the prayers with messianic content. Here they touched the most vulnerable part of the Temple's prayer book. True, the question of the binding nature of the belief in the Messiah in its traditional form was in flux. But what exactly was the true content of the messianic idea and what might actually be expressed about it in prayer were problems that had scarcely been taken up and had certainly not yet found a definitive solution: It was too soon to justify any alteration. What was decisive was not theological considerations, such as those that later led to the revision of the whole messianic idea, but an exaggerated concern for the attainment of emancipation. The opponents of equal rights for Jews, who were never at a loss for good arguments, used the references to the hopes for the future and the faith expressed in the prayers for the establishment of a Jewish kingdom in the Holy Land as a welcome weapon. It was wrongheaded of the reformers then and later to be ready to sacrifice the traditional form of messianic belief to this objection, and to impute to ancient Judaism some deficiency in land-rootedness and patriotism. The political prejudice ought to have been fought with political weapons. Anyone who gave the question honest, unprejudiced thought would be unable to derive from the messianic belief any solid ground to deny the Jews equal rights; irrefutable grounds for these were given by the English statesman Thomas Macaulay in his apologetic treatise on their behalf.[22] Not only in this one point did the founders of the Temple let themselves be guided by opportunism, but everything that they did was determined by external considerations. The men who labored on behalf of reform were not scholars or clergymen striving to develop a new religious conception and to effect a consistent reshaping of the liturgy, but practical men. Nevertheless, they deserve credit for their efforts, for they were the first to find the courage to attempt the renovation of the liturgy. Even the Temple's opponents could not deny that it had "with one blow and without any hesitation removed from the house of God the centuries-old accumulation that no one had dared to touch, purged it with the vehemence of youth, and awakened a sense for order, decorous behavior in worship, taste, and simplicity."[23]

Had the rabbis taken charge of the new movement, as recommended by perceptive traditionalists,[24] had they attempted to influence the reformers and to correct what they saw as errors, who knows what the eventual development of German Jewry would have been? Instead, the rabbis took a decidedly hostile position from the first. Hardly had the first fascicles of the new prayer book appeared when the rabbinical board in Hamburg posted a notice in the synagogue, warning the community members against using the book. By the next day the rabbi of Altona had issued a similar proclamation. One has only to read these half-Hebrew, half-German documents in order to grasp that here was a conflict between two different worldviews, between which no dialogue was possible. The Temple Union did not let itself be intimidated by the threats, but continued the publication of its prayer book and used it regularly in its services, which enjoyed good attendance from the first. The rabbinical board solicited opinions from the most respected rabbis of Germany, Austria, Hungary, and Italy, which it published in the collection *Ele divre haberit*.[25] As the unanimous conclusion, it was announced already on the title page

that it is forbidden to alter even a single word from beginning to end in the order of prayers customary among the Jews, much less to eliminate anything; that it is forbidden to pray in any language other than Hebrew; that any prayer book not printed in accordance with the precepts and customs is invalid; that it is prohibited to pray from such; that, finally, it is forbidden to play any musical instrument in the synagogue on Sabbaths or festivals, even by a non-Jew.

The rabbis' language was strong, for they were used to giving orders and to getting unconditional obedience. For the first time they now encountered a large, unified party that was consciously distancing itself from tradition and rabbinical authority. They went much too far in their charges of heresy, and opposed every demand with an absolute "No." The rabbis faced the innovations in incomprehension and helplessness, although some of them knew from their own experience how widespread were the efforts to abandon traditional Judaism. They were unworldly men who lived only in their books; they controlled the Talmud and codes in minutest detail down to the latest responsum, but they were trapped in their dialectics, and could only hold on to the letter. They were no longer capable of appreciating the spirit of biblical and rabbinic Judaism, and they had no conception of history's influence on the development of religious customs and beliefs. Thus, they united on the position that every innovation was to be rejected, and would not permit even behavior that had never before been prohibited, even practices that could be invalidated only by dint of casuistry and mental gymnastics. They were convinced that not only the text of the prayers, but every liturgical institution without distinction, went back to ancient tradition, that no custom could be altered, for these too were "holy of holies," that "even the slightest deviation in them throws the prayer's efficacy into doubt." The wording of their opinions shows how they were guided by the perspective introduced into legal reasoning by the Kabbalah; they feared that the particular meanings and effects attributed by the Kabbalah to every ritual, even the most insignificant custom, would be jeopardized. Their position toward the organ particularly reveals their helplessness in the face of anything new.[26] Though talmudic texts never spoke of it, the rabbis were certain even before any investigation that the organ could not be permissible. To be sure, they were uncertain whether to prohibit music altogether or only on the Sabbath; and since even uncontested authorities permit music at wedding celebrations, the authors of the opinions were faced with the difficult task of proving that the enhancement of the liturgy was not as great a duty as the enhancement of a private celebration. It was a suicidal dialectic. There was only one positive aspect to the opinions,[27] namely, the unanimous, decisive declaration that the messianic faith and the hopes for the future do not render the Jews unsuited to fulfill any of the duties of citizenship, and that loyalty to the ruler and the fatherland are among the religious precepts of Judaism.

The severity of the rabbis' negative opinion was all the more unjustified in that they themselves had done nothing to ward off the deterioration of religious life. It was by now public knowledge that nearly an entire generation had become alienated from the liturgy because they did not understand its contents and were repelled by its form. The rabbis had observed this indifference untroubled, and made no attempt to examine the motivations of those who were trying to limit the damage. There was absolutely no possibility of an understanding between the two opposing parties because the representatives of tradition showed no inclination to familiarize themselves with the goals and

[301]

wishes of the reformers. By the same token, their arguments and opinions could make no impression on the members of the Temple. Not only did they have several rabbinical opinions in hand that were favorable toward the similar efforts in Berlin and that completely sanctioned the innovations, but one of their most active members had published a sharp satirical refutation of the traditionalists in which he juxtaposed their opinions against the contrary statements of the rabbinic sources.[28] But this was not decisive. Even if the *Shulhan ᶜarukh* and its most authoritative commentators had been united in opposition to them, the Temple congregation would not have been restrained. Times had changed; the Talmud's authority had been overthrown. Decisions would no longer be made on the basis of formalistic decrees and the dialectical reasoning of the rabbinic sources. Even principles of faith and religious institutions had to submit to the judgment of reason. They were no longer revered simply because they were handed down from the ancestors, but had to be tested for inner value and practicality. The old liturgy was superannuated, and had become an empty formality: The mumbling of unintelligible prayers, the revolting singing of the precentor, and the noisy bustle in the synagogue were no longer in the spirit of the times; they were not edifying and did not satisfy the need for piety and reverence. These were unfamiliar, long unheard demands, but they were raised by a new generation living under completely altered circumstances. It could certainly not be seen as a crime against the spirit of the Jewish religion if steps were taken to simplify the liturgy and restore inspiration and solemnity. In one of the opinions against the Temple, the "defection" of the new congregation was declared to be a punishment for the abuses against the liturgy in Germany, for the fact that worshipers disturbed the service by talking and even by arguing and quarreling.[29] That was, in fact, the very core of the problem, and the proponents of reform themselves could not have found a more incisive justification for their actions. But the rabbis, in their pitiable ignorance of the world, did not grasp that the problems were the result of clinging to those very customs that they would not touch because of their supposed sanctity.

By their protest, the rabbis abandoned any influence they might have had on the educated, progressive part of the Jewish population, but did not prevent the Temple from coming into being and prospering. It may be doubted that the members of the Hamburg community were fully conscious of the implications of what they had done or whether they saw themselves as standing for a new principle; but the Temple did not justify either the hopes or the fears that had been attached to its origins. The revolutionary spirit that may have dominated it at the beginning soon dissipated, for the members liked their peace and quiet. They thought more about their businesses than about reorganizing their religion, and they were satisfied with the new institution, having no taste for battle-happy impulsiveness or self-sacrificing enthusiasm.[30] Nor were the Temple's preachers men of outstanding significance. They performed their duties for the congregation, but no more. They limited their activity to preaching and teaching, neither feeling themselves called to be spiritual leaders of the Jews, nor possessing the ability to be such. The impression of their personalities was disappointing; it was summarized in Leopold Zunz's acid comment that "one could learn more Judaism from a stuffed rabbi in a zoological museum than from a live Temple preacher." By the time a few years had passed, no one expected any longer that the Temple could bring about a revitalization of Judaism. It seemed to be no more than an attempt to dress up a structure that no one really believed could survive, one that would not repay the effort and trouble of making fundamental improvements. "The people of Hamburg are badly deluding themselves if they attach universal significance to their idea of reform, but it is a delusion in which they may just as well be indulged. Why do they have to know that they themselves are merely a transitional stage?" This was written already in 1824 by Moritz Moser,[31] the last person in the world to be prejudiced against the progressive movement.

Though the Temple may be considered a not-unimportant episode, the historian cannot call it "a new epoch in the history of the Jewish religion." "We wanted to improve the liturgy, and this is what has happened; I do not feel myself called to be a reformer." These words of the most energetic and cleverest of the Temple's founders[32] show clearly the narrow limits of the undertaking, and are confirmed by the outcome. Within its own circle the Temple contributed to the combat against indifference; it strengthened the faith of those who participated in the new service; it reawakened and sustained religious enthusiasm in some who were nearly completely alienated from the synagogue. But beyond that its accomplishments and successes were few. The most significant act of the Temple Union was the establishement, in 1820, of a branch in Leipzig,[33] where many merchants from Hamburg would stay during the holidays, which usually coincided with the Easter and autumn fairs. Here, visitors from many lands, especially including those from Poland, Russia, and Hungary, came to know and to appreciate many aspects of the new form of liturgy. Back in their homelands they reported on what they had seen, and thus disseminated in numerous places the feeling and understanding for an appealing liturgy. The inclusion of a sermon and choral music, elimination of the unintelligible parts of the prayer book and the liturgical poetry, and above all the introduction of peace and order into the synagogue service came to be seen as an urgent necessity in many congregations.

In great communities like Vienna and Prague, special temples were founded where the service included a sermon. When the temple in Prague was dedicated in 1837, despite the choir and organ, the entire rabbinate was present. In Germany, the governments of several small states issued synagogue regulations aimed at a dignified and proper liturgy, and saw that they were put into effect even against the will of the congregation. In Saxony-Weimar the intervention of the Jewish regulations was severe, in that, alongside other changes in liturgical practices, it stipulated that all prayers must be recited only in the German language.[34] District-Rabbi Hess was so filled with fanatical hatred for traditional Judaism that he encouraged the government in its activity, even though at the same time it was worsening the legal status of the Jews. But the communities opposed the reforms so decisively that they could only be put into effect fifteen years later. In Prussia, too, the prohibition of 1823 (above, p. 302) gradually fell into [303] desuetude, and the congregations were able to introduce the German sermon as a regular institution. Thus the desire for innovation was aroused everywhere, above all for shorter, more beautiful services, and for religious instruction. Here and there battles were fought against the elimination of an abuse or the deletion of a liturgical poem; but in general a tranquil torpor prevailed, and the revelation of a new spirit was nowhere to be found. Despite all efforts for renewal, nothing sweeping was done to prevent the deterioration from continuing.

§ 46 *The Reform Movement at Its Height*

(1)   The founding of the Hamburg Temple was followed by dark years for German Jewry. Their messianic dream was suddenly ruptured, and a great flood of abusive writings and the Hep-Hep movement reminded them that, at least for Jews, the Middle Ages had not yet come to an end. As a consequence of the growing reaction in all the German states,[1] the outlook for attainment of equal rights receded into the distance. Two generations had expended all their efforts to realize an ideal that was now destroyed, and the hope that had given them encouragement and support had vanished. The majority of educated Jews lost their confidence in the future of their religion. Many sought to attach themselves to the prevailing religion; others simply gave up and lived on with no care for their coreligionists. Religious conditions became desperate, and traditional Judaism continued to deteriorate in dearth of both leaders and faithful. Its teachers had no understanding of the language or the aspirations of their contemporaries. Its adherents practiced the traditional precepts with the strictest conscientiousness, but without any inner participation, and therefore without the desire to bequeath these precepts to their descendants. A generation arose that "lived on without God or morality for nothing but sensual pleasures, without religious instruction, without good models, merely mocking everything good, in complete ignorance."[2] People of more penetrating vision could not be unaware that the lack of sincere faith and mindless ritualism must necessarily lead to disaster without the intervention of a timely and complete overhaul of the Jewish spirit and a thorough reform. Samson Raphael Hirsch's *Nineteen Letters* was such a warning, one that made a powerful impression on contemporaries with its warmth of emotion and depth of perception.[3] It represented a new outlook on the development and purposes of the Jewish religion, and distanced itself conceptually from the dominant teaching. But the minute it came to the shaping of life, Hirsch went beyond the *Shulḥan ʿarukh* with the principle of stability, for in his teaching, Judaism begins and ends with the *Shulḥan ʿarukh* and the rite book. Thus his book could not effect any change in religious life. At about the same time, Abraham Geiger developed the concept of a Jewish theology on the basis of historical criticism.[4] He, too, had called for reform, not for individual alterations and small changes in the liturgy, but for a complete reshaping of religious thought and life as a whole. Reform, for him, meant "a complete change of shape, a rejuvenation, forms saturated and permeated with spirit. The heavy and the light, the whole and the particular, should have meaning and significance, should lift the spirit, and warm the heart so that it may influence all manifestations of life." Gradually times improved, and people became more open to the demands made by ideals. With the progressive successes of the bourgeoisie after 1830 the prospects for the Jews also improved. In Gabriel Riesser there arose for the Jews an enthusiastic exponent of high moral pathos.[5] Thanks to him, the self-assurance of the Jews reasserted itself and their confidence in their own convictions grew. Riesser rejected decisively every reform in the religious domain that was intended to ease civil emancipation. His example made itself felt; when the governments of Baden and Bavaria made certain changes in religious life and liturgical usage preconditions for the granting of civil rights, their demand was emphatically rejected.

[304]

(2)   Although the mood had changed and the harbingers of a new age could be

seen everywhere, the movement did not at first take definite shape anywhere until the peace was again broken by the Hamburg Temple. But this time a storm was unleashed that raged far and wide, swept over all the Jewish people, and gave the occasion for a fundamental reform of the liturgy.[6] As a result of the growth in its membership, the Temple congregation saw the need to expand its quarters and decided "in accordance with the progress of the times" to take advantage of this occasion to revise its prayer book. For the fall holidays of 1841, the new edition appeared under the double title סדר עבודה, *Gebetbuch für die öffentliche und häusliche Andacht, nach dem Gebrauch des neuen Israelitischen Tempels in Hamburg* (*Book of Service: Prayer Book for Public and Domestic Worship, in Accordance with the Usage of the New Israelite Temple in Hamburg*). The revision consisted mainly of replacing the rather banal German prayers with more moving and convincing ones. The liturgical poems, which had proved to be too numerous, and therefore unsuitable for use, were left out. By contrast, the statutory prayers were expanded and presented more fully, and much that had earlier fallen out of use was restored. Thus, above all the weekday prayers reappeared; the Morning Benedictions were abbreviated and in German; the Verses of Song were slightly abbreviated and in Hebrew; the *Shema*ᶜ was as before; of the ᶜAmida, the first three and the last three benedictions together with the Kedushah were given in Hebrew, and the others in German; to conclude came the Kaddish and a German hymn. The insertions and Torah readings were retained in the old way. There were no great innovations in details, but rather "every deviation is to be avoided wherever possible; the Hebrew wording was treated with special protection; the wording sanctified by time was in every case preferred over even a better new one." In the ᶜAmida, for example, the translation of Benedictions 14 and 15, on national hopes, was spiritualized, and the reading of the ancient sources was inserted into the eulogy of Benediction 17. In general the changes with respect to the first edition were few and conservative in spirit. It did not occur to anyone that the appearance of the prayer book could cause any upset, and it was used throughout the festival period without protest. Hardly were the holidays over, however, when there appeared a long proclamation of the "Hakham" Bernays,[7] recalling the rabbinical decision of 1819 and declaring that services using the new prayer book were prohibited. The prayer book was spoken of in the crudest terms; it was accused of "arbitrary mutilations, omissions, deviations, frivolous treatment of the divine promises for our future, fragmentation and ruining of nearly all the prayers." A proclamation of this type was not expected of Bernays. He was not an old-fashioned rabbi, but was knowledgeable about the sciences, philosophy, and Kabbalah: He had made statements about the historical development of Judaism that would have sounded to a rabbi of the old type, had he been capable of understanding them, like heresy. One would have expected of him more understanding and impartiality. Actually, he is said to have been induced to make his proclamation by pressure from his own followers, who were irritated by the growth of the Temple. But in his attacks he exceeded the limits of the permissible and, what is worse, of the truth; not surprisingly, his action met with criticism from the widest circles. Not only did the Temple congregation defend itself in a furious declaration of its own, but the theologians, who had much to find fault with in the Temple prayer book, declared their outrage over Bernays's calumniation of a congregation in whose inner religious life he had till then shown no interest at all. As a result of the opponents' indiscretion, the appearance of the new prayer book was the occasion for a renewed

[305]

battle, which, however, did not merely remain at its starting point, but led to a basic split, with weighty consequences.

(3)   The situation was no longer what it had been in 1819, when the negative opinion of the rabbis was accepted without demur; in the meanwhile a new generation with different opinions and aspirations had arisen. Progress was no longer represented by men "who were not sufficiently knowledgeable about the religion and who indulged themselves with superficial talk of enlightenment."[8] Since then the Science of Judaism had come into being, and the way had been found to the historical understanding of Judaism. Zunz's *Die Gottesdienstliche Vorträge der Juden historisch entwickelt (Haderashot)* had proved irrefutably, using classic methods, that religious institutions had evolved. It had shown that the Jewish liturgy did not originally have the same fixed form nor was it of the same extent, but that the liturgy had been subject to continual alteration, and that only through constant additions had it become what was now seen as eternally unchanging and immutable. Zunz had also taken a position in the controversies of the day, summarizing the outcome of his research by saying, "There can be no contesting the right of any organized Jewish authority or community to introduce new prayers or to remove such additions to the prayer book as have become, through their length, incomprehensibility, or offensive content, more a hindrance than a furtherance to improvement." To him it seemed that the most important part of the improvement was the need for "restoration, to replace abuses by proper usages, to replace the fossilized with living forms."[9] On the foundation of Zunz's research, Geiger had built Jewish theology; for him, the reformation of the liturgy was not a goal in itself, but a branch of a great reform program that was a matter of life or death for Judaism. One could no longer be satisfied with formal alterations. The entire view of religion was placed on a new basis, and the question that arose was, To what extent did the religious opinions represented by the prayers conform to the refined conceptions? A Jewish press had arisen in which the points of contention were subjected to vigorous discussion, and a public opinion had emerged, taking lively positions for and against the proposed reform.[10] Above all, and most important for the Hamburg prayer book controversy, there was by now a great number of rabbis with modern academic education,[11] who were convinced of the need for liturgical reform and who had put it into effect in their congregations to a greater or lesser extent. This time, therefore, it was the Temple congregation that sought theological opinions on the book under attack, to ascertain "whether it is really contrary to the teachings of the Jewish religion, and therefore not permitted for use in the liturgy." The opinions were far from paying the prayer book unqualified praise; some took offense at the deviations from the traditional text or at the arbitrary conflation of different texts, while others, missing a consistent application of the reform principle, thought the changes did not go far enough. But all agreed in condemning Bernays's behavior. They not only accused him of not respecting freedom of conscience, but they also denied him, as a rabbi who had done nothing for the correction of the liturgical abuses, the right to take the role of judge in this matter.

[306]

(4)   This settled the matter as far as Hamburg was concerned, but the polemics and the public attention that they attracted made it a matter for the Jewish community as a whole, one that had to be brought to a comprehensive solution. From many quar-

ters there had long been calls for the convening of a rabbinical conference, and the Temple controversy contributed to speeding its convocation. On June 12, 1844, the first was held in Brunswick.[12] The rabbinical conferences were intended as nonpartisan conventions in which representatives of all approaches would convene to take common counsel as to ways and means for correcting the flaws in contemporary Judaism, to put an end to arbitrariness and fragmentation, and to seek expedients acceptable to the community at large for the resolution of problems that were accumulating daily. But that portion of the rabbinate that saw adherence to tradition as the only cure kept assiduously away from the assemblies and renounced any influence on the future shaping of the conditions of the great mass of German Jewry; they were at fault for the representatives of radical reform gaining the upper hand.[13] In accordance with their importance, liturgical problems took first place in the consultations on the reshaping of Judaism. Of the resolutions of the first rabbinical conference,[14] only one was relevant to the liturgy, the recommendation that "all vows" be eliminated.[15] But perversely, this occurred in connection with the question of the Jewish oath, so that once again a religious tradition was sacrificed to a political goal. At first the liturgy itself received nothing more than an extended discussion, and a commission was charged with studying the following six points:

1.   "Whether and to what extent the Hebrew language is necessary in the liturgy, and if not actually necessary, does its retention seem temporarily advisable?

2.   To what extent must the doctrine of the messiah and everything connected to it be included in the prayers?

3.   Is the repetition of the ʿAmida necessary, and must the Additional Services be retained?

4.   How should the reading of the Torah and the calling up to the Torah be performed?

5.   In what way should the sounding of the shofar and the carrying of the Four Species be performed?

6.   Is the organ advisable and permissible in the Jewish liturgy?"[16]

The assignment that fell to the commission was no light one, for the differences of opinion already expressed at the conference permitted the inference that in these questions lay the seed of difficult complications.

(5)   The consultations over the liturgy occupied the greater part of the sessions of the second rabbinical conference, which took place in Frankfurt am Main from July 15 to 28, 1845.[17] The commission, which consisted of five members, presented a comprehensive report, which "dealt at length with the principles that might come into consideration in connection with a reform of the ritual, at the same time giving a very exact and detailed survey of the liturgy that could be proposed for the entire year." The difficulties began right here, for one member of the commission declared himself against every proposed change of the public liturgy, while the others were not in agreement on all points and explicitly resisted taking responsibility for the full contents of the report. From within the conference the complaint was raised that the commission had exceeded the limits of its assignment, that instead of contenting itself with consultations on the six questions, it had set forth a comprehensive reform program. The commission was therefore assigned the task of so altering the report that it would contain

[307]

only the decisions on those questions. If such dissension could arise in dealing with the purely formal and external side, it was predictable that violent clashes of opinion would characterize the theoretical discussion. The report of the commission started with the assumption that a reform of the liturgy in the sense it had been till then understood was not sufficient, but rather that "a new organic reformation of the same was needed." The "failings of the synagogue service" were presented as "the most important reasons for the lack of participation in religious life"; by removing them the synagogue would be restored to its dignity and hearts would be returned to it.[18]

The debates were violent and disagreeable, and opinion was no more clarified than the year before in Brunswick; the short period in between was in fact insufficient to work through a question so far-reaching and of such import. The reformation of the liturgy had to be determined by the overall conception of religious questions as a whole, but Jewish theology was as yet too new a science to be able to deliver settled answers for so numerous important questions. In all the following votes the consequences of this lack of a guiding principle were unpleasantly plain to see; the majority held it to be more important to take resolutions than to linger over settling questions of principle.[19] The first question had to be subdivided, for otherwise no decision could have been reached. The commission had denied the objective necessity of praying in Hebrew, but it had considered this solely from the standpoint of the Talmud and the codes, where it found no contradiction. But the real question was whether an objective necessity existed for retaining the Hebrew language not on purely legal, but on religious and historical grounds. Here opinions were divided: only thirteen were in favor, three were undecided, and the majority of fifteen took the position that, while the goal must still be to have the prayers completely in the mother tongue, for the time being it was advisable to retain Hebrew prayers as well.[20] The vote resulted in the second split in the conference; Zacharias Frankel saw himself forced to withdraw and to go his own way in resolving the question of reform.[21]

As soon as the details were discussed, the result was total disunity. It was not the conference's intention to create a new liturgy, but rather to retain of the tradition whatever could be retained; but there was no agreement as to how much this was. The commission set forth the complete sketch of a prayer book,[22] but hardly any member of the conference was prepared to accept it unaltered. The commission had reduced the Hebrew prayers to a very small scale, proposing that only the first part of the *Shema*ᶜ and the first and last benedictions of the *ʿAmida* be recited in Hebrew; that was accepted as good counsel, but almost unanimously declared to be too little. In the messianic question lurked difficult, as yet unresolved theological problems; there was unity only about the one point "that the prayers for our return to the land of our fathers and for the restoration of the Jewish state be removed from our worship." Beyond that, attitudes on the origin and contents of the messianic idea were so diverse that one had to be content with the general resolution that "the messianic idea deserves an important place in the prayers." This signified progress from the doctrine of the early reformers, in that explicit exception was taken to the idea that the ancient form of messianic belief was in conflict with patriotism.[23] It was characteristic of the spirit that filled the conference that several speakers declared the messianic age of universal love of mankind to have already arrived, a blessed time in which one could be confident of the imminent victory of justice, truth, and humanity. The proposal to eliminate the repetition of the ʿAmida was adopted without dissent;[24] the will of the majority was that on weekdays only the beginning and end, and on the Sabbaths and festivals the whole prayer, should be recited aloud immediately by the precentor. The majority of the commission had declared the Additional Service not permitted;[25]the conference was decidedly opposed to retaining the prayer for the restoration of sacrifices, but it was equally opposed to eliminating the entire service. A majority desired the insertion of a remembrance of the sacrifices of ancient times, even the retention of the biblical verses of the sacrifices, "if the text remains in Hebrew," an addendum hard to reconcile with the general attitude toward the Hebrew language. The Torah reading should be retained in Hebrew, but shortened and done so as not to cause disruption. The commission had proposed the introduction of the triennial cycle; this was accepted with a great majority. The festival of the Joy of the Torah was therefore to be celebrated only once in three years.[26] The reading should be done without trope, and then translated into the vernacular; there was considerable disagreement as to how this "modern Targum" should be done. Besides the Torah, not only the Prophets, but also the Hagiographa[27] should be read, but only in German and, according to the majority view, in the Morning Service. The Book of Esther should be read only once. In opposition to the commission, the great majority wanted to retain the calling of congregants up to the Torah,[28] but they wanted to eliminate the reading of a passage from the Torah for the reader of the Haftara. The question of the shofar and the Four Species was tabled. Finally, it was unanimously resolved that the organ is not only permitted in the synagogue but that it may and should be played, even by a Jew.[29] A commission was appointed to develop a prayer book based on the resolutions that had been taken. The choice again betrayed the great disunity within the conference, which was repeated in a shocking way in the consultations of the commission. It never completed its assignment, for the rabbinical conference met only once more. In Breslau (July 13–24, 1846),[30] the question of the Sabbath was in the forefront. Liturgy was dealt with only insofar as the proposal was raised to introduce Sunday services,[31] but this had no majority. It was also resolved that the second days of festivals could be eliminated,[32] and that the blowing of the shofar on the New Year and the use of the Four Species on Tabernacles should not be omitted even when the festival coincides with the Sabbath.[33]

{309}

The resolutions of the rabbinical conference had a fate similar to that of the Temple prayer book: eager to please all, they pleased no one. For the positivists they left too little of the old liturgy; for the radicals they left too much. Those who were conversant with the traditional liturgy rejected the proposals because they went too far for them—the others, because the proposals did not go far enough.[34] The theories represented by the speakers in the rabbinical conference awakened in the representatives of radical reform the hope for a complete break with rabbinic Judaism, a hope that was not fulfilled; the expected agreement between the assembled rabbis and the supporters of reform did not occur. The first act of defiance against the rabbinical conference was the establishment of services for the fall festivals of 1845 by the *Genossenschaft für Reform in Judenthume*, "Association for Reform in Judaism," in Berlin.

(6)   The history of the formation of this association, which later adopted the name *Jüdische Reformgemeinde*, "Jewish Reform Congregation," is well known.[35] Above all it was dissatisfaction with the condition of the community in Berlin and the desire

for religious renewal that led to its foundation. [The following passage is from a proclamation of the Association.—*Engl. trans.*]

> Many aspects of the religious conditions of the Berlin community could be called rotten. The stiff-necked, strictly conservative party opposed with stubbornness even the most innocent innovations that some sought to introduce as a modest gesture toward aesthetic needs and healthy human understanding. At the same time, those who remained true to the spirit and essence of Judaism, who longed for an inner regeneration of its eternal ideals and the union of these with the highest religious consciousness of the present: such persons found no deep satisfaction in a movement toward completely formal restoration of the ceremonial institutions, even if dressed up in modern garb.[36]

The community was in a sorry state; observers from every religious camp all lamented the worsening deterioration and the increasing alienation of wide circles of people. Sachs, because of his rigid conservatism, could not have the powerful effect on those who were far from religious life to which his talent as a preacher and his classic personality suited him. The unsatisfied longing for an attractive form of religious activity sought fulfillment in the radical solution with which the Association for Reform in Judaism came into being. It was a deep and earnest religious striving that filled the Association's founders:

> We want faith; we want positive religion; we want Judaism. We hold firmly to the spirit of the Holy Scriptures, which we see as a testimony to divine revelation by which the spirit of our ancestors was enlightened. We hold fast to all that belongs to a true reverence for God rooted in the spirit of our religion. We hold fast to the conviction that Judaism's teaching about God is the eternally true one, and to the promise that this teaching will some day become the property of all mankind.

This comprehensive creed lost much of its value through the principles by which it was interpreted. The first of these was the unlimited right of self-determination; the "compromise between life and doctrine" so eagerly sought was effected unequally, for only life with all its errors and absurdities had authority, while religious forms had to give way to the habits of a Jewish community that was alienated from its history. It only compounded the error that the community took its starting point from political conditions in Germany, and wanted to limit itself to German coreligionists. The conflict between religious and patriotic attitudes had no inner justification; a true reform ought to have been applicable to all Jews. Finally, it was a denial of reality for the community to make an exclusive claim on the fulfillment of the messianic calling of Judaism; this was the aspiration of the entire Jewish people, though on the basis of historical Judaism, not on that of humanity at large, as proclaimed by the Association's spokesmen.

[310]

Soon after the Association's founding, the resolution was taken "to hold for the time being provisional services for the coming High Holidays, to satisfy the religious needs expressed therein."[37] The service was fundamentally different from the traditional one. Men and women sat in the same hall, the former on the right, the latter on the left. The men appeared without head covering and were not permitted to wear the *talit*. The service was held completely in German, with only a few biblical passages like the *Shemaʿ*, the Kedushah, and the Priestly Blessing being done in Hebrew and German; the service was accompanied by choral singing and instrumental music. The prerogatives of the priests were eliminated, the Priestly Blessing being recited by the preacher and repeated by the choir. It was further decided to omit the shofar blowing on the New Year, and to interrupt the service on the Day of Atonement for an intermission of several hours.

For this liturgy, a new one of its kind, the prayers had to be specially rewritten. The most important ancient prayers[38] were accepted and new ones were inserted "that particularly brought before the soul of the worshiper the historical memories and the deep festival ideas in the elevated tone of the ancient prayers." The predominant ideas of the prayers were those that stood in the first place in the congregation's program—that is, the thought of Israel's self-sacrificing devotion, its priestly calling, and its mission among the nations. Precisely on the New Year, when the messianic idea stands in the middle of the traditional liturgy, it was easy to put this idea into effect. Since it had been determined that the service was not to be too long, and since besides, every service had a reading from Scripture in Hebrew and German and a sermon, the actual prayers had to be few. The service for the eve of the New Year was of about the same duration as in the old prayer book. In the morning only one service was held, corresponding to the Morning Service; prayers borrowed from the traditional "Creator" and ʿAmida were grouped around the Hebrew passages that were retained, the *Shemaʿ* and the Kedushah. Since the Additional Service was eliminated, part of its content was also taken over. In addition, there were long expositions and meditations in the spirit of the basic ideas of the congregation. The service was read by the precentor "in a strictly oratorical form, without any melody," interrupted here and there by a silent prayer of the congregation or choral singing. The impression made by the service was a deep one; six hundred participants attended and were all filled with enthusiasm for the edification that so long had been lacking. The effect was extremely favorable for the congregation, which then numbered 327 in Berlin and 426 elsewhere, a size that it never again reached.

The most significant consequence, however, was that the members desired to have the service repeated, and they proposed that it be made into a permanent institution. On April 2, 1846, the congregation moved into its own synagogue building, and after a long struggle it was decided to hold services twice a week, on Saturday and on Sunday. The leadership of the congregation declared themselves in favor of Saturday services and voted decisively against shifting the Sabbath to Sunday; in the end they came to an agreement that services of identical status should be held on both days, and that neither day should be treated as a solemn one. By 1849 the Saturday service was cancelled for lack of attendance. The idea that Sunday was the community's real day of rest won more and more ground, and the Sunday service acquired a more explicitly festive character. Of the festivals, except for the New Year, only the first day was observed,[39] as well as the seventh day of Passover and the eighth day of Tabernacles. No attention was paid to other memorial days of the Jewish calendar. On the other hand, confirmation was introduced as a solemn liturgical act. As the liturgy progressed, the prayer book was reissued when needed, usually rather hastily reworked. When Rabbi Samuel Holdheim became the congregation's preacher in 1847 and reworked its teaching from a theological point of view, he immediately recognized the necessity of subjecting the prayer book to revision, but not until 1856 was this thorough revision

[311]

undertaken.[40] Even Holdheim had found fault with the fact that the congregation at first proceeded in a revolutionary, negative manner. He complained of their failure to consider historical facts, resulting in a liturgy but "half-Jewish" in character; he recognized finally that "in the newly-introduced prayers there were fewer great creations of the spirit than modern phrases." He demanded a revision of the prayer book in the interest of historical Judaism, in order to allow the points of contact with history and the Jewish community at large to come more to the fore. In the prayers, biblical spirit and biblical form should predominate, and the driving ideals of the reform should also find clear expression. In Holdheim's revision, each service consisted of three parts. He began with a chorale, then followed with the actual prayers, and finally, after the reading of the Torah and the sermon, with a closing hymn. The prayers were offered in several versions, nine cycles alternating with each other, "through which an indirect admission seemed to be made that prayers in the vernacular become tiresome in their effect over time." The structure of the prayers that was established at the congregation's beginnings remained; even the external form and the arrangement of the service remained unchanged. The prayer book was later subjected to many small changes that did not affect the essence of the liturgy.

The prayer book received a thoroughgoing revision in 1885, but especially in the revised edition by M. Levin on the occasion of the fiftieth anniversary of the congregation. The chorales were completely dropped and replaced by biblical psalms. The prayers, too, were made uniform, with the same text established for every Sunday. The order of prayers basically followed that of the old prayer book; the guiding ideas of the congregation continued to assert themselves, but the structure of the prayers followed the traditional form, and the old version of the benedictions in all its simplicity was again adopted. The *Shemaᶜ*, reduced to its first two sentences, was again enclosed by benedictions, as in the earliest period; the ᶜ*Amida* appeared again in its seven-benediction form; and the Kedushah verses were in Hebrew. For the taking out and

[312] returning of the Torah, biblical verses replaced the earlier chorales, and the service ended with a shortened version of "It is our duty" and the Priestly Benediction in Hebrew. There was also a fundamental deviation from the earlier outlook in that the service for Sunday was not seen as that of a solemn day. The service for festivals was developed according to the same principles, each festival service having its characteristic stamp. A comparison, for example, of the liturgy for the Day of Atonement with the earlier version makes clear that the new one is much closer to the Jewish tradition.[41]

The tremendous influence on the reshaping of German Jewry for which the founders of the Reform congregation had hoped and that the opponents feared did not happen. The congregation's expansion remained modest. Except in Berlin, no similar liturgy was introduced anywhere in Germany, and the membership outside of Berlin gradually fell off. Even in Berlin the congregation lost its attractiveness; from 1854 on, its membership always stayed at about the same level, and the initial enthusiasm gradually gave way to growing apathy. The great mass of German Jewry did not provide a following for the Reform congregation. Its radical changes in the existing liturgical institutions signified a violent break with tradition and the abandonment of all links with history; the few thoughts that the congregation's founders had taken over from ancient Judaism could not suffice to fill in the tremendous gulf that separated them from their ancestors. The congregation's founders let themselves be too much guided by rational considerations and neglected the demands of feeling. Thus, they could not achieve long-term success with their innovations.

(7)   The radicalism with which the Reform congregation developed its liturgical institutions was easy to put into effect, when the congregation was founded for this purpose. But conditions were much harder in the existing congregations in which the new liturgy was to be introduced in accordance with the resolutions of the rabbinical conference. Congregations differed from one another, and the majority were not inclined to reform. Nowhere could one speak of enthusiasm for the all-too-stormy proceedings in which the Frankfurt decisions were taken. On the contrary, the old reverence for customary practice persisted in full force, necessitating mighty battles within the congregations over every deviation from tradition. Violent disputes were unleashed even by matters of no importance at all, like calling people up to the Torah by name or the elimination of the first "May salvation arise," the prayer for the ancient Babylonian authorities who had not existed for centuries.[42] Even in Poland, generally decried in Germany as a land of darkness, it was much easier for people to agree on eliminating certain abuses or the omission of liturgical poems.[43] The difference was that there the people affected were mostly learned in the Talmud and more or less familiar with the history of the prayer book's development; they had not fallen into the ossification and pedantry that often prevailed in the German communities. The worst problem that has arisen repeatedly then and since, especially in the big congregations, was that men who themselves had broken completely with the observance of traditional Jewish law took definite positions against changing even the most insubstantial customs in the synagogue as if the very existence of Judaism was thereby endangered. Nowhere was it even possible to speak of putting the resolutions of the rabbinical conference into effect; even where the government supported the reformers and favored the introduction of synagogue constitutions,[44] no one dared to propose such far-reaching reforms. In most German congregations, it got no farther than the shortening of the service by the elimination of a few particularly incomprehensible prayers, and the partial or complete elimination of liturgical poems, which, however, were retained on the Days of Awe. Further, efforts were made to create formal order in the synagogue, dignity, decorum, and quiet; in most congregations, choral music was introduced. The German sermon was joined by a few German prayers for the government and for special occasions like the taking out and putting back of the Torah. To this degree, reforms were accepted even in orthodox-led congregations.

[313]

(8)   The boundary defining the parties was the organ or other instrumental music;[45] in the early period of the Reform the most violent battles were fought over its acceptance. In nearly all the great communities the liturgy little by little came to be accompanied by music, and the consequence was nearly always that a part of the community held its own service in the traditional manner. The use of the organ did not absolutely mean a change in the prayers; usually at first only a few German hymns were added. The reform of the prayer book occurred only gradually. In 1854 Abraham Geiger published the first reformed prayer book that was intended for the actual use of a congregation.[46] This prayer book did not at all conform to the principles of the rabbinic conference, for the entire liturgy remained in Hebrew, and the prayer book as

a whole was the traditional one, though with the prayers somewhat shortened and the liturgical poems omitted. Changes were made only in places that did not fit with Geiger's general outlook. Thus, hostile expressions against adherents of other religions were struck, and the prayers for the restoration of sacrifices and the Jewish state were eliminated, replaced by prayers of purely spiritual content; references to the election of Israel were softened. What was really new in the prayer book was the German text, for it gave not a literal rendition of the Hebrew but a completely free reworking in a classic, modern form; but the German text was intended for individual worship rather than for congregational services. The Torah reading was according to the triennial cycle; the Haftara was only in German, and for it a new selection of texts was provided. On the entrance of the Sabbath and festivals, before and after the sermon as well as at the points mentioned above, prayers and hymns in German were added. Geiger himself had at first much further-reaching wishes for the prayer book reform, but in the course of the work he saw himself called to compromise with the views and needs of his congregation. In later years he undertook a new revision of the prayer book for his new circle of operations in Frankfurt and Berlin: It appeared in two editions, one for western and the other for eastern Germany.[47] In this edition, the German element was given more attention, many parts were more throroughly abbreviated, and a few pieces were more reworked in accordance with advanced theological views. On the whole, however, this prayer book, too, which was introduced into many congregations, retained a traditional character.

[314] Geiger's Breslau prayer book was later adapted more to tradition by M. Joel,[48] and many of Geiger's changes, such as those involving the election of Israel and the sacrificial passages, were reduced in extent. But what above all determined the character of this revision was the contrivance of printing the traditional text in small type alongside the altered text, so that while the precentor recited aloud the reformed version, every individual was free to recite the traditional one. In Joel's form, the prayer book was spread to numerous large and small congregations; for the most part it represented the position of positive historical reform that, through Frankel's school, became the prevailing one in Germany. Geiger's and Joel's prayer books remained the model according to which German Reform prayer books were prepared, but in details of wording and in the inserted German prayers there was great variety.

(9)   Enthusiasm for reform diminished quickly; the living movement receded, and the people declared themselves satisfied with what had already been achieved. Even when new proposals for liturgical reform were made at the rabbinical conference in Kassel in 1868 and the Leipzig synod of 1869, they did not make a deep impression. The resolutions of the synod were extremely moderate,[49] and betrayed a much more positive spirit than those of the rabbinical conference of 1845. The synod came out in favor of retaining the Torah reading in Hebrew; while it favored the shortening of the weekly readings, it wanted to retain the annual cycle, leaving it to the congregation to decide how to reconcile both requirements. The Haftara was to be read in the vernacular, and was to be chosen not only from the Prophets, but also from the Hagiographa. In the revision of the prayers, it accepted the principles already followed by Geiger. It came out against the repetition of the ʿAmida. The festival prayers were by and large to remain the traditional ones; liturgical poems were to be omitted on Sabbaths and festi-

vals, but on the New Year and the Day of Atonement a few particularly rich in content should be retained, alternating with expressive German prayers. The prayer book published in 1894 by H. Vogelstein,[50] under commission from the Westphalian communities, went far beyond the reforms generally recognized. The German element came strongly to the fore, and the Hebrew part was proportionally reduced; the prayer texts were altered even more than before in connection with some points, like the election of Israel and messianism. An important innovation in this prayer book was the simultaneous publication of a school edition, with which the youth should be prepared from the beginning for the community's services. Here, for the first time in the Reform movement, a uniform prayer book was produced for a large circle of congregations. A similar attempt to introduce a uniform prayer book in the spirit of modern requirements for a whole country, though a small one, was undertaken in 1905 by the Grand Ducal High Counsel of Jews in Baden.[51] But the adoption of this work, which was prepared with great care and with the avoidance of many mistakes of previous prayer books, collapsed against the vigorous resistance of the orthodox party, which set its old *non possumus* against every alteration, and which fought the deviations from the customary text partly with the same arguments that had been brought in 1819 against the first prayer book of the Hamburg Temple.[52]

§ 47 *The Reform Movement Outside of Germany*

(1)   In nearly all advanced countries the living conditions of the Jews in the nineteenth century took similar shape to those in Germany, and thus the same movements—and the same battles—arose everywhere. As the spiritual and social ghettos were overcome, as education improved and the range of vision broadened, dissatisfaction with the traditional liturgy made itself felt among the Jews. The inappropriate external form was felt to be disturbing, and the unintelligible content gave grounds for complaint. The generations that had grown up under more favorable external conditions felt alienated from the liturgy. The question was whether they would sink into total apathy or whether they could be won back by a correction of the flaws and the development of a suitable form of liturgy. Liturgical reform became a life-and-death question for the survival of the religious community. In all civilized countries the external form of the liturgy underwent more or less fundamental improvements. Choral singing was introduced everywhere, accompanied by organ in France and Italy, while the liturgy itself remained unchanged. In Hungary and many other countries the demand was made that the Jews become completely naturalized in exchange for equal rights. This meant holding the sermon in the vernacular instead of in the common German-Jewish jargon, which was introduced over the strong opposition of the Orthodox. Under the influence of the 1848 revolution, a congregation was formed in Budapest on the model of the Reform congregation in Berlin; it was of only short duration, as the country was not ripe for such a sudden leap. Bitter, sometimes bloody battles were fought over the most insignificant minutiae of synagogue construction and liturgical

[315]

custom. It was thus an achievement merely that in many congregations the liturgy was shortened, the poetry was eliminated, and a regular sermon in Hungarian was introduced.[1]

(2)   The Reform movement in England and America developed under the direct influence of the Hamburg Temple. In London the demand for reforms began with the Portuguese. Stringent regulations prevailed in this community, binding its members completely not only in their religious life but in their private lives as well. The liturgy left much to be desired in the areas of aesthetics, dignity, and reverence. Hence it was proposed as early as 1828 to elevate the service by shortening it as much as possible and by holding every Saturday afternoon a sermon on a biblical text in English—for until then anything not in Hebrew was in Portuguese. The sermons were held for a time, but then discontinued. At the end of 1836 a revision of the liturgy along the lines of that used in the Hamburg Temple was demanded, but the congregation refused to do this out of fear of creating a sectarian split.[2] Among the Ashkenazic community, too, the first signs of dissatisfaction come into view, with special offense being taken at the bad conduct of the Torah reading. In addition, the well-off Jewish population had given up their former homes in the center of town and aspired to a service nearer their new homes; but the Portuguese congregation would not consent to the proposal that it should found a synagogue with a revised liturgy in the West End of London The consequence was that in 1840 a new congregation was formed as a synagogue for English Jews, eliminating the distinction between Sepharadim and Ashkenazim. Its charter required a Hebrew liturgy conforming with the principles of the Jewish religion, but so revised and performed as to awaken feelings of reverence, and with regular sermons in English besides. One reform that was introduced immediately was the elimination of

[316]

the second day of the festivals. A special prayer book was issued; the changes it contained consisted mainly of the abridgement and deletion of the prayers that aroused the most opposition. In the Additional Service the 'Amida was substantially shortened. The most striking deviations were the formulation of Kaddish in Hebrew and the elimination of the prayer for the restoration of sacrifices. The petitions for the return to Zion and for the coming of the Messiah were retained. In 1859 organ accompaniment was introduced.

The founding of the new congregation unleashed the most extreme passions among the recognized religious authorities. Its members were immediately expelled from the Portuguese congregation and denied burial in its cemetery; marriages performed in the new synagogue did not obtain the recognition required by English law, and marriages with members of the community were denied religious solemnities. All the community's declarations and protestations that it wanted only to serve the religion, and to work for the dissemination and increasing of piety, were of no avail. The congregation only worsened the situation when it tried to defend its reforms by denying the authority of the Talmud; the rabbinate warned all the congregations of England against the innovators, though it received rather rude replies from the country's most important communities. Despite all challenges, the community remained in existence, and was recognized by an act of Parliament in 1856. It had retained its principles and its liturgy unchanged, but had not undertaken any further reforms. Its founding had a beneficial effect even on other congregations in the country. In official synagogue ordinances, decorum in the service was now urged, a regular English sermon was recommended, and choral singing was instituted. On the whole, however, English Jewry stayed with the traditional liturgy. Besides the one in London, Reform congregations were formed only in Manchester and Bradford, and these, too, long ago lost their oppositional character. An extensive reform was only recently introduced in London. But in order to understand it, we must first examine the situation in America.

(3)   In the United States, the number of Jews a century ago was extremely small, and the organization of the community, other than the Portuguese, was very weak. The man to whom the American communities owe their cohesiveness and their English character is Isaac Leeser in Philadelphia.[3] Through him the English sermon was introduced in 1830 as a significant part of the liturgy. He translated the prayer book and the Bible into English, thereby performing a valuable service to the understanding of the liturgy. He took his stand on tradition, believing that the Reform movement would be of only short duration. When Leeser began his career, a very serious drive had already been undertaken by radical reformers. In Charleston, South Carolina, then the most populous Jewish community in the United States, an attempt had been made as early as 1824 to revise the liturgy.[4] This time, too, the impetus came from Germany, and reform was demanded in the name of the Enlightenment. In order to enhance devotion and the understanding of the prayers, the precentor was to repeat the most important parts of the liturgy in English, and where possible the prayers were to be shortened so that they could all be recited both in Hebrew and in English. Finally, the scriptural readings should be made more fruitful by having an edifying sermon attached to them every week. When the demands were rejected, a small group of twelve men united to form The Reformed Society of Israelites. Out of the modest Reform program, which demanded no more than that the mother tongue be taken into account in the liturgy, emerged a full-fledged opponent of rabbinic Judaism. The community immediately established its statement of creed, which was based on the thirteen articles of Maimonides, but replaced some of the most important of these with their own principles. They recognized only the Ten Commandments as revealed, denied corporeal resurrection and retained only the belief in the immortality of the soul; they eliminated the belief in a Messiah and instead demanded love of God as the only redeemer, and acts of charity. They established a liturgy in conformity with these principles; at that time such a radical reformation had never yet taken place. At the beginning of the Sabbath, they read Pss. 92 and 93 in English, the *Shemaʿ* in Hebrew and English, the *ʿAmida* in English—much abridged—with only the conclusion "My God, protect" in Hebrew and English, and, finally, "It is our duty" in English. Next, a chapter was read from the Prophets, a hymn was sung, the precentor recited a prayer of his own composition, and the Priestly Blessing was recited. On the Sabbath morning, the service began again with an English hymn and prayer; then followed Ps. 33, "My God, the soul" and "You sanctified" in English, the *Shemaʿ* and the *ʿAmida* as in the evening, selected verses from the Psalms in Hebrew and English, a prayer for the country, reading of the Torah, a sermon, an English hymn, a prayer, and the Priestly Blessing. On festivals, special prayers with references to the festive occasion were inserted. The liturgy was accompanied by music, and the congregation appeared bareheaded.

Lacking a spiritual leader, the community did not long survive. But it is of great

[317]

historical interest, because it displayed so early all the elements of the American Reform movement, and the clear influence of the formal organization of the Protestant liturgy. About ten years after the demise of the first Reform congregation, reforms after the manner of the Hamburg Temple were introduced into the old congregation of Charleston. The same battles were fought as in Europe, sometimes in even more violent form.

(4)   The great Jewish emigration from Germany [to the United States] that set in around 1840 resulted in the formation of numerous new communities in which a reformed liturgy, usually based on the Hamburg prayer book, was instituted from the very first. The United States had no obligatory community affiliation; from the point of view of civil law there was not, and is not to this day, any impediment to the foundation of any number of religious unions. Young communities with no past, bound to no tradition, having voluntary membership, and therefore consisting of like-minded people, could easily develop religious institutions after their own hearts. Thus the American congregations introduced liturgical reforms with ease, often changing the liturgy to such an extent that its Jewish character is hardly to be recognized. Until 1840 the liturgy remained in its traditional form everywhere, but within the existing communities reform societies formed, which, when they felt strong enough, founded new communities with more or less deviant forms of liturgy. The members and their spiritual leaders had mostly come from Germany, and so German sermons and German prayers were

[318]   introduced. The changes in the Hebrew prayers stayed within narrow limits, usually affecting only the petitions for the restoration of the sacrifices and the return to Zion; but opposition soon arose to the doctrine of resurrection. It was an innovation unknown till then in Jewish circles when Isaac M. Wise introduced in Albany, New York the Protestant custom of family pews, and thereby the practice of both sexes sitting together.

With Wise's intervention began the radical American Reform movement, which then received its theological and philosophical grounding through David Einhorn and Samuel Hirsch, both participants in the rabbinical conferences in Germany. The basic ideas of this reform can be understood only out of the extreme self-confidence that the unprecedented success of the United States bestowed on all its inhabitants. The immigrants who had fled oppression and poverty in Germany were especially dazzled by the laws guaranteeing freedom and by the increasing prosperity of the New World. Thus, Wise could declare that American Judaism introduced a new epoch in Jewish history, that religious forms had to conform with the requirements of American life and thought. Bringing religion into conformity with the present and with the surroundings became the guiding principles of the Reform, and the demands of the times were declared to be the highest law even of religion. True to these views, the liturgy was given whatever form was the most modern and the most suitable at any given time; but clearly the principles that were being introduced were of very doubtful value for religion. A movement that strives to bring the eternal core of religion to its purest expression here throws itself into total dependency on purely secular considerations and makes as its criterion practical goals of a most dangerous and transitory sort. The American reformers pushed to the limit the principle, already often put forward in Germany, that forms lose their justification when they become foreign to the community's consciousness;

but they did not examine the possibility that they may also retain very high value that would repay the struggle for their retention and revivification. Einhorn brought about a significant deepening of the Reform movement when he placed Israel's messianic calling to all mankind at the center of religious thought and attempted to reshape religious life on the basis of this principle, but even he could not sufficiently repress Americanization as a central idea.[5]

Liturgical reform in America was accomplished in accordance with the guiding principles just summarized, but it was not uniformly put into practice in the synagogues that adopted it; even in the congregations that joined the Union of American Congregations, a great variety of degrees of reform can be found. As to external form, all synagogues use musical accompaniment and mixed choir, and have eliminated the women's gallery; bareheadedness is not universal, nor is the leading of the prayers by the rabbi instead of a precentor. Many congregations hold their service on Friday night, Saturday, and Sunday, with but few holding services only on Sunday. The second day of the festivals has been eliminated everywhere. The liturgy, too, is not the same everywhere. In some congregations the prayers have been completely reworked and contain scarcely more than a faint recollection of the old Jewish order of prayer. But the most widely used prayer books are based on the traditional liturgy, even though they reshape it quite freely. In 1857 Wise published a prayer book under the title מנהג אמעריקא תפלות בני ישורון (*The American Rite: The Prayers of Jeshurun*), which found wide distribution in the congregations of the West and South. The prayer book was completely in Hebrew, and, though slightly abbreviated in its introductory and concluding parts, was otherwise completely founded on tradition. Only in passages mentioning the Messiah and the upheavals connected with his advent were radical changes made. Interestingly, all headings and instructions are given in Hebrew, and unpointed at that; such advanced knowledge of Hebrew could still be presupposed in America in those days. In 1858 Einhorn published his עולת תמיד: *Gebetbuch für israelitische Reformgemeinde* (*The Daily Offering: Prayer Book for Israelite Reform Congregations*), which followed Holdheim's model in the structure of the prayers and in the emphasis on the leading religious ideas of the Reform movement.

{319}

> While he relied as much as possible on the old liturgy as set forth by Zunz, yet in every service he sounded the notes of joyful gratitude for God's wonders in Jewish history. Particularly the Day of Atonement liturgy proclaims with unsurpassed artistry the lofty truth of Israel's mission to the world as a nation of priests, and expresses with enthusiasm proceeding from a passionate Jewish sensibility the ancient and the modern conception of sin, repentance, and divine forgiveness. The whole is the work of a master, whose greatness can be perceived in every detail.

The prayer book was composed in Hebrew and German, and therefore was of use only to German-speaking congregations; only in 1896 did it appear in an English edition. In the meantime, however, the prayer book of the Central Conference of American Rabbis, סדר תפלות ישראל: *The Union Prayer Book for Jewish Worship*, had appeared in 1894, a book that since then has been adopted by about 250 congregations in the United States. The publishers indicate that their goal is to unite the moving memories of the past with the pressing demands of the present, and to enhance the solemnity of the liturgy by bringing together both important elements, the honorable formulas of the past as well as modern prayers and reflections in the vernacular. In its non-Hebrew part, in the theological reflections, as well as in the changes in the Hebrew text following from these, the prayer book follows Einhorn's model. The Hebrew portion is ampler than that of its predecessors. The prayer book falls into two parts; the first contains the prayers for the Sabbaths, pilgrim festivals, and home observances, together with the scriptural readings, and the second contains the prayers for the Days of Awe. All Hebrew prayers are accompanied by an English translation. The structure of the prayers is as follows: The Evening Service begins with a Hebrew psalm and an English selection of biblical verses recited alternately by precentor and congregation. Then follows the Hebrew Evening Service in its traditional structure, but with the text abridged; of the *Shema*, only the first paragraph and one sentence from the third (Num. 15:40) are retained; "Make us lie down" is lacking. The *Amida* on Sabbaths and festivals consists of the first two benedictions and a portion of the middle one in Hebrew, as well as a closing English petition; on weekdays it is entirely in English. It is followed by another English selection of biblical passages, an English prayer by the precentor, a congregational hymn, an English version of "It is our duty," an address to the mourners, and Mourner's Kaddish in the version customary in the Hamburg Temple; the service concludes with the hymn "There is none like our God." A great deal of attention was devoted to prayers for mourners, and a special liturgy was created for services to be held at home during the week of mourning. On the mornings of Sabbaths and festivals the most noticeable deviation from tradition is the absence of the Additional Service. The structure is similar to that of the Evening Service. Some biblical verses are [320] sung in Hebrew as an introduction, then follow a few English prayers from the old prayer book, the *Shema* with its benedictions in shortened form, the *Amida* with the Kedushah and the middle benediction in Hebrew, an English selection of biblical passages, the prayer of the precentor, and the last benedictions of the *Amida* in English. On festivals, "The living God be exalted" and the Priestly Blessing, as well as a selection of Hallel psalms (Pss. 113, 117, 118) are recited in Hebrew. The taking out and replacing of the Torah are accompanied by Hebrew hymns; the Torah reading is short and is translated into English, and the Haftarot are done only in English, with the selections being taken both from the Prophets and the Hagiographa. In this part of the service, the usages of the congregations diverge widely in detail. The scriptural reading is followed by the sermon, with an introductory and concluding hymn. The end of the service is the same as in the evening, except that at the end the rabbi pronounces the Priestly Blessing. The Sabbaths have also an Afternoon Service consisting of an introductory Hebrew hymn and Ps. 145, the Torah reading, English *Amida* with Hebrew Kedushah, sermon, scriptural verses, English reading from *Avot*, and a blessing. The special occasions recognized by the prayer book are the announcement of the New Moon, the New Moon day itself, Hanukkah, the Ninth of Av, and the prayer for rain on the Eighth Day of Assembly. Since only the first days of the festivals are observed, the Joy of the Torah is completely lacking. The *Union Prayer Book* thus adheres consistently to its theological line, but in the selection of prayers and the occasions that it takes into consideration, it is very much guided by the demands of the congregations, to which it has sacrificed the theories of the radical theologians.[6]

The American Reform could not have failed to influence Europe in turn; the liturgy of the Jewish Religious Union in London[7] and the Reform congregation in Paris[8] have been recently established following its example. In Germany, Einhorn's influence could already be observed in the Westphalian prayer book. The recently revised *Israelitisches Gebetbuch für die neue Synagoge in Frankfurt am Main* by Caesar Seligmann follows the American model in structure, though it reproduces those Hebrew prayers that it retains almost unchanged, and, in contrast to the American prayer book, includes more Hebrew on weekdays than on Sabbath and festivals.[9] These are most recent innovations, so recent that history does not yet have the right to pass final judgment on them.

(5)   We have followed the Reform movement down to the immediate present and have acquainted ourselves with its demands and the shape it took in the different countries. We must now draw together the common elements within these variations and evaluate them as a whole from an historical perspective. The starting points of the Reform movement are everywhere the same: With the changed social condition and the rise in the educational level of the Jews, dissatisfaction sets in with the traditional liturgy. The complaint is first about the obvious external defects: the restless, often undignified behavior of the congregation, and the irreverent, often revolting manner in which the prayers are recited. Criticism of these faults, and thereby recognition of them as faults—had this occurred—would have been enough to bring about their eventual elimination; the timing of their disappearance was only a question of the progress of education. Quiet and order, dignity and reverence in worship are such self-explanatory requirements for civilized people, and approach so nearly the precepts of traditional Judaism, that the most conservative circles recognized that they were justified, and everywhere efforts were made to realize them. The refinement of the cantorial rendition and the introduction of harmonic choral singing were also demanded from every quarter and were put everywhere into effect for the beautification of the service. Whether organ accompaniment is permitted was in dispute. In some countries, like Italy and France, it has been introduced without opposition, even where the tradition is most strictly adhered to. In others countries, like England, it is viewed as a declaration of war against the congregation. In Germany it is the boundary line between the parties; it has become more and more acceptable to congregations, and such opposition as still exists is not directed so much against the instrument itself as against playing it on the Sabbath and festivals.

[321]

Complaints are also generally raised about the length of the service, which results partly from the external flaws mentioned above, but mostly derives from the fact that in the course of the centuries the prayers have grown far beyond their original bulk and have become laden with numerous liturgical poems. It was impossible to grasp the meaning of the piyyutim, for even much of the statutory prayers remained inaccessible to the laity. But as knowledge of Hebrew receded, it became harder to understand even the simple prayers and Torah readings. The women, especially, who wished more than in the past to participate in the public liturgy, lagged far behind in the necessary knowledge of Hebrew. The natural consequence was the desire to shorten the service, to eliminate unintelligible prayers and poems, and to introduce prayers and edifying sermons in the vernacular. Broad agreement was reached about many of these demands. The vernacular sermon has been recognized and introduced in civilized countries by all factions as a beneficial and fruitful institution. Even if it does not accompany every scriptural reading on every single Sabbath and festival, it does take place regularly and at brief intervals. The elimination of the poetry and the unintelligible parts of the service is opposed only by those few stubborn persons who cannot tolerate deviation from the rite book in any point whatever. It was even possible to reach a general consensus for shortening the statutory prayers, as long as the changes were slight. Like the sermon, prayers in the vernacular have gained admission into the synagogue and, for the liturgy in the narrow sense of the word, have received the approbation of all parties. But more extreme change in the traditional order of prayer has been adopted only by synagogues with a consciously progressive tendency. Such changes are the abridging of the Torah reading, the abridging of the introductory and concluding portions of the Morning Service, and the interruption of Hebrew prayers by prayers in the vernacular. Even these changes have received a positive response among a large part of the communities. Only with the next stage of reform do the significant attacks on the main parts of the liturgy begin, until they reach those radical revisions that leave little of the traditional type of liturgy standing, and as good as nothing of the Hebrew language.

[322]

The Reform in its true sense does not consist of abridging the prayers and suppressing the Hebrew language; it consists of alterations in the text that proceed from dogmatic considerations, contesting or reinterpreting religious doctrines. It concerns mainly the teaching of the bodily resurrection and belief in a personal Messiah, with whose appearance the prayers connect the restoration of the Temple and the sacrificial cult, the gathering of scattered Israel, and their restoration to Zion. In contrast to the above-mentioned demands, which have been met with understanding by nearly all strata, the dogmatic reconsiderations have been raised mainly by theologically educated persons. They have not enjoyed much popularity, and beyond the alterations already introduced in the Hamburg Temple they have never aroused great interest.

In this split between the efforts of the theologians and the understanding of the communities lies the main reason for the disproportion between the expenditure in effort, energy, and congregational upheaval on the one hand, and the Reform movement's success on the other. In their idealistic enthusiasm, the leaders of the movement have lost sight of actual conditions, seriously overestimating the general progress of the age, and especially the improvement in religious education among the Jews. Just as the "spring of nations" of 1848 failed to bring about the hoped-for age of perfected mankind, so the opinions aired in the rabbinic conference did little to effect a thoroughgoing enlightenment among the Jews. The thin upper class of educated people who adopted those theories were completely occupied with their general cultural interests. They maintained a rather apathetic stance toward the religious movement, and their support had but minimal force. Meanwhile, the broad masses, whose lives were anchored in the views and forms of the past, lost out in both directions: The theological Reform was not strong enough to carry them along, and its dogmatic decisions did not have the force to awaken their enthusiasm. Moreover, the conditions of the times were very unfavorable, for they set people off on the pursuit of wealth and pleasure, and alienated them from pursuit of the messianic ideal. That the reformers did not indulge in lengthy theoretical debates, but threw themselves into their attempt to reshape life, trusting in their example and precept to carry the day, testifies to their courage and competence; but the disadvantage of their hasty action was not long in showing itself. The Reform was accomplished with cool, appraising reason, and much of the poetry and emotional character of the liturgy was sacrificed to sober rationality. Only recently had a beginning been made in establishing the new concepts based on a scientific foundation, and theology grounded itself over-hastily in views that could not hold up permanently in the face of scholarship and that came up against determined oppostion in the congregations. History has passed its judgment on all radical upheavals and has shown that only a steady development rooted in the past is justified.

The mistakes made at the movement's beginnings have impeded its development continually, even though the signs are growing that the situation is improving. There is still much to be done; little is accomplished by changing and wholesale striking-out of prayers if in the process enthusiasm and understanding for liturgy are not awakened. But this is the chief thing that has been heretofore lacking; the Reform movement has remained furthest from its main goals. It has not succeeded in effecting the sought-for freedom in liturgical forms; its adherents did not have the understanding or the loving profundity. Nor did the reformed [sic] liturgy escape the danger of formalism, for its program turned out to be just as strong a bondage as the old order of prayers. In the end, the fears expressed a century ago at the movement's beginnings have been shockingly realized. Simplifying the liturgy did not increase its familiarity; apathy toward its institutions has grown, and is greatest, in fact, just where the demand for revision in the spirit of the times has been most attended to. Here, however, lies the most important task for the future: to reawaken the old enthusiasm for worship and the intensity of the prayerful spirit. Liturgy must become again what it was to our ancestors: the center of religious life, the focus of religious assembly and devotion.

[323]

[1. *The History of the Reform Movement in the Past Thirty-Five Years*

The tremendous changes that have occurred in Jewish life since the late Professor Elbogen completed his book on the Jewish liturgy have, of course, had a great effect on the Reform movement as well. With the elimination of the German center, the focus of Reform Judaism shifted mainly to the United States, despite the revival of progressive Judaism in England (with the help of Holocaust refugees)—though new Reform congregations were founded also in Australia, South Africa, South America, and Israel (most of them also with the participation of refugees from central Europe).

The development of Reform Judaism in Germany of the past differs greatly from its development in other countries, especially in the Anglo-Saxon world. In Germany, synagogues founded on an absolute reform basis existed in only two places—the Hamburg Temple (1818) and the *Reformgemeinde* in Berlin (1845)—whereas in most places the reform grew out of existing congregations. In Frankfurt am Main, Berlin, Munich, Breslau, and elsewhere, the organ and "reformed" prayer ceremonies were introduced on the authority of the congregation itself, not as a schismatic phenomenon, and a special place was given to the extreme traditionalists who refused to participate in the "reformed" service, so that they could worship as they wished. Under these circumstances, the reformers had to take into consideration the local customs and traditional prayers in general, and thus they did not go to extremes. They continued to recite most of the prayers in Hebrew, and did not introduce radical changes into the text of the prayers. This was not the case in the Anglo-Saxon world. There all the Jewish congregations, like those of other religions, were free organizations. Anyone who wanted to set up a religious organization, of any program whatsoever, could do so, without taking into consideration governmental requirements or the opinions of those who did not wish to take part. In such a climate the Reform movement grew and developed in America in the nineteenth century; and its attachment to tradition continually declined. This reform was a radical one. Not only did it eliminate the observance of most commandments, but it explicitly repudiated several doctrines that were considered among the "articles of the faith" of traditional Judaism, such as divine revelation of the Torah, the Messiah, the Resurrection, and so on. In short, this Judaism sought to be completely "universalistic," and rejected "particularism." On this principle the prayer books of Reform Judaism in America were built.

A change in this situation in the United States began in the twenties and thirties of this century, as a reaction to the new anti-Semitism in Europe and under the influence of the building up of Palestine, but also as a consequence of change in the composition of the membership of the Reform movement. Most of the rabbis and members today are the children and grandchildren of Eastern European immigrants, to whom the "particularism" rejected by the early Reform movement is actually attractive. This strange circumstance found expression in 1937 in the "Columbus Platform" of the Reform rabbis of the United States, which spoke of the "people of Israel" and also of "the obligation of all Jewry to aid in [Palestine's] upbuilding as a Jewish homeland by endeavoring to make it not only a haven of refuge for the oppressed but also a center of Jewish culture and spiritual life." It also spoke of "Jewish requirements" involving Sabbath and festival observance and the use of the Hebrew language.

This has been the direction of the American Reform in the last thirty years, and it has had an influence on all Reform congregations in other countries. But it must be noted that [324] progressive Judaism has no supreme authority (like a chief rabbinate), and every congregation chooses the means it deems appropriate to put the "Columbus Platform" into effect. Therefore, Reform Judaism includes all kinds of combinations of faith and heresy, observance of the commandments and nonobservance. In recent years two contradictory streams have taken shape within Reform Judaism, but each acknowledges the right of the other to exist: On the one hand, a humanistic, nontheistic approach has developed, and on the other, the voices of thinkers influenced by Martin Buber and especially by Franz Rosenzweig are more and more to be heard. These thinkers within Reform Judaism aspire to an authentic Judaism (even a halakhic Judaism, though not in the orthodox sense).

Since the principal criterion in our discussion is the "reform" of the prayer book, we must also include the American Conservative movement. This movement has never made a declaration of its beliefs and disbeliefs as has the Reform movement, but in general it aspires to be more "traditional" than Reform Judaism. Nevertheless, it has many points of contact with Reform Judaism, especially with the liberal Judaism of Europe described by Elbogen. Most of the Conservative service is in Hebrew, though some prayers are recited in the vernacular. The organ has been introduced in many synagogues, and like the Reform Jews in the United States the Conservatives have also eliminated the separation of the sexes in the synagogue. The Conservatives have also abbreviated the prayers, especially by deleting liturgical poetry, and they do not pray for the restoration of sacrifices. They have retained the personal Messiah and the kingdom of David in the Hebrew text of the *ʿAmida*, but in the English translation they "interpret" these matters allegorically.

Within the Conservative movement, the Reconstructionist movement was founded in 1935, under the inspiration of Professor Mordecai Kaplan. This is the left wing, so to speak, of the Conservatives. (In recent years the Reconstructionists have begun to see themselves as a "fourth movement," parallel to the Orthodox, Reform, and Conservative movements in the United States, but most of their rabbis still belong to the Conservative rabbinate.) This new movement, affirming the value of tradition and the observance of the practical commandments insofar as they are compatible with American Jewish life, has reservations about the moderate theology of Conservative Judaism. Like the Reforms, the Reconstructionists deny the divine revelation of the Torah (in its literal sense), resurrection of the dead, a personal Messiah, the restoration of sacrifices, and so forth; they have even gone further than the Reformers in denying also a personal God (in their view, God is a "process") and the election of Israel. They have published a new prayer book (1946), which is at once more traditional—from the point of view of form—and more radical—from the point of view of its theological tenets—than the prayer books of the Reform movement. (But several Reform rabbis belong to the Reconstructionist movement.)

2. The Patterns of Reform Worship in Their Development

From 1816 until 1967 about fifty different prayer books of a reform or liberal nature appeared in Europe, and if we count the various editions of these prayer books (often a new edition means numerous changes not only in the prayers themselves, but also in matters of doctrine) the number of prayer books is more than 175. A nearly complete bibliography of Reform prayer books in Europe is found in Jakob Petuchowski, *Prayerbook Reform in Europe* (New York: World Union for Progressive Judaism, 1968). This book also provides a description of the prayer books and how they came into being. The American prayer books of the Reform, Conservative, and Reconstructionist movements are analyzed by Eric Friedland in *The Historical and Theological Development of the Non-Orthodox Prayerbooks in the United States* (Ann Arbor: University Microfilm, 1967). In America, too, these prayer books (in all their editions) numbered more than fifty.

In general, it may be said that the development of the series of Reform prayer books [325] is characterized by a dual tendency: On the one hand, there is an increase in the logical consistency with which the Reform idea finds expression in the text of the prayers; on the other, the Reform liturgy is progressively coming nearer to the external form and style of the traditional liturgy.

True, the Reform liturgy contains great variety, and many attempts have been made to find a way to unite the majority of Reform worshipers. Reform liturgy in England is not the same as Liberal liturgy in England, and the American *Union Prayer Book* is not the same as the *Einheitsgebetbuch* of Germany. Nevertheless, in the various versions of the Reform prayer book, three main streams can be distinguished.

a.   The first stream is content to abridge the traditional material and to make minor changes in wording as necessitated by the beliefs of the age. In addition, this group has inserted some prayers in the vernacular—for taking the Torah out and putting it back, memorial prayers, the prayer for the government, and so forth. But it introduces few new prayers, and in general maintains the traditional form of public worship. To this stream belonged almost all the German Reform prayer books; in the nineteenth century there was hardly a congregation that did not put out its own special prayer book. Only in the twentieth century did the liberal Jews in Germany begin to use the *Einheitsgebetbuch* (1929), the reformed [*sic*] prayer book that, despite its traditional character, allowed every congregation to continue its own local practices. To this stream belongs also the prayer book of the English reformers published in 1841, and the prayer book *Minhag amerika* (1859), published by Isaac Meyer Wise, the great organizer of Reform Judaism in the United States. In addition, the founders of the Conservative movement in the United States also published prayer books. Remarkably, these Conservatives, rabbis like Marcus Jastrow and Benjamin Szold, were even more extreme in the changes that they introduced than was Isaac Meyer Wise!

b. The second stream hardly takes the tradition into account at all. Not only does it largely remove the Hebrew language from the prayer book, but it makes no attempt to shape its form and content after the rabbinic liturgical patterns. This group aimed to place in the worshiper's hands material for prayer and contemplation suitable, in the authors' view, for the aesthetic sensibilities and educational level of a modern person. Actually, they also made use of material from the traditional prayer book, but this was supposedly only incidental. They were not interested in building a "museum" out of the ancient Jewish prayers or in stimulating memories of Israel's past. The main representatives of this stream are the prayer books of the *Reformgemeinde* in Berlin—the congregation of the radical Rabbi Samuel Holdheim—which began to appear in 1845 and continued into many editions, each one different from the others, until the thirties of this century, the prayer books of the Liberal congregation in London, edited by Rabbi Israel Mattuck, beginning in 1912, with several expanded editions afterward, and those of several of the Reform rabbis in America in the nineteenth century, each of whom published his own prayer book.

c. Between these two streams a third one formed, one that tried to be "satisfactory to both sides"—that is, true to tradition, yet alert to the demands of the modern age. The first representative of this stream was Rabbi David Einhorn, who came from Germany to the United States in the last century and served as a rabbi in Baltimore. There he published his prayer book entitled עולת תמיד, "Daily Offering," in Hebrew and German (1848). In this prayer book we find, though abridged and altered in line with the author's theological outlook, the majority of the most ancient prayers from the tannaitic period, like the *Shemaᶜ* with its benedictions and the ᶜ*Amida*, both in English and German. But besides these, Einhorn included in his prayer book much new material, which he himself composed in German. While these new prayers had their origin in the traditional Jewish prayers, Einhorn gave them a completely new form in which the ideas, feelings, and aspirations of the nineteenth century found expression. Furthermore, Einhorn's prayer book, rather than Isaac Meyer Wise's *Minhag amerika*, became the basis of the most widely accepted prayer book of Reform congregations in America. סדר תפלות ישראל is the Hebrew name of the *Union Prayer-Book* (first edition, 1894; revised edition, 1918; newly revised edition, 1940), the official prayer book of the Reform congregations in the United States. It follows the same method, in Hebrew and English, as Einhorn followed in his ᶜ*Olat tamid*, allowing both for tradition and the demands of the times. For its part, the *Union Prayer-Book* influenced other Reform prayer books that appeared later, not just its own special editions, such as

[326]

the ones for Australia and South Africa, but also prayer books like the *Israelitisches Gebetbuch* of Caesar Seligmann (Frankfurt am Main, 1910), *Rituel des prières journalièrs* published by the liberals in Paris in 1925, *Sidur hatefilot leshabat* published by the Circle for Progressive Judaism in the State of Israel (Jerusalem, 1961/2), and the prayer book *ʿAvoda shebalev* published by the liberals in England in 1967 to replace the prayer book of Israel Mattuck, which had been in use until then.

3. *The Main Characteristics of Reform Prayer*

a.   **Abridgement of the Traditional Prayers.** All Reform prayer books seek to shorten the traditional prayers to a greater or lesser extent. All repetitions, as of "Happy," Kaddish, and Kedushah are eliminated. (In the case of this last, the Kedushah of the ʿAmida is considered sufficient, and the other two are omitted.) Usually the ʿAmida is recited only once. (Either the precentor and the congregation recite the whole ʿAmida together, or the precentor recites the first three and the last three benedictions aloud and the middle benedictions are recited silently.) Above all, the liturgical poems are eliminated, nearly all on the pilgrim festivals, and most of them on the Days of Awe. On the other hand, several poems of the Sephardic rite by Ibn Gabirol, Judah Halevi, and others have been introduced into the Reform liturgy of the Days of Awe.

b.   **Use of the Vernacular.** All Reform congregations acknowledge the legitimacy of the local language for public worship, but congregations differ in the extent to which they put this theoretical legitimacy to use. In Germany the service was 90 percent in Hebrew, except for the congregation of Holdheim in Berlin, where the service was entirely in German (except for the first verse of the *Shemaʿ*, the biblical verses of the Kedushah, and the Priestly Blessing). In Reform congregations in England about half the service is in Hebrew, and in the Liberal congregations in England most of the service is in English, but the prayer books of both movements include also the Hebrew text of those prayers that are recited in the vernacular. In the state of Israel the services of Progressive congregations are in the local language, but here that language is Hebrew.

c.   **Elimination of Angels.** All Reform prayer books eliminate the references to angels in prayers (as in "Creator of light," the Kedushah of the ʿAmida, and so on, not to mention the additions of the Kabbalists in the blowing of the shofar, and the like). In Europe, for the most part, such references were merely reduced, while in the United States they have been eliminated altogether.

d.   **Reduction of Particularism.** Traditional prayers that create the impression of an unfavorable comparison between Jews and non-Jews—for example, ורוממנו מכל לשון, "Who elevated us above every language"; שלא עשנו כגויי הארצות, "Who has not made us like the nations of the lands"; and the like, have been eliminated or "emended" to a more universalistic language.

e.   **Elimination of the Petitions for the Gathering of the Exiled Communities and the Return to Zion.** Several Reform prayer books retain the references to Jerusalem (and some have restored these references after they had been eliminated in earlier editions). But no Reform prayer book includes petitions for the liquidation of the Diaspora and the assembling of all Jews of the world in Palestine, except for the prayer book of Progressive Judaism in the state of Israel and the new prayer book (*Seder tov lehodot*, 1964) of Liberal Judaism in Holland, which includes the prayer והביאנו לשלום מארבע כנפות הארץ ותוליכנו קוממיות לארצנו, ''Bring us in peace from the four corners of the earth and lead us upright to our land.'' On the other hand, since the rise of the state of Israel, prayers are recited in many Reform congregations in all countries for Israel's welfare. As early as eight years before the State came into being (1940), the American Reform's *Union Prayer Book* included an English prayer saying:

[327]

> Uphold also the hands of our brothers who toil to rebuild Zion . . . Grant us strength that with Thy help we may bring a new light to shine upon Zion. Imbue us who live in lands of freedom with a sense of Israel's spiritual unity that we may share joyously in the work of redemption so that from Zion shall go forth the law and the word of God from Jerusalem (1:68–69).

f. **Elimination of Prayers for the Reinstitution of Sacrifices.** Even the prayer books of Liberal Judaism in Germany, which all contain the Additional Service, have eliminated the prayer for the restoration of sacrifices. Some do not refer to sacrifices at all; others mention them as a purely historical matter, without reference to the future. Neither in the Anglo-Saxon world nor in Israel does Reform Judaism have the Additional Service at all, except for a few congregations that have it on the Days of Awe.

g. **''Messianic Age,'' ''Redemption'' as a Substitute for Personal Messiah and ''Redeemer.''** Only the Reform prayer books in the United States and the Liberal prayer book in England have gone to the logical extreme in this matter. In Europe the traditional Hebrew text has mostly been considered adequate, though the translations have made use of the impersonal substitutes.

h. **''Eternity of the Soul'' as a Substitute for Resurrection.** Here, too, the Americans have taken the extreme position, while the European prayer books (except for that of the English liberals, 1967) have not eliminated the words ''Who revives the dead'' from the Hebrew text, though in the translations they stress the eternity of the soul.

i. **Variety.** The Reform prayer books distribute among several services prayers and psalms that, in the traditional prayer book, belong to a single service. Likewise, these prayer books distribute the psalms for the Welcoming of the Sabbath among the Sabbaths of the month and those of the Verses of Song in the Morning Service among the days of the week. This method not only permits the shortening of the service, but sometimes permits giving each ritual occasion its own special character.

j. **Addition of New Prayers Expressing the Aspirations of the Modern Age.** Great differences exist among the various Reform prayer books as to the extent of the new prayers that they include, but all agree as to the legitimacy of such additions.

4. Bibliography

Bemporad, Jack, ed. *The Theological Foundations of Prayer: A Reform Perspective.* New York: Union of American Hebrew Congregations, 1967.

Blau, Joseph L. *Modern Varieties of Judaism.* New York: Columbia University Press, 1966.

C.C.A.R. Journal: A Special Issue on Worship and Liturgy. New York: Central Conference of American Rabbis, 1967.

Central Conference of American Rabbis. *Yearbook Index, Volumes I–L.* New York: Central Conference of American Rabbis, 1941.

Davis, Moshe. *Yehadut ameriqa behitpathuta.* New York: Jewish Theological Seminary, 1951.

Eisenstein, Ira, ed. *Varieties of Jewish Belief.* New York: Reconstructionist Press, 1966.

Freehof, Solomon B. "Reform Judaism and Prayer." In *Reform Judaism: Essays by Hebrew Union College Alumni.* Cincinnati: Hebrew Union College Press, 1949.

Friedland, Eric Lewis. *The Historical and Theological Development of the Non-Orthodox* "Prayerbooks in the United States." Ph. D. dissertation, Brandeis University, 1967. Ann Arbor: University Microfilms, 1967.

Friedman, Theodore. "Jewish Tradition in Twentieth Century America: The Conservative Approach." *Judaism* 3 (1954): 310–20.

Idelsohn, Abraham Z. *Jewish Liturgy and Its Development.* New York: Henry Holt, 1929.

Kaplan, Mordecai M. *Judaism as a Civilization.* Enlarged edition. New York: Thomas Yoseloff, 1957.

Petuchowski, Jakob J. "From Censorship Prevention to Theological Reform." *HUCA* 50–51 (1969–70): 299–324.

———. "Karaite Tendencies in an Early Reform Haggadah." *HUCA* 31 (1960): 223–49.

———. "New Directions in Reform Liturgy." *C.C.A.R. Journal* 16 (April 1969): 26–34.

———. "The New Prayerbook of English Liberal Judaism." *C.C.A.R. Journal* 15 (June 1968): 94–99, 103.

———. "New Trends in the Liturgy of British Reform Judaism." *Judaism* 15 (1966): 492–96.

———. *Prayerbook Reform in Europe.* New York: World Union for Progressive Judaism, 1968.

———. "Reform Benedictions for Rabbinic Ordinances." *HUCA* 37 (1966): 175–89.

———. "Reform Prayer out of Zion." *C.C.A.R. Journal* 10 (1963): 31–37.

Philipson, David. *The Reform Movement in Judaism.* Reissue of new and revised edition. Introduction by Solomon B. Freehof. New York: Ktav Publishing House, 1967.

Plaut, W. Gunther. *The Growth of Reform Judaism.* New York: World Union for Progressive Judaism, 1965.

———. *The Rise of Reform Judaism.* New York: World Union for Progressive Judaism, 1963.

Schulweis, Harold M. "The Temper of Reconstructionism." *Judaism* 3 (1954): 321–32.

Silberman, Lou H. "The Union Prayer Book: A Study in Liturgical Development." In *Retrospect and Prospect,* ed. Bertram Wallace Korn, 46–80. New York: Central Conference of American Rabbis, 1965.

Waxman, Mordecai, ed. *Tradition and Change: The Development of Conservative Judaism.* New York: Burning Bush Press, 1958.

Wolf, Arnold J., ed. *Rediscovering Judaism: Reflections on a New Theology.* Chicago: Quadrangle Books, 1965.]

PART THREE

The Organization of the Jewish Liturgy

CHAPTER ONE

The Synagogues

§ 48 Synagogues: Name, Age, Distribution, and Location

(1)   The holding of services was not bound to fixed sites or buildings; anyone was permitted to worship alone (בינו לבין עצמו, ביחיד) like Daniel, who worshiped in his room (Dan. 6:11: עליתא). But the reading of the Torah and religious instruction demanded a public—that is, a congregation. It seems likely that the congregation always assembled in the same place and that a special site was set aside for the purpose of the liturgy. The oldest name customarily used for such a place is בית העם, "House of the People" (Jer. 39:8),[1] which in the pre-exilic period meant a public building. This expression remained long currrent in popular usage; as late as the end of the second century C.E., the Aramaic equivalent בית עמא, "House of the People," was current among the lower classes, though the sages were unhappy with this expression and considered its use a capital offense (B. *Shab.* 32a).[2] Another biblical name is בית התפלה, "House of Prayer" (Is. 56:7), for it is written that the Second Temple will be "a house of prayer for all nations." It is generally assumed that מועדי אל, "God's tabernacles in the land" (Ps. 74:8) and perhaps also בית מועד, "The house assigned for all the living" (Job 30:23) refer to the sites of assembly for prayer located throughout the land; at least so Aquila understood the expression and translated it συναγωγάς. This Greek expression eventually prevailed over the others. In the Septuagint it corresponds to עדה, which in the Aramaic targumim is rendered כנשתא; the verb כנש is used as the translation for הקהיל and אסף ["to assemble, to gather"—*Engl. trans.*]; thus, the expression בי כנשתא or simply כנשתא came to mean the communal assembly house. Since this root occurs also in Hebrew in the form כנס (Esth. 4:17), Rabbinic Hebrew uses כנסת for "assembly"; hence, the building that serves the purpose of liturgical assembly is called בית כנסת, plural, בתי כנסיות. The same shift occurred in the word συναγωγή, which, like כנשתא, originally designated the congregation, and therefore is sometimes used to refer to societies, until eventually it also became the name for sites of communal assembly, the building set aside for the holding of services.[3] By way of Latin, the Greek word passed as a loan word into Italian, French, German, and English; in Spanish it took the form *Esnoga*.[4]

[332]

337

Among Hellenistic Jews we find most often the expression προσευχή, προσ-ευκτήριον, equivalent to בית תפלה (LXX: οἶκος τῆς προσευχῆς), to which Juvenal even gave the Latin form *proseucha*. The difference in usage between Palestine and the Hellenistic diaspora becomes very clear when Philo, in speaking about the Essenes, stresses that they call their sacred places συναγωγαί. Very rare is the name σαββατεῖον, alluding to the assemblies held every Sabbath and paralleled by the Syriac expression בית שבתא דיהודיי, plural, בית שבי דיהודיי.[5] Pagans call the synagogues of the Jews also τὰ ἱερά, the customary designation of their sanctuaries. Among Arabic-speaking Jews, בית כנסת survived in *al-kanīs*, corresponding in meaning with *al-jumʿa*, and found in documents from Provence in the form *aljama*. But Maqrīzī also says *ṣalawāt*, which corresponds to בית תפלה. In medieval Sicily the word *meskita*—that is, mosque (Arabic *masjid*)—was common; the Falashas, too, call their synagogues *masjid*. It is likely that this is an ancient word going back to בית השתחוות found in recently discovered texts.[6] The Turks call synagogues *havras*, a term derived from the Hebrew word for "company" (חברה).[7]

In Rumanian and Slavic lands, as well as in Hungary, the local word for synagogue is derived from the Latin *templum*, but other terms are also found alongside this, like *synagogue* or expressions equivalent to "house of prayer." In Rome, the Jews, like members of other groups, called their community organization *schola*; the first notice of this usage is from the year 1111. Hence, the places where they used to assemble were also called in Italian *schola*,[8] and in German *Schule*, or *Schul*. Luther ordinarily translates the word συναγωγή in the New Testament as *Schule*, and in Yiddish the synagogue is called *shul* to this day. A century ago the word *temple* was introduced for modern synagogues. In Austria this term took root, while in Germany the term *synagogue* is preferred.

(2) We do not know when permanent synagogues were first established; opinions on this question are in part dependent on the interpretation of the above-mentioned terminology. If, following the ancient Jewish tradition,[9] we view the biblical "House of the People" as a synagogue, this institution must have existed prior to the Babylonian exile. However, since nowhere else in this ancient period do we find the slightest reference to fixed communal services or to buildings set aside for this purpose, and since the name in itself does not at all suggest that the structure served especially for such prayer meetings, this conjecture has no basis. On the other hand, it is nearly certain that special places were established for prayer meetings in the Diaspora. The house in which a prophet like Ezekiel lived certainly served as a natural gathering point (see Ezek. 8:1), but in other places it was necessary to seek a suitable site for assembly. In the talmudic period it was claimed that several synagogues in Babylonia, like the one in Shefitiv[10] near Nehardea and the one in Hutzal, existed since the time of the Babylonian exile. When public worship was introduced in Palestine, especially after Ezra's [333] arrival, the number of synagogues in the Holy Land increased, and by the time of the Syrian oppression, the subject of Ps. 74, it could already be said that "they burned all God's tabernacles in the land."

The first datable information about the existence of Jewish places of worship has reached us from Egypt. An inscription from Schedia[11] near Alexandria reports the dedication of the Jewish *proseuche* "to King Ptolemy III Euergetes (247–221) and Queen Bernice"; likewise, in another inscription and in a papyrus from the third century, the

Jewish *proseuchai* in Egypt are mentioned. Thus, there is no room to doubt their existence in the mid-third century. And if we consider the synagogue in Schedia as a branch of the great *proseuche* in Alexandria, it would seem that the latter was established considerably earlier—that is, around the time of the migration of the Jews to this new and flourishing city. Some hold the opinion that the very institution of the synagogue arose in the Hellenistic lands, whence it was transferred to Palestine,[12] but this is contrary to all the other known facts. The Jews of Alexandria were entirely dependent on their homeland in matters of religion; it is therefore more reasonable to assume that the development was in the opposite direction—that is, that the synagogues, which had long been widespread in Palestine, were transferred to Egypt. From the above-mentioned attestations we may deduce that this happened rather early. The spread of the synagogue occurred with astonishing rapidity; wherever the Jews wandered they set one up. We may therefore apply to the synagogue Strabo's statement that there is no place in the οἰκουμένη that has not absorbed the tribe of the Jews and been conquered by them.[13] Wherever a significant number of Jews dwelt, they established a religious community and synagogues. Thus, even before the destruction of the Temple we find synagogues everywhere, not only in Palestine, but throughout the Diaspora; we have much information about their existence especially from the Hellenistic-Roman world. Josephus mentions synagogues in Dora, Tiberias, Caesaria, and Antioch; the Gospels mention those of Nazareth and Capernaum; Acts, those of Jerusalem, Damascus, Salamis in Cyprus, Antioch in Pisidia, Ikonion, Philippi in Macedonia, Thessalonica, Beroa, Athens, Corinth, Ephesus. Papyri and inscriptions attest to the existence of synagogues in various places and districts in Egypt; and in Rome the catacomb inscriptions serve as testimony to their existence. Wherever Jews are found, from the Persian Gulf to the Pillars of Hercules, we find the traces of these new centers of their religious life. For Philo and Josephus they are an ancient institution from the time of Moses, and a rabbinic tradition preserved in the Targumim[14] also carries them back to the very beginnings of the Jewish people. Christianity was always able to make use of the synagogue for propaganda purposes; they were not only the *fontes persecutionum*, "sources of persecution," as Tertullian calls them, but also, as Harnack writes, "the most important precondition for the rise and growth of Christian congregations in the Roman empire."[15] The establishment of synagogues did not cease even after the Christian victory. Whenever local or church law did not prohibit them, they were established wherever the Jews came. Even where they were not permitted, places of worship were established in secret and illegally. So it is to this day; the synagogue is the phenomenon that constantly accompanies the Jewish community everywhere.[16]

(3)   In Palestine synagogues were an inseparable part of the structure of the city. [334]
They were built in its center, the place that seemed most appropriate. This does not seem to have been the case in the Diaspora; Paul finds the synagogue of Philippi outside the city by the river: ἔξω τῆς πύλης παρὰ ποταμὸν οὗ ἐνομίζομεν προσευχὴν εἶναι (Acts 16:13). Is it by chance or intention that the synagogue stands by a river?[17] Josephus also speaks of the decision of the people's assembly of the citizens of Halicarnassus,[18] apparently from the period of Julius Caesar, permitting the Jews to build a synagogue on the seashore, in accordance with their ancestral custom, προσευχὰς ποιεῖσθαι πρὸς τῇ θαλάσσῃ κατὰ τὸ πατρίον ἔθος (Antiquities, 14.10.23). Likewise, the προσευχὴ τῶν

Ἰουδαίων, mentioned in a papyrus from the Egyptian city Tebtunis from the end of the second century B.C.E., was located by the water. Yet rabbinic sources mention only that the place where God appeared to the prophets of the Diaspora was always by the water. We know of no halakha stipulating that the synagogue be built by water, and in fact in Palestine the synagogues were not. For ritual washing of the hands before prayer, water from a well or basin, as is found today in every synagogue and mosque, was probably considered adequate, and is easier than being near a river or ocean. It does not seem at all likely that even in the Diaspora the synagogues were always located beside a source of water. Of the synagogues in Rome, it is not likely that even one was near the river. Nor is this reported of the great basilica in Alexandria; and it is most unlikely that the numerous other synagogues scattered throughout the city were on the water.[19] Probably even in the Diaspora there was no uniform custom in this matter. In the halakhic sources there is no mention of the whole subject before the fourteenth century, when Jacob b. Asher is the first to note that it is advisable to worship beside the water. In the nineteenth century Hayim Palaggi of Smyrna (1788–1869) finds particular virtue in the synagogue of Constantinople in that it is beside the water,[20] but he adds apologetically that the recommendation of worshiping beside the water was intended to apply only to individual worship. Nor, as far as we know, has anyone ever expressed conscientious regret over the fact that a synagogue was not directly by the water.

It is also probably not by chance that another location is mentioned as the site of the synagogue of Philippi, namely that it stood before the city gate. It seems that as a rule synagogues in the Diaspora mostly stood outside the city. The Jews avoided worshiping inside cities that contained pagan sanctuaries; only if special Jewish quarters existed, as in Alexandria, were synagogues established in them. But probably there was no completely uniform practice, and there were always exceptions; in Corinth, for example, it is hard to imagine that the synagogue stood outside the city, if the house of Titius Justus, where Paul stayed, was next to it (Acts 18:7). In Rome,[21] and probably in other cities as well, it was forbidden by law to establish foreign cultic sites inside the Pomerium. It is nearly certain that a similar difficulty existed in Babylonia as well.[22] It must be assumed that synagogues were not tolerated within the city by the Persian fire-worshipers—"they tear down the synagogue" (B. *Yoma* 10a)—and therefore they had to be built at some distance. In the Talmud a synagogue standing near a city

(B. *Qid.* 73b) is considered exceptional,[23] for it was ordinarily at a distance. Thus, also the midrash (*Tanh. B.*, Gen., 61b) assumes that when one goes to the synagogue he is going some distance ("Come, let us go out to the synagogue"), makes rest-stops, and does the trip in stages. In rain or burning sun one would seek refuge in the synagogues because no other shelter was nearby, though this was prohibited (B. *Meg.* 28b). We frequently hear about measures adopted so that the worshipers did not have to remain alone or only in a small number in the synagogue. In the Middle Ages, we find the opinion among the sages of the Franco-German school from Rashi's time on that the synagogues in Babylonia stood in the fields outside the cities. This idea must rest on a direct tradition, for they did not know of synagogues in the fields from their own experience,[24] yet it is expressed with such certainty that it cannot have arisen from a mere conjecture. Even in Babylonia there must have been exceptions, and even there some synagogues must have been inside the cities.

(4)   Diaspora synagogues stood under government protection. In Egypt they were dedicated to the king and declared inviolable. Old inscriptions to this effect, when they became worn out with time, were restored by the government. It is reported that the synagogue of Shefitiv near Nehardea[25] even had a statue of the king; it was probably intended as witness to the dedication of the structure, and therefore not considered a desecration of the site's sanctity. Likewise the synagogue in Casium in the Upper Galilee[26] was established, according to an inscription found in it, "for the welfare of the emperor Septimius Severus and his sons Caracalla and Geta" (ca. 197). Calling the synagogue by the emperor's name was another form of honor (συναγωγὴ 'Αυγουστ– ησίων, כנשתא דאסוירוס, "Synagogue of Augustus, Synagogue of Severus"). The Chinese Jews of Kai-feng-fu set up a table in the middle of their synagogue on which the emperor's name was written in golden letters, together with a prayer for his long life.[27]

Since the Jews were granted freedom to practice their religion, the synagogues were under the protection of the law.[28] Anyone who destroyed or desecrated them by violence was subject to severe punishment, and usually was obliged to pay restitution for the damage. But from the patristic age on,[29] plenty of Christian clergymen saw religious merit in destroying synagogues or turning them into churches. The last emperors of the western Roman Empire were repeatedly forced to impose punishments on account of such disturbances. Likewise Pope Gregory the Great proclaimed that the illegal destruction or misappropriation of a synagogue is a punishable act. Even though he, too, believed that once a site had been consecrated as a church it could never be restored, he did insist that the Jews be paid full compensation. The first case of the forcible turning of a synagogue into a church occurred in Byzantium, and this malicious act was recognized as state policy. When the Vandal kingdom was conquered in 535, the emperor Justinian ordered that its many synagogues be turned into churches.[30] This example was followed throughout the Middle Ages, especially in Roman territory; in Spain many churches that were once synagogues are standing today, among them the two splendid buildings *el Transito* and *Santa María la Blanca* in Toledo,[31] which, because of their great architectural value, were recently renovated out of state funds and declared national property. In Germany a different practice was followed: When a Jewish community was destroyed, the synagogue was demolished and a church erected in its place.[32] The last example of such use of synagogues on German soil occurred in Vienna, where—as tastefully proclaimed in an inscription plaque—on August 18, 1670, the emperor Leopold I "rebuilt the synagogue, that den of iniquity, as a 'house of God.'" It happened more than once that during a persecution the members of a community assembled in their synagogue, set fire to the structure, and went up in flames together with it—man, woman, and child.

[336]

(5)   In many cities the number of synagogues was considerable. Since the buildings were usually small, a goodly number was needed to serve a large Jewish population. Other reasons also accounted for this, as, for example, when separate synagogues were maintained for summer and winter (B. *B.B.* 3a). It is said hyperbolically of Jerusalem that at the time of the destruction of the Temple it had 394 or even 480 synagogues;[33] a similarly unlikely number is reported of Betar, but even in reliable reports high numbers are found. Thus, it is reported that there were thirteen synagogues in Tiberias around the year 300;[34] Philo mentions the existence of many *proseuchai* in Alexan-

dria,[35] and in Rome we now know from grave inscriptions of eleven congregations in the imperial age.[36] Under the pagan government there was unlimited freedom to establish congregations and synagogues. From the time of the emperor Theodosius II (408–450),[37] the Christian emperors no longer granted permission to build new synagogues, but only to repair old ones. Later Christian legislation decreed that the Jews of one city would never be permitted to maintain more than one synagogue.[38] This matched the Islamic legislation, for according to the regulations of Omar,[39] it was forbidden to build more than one synagogue in a single city. But actually, many exceptions were tolerated. Wherever legislation of Jewish affairs was under the influence of the church, the government adhered to this limitation, and only in the modern period, with the proclamation of the principle of freedom of conscience, did it become possible to restore the ancient practice.

(6)   The synagogues were a kind of "little Temple" (מקדש מעט); they had sacred character,[40] meaning that it was prohibited to make use of them for individual purposes other than prayer and study of the Torah. It was not even permitted to enter the synagogue except to pray; it could not be used as a shortcut, for example. But either these regulations were not strictly enforced, or we have to assume that the synagogues had side rooms, which could be used for other purposes, alongside the prayer hall. For according to everything we know, the synagogues served as community buildings in the broadest sense of the word. Besides prayer assemblies, they were used, for example, for the holding of eulogies for distinguished persons, both men and women.[41] The Talmud refers to a כנשתא דמרדתא—that is, "the synagogue of the rebellion" in Caesaria;[42] this designation agrees with the story told by Josephus, that in the time of the Jewish war political meetings were held in the synagogue. In the city of Panticapaeum,[43] today Kerch in the Crimean peninsula, in the year 81, the emancipation of a slave was held in the synagogue (ἐπὶ τῆς προσευχῆς). Further, the Talmud frequently speaks of court enactments and judicial activities being conducted in the synagogue buildings. It was probably not the prayer hall but a specially designated room that was used for these

[337] purposes; but as the center of social life, the synagogue was the suitable place for all such proclamations. R. Joshua b. Levi (third century) claimed for the sages and their disciples the right to make use of the synagogue building, and this was widely the practice in Palestine (Y. *Meg.* 3:4, 74a). A residence for the sexton was also often attached to the synagogue building. In Babylonia the side rooms were used as a hostel for travelers. But more important than all these was the use of the synagogue building as a school; from earliest times it was customary to attach to the synagogue rooms for teaching, so that school and synagogue came to be twin concepts.[44]

In the Middle Ages the synagogue became not only the Jews' place of worship but the actual center of all their community life. Therefore, the synagogue and its side rooms were used not only for conducting the affairs of the community, but, as in ancient times, also for proclamations and announcements of all kinds; often the government authorities demanded that proclamations be communicated there because this was the best guarantee that they would be fully publicized. The Jews were also required to swear their oaths in the synagogue. The synagogue had another peculiarly legal function: Anyone who believed that he had suffered an injustice for which the authorities had not provided satisfaction was entitled to interrupt the service and prevent its continuation until the injustice done to him had been redressed. Probably this right was sometimes abused, so that it was necessary to take severe steps against this practice. In the Middle Ages, as in antiquity, the school often found a home in the synagogue. In general this situation has obtained down to the present, the synagogue structure containing both the school and the community administration.[45]

§ 49 *Synagogue Construction*

(1)   It was not necessary to erect whole buildings for the purposes of public worship; a single room in which the congregation could perform their prayers undisturbed was enough. Especially in the Diaspora, private houses were probably first used in most cases for prayer assemblies, before the first synagogues were built. As to the shape of the building, the congregation had absolute freedom. The Mishnah does not contain even a single regulation as to the details of the building for public worship, and the Tosefta contains no more than two, one bearing on the building's location and the other on its orientation. As to location, it says that the synagogue should be built "at the city's highest point,"[1] and as for orientation, that the entrance should be on the eastern side,[2] with the congregation facing west (T. *Meg.* 4:22–23).

The Bible says that in the upper chamber of the house where Daniel prayed, the windows faced Jerusalem (Dan. 6:11). On the basis of this, a baraita prescribes for private prayer that in the Diaspora one should face the Holy Land; in Palestine, one should face Jerusalem; in Jerusalem, the Temple; and in the Temple, the Holy of Holies, so that the entire Jewish people face the same spot in prayer (B. *Ber.* 30a).[3] The Mishnah, too (*Ber.* 4:4), presupposes this rule, but, as mentioned, only in connection with the prayer of the individual; nowhere does it speak of the orientation of the synagogue.

[338]

(2)   In the absence of any literary documents concerning the character and construction of synagogues, great importance attaches to the form of the extant remains of synagogue buildings from antiquity. Here we must turn first to the eleven synagogue ruins in the Galilee,[4] whose constantly deteriorating vestiges were excavated minutely ten years ago by a mission of the *Deutsche Orientgesellschaft*. As to the results of their study, we have for the time being only a provisional survey [see supplementary material, below, pp. 345–350], but this is sufficient for our purposes. The synagogues are near the Sea of Galilee, around the cities Meron, Tiberias, and Capernaum. The main outcome of the study was that the plan of construction has been determined, and that all the ruins have a single ground plan: a broad nave with a row of columns on three or four sides, bearing a gallery.

Of the largest of these synagogues, that of Tel Ḥūm, the ancient Capernaum, the survey says:

Of the outer walls of the structure, whose area is 18x25m, only little has been preserved, but this little is enough to show that all the external walls were divided by pilasters, that the southern wall was broken by one main gate and two secondary gates, and the eastern wall, by a side door. This side door led to a court paved with large stones, the eastern and northern boundaries of which could not be determined. On its southern side and in front of the synagogue facade lay a porch 3.3m in width and nearly 2m in height, which was ascended on the western side by four steps and, on the east, by fourteen. That the unroofed porch had a narrow parapet may only be deduced from traces of its base. The area was on a west-to-east slope; the eastern part of the porch and the eastern court stood on a firm base of hewn stones as high as three meters above the outer level. In front of the two staircases begins a pavement of basalt stones leading, apparently, from the eastern staircase to the Sea of Galilee, about 80m distant from the synagogue.

On the inside, a colonnade on a raised stylobate surrounding the synagogue on three sides has been determined. The pedestals of the columns with the bases attached to them are mostly still in place. Originally there were six square foundations for each of the full columns on the eastern and western sides and two for the columns on the north, while at the corners formed by the junction of the northern row of columns with those of the east and west stood special corner pedestals for pilasters with attached half-columns. The floor of the colonnade, 3.5m in width, is at the same level as the floor of the 8m-wide nave. Both were paved with large sandstones. The long walls were accompanied by two rows of benches; the upper one, where it met the side walls and the sides of the eastern door, ended with a stone cushion. The cushion on the south-western corner has been preserved: its end is shaped like a head.

For the building's internal construction, monolithic sandstone pillars were found, 3.74m in length; Corinthian capitals were found and architraves with frieze attached, nearly 3m in length, belonging to a lower row of columns. Pillars of a somewhat smaller diameter, capitals with torus and scotia belonging to them, and matching architraves originated from an upper row of columns. The depressions for beams on the rear of the architraves show that the colonnade had two stories. Thus the central nave was surrounded on three sides by a balcony.

[339]

The pieces of the splendidly worked wall-architecture seem to have come from the walls of the balconies. These walls were composed of pilasters with Attic bases and Corinthian capitals, a richly ornamented frieze whose corner molding protruded above the half-columns, forming a cornice with a cyma. In the numerous frieze-fragments, which have in part been well preserved, various decorations are visible in the circular troughs, closed by thickets of acanthus: leaves, buds of all kinds, rosettes, stones, pentagrams, and hexagrams, two kinds of grape-clusters, and pomegranates. Fragments of the frieze found near the northern wall contain the front parts of animals—lions or sheep—leaping out of acanthus leaves, but these have unfortunately been purposely broken off. On the cyma, decorated with acanthus and palm fronds, a row of figures has been preserved: two eagles bearing a garland in their beaks, and a porpoise.

Many smaller building stones apparently originated in the aedicula-type decoration of the inner southern wall. To it belong parts of a gable, two to three conch-shells that were arrayed inside the gable, and above which stretched in an arc a frieze of animals as well as little twisted pillars with Corinthian capitals. This may also be the source of the remnants of the colored plaster decorations found near the building facade.

The figures portrayed on the three lintels can only be guessed from their outlines: above the central gate an eagle and Erotes bearing garlands, and above the side gates, four- and two-legged animals between palm trees. In the center of the western lintel was a vase, and in the center of the eastern lintel a wreath probably borne by an eagle. To the main gate belong two door consoles, which on the facade side bear a decorative palm tree. Above, on one side, is a window originally roofed over by a gable with conches and closed with lattice-work. As the upper conclusion of the facade, apparently a large gable served, whose horizontal, richly decorated beams ended with an arch in the Roman-Syrian style. The animals bounding out of the acanthus leaves have all been cut away.

[At a little distance to the north of Capernaum was the Jewish city Khorazin, where another synagogue, one of the most splendid of those in the Galilee, has been discovered. This synagogue was first surveyed and described by Kohl and Watzinger at the beginning of the century; partial excavations were performed by the Department of Antiquities of the Mandate in 1926 and later by the antiquities division of the Office of Education and Culture. Like the other Galilean synagogues, its facade also faces south. The length of the building is 20m, and its width is 13m. Two rows of columns and the corner column in every row divide the building into a central nave 6.6m in width and two aisles, each 3.2m in width. Two columns in the north of the hall create a third aisle, as in Capernaum. Around the building's walls, except for the southern wall, stone benches were built. On the building's southern facade there were three openings, and in front of them an elevated terrace approached by steps. On the western and eastern sides of the building there were annexed rooms. Especially important is a small room, 3x3m in dimension, adjacent to the northwest corner of the building. In this room steps were discovered, apparently leading to a women's gallery in the balcony over the columns. Unlike the synagogue of Capernaum, [340] which was built of hard, light-colored limestone, the synagogue of Khorazin was built of black local basalt.

In the debris of the building many decorated stones were found, by which the building's interior decoration and that of its facade may be reconstructed. It seems that the wall of the balcony was decorated with a frieze on which were geometric and floral subjects, and images of men and beasts. On one of the fragments of the frieze, a harvest scene is depicted: A man stands with a staff in his raised right hand and a heavy grape cluster in his left; a man and a woman are sitting with a grape cluster suspended between them. On other stones are depicted a medusa, an animal suckling two cubs, and a battle between a centaur and a lion. In the building rubbish a statue of a lion was discovered, perhaps one of those that guarded the ark, and a Moses throne, both made of basalt. Over the throne is inscribed:

דכיר לטב יודן בר ישמעל
דעבד הדן סטוה
ודרגוה בפעלה יהי
לה חולק עם צדיקים

"May Judah b. Ishmael be remembered for good,
who contributed this colonnade
and its stairs from his property. May
he have a portion with the righteous."

Apparently, the facade decoration of the Khorazin synagogue was similar to that of Capernaum.

Another synagogue, also a magnificent one, was discovered in Kefar Barʿam. This building is smaller than those of Capernaum and Khorazin. Its dimensions are 13.95x18.10m, and its facade is also oriented to the south. The inside of the hall is here divided into a central nave and four aisles, as against the three in the above synagogues. Against the building's facade stood a portico supported by two rows of six columns. (According to an available plan of the synagogue, the portico had one row of six columns across the front and two columns on the sides—*Engl. transl.*) The portico was roofed with a gable with an arch in its center (Syrian gable). On the southern wall of the building were three doors with decorated lintels and an arch rising above the middle door. The lintel of this door was decorated with a garland bound in a Hercules knot. Next to the garland were two figures that have been purposely destroyed, as was done at Capernaum. (In Khorazin the figures were not destroyed; hence, scholars conjecture that this synagogue was destroyed by an earthquake before the Jews were taken by the spirit of religious fanaticism around the middle of the fourth century C.E., after the persecutions of the period of the Gallus rebellion.)

In the synagogues surveyed above and in the other Galilean synagogues there was no fixed place for the ark. Scholars conjecture that in this period, the third and fourth centuries C.E., the ark was a portable wooden structure. After the congregants entered the building by way of the doors on the southern side (which was also the orientation of prayer) and took their places on the benches built along the building's walls, they would bring the ark, which had been kept in a side room (perhaps the room on the northwestern corner of the building in Capernaum and Khorazin), and set it up in front of the middle door in the southern wall. At the end of the service, before the congregation left, they would apparently return the ark to the little room where it was kept.

During the third and fourth centuries there existed in Palestine a type of synagogue on a different plan from that of the Galilean synagogues. Scholars call these *synagogues of the transitional type*, or *of the transitional period*, because they are seen as a transitional type from the Galilean synagogues, which lacked a fixed place for the ark, and the later synagogues of the fifth to seventh centuries, in which an apse was provided for this purpose. The outstanding example of a synagogue of the transitional type is the synagogue of Beth Shearim. The core of this synagogue is a long hall with two rows along the length, lending it the form of a basilica. The dimensions of this hall are 15x35m. Archaeologists discern in this building two stages of construction and use. When it was built, in the first half of the third century, its facade faced Jerusalem and had three doors, as was customary in the Galilean synagogues. This synagogue did not have a fixed place for the ark, but in its northern part, opposite the door, there was a bema, upon which, as the scholars believe, part of the prayer rite was held. The congregants would sit on the benches along the long walls of the hall. From the decorative fragments discovered in the building's debris, it seems that this synagogue was not inferior to the Galilean synagogues. At the beginning of the fourth century the synagogue's plan was altered. The middle door in the southern facade was closed up and a niche was set in front of it, in which the scholars conjecture that an ark was permanently placed.

The synagogue of Eshtemoa, south of Hebron, is also assigned to this type. This synagogue is a broadhouse, 21.3x13.3m in dimension. The entrance to the building was in the eastern wall, while in the northern wall, which faced Jerusalem, a niche was set for the ark. Lampstands were set in two smaller niches on each side of the ark niche.

It seems that a fixed place was set for the ark also in the synagogues of Arbel, Hamath

Tiberias, and Ḥusifa (Isfiya on Mount Carmel), which also belong to the transitional type. The last two synagogues also had mosaics.

The synagogue discovered in recent years in Sardis in Asia Minor indicates that a synagogue built according to the plan of the Beth Shearim synagogue is not an isolated phenomenon. Mr. G. Barkai, a student of the author of these notes, proposed in a recent study that this group of synagogues is not to be seen as a transitional type devised in search of a better solution to orientation and fixing of a permanent place for the ark, but rather that the source of this plan is to be sought in the Diaspora, and that perhaps these synagogues were erected by Diaspora Jews who came to Palestine. In connection with Beth Shearim, where many Diaspora Jews were buried, this conjecture seems reasonable. Analyzing the conduct of the service in the synagogue of Sardis, Mr. Barkai comes to the conclusion that the orientation of the service itself was toward the main facade of the building—that is, toward Jerusalem, while the elders would sit in a semicircular colonnade in the wall opposite the entry. In front of the colonnade was an elevated bema for the reading of the Torah. The congregants would sit on benches along the walls. At first they would turn their heads toward the direction of prayer, later to the place of the Torah reading and where the elders sat. The synagogue of Sardis was built at the end of the second century C.E. East of the building is a large court, 20x20m in dimension. Three doors lead from the court to the interior of the basilica, which was 63x20m. The building was completely covered with marble, its columns were marble, and their capitals were decorated with seven-branched lampstands. The whole floor of the synagogue is paved with splendid mosaics. The synagogue is in the midst of excavation now, and doubtless many conceptions that we hold in connection with the construction and plans of Palestinian synagogues are destined to change.

At the end of the fourth century mosaic floors were first provided for the synagogues in Palestine. This phenomenon became a regular one in the fifth and sixth centuries. The synagogues decorated with mosaic belong to the late type. Their characteristics are an entry into the building that is on the wall opposite the one facing Jerusalem, an elevated bema and an apse as a fixed place for the ark in the wall facing Jerusalem, and the floor of the central nave and the aisles decorated with mosaic. In general, the construction of the later synagogues is poorer than that of the early ones; hence, in most cases only the mosaic floor and a little of the walls have been preserved.

Several types of decorations can be distinguished in the later synagogues: (1) depictions of a biblical scene, the wheel of the zodiac, the seasons of the year, the ark, and a seven-branched candelabrum; (2) the ark, candelabrum, and wheel of the zodiac together with subjects from the animal world, and floral and geometric decorations. In this last category it is not necessary for all the subjects to occur together, but sometimes only a few are found.

Among the biblical scenes we find the binding of Isaac (Beth Alpha), Daniel in the lion's den (Naaran), and the exit from Noah's ark (Gerasa, in the Transjordan). All these images are connected with acts of rescue.

We now describe some of the most important mosaic floors. One of the fullest depictions is found in the synagogue of Beth Alpha in Kibbutz Ḥefẓi Bah. The synagogue is entered by a door that was opened in the western wall of a large court surrounded by a wall. Two entrances lead from the outer court to the narrow narthex. The court and inner narthex were paved with crude mosaics. Three entrances lead from the inner court to the

[342]

basilica, which is 14x28m in dimension. Next to the entrance, inside the hall, there is a dedicatory inscription in Aramaic, the first two lines of which help to determine the date of the mosaic: "(This mos)aic was set in the year (. . . of the r)eign of King Justin." Since two emperors bore this name, the mosaic may have been made in the time of Justin I (518–527) or Justin II (565–578). In a second inscription, in Greek, located beside the first one, the builders Marianus and Hanina his son, who did the work, are commemorated. Next to the inscriptions are a lion and an ox.

On the first panel in the nave the binding of Isaac is depicted. The depiction goes from left to right: two boys and the donkey; the ram caught in the thicket, with the inscription "Lo, a ram" above it; Abraham with a knife in his right hand and Isaac in his left, with the inscriptions "Abraham" and "Isaac" above them; the altar, with flames leaping up from it; the sky with palm trees, from which a hand is emerging, and above it the inscription "Do not send."

A chart in the middle portion of the floor depicts the twelve signs of the zodiac, each with its symbol and name in Hebrew. In the center of the chart is a medallion in which Helios, the god of the sun, drives a chariot harnessed to four horses. In the four corners of the panel are the four seasons, portrayed as young women, each season with its fruits and its name alongside it. "The season of Tishre," "The season of Tevet," "The season of Nisan," and "The season of Tammuz." The seasons are not arranged alongside the corresponding constellations.

The third panel, near the apse, has a splendid ark in its center. In an arch over it, an eternal light may be seen, and beside it two lions guarding the ark and two seven-branched lampstands with their lamps lit. Beside each lampstand is a ram's horn and an incense shovel, a palm branch, and a citron. It is nearly certain that this part of the panel was meant to depict the ark and its decorations as the artist saw them in this very synagogue. To stress the realism of the depiction, the artist added on the ends of the panel the open curtain, revealing the whole scene.

All around the floor are geometric designs and scenes of wildlife: various birds, animals, and twining vines.

As stated, the dedication inscription in the mosaic floor fixes the date of the Beth Alpha synagogue as the beginning of the sixth century. Nearly two hundred years earlier is the synagogue of Hamath Tiberias, which was discovered and excavated a few years ago. The place of the biblical scene is taken by the many dedicatory inscriptions in Greek. In the center of the floor is a medallion with Helios riding the sun chariot, surrounded by the wheel of the zodiac. Here, too, the names of the constellations are in Hebrew, but it seems that the artist was not versed in this language, and one of the inscriptions, Aquarius, came out backwards. That the artist was not Jewish is also indicated by the fact that the boy holding the balance is uncircumcised. In the corners of the zodiac wheel the seasons are depicted. In the southern part of the mosaic the ark is depicted, with lampstands and holiday symbols beside it. In its details this depiction is not different from the one on the floor in Beth Alpha, but the quality of the workmanship is considerably better than that in the floor of the village settlement, and it may be conjectured that the mosaic artists who made the floor in Hamath Tiberias came from Antioch in Syria, which at that time—the fourth century—was one of the leading centers of mosaic art in the Roman empire.

After the destruction of the synagogue in the fourth century another synagogue was built in its place in the fifth. This synagogue too was paved with mosaic, but the main subjects of this floor were geometric figures and animals.

Another synagogue in the north of the country is the one of Beth Shean, also recently discovered. Here a synagogue was first built in the fourth to fifth centuries. This synagogue too is a basilica with an apse in the wall facing west, even though Beth Shean lies north of Jerusalem. It seems that the builders followed the practice customary in the Transjordan, where most of the synagogues faced west, even if that was not the direction of Jerusalem. Perhaps the reason is that Beth Shean formerly belonged to the Decapolis, all of whose cities with the exception of Beth Shean were east of the Jordan.

Of the original floor few fragments remain, so it cannot be determined how they were decorated. In the fifth to sixth centuries, the synagogue was renovated and the mosaic floor rebuilt. East of the building was an inner court paved with mosaics in geometric patterns. [343] Here, too, the floor of the central nave was divided into three fields. In the two eastern fields there is a combination of geometric and vegetal patterns, while in the third field, next to the apse, an ark is depicted standing within a temple, with two lampstands at its sides, and with a ram's horn and an incense shovel beside each lampstand. This synagogue was renovated in the sixth century and existed until the seventh century. According to the testimony of the inscription, the renovation of the mosaic was done by Marianus and Hanina, the artisans who made the mosaic of Beth Alpha. The building was surrounded with many annex rooms, which probably served for Torah study and as guest accommodations.

Completely different in its decorations from these synagogues is the one in Maʿon (today near Nirim in the northwest Negev). This synagogue was discovered by accident about ten years ago. The building's dimensions are 11.8x14.8m, and it is oriented to the northeast, facing Jerusalem. The southern portion of the building and its aisles are paved with stone slabs, but the main portion of the decoration is in the central nave. The western half of the floor was mostly destroyed at the time of its discovery by a bulldozer that was clearing a path at the site. But the remaining northern portion permits its complete reconstruction. On the southern borders of the floor, a jar is depicted, with two peacocks at its two sides. From the jar extends a twisting vine, which forms fifty-six medallions arranged in five rows. On the four side rows, there are alternating birds and beasts of various kinds, while in the middle row there are baskets of fruit, goblets, laying hens, and so forth. Only the north side of the floor next to the apse shows that this is a synagogue floor. Here, between two tall palm trees, is a seven-branched lampstand, flanked by a ram's horn and a palm branch. Beside the branches of the lampstand stand two fearsome lions. Outside the panel, opposite the apse, is a dedication inscription in Aramaic, commemorating all the members of the congregation.

Scholars have dated this synagogue in the sixth century. For the time being, its floor is unique in its decoration among Palestinian synagogues. A close analogue to this floor is found in the mosaic of the church of Shellal, near Nirim, and it is not impossible that a single artisan made both floors.

The latest synagogue in Palestine, according to the scholars, is that of Jericho, the decorations of which are lacking in depictions of men and beasts. This small building was discovered many years ago not far from Tel es-Sultan, the mound of ancient Jericho. The building is a small basilica, 10x13m in dimension. The nave and aisles were paved with mosaic. By the entrance to the nave there is an Aramaic dedication inscription:

דכירן לטב יהוי דכרונהון לטב כל
קהלה קד(י)שה רביה וזעוריה דסייע
יתהון מלכיה דעלמה ואתחזקון ועבדון
פסיפסה דידע שמתהון ודבניהון ודאנשי
בתיהון יכתוב יתהון בספר חיים (עם)
צדיקיה חברין לכל ישראל שלום (אמן סלה) .

"... remembered for good. May all this holy congregation be remembered for good, old and young, whom the King of the World helped so that they took strength and made the mosaic. May He Who knows their names and (the names) of their children and (the names) of their households write them in the Book of Life together with all the just. All Israel are comrades. (Amen, *sela.*)"

Most of the surface of the floor between the inscription and the apse is decorated with circles, squares, and other geometric patterns. Next to the apse is a circle in which a seven-branched lampstand is depicted, flanked by a ram's horn and an incense shovel; beneath them is the inscription שלום על ישראל, "Peace upon Israel." Between this circle and the apse is a depiction of a splendid ark standing on four feet, surmounted by a conch. From analysis of the form of the writing, the scholars believe that the synagogue was built in the eighth century.

Scholars have attempted to classify Palestinian synagogue mosaics according to their decorative subjects. According to this opinion, the earliest floors are those with geometric and simple vegetal decorations. Later came the subjects that include depictions of men and beasts; and at the end of the period there was a return to depictions without images of men or beasts. The new discoveries of recent years show that this conjecture is unfounded, and that apparently the manner of floor decoration was completely at the discretion of the builders of the synagogues.

[344]

In this survey we have reviewed the development of the synagogue from the third to the seventh–eighth centuries. From epigraphic evidence it is known that synagogues existed in Palestine even while the Temple was standing, but until recently no remnants at all had been discovered from that period. Recently a building was discovered on Masada that the excavators conjecture may have been a synagogue. This little building is situated in the northwest wall of the fortress. It is a kind of basilica with two rows of columns, three to a row. The entrance to the building is on the east, and it faces west. Along three of its walls are four-tiered benches. This was the state of the building in the time of Herod. At a later period, apparently at the time of the great revolt against the Romans, a little chamber was built in the northwest corner of the building. On the building's stone flooring many coins from the period of the rebellion were found, while in the wells dug in the floor, fragments of Deuteronomy and Ezekiel scrolls were found. According to the excavators, these finds strengthen the assumption that the building served as a synagogue during the rebellion, and perhaps even in the time of Herod. A similar building was discovered at Herodium, another fortress built in Herod's time. This building, too, shows signs of having been altered during the time it was in the hands of the rebels.]

Very important because it was well preserved and because it provides an example of the building style of the Diaspora is the synagogue ruin at Ḥammam-Lif,[5] ancient Naro, in North Africa, near Carthage at the foot of Jebel bu-Qairawan. From the ruins, the plan and organization of the extensive building can still be discerned. A French scholar describes it as follows:

The building forms an almost perfect square of about 20m per side. Apparently there was a side entrance in the middle of the southeast side at the farthest end of a long passage and an exit door on the northwest side; but the main facade, faced by a court, was situated in the southwest. The facade was decorated with two columns, above which a gable may be seen to be set. The monumental door led to a colonnade, which had a massive wall on its right and two small rooms on the left. Through the colonnade one could reach a rectangular vestibule, equal to it in width but not as deep. Left of the vestibule a small door led into a room; opposite the main entrance a large door connected the vestibule with the sanctuary. On the threshold was an inscription with the name of the donor of the mosaic. The actual sanctuary was a long rectangle about 10x6m in dimension. It displayed on the western side a rounded niche, reminiscent of the *mihrāb* of mosques. The floor was completely covered with mosaics, which were divided on the width-side into three fields of varying length. Near the entrance and in the background were depicted birds, quadrupeds, flowers, and fruits, the whole surrounded by boughs. The middle portion of the mosaic exceeded both of the others together in size. It, too, was divided into three parts arranged in the opposite direction—that is, according to length. At the top one could see a landscape with water, fish, and aquatic birds; below there was a pure landscape with palm trees shading a dish, on the handles of which two peacocks stood facing one another. In the middle section, within the framework of swallow-tails and between two seven-branched lampstands and other cultic objects, was a dedication inscription informing the worshipers that the sanctuary's mosaic floor had been made at the expense of a lady named Juliana.

In the northwest part of the sanctuary, but not connected to it, behind the niche, extended a large rectangular room facing outward. In the southwest corner of the sanctuary was an opening to a long passage that led into several halls, two on the left, three on the right. In the east wall, opposite the niche, three doors were broken through, leading to the same number of rooms. The first room served as a storage place for cultic objects and holy books; this is indicated by an inscription set in the mosaic floor.

Thus, the synagogue contained, apart from the annexes, about fifteen rooms grouped around the main entrance, a long passage, and the sanctuary. The purpose of most of the rooms is unknown. Many were decorated with mosaic. Besides the images already mentioned, remains with the following depictions have been found: seven-branched lampstands, various animals, lions, hyenas, roosters, partridges, guinea-fowl, ducks, fish, trees, and fruit baskets; also, the bust of a young man with long hair with a bent stick on his shoulder, the bust of a woman with a helmet bearing a spear, and more. In its motifs and the character of its decorations the synagogue of Naro recalls the African villas of the Roman Empire, and seems to hail from the third or fourth century of our era.

|345|

(3)   Let us add to this what is known from literary sources or synagogue inscriptions about synagogues of antiquity. We must think first of the descriptions sketched by the Talmud of the great *proseuche* in Alexandria (Philo: μεγίστη καὶ περισημοτόμη):

Whoever has not seen the double stoa of Alexandria has not seen the splendor of Israel. It was built like a great basilica, one row of columns within the other. Sometimes it held twice as many people as the troop that marched out of Egypt. Corresponding to the seventy-one elders in it, it had seventy-one thrones of gold set with gems and pearls, each one worth 250,000 (gold dinarii). In the middle was a wooden daïs . . ." (T. *Suk.* 4:6).[6]

Philo[7] complains that when in the time of Flaccus the *proseuchai* in Egypt were destroyed, the shields, golden wreaths, and stelae with inscriptions erected in honor of the emperor were also destroyed, and that without their περίβολοι, "sacred precincts," in which to place the signs of their gratitude, they had no opportunity to express their thanks to their benefactors. This same designation, περίβολοι, is used also for the forecourts of the synagogues in Phocaea[8] on the Ionian coast, where the woman who donated the synagogue and the περίβολος was honored with a golden tiara and the προεδρία. The Palestinian Talmud mentions a פרורה,[9] which is also a large courtyard next to the synagogue building. Finally, in Mantinea a πρόναος, "atrium," was donated for the synagogue.[9a]

(4)   The above descriptions of ancient ruins have much to teach us about the later development of synagogue construction. Most of the buildings mentioned are striking in their height. This recalls the precept of the Tosefta discussed earlier. It was not possible everywhere to build on a terrace. In such a case, Rav, who held a very strict opinion in this matter, at least with respect to Babylonia, demanded that the roofs of private houses not rise above that of the synagogue, and R. Ashi actually built a synagogue for the site of the academy Mata Mehasia that rose above all the buildings of the town (B. *Shab.* 11a). At a later time this law could not be observed, and already [346] the midrash reports that formerly, in olden times, the synagogues were tall buildings.[10] Where the church took pains to see that the Jews did not become presumptuous, it did not permit monumental synagogues; it complained particularly when Jewish houses of prayer stood out against neighboring churches,[11] which did occur here and there, even in the High Middle Ages.[12] The civil law was influenced by the outlook of the church and set all kinds of impediments to the construction of monumental synagogues. Nonetheless, the old precepts about the height of the building remained in force, and in the High Middle Ages the talmudists began to give thought to the problem of their unenforceability. Some required the Jewish owners of adjacent buildings to lower their premises; others found a justification in the fact that in northern Europe the roofs are not flat as they are in the Orient, and that from our sloping roofs one could not peer into the synagogue while working and thereby disturb the service. But we know of cases of outstanding authorities demanding the partial elevation of the synagogue, at least so that the garrets under the roofs of the surrounding houses not lie higher than the synagogue gables. In a non-Jewish environment it was impossible to put the talmudic precept strictly into practice; in both Christian and Muslim lands it was openly acknowledged that out of consideration for the ruling population it was necessary to renounce observing this particular law. In Poland, at least ca. 1650, it was customary to attach to the roof of the synagogue one beam rising above the residential houses; this custom went over into Germany and has been widely retained, though artistically executed, until the present day, even though the liturgical buildings of the present are not in need of this kind of elevation, thanks to their monumental form.

(5)   The orientation of the building-site was quite varied. The above-mentioned rule of the Tosefta that the entrance door should be set in the east and the building oriented toward the west is followed only in the ruins in Irbid.[12*] The Talmud never speaks of the orientation of the synagogue; for individual worship, here and there different directions are recommended, mostly toward the east.[13] Christendom early took over this practice,[14] which is observed to this day in church construction. Although no binding precept about this matter is mentioned, the custom must have arisen early to choose the direction of the Holy Land and to build the synagogues accordingly.[15] This was suggested by the example of Daniel, and the material in Solomon's prayer at the time of the dedication of the Temple (I Kgs. 8:44, 48) was so interpreted. Jerome testifies that it was the Jewish custom to pray in the direction of the Temple. Apion, too, mentions that the synagogues are situated facing east. The ruins of Hammam-Lif have their main facade facing southwest, so that the worshipers sat facing northeast—that is, in the direction of Jerusalem. Finally, it is to be noted that the Samaritans, too, pray in the direction of Mount Gerizim, and that in this, as in other religious customs, they follow Jewish institutions. Despite all this evidence there can be no doubt that the practice was not uniform. The Galilean ruins are, with one exception, oriented from south to north—that is, away from Jerusalem. It is hard to assume that this continues an older architectural principle or that the congregation sat facing the door; rather, the building plan for some buildings was obviously chosen out of consideration for how the building would look from a distance. In Capernaum and Khorazin the richly decorated facades   [347] dominated the Sea of Galilee[16] and afforded those sailing on it a most splendid view. Likewise one could enjoy the magnificent view from the terraces or through the opened doors. The ruins of Nabratein lie "on an outrunner of the hills of Safed on an especially beautiful site with a view of Lake Hula, the Jordan plain north of it, and the whole mighty Hermon range."[17] In Meron[18] the platform for the synagogue structure is hewn out of a small, steep peak of rock, which also affords a lovely view of the lake.

Custom decided in favor of orientation toward Jerusalem. At the same time, however, the precept remained in force that the entrance of the synagogue should be in the east. Maimonides codified this as formulated by Alfasi, but he does not attach the worshiper's orientation to it;[19] rather, he prescribes that the worshiper should face the ark, which should derive its location from the geographical location of the town. But in France and Germany[20] no attention was paid to the stipulations about the doors, and only the orientation toward Palestine was observed; the synagogues were built so that they lay toward the east with the entrance on the western wall. In the *Shulḥan ʿarukh* the two views are combined,[21] resulting in the stipulation that the entrance door must be located opposite the direction indicated by the location of the ark. The orientation toward the east generally observed in Europe was geographically not exact; Mordecai Jaffe therefore required a southeastern orientation, but although his demand was later renewed, the orientation remained toward the east. The building sites of the synagogues were very carefully marked out, often without regard to other advantages, in order to obtain an eastward orientation. The congregations were even less flexible than even the strictest rabbis, who, through studying the sources, did not read out any deviation from the tradition.

(6)   The number of doors leading into the synagogue must have varied greatly.

In the Galilean ruins we regularly find a main door in the center and two side doors,[22] and the midrash, too, mentions a middle door.[23] It is therefore not impossible that this was a standing arrangement, perhaps with symbolic significance. Alongside the doors on the entrance wall the ruins display side doors,[24] known also to the Talmud—פתחא אחרינא (B. *Sota* 39b)—which probably led into side rooms.

In Irbid the flooring is supposed to have lain much lower than the threshold of the entrance door.[25] Unless there was some particular reason for such an arrangement, we would be seeing here for the first time a case of the observation of the talmudic precept that, during prayer, one should stand in a low place so as to call out to God from the depths (see Ps. 130:1). According to the simple meaning of that passage (B. *Ber.* 10b), there can be no doubt that this rule applies only to individual worship in a private house. But in talmudic Babylonia, it was already taken into consideration, and the precentor stood at a lower spot than the congregation. In the Middle Ages, synagogues were so built that one had to descend into them by one or two steps;[26] only in the modern period is this tradition mostly overlooked.

(7)   The floors of the Galilean synagogue ruins are nearly always covered with simple stone paving.[27] Only in Umm al-Amad was it covered with a simple mosaic of limestone cubes, and at Hammam-Lif and Pontus a rich and artistic mosaic decoration has been discovered.[28] Here the Diaspora seems to have adopted Greek taste, while in Palestine the stricter view interdicting mosaic was generally followed, though the Temple in Jerusalem had an artistic pavement. In Babylonia there was no reservation even about a stone pavement—רצפה של אבנים (B. *Meg.* 22b), for it was considered forbidden to prostrate oneself (השתחויה) on such; and where this was done it was explained away as an inauthentic form of prostration.[29] In the end, caution reached the point that even prostration on a wood floor was avoided. In Germany, where the custom prevailed of prostration during the ʿAvoda on the Day of Atonement, mats were spread,[30] even straw in poor regions, to avert any appearance of prostration on the floor itself.

(8)   The inner space as a rule had the rectangular form of a Roman basilica.[31] The Talmud calls the *proseuche* in Alexandria בסיליקי, and the Galilean ruins as well as those of Hammam-Lif all have the sanctuary in the form of a lengthened rectangle. In the Galilean ruins, columns run along the two long sides, usually along the third side as well, so that a complete ambulatory is present, and the space is divided into a wide central nave and two narrower side naves. The division into three naves is retained in most synagogues, even in Kai-Fung-Fu. In Galilee remains of a double row of columns are usually preserved,[32] and probably the colonnade was surrounded by a gallery. In plan and style the ancient synagogues betray the influence of Roman monumental construction.[33] The execution and organization of the facade, the arrangement of the portals, the placement and working-out of the columns, the shaping and decoration of the gables reflect the common usage of the empire. In certain details—for example, the particular formation of the Ionic capitals[34]—specifically Jewish influence may be recognized. This union of foreign and native may be seen as a basic rule of synagogue construction in all ages.[35] The effort was generally directed at erecting as beautiful and dignified a synagogue as the community's needs permitted. Hostile legislation saw to it that they would not be too splendid. For architectural style the dominant taste of

the environment was always decisive, but deviations were made in detail in favor of tradition and the characteristic shape of the synagogue. A typical example is provided by the synagogue in Worms.[36] Its oldest component (completed in 1034) is in Romanesque style, like the synagogue built ca. 1100 in Speyer.[37] The annexed part in Worms from 1213 already shows the influence of early Gothic. The still extant Spanish synagogues[38] are built in Moorish style, but with marked deviations that imply a very happy development of art among the Jews of Spain. In the Orient the synagogues often recall the *qubba* of the Muslims,[39] the chapels built over graves that serve pilgrims as sites of devotion. Thus it was in every age: Synagogues were built in the style prevailing in that country at that time, and every possible exertion was made to achieve the highest possible degree of artistic perfection. Especially telling in this regard are the wooden synagogues of Poland and Russia,[40] which have recently been the object of attention; these also show a more or less noticeable affinity with the general style of construction of the local churches. They are also conclusive proof that even where no artistic influence flowed from the environment, great value was laid on the careful execution of the place of worship.

[349]

In the modern period numerous new congregations have formed in the great cities, which have willingly offered rich resources for the building of synagogues. In most countries the legal limitations have vanished, and architects can let their artistic inclinations guide them without hindrance. Thus, in all parts of the globe, splendid synagogues have arisen, many of which do honor to their surroundings. No typical style of synagogue construction has yet emerged; depending on whatever style was fashionable, a Moorish, Byzantine, Gothic, Romanesque, or classical architectural style—or an eclectic style—was used. A new phenomenon in modern synagogue buildings is their decoration with one or several domes, which sometimes serve to increase the building's height. Their appropriateness for the synagogues' interiors must be decided by specialists; but for worship they are usually a disturbance, as they noticeably affect the acoustics.

(9)   According to talmudic precept, one should only pray in a house with windows (B. *Ber.* 31a),[41] something that could not be taken for granted in the houses of antiquity and in the Orient. It seems logical that this rule applies also to synagogues, and in fact it has generally been so interpreted. In the ruins, recesses for windows have frequently been preserved. In the Zohar,[42] twelve windows are required for a synagogue; the *Shulḥan ʿarukh* recommends the same number, a recommendation that has often been followed in the last centuries. But in antiquity some synagogues had no windows; instead, they were without roofs, so that prayer was held under the open sky. R. Ami and R. Assi in Tiberias (300) liked to pray in their houses of study, which were not roofed—ביני עמודי (B. *Ber.* 8a). Epiphanius also reports that the Samaritans, following the example of the Jews, hold their services under the open sky in sunny spots.[43] Roofless synagogues are attested in the Orient in every century. Maimonides ruled that windows were not even necessary for a synagogue,[44] for the talmudic precept related only to individual worship, and was intended as an enhancement of devotion. In the seventeenth century Pietro dalla Valle relates that in Aleppo the service as a rule was held in the synagogue court,[45] which was surrounded by colonnades, and that a hall was used only in rainy or cold weather.[46] Ḥayim Y.D. Azulai (d. 1806) also knew still of unroofed synagogues in Jerusalem, which were sanctioned even by the strictest rabbis.[47]

[350]

(10)   The Galilean synagogues stand out for their rich and abundant ornaments on the columns, friezes, door jambs, and gables.[48] Among them are the characteristic Jewish ornaments like the seven-branched lampstand, vine leaves and grapes, pomegranates, palm leaves and branches, goblets and oil vessels, pentagrams and hexagrams. Surprising are the many pictorial representations of animals and even here and there human heads, which are found in all ruins, even those from Galilee. Quite typically the figures have been mutilated, almost without exception. Whether the vandalism is to be traced to Jewish or Muslim fanatics cannot be determined. As things are, even the Jews must be owned capable of such; according to the opinion that has become current, the ornaments offended Jewish religious beliefs. Actually, this doctrine was never taught in such severity, and synagogues were never without figurative depictions. "The fable of the synagogue's hatred for all art down to the Middle Ages and the modern period must fade away in the face of the facts of life and the testimony of literature." With the end of the fear that the depictions would be the objects of idolatrous adoration, the Jewish distaste for artistic imitation also ended. Forbidden only were human figures, the cherubim and the combined animal figures that Ezekiel had seen in the divine throne-chariot; all other ornaments, plant and animal figures, whether represented in painted or plastic form, could be produced without disturbance. Thus Ephraim b. Joseph (twelfth century) permitted the painting of synagogues with animal figures like birds and horses. The windows of the synagogue of Cologne were then adorned with stained-glass paintings of lions and snakes, and that of Meissen with trees and birds. Lions, especially, are represented at all times in synagogue decoration in the most varied forms, whether in painting, embroidery, or plastic. Against the freer practice stood an opinion of Maimonides, who did not actually prohibit the pictorial decoration of synagogues, but who personally followed the practice of closing his eyes whenever he prayed facing a wall decorated with pictures, because he feared being distracted by it. This raised fears in the hearts of anxious souls, so that individual rabbis even prohibited the painting of the walls with leaves, flowers, and trees. But the examples of such decorations were too numerous and too well known, so that even where new ornamentation was declared prohibited, the old was tolerated. They were preserved even in regions and centuries that are generally considered dark and hostile to culture. Johann Christoff Wagenseil knows of flowers, palm branches, pictures of the Temple in Jerusalem, Hebrew prayers and biblical verses, and similar decorations as being widespread in synagogues in Germany. Even more telling are the reports from some of the above-mentioned wooden synagogues of Poland. In one of them there are, to be sure, no paintings; but on the ark and on the balustrade of the women's gallery there are even animal heads in bas-relief. In another, the walls are decorated with prayers and biblical verses, which, however, are all surrounded by paintings, among which all kinds of birds and animals are not lacking.[49] Under the influence of talmudists hostile to art, the decoration of synagogues had become in the last century rather monotonous; decoration with biblical verses and prayers, with memorial tablets for benefactors, or meaningless patterns became general. The improvement of taste in the modern period and the richer architectural form of the synagogues have brought more variety into the ornamentation, but as for the appropriate subjects, the artists are mostly in great confusion. A model of artistic decoration of synagogue walls and windows with motifs that are completely in the spirit of the Jewish religion is provided by the new synagogue in Szegedin in Hungary.[50]

(11)   A characteristic form is lent the interior structure of the synagogue of today by the women's section, which is usually located on a gallery.[51] This was not always so, for old synagogues have the space for the women behind that for the men on the same floor. The question arises as to what is exactly the status of the separation of the sexes in the service. It cannot have originated in the institution of the Court of Women (עזרת נשים) in the Temple, for that court served only to bound the area that the women were permitted to enter; it did not belong exclusively to women, for men could also stay in it, and actually had to use it as a passage if they wanted to gain access to the sacrificial altar. Only on one occasion was the separation of the sexes strictly enforced: On the feast of the Drawing of Water (שמחת בית השואבה),[52] the female spectators had to take their places on special platforms (גזוזטרא or ἐξῶστρα)—not so as to keep apart from the men but only to protect them from the extravagant behavior anticipated due to the exuberant joy of the festival. At the service of the synagogue the women originally took part as members of the congregation with full rights.[53] In the most ancient period there was no objection to a woman reading from the Torah, and only later was it prohibited, out of consideration for the congregation. The sources repeatedly report that women attended liturgical gatherings; on the other hand, nowhere do they mention that women had to stay in a separate area. From antiquity it is reported only of the Therapeutai that their prayer rooms were provided with a double wall,[54] the inner one being three or four cubits above the floor to serve as a partition between men and women. The Mishnah knows nothing of this; it knows only of a separate area for lepers. When one of these attends the synagogue an enclosure is thrown up for him; he must enter first and be the last to leave (*Negaʿim*), a regulation that makes perfect sense on hygienic grounds. But of a permanent separation of women, the Mishnah knows nothing. Nor does the Talmud know of the women's gallery. It reports that Abaye had earthenware jars and Rava had dried-out reed staves set out to separate women and men, so as to prevent them from being alone together (B. *Qid.* 81a).[55] From this it follows that even in the synagogues in Babylonia, which were certainly run according to the strictest principles, there were, as in the ancient Christian churches,[56] separate rows of places for men and women, but that these were very close to each other. It must have been the same everywhere. Therefore when we find special galleries with rows of seats in synagogue ruins both in the Galilee and in Ḥammam-Lif,[57] it may not be unjustified to suppose these to be places for women; but we cannot be absolutely certain that these ancient synagogues had women's galleries.

In the Orient, in general, it was probably unusual for women to frequent the service; therefore, Maimonides, in the section on synagogue construction, cites no stipulations about the places for women. It was different in the West. Here, women attended the synagogues in great numbers especially when there was to be a sermon. Respected teachers like Rashi spoke out against degrading or insulting women.[58] R. Eleazar b. Joel Halevi of Bonn (ca. 1200) reports that on the Sabbath before there was to be a sermon, curtains were spread between the seats of men and women, permitting the conclusion that the seats were in the same room.[59] Gradually the transition was made, probably because of insufficient space, to building a separate hall onto the synagogue for women (בית כנסת של נשים). In Worms,[60] for example, the men's synagogue dates from the year 1034, while the one for women was erected only in 1213. In the Prague Altneuschul,[61] the women's synagogue forms an annex; the examples of the few remaining old syna-

[351]

gogues can be multiplied. The rooms for women lay close to the synagogue or a little higher and were connected with the men's rooms by balustrades[62] or windows. The elevation evolved in the course of time into a whole story; the separation, too, became stricter in the course of the Middle Ages, with thick grating or glass panels provided and curtains blocking the view of the worshiping women; and the complete separation was believed to be a strict religious commandment. In most cases the galleries had an adverse effect on the architectural structure of the synagogue, but there are also examples, as in the Portuguese synagogue in Venice,[62*] where the installation of the women's gallery is what lent the architecture of the building its full artistic perfection.

In the modern period, a fundamental change occurred in connection with the building of the women's gallery. In modern synagogues the grating has been completely removed, which has often led to violent battles,[63] for in the course of time people had come to believe that a religious basis and reliable authorities could be found even for the height and thickness of the grating. Even in places where there was a desire to observe the tradition as much as possible, the separation of the women's gallery was ameliorated considerably and the gratings metamorphosed into artistic decoration. In the Berlin Reform congregation, the women's gallery was removed from the first, and a section in the lower floor of the synagogue, the only one, was set aside for the women. In Europe this example found only isolated imitation, but in America the new arrangement was taken over with great approval, and synagogues with women's galleries are in the minority in the New World.[64] Wise introduced family pews, after the model of the Christian churches, and since then men and women sit together in many American Reform congregations. Naturally, the partitioning and architecture of the synagogues has undergone great change as a result of this innovation.

(12)   Besides the sanctuary, all synagogue ruins include several side rooms. In Hammam-Lif their number is so great that the building could satisfy the most varied needs of the community and probably was used also for meetings, and for administrative and instructional purposes; one room served for storing ritual objects. In the Galilean synagogues,[65] we find broad terraces with places for sitting and splendid vistas that served for the community's relaxation. Around the synagogues there was often a promenade enclosed by columns, the double-stoa (דיפלסטון) also mentioned in rabbinic texts.[66] In the halls, places for sitting were installed, as in the Roman Exedra (אכסדרא),[67] where the congregation spent their leisure time. Sometimes only a few columns were found at the entrance, forming a vestibule (πρόναος, "atrium"), a room still found in the present-day synagogue, and which in the Middle Ages in Germany was called *Polisch*.[68] In the halls there were often plaques of honor and memorial tablets for the lords of the land and the benefactors of the community.[69] As still exists today, there was also found in ancient times in the synagogue vestibule or in the court enclosed by columns, a basin (called גורנה),[70] at which the faithful washed before prayer; it is interesting that on a papyrus from the year 113 there is a bill for the heavy use of water in the synagogue of Thebans in Upper Egypt.[71] From the oldest Christian basilicas, which follow fairly exactly the manner of construction and the arrangements of the synagogues,[72] much can be learned about the character of the Jewish houses of worship in antiquity. Most of the component parts of the ancient buildings have survived into the present, insofar as that was possible given the changes of building style.

§ 50   *The Furnishing of the Synagogue*   [353]

(1)   The inner furnishings of the synagogue were at first very simple, consisting only of a single object: the shrine containing the Torah scrolls. Like Noah's ark, this is called תיבה (M. *Ta.* 2:1, *Meg.* 3:1), more fully תיבה של ספרים (T. *Yad.* 2:12), Aramaic תיבותא (Y. *Ber.* 5:4, 9c), Greek κιβωτός (LXX Gen. 6:14).[1] The ark was made of wood; when it wore out, a new one was built out of the undamaged remains (B. *Meg.* 26b). It was portable, and was carried out to the marketplace for prayer assemblies on fast days (M. *Ta.* 2:1). It probably stood in place in the synagogues only during the service, and at other times behind a curtain in a side room.[2] The most ancient synagogues did not have a "sanctuarium,"[3] but the direction of prayer was determined by the place where the ark stood. The precentor stood before it (§53), and the biblical scrolls lay on it when being read.[4] The word תיבה later came to mean the place where the precentor stood,[5] but it continued long in use as the term for the shrine, especially in Babylonia. Thus we find it in Amram, and from there it was taken over into *Vitry.*

In the Tosefta (*Meg.* 4:21), the place where the Scriptures are kept is called קדש, "Sanctuarium."[6] It may be that this term already denotes the niche in the wall known in the church as *apse*[7] and in the mosque as *miḥrāb*, and which is found in the ruins of Khorazin and Hammam-Lif. Or perhaps קדש is merely short for ארון הקדש, as the ark is called to this day. ארון is the biblical name for the ark of the covenant; hence, in popular usage, the ark was called ארנא. At the end of the second century the use of this designation was declared a capital sin (B. *Shab.* 32a),[8] but this did not prevent the Palestinian Talmud from regularly calling the ark ארונא (without qualification). The expression ארון continued in later usage among Italian, French, and German Jews, to some extent alongside תיבה, while among Spanish and Oriental Jews the usual word was היכל, which in the Solomonic Temple designated the sanctuary.

In the oldest Roman synagogues of Germany, the ark was still in the form of a niche built into the wall. Because the Torah scrolls were damaged by the moistness of the walls, wooden boxes were introduced,[9] and these came to be so customary that by 1200 the ark built into the wall was no longer known. Later the ark was also made of marble. The "Holy Ark" stood by the wall facing Jerusalem and it determined the orientation of the synagogue. But in some synagogues in the East—for example, in Constantinople—the ark was set on the south or north side, and therefore the eastward orientation was not adhered to even during prayer. Later, the emigré rabbis from Spain decided to place the precentor's desk on the eastern side, so that the congregation no longer faced the ark during prayer. In general, however, the ark continued to stand on the eastern side, and only in modern times can a few rare exceptions be cited.[10]

The ark was, according to the Talmud, sheltered by a baldachin (כילה, Y. *Meg.* 3:1, 73d)[11] or a curtain (פריסא, B. *Meg.* 26b); the latter was taken down and used as a mat under the scroll when it was laid on the reading desk (לווחין, Y. *Meg.* 3:1, 73d or לוחות, B. *Meg.* 32a). The ark was elevated, so that one had to ascend to it by a few steps; the Zohar even saw to it that their number was stipulated. The greatest care was expended on the architectural execution of the ark from earliest times. On some ancient glass vessels[12] and in Roman catacombs one may see depictions of an ark with additional decorations and the doors standing open, with the interior divided by boards into compartments in which the scrolls lie. Sometimes only some of the compartments were used

[354]

for biblical texts, while the other spaces were used for other things. Already in antiquity arks with figurative decorations can be found, flanked by doves bearing olive branches, or by lions; the decorative use of lions was long-lived. Even later the ark was the most highly decorated furnishing of the synagogue. Even in simple buildings, arks outstanding in their artistic execution are found. In famous buildings, like the Portuguese synagogue in Amsterdam or the synagogue of Florence, masterworks of architecture or cabinet-making were fashioned (see the illustrations in *J.E.* 2:110f.). For the decoration of the Holy Ark, some typical characteristics emerged. As a rule the upper part shows the two tablets of the Law,[13] which, however, is not attested before the seventeenth century. The ark itself is covered with a curtain (פרכת),[14] which in Ashkenazic congregations is found in front of the doors, and in Sephardic congregations, behind them. The curtains are artistically woven and embroidered, often with figurative representations, especially of lions. The permissibility of these gave rise to frequent halakhic discussion and debate.

(2)   In the ark are found the Holy Scriptures. In ancient times, this meant scrolls of the Torah and Prophets, later of Torah scrolls alone. The Torah must be complete. In antiquity it was permitted to read even from a defective copy, but later this was prohibited as an inducement to the congregation to expedite the restoration of scrolls destroyed by violence or damaged through use.[15] In antiquity the scrolls were wrapped in cloths (מטפחות)[16] and placed in a bag (תיק);[17] the cloths were often colorful ones, decorated with little bells.[18] On the Joy of the Torah,[19] it was customary to dress the Torah splendidly and to deck it out like a bride. In Babylonia crowns of gold, silver, or myrtle leaves were set on the scrolls, while in Spain and southern France they were adorned with elegant veils and women's ornaments. From these gradually developed the dressing of the Torah in decorative pieces (כלי קדש), which is encountered with minor variations everywhere since the Middle Ages [in Ashkenazic congregations]. Both ends of the Torah scrolls are attached to wooden columns (עץ חיים) on which they may be rolled; the scroll is bound with a strip of cloth or wimple (מפה), and covered with a mantle (מעיל). On the mantle a breastplate (טס) is hung by a chain, after the manner of the breastplate of the high priest; it is usually adorned with figurative decorations and the tablets of the Law. Also hung on the scroll is a hand with outstretched index finger used to indicate the place to be read. On top of the wooden columns gleams a crown (כתר, עטרה) or a pair of pomegranates, which are mentioned in the Bible as decoration for the garments of the high priest (רמונים, also תפוחים). Not always are all the Torah's adornments used, but they are graduated according to the solemnity of the day; most congregations possess Torah ornaments in simpler and more costly versions to distinguish between weekdays, Sabbath, and festivals. The manner of their execution depends on the available means and taste. The good will to engage the best craftsmen for this work was never lacking. Since attention has again been drawn to these antique ritual objects, outstanding artistic productions have come to light.[20]

[355]

(3)   The ancient basilica ended in an elevated platform on which the judges sat. This is reproduced in the ancient synagogue as well, for to the ark is attached a platform, called בימה, βῆμα.[21] In the Mishnah, בימה denotes the elevated platform that, for example, was erected for the king, when he would read Deuteronomy to the assembled

people at the end of the Sabbatical year (M. *Sota* 7:7); the Greek word corresponds to the Hebrew מגדל, from which Ezra read the book of the Torah (Neh. 8:4). In the middle of the unusually big basilica in Alexandria there was a dais of this kind, from which the sexton signaled the congregation. This was why in many synagogues the dais for the reading of Scripture and the sermon was built in the middle. Maimonides, in fact, declares it a religious obligation to erect such a dais in the middle of the synagogue.[22]

Others used the biblical מגדל for the place at which the reading was held,[23] while yet others used the term employed in the Temple, דוכן;[24] in each place a different term was used based on biblical or talmudic authority. In China the dais was called "the seat of Moses,"[25] for which the midrash offers the analogous קתדרא דמשה. For a German translation, Jacob Weil (ca. 1400) chose the church term *altar* (עלטאר).[26] But the most widespread term, which is found already in Rashi's Talmud commentary, is *almemor* (*almemar*),[27] a garbled form of the Arabic *al-minbar*, the speaker's platform in a mosque. On the dais there must be a table or desk for reading the Torah; this is called most simply שלחן or כסא, but often also תיבה.[28] This last term was used with so many different meanings that scholars have difficulty distinguishing them;[29] terminology fluctuated because synagogue construction varied. In the course of time we find several arrangements of the dais. The dais and precentor's desk may be separate, with the desk next to the steps leading up to the ark, and the dais next to the ark or in the middle of the room. Or they may be joined,[30] with either both of them right next to the ark, or with the precentor's desk and the reading table in the middle of the room. The position in the center was especially appropriate when the synagogue was large or consisted of several adjoining spaces, for then the precentor could be heard in every direction. Joseph Caro[31] knew from his own experience of numerous synagogues in which the dais was not in the center but at one end; he considered this very practical for smaller rooms, and therefore avoided setting a rule for this matter in the *Shulhan 'arukh*. His glossator Moses Iserles, however, added Maimonides' precept verbatim; therefore, in Germany and Poland it was universally seen as a religious duty to erect an almemor in the middle of the synagogue for the reading of the Torah and for the recitation of certain prayers.

For the eye, the almemor was and still is the cynosure of the synagogue. They were usually made with high craftsmanship, often out of precious materials. Already in antiquity the use of marble for this purpose is reported.[32] Furthermore, the solemn procession from the ark to the almemor and back was a thrilling sight. On the other hand, the erection of the almemor also caused certain intolerable problems. The dais occupied a great deal of room, preventing those whose place was behind it from seeing and hearing. In order to eliminate both problems, most modern synagogues have no almemor in the middle; thus, more room for seating is available for worshipers, and everyone has an unobstructed view of the precentor's desk and the ark. The new arrangement came up against considerable opposition,[33] and had to be justified by numerous rabbinical opinions, but in view of its practicality it has come in nearly everywhere. In America, Germany, and Austria-Hungary, synagogues are only rarely built with the almemor in the middle, but rather the dais is placed directly before the steps leading up to the ark. On it stand the precentor's desk (also called עמוד) and the reader's table, with the former facing the ark and the latter, the congregation. In a few rare exceptional cases these are the same. Another furnishing of the dais, since ancient

[356]

times, is a chair (כסא) or bench on which the person sits who holds the Torah while
it is being rolled and awaiting its return to the ark. In ancient times the sermon was
delivered from the dais, and in the Greek synagogues the speaker used a special platform (ἄμβων); in recent times the platform is situated directly before the ark or, in individual cases, on a pillar by one of the side walls.

(4)　Places for sitting (ספסלא or *subsellium*)[34] were very few in antiquity; ordinarily
the congregation probably sat on mats spread out on the floor—ציפי (B. *B.B.* 8a).[35] A
few benches set in the walls are still visible in some ruins in the Galilee.[36] There were
places of honor in the synagogue (προεδρία),[37] which could be assigned to benefactors
of the congregation, including women. Perhaps the places in the ruins with still-visible
cushions served this purpose. Places of honor were accorded also to the scholars. In
the Tosefta, the seating order in the synagogue is described as follows: The elders (זקנים)
sit with their faces to the congregation and their backs to the ark; the reader's desk faces
the same way; likewise the priests, when they pronounce the blessing; but the congregation and the sexton face the ark (M. *Meg.* 4:21). The seating of scholars in places of
honor was not always viewed favorably: In the Gospels they are reproached for pushing
their way to the πρωτοκαθεδρία (Mark 12:39 and parallels). This did not hinder the
bishop from having his cathedra and the clergy from having their benches on the dais
by the altar in church.[38] The same word, קתדרא, is used for the choice seats.[39] In the
great *proseuche* in Alexandria there were said to be seventy-one such seats of gold. Likewise in the Middle Ages the seats of honor in German synagogues were called קטידרא.[40]

The seating order in the *proseuche* in Alexandria is also interesting in that the
places for the various professions were together, so that each occupation had its own
separate section: "the goldsmiths apart, the silversmiths apart, the smiths, and various
kinds of weavers apart."[41] Later, such distinctions were declared inappropriate.[42] In
European synagogues seating was introduced for all worshipers, who then sat on chairs
or benches; while in the Muslim lands seating on mats spread out on the ground was
long the widespread practice, and may still be seen in the East. In general the number
of places for sitting in the Portuguese synagogues is small. The places on the east wall
(מזרח) to the right and left of the ark are still coveted. In time the communities had
to come around to selling and renting the places in order to cover their expenses; but
care was always taken that the places seen as the most prestigious ones were reserved
for the most worthy. The rabbi was always given a place by the ark. As prayer books
came to be more easily acquired and as they were more commonly found in the hands
of the worshipers, special desks (עמודים) had to be fashioned for them, which have often
been retained into the modern period. Since they were movable, they proved to be a
very disturbing element in the service, and because of their size they took up excessive
space. Modern synagogues cannot afford to allot so much space to the individual, so
they have been removed. Even in quite orthodox congregations today fixed benches
with immovable reading desks are erected. Even this deviation from tradition could not
be accomplished unopposed.

(5)　Finally, the illumination of the synagogue must be mentioned. The Talmud
already mentions lamps and candelabra (נר, מנורה) and knows that on as important a

[357]

day as the Day of Atonement more lamps must be lighted than usual.[43] On festivals
the synagogues were illuminated even by day, so that they would look festive. In antiquity the fuel was oil, and this continued into the Middle Ages as well. Since, however,
the oil in western lands was of poor quality for burning and produced much smoke,
a shift was made to tallow and wax candles (צירא);[44] but the very punctilious thought
it right to add to these a little oil as prescribed in the ancient sources. In the modern
period, the technical progress in illumination was put to the service of the synagogue
without opposition. In conformity with tradition, two candles still burn before the precentor's desk. In front of the ark is found the eternal light (נר תמיד),[45] in which even
today oil is burned, a memorial to the never-extinguished lamp in the sanctuary. But
there is no literary evidence for the existence of the eternal light before the seventeenth
century. The cost of illuminating the synagogue was formerly met through donations,
and the donor was mentioned in the prayers.

The Liturgical Community

§ 51   *Congregation and Synagogue*

(1)   The existence of synagogues in Palestine in the time of the Mishnah is taken for granted. A scholar is advised not even to live in a place without a synagogue (B. *Sanh.* 17b). There were synagogues even in little villages (כפר) where the necessary number of men assembled only on market days (ימי הכניסה),[1] and certainly in bigger places (עיר גדולה), where ten men free of other occupation (בטלנים) could be counted on,[2] and in the main cities (כרך), where strangers from the surrounding areas also took part in the service. The inhabitants of a city could be compelled by a tax assessment to build a synagogue and to purchase a copy of Scriptures.[3] This is how the law reads in the legal sources, and so it stands today, with the modifications due to civil law. The communities did not often have to make use of the compulsory assessment, for the members gladly made the necessary sacrifices. In the Diaspora the possibility of compelling the payment of the tax was available only in the rarest cases. Except in Babylonia, where the communities were well organized, recourse could be had only to free-will contributions. But as we see, these were never lacking.

(2)   Sometimes an individual would erect a synagogue and place it at the community's disposal, or he would dedicate (הקדיש) a building intended as a dwelling for liturgical purposes.[4] Even heathens gave such gifts.[5] Just as the Gospel tells that a Roman centurion built the synagogue for the Jews of Capernaum (Luke 7:5), so the Talmud repeatedly relates that heathens supported synagogue construction. A Greek inscription in Akmonia in Phrygia[6] gives notice that a priestess of the emperor cult, Julia Severa, donated the synagogue. So it was, mutatis mutandis, in every age: Individual members of the community frequently donated synagogue buildings to their coreligionists, and in isolated cases non-Jews placed at the community's disposal whole buildings or substantial support for liturgical purposes. Not always was the whole building given; in such cases at least some parts were built through donations (εὐχαί or נדבה),[7] or a campaign for funds was instituted,[8] and the existing assets of the community were also used. Especially in large places many contributions came in from outside, namely from coreli-

gionists who frequently visited the town and attended the service there. When synagogues became dilapidated or needed to be expanded, the means were accumulated in the same way. Sometimes the money came in such quantities that there was a surplus, for which another suitable use had to be found. The names of the donors were perpetuated by inscriptions on the wall of the synagogue building or on the portion that they had donated.[9] In Barʿam[10] an inscription reports that Joseph the Levite had the lintel made; in Ḥammam-Lif, Asterius the son of Rusticus together with Margerita the daughter of Riddeus decorated part of the foyer with mosaic, while in the interior a young lady named Juliana had the floor decorated with mosaic "for her own salvation." Such reports can be assembled in great numbers from every century, demonstrating extraordinary generosity and readiness to sacrifice. It was no different with the individual items of the internal furnishings. All the objects that stood in the synagogue's interior, from the simplest chair to the Torah scroll and its ornaments, could be, and were, donated. These, too, were donated by Jews and non-Jews. Since antiquity the donors' names have been perpetuated on the objects donated. In many congregations on the memorial days of individual families, it is still customary to make use of the objects donated to the synagogue through their generosity. In western Germany, when a boy was first brought to the synagogue a wimple was brought with him with his name and birth date worked into its design,[11] so that the communities had in their wimple collections an exact duplicate of their birth registers. A prayer was recited for synagogue benefactors on the Sabbath since the early Middle Ages.

(3)   The right to determine the use of funds collected for the building of a synagogue and the furnishing of its interior depended on the manner in which those funds were raised. In general, the synagogue may not be used for other than liturgical purposes;[12] only the house of study has higher status. The furnishings have a greater degree of sanctity than the building, and the Torah has the highest degree. According to ancient regulations, the synagogue should not be sold at all or at least only under the condition that it be used for a dignified purpose.[13] This rule could not, however, be completely enforced at all times. When individuals or small organizations erected a synagogue out of their own funds, they were granted full rights of disposal. Communities could not operate thus unrestricted, but its representatives generally had to assure themselves of the community's agreement.[14] In big cities, where some of the money for the building of the synagogue had come from the outside, it could not be sold at all.[15] Donations could be used only in the manner intended by the donor; only when their names no longer could be recognized on the objects or when they had completely vanished from memory could their donations be used for other purposes, though always for similar ones. In the Middle Ages, individual donors and their heirs often retained the right in perpetuity to finance the necessary synagogue repairs from their own means.[16] Sometimes the heirs would want to transfer the right to others, but the communities would not agree to this if the new possessors of the right did not seem to them equally worthy. In general the use of the building and its materials was strictly controlled.[17] It was not even permitted to use the materials of an old synagogue to build a new one. Only when the new building was completely finished and suitable for use could the reuse of the old synagogue be considered.

(4)   As in big cities the synagogue was used not only by residents of the city but [360]
also by people from outside it, so it often happened that not all the inhabitants of a
big city belonged to the same synagogue, but that a number of congregations and synagogues existed. This was true of Palestine no less than of the Diaspora. The congregations were often differentiated by place of origin. "Then some of those who belonged
to the synagogue of the Freedmen (as it was called), and of the Cyrenians, and of the
Alexandrians, and of those from Cilicia and Asia arose." What Acts (6:9) here reports
is confirmed by other ancient sources. The Talmud tells of a synagogue of the Alexandrians in Jerusalem,[18] of the Babylonians in Sepphoris,[19] and of the Roman Jews in
Maḥoza.[20] Inscriptions tell of a synagogue of Hebrews in Rome,[21] opposite which stood
that of the Vernaclesians,[22] so that we must assume that there was a distinction
between those who retained their mother tongue and those who preferred the language
of their surroundings. In one Egyptian metropolis, the Thebans had their own synagogue,[23] and in Tarsus, so did the Cappadocians.[24] This custom of people of similar
origin gathering together for prayer was retained even later, though then the determining factor was not simply the place of origin but the rite that was bound up with it. So,
just to name a very few examples, we find that in medieval Cairo there was a synagogue
of the Palestinians (*al-shāmiyīn*) and one of the Babylonians (*al-ʿirāqiyīn*);[25] in Rome,
a synagogue of the Sicilians, Castilians, and Catalonians;[26] in Salonica, a synagogue
of Aragonians, Barcelonans, and so on.[27] Or synagogues could be formed in great com-
mercial cities by people of the same origin who spent time there for business purposes.
This is how, for example, in Breslau the synagogues of Glogau, Lissa, Lemberg, and
the villagers came into being.[28]

Another reason for the separation of the congregations was membership in a particular profession. In Alexandria, as we saw, the individual crafts had their own separate
sections in the synagogue, and the Libertines in Jerusalem means people of a particular
class. In Tarsus we find a synagogue of the linen dealers, and in Rome, one of the lime
burners.[29] The division of communities by profession was widely retained into the later
periods, and had great social significance.[30] It is said of Alexandria that when a stranger
came to the city he could easily make contact with the fellows of his profession in the
synagogue, and thereby could find opportunities for work. The synagogue served a
social function even where the congregation was composed of members of all professions. A stranger, especially a poor one, could always count on finding protectors after
the service who would undertake to provide him with shelter, food, and if possible,
work.

Synagogues were distinguished by external markings, for example, emblems
depicted on them. In Sepphoris there was a synagogue of the vine (כנשתא דגופנא),[31] and
in Rome, a synagogue of the olive tree (ἐλαίας);[32] perhaps the seven-branched candelabrum above the portal in Nebratein[33] served to make such a distinction.

Many congregations got their name from famous men or outstanding patrons. In
Rome we find the synagogue of the Augustesians,[34] which got its name either from the
emperor Octavian or some other reigning Augustus, or from being composed mainly [361]
of Octavian's slaves and freedmen. Another synagogue was named for Alexander Severus.[35] It was said to contain a Torah scroll brought by Titus to Rome and given by the
emperor to the Jews as a gift. Synagogues were also named after Jewish princes: A
Roman congregation was named after Herod,[36] and another, most likely, after King
Agrippa.[37]

In the Islamic countries,[38] there was the custom of naming synagogues after biblical personalities, usually on the basis of some connection between these men and the place in question. Thus there was a Moses synagogue in Fustat and Damwah in Egypt, Aleppo, and so on. Elijah synagogues were especially common: We find them in Jaujar and Fustat, in Damascus and Byblus, Laodicea and Hama, and perhaps also ca. 600 in Sicily. In Palestine and Babylonia the names of synagogues were derived from tannaim and amoraim. The name of Simon b. Yohai enjoyed particular popularity. In most cases such synagogues are found beside the assumed grave-site of the master, recalling the *qubba* that the Muslims erect over the graves of saints. The custom of naming synagogues after famous men of old has also never been completely abandoned, though it has become rare with time. It is partially recalled by the lovely custom of North American communities of giving synagogues a byname deriving from a biblical concept.

By contrast, the names chosen in Europe are plain ones. Where several synagogues exist, they are distinguished by their location or at least by being called "old synagogue" and "new synagogue" (even in the Middle Ages we already hear of an "old synagogue").[39] This practice, too, can be traced back to ancient models; in Rome, for example, we find the congregation of the Campesians, whose synagogue was in the Campus Martius, and that of the Subursians, in the vicinity of the Subura.[40]

§ 52 The Officials of the Community

(1) The administration of the community was not the same in all places and at all times. Though it was kept as much as possible in line with the conditions of the oldest period, certain changes were unavoidable; the differences are marked not only in the substance but also in the designation of the functions. But since the sources are not always conscious of the changes, the reports from antiquity are often interpreted in a distorted way. It even happens that the text is inaccurately reported because in the intervening period a different meaning was attributed to the words.

The congregation (בני הכנסת) is, as we have seen, not identical with the community (בני העיר). The administration of the religious congregation, therefore, was not in the hands of the city leadership (פרנסי העיר).[1] Where the local authorities have control, a special committee is charged with the affairs of the synagogue and the liturgy. So it was at least in Palestine and in those places in Babylonia whose inhabitants were predominantly Jewish. In the Diaspora the external administration of the congregation was in the hands of the *arkhontes*,[2] headed by the *gerousiarch*. We shall concern ourselves here only with the liturgy, which was directed, according to the ancient sources, by no more than two officials, the president and the sexton of the synagogue.

[362]

(2) The president of the synagogue was called in Palestine ראש הכנסת, and in the Greco-Roman diaspora ἀρχισυνάγωγος, ἄρχων τῆς συναγωγῆς—Archisynagogos (Arcosinagogus).[3] He had to direct the liturgy and to distribute the liturgical functions. He would direct one of those in attendance at the service, whether that person was a member of the community or not, to recite the prayers aloud.[4] When the Torah was to be read, it was handed to him[5] and he would choose those who were to come forward

to read; afterwards he would honor one by directing him to preach.[6] He would also see to the external order of the synagogue; if someone did something improper, he would admonish him (compare Luke 13:14). The care of the synagogue building may not have been among his duties in every locality, but it does suit his office that he should have been responsible for keeping up its condition and, when necessary, for raising the money for its improvement, expansion, or reconstruction.[7] The office was an esteemed one, perhaps the highest the community had to offer.[8] The presidents (ראשי כנסיות) stand in rank behind the scholars (תלמידי חכמים) and the "chief men of the age" (גדולי הדור), but ahead of the alms collectors (גבאי צדקה; B. *Pes.* 49a).[9] They also take precedence in reading from the Torah, though etiquette permits them to read only when invited by the members of the congregation (T. *Meg.* 4:21). At funerals it was customary for a time to drink in honor of the president and to recite a blessing.[10] The office was not a light one, but made demands of time; accordingly the imperial law[11] freed the archisynagogos from all personal service to the state and local government. We cannot tell from the sources whether there was always just one archisynagogos or whether several functioned at the same time.[12] Many individuals held other offices simultaneously,[13] like that of arkhon. It also seems that once someone had held this office, he retained the title for life. The office was assigned by election;[14] the incumbent could be reelected, even for life (διὰ βίου).[15] It sometimes happened that a son followed his father. Despite all democratic principles, it was generally viewed favorably for fathers to bequeath their offices to their sons, and it seems that the office under discussion was also often transmitted by inheritance. It is certain that the title was even bestowed upon minors, who were designated as future archisynagogoi (ἀρχισυνάγωγος νήπιος).[16]

In this way, the term archisynagogos became an honorary title unconnected with an office. Thus, women too could later bear it:[17] A column in Myndos mentions an archisynagoga Theopemptes, and a gravestone in Smyrna was erected by a Jewess Rufina who bore the same title. On the other hand, the word was used also as a derisive name: the emperor Alexander Severus is called a "Syrus Archisynagogos,"[18] probably because he showed favor to the Jews, perhaps even endowed their synagogues.

The relationship has not been clarified between them and the πρεσβύτεροι,[19] whom Eusebius calls the leaders of the Jewish-Christian communities and which the Theodosian Code names together with the archisynagogoi. Πρεσβύτεροι is the translation of זקנים, who, according to the Talmud, took the places of honor in the synagogue. We are just as little informed as to the meaning of similar titles like προστάτης and ἐπιστάτης.

Also connected with activities on behalf of the congregation are the titles πατὴρ συναγωγῆς and μήτηρ συναγωγῆς, which also appear in Latin as mater synagogae and even Pateressa.[20] No office was attached to these; they were titles of honor for individuals who had performed service and whom the congregation wished to honor, in the same way that we bestow honorary citizenship. From a few examples it may be inferred that the title was bestowed upon particularly deserving and elderly members. It is interesting that one and the same person could hold the distinction from several synagogues. How highly this honor was esteemed is best shown by a Roman grave inscription in which the husband of the deceased is called the brother of a "father of the synagogue."[21]

The material from talmudic sources is not as rich as that coming from the Dias-

[363]

pora. The title ראש הכנסת does not appear in post-talmudic times; it is also questionable how long this separation of offices, with the leader of the synagogue not belonging to the local administration, remained in effect. In the Tosefta, the פרנסי העיר already appear as the ones who have authority over synagogue property (M. *Meg.* 3:1), for which Rava uses שבעה טובי העיר (B. *Meg.* 26a). In later times, the new name was retained. Circumstances often demanded that the president direct not only the synagogue but all communal affairs. The community committee was called טובי הקהל or מנהיגים, פרנסים. Even later it was composed of seven members, but often more—for example, twelve, of which each had to function one month in a year (פרנסי החודש). For special purposes special commissions were chosen; where a smaller group was charged with the direction of the synagogue, its members were called גבאי בית הכנסת.[22] The office was always unsalaried; it was bestowed by elections among the community members, all of whom were eligible. The elections were ordinarily held, as in ancient times, in the fall. In modern times the administration of the communities and the distribution of offices are regulated by government-recognized statutes. The honorary titles of ancient times are no longer in use. The only distinction available to deserving members was to be elected to the congregation's administrative body or, in very rare cases, freedom from taxation.[23]

(3)   By the side of the president stood the sexton. He is called in Hebrew חזן הכנסת, Aramaic חזנא, Greek, ὑπηρέτης.[24] We find him in the same sources as the ראש הכנסת, and even on gravestones we find noted that the deceased had held this office.[25] The office must, therefore, have been seen as an honor, and as having higher status than the title of "sexton" connotes to us. In antiquity this official, too, was honored at funeral meals with a blessing recited on his behalf.[26] The most important distinction would have been [364] that this office in all likelihood was a salaried one. The sexton had to execute the directions of the president at religious services; he conveyed the invitations to congregants to lead the prayers, read the Torah, or deliver the sermon. He had to bring the biblical scrolls out of the ark and to put them back, and he had to open the scrolls to the place to be read. In the synagogue he had a special place, which always had to be occupied. When, he, for example, read from the Torah, someone else had to come and sit there in his place. In the great *proseuche* in Alexandria he stood during the service on the dais in the middle holding a banner, with which he would give a signal to the congregation whenever they had to chime in with "amen" (T. *Suk.* 4:6). In one version of this report, the official is called ממונה (Y. *Suk.* 5:1, 55b).

The sexton's functions were numerous.[27] He had to watch over the synagogue building and keep it in order; for this purpose an apartment in it was provided for him. He is also mentioned as city watchman; as a municipal official he had to accompany the residents to Jerusalem when they brought their firstlings. Finally, as servant of the court, he had, among other duties, to execute corporal punishment. Administration and supervision are part of the root meaning of the word. Epiphanius is right in a certain sense when he compares the ἀζανῖται with the deacons, for in fact they served as administrators. It can hardly be assumed that one and the same official could perform all the above-mentioned activities; probably in most cases the word הכנסת was added to חזן by mistake. Otherwise, the congregational sexton would actually have to serve all the offices that were located in the synagogue.

Only with difficulty can the functions named above be harmonized with the report according to which the sexton is identified as teacher of children, in charge of their first instruction in reading and responsible for drilling them in the weekly pericope; as such he is also called סופר, "scribe." Nakkai,[28] one of the founders of masoretic studies, is called, in one tradition, a sexton, who had to put the lamps in order, and in another, a scribe. But the expression for sexton in this source is שמש, for the later sources did not know the terminology and did not make exact distinctions. Therefore, it is said in a much quoted report (Y. *Yev.* 12, 13a) that the community in Simonias asked Judah I to recommend a man "to give sermons, judge, act as sexton, scribe, teacher of tannaitic law, and do everything we need" (דריש דיין וחזן ספר מתניין ועבד לן כל צורכינן). Only with difficulty could we say that such a small community needed such a man for all seasons to perform such varied functions; probably the parallel source is more accurate: "who can read the Bible for us, and teach us tannaitic law and serve as our judge" (שיהא מקרא אותנו ושונה אותנו ודן את דיננו). Thus, he only had to teach and judge (דיין ספר מתניין).

The connection between sexton and scribe leads us to another conjecture. In a group of Roman inscriptions we find the title γραμματεύς, often in connection with communities, so that he must be seen as a community official. It is not impossible that γραμματεύς is the translation of סופר, and corresponds to one of the functions of the חזן.[29]

In the post-talmudic period the sexton is called שמש;[30] his functions in the synagogue remained on the whole the same. Secondary offices were nearly always attached to his position so that he would earn enough to survive. Later as well this office enjoyed a certain amount of respect, and was frequently filled by learned men. What gave the sexton particular status was his great involvement with members of the community, with whom he came into contact on both joyous and sad occasions.

In large congregations a second sexton was employed, the *Schulklopfer* (*Schulklöpper*),[31] whose task it was to knock with a hammer on the door of the synagogue or of every member of the congregation to summon them to prayer. Since his task was equivalent to that of the bell-ringer in the church, he is called *Campanator* or *Glockenere* in the documents. The office is an old one, for as early as 200 a מקושא is mentioned (Y. *Beṣ.* 5:2, 63a).[32] In some congregations the hammer was seen as such an important instrument that it was permitted to be stored in the Holy Ark (Y. *Meg.* 3:1, 73d). In the Middle Ages the *Schulklopfer* was the best-known man of the Jewish community, even in Christian circles. His function was considered so important that even the number of strokes that he would beat in the various neighborhoods during his rounds was handed down as a tradition. The court officials often made use of him as a bailiff to execute police functions.

⌊365⌋

(4) Other than the president and the sexton, the ancient synagogue knew no other officials. The recitation of the prayers and the reading and exegesis of Scripture were all performed by members of the congregation; the president determined who would have the honor of leading the prayers, reading and translating the Torah and Prophets, and preaching. Every worshiper present was eligible to perform all the functions. The determination was made solely on the basis of personal worthiness, no precedence being given on account of birth or special training. If in the most ancient sources the precentor already appears as the agent of the community (שליח צבור), this does not designate a standing office but only the function that he was at the moment filling. In

principle the old democratic rule still exists in the synagogue. Even today, in many synagogues one may hear ordinary individuals leading the prayers and reading from the Torah. Judaism does not know a distinction between laymen and specialists or even priests, though circumstances have widely enforced deviation from tradition and placed the leading of the service in the hands of professional officials. It was not possible to rely permanently on volunteers, for often the qualified laymen were lacking, and the unqualified forced their way into the functions. The first office that had to be created was that of תורגמן, "translator,"[33] of the scriptural reading; he was first to be permitted to be paid for his efforts. Though it was repeatedly warned that there was no blessing in the wages he received, the warning itself proves that this work was often paid for. Probably the sexton, whose regular duties involved teaching, had to take over the translating of the reading. Even so, it was not always easy to find the necessary number of congregants who knew how to read from the Torah; thus, gradually, the reading of the Torah, too, was assigned to an employed official (קורא). Exceptions are still known to this day, and the Haftara is in the overwhelming majority of cases still read by lay worshipers, often even by boys.

[366]   (5)   The most important office that the synagogue developed was that of the precentor. We have no information as to when precentors were first appointed to a regular position. To judge by the sources, this must have happened already in amoraic times. In the Palestinian Talmud, the precentor often appears with the title *hazan*,[34] which the office later bore, but it can be proved that the texts have been altered on the basis of later usage. In *Soferim*, too, we find the precentor called *hazan*, and it is therefore not impossible that the passages in question are late insertions. But by the time of the composition of *Soferim*, the custom of employing a professional precentor may already have been widespread. The liturgy had grown with time, and to master it demanded considerable knowledge; yet familiarity with the Hebrew language had largely declined. Further, the desire to hear the prayers recited by a pleasant voice was widespread. " 'Honor God with your means'—this means that if you have a pleasant voice and are sitting in the synagogue, get up and give honor to God."[35] This exegesis still presupposes a voluntary performance by the precentor, but the demand for a vocally beautiful performance must necessarily have led to the quest for someone qualified to fill this position on a long-term basis. The introduction of the liturgical poetry would have been decisive. The *hazan* was the singer and the poet who composed the *hizāna* and performed it; in this capacity he at first stood forth by the side of the שליח צבור, but soon supplanted him. The *hazan* took over not only the poetry, but the statutory prayers as well. With the expansion of the public liturgy the significance of the precentor increased; the more the liturgy grew the more extensive was his activity and the more influential his post. The precentor was usually the only one in the congregation who had at his disposal a prayer book with the numerous poetic inserts; the congregation hung on his words and was in his hands, for better or worse. The precentor was so indispensable in the Middle Ages that the women, too, in their section of the synagogue, had their own female precentor (המתפללת לנשים). The chore was gladly undertaken; the precentor's vocal artistry enjoyed general popularity, and its position became strong. Even famous sages could do nothing to reduce their often independent proceedings. The precentors became the determining factor in the shaping of the liturgy. In time,

leading the prayers took second place to singing; the ḥazan became ever more a singer, or cantor, as he was called in the romance-speaking lands. He had to have a good voice and had to be able to sing well, and in the end he could even have himself accompanied when singing. The congregations spared no cost in order to employ a vocally gifted cantor; able singers went on tour to appear for a fee in the synagogues on a Sabbath or a festival.

From the beginning certain demands were made of the precentor.[36] He had to have clear diction: Whoever could not audibly distinguish א and ע, ה and ח was not admitted, even in the age of the voluntary precentor (B. *Meg.* 24b). Of course, knowledge of the prayers, Scriptures, and liturgical customs were presupposed. In addition, although the Mishnah considers a boy of thirteen to be suitable for the office, mature years were also demanded (B. *Ḥul.* 24a).[37] Above all, however, the precentor must be distinguished by moral impeccability and deep religiosity. The community's representative in prayer must be a man who commands general respect and, if at all possible, a man of general popularity. At least he should have no enemies in the congregation, for even a single opponent is enough to call his appointment into question. Since this extreme freedom was all too often misused and gave rise to strife, the decision was finally given over to the majority of the congregation's membership. Especially high demands were laid by the Talmud on the precentor who officiated on public fast days (M. *Ta.* 2:2); hence, even at synagogue services on the Days of Awe and the days preparatory to them, only the choice precentors were admitted, men of blameless conduct, of uncontested respect, and possessing the ability to give a fully expressive and moving rendition of the service. Even music lovers agreed to dispense with the display of a beautiful voice on these days and to give precedence to the most worthy.

[367]

Many precentors fulfilled the high demands of their office in every respect and enjoyed the admiration of their contemporaries and the recognition of posterity. Holders of the office often distinguished themselves through exceptional learning and took a leadership role in their age: One need only think of Meir b. Isaac of Worms and Jacob Möllin. But there was also no lack of exceptions; in fact, they were probably the majority. From the moment when the congregations began to put the emphasis on singing they tended to overlook all shortcomings as long as the possessor of the office compensated with a beautiful voice. Only too often strife and anger arose over the precentors, for their conduct both inside and outside the synagogue often left much to be desired.[38] In Spain by 1300, the office had lost all of its prestige. The professional work itself of many precentors was not always satisfactory; they took the liberty of shortening prayers arbitrarily,[39] of reciting the prayers too rapidly and without devotion, and of introducing foreign melodies. Above all, however, they were criticized for vanity. The endless singing with which they dragged out the prayers was dubbed "The song of the fools" (Ecc. 7:5); it was said that in their singing they were thinking more of the approval of the audience than of the honor of God. The attacks against their proverbial foolishness and crudeness increased from generation to generation. But with all the accusations and scorn directed against them, they were left alone, because song was considered a necessary component of worship. Even in the hearts of the unfortunate Jews, tormented from every side and blocked from joy, there lived the longing for the noble world of art. The synagogue was the only place in which they felt free, and the song of the precentor the only—if often quite doubtful—art that they might enjoy.

With the invention of the printing press, more prayer books came into the hands of the public, and with that the congregation's dependency on the precentor declined. The congregation could now pray independently, and the cantor's importance receded. But at the same time the ignorance and boorishness of the precentors increased, and they performed their office with little dignity and growing arrogance. There were always exceptions, and among the Portuguese the extreme behavior of the precentors stayed within reasonable limits, but in the realm of the Ashkenazim, in Germany and Poland, the cantor became more and more the bane of the serious worshiper. The low estate of the liturgy on the threshold of the modern age was not least owing to the bad behavior of the cantors.[40] It necessitated the long, wearying labors of zealous cantors and the appearance of some inspired artists to restore the honorable position of the cantor in the liturgy under the altered conditions of the modern period.

[368] (6)   Only since the last century has the rabbi, too, emerged as one of the synagogue officials. Until deep in the Middle Ages rabbis were not appointed by congregations, but were voluntary popular teachers recognized for their learning; private individuals who kept a house of study and placed their knowledge at the disposal of the community; men in whom the community placed their trust and whom they freely accepted as their authority. But even after 1350, when they became salaried community officials,[41] the rabbis appeared only rarely at public worship; they observed private devotions, preferring to pray with their disciples in the house of study. In the synagogue they were disturbed by the endless singing, against which they were helpless; therefore they came to the community synagogue only on the Days of Awe, or when they preached, which was seldom. Here the modern age brought about a fundamental change. The sermon regained its original status, becoming again, as in antiquity, an important part of the service. But the simple type of scriptural exegesis in ancient times allowed everyone to take the floor and address the congregation, a practice that has been retained in some countries, like England and Italy, until the present; whereas in our day the sermon is the exclusive province of the specialist. The growing significance of the sermon in the last century has lent the rabbi an important function in the liturgy. In western Europe and America he must deliver edifying sermons at regular intervals, and those prayers that are recited in the vernacular are recited by him. In Reform congregations the tendency is to give more and more of the liturgy to the rabbi; in the Berlin Reform congregation and in the many Reform congregations in America, the office of the precentor has been completely eliminated, and the sung part of the service is performed by the choir instead. This elevation of the rabbi out of the congregation into the role of an "ecclesiastic" is an unfortunate aspect of the development of the Reform.

The Conduct of the Service

§ 53 The Precentor and the Community

(1)   The liturgy is intended as a community service, and is unthinkable without a congregation. The individual prayers and readings of which the liturgy is composed may be recited only before a particular public. The congregation as a public, or collectivity, is called צבור (from צבר, Gen. 41:35, "to gather"); the word denotes the collectivity, as opposed to the individual (יחיד),[1] and to worship in a congregation is התפלל עם הצבור or התפלל בצבור. The congregation is composed of ten mature males (מנין).[2] The Talmud derives the number from the biblical עדה, and we actually do find in the Bible that ten persons is often the minimum size of a public group. Thus, it is the more surprising that according to a Palestinian tradition in *Soferim*,[3] as few as seven men satisfy the requirement for public worship. The Mishnah defines a large city as one in which seven men are always free of work so that they may attend the service (עשרה בטלנים; *Meg.* 1:6). These are not community employees, but volunteers, whose presence at the service can be counted on (Y. *Meg.* 1:6, 70b). It follows that attendance at services on weekdays was not particularly good,[4] and that only on Sabbaths and festivals, when people were free from work, did all attend. That is also why in many places the synagogue was called the Sabbath house. If it was so difficult to hold daily services in ancient Palestine, we can infer that it must often have been even more difficult in the Diaspora to draw together the necessary number of worshipers into the synagogue, especially in the Middle Ages, when congregations were small and people worked far away from home. So that the service not go too often unperformed, it was then customary for the community to pay some people as regular employees with the duty of attending services. Where it was absolutely impossible to assemble the necessary number throughout the year, an effort was made at least for festivals, especially the Days of Awe.[5] The communities did everything in their power to enable themselves to hold services on special days. It aroused great bitterness when individuals from such small communities traveled to bigger places, thereby making it harder to hold services. Although the structure of congregations has changed greatly in the modern period, the practice of employing professional worshipers has not become completely superfluous even today. In most

recent times, however, the traditional number has here and there come to be overlooked, and services are being held with fewer than ten participants.

[370]

(2)   The leader of the congregation in prayer is the שליח צבור. He is their speaker, not their representative, and is chosen from among them as spokesman, not as intercessor. Thus the activity of the precentor was understood in antiquity: "The eyes of the community are raised to him, and his eyes are raised to God,"[6] as it says in a midrash and in an ancient prayer. Only when prayer was dealt with from a halakhic point of view did the doctrine arise that the precentor represented the congregation (*R.H.*, end), but he was never considered a priestly intermediary. Throughout the Middle Ages the conception persisted that the precentor was the congregation's representative. This had very healthy consequences, for it set a high standard for the precentor, but obviously a great deal of religious unclarity was connected with it. The modern period has quite properly reverted to the old conception.

Though the precentor was the congregation's spokesman, the people were not a mute audience, but participated in the service by chiming in with responses at certain points (ענה). These responses were a heritage from the Temple, for eulogies were customary when the psalms were recited. The simplest form is retained in Ps. 89:53: "Blessed is the Lord forever; amen and amen." In an expanded form it went, "Blessed is the Lord, God of Israel, from eternity," but finally, in order to stress the belief in the next world (*Ber.*, end), "Blessed is the Lord, God of Israel from eternity to eternity" as in Pss. 41:14; 106:39 (I Chron. 16:36). The ancient doxologies have all passed into the prayer book, but not as responses. In public worship they were used in ancient times on the occasion of public fasts, but this occurred exclusively within the Temple precincts (M. *Ta.* 2:2). As congregational responses in the synagogue, it was customary to use the same words with which the people in the Temple responded to the song of the Levites, "amen" and "hallelujah" (Ps. 105; I Chron. 16:36). "Amen" is the most important and most often repeated response. It is said immediately after the precentor or Torah reader recites a benediction or when the priests pronounce their blessing. In Alexandria the sexton would stand on the dais in the center and wave the banner to give the congregation the signal to say "amen." This response was seen as so important that it was considered to be of value even where, as in the huge *proseuche* of Alexandria, the worshipers could not even hear the benediction. "Amen" had the same meaning as in the Bible, expressing an acknowledgment and reinforcement of what had been said. "Amen" after a benediction usually corresponds to Jeremiah's "Amen! May the Lord do so! May the Lord fulfill what you have prophesied" (28:6).

In the Temple in Jerusalem the response "amen" was not permitted; instead the eulogies were answered with "Blessed be the name of His majestic glory forever." The same response is found in the ritual of the high priest on the Day of Atonement: Each time the high priest pronounced God's name, the congregation would respond with "Blessed be the Name. . . ."[7] In prayer we find this exact response in only one place, between the first two verses of the *Shema*; it is probably the oldest response in the whole liturgy. In meaning it corresponds to ברוך הוא וברוך שמו, "Blessed is He and blessed is His Name," which is said by the congregation after the precentor pronounces the name of God; it is a combination of the two eulogies "Blessed is He" and "Blessed is His Name," which we find in "Blessed is He Who spoke."

The other response mentioned in the Psalms, "Hallelujah" also passed into the liturgy, and is used during the recitation of Hallel.

[371]

(3) The manner of the response and of congregational participation in the various parts of the service was not uniform in ancient times. Simplest was the performance of the ʿAmida, which the precentor recited alone while the congregation listened and answered "amen," verse by verse. When the practice was later introduced of reciting the ʿAmida silently before the recitation aloud, the manner of recitation did not change; the precentor spoke the text just as in ancient times, and the congregation had to respond in the same way. New responses were provided the congregation by the Kedushah, in which the congregation spoke the biblical verses in unison with the precentor. During the Priestly Blessing, the congregation answered "amen" after each sentence.[8]

Similar by virtue of the constant refrains, but not identical, was the recitation of Hallel. The precentor began with "Hallelujah"; the congregation repeated it, and then responded after each half-verse with the same word, altogether 123 times, as reported in the ancient sources (Y. *Shab.* 16:1, 15c). The manner of reciting Hallel (B. *Suk.* 38b) was often changed in the course of time. In many regions it was customary to repeat the last verses, from Ps. 118:21 on, while in others these verses were recited only once. In Babylonia around 350 the congregation said "Hallelujah" only twice more at the beginning; then Pss. 113–117 were recited without interruption; "Praise the Lord for He is good" (Ps. 118:1) and "O Lord deliver us" (Ps. 118:25) were repeated; and finally "May he who enters be blessed" (Ps. 118:26) was recited antiphonally. In the course of time, every trace of this old recitation disappeared. From the Middle Ages we begin to hear that after the three verses beginning "Let . . . declare" (Ps. 118:2ff.), Ps. 118:1 is repeated, as is done today.[9] There is a slight reminiscence of the old procedure in the manner common in western Ashkenaz of reciting the psalms alternately between precentor and congregation. The repetition of Ps. 118:21ff. is accepted everywhere.

For the *Shemaʿ* and its benedictions, antiphonal recitation was customary. The precentor began the prayer, and the congregation repeated the half-verse that he had recited and continued to the end of the verse. In this way the entire passage was recited. When the precentor had said "Hear, Israel" and heard the entire verse recited to the end by the congregation, he would quietly insert the above-mentioned response, "Blessed be the Name of His majestic glory forever." From the division of the verses, this manner of recitation was called פרס על שמע, "to divide the *Shemaʿ*." The same manner of recitation was not customary everywhere: The procedure in use among the people of Jericho, for example, was called כרך את שמע, "to wrap the *Shemaʿ*." There the precentor recited the entire passage without interruption, and the congregation listened or recited along with him; there was no interruption with "Blessed be the Name. . . ."[10] Reciting the *Shemaʿ* straight through, originally only an isolated practice, later became the general one; the response with "Blessed be the Name . . ." was retained, though it had to be said silently. In Ashkenaz it was usual to recite the biblical passages silently; since it could be presumed that the congregation knew them well, the precentor was not needed.

(4) Various names were used for those who conducted the parts of the service, depending on which part they led. One who read from the Torah was called קורא; one who concluded the reading with a passage from the Prophets was called מפטיר בנביא.[11] One who led the Hallel or recited the words of the Priestly Blessing for the priests was called מקרא.[12] Because the public reading of biblical passages was always referred to by use of the verb קרא, this word was used for the liturgy as well, though prayers were never read but always recited from memory (קרא על פה). The precentor for the *Shema'* was called "he who divides the *Shema'*,"[13] even when the manner of recitation that had given rise to the name was long forgotten. Finally, the one who conducted the *'Amida* was called "he who passes before the ark,"[14] because he stepped before the ark with the Torah scrolls. The name continued in use even when the precentor had to take his place long before the *'Amida*. Where his place was lower than the floor-level of the synagogue the term used was יורד לפני התיבה, or ההוא דנחית. Because he had to change his place and step forward he was also called קרובא. The precentor for the *'Amida* was simply called the precentor with no further qualification (שליח צבור), because he was the only one who stepped up to a place where he could be seen and recited the prayer for the congregation to hear with hardly any participation on their part. There were no other precentors, because in the earliest period the service consisted only of the three parts named, each part with a different precentor. On days when two *'Amidot* had to be recited there were two precentors, and in that case the first recited Hallel. If the shofar was to be blown, this was done by the second.[15] [The precentor does not actually blow the shofar, but prompts the shofar blower (מתקיע).]

The service began with the president of the synagogue having one of those present instructed פרוס על שמע, "Lead the recitation of the *Shema'*." When this act was completed, he had another instructed עבור לפני התיבה, "Pass before the ark," or בא וקרב, "Come and approach."[16] It was considered polite to decline such an invitation out of modesty and to wait for a second or third invitation; on the other hand it was considered unseemly to resist too long, thereby wearying the congregation. It could also happen, however, that the one chosen had to refuse the honor because he was unable to deliver the prayers from memory. The recitation of the *'Amida* was the most difficult. It was relatively long, the sequence of its various passages was rigidly fixed, and the precentor did not have the foothold provided in the other prayers by the congregational responses. Therefore, the precentor was given time to prepare his *'Amida* (תקן תפלתו הסדיר,).[17] On the Days of Awe, which recur infrequently and have an unusually long *'Amida*, the medieval manuscripts still prescribe that the precentor should first prepare his text, a rule that became completely superfluous after the introduction of prayer books. It could easily happen that the precentor would lose the thread (טרוף הדעת),[18] or, as happened often, recite incorrect texts. According to the oldest regulations, in such a case he is supposed to give his place to another, but authorities were more patient and allowed him time to find his way again. Only in connection with particular passages that were touchstones of religious probity did they continue to insist firmly that he recite the correct text or step down.[19] On ordinary days the precentor stood alone; on fast days, two congregants stood by his side, one to the right and one to the left.[20] Recent writers have erroneously applied these regulations to every day of the year. Until this day it is the custom in the Italian and Portuguese synagogues for two congregants to stand by the precentor's side throughout the entire Day of Atonement. In the

[372]

Middle Ages this was customary also in Germany, and it was often done also on the New Year.

(5)   As to the posture of the congregation in prayer, Agatharchides of Cnidos reports that the Jews pray seated with outstretched hands (ἐκτετακότες τὰς χεῖρας).[21] In the biblical period this must have been the general practice, but it can nowhere be documented that such a practice also prevailed in the synagogue. At most, among the ecstatics of the later period we find, alongside other bodily motions, also the stretching out of the hands. In general a sedate posture was prescribed for the congregation. During the *Shema* they sat, with the precentor remaining among them. Even in the Middle Ages, when the precentor already had a special place, he sometimes remained seated during this passage. For the *Amida* the precentor and the congregation both stood; in certain passages they bowed (שחה), but excessive bowing was viewed with disfavor.[22] Finally, for the silent prayer following the *Amida* [that is, the Supplications], the congregation threw itself upon the ground. The mystics introduced new motions. With them originated the custom of hopping during the Kedushah, which in Europe is first observed in France. They must also be the source of the practice in France and Germany of looking upward, and in Spain, downward. The custom of shaking the whole body during the *Amida* was also first noted among the pietists in France (נענע, התנועע, את עצמו);[23] this also probably originated among the mystics, and is supposedly even recommended in the midrash. Swaying was originally customary only during study; Judah Halevi tried to explain it by the fact that due to the scarcity of books many people had to share one book, and they therefore had to lean over one after the other. For prayer a different explanation is doubtless more appropriate: The motion of the body stirs up the blood, a genuine demand of the mystics. The casuists argued a good deal over the question of whether one should sway during prayer and at what points; in the end the ecstatics won the day for swaying.

Someone who was to step out of the ranks of worshipers to perform a liturgical function had to be properly dressed;[24] he owed this to the dignity of the congregation. Not only defects in one's clothing, but certain kinds of clothing were considered improper and rendered the wearer unsuited to serve as precentor (M. *Meg.* 4:8; T. *Meg.* 4:30). The precentor used to wrap himself in his coat (התעטף בטליתו כשליח צבור).[25] From this, scholars became accustomed to put on special clothing whenever they visited the synagogue or set about praying anywhere else. The sash, which in those days held together the hanging upper garment, was preferred in Babylonia. In particular they used to put on the particular type of coat that in the Talmud is called טלית (*talit*). As a result the general custom arose of putting on for the Morning Service a garment corresponding to the *talit*, worn always by the precentor. In general they were particular about retaining old customs; people had special clothes for the synagogue.[26] In the Middle Ages, when generally little care was invested in clothing, this was extremely beneficial. Often, to be sure, the reports of old sources and the customs of beloved teachers were slavishly and pedantically imitated, even when the clothing they wore had long ceased to correspond to current fashions. Such a vestige of an ancient garment is the white *kittel*, which often is still worn in Germany on the Day of Atonement, and which in western Germany still bears the Middle High German name *Sargenes*. The newly introduced special official garments for the rabbi and cantor may be seen as continuing this old custom.

[373]

[374]

The covering of the head during prayer was related to the wearing of the *ṭalit*, which had a hood attached to it. It was understood as an expression of submissive respect for the divine majesty; it was also seen as the privilege of a free man that he could remain with covered head.[27] It is Israel's privilege to participate in the revelation of the King of Kings [that is, the *Shemaʿ*] sitting comfortably with covered head, while the servants of earthly powers must hear all royal proclamations bareheaded in fear and trembling. Covering the head was particularly insisted upon in Babylonia; it corresponded to the general custom, but was never prescribed as a religious duty. So it could happen that in post-talmudic Palestine portions of the service or the Blessing of the Priests could be recited bareheaded, though this did not generally meet with favor, for it was generally considered impermissible to pronounce God's name with uncovered head.[28] In Europe, too, the covering of the head seems first to have been strictly enforced only in Islamic Spain. At the beginning of the thirteenth century we hear that in France[29] the Grace after Meals was recited without the head being covered and that it was even customary to call the children bareheaded to the Torah on the Joy of the Torah. Even then this was not generally regarded as proper, and later the covering of the head was elevated to the status of law. Bareheadedness never again occurred in the synagogue until Ahron Chorin (1766–1844)[30] recommended it in 1826 and the Berlin Reform congregation prescribed it for its services.[31] In Europe this institution of Reform worship was never imitated: "Praying with uncovered head particularly marked it as foreign in style and repelled even those who were inwardly sympathetic."[32] But in America in many congregations, head-covering has been dispensed with, and in others it has been left to the discretion of the worshiper.[33]

The discussion of conduct in prayer has often reached back into antiquity, because the customs mentioned in the Talmud never lost their significance. Later authors paid close attention to them and codified them; and thus they were scrupulously observed as far as possible, even when circumstances changed.

(6)   The liturgy underwent a complete revolution through the development of the office of precentor.[34] The service became longer, and the whole style in which it was rendered suffered distortion. In the most ancient period the precentor stepped before the ark only to recite the ʿAmida aloud; later he began with the Kaddish before "Bless the Lord," where Maimonides, for example, has him begin. In the meanwhile, however, he had taken over the preceding psalms in many countries, and in the end even the Morning Benedictions were not only recited in the synagogue but were also recited aloud. Also in the end the liturgy no longer concluded with the ʿAmida, but the Supplications became part of the public service and became longer and longer. The precentor led the entire service, reciting it aloud from beginning to end.[35] Where the congregation knew the prayers thoroughly they recited it along with him in an undertone, and gradually they came to pray together with the precentor. In France and Germany, more people were knowledgeable (בקיאים) about the prayers than in the Orient and in Spain, and printed books were in wider circulation.[36] Therefore, in these countries the precentor raises his voice only at the end of each section, except for the ʿAmida, which he recites aloud from beginning to end; whereas outside Ashkenaz he recites the entire liturgy aloud to the accompaniment of the congregation.

Although the congregation had become habituated to praying along with the precentor, the old responses were still prescribed; new ones were even added, and much weight accorded them. Under the influence of the mystics, the significance of the responses in Kaddish and the Kedushah was very much exaggerated. For the poetry, the community was dependent on the precentor not only all throughout the Middle Ages but even later; he would recite the text, and the congregation would answer only with a refrain wherever possible. Thus, the *pizmon* enjoyed great popularity because it nearly always had a refrain. Merely listening did not satisfy the congregation; they wanted to pray along with the precentor or they sought to pass the time in other ways. The result of both was disruptive,[37] necessitating a thorough revision in the modern period.

§ 54 *Synagogue Song*[1]

(1)   Plain and simple delivery of the prayers was replaced in the course of time with an artistic and more varied musical rendition. How this shift came about and the origin of the melodies used in the liturgy are much disputed questions that are not likely to be clarified. One may be justified in thinking of a relationship with the song of the Levitical choir in the Temple of Jerusalem, but we do not know whether the songs of the Levites consisted of recitative or melodies or how much was transmitted to later generations.[2] It is certain that annotated melodies never existed,[3] and that after the destruction of the Temple most of the opportunities to perform traditional song vanished. It is, however, entirely possible that some melodies have been preserved by tradition for those parts of the liturgy that have a connection with the Temple service, like the recitation of psalms, the Priestly Blessing, or the procession of Tabernacles.[4] Since every aspect of the Temple cult was the object of lively interest, this is very likely, but no certain proof can be cited. From the Talmud it seems fairly certain that the collapse of the independent state made the dominant mood of the times one of depression, that the joy went out of music, and that in general every kind of music was prohibited.[5] We have certain information about the cultivation of music in antiquity only from the circles of the Therapeutai,[6] who were somewhat apart from official Judaism; they performed their hymns in artistic, choral singing in many voices.[7] It can hardly be assumed that choral singing was generally practiced in the Hellenistic diaspora, for in that case some report about it would have reached us.

(2)   The synagogue was never completely without music; even the simplest rendition must have been somehow connected with music, for experience shows that even unschooled recitation always ends in singing. If the precentor recited the prayer in a raised voice and with inner emotion, his voice must often have taken on a solemn tone. The requirement of a beautiful voice for the precentor was first set for the fast-day liturgy;[8] he had to be in lowly spirits and deeply pained over the suffering of the community. The knowledge that a beautiful voice enhanced the liturgy's solemnity resulted in this being valued in daily prayer as well, and thus the use of a precentor with a lovely voice was warmly recommended. As with prayer, so with the reading of Scripture: The intention that the text be reproduced in accordance with its meaning and in an impres-

[376]

sive manner led to a flexible style of performance and to cantillation. We are still quite far from melodies, but a recitative style was introduced quite early.

(3)   The requirement of a melodic rendition first arose in connection with the reading of religious literature: "Whoever reads Scripture without melody and recites traditions without song, of him Scripture says, 'And I have given him laws that are not good.' " So says R. Yoḥanan (B. *Meg.* 32a). Accordingly, the Bible and the traditional literature were provided with accent marks that guided the singing.[9] The accents, which are still printed in all Bible editions, were long seen as an ancient component of the biblical text, but the marks themselves are no older than about the sixth or seventh centuries, and the system customary among us evolved slowly. That does not, however, mean that the melody indicated by the accents (נגון, נעימה) is not older.[10] The accents have more hermeneutical than musical significance,[11] but the traditional cantillation could very well be connected with the accents, with which they share the sentence division and the rhythm. Thus every accent signifies a note, or rather, usually a musical phrase. The books of the Bible are not all rendered in the same manner. The cantillation of the Torah is different from that for the Prophets, and both are different from that for Lamentations and Esther. Even within the Torah, there is a special cantillation for certain passages and certain days. From this it follows that a particular accent does not always have the same musical meaning. Further, varied realizations emerged in different countries. One used to distinguish between the German-Polish cantillation and the Sephardic and Oriental cantillation, but this does not at all exhaust the existing styles. In the Middle Ages the cantillation was called "trope," just as in the church the rich, florid melody was called "tropus."[12] In teaching children, a special melody known as *Stubentrop*, "school-trope," was used.[13] Jacob Möllin performed the Torah reading on the New Year and the Day of Atonement in this style, which is still used today. The extent to which the various types of scriptural cantillation were influenced by the environment and whether a common feature can be recognized in their phrasing have not yet been clarified. The available material is for the time being too scanty to permit a clear judgment.[14]

(4)   The prayers were also long recited in the traditional style of cantillation, and appreciation for beautiful-sounding voices continues to grow the closer we come to the end of the talmudic period. In *Soferim* beautiful singing (נעימה) is prescribed for taking the Torah from the ark.[15] The Targum of the Prophets translates the biblical expression for singing, נגן, with פייט, and the noun חזן, which in the end came to be the regular term for the precentor, is derived from חזנות (ḥizāna). This is the key to explaining the introduction of melodic singing into the prayers. It was the composers of liturgical poetry who enriched the liturgy not only with poems but with a new manner of recitation. Their creations were songs in the true sense of the word, and they were sung by the authors themselves. The impetus to do this came in all probability from the eastern church. "Just as the dissemination of Syriac, Greek, and Latin church poetry awakened within Judaism the desire to give polish to the liturgy by means of poetic prayers, so the sound of church singing with its solemn melodies certainly was a stimulus to synagogue music."[16] The efforts of the mystics in the first centuries of the geonic period also had the effect of encouraging the dissemination and recognition of music.[17] Mys-

tics in all periods liked to sing hymns. "Israel's zeal in emulating the harmonious song of the heavenly hosts is a favorite theme of the *hekhalot*, according to which even God's throne sings." At a later time Judah the Pious likewise recommends the use of "melodies that are pleasing and sweet to you,"[18] melodies that contribute to the heightening of feelings of reverence, melodies that induce the heart to weep and shout with joy.

Synagogue song achieved recognition owing to its effect on emotional life. Because it elevated the worshipers and put their hearts to flight, aroused and deepened in them moods of piety, pain, and joy, they looked aside from the traditions that were hostile to music. The most respected legal authorities declared music for liturgical purposes and for the glory of God to be permitted, and later they even declared it to be commanded.[19] Even Maimonides, the implacable foe of every kind of music, could not withstand the general opinion, and had to sanction the melodies that rang out the praise of God.[20] Complaints were often raised over the faulty and overdone practices of the singers, but singing itself was not only tolerated but generally recommended "because it moves the heart." "*Piyyut* and *pizmon* were not simply read, but were executed in recitative-like manner, and partly sung. There was a manner of singing *yoser*, *ofan*, *meʾora*, etc., *qerova*, Aramaic poems, etc., likewise *ʿavoda*, *seliḥa*, and *qina*."[21] The melodies to which the individual pieces were to be sung were noted at the beginning; in printed prayer books some such notations are still present. It got to the point that sometimes the recitation of a poem was given up altogether because the melody had been forgotten. The melodies prescribed for the poems came from a great variety of sources.[22] Melodies of folk songs and love songs from every country can be found among them, and it is not to be doubted that the settings of church hymns were occasionally taken over. Art knows no boundaries, and cannot be restricted to a particular circle. The precentors took their tunes unconsciously wherever they found them. The criticism was raised early that too many foreign songs had been introduced into the synagogue.[23] But the Jews are not alone even in this complaint. Church writers also raise the reproach that too much secular music is mixed with the Christian liturgy.[24] There were archetypal melodies; well-known Hebrew and foreign songs were used as melodies for many other songs. The fact that much of the music used for liturgical poetry is borrowed from non-Jewish sources is proved and undisputed; the question that arises is how much synagogue music goes back to Jewish tradition. For it also cannot be overlooked that many melodies display a certain peculiarity not to be found elsewhere, and which must rest on an old tradition.[25]

[378]

(5) Nor did the statutory prayers have to do without the joy of song.[26] Certain piyyut melodies were transferred to individual prayers, the melodies of the scriptural readings were employed, and new melodies were composed. For nearly every prayer an individual melody was formed, and a special recitative for Sabbaths and festivals. Special pleasure was taken in singing the Verses of Song in the Morning Service, which was done at length. In Regensburg a full hour was needed just for the prayer "Blessed is He Who spoke," and the same amount of time was used by Isserlein in Wiener Neustadt during the period from the first of Elul to the Day of Atonement. In the Orient, too, the recitation of the psalms required a full hour around the year 1200. Immanuel of Rome gives a revealing picture of the rich program of a cantor and his activity around 1300:

When I recite the great Kedushah, a *yoṣer*, or the *qerova*, the wellsprings of the great abyss are broken open; and when I pray on the Day of Atonement or read the scroll on Purim, even the Mighty Ones tremble; and when I recite the vision of Isaiah or read Lamentations or the bad prophecies in Jeremiah you may see every tongue silent, every eye weeping.[27]

The melodies of the statutory prayers impressed themselves in the minds of the congregants, and though not notated, they took on a fixed form, so that there was no further deviation from the traditional melodies. In Germany already in the fourteenth and fifteenth centuries one distinguished the tunes used in the Rhineland from those of Regensburg and Austria. Jacob Möllin recommends holding fast to the local melodies and not changing them for foreign ones, and the later halakhists took this rule very seriously. His disciples noted exactly the way in which he executed the individual prayers on the various festivals. Since his model was emulated, he can claim the credit of being the creator of the synagogue musical tradition of Germany and Poland. The Portuguese, too, paid great attention to the prayer melodies. They distinguished eighteen basic melodies, of which each could be sung in four variations.[28] In Germany, this would not have sufficed. From Worms, for example, in the seventeenth century, melodies are mentioned for the *Shemaʿ* before "Blessed be He Who spoke," for "Blessed be He Who spoke" of Sabbaths and festivals, for the following psalms for Sabbaths, for the first and eighth days of Passover, for the Twenty-third of Iyyar (the day commemorating the persecution of 1096),[29] for the month of Av, and so on. In Poland, they were even more enthusiastic about melodies;[30] precentors could let their imaginations range unbridled, and they produced a kind of melody that has been called "a *pilpul* set to music." Like *pilpul*, synagogue melody was transplanted to the West, to the detriment of the congregations and the liturgy.[31] For those precentors schooled neither in the Hebrew language nor in music, the "melody" became the main thing, and prayer was forced into the background, its text mercilessly corrupted.[32]

(6) Synagogue music was in general solo music. The congregation did, however, often accompany the precentor, not as a trained choir, but with undisciplined and arbitrary interruptions that disturbed the singing. The responses, too, were without order or uniformity. Quite rarely, on special occasions—for example, at the installation of an Exilarch—a choir (בחורים)[33] was employed for the Sabbath service. This happened occasionally in the Middle Ages, too; for example, in Italy a few singers assisted the precentor on the Days of Awe.[34] A strange error was the introduction of choir boys in Poland,[35] a practice perhaps still known to this day in the East, and which even in Germany had for centuries the most harmful influence on the liturgy. On either side of the precentor stood a singer, who accompanied his singing in a higher or lower voice—and who was therefore called *singer* and *bass*—sounding harmonic intervals and sometimes performing small solo passages. This kind of singing could generally be heard everywhere until the middle of the last century (it was still customary in Berlin until 1840);[36] it intensified the disorder and tastelessness in the extreme.[37]

Among the Jews polyphonic music on artistic principles was first cultivated in Italy. In 1620 Solomon de' Rossi printed thirty[-three] pieces from the prayer book [including

[379]

psalms, prayers, and poems] with melodies for several voices in his *Hashirim asher lishelomo*, the first notated publication of Hebrew music.[38] From this it is evident that his efforts were directed primarily at introducing organized choral singing.[39] What success these efforts enjoyed can no longer be determined. But the music of the Italian communities was never as disorderly as that of the northern synagogues.[40]

(7)   In Germany the revolution occurred in the period after Mendelssohn. Then the Jews' taste became more refined and they came to be repelled by the traditional Polish music; the need was now felt to restore order and dignity into the performance of the synagogue service. Among the means for improving the music came first the introduction of congregational singing and organ accompaniment.[41] Among all the innovations attached to the name of Israel Jacobsohn, none has called forth such determined opposition as that of the introduction of the organ [§45(3)—*Engl. trans.*]. It was seen as a lethal attack on traditional Judaism, as a disruption of the essence of the Jewish liturgy. The battle has now been going on for nearly a century, but it has lost none of its intensity. The organ thus acquired a significance that it does not deserve. Instead of being seen as a measure to be judged for aesthetics and practicality, it became a question of a party program, and a bone of contention between battling religious movements. Jacobsohn's intention was to replace the precentor's singing with congregational hymns, and to lend to the part-singing the firm support of organ accompaniment as well as a purer, more rhythmical shape. This meant the complete destruction of traditional synagogue music, for the new congregational hymns had no connection with either the responses or the melodies of tradition. The new congregational singing was unquestionably an enrichment of the service, but its consequence was an impoverishment in melodies.

The true regeneration of synagogue music is to be credited to Solomon Sulzer (1804–90), in whose person all the abilities necessary for this purpose were harmoniously combined: musical genius, a phenomenal voice, and profound knowledge of the traditional music. Fate set him down in an auspicious place, determining that the locus of his activity should be the Vienna of Beethoven and Schubert. Sulzer became the trailblazer of modern synagogue music, and his *Shir zion* the fundamental work that inspired all his followers. Sulzer's significance rests in his being the first to make a critical selection from among the traditional melodies, removing what was not usable and supplying what was lacking with his own compositions. He also reproduced the ancient Jewish melodies in musical notation, revising them in accordance with the rules of musical science so that they became both melodic and rhythmical. Finally, he brought the institution of the synagogue choir to an extraordinarily high level, by creating pieces that were at once artistically correct and permeated with the old Jewish spirit and true religious devotion. Sulzer's music resounded in synagogues throughout the world and gave his colleagues the impetus to undertake similar efforts. Moritz Deutsch in Breslau (1818–92) worked in the same vein; he made his special province the theoretical and practical training of cantors, and in his *Vorbeterschule* offered a complete collection of the "ancient synagogue intonations." The *Gesänge für Synagogen: Eingeführt in der Synagoge zu Braunschweig* (Brunswick, 1853) of H. Goldberg provided for congregational singing by offering uncomplicated one- or at most two-part musical settings of the prayers, thereby making possible congregational singing even in communities that

[380]

could not or would not establish a choir. A worthy successor to Sulzer was Louis Lewandowski (1823–94), who, as choir director in Berlin (since 1840), did pioneering work for the development of choir and congregational singing. In his *Qol rina utefila* (Berlin, 1882) he first attended with particular care to the recitative for the cantor, which he reproduced in exact musical notation, without stripping it of its peculiar Jewish character; but at the same time he offered for the use of smaller congregations two-part pieces "which excel by virtue of their flowing melody and harmony." He displayed his greatness as a musician in the four-part choruses for Sabbaths and festivals contained in his two-volume work *Toda vezimra* (Berlin, 1876–82). Here he created a great number of pieces distinguished by their perfect beauty and suffused with deep religious spirit. He set the entire liturgy for the Berlin community, for cantor, choir, and organ; his pieces became widely known and popular in the best sense. Lewandowski's pieces brought the religious community near to their ancestral treasures of thought; they became the most faithful interpreters of the prophetic revelation, in which our liturgy is steeped.

In a similar way numerous other masters have labored to elevate the liturgy through the reworking of old compositions and the composition of new ones. The melodies of the Portuguese Jews have found in Federigo Consolo an interpreter equally enthusiastic for and accomplished in his art.[42] Thus, for decades the work of ennobling the synagogue music has been zealously pursued, and the highest value placed on the musical training of the cantor and the establishment of a well-trained choir. Experience has taught that the soulful old melodies of previous generations are deeply rooted and form an indispensable part of the liturgy. At the same time, the progressive tendency leads to the suppression of singing through the richer development of instrumental accompaniment and the simplification of the liturgy. Whatever shape this development will take, music in the synagogue does not exist for its own sake, but as a means for reaching the goal of the liturgy. The task of liturgy is and remains the assembling of the community for collective devotion, to elevate its spirit toward our Father in Heaven, and to instruct it from the eternally flowing well of revelation.

Notes

Selected Bibliography

Appendix

SECTION BIBLIOGRAPHIES

Index of Prayers

HEBREW INCIPITS

ENGLISH INCIPITS

Index of Names and Subjects

Notes

§1–5   Introduction

1. The history of the liturgy is covered at length, and sources are cited below, in the notes for §34ff.

2. The inner meaning of synagogue worship is treated from a history of religion perspective by Bousset, *Judentums*, 201f.; new edition, revised by H. Gressmann, entitled *Religion des Judentums im späthellenistischen Zeitalter* (Tübingen, 1926).

[3. On the essential meaning of the creation of public prayer as a new kind of service of God, see also Spiegel, *Poetry* and Heinemann, *Prayer*, 17ff.]

4. Cf. below, §31(2).

5. On the occurrences of the word λειτουργεῖν in the Septuagint, see E. Hatch and H. Redpath, *Concordance to the Septuagint* (Oxford, 1906), 872f.; for לטרגיה in the midrash, see Perles, *Beiträge*, 68f.

6. H. Achelis, in his book *Praktische Theologie*, vol. 1, cannot explain the connection between the various meanings of liturgy because he misses the connecting link, the word עבודה, in which the same shift of meaning occurred. The New Testament material needs to be re-examined from this point of view. Likewise, Rietschel, *Liturgik*, 1:27f., was not deterred by his own ignorance from pronouncing a disparaging judgment against the word עבודה and the meaning of the Jewish cult; the word does not imply "enslavement to the world of law" any more than does the German expression *Gottesdienst*.

7. On the reading of the *Sifre*, see *Sifre* (edited by Meir Friedmann), *Sifre* Deut., 80a, §41; *Midrash tanaim*, 35; cf. also Y. *Ber.* 4:1, 7a and *Midrash tehilim* 157b, §66.

8. *Sifre* Deut., 70b, §26 enumerates ten expressions for prayer; cf. the literature cited by Friedmann in *Sifre* (*Sifre* Deut., 80a, §41).

9. ברך is a loan word from Egyptian; cf. Gesenius, *Handwörterbuch*, 15th ed., 117.

10. On the requirements of a benediction, see B. *Ber.* 40b; instructive notes in Jawitz, *Meqor*, 4f. ["The mention of God's name" in the benediction formula refers to the name *adonai*, which is considered the *qeri* of the tetragrammaton; cf. Y. *Ber.* 9:1, 12d and T. *Ber.* 7:20; see Lieberman, *Tosefta*, 1:122. Various scholars have dealt with the gradual formation of the benediction formula. In the early stages of the formula's use, it seems that not all circles insisted that only the tetragrammaton be used, as demonstrated by the above-mentioned *baraita* in Y. (cf. also T. *Ber.* 4:4–5 and parallels); likewise, a "benediction formula" using *adonai* is found in a few texts of the Judean desert scrolls; see S. Liebermann's article in *PAAJR* 20 (1951): 395f.; Heinemann, *Prayer*, 76 and n. 37. As for the use of אתה, "you," in the benediction formula, see A. Spanier, "Zur Formengeschichte des altjüdischen Gebetes," *MGWJ* 78 (1934): 438f.; Heinemann, *Prayer*, 52ff. On the significance of the requirement of *kingdom*, see J.G. Weiss, "On the Formula *melekh ha-ʿolam* as anti-Gnostic Protest," *JJS* 10 (1959): 169; C. Roth, "*Melekh ha-ʿolam*: Zealot Influence on the Liturgy," *JJS* 11 (1960): 173–75; J. Heinemann, "The Formula *Melekh ha-ʿolam*," *JJS* 11 (1960): 177–79; E.J. Wiesenberg, "The Liturgical Term *Melekh ha-ʿolam*," *JJS* 15 (1964): 1–56; J. Heinemann, "Once Again, *Melekh ha-ʿolam*," *JJS* 15 (1964): 149–54; E.J. Wiesenberg, "Gleanings of the Liturgical Term *Melekh ha-ʿolam*," *JJS* 17 (1966): 47–72; and Heinemann, *Prayer*, 61ff. The various rules for the benediction formula were at first fully applicable only to the fixed statutory public prayers, not to the individual, optional prayers; see Heinemann, *Prayer*, 100f.]

11. The meaning of the dictum, "A biblical verse may not serve as a benediction" (Y. *Ber.* 1:8, 3d),

is that a verse can serve as a benediction only if it receives a eulogy, like Psalms 120 in the fast-day benedictions. [Detailed discussion of the meaning of this dictum appears in Ginzberg, *Perushim*, 1:209f.]

12. The etymology of תפלה in Ignaz Goldziher, *Abhandlungen zur arabischen Philologie* (Leiden, 1899), 36. Döller, *Gebet*, 17, relying on earlier explanations, takes פלל as having to do with mediation, and התפלל as meaning prayer on someone's behalf; he explains צלא from the Assyrian *sullu*, meaning "to plead to," and the Ethiopic *ṣalaya*, "to pray." That תפלה is used only for the ʿAmida is demonstrated in Elbogen, *Studien*, 36.

13. Cf. *Rivista Israelita* 5 (1907): 98–102. For evidence of the use of סדור for a prayer book, see Zunz, *Ritus*, 19e, 33g; מחזור ibid., 19f.; cf. also Zunz, *Ritus*, 33. Outside the Ashkenazic regions the words סדור and מחזור were not always used as here described.

14. Cf. Elbogen, *Studien*, 1.

15. Zunz, *Ritus*, 18.

16. Ginzberg, *Geonica*, 2:114f.; cf. ibid., 109f.

17. The complete Amram text is available in Frumkin, *Seder*. Marx's work also appeared separately, and this is the edition cited. Much data from Saadia in Bondi, *Saadia*, and in Frumkin's commentary. *Maḥzor Vitry* was published by S. Hurwitz after cod. Br. Mus. Add. 27, 200, 201; selected passages from the better Oxford manuscript in Steinschneider, *Catalogus*, no. 1100 in Frumkin, *Seder*. Rashi's prayer book was prepared for the press by S. Buber; after his death it was published by J. Freimann [see *Siddur Rashi*]. For smaller collections, see Zunz, *Ritus*, 33. [For additional manuscripts of *Vitry* and of a prayer book from Rashi's school, see *REJ* 125 (1966): 63f., 127f., 245f.]

18. See below, §43(3)f. Zunz, *Ritus*, 38 describes the peculiar character of each rite. See also Luzzatto, *Mavo*, 15f.

19. On the geniza, see Schechter, *Studies*, 2:1–3. Manuscripts of prayer books, especially for the festivals, are extant in the thousands. Especially rich collections can be found in the libraries of Hamburg, London (British Museum and Jews' College), Munich, New York (Jewish Theological Seminary), Oxford, Paris, Parma, and Rome. The great majority of geniza fragments are deposited in Cambridge, but Oxford, the British Museum, Leningrad, New York, and the Academy in Budapest also have many that originated there; cf. *REJ* 63 (1912): 112ff.; *JQR* NS 14 (1923–24): 189f.—The bibliography of prayer books is still in a poor state. In general, cf. Steinschneider, *Catalogus*, 303–484; Zedner, *Catalogue*, s.v. "maḥzor," "tefilot"; *J.E.*, s.v. "Prayer Books." The first edition of Ashkenaz in Zedner, *Catalogue*, 458; of Poland, Steinschneider, *Catalogus*, no. 2064. For Asti, Fossano, and Montecalvo, see Zunz, *Ritus*, 59f.; Luzzatto, *Mavo*, 16. This prayer book has never been printed. In the Leghorn edition of the Italian rite, only the introduction is by Luzzatto; for the first edition, see Steinschneider, *Catalogus*, no. 2061.

20. The title of the Romaniot rite is also ספר חונא (Ben Jacob, *Oṣar sefarim* [Vilna, 1880], 664). A single copy of the edition of Constantinople, 1510, entitled ספר תפלות השנה (A. Berliner, *Aus meiner Bibliothek* [Frankfurt am Main, 1898], no. 1) is in the possession of the municipal library of Frankfurt. The first well-known edition is Venice, 1524; the other is 1573–76, according to Zedner, *Catalogue*, 483. My friend Felix Perles in Königsberg kindly enabled me to use a nearly complete copy of the latter edition.

21. *Sepharad* first appeared under the title תמונות תחנות תפלות. An unknown edition of 1517 is listed in Steinschneider, *Catalogus*, 305, no. 2066; the first known edition, ibid., 1524, no. 2067.

22. On the prayer book of southern Arabia, cf. W. Bacher in "Der Südarabische Siddur und Jaḥjā Ṣāliḥ's Commentar zu Demselben," *JQR* 14 (1902): 581–621.

23. Complete editions of Provence do not exist; the prayers for each of the three cities appeared in separate parts. See the bibliographies.

§6 The Morning Service of Weekdays

1. The structure of the Morning Service in Sachs, *Poesie*, 168.

2. Cf. Elbogen, *Studien*, 78, 81.

3. See, e.g., *JQR* 10 (1898): 654.

4. Berliner, *Randbemerkungen*, 1:10.

5. The kabbalistic conception in Lewysohn, *Meqore*, 24f.

§7 The Shemaʿ and Its Benedictions

1. The name קריאת שמע is the usual one in the Talmud, midrash, and halakhic literature (M. *Ber.* 2:1 has מקרא). תפלת יוצר occurs in manuscripts and in printed books from Oriental lands. ברכת המאורות is found

in Abudarham, among others.—As for the benediction before the *Shemaᶜ* (ברוך אתה ה' אלהינו מלך העולם אשר קדשנו במצותיו וצונו על מצות קריאת שמע להמליכו בלבב שלם וליחדו בלב טוב ולעבדו בנפש חפיצה, "Blessed are You, Lord our God, King of the world, Who sanctified us by His commandments and commanded us concerning the Recitation of the *Shemaᶜ*, to declare His Kingship with a whole heart, and to declare His unity with a willing heart, and to serve Him with a willing soul"), see *JQR* 10 (1898): 654 and *REJ* 53 (1907): 240f.; cf. Abudarham 47a; Ginzberg, *Geonica*, 1:136f. The benediction has meanwhile been found a few times in the fragments, not only for the Morning Service but for the Evening Service as well, and not only for weekdays but also for Tabernacles; cf. Mann, *Palestinian*, 286, 308, 332. But the benediction is not found in all the fragments, and whether it is optional or mandatory is disputed; Mann, *Palestinian*, 287, assumes that the Kaddish before "Creator" belongs to "Creator" and that in Palestine the benediction served as a substitute for it.

2. *Y. Ber.* 7:3, 11c; *B. Ber.* 50a (Elbogen, *Studien*, 19).

3. *Ṭur, O.Ḥ.* §57 and Abudarham; cf. Zunz, *Literaturgeschichte*, 13. In Amram 4a the words " 'Bless the Lord' for the individual" are inserted here, but this is a late addition; cf. Marx, *Untersuchungen*, 4; Frumkin, *Seder*, 1:185.

4. Elbogen, *Studien*, 19.

5. New "Creator" texts were published by Mann, *Palestinian*, 273, 293, 320f., 323 (these last, for the Sabbath).

6. Analyses of "Creator" in Rapoport, *Qalir*; Jawitz, *Meqor*; Elbogen, *Studien*, 20f.—Manhig, "Laws of Prayer," §30 defends the reading בטובו מחדש, "in His goodness He renews," as against טובו מחדש, "His Goodness renews" [but this is the reading of Saadia, *Siddur*, 13]; see also *Rivista Israelita* 4 (1907): 194f. and *B. Ber.* 50a.

7. Saadia's text [ibid.], Amram 4b f.; Frumkin, *Seder*, 1:193f.; Bondi, *Saadia*, 13; Elbogen, *Studien*, 21. In Saadia [*Siddur*, 36] the passage from מה טוב to אדון עוזן (Bondi, *Saadia*, 17) is lacking, but he has, alongside "Blessed God," another alphabetical acrostic [ibid., 37]; Zunz, *Literaturgeschichte*, 13; Bondi, *Saadia*, 17; Elbogen, *Studien*, 22 and n. 1, also on the chain-rhyme.

8. The letters with final form are now represented only by the words תמיד מספרים כבוד, while Saadia reads תמיד יספרו לאל קדושתו (ibid.); it appears that our text was not changed unintentionally. There were also some who sought in the words מספרים כבוד an acrostic of the name Michael (Baer, ᶜAvodat, 77).

9. *All are beloved*: for Saadia, cf. Bondi, *Saadia*, 17. For Kaffa in Crimea, see Baer, ᶜAvodat, 78; Zunz, *Ritus*, 82 demonstrates that its rite belongs to Romaniot; see I. Markon, "Maʾamar ᶜal odot mahzor minhag kafa" in *Zikaron leʾavraham eliyahu*, Festschrift for A. Harkavy, ed. I. Markon and D. Günzberg (St. Petersburg, 1908), 449f. The expanded acrostic was known also in Persia; cf. *JQR* 10 (1898): 608.

10. On the Merkava mystics, see below, §44(4)f. The text in Amram 4a did not originate there (Marx, *Untersuchungen*, 18, Hebrew section, 4), but is taken from the *Hekhalot*; cf. Bloch, *Merkava*, 20.

11. Ginzberg, *Geonica*, 2:48; see now also *REJ* 70 (1920): 135f.; *Tarbiz* 2 (1930/1): 383f.; Elbogen, *Studien*, 22f.

12. [Saadia's attack on the recitation of "Cause a new light" is not in his *Siddur* as printed, but it is found in a fragment published by N. Wieder, *Saadia Studies* (Manchester, 1943), 262; on the whole matter, see ibid. On Saadia's position of principle vis-à-vis changes in the wording of the prayers, see Heinemann in *Annual of Bar-Ilan University* 1 (1962/3): 220f.]

13. On the conclusion of "Creator," see Baer, ᶜAvodat, 79; Elbogen, *Studien*, 23. The following summary displays the development in the Reform prayer books: "Cause a new light" is lacking in the Hamburg Temple; "Be blessed, our Rock" and the Kedushah are lacking in the prayer book published by Heinemann (Vogelstein); a shorter version is found in D. Einhorn, *Book of Prayers for Jewish Congregations* (Chicago, 1896), the *Union Prayer-Book*, and the Baden prayer book.

14. The quotation in Mann, *Palestinian*, 293, n. 63 does not contradict the above; while the idea of Zion is strongly stressed, the text under discussion is a poetically elaborated one. Nor does the version mentioned in Mann, *Palestinian*, 295 constitute an absolute contradiction. It seems that this is an area of religious development and expression that has not yet been explored.

15. On the text of "With great love," cf. Zunz, *Haderashot*, 179; *REJ* 50 (1904): 145f.; Elbogen, *Studien*, 26f.; *Haqedem* 2 (1908): 85, 88f. [; Heinemann, *Prayer*, 43, n. 34]. Expansions of the version current in France were rejected by R. Judah the Pious; cf. J. Perles's article in *Graetz Festschrift*, 17.

16. A hitherto unknown variant of "Who loves His people Israel" appears in Mann, *Palestinian*, 288.

17. On *amen*, cf. Frumkin, *Seder*, 1:196; Ginzberg, *Geonica*, 1:138 derives *amen* from the benediction mentioned above in §7, n. 1, which seems unlikely. Mann, *Palestinian*, 295, points to the Palestinian fragment, which reads here *amen*, but he himself admits that the problem has not been completely resolved. Y. variants cited in medieval works are not decisive, for we know that these often cite Y. even though it was not actually a source, as Mann himself admits (Mann, *Palestinian*, 291, n. 60).

18. On the word count, cf. Manhig, "Laws of Prayer," §33; *Ṭur, O.Ḥ.* §61, and commentators; see also Baer, ᶜAvodat, 81.

19. On "Blessed be the Name," see Blau in *REJ* 31 (1895): 189 and Elbogen, *Studien*, 10.—Supplementary material to the third edition: With this reference to Blau, I meant only that at the moment we can say no more about the development of the text. According to Aptowitzer in *MGWJ* 73 (1929): 192, it came into being ca. 100 B.C.E., as a protest against the Hasmoneans and the Sadducees. Not all will agree that this is "beyond all doubt," especially since it remains unresolved why the text was not eliminated or changed when the time for that protest had passed. On the other hand, the emergence of the text can be easily explained from the parallels in Pss. 72:19 and 145:11 cited by the author. According to Aptowitzer, the text was inserted into the recitation of the *Shemaʿ* not out of liturgical, but out of political considerations. According to him, only one person would recite the *Shemaʿ*, while the congregation would merely respond. Eventually, when individuals began to recite it with the reader, they all said the response "Blessed be the name" (Aptowitzer, op. cit., 106). This implies that at that time the entire text was always recited aloud. The reason that it was later said silently was that, in the meanwhile, the cause for protest had ceased to exist. But still later a time came when the protest was again called for; hence, the need to proclaim the responses aloud was stressed. This would have been ca. 250, when the trinity dogma was being developed, and the *Shemaʿ* with the proclamation "Blessed be the Name" attached to it was a kind of formal manifesto of pure monotheism. But this institution had only local force, and did not prevail everywhere (Aptowitzer, op. cit., 118). This rather complex construction does not shrink even from the assumption that changing times bring about changes in the manner of reciting the prayers; but at the same time, it does not take into consideration the fact that times change also with respect to their political and religious goals as well as in the availability of opportunities for protest. Furthermore, Aptowitzer does not give attention to such technical terms as פרס על שמע and ברך את שמע. [Cf. also Heinemann, *Prayer*, 84f.]

20. On the composition of "True and Certain," see Elbogen, *Studien*, 28f. On the text of Saadia, see Bondi, *Saadia*, 13 [Saadia, *Siddur*, 15; cf. also *Tarbiz* 34 (1964/5): 363f.]; Rashi, cf. *Pardes* 55a; Palestine, see *JQR* 10 (1898): 656; Ashkenaz's version for use with piyyutim, see Baer, *ʿAvodat*, 216.—Poetic expansions of the text, both of the Morning and Evening services for weekdays and Sabbaths in Mann, *Palestinian*, 294f., 305, 321; they are even more extreme than the versions reported in Elbogen, *Studien*, 31. But it must be noted that these expanded texts, though prolix, contain no conceptual innovations; only in the liturgical poem cited in Mann, *Palestinian*, 294f. and attached to the daily psalm is a refrence made to the Resurrection.

21. The words קיים עלינו, "fulfill for us," are rejected in Ginzberg, *Geonica*, 2:91, since this is no place to refer to Redemption.—How "Help of our fathers" took shape can be seen from the facsimile in Elbogen, *Studien*, 32; cf. ibid., 31 and *REJ* 53 (1907): 236, 241 on the end of "Redemption." The critique of R. Judah the Pious of other additions may be found in Perles's article in *Graetz Festschrift*. In Worms, גואלנו was introduced only by R. Meir b. Isaac. See Epstein in *Hagoren* 4 (1903): 91f.

[22. On the eulogy "Who redeemed Israel," see Goldschmidt, *Hagada*, 58. But it cannot be excluded that this eulogy text existed before Rava's time; perhaps it is only an alternate Palestinian eulogy. See *Tarbiz* 30 (1960/1): 406f.; Heinemann, *Prayer*, 62 and n. 28. Evidence has survived that some used to say גואל ישראל, "Redeemer of Israel," at the end of the Redeemer benediction after the *Shemaʿ*. Cf. *Qiryat sefer* 29 (1952–54): 172. The conjecture of Z. Ben-Hayim in *Leshonenu* 22 (1957/8): 223f. must also be considered: that this eulogy originally read גאל ישראל, "Redeemer of Israel," participle of the form *paʿel*.

On the rhyming "Rock of Israel," see Heinemann in *Annual of Bar-Ilan University* 4–5 (1966/7): 132f.]

23. Cf. Elbogen, *Studien*, 13f. As a declaration of faith, the passage came to be called "the acceptance of the yoke of the kingdom of heaven" (cf. M. *Ber.* 2:3). On individual prayer: Elbogen, *Studien*, 40f.; below, §10.

24. Detailed discussion of the reason in Elbogen, *Studien*, 7f. Against my approach, Blau, *REJ* 55 (1909): 201f.; Blau, *REJ*, 59 (1913): 198f.; Bacher, *REJ* 57 (1911): 100f.; and my reply, *REJ* 56 (1910): 222f.; a compromise approach is advanced by Lieber, *REJ* 57 (1911): 161f.; Lieber, *REJ* 58 (1912): 1f. (also appeared separately under the title *La récitation du Schema et les bénédictions*), with which Brody agrees, *MGWJ* 54 (1910): 491f. But despite the strong opposition, I see myself compelled to hold my ground. First, no evidence is found that the Talmud anywhere refers to reciting the benediction, or the benediction over bread, by the expression פרס. This term is used only for breaking the bread itself, and a piece of bread broken from the loaf is called פרוסה. The same is the case with the verb בצע, and the statement לא בצע על פרוסה שאינה שלו in B. *Ḥul* in 7b is no exception. Bacher relies, to be sure, on Rashi's comment לא היה מברך; but R. Gershom's comment on the passage, כלומר לא היה נהגה, shows that this is unnecessary. Thus, neither the word בצע nor פרוסה refers to the benediction. It is true that a pious Jew would not break bread or eat it without saying a benediction over it, but this has nothing to do with the original meaning of the word. True, Rashi and all later commentators and decisors no longer made these distinctions, and most of the criticism of those who disagree with me depends on such inexact interpretations of the later rabbis. We would easily be able to come to an agreement as to how the expression פרס על שמע was understood by *Soferim* (the sources were assembled by Blau, *REJ* 73 [1921]: 140f.), for the sources speak quite clearly; but we must not pay attention

to late commentaries of any kind, and must follow the original meaning of the earliest sources. From these, I am unable to reach any other conclusion than the one that I explained in *Studien*, 7f. Even today I am unable to find an attestation for the combination of פרס and על, but I do not think, as does Bacher, that my explanation collapses on that account. We must accept the fact that this is a unique expression that occurs only in connection with the Recitation of the *Shemaʿ*. Thus, one says, for example, in the often-cited baraita T. *Meg.* 4:27, הפורס על שמע, but המברך על המצוות. We all agree that the term refers to the three passages of the *Shemaʿ* together with the benedictions, and that the *Shemaʿ* was recited verse by verse antiphonally. Wherein lies our disagreement? My opponents insist on deriving פרס from the benedictions, whereas I derive it from the meaning "to divide in half." Lieber goes too far in trying to connect the antiphonal rendition with the text in the present prayer book and in finding in all the functions named in M. *Meg.* 4:5 the same scheme and, wherever possible, the same internal structure of the benedictions.

[See lately also Albeck, *Mishnah*, 1:328. He believes that the congregation would respond "Blessed be the Name" after hearing the first verse and the name of God included therein from the precentor. This seems likely in light of the fact that we always find this formula as a congregational response. See Albeck, *Mishnah*, 2:502f. Lieberman, *Tosefta*, 5:1206f. upholds the interpretation of the expression הפורס את שמע as "the one who announces the *Shemaʿ*." But despite the disagreements as to the meaning of the term פרס and as to the exact distribution of the recitation between the precentor and the congregation, no one disagrees that the *Shemaʿ* was recited antiphonally in antiquity, as implied by R. Nehemiah in the baraita, "As a scribe הפורס את שמע in the synagogue: He begins and they respond" (B. *Soṭa* 30b, T. *Soṭa* 6:3).]

§ 8 The ʿAmida: *Composition and Structure*

1. Kohler, *Ursprünge* derives the ʿAmida, like all the prayers, from the circles of the early pietists whom he identifies as probably being the Essenes. Accordingly, he holds that the original form of the prayer was entirely hymnic, as it is on Sabbaths and festivals. He takes no note of the fact that these ʿAmidot, too, are not hymnic in their entirety, and that the word תפילה points to petitions. On the basis of his assumptions, Kohler hypothesizes that the weekday ʿAmida developed out of the fast-day prayer ritual and that it was created by worshipers of the circle of Honi the Circle-Maker. This is possible for some of the benedictions, but is unlikely for the group as a whole.—A completely new conception about the rise of the ʿAmida is set forth in Finkelstein, ʿAmida. He believes he is able to fix all the stages and to clarify exactly the period from which the various parts come. One of his claims is incontrovertible: that the Palestinian version has the address יי אלהינו, "Lord our God," in several places. But the extant material is not sufficient to bring us to secure conclusions; the prayers of Rabban Gamaliel and of Rabbi Akiva or Ben Azzai, which he cites, have a completely different character and cannot be compared with each other; likewise, he does not explain why the changes in the ritual occurred. The material available as evidence (pp. 6f.) is insufficient, and it is not entirely certain that Palestine is always the source of the earliest form of the text. On p. 137 he mentions that Romaniot and others include in this benediction the words "Lord our God" in places where they do not occur in other texts; but in all rites such terms of address are customarily added freely, and in Benedictions 13 and 19 of the Babylonian text Finkelstein shows them to be late additions. In Benediction 5 Finkelstein, for the sake of his theory, proclaims the version based on Lam. 5:21 not original and prefers the ordinary version "Our Father." He correctly points out that some of the benedictions contain seven words, but we have no proof that this came about out of consideration for the mystics and Hillel's mystical inclinations. For had they been able to do so, would not the mystics have changed the wording of the other benedictions so that they too would number seven words? Surely it may be assumed that these zealots would not have been satisfied with adding a few biblical expressions, but would have changed the entire text to accord with their demands. Likewise, it does not seem that Benediction 11 was introduced only in the aftermath of the Jews' loss of the right to judge capital cases; and from the account that Rabbi Akiva once said on a fast-day, "Our Father, our King," it cannot be proved that every time the kingdom of heaven is stressed it must be dated between the years 117 and 135! And the claims that the petition for peace in Benediction 18 (19) attests to a preceding period of disorder, and that the stress on resurrection in Benediction 2 must follow a period of war, underestimate the value of religious longings and exaggerate the value of external events.

[Finkelstein's central claim, which serves as the foundation and starting point for the 'textual criticism' and for the separation of the 'layers' in the ʿAmida, namely, that in the time of Rabban Gamaliel II the epithet "Lord our God" was no longer in use in prayer, has already been overturned by A. Marmorstein in his book *The Old Rabbinic Doctrine of God* (London: Oxford, 1927), 70. On the entire matter, see further Heinemann, *Prayer*, 10ff., 32ff., 45ff.]

2. Cf. Elbogen, *Studien*, 36. On "Pass before the ark," ibid., 33f.; on ʿAmida, see *Soferim*, 16, end.

3. On the elimination of the precentor's repetition by Maimonides, see David b. Zimra, *Responsa*, nos. 5

and 94 (Venice, l749) and thereon A. Geiger, *Melo ḥofnayim* (Berlin, 1840), 70f. and the responsum published by Friedlander in *JQR* NS 5 (1914–15): 1f.

4. The internal structure of the ʿAmida, B. *Ber.* 34a, quoting R. Hanina (third century), and Y. 2:4, 4d, quoting R. Aḥa in the name of R. Joshua b. Levi (same generation).

5. On the origin of the ʿAmida, see B. *Ber.* 22b; Y. 4:1, 7a f.

6. For the explanation of the word הפקולי, compare the word λινόπωλος, which occurs in an inscription that was found in Jaffa; see *Palestine Exploration Fund Quarterly Series* (1900): 118, 122; Schürer, *History*, 3:35. Klein, in *MGWJ* 64 (1920): 195, derives the word from the name Φικόλα mentioned in Josephus, *Antiquities*, 12.4.2.

7. I have made significant changes in connection with the origin of the ʿAmida from what I wrote in *Achzehngebets*. First, I have particularly clarified here the various groups of benedictions of which the ʿAmida is composed; further, I have relied here throughout on the most ancient form of the text known to us. The main error in the claims of Loeb, Israel Levi, Schwab, and Tchernowitz is that they are based on the current version. I am unable to agree today with Levi's conception of a connection between the Psalms of Solomon and the ʿAmida. Other than the number eighteen, which is common to them, and the dependence of both on biblical expressions, I am unable, despite repeated examinations, to discover any relationship between them. The severe denunciations in the Psalms of Solomon of the caste of the priests has nothing to do with Benediction l2, and there is no point to the claim that the Benediction of the Sectarians was originally directed against the Sadducees. The relationship between the ʿAmida and the psalm that concludes the Hebrew Ben Sira, from which I have quoted parallels in several places, is another question. Here there is no mistaking the strong influence. From Ben Sira it seems that in those days similar groups of thoughts were developed in different forms. Loeb found similar relationships between certain Psalms, Deuteronomy, Isaiah, etc. and the ʿAmida, but his claim is too one-sided and therefore many parts of it cannot be accepted. Worthy of attention is Schwab's demonstration that prayers were customary in small, private circles before they were recognized as public prayers.

8. E.g., Rashi to B. *Ber.* 11b [s.v. עבודה].

9. I have treated M. *Tam.* 5:1 at length in *Studies in Jewish Literature in Honor of K. Kohler* (Berlin: G. Riemer, 1913), 78f. That the "Benediction of the Priests" does not here denote the priestly benediction, see ibid., 80 and Elbogen, *Achtzehngebets*, 16, n. 3.

10. There is a petition on behalf of Jerusalem also in Ben Sira 36:17f.

11. According to the above Yerushalmi passage, השוכן בציון is simply one of the eulogies of the benediction for the Temple. But earlier it was probably the eulogy of Benediction 16 (17), for in the ancient Palestinian version the petition "and dwell in Zion," corresponding to this eulogy, occurs in this benediction; and even the eulogy familiar today, "Who restores His presence to Zion," is apparently merely the consequence of the adaptation of this eulogy to post-Destruction conditions. On the mutual similarity and partial congruence between the benediction of Jerusalem and the "Benediction of the Temple" on the one hand, and Benediction 16 (17) on the other, see Heinemann, *Blessing*. On the several eulogies of the benediction "Builder of Jerusalem" (in various rites and periods), cf. Heinemann, *Prayer*, 36f. and 50f.

12. For the opinion that the ʿAmida was originally composed of only six benedictions, see Zunz, *Haderashot*, 179, from which it has been widely adopted.

13. For the connection of the national petitions with Ezek. 20:34f., see I. Loeb, "Les dix-huit bénédictions," *REJ* 19 (1889): 38. A petition for the assembling of the exiles is found also in Ben Sira 36:13, 55:12f. The Didache 10:5 quotes a prayer that "the holy church be brought by the four winds into the kingdom of God"; the context is the Grace after Meals, which contains a national petition to this very day.

14. *Contra* Levi in *REJ* 32 (1896): 171. Hoffmann, *Synagogen*, 51f., 55f. also assumes a connection between Benediction 11 and the wicked. On "Give us Understanding," see B. *Ber.* 29a; Y. ibid. 4:3, 8a, and the summary in B. *Meg.* 17b; cf. Loeb, "Les dix-huit bénédictions," 38.

15. For details on "Look at our misery," see Elbogen, *Achtzengebets*, 22f., and, for a contrary view, see Levi in *REJ* 47 (1903): 166. But it should be noted that in M. *Ta.* 2, the Remembrance verses are counted as the first addition, so that only the second eulogy corresponds to them; while it says "One expands 'Redeemer of Israel'" (B. *Ta.* 16b).

16. V. Aptowitzer, in *Die Parteipolitik der Hasmonärzeiten im rabbinischen und pseudepigraphischen Schriftum* (Vienna: Kohut Foundation, 1927), 51, conjectures that to the six fast-day benedictions another was added at a later stage (i.e., in the time of Alexander Jannaeus); but he thinks that this additional benediction was בא״ה המרחם על הארץ, ". . . Who has mercy on the earth" (or בא״ה משפיל רמים, ". . . Who lowers the haughty," Y. *Ta.* 17a), in which he sees a protest against the Hasmonean kingdom. This conjecture is totally unfounded. He even seeks in this manner to resolve the "contradiction" in the Mishnah between six and seven additional benedictions, but he creates an enormous new difficulty. For if the benediction "Redeemer of Israel" was always one of the six (!) additional benedictions, the clause in the Mishnah "the eighteen bene-

dictions of every day, and he adds to them six more" would be meaningless, for without the benediction "Redeemer of Israel" there would not be "eighteeen benedictions of every day."

17. On the Benediction against the Sectarians there exists a ramified literature listed in Schürer, *History*, 2:462–63; Strack, *Einleitung*, 179; Strack, *Jesus*, §21a–d, §25. To this, add Berliner, *Randbemerkungen*, 1:50f. On the meaning of "sectarian," cf. also J. Bergmann, *Jüdische Apologetik in neutestamentlichen Zeitalter* (Berlin: G. Reimer, 1908), 7f. For the sources in the church fathers, see Schürer, *History*, 462, n. 164.—On the sectarians, cf. *MGWJ* 73 (1930): 109f., where an attempt is made to demonstrate that the struggle with the early Christians was going on as early as the first century, even before the destruction of the Temple.

18. All descriptions of the Christian liturgy begin with the Mass; the earliest signs of the prayer rite are shrouded in darkness. Louis Duchesne, *Origines du culte Chrétien*, 4th ed., 47f. also assumes that originally the Christians continued to worship in the same manner as the Jews. Even Rietschel, whose knowledge of Jewish institutions is very limited, is forced to admit this (Rietschel, *Liturgik*, 1:232f.).

19. On sectarians acting as informers, cf. Manuel Joel, *Blicke in die Religionsgeschichte zu Anfang des zweiten christlichen Jahrhunderts* (Breslau: S. Schottländer, 1880–83), 1:32f., 2:49f.

20. That Jewish Christians served as precentors must be assumed based on M. *Meg.*, end.

21. For errors by the precentor, see M. *Ber.* 5:3 and Y. *Ber.* 5:3, 9c. Samuel the Lesser is an exception, ibid. Instead of "The sages did not have this in mind," the reading should be "The sages did not have you in mind"; thus, Ginzberg, *Seride*, 1:22 and Y. *Ber.*, ed. Luncz, 55a; cf. Strack, *Jesus*, 66.*

22. "One includes the Benediction against the Sectarians (מינים)": The text follows Y. *Ber.* 4:3, 8a and Y. *Ta.* 2:2, 65c; in Y. *Ber.* 2:4, 5a our versions read רשעים, while the Vatican manuscript (Luncz 19b), Ginzberg, *Seride*, 1:348 also reads פושעים; cf. Strack, *Jesus*, 65.* Perles, in *OLZ* 16 (1913): 73f., attempts to defend the reading פרושים, but in my opinion, his reasons are not decisive. [But Lieberman, *Tosefta*, 1:53 retains and explains this reading.]

23. On the Benediction against the Sectarians, see also A. Marmorstein, "The ʿAmida of the Public Fast Days," *JQR* NS 15 (1924–25): 414f.; S. Krauss, "Zur Literatur der Siddurim," *Festschrift für Aron Freimann*, eds. Alexander Marx and Hermann Meyer (Berlin, 1935), 125f.; M.H. Gvariahu, "Birkat haminim," *Sinai* 44 (1959): 367.

24. For support for the number eighteen, see Y. *Ber.* 4:3, 8a f.; Y. *Ta.* 2:2, 65c; B. *Ber.* 29a; *Num. R.*, §2; *Midrash tehilim*, 231 (to Psalms 29) and the parallels cited there; cf. Baer, *ʿAvodat*, 87.

25. To the supports cited in Elbogen, *Achtzehngebets*, 24, we may add also the reference to Pal., p. 57, and to an ʿAmida from Egypt from the year 1022 (see *Hasofe* 6 [1922]: 13). Typical is the regulation of R. Samuel b. Ḥofni that those who say the eulogy אלהי דוד בונה ירושלים may omit את צמח (Harkavy, *Studien*, 3:34, n. 89; cf. *JQR* 20 [1908]: 807). Thus as late as the eleventh century it was known in Sura that את צמח entered the ʿAmida only with the elimination of the ancient eulogy of Benediction 14.—Palestinian texts and piyyutim composed under its influence without את צמח abound in texts recently published by Mann, Marmorstein, and Marx in places cited in §9, as well as in Davidson, *Ginze*. Untenable is Mishcon's opinion (*JQR* NS 17 [1926/7], 37ff.) that this petition is directed against the acknowledgment of Jesus as the Messiah, which was long unknown in Babylonia and was introduced there only in the fourth century, with the spread there of Christianity.

§9 The ʿAmida: Text

1. For deviations, see Luzzatto, *Mavo*, 5f [, 18f.].

2. For word count, see *Ṭur, O.H.*, §113. Baer (*ʿAvodat*), too, indicates the number of words each time. The number of words in every benediction is found also in R. Israel Alnaqawa, *Menorat hamaʾor*, ed. H.G. Enelow (New York: Bloch, 1929–32), 115f.

3. *REJ* 14 (1887): 26f.

4. Numerous variants to the Palestinian version are cited in Mann, *Palestinian*; their version does not always seem consistent, since the Jews were often subjected by their wanderings to non-Palestinian influences. Finkelstein, *ʿAmida*, 142f., offers textual material of an abundance never before assembled; in general he understood correctly the relationships between the various rites, but he did not always make note of the fact that the texts known to us are influenced by existing halakha and have been diverted in the direction of the Babylonian ʿAmida (which he calls "the Diaspora ʿAmida," 139), and that the traces of the Palestinian tradition were effaced to a great extent, having been preserved to but a small degree. Add to these differences arising at the source the influences to which the various rites were subjected through the migrations and wanderings of the Jews, with all the random developments thereto appertaining. Finkelstein's attempt at reconstructing the original text of the ʿAmida is, of course, founded on his views concerning the origin of this prayer that have been sketched above. Details on the text are given also in Schechter, *Liturgy*, 85f. The Palestinian

text [in a geniza version], which was first published in *JQR* 10 (1898): 656, is of such decisive importance that it is worth providing here:

א. ברוך אתה ה' אלהינו ואלהי אבותינו אלהי אברהם אלהי יצחק ואלהי יעקב האל הגדול הגבור והנורא אל עליון קונה שמים וארץ מגננו ומגן אבותינו מבטחנו בכל דור ודור ברוך אתה ה' מגן אברהם. ב. אתה גבור משפיל גאים חזק ומדין עריצים חי עולמים מקים מתים משיב הרוח ומוריד הטל מכלכל חיים מחיה המתים כהרף עין ישועה לנו תצמיח. ברוך אתה ה' מחיה המתים.

ג. קדוש אתה ונורא שמך ואין אלוה מבלעדיך. ברוך אתה ה' האל הקדוש. ד. חננו אבינו דעה מאתך ובינה והשכל מתורתך. ברוך אתה ה' חונן הדעת. ה. השיבנו ה' אליך ונשובה חדש ימינו כקדם. ברוך אתה ה' הרוצה בתשובה. ו. סלח לנו אבינו כי חטאנו לך מחה והעבר פשעינו מנגד עיניך כי רבים רחמיך. ברוך אתה ה' המרבה לסלוח.

ז. ראה בעניינו וריבה ריבנו וגאלנו למען שמך. ברוך אתה ה' גואל ישראל. ח. רפאנו ה' אלהינו ממכאוב לבנו ויגון ואנחה העבר ממנו והעלה רפואה למכותינו. ברוך אתה ה' רופא חולי עמו ישראל.

ט. ברך עלינו ה' אלהינו את השנה הזאת לטובה בכל מיני תבואתה וקרב מהרה שנת קץ גאלתנו ותן טל ומטר על פני האדמה ושבע עולם מאוצרות טובך ותן ברכה במעשה ידינו. ברוך אתה ה' מברך השנים. י. תקע בשופר גדול לחרותנו ושא נס לקבוץ גליותינו. ברוך אתה ה' מקבץ נדחי עמו ישראל.

יא. השיבה שופטינו כבראשונה ויועצינו כבתחלה ומלוך עלינו אתה לבדך. ברוך אתה ה' אוהב המשפט. יב. למשמדים אל תהי תקוה ומלכות זדון מהרה תעקר בימינו והנוצרים והמינים כרגע יאבדו ימחו מספר החיים ועם צדיקים אל יכתבו. ברוך אתה ה' מכניע זדים.

יג. על גרי הצדק יהמו רחמיך ותן לנו שכר טוב עם עושי רצונך. ברוך אתה ה' מבטח לצדיקים. יד. (טו) רחם ה' אלהינו ברחמיך הרבים על ישראל עמך ועל ירושלים עירך ועל ציון משכן כבודך ועל היכלך ועל מעונך ועל מלכות בית דוד משיח צדקך. ברוך אתה ה' אלהי דוד בונה ירושלים.

טו. שמע ה' אלהינו בקול תפלתנו ורחם עליו כי אל חנון ורחום אתה. ברוך אתה ה' שומע תפלה. טז. רצה ה' אלהינו ושכון בציון ויעבדוך עבדיך בירושלם. ברוך אתה ה' שאתך ביראה נעבד. יז. מודים אנחנו לך אתה הוא ה' אלהינו ואלהי אבותינו על כל הטובות החסד והרחמים שגמלתנו ושעשיתה עמנו ועם אבותינו ואם אמרנו מטה רגלנו חסדך ה' יסעדנו. ברוך אתה ה' הטוב לך להודות.

יח. שים שלום על ישראל עמך ועל עירך ועל נחלתך וברכנו כלנו כאחד. ברוך אתה ה' עושה השלום.

5. Numerous variants and biblical parallels are reported in Elbogen, *Achtzehngebets*, 49f. (see also *MGWJ* 46 [1902]: 515f.); below we refer generally to this material.

6. A few verses appear before the beginning of the 'Amida also in Persia; see *JQR* 10 (1898): 609.

7. Also *REJ* 53 (1907): 237. *Tosafot*, B. *Ber.* 49a s.v. ברוך indicates that the conclusion of Benediction 1 is אל חי וקים, "living and eternal God."

8. H. Brody, *MGWJ* 54 (1910): 500, surmised that the ancient eulogy was בא"ה מגן אבות, "Blessed are You, O Lord, Shield of the patriarchs"; Ben Sira 51 does not support any objection to this, for there we find alongside מגן אברהם, "Shield of Abraham," צור יצחק, "Rock of Isaac," אביר יעקב, "Champion of Jacob." This benediction thus may have undergone three stages: In the first, each of the three patriarchs was mentioned separately; in the second, all were combined in "Shield of the patriarchs," while in the third it was considered sufficient to name only Abraham in the eulogy, on the basis of the homily of Resh Lakish (B. *Pes.* 117b). See the article by Heinemann in *REJ* 125 (1966): 107f.

9. On "Remember us," cf. Elbogen, *Achtzehngebets*, 45, 50 (see also *MGWJ* 54 [1910]: 437). *Manhig*, *R.H.*, 41b, §2 calls it "the custom of the French"; and, in fact, French authorities declare it obligatory. Tosafot, B. *Ber.* 12b, s.v. והלכתא. There they attempt to justify the existing custom, as is shown by the detailed discussion in *Vitry*, 362f. (see also *S.L.* 13, bottom). See also R. Hai in *'Itim*, 252; Maimonides, M.T., "Laws of Prayer," 2:9.

[There is reason to assume that "Remember us" is an ancient quasi-piyyut composed in Palestine, even though it is not found in Palestinian (or Egyptian) versions known to us from the Cairo geniza; see the article by Heinemann in the *Annual of Bar-Ilan University* 4–5 (1966/7): 132f. But cf. the opinion of N. Wieder in *Tarbiz* 37 (1967/8): 146f. that "Remember us" originated in Babylonia.]

10. This is the supposition of Loeb in *REJ* 19 (1889): 19.

11. For variants, see Elbogen, *Achtzehngebets*, 50 (517); *JQR* 10 (1898): 658; Elbogen, *Studien*, 46. ורב להושיע, "and mighty to save," is also one of the phrases that recurs in nearly all the texts. If we assumed a brief version, it would seem that *Sifre*, Deut., 142, §343 contradicts this assumption, but the text there seems to be corrupt; cf. *Midrash tanaim*, 209 [and see above, p. 31, for a different interpretation of the *Sifre* passage].

12. "Who makes the dew fall" appears in Palestine, but these words are lacking in Amram; see Marx, *Untersuchungen*, 5 and Frumkin, *Seder*, 1:237. On the Palestinian rite, see Rapoport, ʿErekh, 228a. Saadia knows additions like מלך מחיה כל בטל, "King Who revives everything with dew" or בגשם, "with rain," and permits their place seems to have been at the end of Benediction 2; Bondi, *Saadia*, 14.

["King Who revives everything with dew": See N. Wieder in *Tarbiz* 34 (1964/5): 45, n. 10 and *Tarbiz* 37 (1967/8): 138.]

"Who makes the dew fall" does not exist in Germany: See the gloss on *S.A., O.Ḥ.* §113:3. For *Manhig*, cf. also Tosafot, B. *Ta.* 3a, s.v. בטל. Cf. also Tosafot, ibid., 3a, s.v. בימות; Zunz, *Ritus*, 40.

13. אב הרחמן is also in Amram 44b; Frumkin, *Seder*, 2:292; but cf. Marx, *Untersuchungen*, 27, with Amram 46a, where אב הרחמן is cited.

14. See Elbogen, *Achtzehngebets*, 52f.; cf. also Bloch, *MGWJ* 37 (1893): 305f. The eulogy המלך הקדוש, see Ginzberg, *Geonica*, 2:50; *REJ* 52 (1906): 132; *REJ* 55 (1909): 184. On המלך הקדוש, cf. Ginzberg, *Ginze*, 550 n.—On the word סלה, Perles, in *REJ* 80 (1925): 99 correctly notes that the word comes at this point under the influence of Ps. 84:5, just as later, at the end of the ʿAmida, it is recognizably influenced by Pss. 88:11 and 68:20. In a letter, Perles points to וקרבתנו לשמך הגדול סלה, "and bring us near to Your great name, sela," in the benediction "With great love" and Josh. 7:9.

[As the eulogy of the benediction for the Additional Service of the New Year, when Kingship verses were inserted in accordance with the opinion of R. Yoḥanan b. Nuri (M. *R.H.* 4:5), the version אדיר המלוכה והאל הקדוש, "The Mighty in kingdom, the holy God" (Y. *R.H.* 4:6, 59c) is mentioned. This eulogy is customary in Persian and Romaniot, and it is also found in a geniza fragment published by I. Elbogen in *MGWJ* 55 (1911): 595; see also 590.

On the Palestinian source of the version "Holy are You" and the way in which it came to be part of the ʿAmida of the Days of Awe in the Babylonian rite, together with Is. 5:16, see N. Wieder, *Tarbiz* 34 (1964/5): 43f.; A. Mirsky, *Tarbiz* 34 (1964/5): 285f.; and N. Wieder, *Tarbiz* 37 (1967/8): 147, 256f.]

15. On its meaning, see Kohler, *Ursprünge*, 447. "You bestow" is found already in *Halakhot gedolot*, 32; cf. also *REJ* 53 (1907): 227. On the version of Y. *Ber.*, cf. Ginzberg, *Seride*, 19; Ratner, *Ahavat*, 128. On "You distinguished," see Jawitz, *Meqor*, 45. Frumkin, *Seder*, also has first "You bestow" and afterward "You distinguished"; cf. the literature cited there.

16. A fragment in Mann, *Palestinian*, 306, cites after the Palestinian verse also Ezek. 33:11.

17. "God" is found also in both manuscripts of Amram; see Marx, *Untersuchungen*, 5.

18. "Who is a God like You," which is usually abridged in Ashkenaz, but which is preserved in its entirety in Romaniot and Rome, is found at the end of nearly all the Yom Kippur ʿAmidot.

19. "And may He not prevent" also in Amram; cf. Marx, *Untersuchungen*, 26 and Saadia in Bondi, *Saadia*, 39; and cf. *Responsa Ḥemda genuza*, 160f.

20. Although the beginning is taken from a biblical verse, in the Middle Ages the word נא was added; cf. *Vitry*, 66; Judah Halevi, *Kuzari* 3:19; *Ṭur*; Abudarham; Sepharad; and Rome.

21. Amram does not have the text of "Answer us"; the text of Saadia is found in Frumkin, *Seder*, 1:243 [and in Saadia, *Siddur*, 317].

22. For Amram, cf. Marx, *Untersuchungen*, 5 and Frumkin, *Seder*, 1: 242; *Oṣar ṭov* also reads "for all of our pains."

23. The petition for rain is mentioned in Gen. R., 45, §6:5: "If you go to the synagogue and hear them praying for rain . . . ."

24. The exact version of Amram: Frumkin, *Seder*, 1:245 and cf. Marx, *Untersuchungen*, 5.

25. Marmorstein, in *JQR* NS 20 (1929/30): 318, notes on this benediction that Palestine hints at the future Redemption, thus preparing the transition to the national petitions. In the first benediction of the ʿAmida the situation is the reverse: The Babylonian text mentions the Redeemer, and Palestine does not.

26. Cf. Marx, *Untersuchungen*, 5 and Frumkin, *Seder*, 1:246; the same text is in *REJ* 53 (1907): 237.

27. Alfasi, ad loc. and cf. *Manhig, R.H.*, §2; *Ṭur, O.Ḥ.*, §108 and Rome. Since *the holy God* is changed to *the holy King*, analogy would suggest that underlying *the king of justice* there was a version *the God of justice*. The Munich manuscript of B. *Ber.* 12b reads מאי הוה עלה רב יוסף אמר האל הקדוש והאל המשפט; cf. *Diqduqe soferim*, 1:55.

28. Cf. Baer, ʿAvodat, 93f. (who accounts for many ancient texts), Berliner, Strack, Amram in Marx, *Untersuchungen*, 5 and Frumkin, *Seder*, 1:246, 253; cf. also Davidson, *Oṣar*, 2:192, and Marmorstein in *JQR* NS 15 (1924/5): 415f.

29. Cf. L. Geiger, *Johann Reuchlin, sein Leben und seine Werk* (Leipzig: Duncker und Humblot, 1871), 229, n. 3.

30. The beginning, *To the apostates*, in a greatly expanded version appears also in Persia; see *JQR* 10 (1898): 610.

31. *Malkhut zadon: Shevet Yehuda*, ed. A. Shochat, 51, §9; 128 ff., §64, where an apologetic explanation is also given.

32. *To the informers* appears together with the *sectarians*, e.g., in Rome, Yemen, and *Oṣar ṭov*.

33. There is reason to connect the words פליטת סופריהם with פליטת ספריא mentioned in Hans Lichtenstein's edition of *Megilat taʿanit*; see Hans Lichtenstein, "Die Fastenrolle: Eine Untersuchung zur jüdisch-hellenistischen Geschichte," *HUCA* 8–9 (1931–32): 347. If so, this expression and perhaps the others at the beginning of this benediction like חסידים and זקני ישראל should be explained against the background of Alexander Jannaeus. Cf. Lieberman, *Tosefta*, 1:54; E.E. Urbach in *Tarbiz* 27 (1957/8): 175; L.J. Liebreich in *HUCA* 35 (1964): 99, and the references there.

34. T. *Ber.*, ed. Zuckermandel [see *Tosefta—Engl. trans.*], reads כולל של גרים בשל זקנים, "One includes (the benediction) of the proselytes in that of the elders," while the other editions like Y. *Ber.* 2:4, 5a and parallels read כולל של גרים ושל זקנים במבטח לצדיקים, "One includes (the benediction) of the proselytes and of the elders in 'the trust of the righteous.'"—Rashi to *Nid.* 49b, s.v. מריעי.—Amram, Oxford manuscript; Marx, *Untersuchungen*, 6; Frumkin, *Seder*, 1:253—For the version "And may we never be shamed," cf. also Berliner, *Randbemerkungen*, 1:63. Additions in Persia, *JQR* 10 (1898): 610. [See also Heinemann, *Prayer*, 43 and n. 34.]

35. Saadia in Frumkin, *Seder*, 1:242, and cf. *REJ* 53 (1907): 238. [This is merely Saadia's own version; cf. *Tarbiz* 34 (1964/5): 363f.] On "Have mercy," see Marx, *Untersuchungen*, 27, and Saadia in Frumkin, *Seder*, 2:263.

36. Cf. *Eshkol*, 2:17; *Tur, O.Ḥ.*, §557.

37. On the eulogy "Who consoles Zion," cf. Buechler, *JQR* 20 (1908): 779f.

[On the various versions and the evolution of the benediction "Who builds Jerusalem," see Heinemann, *Prayer*, 35f., 39, 48f. and Heinemann, *Blessing*.]

[38. On the special construction of the *qerovot* for the Ninth of Av concluding with this benediction, in which the *qinot* are inserted, see lately Fleischer in *Sinai* 62 (1967/8): 13f. and D. Goldschmidt, *Seder haqinot letishʿa beʾav* (Jerusalem: Mossad Harav Kook, 1968), 8f.]

39. Amram in Frumkin, *Seder*, 1:253 reads כי לישועתך, but these words are lacking in manuscript S in Marx, *Untersuchungen*, 6. The expression לישועתך קויתי is from Ps. 25:5 and Gen. 49:18.

40. In Marx, *Untersuchungen*, 6 and Frumkin, *Seder*, 1:253, שמע קולנו ה' אלהינו וקבל ברחמים וברצון את תפילתנו כי אל שומע תפילותינו ותחנונינו אתה מעולם. בא'ה וגו', "Hear our voice O Lord our God and accept our prayer in mercy and satisfaction, for You are a God Who hears our prayers and our supplications."

41. Elbogen, *Achtzehngebets*, 60f. ובתפילתם שעה also in Marx, *Untersuchungen*, 6.

42. "And may our eyes behold" is still lacking in *REJ* 53 (1907): 237.

43. *Qoveṣ teshuvot*, 1:20a, no. 98 [*R. Moses b. Maimon*, 2:336–40], and cf. thereon, Schechter, *Saadyana*, 42, §14.

44. Saadia, *Oeuvres*, 9:156.

45. *Manhig*, "Laws of Prayer," §59.

46. *Bet Yosef* to *Ṭur, O.Ḥ.*, §120.

[47. On the basis of allusions to the wording of the benediction's eulogy, which occur frequently in the conclusions of the verses of early *qerovot*, E. Fleischer attempts to reconstruct a different ancient eulogy for this benediction, including an expression of satisfaction, such as הרוצה בעבודה, "Who is pleased with the Temple service"; see *Sinai* 60 (1966/7): 269f.

On "Ascend and come," cf. lately L. J. Liebreich, *HUCA* 34 (1963): 125f.; he distinguishes between the Palestinian and Babylonian versions of this prayer and rejects the conjecture that it was originally intended to be recited on the New Year. On the other hand, see Heinemann, *Blessing*, 99f., showing that this prayer was likely composed as a special version of the third benediction of Grace after Meals for the New Year.]

48. *Manhig, R.H.*, §5.

49. Given in Mann, *Palestinian*, 307f. in abbreviated form. But it deserves mention that the full text of "We give thanks" was also inserted into the short versified versions of the ʿAmida (see below); cf. Mann, *Palestinian*, 309 and 310.

50. *Igrot shadal*, ed. Eisig Graeber, 2 vols. (Przemysl: Zupnick et Knoller, 1882–94), 465.

51. Cf. Müller, *Soferim*, 286, nn. 27, 28.

52. Abudarham 54c.

53. Cf. ʿItim, 252; Tosafot, B. *Meg.* 4a, s.v. פסק.

54. Amram 44b; Frumkin, *Seder*, 2:249, without טובים; זכור רחמיך in Amram 44b, before ועל כולם; for סלה see above, n. 14.

55. See Berliner, *Randbemerkungen*, 1:30.

["Your mercy extends to the bird's nest": cf. Heinemann, *Prayer*, 126.

"For the miracles": cf. S. Stern in *JJS* 5 (1954): 110f., 48f.; also Heinemann, *Prayer*, 150.]

56. "Great peace" appears first in *Pardes* 44c, R. Meir of Rothenburg in *Hagahot maimoniyot* to the text of the prayer. For the Afternoon Service it is also found in Amram 18a; Marx, *Untersuchungen*, 11; Frumkin, *Seder*, 1:188. In Yemen it was also heard by Sapir 1:57a, but the printed prayer book reads "Grant peace." [The version "Great peace" is first mentioned in a responsum of the geonic period: *Teshuvot ge'one mizraḥ uma'arav*, no. 126, ed. J. Müller (Berlin: P. Deutsch, 1888); cf. Ginzberg, *Perushim*, 4:170. There is reason to assume that this version is ancient and of Palestinian origin; cf. *REJ* 125 (1966): 109. In Sepharad yet another version of this benediction is in use on the Ninth of Av: עושה השלום. ברכנו ברוב עז ושלום. כי אתה אדון השלום, "O You Who make peace, bless us with much might and peace, for You are the Lord of peace." The concluding verse in this version and in "Great peace" apparently reflects an alternate version of the eulogy: בא"ה אדון השלום, ". . . Lord of peace"; see the above-mentioned article and J. Heinemann in *Annual of Bar-Ilan University* 4–5 (1966/7): 132. It seems that the custom of concluding on the Ten Days of Repentance with מלך עושה השלום, "King, maker of peace," instead of המברך את עמו ישראל בשלום, "Who blesses His people Israel with peace," is a Babylonian custom of the geonic period, to which, however, the geonim were opposed; cf. N. Wieder, *Tarbiz* 37 (1967/8): 254f.]

57. The eulogy עושה השלום, "Who makes peace," was first used in Ashkenaz on the New Year since ed. Thiengen (1560), but for kabbalistic reasons it was soon thereafter introduced into the Ten Days of Repentance; Berliner, *Randbemerkungen*, 1:34.

["Who makes peace": the style of this sentence, especially the addition of the address to the congregation "and say, 'amen' " at the end, suits its being said at the end of Kaddish, but not at the end of the silent 'Amida; cf. Pool, Kaddish, 76; Heinemann, *Prayer*, 163f.]

58. In Ashkenaz, ed. Prague and Turin, עשה למען שמך is lacking; cf. Baer, 'Avodat, 104. Its source is derived in the *Manhig*, "Laws of Prayer," §62, from an unknown aggadah. מלכנו אלהינו, Amram 9a; Frumkin, *Seder*, 1:264f. For other additions, see Baer, 'Avodat, 105.—In Mann, *Palestinian*, 308 and 310 other versified texts are found at the end of the 'Amida.

Poetic abridgements, Elbogen, *Achtzehngebets*, 47, have been preserved in manuscripts in various editions for the entire 'Amida; for expansions, see Elbogen, *Studien*, 47–48. Supplement to the third edition: On the subject of the poetic versions of the 'Amida treated briefly in Elbogen, *Studien*, 47f. we have more material today. We have short versions, most of them alphabetical, that completely overlook the traditional text and include only its eulogies; all of them belong to the Palestinian realm; whenever they are used in the other rites, the missing text of "The plant" is supplied. The simplest example of a short version of this type is the rewording of Psalm 34 published by Marmorstein in *MGWJ* 69 (1925): 38f. Besides this we have the version whose opening I noted in *Achtzehngebets*, 47, attributed to "early precentors," and used even in Babylonia on the eves of Sabbath and festivals; the full text has now been published by Marmorstein, op. cit., 36f.; Mann, *Palestinian*, 310f.; Marx, *Ginze qedem* 3 (1925): 65f.; Schechter, *Liturgy*, 97; with certain variants among all these publications. A still shorter version of this text for the Afternoon Service appears in Mann, *Palestinian*, 308f. and Marmorstein, op. cit., 37, n. 2. A different poetic summary is in Mann, *Palestinian*, 309f. and yet another in Marmorstein, op. cit., 39. [Cf. also A.M. Haberman, *Tefilot me'en shemone 'esre* (Berlin: Schocken, 1932/3).] As for the expansions, besides the one listed above, §8, n. 25, published by J. Mann in *Hasofe* 6 (1922): 13 (and because of its special purpose, which is not relevant here), the piyyut in Elbogen, *Studien*, 47f. should be mentioned. The fragment published in *Hagoren* 10 (1928): 91f., joining another fragment published earlier by Marmorstein in *JQR* NS 15 (1924/5): 414f., should also be noted. Here we have a much-expanded hymnic reworking of the traditional text; in the manner of the fast-day liturgy, this piyyut mentions in every benediction one of the heroes of antiquity and begs that just as he was answered in time of trouble, so may we too be answered. To these expanded hymns one should perhaps compare the text from the *Apostolic Constitutions* 7:33f., translated by Kohler in "The Origin and Composition of the Eighteen Benedictions," *HUCA* 1 (1924): 387ff. Because of its great importance, the fragment is reproduced here:

ברוך שמך יי' צבאות אלהי ישראל

שאתה הוא אל מברך השנים הטובות ומברכות

טוביך יתברכו ויחיו כל בריותיך וגם עמך

ואני עמם ואתה שמעת תפלת דוד משיח

צדקך בבנותו מזבח בגרן ארנן היבוסי

כן תשמע תפלתי למענך ולמען שמך

ולמען דוד נגידך ולא למע' עונו' ברכנו ה' אלהי בכל מעשה

ידי והעתר לי בכל צרכי ותרויח לי במזונותי
בברכה והצלחה ורחמים ואמת ותן ברכה
בכל צאתי ובואי ותהא השנה הזאת שנת
גשומה ושחונה וטלולה והצלחה בתבואת׳
ודגן ופירות ותקרב שנת ישועה לעמך ישר׳
וארץ תתן יבולה יברכנו אלהים אלהינו ב׳ מברך
ברוך שמך יי׳ צבאות אלהי ישראל
שאתה הוא אל רועה ישראל ונהגתה אותם
כצאן אש׳ א׳ ל׳ רועה והבטחת אותם לקבץ
נדוחיהם מארבע כנפות הארץ ואתה שמעת
תפלת שלמה המלך בבנותו מקדש לשמך
כן תשמע תפלתי למענך ולמען שמך ולמען
ידידות מקדשך ולא למען עונות׳ הושיעני ה׳ אלהינו וקבצ׳
והצי׳ מ׳ הגו׳ להו׳ לש׳ קר׳ להש׳ בתה׳ ב׳ מקבץ
ברוך שמך ה׳ צבאות אלהי ישראל
שאתה הוא אל אוהב צדקה ומשפט והודעת
משפטי צדקך לישראל עמך משפט וצדקה
ביעקב אתה עשית ושמעת תפלת אליהו עבדך
שקרא לשמך יי׳ צבאות אלהי אבר׳ יצ׳ וישר׳
באש ובגשם מן השמים עניתו כן תשמע
תפלתי ותעניני למענך ולמען שמך ולמען
אליהו עבדך ולא למען עונות׳ והצדיקנו במשפט ואל תרשיענו
והוציא כאור צדקינו ומש׳ כצהרים ב׳ אוהב
ברוך שמך יי׳ צבאות אלהי ישראל
שאתה הוא אל מגדע קרני רשעים ומעבד
בני עולה מן הארץ ומלכות זדון תעקר ותופיע בהדר מלכותך על עולמך
ויאמרו כל אשר נשמה באפו יי׳ אלהי ישראל מלך ומלכותו בכל משלה
כב׳ יי מלך תגל הארץ ישמחו השמים יי מלך יי ימלוך לעולם
ועד יי מלך עולם ועד אבדו גויים מארצו יי מלך גאות לבש מלך אלהים
על גויים יי מלך ירגזו עמים יי למבול ישב וישב יי [מלך לעולם] כי ליי
המלוכה ומושל ועלו מושיעים והיה יי למלך וחפרה הלבנה
והאלילים ועובדיהם כליל תחלוף יבשו ויבהלו עדי עד וידעו כי אתה
שמך ברוך אתה יי׳ שובר רשעים ומכניע זדים ברוך שמך יי צבאות
אלהי ישראל שאתה אל צדיק ואוהב צדקות ואתה משען לחוסים בך
ומבטח לבוטחים בשמך ומחסה ליראיך ומשגב לחסידיך ומנוס לעבדיך
ומפלט לאוהביך ומעוז לידידיך ורב חסד לכל קוראיך ואתה שמעת
זעקת יהושפט במלחמה כב׳ ויזעק יהושפט ויי׳ עזרו כן תשמע תפלתי
למענך ולמען שמך ולמען יהושפט עבדך היה לי למבטח ומשגב ולמפלט

[Other portions of this hymnic version, including its opening, have since been found in various manuscripts, some of which attribute it to Saadia; see M. Zulay, "Shemone ʿesre lerebenu saʿadia gaʾon," *Tarbiz* 16 (1944/5): 57f. and now also in his book *Haʾaskhola hapayetanit shel rav saʿadia gaʾon* (Jerusalem: Schocken, 1964), 248f. On the nature of this prayer and the problems it raises with regard to Saadia's position on deviations from the statutory text of the liturgy, see Heinemann in *Annual of Bar-Ilan University* 1 (1963): 229f. Lately, E. Fleischer has again expressed doubts about the attribution of the prayer to Saadia, and assumes that it is very ancient; see *Sinai* 60 (1966/7): 274.]

§9a The Kedushah

1. For literature, cf. J. Mann in *REJ* 70 (1920): 122f. Aptowitzer has written on the origin of the

Kedushah. He, too, believes that the Kedushah of the ʿAmida is the original one, but he imagines that it was introduced in such a way that the verse from Isaiah was originally recited after Benediction 3 as the language of the angels' praise. According to him, the verse Ezek. 3:12 does not occur in the ancient Kedushah in Enoch because when the latter was composed the wording of the verse was still ברום and not ברוך. But the Kedushah originally cited the verse ברוך שם כבודו, "Blessed be the name of His glory," which was eventually expanded to ברוך שם כבוד מלכותו לעולם ועד, "Blessed be the name of His majestic glory forever"; only when the reading in Ezekiel was changed was the verse brought in from there. Aptowitzer explains the difficult language of T. *Ber.* 1:9 as meaning that R. Judah recited the verses together with the one who sang the Kedushah after the benediction—i.e., one of the congregation, his intention being to fulfill literally the words "And they called one to another."

2. The 'trishagion' (Is. 6:3) has existed in the Christian liturgy since the time of Clement Romanus; see *Realencyklopädie*, 20:125f.; Thalhofer, *Handbuch der Katholischen Liturgie* (Freiburg im Breisgau: Herder, 1883), 155f.

3. By contrast to this term, Baer, ʿAvodat calls the Kedushah of "Creator" קדושה דישיבה; he constructed the name on the pattern of *Soferim* 10:8, but it is not found in ancient sources. *Eshkol* 1:12f. speaks of קדושה מיושב (Kedushah recited while sitting).

4. Following Rapoport, *Qalir*, 119, n. 20, many derive the Kedushah from Essene influence, a view championed especially by Kohler and Ginzberg; and from the Christian side, Baumstark has attacked my arguments (*Oriens Christianus* NS 9 [1920]: 139). But after reexamining the sources, I have to note that in the places that mention the Morning Service of the Essenes and the special favor in which hymns were held among them, I cannot uncover any clear reference at all to the Kedushah. Is. 6 does not contain anything that would directly suit it to serve as a morning prayer. Ezek. 3:12 would be more suitable, but it lacks the concept of the Kedushah. Conversely, wherever we find the Kedushah clearly, as in Enoch 39:12, there is no reference to a morning prayer. In Revelations 4:8–11 one finds at least a slight connection between the Kedushah and a hymn to the glory of the Creator. I imagine the development to have been that in Benediction 3 of the ʿAmida, the Kedushah of Israel was mentioned, with Is. 6:3; to this foundation inspired poets added dramatic reworkings, such as those in B. *Hul*, 91b; *Pirqe derabi eliʿezer*, chap. 4; *Pesiqta rabati* 97a, §20, and such as were disseminated by the mystics of the geonic period. In Babylonia they succeeded in introducing the Kedushah, while in Palestine the immigrants from Babylonia around the year 800 fought until they got the Kedushah accepted for the daily service. In the report in Ginzberg, *Geonica*, 2:50f. and *REJ* 70 (1920): 133f., one must distinguish between what the polemicist [Pirqoi ben Baboi; see also *Tarbiz* 2 (1930/1): 383f.] reports as facts from Palestine and what he reports as the opinion of R. Yehudai Gaon; these two are not identical, just as his attacks on the Babylonians do not match his praise for the Babylonian R. Yehudai Gaon. The material in *Geonica* 2:50, has now been printed in Ginzberg, *Ginze*, 551f. in a more complete version; there is also a detailed discussion of it in Ginzberg, *Ginze*, 524.

5. המברך: According to the context, the word refers to the precentor; thus, Aptowitzer in *Hilkhot ravya*, 3 vols (Berlin: Mekiṣe nirdamim, 1912–36), 1:42, n. 2, to B. *Ber.* 21b, *contra* Ginzberg, *Geonica*, 1:129. [There is a tannaitic source in which the root ברך designates someone reciting the ʿAmida—i.e., M. *R.H.* 4:9: "One who recited the benedictions and then came into possession of a shofar . . ."] This early testimony is paralleled by the Kedushah in the *Apostolic Constitutions* 7:35, to which W. Bousset called attention in *Nachrichten der Gel. Gesellschaft* (Göttingen, 1915), phil.-hist. Klasse, pp. 35f. The redacting of the *Constitutions* occurred in the generation of R. Abun. With this Kedushah, compare Kohler, *HUCA* 1 (1924): 415f.

6. Instead of Kedushah, ancient texts of B. *Ber.* 21b read לקדוש, but the meaning is probably the same.

7. R. Abun: cf. A. Hyman, *Toledot tanaʿim vaʾamoraʾim* (London, 1910), 1:49; for the text, cf. Ratner, *Ahavat*, 131.

8. זה שעובר: cf. Elbogen, *Studien*, 33f.

9. Cf. also Jellinek, *Bet hamidrash* 5 (1872), 162; Tosafot to B. *Sanh.* 37b, s.v. מכנף. In *Soferim* 20:7 the Kedushah is mentioned in a *baraita* beginning "R. Hiyya taught."

10. Ginzberg, *Geonica*, 2:50; see above. According to *Soferim*, the Kedushah is recited on every day when there is an Additional Service, and on Hanuka.

11. *Shemaʿ* in the Kedushah: cf. Amram 11a; Frumkin, *Seder*, 1:278; and Rapoport, *ʿErekh*, 37b; clearer is the report in Ginzberg, *Geonica*, 2:50f. and *Pardes* 56b, where the "kingdom of Edom" is mentioned explicitly as the author of the prohibition. This very passage militates against Ginzberg's conception, for all that is spoken of is a prohibition directed against Palestine and the replacing of the *Shemaʿ* with the Kedushah of the ʿAmida. Mann, in *HUCA* 4 (1927): 254f., wants to explain the *Shemaʿ* of the Kedushah as the result of the Persian persecutions under Yazdagard (ca. 450). According to him, the reciting of the *Shemaʿ* was prohibited there. When in the time of the emperor Heraclius (612) the prohibition of the reciting of the *Shemaʿ*, which may have been issued long before, was renewed, the Babylonian custom of inserting the *Shemaʿ* into the Kedushah was adopted there. When the Arabs came into power, the Babylonians still retained the *Shemaʿ*

only in the Kedushah of the Additional Service, and the Palestinians, in the Morning Service [for there the Kedushah was in use only in the Morning Service of Sabbaths and festivals].] According to Ginzberg, *Geonica*, 2:525, the practice in Babylonia was not at all uniform: In Sura the *Shemaʿ* was inserted into the Kedushah, but not in Pumbedita. But these theories have no certainty. In connection with Mann's theories about changes in the prayer rites in consequence of persecution, which we mention several times, we refer generally to the critique of Y. Bergman in *MGWJ*, 70 (1928): 449f., who sees the explanation of prayers and other practices by persecution, which is very common in the tradition, as a farfetched explanation of the aggadic type.

12. For the texts, cf. Zunz, *Literaturgeschichte*, 13f.; Saadia's Kedushah in Bondi, *Saadia*, 17.

13. In the expression נמליכך, in Maimonides, there may perhaps be detected a bit of the spirit that gave rise to the inserting of Ps. 136:10. [M. Liber, *JQR* NS 40 (1949/50): 316 claims that originally Benediction 3 of the *ʿAmida* stressed the motif of the kingdom of God (in the eschatological sense) and not the Kedushah of the angels—hence, the use of Ps. 136:10 and the expressions denoting kingship in the various passages quoted in the Kedushah and in some of the versions of the benediction itself. Similarly this relationship between the Kedushah and God's kingdom led to the placing of the recitation of the Kingship verses on the New Year in this benediction (according to the practice of R. Yohanan b. Nuri), a vestige of which has been preserved till this day in the prayer ובכן תן פחדך, "And so set your fear"; this prayer is merely an introduction to the Kingship verses inserted in this benediction on the Days of Awe. See also L.J. Liebreich in *HUCA* 35 (1964): 89f.; cf. also above, §9, p. 40.]

14. כתר: This version existed also in Rome, as can be inferred from *S.L.*, 13. *Oṣar ṭov*, too, has this reading. [Also in the version of the *ʿAmida* of the Morning Service for Rosh Hashana from the geniza (T.-S. H 8/7), which has a distinctively Palestinian character (as is proved, *inter alia*, by the eulogy of Benediction 3; "the holy God" rather than "the holy King"), the Kedushah begins with "crown," as follows: כתר קדושתך יתנו המוני מעלה עם קבוצי, "מטה יחד ישלשו לך כב', וקרא זה אל זה וכו', "The crown of Your holiness is given by the throngs on high with those gathered below; together they say thrice to You, as it is written, 'And they called one to another'."]

15. Amram 10b; *Vitry* 156.

16. "Twice" with no preface is mentioned also in the geonic responsa; e.g., Amram 10b f.; Frumkin, *Seder*, 1:278. It was particularly the insertion of "twice" that aroused vehement opposition; see Ginzberg, *Geonica*, 2:52.

17. Cf. *Pardes* 42a; according to this, *adir* was used at first only on Rosh Hashana and Yom Kippur until R. Eliakim of Speyer, who ordered its recitation on Pentecost as well; *Sefer Ḥasidim*, §501, knows this custom already for all three pilgrim festivals. R. Meshulam b. Kalonymus is the author of the *qerova* for the Morning Service of the Day of Atonement in Ashkenaz, in which the word *adir* plays a special role; particular notice should be paid to the last part of the version of the Kedushah in which the repeating words are ה' אדיר שמך and אדונינו.

18. The time of the additions to the Kedushah verses is determined by the fact that "Let us sanctify" is mentioned already in *Soferim* 16:12.

19. The best-known such reworking in German is that of Abraham Geiger, which was set to music by Lewandowski. An English version is found in the *Union Prayerbook*.

20. Above, §7, p. 18, I cited the grounds for the opinion that the Kedushah of "Creator" is the later one; to these is to be added the fact that the mystics strove forcefully to allow individuals, too, to recite the Kedushah, or at least a substitute, the קדושה ליחיד, "Kedushah of the individual." The rule is that even in "Creator" the individual should omit the Kedushah; and since the authorities make this point repeatedly, it seems that the mystics from time to time renewed their campaign until they finally won. The sources for the struggle were assembled by Büchler in *REJ* 53 (1907): 220f. (cf. Elbogen, *Studien*, 20f.). In fact, in Saadia hardly anything remains of "Creator" for the individual; he would not have dared to abridge the text so drastically had he not been able to rely on an ancient version. This version was the old Palestinian "Creator" that in the course of time was reduced in status to that of the "Creator" for the individual.

§9b The Priestly Blessing

1. For the meaning of the expression *the steps of the porch* and *dukhan* in the Mishnah, see Adolf Büchler, *Priester*, 126 and the sources listed there, n. 1.

2. "Went up to the platform" is placed in the mouths of tannaim in the Talmud, but the expression is exclusively from the amoraic period.

3. נשיאות appears in *Sifre* Num., 11b, §39 and B. *Sota*, 39a, but among the late legal authorities it is generally נשיאת, as is the reading, incorrectly, in several editions of the Talmud.

4. The significance of the transfer of the Priestly Blessing from the Temple to the syngagogue from the

point of view of the history of religion has been brought out strongly by Israel Levi in *REJ* 30 (1895): 142. *Sifre zuta*, ibid., derives this from Ex. 20:24.

5. The reference is only to blemishes of the face, hands, and feet, because the people ordinarily look at them. T. *Soṭa* 8:8; and cf. T. *Meg.* 4:29, B. *Meg.* 24b; Y. *Meg.* 4:8, 75b, etc.

6. The obligation of the priests is stressed by R. Judah b. Pazi (ca. 300) in the name of R. Eleazar; cf. B. *Soṭa* 38b and *O.Z.* 2:165. In the Christian church the Priestly Blessing became a part of the service only in the wake of the Reformation; earlier, only occasional traces of its use are found; Achelis, *Theologie*, 365 (where the words ". . . the Priestly Blessing, with which the entire synagogue service concluded" need to be corrected); Rietschel, *Liturgik*, 1:326, 402, etc.

7. On the priests' fingers, cf. I. Löw in the *Kaufmann Memorial Volume*, 68; Berliner, *Randbemerkungen*, 1:4l. Spread-out hands on gravestones are the sign of a priest's grave.—The view that this blessing has magic effect was much strengthened by the Kabbalah. That the priests should turn their backs to the shrine and their faces toward the congregation is required also by T. *Meg.* 3:24; this is in accordance with the Babylonian custom, while in Palestine they stood with their faces toward the ark; see *Ḥiluf minhagim* 34, §36.—To *Sifre* Num., 11b, §39, cf. *Sifre zuta*, 247, §23 and B. *Soṭa* 39b.

8. In the early period the call was given by the *ḥazan*, i.e., the sexton; so R. Tam still understood the sources, *Tosafot*, B. *Ber.* 34a, s.v. לא יענה. If later the precentor filled this role, it may be that this is one of the many confusions that resulted from the late usage in which *ḥazan* came to mean precentor. Cf. *O.Z.*, ibid., and *'Arukh*, s.v. חזן.

9. The verses are first found in the *Laws of the Blessing of the Priests* by Rashi (MS Vatican, 318); cf. *Vitry*, 101; Berliner, *Randbemerkungen*, 1:40. But since all rites adopted the verses, it seems that their introduction occurred rather early. Against the interruption of the benediction by the recitation of the verses, cf., for example, Abudarham 33a, *Bet Yosef* to *Tur, O.H.*, §128.—For the healing of a dream, cf. R. Nisim b. Jacob, *Mafteaḥ* to B. *Ber.* 55b. The prayer was already adopted by Amram 11b; Frumkin, *Seder*, 1:287, but the regulation to recite it whenever the Blessing of the Priests is said comes only from R. Meir of Rothenburg (*Hagahot Maimoniyot* to M.T., "Laws of Prayer," 14:7). Even R. Isaiah Horwitz (*Shene luḥot haberit*, 390) expressed his opposition; Berliner, *Randbemerkungen*, 1:41.

10. The text of "May it be your will" at the end comes from R. Nathan Hanover, *Sha'are ṣion* (Amsterdam, 1720); Berliner, *Randbemerkungen*, 1:41. For the explanation of the odd expression אנקתם וכו', cf. B. Heller in *REJ* 55 (1909): 60f.; S. Krauss in *REJ* 56 (1910): 251f.

11. Singing in the performance of the Blessing already in *Orḥot* 109b; *Responsa of Maharil*, no. 148 (Slopkowiecz, 1807).

12. Daily Blessing of the Priests also in Saadia: Bondi, *Saadia*, 17; Yemen (*Sapir* 1:57a); Jerusalem (Zunz, *Ritus*, 54). For the elimination of the Blessing, L. Löw, ibid.; cf. *Orḥot* and Maharil ad loc.; commentaries to *Tur, O.H.*, §128, end.

13. *J.E.* 1:538f.

14. *Ḥiluf minhagim*, 28, §29; *Manhig*, "Laws of Prayer," §64.

15. In the Morning Service of the Ninth of Av there is no Blessing of the Priests; in Amram (Frumkin, *Seder*, 2:268), it was still in use.

16. *Responsa of Maharam*, no. 648 (Prague, 1608); Mordekhai, *Meg.*, §817; *Bet Yosef*, ad loc.

17. R. Joseph Kimhi: see Abudarham 32d.

18. Causes of opposition to the Benediction: See Geiger, *Juedische Zeitschrift* 11 (1888), 284; Philipson, *Reform*, 347, 351.

§10   The Supplications

1. For the terminology, cf. Maimonides, M.T., "Laws of Prayer," 5:13; 14.

2. In Elbogen, *Studien*, 40f. we have demonstrated in detail that the meaning of "Supplications" is the prayer of the individual. In Arabic the expression *tanaffala* is used in this sense, and Judah Ibn Tibbon translates this word as התנפל, "to fall prostrate," but also "to offer a voluntary prayer" or "an optional prayer"; cf. Bacher's introduction to *Sefer hashorashim*, x, n. 4.

3. Yemen in *Sapir* 1:57a; Saadia in Bondi, *Saadia*, 15.

4. Among the legal authorities of the last centuries and in all calendars.

5. From geonic literature, e.g., "He fell to his face and asked for mercy," *Halakhot gedolot*, 22. See also Natronai in Amram 9a; Frumkin, *Seder*, 1:264.

6. *S.A., O.H.*, 131.

7. Amram 12a, and cf. Marx, *Untersuchungen*, 6f.; Frumkin, *Seder*, 1:299.—Passages of supplication in Zunz, *Literaturgeschichte*, 15f.; Saadia in Frumkin, *Seder*, 1:298; Bondi, *Saadia*, 15 [Cf. also the supplications

for the individual composed by Saadia, *Siddur*, 45f.]; Maimonides, M.T., "Laws of Prayer"; cf. *Qoves teshuvot* 1:330.—*Vitry*, 78; Frumkin, *Seder*, 1:298, where still other variants are reported. Very interesting is the report of Abu 'l- Walīd that his teacher, R. Isaac b. Saul, used to recite Ps. 143 in the evening as a supplication, "and when he examined himself and did not understand clearly the meaning of the word כסיתי (v. 9), he refrained from saying the psalm" (*Sefer hashorashim* 226, s.v. כסה and introduction). Abudarham is still aware that several valid versions exist. Ps. 6 was introduced in Ashkenaz only 150 years ago; Berliner, *Randbemerkungen*, 1:24.

8. "Merciful and clement one," also in Saadia; cf. Frumkin, *Seder*, 1:297f. "And David said" comes from Sha'are șion; see Berliner, *Randbemerkungen*, 1:24; Baer, 'Avodat, 166; Frumkin, *Seder*, 1:297f.

9. "Guardian of Israel": Zunz, *Ritus*, 131; Zunz, *Literaturgeschichte*, 18; Frumkin, *Seder*, 1:300. [See also J. Heinemann in the *Annual of Bar-Ilan University* 4–5 (1966/7): 132.]

10. The confession is present only in recent centuries, and was apparently introduced under the influence of the Lurianic Kabbalah; but cf. *JQR* NS 9 (1918–19): 287f.

11. For the text, see *Megilat ta'anit*, 22.

12. See G. Klein, *Der älteste christliche Katechismus und die jüdieche Propaganda-Literatur* (Berlin: G. Reimer, 1909), 212.

13. M. *Ta.* 1:4f. For the other fasts, T. *Ta.* 2:4: "On Monday and Thursday the individual observes the public fast"; the Fast of Esther was also held on Monday and Thursday; see *Soferim* 17:4.

14. "Days of Assembly": M. *Meg.* 1:1.

15. Cf. *Seder 'olam raba*, ed. A. Marx (Berlin, 1933), German part, 20; *Manhig*, "Laws of Prayer," §70.

16. Amram 19b (Frumkin, *Seder*, 1:393); Rome also in Frumkin, *Seder*, 1:301.

17. For "And He, being merciful," cf. Baer, 'Avodat, 112, Zunz, *Literaturgeschichte*, 16; H. Gross, *Gallia Judaica* (Paris: L. Cerf, 1897), 74f.; Berliner, *Randbemerkungen*, 1:70f.; cf. the literature listed in Davidson, *Oṣar*, 2:183. If Zunz is referring to *Vitry*, he is thinking of the Bodleian manuscript, where the story is actually found; cf. Frumkin, *Seder*, 1:293 (*contra* Berliner). That "And He, being merciful" is spurious in Amram is shown by Marx, *Untersuchungen*, 11. For variants to this prayer, see Baer, 'Avodat; Frumkin, *Seder*, 1:294. This text deserves a special study. Petition: Amram 23b; Frumkin, *Seder*, 1:395.

18. "Lord, God of Israel": Zunz, *Ritus*, 123 was in use as early as the eleventh century; see Zunz, *Literaturgeschichte*, 17.

19. Other liturgical poems in Amram; cf. Marx, *Untersuchungen*, 11.

20. *Vitry*, 71.

21. "God, the patient": Zunz, *Literaturgeschichte*, 17; Berliner, *Randbemerkungen*, 1:29. Amram does not yet know it.

22. Cf. S.A., O.H., 131:4, but they went beyond the number stipulated there; a list of all the festive days appears in Baer, 'Avodat, 112. The influence of private celebrations is discussed in Berliner, *Leben*, 114. Waagena, *Jeschurun* 10 (1923): Hebrew section, 9, concludes from Y. *Ber.* 4:1, 7b and Y. *Ta.* 2:14, 4:1, that in Palestine the Supplications were recited on the New Moon, as well.

23. See *Teshuvot hage'onim*, no. 90, where two responsa have been confused; Amram 14b; *'Itim*, 253; *Vitry*, 26. Ginzberg, in his conception (*Geonica*, 2:299) of the *Qedusha desidra* as a kind of Haftara benediction, overlooks the text's assumption that the study of Torah had preceded. An attempt was made to prohibit the individual worshiper from reciting this Kedushah as well. Amram in Frumkin, *Seder*, 1:330 and Bondi, *Saadia*, 15; Saadia in Bondi, *Saadia*, 17f.; and Maimonides have a rather different text, as does *JQR* NS 9 (1918/9): 282.—Mann's explanation that the expression *Qedusha desidra* originated in the recitation of the trishagion when the Torah is taken out, a practice ultimately prohibited (about the time of the emperor Constantius) and replaced by being brought into "A redeemer will come to Zion" (*HUCA* 4 [1927]: 270–76), seems unlikely to me and totally unproved. Even if this Kedushah was completely unknown in Palestine, it would not speak for his conjecture. The whole passage in Amram gives the impression of an originally Babylonian custom, and the other uses of the prayer also suit in every way the usual conception reported in the text. Cf. Bergman in *MGWJ* 70 (1928): 454.—Babylonian practice: see Amram and *Teshuvot hage'onim*, no. 90. [Cf. also the analysis of "And a redeemer will come to Zion" in L. J. Liebreich, *HUCA* 21 (1948): 176f. Heinemann, *Prayer*, 166f., 171f. studies the stylistic properties of the passage "Blessed is the Lord . . . ," which also indicates that this prayer was once connected to the public homily. D. Flusser, in his article "Sanktus und Gloria" in the Festschrift for Otto Michel, *Abraham unser Vater*, ed. Otto Betz et al. (Leiden: E.J. Brill, 1963), 129f. connects the translation of Is. 6:3 in the Kedushah of the Lesson with the Gospel of Luke 2:14. In his opinion, other extremely ancient fragments have been preserved in the prayer "A redeemer will come to Zion"; among them are the Benediction of the Torah in the passage "Blessed is our God. . . ." and the fragment that begins "He will open our heart to his Torah," so remarkably parallel to the petition in II Macc. 1:3–5.]

24. Amram 14a; Frumkin, *Seder*, 1:317, 327; *Vitry*, 74; *Orḥot*, 21b, §4f. On the psalms that were customary in Toledo, see *Manhig*, "Laws of Prayer," §77. Saadia at this point cites his two well-known prayers.

"There is none like our God": It would have been more logical for "Who is like our God" to be the first stanza; the order was changed in order to get the acrostic "AMeN"; cf. *JQR* 13 (1901): 160. Other additions are in Baer, ʿ*Avodat*, 154f.

25. "It is our duty" I find first in *Ṭur, O.Ḥ.*, 133; according to Berliner, *Randbemerkungen*, 1:49, *Roqeaḥ* already included it in the Morning Service. As for the denunciations of this prayer, see *J.E.* 1:336f.; Berliner, ibid. Prussia: Cf. the literature listed in L. Geiger, *Geschichte der Juden in Berlin* (Berlin: J. Guttentag, 1871), 2:27f.

26. Even the Vilna Gaon came out against the Song of Unity and against excessive repetiton of Kaddish; see Frumkin, *Seder*, 1:114. Spurious verses at the end of the Song of Glory have been demonstrated by Simonson in *MGWJ* 37 (1893): 463f.

§11   *The Morning Psalms*

1. Amram (Frumkin, *Seder*, 1:138) begins the public worship here; "And when Israel enters the synagogue to pray in the villages, the *ḥazan* of the synagogue stands and begins with 'Blessed is He Who spoke.' "

2. On the text of B. *Shab.* 118b, cf. Aptowitzer in *Hasofe meʾeres hagar* 1 (1911): 84f.; the relationship with Ps. 145f. already in R. Moses Gaon, ʿ*Arukh*, s.v. תפל and Alfasi, ad. loc.

3. Ps. 30 may have been introduced on the initiative of R. Isaac Luria (see Berliner, *Randbemerkungen*, 1:22); the opposition of the Gaon of Vilna, see Frumkin, *Seder*, 1:114.

4. Bloch, *Merkava*, 262, also emphasizes that "Blessed is He Who spoke" is composed of two heterogeneous parts. The first is lacking in many geniza fragments (Saadia knows it only for the Sabbath); Bondi, *Saadia*, 16; Frumkin, *Seder*, 1:154. It is lacking also in Mann, *Palestinian*, 279. According to the survey in Marx, *Untersuchungen*, 3, bottom and Frumkin, *Seder*, 1:167, it ought to have been lacking also in Amram; yet Marx, *Untersuchungen*, 2b (Frumkin, *Seder*, 1:138) begins with it; thus, it seems likely that it is a late addition. As for the style of exposition, cf. Rapoport, *Qalir*, 177, based on the story of R. Nathan Habavli (ca. 960) in *Medieval Jewish Chronicles* 2:83. The meaning of the first part in Margulies, ibid.; *Tana deve eliyahu*, 179. [D. Hoffmann, *Leviticus* (Berlin: M. Poppelauer, 1905–6), 1:95f., points out that the various sections of "Blessed is He Who spoke" each include a homily or other explanation of the tetragrammaton, and he conjectures that this portion was intentionally placed prior to the first mention of the tetragrammaton by the precentor each morning at the beginning of the following benediction. But cf. also Heinemann, *Prayer*, 170.] The eulogy מלך מהולל בתשבחות, "King praised with praises": Amram, ibid.; Bondi, *Saadia*, 16.—R. Moses Gaon: ibid., *Mafteaḥ*, 76; Zunz, *Literaturgeschichte*, 12.

5. On the order of the Morning Psalms themselves and its principles, see L.J. Liebreich in *PAAJR* 18 (1949): 255f. But the whole effort to find signs of a plan or system in this section seems very dubious in light of the constant changes that occurred in it in all times and places; cf. Heinemann, *Prayer*, 14. On the lack of any system or order in the geniza texts in this portion of the Morning Service, including both the Morning Psalms and the Morning Benedictions, see Heinemann, *Prayer*, 103f.

6. In Amram (Frumkin, *Seder*, 1:167) and Saadia, הודו is still lacking; verses after והלל לה׳, "and give praise to the Lord," occur first in Vitry, 61f.; more on these additions in Jawitz, *Meqor*, 63f., Zunz, *Ritus*, 59; in the current text of Amram the verses are found among the Sabbath prayers, 27a, but they are lacking in the manuscripts. ʿ*Itim*, 249, protests strongly against all these additions.

7. For the text of Y. *Ber.* 5:1, 8d, see Ratner, *Ahavat*, 120.

8. Ps. 100 is found neither in Amram nor in Saadia. On this psalm, see *Manhig*, "Laws of Prayer," §21; *Ṭur, O.Ḥ.*, §50. Cf. Berliner, *Randbemerkungen*, 1:22 also on Ps. 20, which many insert here.

9. In Amram, the Morning Psalms begin with ה׳ מלך, "The Lord is King," preceded by "Blessed is he who spoke"; *Manhig*, "Laws of Prayer," §19 knows this only for Sabbath; in Sepharad it opens the Morning Psalms for every day of the year.

10. Other verses beginning with "Happy" are found first in Vitry; cf. Zunz, *Ritus*, 59. They are also found in the manuscripts of Marx, *Untersuchungen*, 3; Frumkin, *Seder*, 1:167.

11. The verses beginning "Blessed is the Lord forever" for the first time in *Roqeaḥ*, §320; "And David blessed" down to verse 13, already in Amram (Frumkin, *Seder*, 1:168; Marx, *Untersuchungen*, 3). The sequel was originally in use only on the Sabbath, at first in the Romaniot lands; it was brought to Germany from Italy by R. Moses b. Kalonymus (Vitry, 226). As for France, see Zunz, *Ritus*, 14. On the whole subject, see Ginzberg, *Geonica*, 1:127. In the Temple, the Song of the Red Sea was sung on Sabbath afternoons as a psalm (B. *R.H.* 31a); its acceptance into the liturgy was attacked by R. Natronai Gaon (see ʿ*Itim*, 249). After "The breath" we find the song still in Persia; see *JQR* 10 (1898): 608.—ʿ*Itim*, 249, requires that this hymnic section be completed before the Song of the Red Sea, and so the Turin manuscript in Mann, *Palestinian*, 284, n. 45.

12. The heaping-up of synonyms in "May Your Name be praised" is attributed by Bloch to the kabbal-

ists, but similar expressions are already found in M. *Pes.* 10:5 and *Mekhilta* to Ex. 14:8, 14. The text of Saadia is shorter, but his conclusion is actually longer (see Bondi, *Saadia,* 16). The eulogy is in Frumkin, *Seder,* 1:178; Saadia reads in the eulogy רוב ההוראות, though Amram objects to it (Frumkin, *Seder,* 1:154).

[On the benedictions before and after the Morning Psalms, their texts and development, see Liebreich in *JQR* 41 (1950): 195f; and cf. N. Wieder in *JJS* 4 (1953): 65f.]

13. Zunz, *Ritus,* 6; Maimonides, M.T., "Laws of Prayer," 9:1. In Persia, one puts on the *talit* only here; *JQR* 10 (1898): 608. Amram (Frumkin, *Seder,* 1:178; Marx, *Untersuchungen,* 3) has an introductory note to "May Your Name be praised": "The precentor stands before the ark and concludes with the eulogy," since only at this point did the precentor rise to his feet, having up to this point been seated; but through the error mentioned above, p. 72, he begins with "May Your Name be praised."

§12 *The Morning Benedictions*

1. In Saadia and Maimonides, the Morning Benedictions are included among the Enjoyment Benedictions, because these, too, were recited at home; see Bondi, *Saadia,* 20; Maimonides, M.T., "Laws of Prayer," 7. [See Saadia, *Siddur,* 68. The organizational principles of his prayer book are different from all other known prayer books; thus, these benedictions, too, are in an unusual place. The Benedictions of the Torah (of the Morning Service, as well) are given in his prayer book, 358, at the beginning of the section dealing with the Torah reading.] For Palestinian versions of the Morning Benedictions, see Mann, *Palestinian,* 272f.; there, too, they are recited as a home prayer. Cf. Schechter, *Liturgy,* 87f.

2. Num. 24:5 and Ps. 5:8 are cited already by Amram among the special benedictions; see Frumkin, *Seder,* 1:38. He knows also Ps. 5:9 and a verse recited when one leaves the synagogue; more verses are found already in *Vitry.* R. Solomon Luria wrote against Num. 24:5, but in general this verse was given a favorable reception; see Berliner, *Randbemerkungen,* 1:11.

3. Cf. Luzzatto, *Mavo,* 20 [Goldschmidt ed., p. 44.]; Berliner, *Randbemerkungen,* 1:13. On its author, see the unacceptable opinion of Hirschfeld in *JQR* NS 11 (1920/1): 86f.

4. On the establishment and literary dissemination of Jewish dogma, cf. Schechter, *Studies,* 1:200f.; Marx in *JQR* NS 9 (1918/9): 305.

5. *Mahbarot,* chap. 4; cf. Chayes in *Rivista Israelita* 7 (1908): 96; *ZHB* 11 (1907): 159.

6. According to Berliner, *Randbemerkungen,* 1:12.

7. Sepharad inserts another line: בלי ערך בלי דמיון וכו', "Without equal, without like" (Frumkin, *Seder,* 1:41). On the content of "Eternal Lord," cf. the lovely article of I. Abrahams in *Festival Studies* (London: Macmillan, 1906), 174f.

8. Zunz, *Poesie,* 216.

9. That the Morning Benedictions were originally intended strictly as occasional prayers emerges clearly when one considers the benedictions that have become separated from them—i.e., those of fringes and phylacteries, which are to this day recited only when one is about to fulfill these commandments. When the Morning Benedictions became part of the daily service, a justification was found in that they acknowledge the might of the Creator. Cf., e.g., *Eshkol* 1:7 (Auerbach ed., p. 10).

10. "On the lifting of the hands" comes first, in accordance with Frumkin, *Seder* 1:47; also Amram and *Vitry,* 56; in the Talmud the order is "My God, the soul" followed by "on the lifting of the hands." The order of the short benedictions diverges from the Talmud not only in Amram, but even more in later periods. Cf. Jawitz, *Meqor,* 5f.; Berliner, *Randbemerkungen,* 1:13f.; Frumkin, *Seder,* 1:53.

11. On the text of Y. *Ber.* 9:2, 12b see Ratner, *Ahavat,* 198. The reading בור, "ignoramus," was invalidated already by Amram (Marx, *Untersuchungen,* 2; Frumkin, *Seder,* 1:85); גוי, "gentile," was changed out of consideration for censorship to נכרי, "foreigner"; Baer, *'Avodat,* 40f. The version שעשני כרצונו, "Who made me according to His will," for women is later than *Vitry;* it first appears in *Tur, O.H.,* §46 and Abudarham 14c. שמתני instead of עשאני (both mean "made me") in Saadia, ibid., and Maimonides, M.T., "Laws of Prayer," 7:6; cf. *Hagahot maimoniyot* ad loc. שלא שמתני עם הארץ, "Who did not make me an *am ha'aretz,*" in S. Schechter, in the *Kaufmann Memorial Volume,* Hebrew part, 53; cf. Persia in *JQR* 10 (1898): 607. The meaning of the three benedictions is given in Kaufmann, *MGWJ* 37 (1893): 14f.

12. In place of לעסוק בדברי תורה, "to work with the words of the Torah," Amram reads על דברי התורה, "concerning the words of the Torah" (Frumkin, *Seder,* 1:70). That great changes have occurred in this group is attested by the different order in the various texts. Amram 1b (Frumkin, *Seder,* 1:72f.) cites it after the one discussed here in §5 and before the one discussed in §7; cf. Ginzberg, *Geonica,* 1:126. *Tur, O.H.,* §46, end, reports that the author himself used to move the Benediction of the Torah to follow "My God, the soul," following it with the Priestly Blessing and the short benedictions; R. Moses Isserles notes that in Ashkenaz the order in the present-day prayer books was customary. But, as correctly noted by the Vilna Gaon, all

ancient prayer books cite the entire group—that is, the Benedictions of the Torah including the double material for study, at the end, after group 7; and this is the order that exists today according to the rite of Frankfurt am Main. Cf. Berliner, *Randbemerkungen*, 1:16 and Frumkin, *Seder*, 1:98 in the commentary.

13. B. *Qid.* 30a.

14. See *Ṭur, O.H.* §1; according to Berliner, *Randbemerkungen*, 1:28, the recitation of the biblical passages on incense, Ex. 30:7–8, 34–36, and "The Compounding of the Incense" in 1589, on the occasion of a plague, show how strange are the factors that influenced the shape of the prayer book.

15. There are myriad variants on M. *Pe.*; cf. the chart compiled by Berliner, *Randbemerkungen*, 1:18.—On the whole Palestinian complex, cf. the collection *Qoveṣ teshuvot* 1:328.

16. Amram concludes the Morning Benedictions *before* "One should ever be," and sees this passage as a transition to "Blessed is He Who spoke," as does Rome. In the prayer books, the sentence beginning "One should ever be" is frequently printed in smaller letters because it was thought not to be part of the prayer; for the same reason the sentence is lacking in the Oxford manuscript of Amram and Frumkin, *Seder*, 1:94 (but it is found in Frumkin, *Seder*, 101). Also, Abudarham 18d prefaces it with the note "In some places it is customary to say," but he himself is opposed. *Ṭur, O.H.*, §46 gives Y. as the source for it; this incorrect reference is often given in the Middle Ages; cf. Aptowitzer in *MGWJ* 55 (1911): 419f.—For the source of "One should ever be," cf. Rapoport, ibid.

17. "Lord of the Worlds": See below, §16, n. 1.—An expression similar to "Happy are we who rise early"; cf. *Midrash tehilim*, 27a (to Ps. 5:6).

18. On the text of Y. *Ber.*, cf. Ratner, *Ahavat*, 1:199.

19. For the recitation of the *Shemaʿ*, cf., among others, *ʿItim*, 253. Palestine knows neither the *Shemaʿ* here nor the entire introduction to it, but has a completely different order; cf. Mann, *Palestinian*, 281. But it may not be concluded from this that the recitation was introduced, as alleged, in Babylonia when the recitation of the *Shemaʿ* was prohibited in the time of Yazdagard (*HUCA* 4 [1927]: 250 and Bergman in *MGWJ* 70 [1928]: 453f.).

20. See *S.L.*, §6; *Manhig*, "Laws of Prayer," §3.

21. For the status of the Morning Benedictions, the following passage is typical: Amram says in the introduction (Frumkin, *Seder*, 1:50), "Thus said R. Natronai, 'The ḥazan begins, and he recites the benedictions seated.' " [On the order and number of the Morning Benedictions in general, which constitute in his opinion a kind of complete "order of prayer" in miniature, S. B. Freehof wrote in *HUCA* 23 (1950–51): Part 2, 339f.; but see Heinemann, *Prayer*, 14 and n. 12. On the origin of the practice of reciting the Morning Benedictions together in the synagogue at the beginning of the public worship, see S. B. Freehof, *Studies and Essays in Honor of Abraham A. Neuman*, ed. M. Ben-Horin et al. (Leiden: E. J. Brill, 1962), 218f. On the lack of stability as to number, order, form, and wording in these benedictions and others that are not in the category of the community's obligatory prayer, see Heinemann, *Prayer*, 99f., and especially 104; in this way we can also understand the phenomenon, so surprising to the legal authorities, that they include a benediction like "My God, the soul" that does not begin with "Blessed," in contradiction to the talmudic rule that "Every benediction begins with 'Blessed' except for . . ." (T. *Ber.* 1:9); see Heinemann, *Prayer*, 108f. On the development and the many versions of the Benediction of the Torah, see Heinemann, *Prayer*, 105f. Among the various versions of the benedictions "Who did not make me a gentile . . . a slave . . . etc.," noteworthy are those that mention not only the negative benefit but also the positive benefit that God has actively performed, each item with its opposite, like those found among the geniza fragments: בא״ה אמ׳ה אשר בראת אותי אדם ולא בהמה איש ולא אשה ישראל ולא גוי מל ולא ערל חופשי ולא עבד, "Blessed are You, Lord our God, King of the universe, who created me a man and not a beast, male and not female, a Jew and not a gentile, circumcised and not uncircumcised, free and not a slave"; *HUCA* 2 (1924): 277, and similarly in *Sefer Dinaburg*, ed. Y. Baer (Jerusalem: Qiryat Sefer), 120; and the one found in the Italian *Seder ḥibur berakhot* (see Schechter, *Liturgy*, 88f.): שלא עשיתני גוי (עובד ע״ז) כגויי הארצות מל ולא ערל שלא עשיתני עבד לבריות שלא עשיתני אשה שלא עשיתני בהמה, "Who did not make me a gentile (idolator) like the nations of the world, circumcised and not uncircumcised, Who did not make me a slave to other creatures, Who did not make me a woman, Who did not make me an animal." On this, see Lieberman, *Tosefta*, 1:120 and nn. 70–71, and Heinemann, *Prayer*, 104 and n. 12.]

§12a Kaddish

1. The sources are all cited in Pool, *Kaddish*, 8f.; cf. Jawitz, *Meqor*, 82. In B. *Ber.* 3a, the assumption is that Kaddish is heard both in the synagogue and in the house of study.

2. Kaddish is first mentioned as a conclusion to aggadic homilies in Zunz, *Haderashot*, 483, n. 64, citing this explanation in the name of Rapoport, but the latter erroneously understands נחמתא as meaning "consolation for the mourners," whereas the reference is actually to the general consolation of Zion. The prayer על הכל, "For everything," before the reading of the Torah is, as correctly noted by Pool, very similar to Kaddish; see below, §30(1).

[It seems that "For everything" was originally intended to be said after the public homily; for prayers following the homily and their formal characteristics, cf. Heinemann, *Prayer*, 158f.; on Kaddish, Heinemann, *Prayer*, 163, 169f. On the "invitation to respond" as one of the characteristics of these prayers, see Heinemann, *Prayer*, 169.]

3. Kaddish and the Lord's Prayer: G. Klein, *Der älteste christliche Katechismus und die jüdische Propaganda-Literatur* (Berlin: G. Reinter, 1909), 256f.; same as *ZNW* 7 (1906): 34f. Kohler's attempted analogy to II Macc. 13:38f. is unfounded.

[On the relationship of the Lord's Prayer in the New Testament to ancient Jewish prayers, see also Heinemann, *Prayer*, 120 and 44.]

4. לעילא מן כל ברכתא, "Above all blessings," is connected with Neh. 9:5.

5. Cf. G. Dalman, *Grammatik des jüdisch-palästinischen Aramäisch*, 2nd ed. (Leipzig: Hinrichs, 1905), 26. The original connection is shown by a fragment containing a longer text and mentioning Babylonian office-holders in Lewin, *Ginze qedem* 2 (1923): 47f.

6. Kaddish was used wherever the intention was to conclude one of the sections of the service, like the Morning Psalms (§11).

7. On *Soferim* 19:2, see *Soferim*, 279. According to *Pirqe derabi eliᶜezer*, chap. 17, the mourners come to the synagogue. As to the manner in which they were received and dismissed, cf. the words of R. Akiva, "Go to your homes in peace" at the conclusion of his words of thanks for sympathy on the death of his sons, B. M.Q. 21b; *Semahot* 8.—בעלמא דעתיד לאתחדתא (*Soferim* 19:2).

8. *Tana deve eliyahu*, 120, §20. For the legend about R. Akiva, see *Tana deve eliyahu zuta*, 23, §17 and the editor's notes; Pool, *Kaddish*, 102. A new version of the legend of R. Akiva appears in Ginzberg, *Ginze*, 238f.

9. According to *Kol bo*, §114, the mourners recited Kaddish for a full year; this period was shortened to eleven months on the basis of the Zohar because "the judgment of the wicked is twelve months in Gehenna" (M. ᶜEd. 2:10), and cf. Isserles to S.A., Y.D., 376:4, and Lewysohn, *Meqore*, 138.

10. O.Z., 2:11.

11. See *J.E.* 7:63f. The Ashkenazic term *Jahrzeit* derives, as stressed by Rieger in *AZdJ* 17 (1853): 468, from the usage of the Catholic church.

12. The movement of R. Isaac Luria had special influence on the development of the Mourner's Kaddish; see Lewysohn, *Meqore*, 138.

13. Pool, *Kaddish*, 107.

14. Kaddish for the individual is frequent in Amram, but consistently lacking in the manuscripts; cf. Marx, *Untersuchungen* and Frumkin, *Seder*, on the appropriate passages.

15. Bloch, *Merkava*, 264 attributes the synonyms in "May the name of the King be blessed" to the influence of the kabbalists. At the end of this sentence, the words שמיה דקודשא בריך הוא, "The name of the Holy One, blessed is He," of course belong together; Sepharad has here the response "amen," while Ashkenaz, since the thirteenth century, has understood the words "blessed is He" as a response to דקודשא, and separated them from it; cf. O.Z., 2:10a.

16. In the order of prayers of the Hamburg Temple and in Frankfurt am Main. The Reform congregation in London has Kaddish in Hebrew translation.

17. *Nathan the Babylonian*, 84, and cf. Schechter in the *Kaufmann Memorial Volume*, 54. A version mentioning the name of the Exilarch Sar Shalom (800) is reported in *Ginze qedem* 3 (1924): 54. Since as gaon R. Zemah b. Paltoi of Pumbedita (872–890) and R. Zemah b. Hayim of Sura (879–885) are named, there is reason to assume that the texts before us come from that period; since Pumbedita is mentioned first, the fragment seems to come from there.

18. Maimonides, in *Qoves teshuvot* 3:9a; cf. *MGWJ* 41 (1897): 214f. After Sir Herbert Samuel was appointed High Commissioner of Palestine, this version was reinstated.

19. Zunz, *Literaturgeschichte*, 19. During the funeral there also occurs the addition beginning, תתכלי חרבא, "May war be ended"; R. Hai Gaon sanctioned its use even on festival days. See Warnheim, *Qevusat hakhamim* (Vienna: A della Torre, 1861), 109.

§13 The Afternoon Service

1. On the meaning of מנחה, cf. Gesenius, *Handwörterbuch*; Levy, *Wörterbuch*, 3:153, and see *Tosafot*, B. *Pes.* 107a, s.v. סמוך. Abudarham points to Targum Onkelos, which translates לרוח היום (Gen. 3:8) as למנח יומא, "at the decline of the day"; accordingly, מנחה should be understood as a prayer recited toward evening, as assumed by Herzfeld, *Tefillat*. If Epiphanius, *Haeres*, 29:9 speaks of one prayer μέσης ἡμέρας and one περὶ τὴν ἑσπέραν, it would seem that the former refers to the "Great Afternoon Service," or perhaps he still knew

of the Additional Service of the ma'amadot (cf. below, §17:1), which was recited in the afternoon.—The mid-point between nine and a half hours, the time of the "Lesser Afternoon Service," and nighttime is called פלג המנחה (T. Ber. 3:1); this time, ten and three-quarters hours, became the actual time of prayer, and to this day it is preferred to connect the Afternoon Service and the Evening Service at this time (§14). The antiquity of the practice of combining the two services may be observed in Teshuvot hage'onim, no. 51, and cf. Vitry, 7; Eshkol 1:56; Tosafot, B. Ber. 2a, s.v. מאמתי; Zunz, Ritus, 8.

2. Cf. also Mann, Palestinian, 300f.; for the texts, see Mann, Palestinian, 308f. and Marx, Ginze qedem 3 (1924): 65.

3. Ps. 145 in Amram, MS Oxford (Marx, Untersuchungen, 11; Frumkin, Seder, 1:375); R. Jonah Gerondi in Igeret hateshuva; cf. Abudarham ad loc.—Vitry, 75f.

4. Cf. Elbogen, Achtzehngebets, 47.

§14 The Evening Service

1. There are complaints against reciting the Evening Service too early already in Teshuvot hage'onim, no. 78; cf. Asheri to M. Ber. 1:1. In Palestine they would, in such a case, recite the Shema' again at dark (Y. Ber. 1:1, 2a).

2. On the benediction preceding the Evening Service in Palestine, cf. above, §7, n. 1.—On the text of the service, cf. Mann, Palestinian, 307. Especially worthy of mention is the versified prayer after the Shema', אתה הכית, "You smote," which is very similar to "Help of our fathers" of the Morning Service; also Mann, Palestinian, 308, but in this version the first benedictions, too, are in versified form.

3. On the reason for "And He, being merciful," see Pardes, 55a; Manhig, "Laws of Prayer," §83. [On "And He, being merciful," see now the detailed study by L.J. Liebreich, "The Liturgical Use of Ps. 78:38," Studies and Essays in Honor of Abraham A. Neuman, ed. M. Ben-Horin et al. (Leiden: E.J. Brill, 1962), 365.]

4. Vitry, 77f.

5. Cf. Baer, 'Avodat, 163.

6. In Saadia, only ה' צבאות שמו ימלוך, "The Lord of hosts is His name—He will rule" (Frumkin, Seder, 1:381). [In his prayer book as actually before us, Siddur, 26, ה' צבאות שמו קדוש ישראל, "The Lord of hosts is His name, the Holy One of Israel."] That the ideas of the section are influenced by the Babylonian world view is stressed by Blau in REJ 70 (1920): 142f.

7. Elbogen, Studien, 26. Text in Frumkin, Seder, 1:381.

8. Cf. Elbogen, Studien, 16f.

9. Rav: B. Ber. 12b.

10. In "True and Certain," all texts but Ashkenaz (but also Vitry, 78) read הגואלנו מלכנו, "Who redeems us, our King"; the sentence העושה גדולות, "Who does great deeds," is found only in Ashkenaz (already in Vitry); cf. Baer, 'Avodat, 166.

11. The passage in Amram 19a, MS Oxford (Frumkin, Seder, 1:382), but the current verse Jer. 31:11 is found in Saadia in Amram (Frumkin, Seder, 1:382).

12. On "Make us lie down," and especially the eulogy, see Büchler, "The Blessing 'bone yerushalayim' in the Liturgy," JQR 20 (1908): 799ff. The short text edited by Büchler matches approximately the one in REJ; Persia, too, has a comparable short one in the Sabbath service. Cf. JQR 10 (1898): 605.

13. For the reading of Y. Ber., cf. MS Rome in Ginzberg, Seride, 305 and Isaiah de Trani in Hamakhria', 77b to B. Ta. 13a.

14. Texts from the geniza in JQR 10 (1898): 656; REJ, ibid. Büchler, ibid., wishes to prove from Song of Songs r. 4:4, §6 that the ancient eulogy was only "Builder of Jerusalem," but he himself refers to Lev. r., §9, end, from which he concludes the opposite. Amram 43a and Manhig, "Laws of Prayer," 23b, §3 do not conclusively attest to Palestinian usage.

15. Cf. Graetz, Divre, 2:175f.; Weiss, Dor dor vedorshav (Vilna: I. Goldenberg, 1911), 2:93.

[16. Today it is clear, especially in view of the great number of qerovot by Palestinian poets for the Evening Service, that there were times and places in which the repetition aloud of the 'Amida was customary in the evening as well; cf., for example, A. M. Haberman, Tefilot me'en shemone 'esre (Berlin: Schocken, 1932/3), 49, n. 2.

On the two traditions, the one of two services and the other of three daily services, both of which are ancient, and which eventually merged, see G. Allon in Talmudic Age, 1:126f.; id., Mehqarim, 1:284f.]

17. Since "Blessed is the Lord forever" is lacking in Palestine, Mann, in HUCA 4 (1927): 278, conjectures that it was introduced in Palestine in the time of Justinian as a replacement for the proscribed 'Amida, and that eventually, when the land was conquered by the Arabs, it was eliminated, remaining in the Babylonian rite; but the question remains as to why the Babylonians adopted a practice that originated out of a Palestinian crisis. Cf. also Bergmann in MGWJ 70 (1928): 454f.

18. *Pardes* 55b; *ʿItim*, 173.

19. *Semag*, Positive Commandments, 19.

20. According to *Baʿal haminhagot* in Abudarham 39a, bottom.

21. Ibn Adret in *Orḥot*, 43a, §52. Similar arrangements are the abridging of the Torah reading on weekdays and the elimination of the Priestly Blessing on weekdays.

22. *Manhig*, "Laws of Prayer," §84 and cf. S.L., §52.

23. Amram 19a, רבנן בתראי and *ʿItim*, 173 explain correctly דבתר הוראה. On the meaning of this expression, cf. I. Halevy, *Dorot rishonim* (Pressburg-Jerusalem: Bamburger, 1897–1937), 3:183f.

24. Cf. *Qoveṣ teshuvot*, 1:323. That they should be eighteen in number is required already by *Pardes* 55b.

25. "All your deeds will praise you" with the eulogy of Romaniot is cited also in Frumkin, *Seder*, 1:384; he cites it alongside "May our eyes behold."

26. *Manhig*, "Laws of Prayer," §84.

27. In Abudarham 39b; apparently he infers from Maimonides' silence in M.T., "Laws of Prayer," 7:18.

28. *JQR* 10 (1898): 609.

29. Cf. *Qoveṣ teshuvot*, 1:329, n. 3; Bondi, *Saadia*, 15; likewise, on the eve of the Sabbath, see Bondi, *Saadia*, 27; Frumkin, *Seder*, 2:7.

The eulogy is cited also by R. Natronai (Ginzberg, *Geonica*, 2:117): המולך בכבודו תמיד על כל מעשיו, "Who rules in His glory forever over all His creations." It seems that this language has been abridged by a copyist. Against the word תמיד, Ibn Adret in *Orḥot hayim*.

30. The regulation of the night prayer is first found in B. *Ber.* 4b: "R. Joshua b. Levi said, 'Even though one has recited [the *Shemaʿ*] in the synagogue, it is obligatory to recite it in bed.' " As a biblical verse, Ps. 31:6 is cited there, too.

31. See *Judaica: Festschrift zu Hermann Cohens siebzigsten Geburtstage* (Berlin: B. Cassirer, 1912), 677.

32. In Abudarham, ibid., also R. Sh. (?) in *Orḥot*, 43b, §4, end.

33. Amram 19a quoting Sar Shalom; Frumkin, *Seder*, 1:386 ("in the house of our master in Babylonia," ibid.), Bondi, *Saadia*, 15.

34. *Vitry*, 79; *Manhig*, "Laws of Prayer," §84.

35. *Kol bo*, §28; the present custom in Ashkenaz: Berliner, *Randbemerkungen*, 1:26.

§15 Friday Night

1. The celebrations of the religious societies were first treated by Geiger, *Urschrift*, 124f. Details are given in Scheiber, *Semitic*, 180f.

[Cf. also Allon, *Meḥqarim*, 1:287; Y. Baer, "Hayesodot hahistoriim shel hahalakha," *Zion* 17 (1952): 33f. and 46f.; id., *Yisraʾel*, 27f. and 43f. Today we are rather well informed about the meals of such societies also from the Dead Sea Scrolls; cf., for example, S. Lieberman's article in *JBL* 71 (1952): 199f.; also Heinemann, *Prayer*, 14f. and the literature cited there.]

[2. On the prayer of R. Zadok, see Lieberman, *Tosefta*, 1:34f. and J. Heinemann in *REJ* 125 (1966): 104f.]

3. The Welcoming of the Sabbath is first found in *Tiqune shabat* and then in the prayer books; cf. Zunz, *Ritus*, 159; Berliner, *Randbemerkungen*, 1:43f.; Schechter, *Studies*, 2:275f.; Maarssen in *Jeschurun* 9 (1923): Hebrew part, 46f.

4. Zunz, *Ritus*, 153; Zunz, *Literaturgeschichte*, Nachtrag, 59f.; J.E. 7:675, s.v. "Lekah Dodi," paragraph "melody."

5. J.G. von Herder, "Lied zur Bewillkommung des grossen Ruhetages der goldenen Zeit," in *Saemtliche Werk* (Carlsruhe, 1820–29), 26:422; Heine, "Uebersetzung eines Sabbatliedes," in *Letzte Gedichte und Gedanken von Heinrich Heine*, ed. A Strodtman (New York: S. Zickel, 1871). That Heine attributes the poem (in his *Prinzessin Sabbath*) to R. Judah Halevi simply reflects his high opinion of the poem.

6. *Qoveṣ teshuvot*, 121c, no. 113 [R. Moses b. Maimon, 326, no. 178]: He [Maimonides—Engl. trans.] is asked whether the "longstanding" existing custom of reciting Ps. 92 and later, "And the heavens," is correct. In Berliner, *Randbemerkungen*, 1:45, the objection to this custom is mentioned.

7. Amram 24a; same as *ʿItim*, 172, but it is lacking in the Oxford manuscript; cf. Marx, *Untersuchungen*, 12; Frumkin, *Seder*, 2:7; Persia has Ps. 25:6 in place of "And He, being merciful." On Spain, see *Manhig*, "Laws of Sabbath," §2; Abudarham 38b, 40a; as opposed to this, *Orḥot*, 1:61b; for Worms, cf. *Vitry*, 81 and 142, where "And He, being merciful" is lacking.

8. The texts of Saadia are in Frumkin, *Seder*, 2:7; Bondi, *Saadia*, 27; the addition to "With Eternal Love" begins למען אהבת עמוסים, "For the sake of those borne"; for "Make us lie down," the short version mentioned above, §14:6, is used, as in Persia. [See ibid., n. 12.]

9. שומר is recited, according to Sar-shalom as quoted in Amram 25a (cf. Marx, *Untersuchungen*, 12; Frumkin, *Seder*, 2:9), in all synagogues except for the academy, i.e., the academy of Sura, and the house of the Exilarch. הפורש, Amram, ibid. *Manhig*, "Laws of Sabbath," §3 mentions שומר as the Sephardic custom. Cf. *Manhig*, "Laws of Sabbath," §4 for France and Provence. According to ʿItim, 172, it would seem that Amram also had ופרוס עלינו סכת שלומך. R. Meir, the Precentor of Worms, insisted vigorously that the eulogy read עלינו ועל כל עמו ישראל, "over us and over all His people Israel" (*Vitry*, 142).

10. "And the Israelites shall keep" was said, according to Abudarham, also in Pumbedita; Persia has also Ex. 16:30.

11. ʿItim, 173.

12. Abudarham 40a; cf. *Manhig*, "Laws of Sabbath," §3.

13. *Manhig*, "Laws of Sabbath"; *Vitry*, 142.

14. In *S.L.*, §65; *Tanya*, §13.

15. For the text, see also *S.A., O.Ḥ.*, §267 and the commentators.—Poetic texts for the benedictions according to the Egyptian rite and MS Turin in Mann, *Palestinian*, 319–21 (cf. 311f.); Schechter, *Studies*, 109f.

16. Possibly the expression קלוס referred only to the petition קדשנו במצוותיך, "Sanctify us with Your commandments."

17. The text of the eulogy in Palestine was מקדש ישראל ואת יום השבת, "Who sanctifies Israel and the Sabbath day"; cf. Y. *Ber.* 8:1, 11d (Ratner, *Ahavat*, 181); Ḥiluf minhagim, §32; astonishingly, *Soferim*, 13 end, reads מקדש השבת, "Who sanctifies the Sabbath"; cf. Müller, *Soferim*, 185.

18. Preserved also in Frankfurt am Main; for the text, see *Orḥot* 61c, §§7–8.

19. In Amram 29b, as a *Haftara* benediction; in the ʿ*Amida* only for the Afternoon Service, 30a [and so Saadia]; *Manhig*, "Laws of Sabbath," §5 quotes from Amram for the Evening Service, והניח לנו שבתות מנוחה, "and grant us Sabbaths of rest," but this version is not found in any manuscript.

20. Amram 25a; Bondi, *Saadia*, 28; also Mann, *Palestinian*, 320, 322; רצה והנחל, "Accept and grant," is also lacking here.

21. Amram, in Marx, *Untersuchungen*; Frumkin, ibid.; Natronai in ʿItim, 174 recommends only ומאהבתך, "And because of Your love," and apparently does not know of אתה קדשת, "You sanctified."

22. Amram 2b, Oxford manuscript (Marx, *Untersuchungen*; Frumkin, ibid.) begins with ויברך, "And God blessed," as does Abudarham 40b; Asheri to *Shabbat* 16:5 has the same opinion; *Tur, O.Ḥ.*, §268.

23. JQR 10 (1898): 606.

24. In full form, Abudarham 40b; only the sentence ובשביעי, "And on the seventh day," *Manhig*, "Laws of Sabbath," §5; in *Kol bo*, the wording of the conclusion is זכר למעשה בראשית וליציאת מצרים, "In memory of the creation of the world and the exodus from Egypt."

25. *Vitry*, 82; in the text of the prayer, on p. 143, no traces are any longer evident.

26. Amram 25b (cf. *Untersuchungen*; Frumkin, *Seder*, 2:19); apparently Saadia did not have it [see Saadia, *Siddur*, 21 and 111]; probably the text in Amram is corrupt; cf. ʿItim, 174. [The version ורצה הנחיל לבניהם וכו׳, "He was pleased and granted to their children . . . ," is found also in geniza manuscripts, not only for the Sabbath, but also for festivals; cf. N. Wieder in *Tarbiz* 37 (1967/8): 144f.]

27. Ginzberg, *Geonica*, 2:51; *Manhig*, "Laws of Sabbath," §8.

28. A poetic version of the ʿ*Amida* (it is not clear which ʿ*Amida*) was published by Marmorstein in *MGWJ* 69 (1925): 39f.

29. The comments of Finkelstein in *JQR* NS 16 (1925/6): 24–27 are totally unfounded.—The doubling of ויכלו caused the legal authorities great confusion. The one to which the Talmud refers is the second, and Amram knows it only in the second position.—The short ʿ*Amida* (ברכת מעין שבע; Amram: קדושתא אחת מעין שבע) is mentioned in B. *Shab.* 24b and discussed in Elbogen, *Studien*, 35. It is very interesting that in S. Wertheimer, *Oṣar hamidrashim* (Jerusalem: Lipschitz, 1913–14), 1:89f., the beginning is cited as מגן אברהם, "Shield of Abraham," and at the end מעון הברכות, "Dwelling of blessings," and אב האמת, "Father of truth." That the "Short ʿ*Amida*" mentioned in Y. *Ber.* 4:2, 7d is identical with the text of "Shield of the patriarchs," as assumed by Mann, *Palestinian*, 2:314, is not at all certain. That this text served as Kiddush is merely an unsuccessful formulation, but it is not impossible that the origin of Kiddush is to be found here; cf. Mann, *Palestinian*, 2:322, עת להקריש in MS Turin. [On "One benediction replacing seven," cf. Ginzberg, *Perushim*, 3:319; Allon, *Meḥqarim*, 2:128; Mann, *Palestinian*, 314f.; Lieberman, *Tosefta*, 1:34; E.D. Goldschmidt, "Qidush vehavdala," *Maḥanayim* 85–86 (1963): 48–53; and J. Heinemann in *REJ* 125 (1966): 101f. The text of this prayer indicates clearly that it is of Palestinian origin. The custom of reciting it as a kind of precentor's repetition of the ʿ*Amida* in the Evening Service is known to us as a Babylonian rite from the evidence of the above-cited Y. passage (which, however, does not quote the text of this prayer): "It is the custom there (in Babylonia) that if there is no wine the precentor goes before the ark and recites 'one benediction replacing seven' and concludes 'Who sanctifies Israel and the Sabbath day.'" In Palestine this prayer must have been created, like that of R. Zadok, as a "short

'Amida'' in place of the 'Amida of the Evening Service, as the practice of those who did not recite the 'Amida on weeknights, but who did not want to do without it on the Sabbath altogether because it contained the Sanctification of the Day.]

30. Cf. *J.E.* 7:483f. and Berliner, *Randbemerkungen*, 1:73f. For the use of Kiddush in the Didache, see Klein, ibid., 316, Rietschel, *Liturgik*, 1:248. On Kiddush in the *Apostolic Constitutions* 7:36, cf. Kohler, ibid., 418f.—On the text of Kiddush (for home recitation): Amram 26a (Frumkin, *Seder*, 2:28).

31. Amram, ibid., cf. *'Itim*, 177 and the following sections as cited in Frumkin, *Seder*, 2:26.

32. *Vitry*, 145f.

33. Berliner, *Randbemerkungen*, 1:64 also recommends the order of Sepharad.

34. Zunz, *Ritus*, 152f.; Berliner, *Randbemerkungen*, 1:45f.—Supplications in the Evening Service are mentioned in Mann, *Palestinian*.

§16 *The Sabbath Morning Service*

1. On the verses of the sacrifices, Amram 27a; Frumkin, *Seder*, 2:38. With respect to the Sabbath, Amram rules explicitly that the precentor begin with "Lord of the worlds." Saadia's opposition in Abudarham 44b.

2. The multiplying of psalms resulted from the fact that people arrived at synagogue long before the beginning of the public service and sang psalms, at first *ad libitum*, and later specified psalms; cf. *Teshuvot hage'onim*, no. 87; *'Itim*, 248. The rites differed on this point, and the text of Amram was changed accordingly; cf. Amram 27a with Marx, *Untersuchungen*, 13 and Frumkin, *Seder*, 2:38, 47. It seems that Ps. 92 in *'Itim*, 249 comes from another source; cf. *Nathan the Babylonian*, 83. Sepharad has Ps. 122, which, according to *Manhig*, "Laws of Sabbath," §22 was customarily recited in the synagogue of Yehosef Ibn Nagdala in Granada (murdered, 1066). The multiplication of psalms appears also in the fragment published by Mann, *Palestinian*, 323. As for the psalms customary in Ashkenaz, see Berliner, *Randbemerkungen*, 1:22f. That Ps. 33 follows Ps. 136, instead of preceding it as in the order of the Book of Psalms, Berliner explains by the fact that in the Passover Haggadah, Ps. 33: 1–3 is said after Ps. 136, as was pointed out by *Tosafot*, B. *Pes.* 118a, s.v. מהודו. Accordingly, we find that the printers customarily print the verses a little apart from the beginning of the line. Surprisingly, the same order is found already in *Vitry*, 62.—R. Natronai would not agree to permit Ex. 15 even on the Sabbath (*'Itim*, 249).

3. [An analysis of "The Breath" and an attempt to prove that it is composed of several sections, each of which was originally a separate version of the Benediction of the Song, is given in E. D. Goldschmidt, *Hagada shel pesah vetoledoteha* (Jerusalem: Bialik Institute, 1960/1), 67f. and 107f.; and cf. J. Heinemann in *Tarbiz* 30 (1960/1): 408f. A detailed stylistic analysis appears in A. Zeidman, *Ma'yanot* 8 (1964): 379f. On certain expressions common to "The Breath" and other prayers, see Heinemann, *Prayer*, 40f. and 43.] Cf. Jawitz, *Meqor*, 67f., but he goes too far in assuming parallels, *J.E.* 9:313f. In Rome, "The Breath" comes only after "May Your Name be praised"; thus, there can be no talk of any reciprocal relationship between them. [See now D. Goldschmidt, *Mahzor layamim hanora'im* (Jerusalem: Qoren, 1970), 1:22, n. 23.]

4. Zunz, *Literaturgeschichte*, 5; Elbogen, *Studien*, 74. Rashi: *Vitry*, 282. In view of this legend, Graetz, *Divre*, 3:166, assumed that there was a liturgical poet named Simeon b. Kefa.

5. Abudarham 45b, bottom. Complex acrostics of this type are not ancient in Jewish literature; see *REJ* 33 (1897): 153.

6. A similar heaping-up of synonyms is in fact found in M. *Pes.* 10:5. The text of Amram 26b is shorter than Frumkin, *Seder*, 2:47; it includes numerous late additions.

7. In Amram 27b (Frumkin, *Seder*, 2:48), there is a congregational response to "Bless the Lord" that is different from the one used on weekdays; it begins ישתבח שמך, "May Your Name be praised." A different one is found in *'Itim*, 250, but the author rejects it.

8. אין ערוך already in Frumkin, *Seder*, 2:48. On the three additions, see Elbogen, *Studien*, 24f. New additions in *REJ* 53 (1907): 241.

9. Romaniot has both "God the Lord" and "Blessed God."

[10. "To the God Who rested" is not unique; a poem in exactly the same form for Thursdays was published from the geniza by Elbogen, *Studien*, 24.]

11. In Bondi, *Saadia*, 29; Barzilai in *'Itim*, 250f.

12. *Orhot*, 65a, §3; *Tur*, *O.H.*, §281; according to Abudarham 46b it must be concluded that the congregations that said "To the God Who rested" were the exception.—Poetic reworkings of "Creator" in Mann, *Palestinian*, 323; in the words אשר ברוב חכמה גדל the word חכמה should be omitted, as it disturbs the alphabetical acrostic; or perhaps it originally read בחכמה.

13. Already Amram 28a (Frumkin, *Seder*, 2:48)—ולא נתתו: cf. Jubilees 2:31.

[Cf. A. Mirsky, "Yesod qerova," *Sinai* 57 (1965): 127f., who sees in "Moses rejoiced" a remnant of an ancient *qerova* with an alphabetical acrostic, of which only the letters י כ, ל, are preserved (instead of ושני לוחות אבנים, a geniza fragment has לוחות אבנים); this would also explain the problem of the verses following this passage, which are not from the Ten Commandments but from a different place.]

§17   *The Additional Service*

1. *Musaf* as an additional service: e.g., B. *Meg.* 22a, where the lengthened service of fast days is called מוסף תפילה.

[On the Additional Service on weekdays, cf. also Albeck, *Mishnah*, 2:495 and Lieberman, *Tosefta*, 5:1086, to lines 34–35.]

2. See Geiger, *Urschrift*, 122; A. Büchler, *Der galilaeische ʿAm haʾarez des zweiten Jahrhunderts* (Vienna: Israel-theol. Lehranstalt, 1906), 212; Y. Horowitz in *Festschrift zu siebzigsten Geburtstage Jacob Guttmans* (Leipzig: G. Fock, 1915), 126. S. Krauss and Y. Horowitz dealt at length with the subject in *Jahrbuch der jued.-liter. Ges.* 18 (1926): 195–312, without succeeding in completely clarifying the matter. In any case, Horowitz now distinguishes between חֶבֶר עיר and חֲבַר עיר, and understands the former as meaning a community organization. It is doubtful that a "higher synagogue" as imagined by Krauss ever existed.

3. M. *Ber.* 4:1 and B. *Ber.* 28a, and cf. Mittwoch, ibid., 30f.

4. The source of the information there is "R. Anan b. Rava in the name of Rav" of the third century, but the division itself is ancient.

5. On the origin of the text of the ʿAmida of the Additional Service, cf. Rosenthal in Graetz, *Geschichte*, 4:470, and *MGWJ* 55 (1911): 428; but it should be noted that Palestine goes without transition from ותתן לנו, "and You gave to us," to the sacrifices, cf. 441f., 446, 586.

6. According to Rashi's ruling, if one says יהי רצון, "May it be Your will," he has fulfilled his obligation; *Pardes*, 55d.

[On the style of "May it be Your will" in the Afternoon Service, which occurs nowhere else in all the other statutory prayers, cf. Heinemann, *Prayer*, 172.]

7. Variants on "You established the Sabbath" in Saadia (Frumkin, *Seder*, 2:88). For אז וכו', *Manhig*, "Laws of Sabbath," §42; *Orhot* 65c, §1; the words are already lacking in *S.L.*, §82; *Tanya*, §17; but also in Amram 29b and Frumkin, *Seder*, 2:70.

8. Cf., e.g., Steinschneider, *Catalogus*, 2716, 36b—In fragments in Mann, *Palestinian*, 323, the ʿAmida of the Additional Service is passed over in silence, but he does report a very interesting poetic version from MS Turin, p. 335, n. 134. Cf. also Schechter, *Liturgy*, 99f., where two other poems of this type are published.

9. Below, §45f. [notes and text—Engl. trans.].

10. *Manhig*, "Laws of Sabbath," §44.

§18   *The Afternoon Service*

1. B. *R.H.* 31a, transmitted by R. Yose b. Ḥalafta, who had reliable information on the Temple service from his father.

2. Cf. *Tanḥuma*, *Vayaqhel* in *S.L.*, §96; *Yalqut*, *Exodus*, §408 from *Midrash abkir*; Rashi to B. *Meg.* 21a, s.v. ואין מוסיפין; Zunz, *Haderashot*, 176. From *Itim*, 289 one can still clearly discern the connection between these homilies and "And You, being holy"; cf. Ginzberg, *Geonica*, 2:299.

3. Information from Dr. I. Abrahams of Cambridge.

4. *S.L.*, §126.

5. MS Oxford in Marx, *Untersuchungen*, 14; Frumkin, *Seder*, 2:100.

6. Explanations: e.g., *Manhig*, "Laws of Sabbath," §60; *S.L.*, §126: עת רצון, Is. 49:8; cf. I Kgs. 18:36f.

7. Cf. Marx, *Untersuchungen*, 14; Frumkin, *Seder*, 2:101.

8. E.g., Steinschneider, *Catalogus*, 2716, 36b.

9. Strange variants and explanations in Baer, ʿ*Avodat*, 262f.; Lewysohn, *Meqore*, 55f. Several vain attempts to explain "Abraham will rejoice . . ." in *Jeschurun* 11 (1924): 475; *Jeschurun* 11 (1924): Hebrew section, 140; *Jeschurun* 12 (1925): 198. Poetic version of the ʿAmida in the Turin manuscript; see Schechter, ibid., 101f.

10. Amram: See Ginzberg, *Geonica*, 1:139; Bondi, *Saadia*, 30; various motivations in Baer, ʿ*Avodat*, 265; Frumkin, *Seder*, 2:104; *REJ* 26 (1803): 132f.

11. *Vitry*, 113.

§19 The End of the Sabbath

1. For Havdala, cf. *J.E.* 6:118 and in the *Lewy Festschrift*, 185f.

2. B. *Pes.* 105a.

3. *Rivista Israelita* 5 (1908): 98f.

4. In Marx, *Untersuchungen*, 15; Frumkin, *Seder*, 2:117; the text is inaccurate in both, for אלהינו should come at the end of the line after ברוך.

5. The text of Saadia now in Frumkin, *Seder*, 2:107, and on this basis it would be possible to expand the data; likewise, before the ʿAmida it has a special conclusion: לך נפאר אל מלך מושל בכל, "You we glorify, God, King, Who rules all," Frumkin, *Seder*, 2:107 and Bondi, *Saadia*, 30.

6. Ibid.; and cf. Mann, *Palestinian*, 323f.

7. Cf. the commentators on the *S.A., O.H.,* §294.

8. Cf. *Ex. r.* 39:43; Ginzberg, *Geonica*, 1:139.

9. *Vitry*, 114.

10. On this, see Baer, ʿ*Avodat*, 305f.

11. *Vitry*, 116, where something is obviously missing. The text resembles that of Rome, except that the petitions are more varied; but later they were abridged.

§20 The New Moon

1. On the solemn nature of the New Month in the ancient world, see *J.E.* 9:243f., s.v. "New Moon." For *Soferim* 19:9, see Müller, *Soferim*, 270f.

2. The existence of such a central authority follows, e.g., from the dispute between Saadia and Ben Meir; cf. Mann, *Egypt*, 1:52f., 2:41f., 2:49f.

3. The first mention of "Thus the honored masters have decreed" in *Sefer yereʾim*, §103 and *Orhot*, 65b, top. The Sephardic versions of "May it be Your will" are found in Amram 33a as a prayer for the New Moon after the reading of the Torah; the correct text is in Marx, *Untersuchungen*, 15. Marmorstein has published liturgical poems by R. Phineas (see §40[4]), which were connected with the announcement of the New Moon under the name קדוש ירחים דר' פנחס in *Hasofe* 5 (1921): 235f.

4. Cf. Zunz, *Ritus*, 150f.; Abeles, *Der kleine Versöhnungstag*.

5. T. *Ber.* 3:14; B. *Ber.* 29b; Y. *Ber.* 4:3, 8a; B. *Shab.* 24a. The beginning of "Ascend and Come" in *Soferim* 19:7: אנא ה' אלהינו יעלה; cf. Müller, *Soferim*, 269, n. 26.—Palestinian text: *MGWJ* 55 (1911): 439. [On the source of "Ascend and Come" and the variant readings between the Palestinian and Babylonian texts, see the detailed article of L.J. Liebreich in *HUCA* 34 (1963): 125f. and Heinemann, *Blessing*, 99f.]

6. According to Saadia (Bondi, *Saadia*, 34), the skip consists in reciting only verses 12–14 and 19 in Ps. 116.

7. B. *Ta.* 28b.

8. The difference between "to recite" and "to complete" does not appear to be very ancient, even though it is claimed (Bondi, *Saadia*, 34) that it already appears in Saadia [*Siddur*, 153]; cf. Tosafot, B. *Suk.* 44b, s.v. כאן.

9. Amram 33a (Frumkin, *Seder*, 2:130).

[10. On "All Your deeds will praise You" and on the Benediction of the Song in general, cf. the article of N. Wieder in *JJS* 4 (1953): 65f., and Goldschmidt, *Hagada*, 64f.]

11. Cf. T. *Ber.* 3:14.

12. See Y. *Ber.* 9:2, 13d; Ginzberg, *Seride*, 253a and Ratner, *Ahavat*, 203; *Pesiqta rabati*, 1a, n. 4. The current eulogy: B. *Ber.* 44a; 49a already in the name of R. Judah the Prince.

13. See Berliner, *Randbemerkungen*, 1:67.—A poetic *shivʿata* for the Additional Service of the New Month that falls on a weekday was published by Marmorstein in *Hasofe* 4 (1922): 56, and, with errors (אותות בוצצת or ביצצת instead of בונגת) in *MGWJ* 69 (1925): 40. —For the Sabbath, *Vitry*, 197, has some additions that are found nowhere else.

14. For the text of Sabbath and the New Moon, cf. Mann, *Palestinian*, 337f.

[15. Various piyyutim for the New Month, especially that of Nisan, in the honor of which the wording of the eulogy was changed to מקדש ישראל וראש ראשי חדשים, "Who sanctifies Israel and the chief of the New Moons," cf. the article of E. Fleischer, "Rosh rashe hodashim," *Tarbiz* 37 (1967/8): 265f.]

16. B. *Suk.* 54b.; *Soferim* 18:1; cf. Müller, *Soferim*, 250, n. 3.

§21 Fast Days

1. See *J.E.* 5:347, s.v. "Fasting"; W. Groenman, *Het Vasten bij Israel* (Leiden, 1906.)

2. *Ḥasofe* 5 (1921): 229; Zunz, *Ritus*, 124f.

3. Amram in Marx, *Untersuchungen*, 17.

4. Warnheim, *Qevuṣat hakhamim* (Vienna: A della Torre, 1861), 107; *Ḥemda genuza*, no. 160–61; *Eshkol*, 2:5f.—Compare Marmorstein in *JQR* NS 15 (1924/5): 411f., who publishes an ʿAmida for fast days beginning with the nineteen ordinary benedictions in poetic form (four alphabetical lines each, beginning, in rotation, with ברוך, and מי אל כמוך, ותשתבח, תתברך; the common concluding verse is based on the language of the ordinary eulogy), while the six additional benedictions mentioned in M. *Ta.* 2 follow as Benedictions 20–25. The name of the author is, as noted by Davidson, ibid., 507, R. Eleazar b. Aaron Fasi. Davidson himself notes in *Ginze qedem* 3 (1925): 46f. the expanded ʿAmida for fast days cited in Abudarham, Fast-day Service, and *Ṭur*, *O.Ḥ.*, §579 from the geonic prayer book. One of the abbreviated reworkings of the ʿAmida (above, notes to §8:6) for fast days, with the repeated beginning אנא אלהינו, "O our God": see Schechter, *Liturgy*, 98f.

[Cf. further: D. Goldschmidt, "Seder taʿniyot ṣibur bemaḥzor roma," in *S. Meir Memorial Volume* (Jerusalem, 1956), 77f.]

5. *Soferim* 18:4f. (*Soferim*, 255f.), Amram 44a (Frumkin, *Seder*, 2:268f).

6. Cf. Ginzberg, *Seride*, 174.

7. Amram, Manuscript S in Marx, *Untersuchungen*, 27.

8. Rome has both a short eulogy, "Who builds Jerusalem," as in Maimonides, and the long version; cf. *Orḥot*, 95d, §16.

9. Thus, R. Isaac Barceloni in *Ṭur*, *O.Ḥ.*, §557; for France, *Manhig*, "Laws of Fasts," §26; against this, *Vitry*, 229.

10. *Eshkol*, 2:17; *Manhig*, "Laws of Fasts," §28; *Orḥot*, 95d, §16; cf. *S.A.*, *O.Ḥ.*, §§552, 559:4.

11. *Vitry*, 226; *Manhig*, "Laws of Fasts," §28, derives it from Palestine, and in fact the influence of the Palestinian leaders on Italy is proved from other sources as well.

12. Cf. Rome and *Orḥot*, 95d, §19.

13. Only in Isserles on *S.A.*, *O.Ḥ.*, §559:4.

[14. On the special structure of the *qerovot* for the Ninth of Av, which have stanzas corresponding only to fourteen benedictions (up to "Who builds Jerusalem"), cf. E. Fleischer in *Sinai* 62 (1967/8): 13f.; also D. Goldschmidt, *Seder haqinot letishʿa beʾav* (Jerusalem: Mossad Harav Kook, 1968), Hebrew part, 8.]

15. *Qinot*; *Orḥot*, 96a, §20.

16. Cf. Romaniot.

§22 Hanukkah and Purim

1. For the place of the addition for the "Reference to the Occasion," cf. T. *Ber.* 3:14.— The text of the addition must be reconstructed on the basis of variant readings in Müller, *Soferim*, 286 on *Soferim* 20:8 as follows: ונודה לשמך לנצח . . . כן עשה עמנו . . . וכנסי פלאות ותשועות כהנגיך אשר עשית, "And like the wonders and salvations such as these which You have done . . . so do for us . . . and we will give thanks to Your name forever." For the dispute as to the legal status of this passage, cf. *Tosafot*, B. *Meg.* 4a, s.v. פסק; *Manhig*, "Laws of Megila," §25.

2. Cf. *Soferim*, ad loc.

3. "To make them forget your Torah" is parallel to I Macc. 1:49; cf. Zunz, *Haderashot*, 227, n. 31 and *REJ* 73 (1921): 174f.; on the text, *Rivista Israelita* 4 (1907): 102.—A shorter version of "For the Miracles" with the wording for Purim, ועשה עמנו (but without וכנסי at the end) in Mann, *Palestinian*, 309.

4. *Soferim* 20:9.

5. For the text of the benediction, cf. *Diqduqe soferim* to B. *Shab.* 23a, *Tosafot* to B. *Suk.* 46a, s.v. העושה.

6. By R. Mordecai b. Isaac, before 1250, Zunz, *Literaturgeschichte*, 580. On the text of "These lamps" and "Fortress, rock," see Baer, *ʿAvodat*, 440.

[A critical analysis of the text of "These lamps" in D. Goldschmidt, *Deʿot* 8 (1954).]

7. Cf. *Soferim* 17:4.

8. Amram 37b; Frumkin, *Seder*, 2:184; as against this, *Manhig*, "Laws of Megila," §23; *Tosafot*; B. *Meg.* 5b, s.v. שאסורים.

9. The whole beginning of Tractate *Megila*, in which the word *megila* serves as a well-known and accepted designation for the Book of Esther, and likewise the casuistic distinctions between unwalled cities and those surrounded by a wall, and all the technical terms testify to a very early origin for the custom.

10. The benedictions were first recited in the time of R. Ashi (ca. 400); on the question whether to repeat the third benediction (known as זמן) in the morning as well, see *Vitry*, 218, Maimonides, *M.T.*, "Laws of Megila," 1:3.

11. The benediction "Who fights our battle," B. *Meg.*, 21b, from the same period; "cursed be Haman" is cited independently of the benediction in the name of Rava, B. *Meg.*, 7b; see Amram 36b and cf. Marx, *Untersuchungen*, 18f. and Frumkin, *Seder*, 2:179.

12. The expansion beginning אשר הניא, "Who annulled," is first mentioned in the name of Rashi in *S.L.*, §200. In *Vitry*, 214 this passage is called "A liturgical poem composed by the men of the Great Assembly." Zunz, *Literaturgeschichte*, 15 fixes its period in the time of the most ancient expansions of the prayer book.

["Who annulled" is not merely a liturgical poem, but a versified benediction that began "Blessed are You, Lord our God, King of the universe, Who annulled...." It seems to have served as an alternative to the benediction following the reading of the *Megila* that begins "Who fights our battle," like the benedictions in the very same versified style after the reading of the Torah on solemn occasions, such as אשר בגלל אבות בנים גידל, "Who for the sake of the ancestors raised up sons ...," after the reading of the Book of Deuteronomy on the Joy of the Torah. See Heinemann, *Prayer*, 106f. and the literature cited there, and Heinemann in the Annual of Bar-Ilan University 1 (1963): 222, n. 6.]

13. The participatory reading of serveral verses, in Amram; cf. Marx, *Untersuchungen*, 18 and Frumkin, *Seder*, 2:179, where there is also an allusion to *Vitry*, 210; *Hagahot maimoniyot* to Maimonides, *M.T.*, "Laws of Megila."

14. The beginnings of interruptions already in Y. *Meg.* 1:5, 70b; noisy interruptions, *S.L.*, §200; Abrahams, *Jewish Life*, ibid.

§23   The Three Pilgrim Festivals

1. In an Amram manuscript in Marx, *Untersuchungen*, 23, וסדר תפילה של ימים טובים ושל מועדות.

2. The Additional Service of the New Year, below, §24(3).

3. E.g., B. *Meg.* 31a, B. *Beṣ.* 6a; Y. *ʿEruv.*, chap. 3, end (21c).

4. *Soferim* 19:3

5. T. *Ber.* 3:13.

6. The version "You chose" is to be preferred to "You chose us" not only on stylistic grounds but also on account of the content, insofar as it touches on revelation as the purpose of chosenness (cf. the dependence on Lev. 18:5).

7. Amram 37b (Marx, *Untersuchungen*, 23).

8. *Shaʿare simḥa*, 2:7.

9. Cf. *Judaica*, 670.

10. Cf. Ratner, *Ahavat*, 203.

11. Amram 43a, *Vitry*, 300.

12. With regard to the verses of the sacrifices they relied on the dictum of Rav, "Once he says 'and in your Torah it is written as follows: ...' " (B. *R.H.* 35a), but this dictum refers to the verses of the Additional Service of the New Year, cf. the commentators, ibid. According to the gaon Sar Shalom the verses were not recited, but according to Natronai and Saadia they were; Amram sees them as optional and not obligatory, see Marx, *Untersuchungen*, 27 and Frumkin, *Seder*, 2:259; *Shaʿare simḥa*, 2:26; Ginzberg, *Geonica*, 2:112–19; *Halakhot pesuqot*, 31; Rashi in *Vitry*, 438f.

13. This baraita is quoted also in B. *Beṣ.* 17a; in Rashi (*Vitry*, 438f.), s.v. מתחיל: המנוחה את יום, while in *Vitry*, 299: המנוח.—Fragments for Tabernacles and the Sabbath in Mann, *Palestinian*, 232.

14. For the text of "And You proclaimed to us," see *Diqduqe soferim*, 1:181.

[Geniza texts reflecting the custom of reciting Havdala in Benediction 18 in the Evening Service of festivals occurring on Saturday night have been published by N. Wieder in *JJS* 4 (1953): 30f.; additional attestations of this custom in the article by E. Fleischer, "שבעתות הבדלה ארץ ישראליית," *Tarbiz* 36 (1966/7): 342f.]

15. In Spain, at first only in Seville and Toledo; cf. Abudarham 40a.

16. The verses are not yet found in Amram, and the variants between them are a sign of their lateness.

17. For the expanded Kiddush for Passover, which *ʿItim*, 288 goes so far as to call "the way of the Karaites," cf. Bondi, *Saadia*, 32; the expansion permitted by Saadia is maintained in Yemen to this day, cf. *JQR* 14 (1923/4): 591f.

[And cf. Goldschmidt, *Hagada*, 91f.]

18. As for the psalms, note must be taken of *Soferim* 18:2: "But on the first days of Passover he must say ..." and it must be explained in connection with *Soferim* 17:11; this obviates the point of Müller, *Soferim*, 252.—The psalms in Amram 41b, according to Marx, *Untersuchungen*, 25 and Frumkin, *Seder*, 2:226.

[Cf. the article of N. Wieder in *JJS* 4 (1953): 65f., where he publishes geniza fragments demonstrating that these benedictions or something like them were recited before and after the psalm of the day on different festivals.]

19. T. *Suk.* 3:2.

20. *Manhig*, "Laws of Sukkot," §57f. [According to the practice of the Vilna Gaon, which is accepted among some of the Ashkenazim in Palestine, when any of the five scrolls is read from a validly written roll of parchment, the benediction is recited בא״ה אמ״ה אקב״ו על מקרא מגילה, "Blessed are You, Lord our God, King of the universe, Who sanctified us with His commandments and commanded us about the reading of the scroll."]

21. B. *Suk.* 55a.

22. Cf. *MGWJ* 55 (1911): 441; *Shaʿare simha*, 2:7.

23. The designations for the festivals used in the liturgy are already found in Amram. In Palestine and *Soferim*, neither "the season of our freedom" and the like, nor "in memory of the exodus from Egypt" are found, but the meaning of the festivals is indicated by the words לשמחה וליום טוב ולמקראי קודש, "For joy and a holiday and holy assembly."

24. *Vitry*, 280, following *Megilat setarim* of R. Nisim, *Manhig*, "Laws of Pesaḥ," §52.

25. Raviah gives as a source, "I found in a responsum."

[Cf. now S. B. Freehof in *Studies and Essays in Honor of Abraham A. Neuman*, ed. Meir Ben-Horin et al. (Leiden: E.J. Brill, 1962), 226f.]

26. Cf. S.A., O.H., §487, end, and commentaries.

27. Neither from Amram nor *Vitry* is it clear whether in those days Hallel was yet recited; in late sources the recitation of Hallel with the omission is always assumed.

28. *Vitry*, 304.

29. Ps. 69 is explained in the aggadah as referring to the Revelation.

30. *Vitry*, 344.

31. Ps. 76, for the sake of v. 3. In Mann, *Palestinian*, 332, Ps. 122. The Talmud lists each time only the beginning of the psalm-reading, so that there is no way of knowing how far it went.

32. M. *Suk.* 4:5. Yemen reports in the name of Saadia that the processions are already held after Hallel.

33. *Vitry* does not yet know the name Hoshana Rabba, but *Manhig*, "Laws of Etrog," §38 does.—The oldest description of the festival in the appendix to *Midrash tehilim*, 128 to Ps. 17:2.

34. *Vitry*, 444; *Manhig*, "Laws of Etrog," §38.

35. Zunz, *Ritus*, 94ff. Luzzatto, *Vikuah ʿal haqabala*, 5ff.; Berliner, *Randbemerkungen*, 2:25ff.

36. *Halakhot gedolot*, 173.

37. See *Sefer Hasidim*, §630; Harkavy, *Studien*, 5:215; Epstein in *MGWJ* 67 (1903), 342ff.; Krauss in *Jahrbuch für jüdische Geschichte und Literatur* 22 (1919): 43ff.

38. B. *R.H.* 4b and elsewhere.

39. Cf. Müller, *Soferim*, 262ff.

40. *MGWJ* 55 (1911): 438ff.

41. *Vitry*, 446.

42. M. *Ta.* 1:1; announcement, Abudarham 81b.

43. Below, §32, p. 172.

44. In a discussion of the falsification of a document in Cologne, 1132, it is called יום תשיעי עצרת and תשיעי ספק שמיני (Ravan, no. 48); in the commentary of R. Solomon Son of the Orphan (twelfth century), ed. Chajes, 115 it is called וזאת הברכה. The familiar name is first found in Ibn Ghiyath, *Shaʿare simha*, 118; *Pardes*, 45b.

§ 24 The Days of Awe

1. The name *Days of Awe* is first found in *Maharil*.

2. On the origin of the New Year, cf. *J.E.* 9:354; D. Hoffmann, *Das Buch Leviticus* (Berlin: M. Poppelauer, 1905–6), 242ff.; B. Eerdmans, *Alttestamentliche Studien* (Giessen: Toepelmann, 1908–12), 4:68; E. Mahler, *Handbuch der jüdischen Chronologie* (Leipzig: G. Fock), 359 and the literature cited there.

3. M. *R.H.* 4:4.

4. *MGWJ* 55 (1911): 434.

5. J. Mann, "Changes in the Divine Service," *HUCA* 4 (1927): 300 attempts to explain the change in the place of the shofar-blowing as evidence of persecution, and it is true that during the [First] World War the shofar-blowing was prohibited in Alsace and other places close to the front of war, out of fear that the soldiers would think it a military signal. [In the opinion of Allon, *Mehqarim*, 124, the rite of shofar-blowing originated in the Temple, where they used to blow it over the daily sacrifice (i.e., over the Additional Sacrifice); and

when they began to blow it outside the Temple as well, they aimed to do so at the same time as in the Temple. But see Lieberman, *Tosefta*, 1:41, to line 58.]

6. B. *R.H.* 16a; the motivation provided by R. Abbahu, "to confuse Satan," has recently been shown to be a reliable Babylonian tradition; cf. *Theologisch Tijdschrift* 38 (1904): 20.

7. Cf. *Judaica*, 672ff.

8. Cf. M. *R.H.* 4:5 and T. *R.H.* 4:5 as well as Y. *R.H.* 4:6, 59c: "In Judea they followed R. Akiva and in the Galilee they followed R. Yohanan b. Nuri . . . ."

9. R. Simeon b. Gamaliel; Y. *R.H.* 4:6; B. *R.H.* 32a.

10. *Orhot*, 99a, §1 expresses the opinion, adopted also by Landshuth, that the three passages beginning "And so" are a short version of the Kingship, Remembrance, and Shofar benedictions. This is not the case, for the content of the Remembrance benediction can only be found there with difficulty, and that of the Shofar benediction is not included at all; rather the entire prayer is equivalent to the Kingship benediction, and this relationship is particularly evident in "And You will rule"; cf. also L.A. Rosenthal in the *Hoffmann Festschrift*, 234ff. The train of thought of "And so set Your fear" is found as early as Ben Sira 36:2ff.; cf. Perles in *OLZ* 10 (1902): 493. ["And so set Your fear" was not customary in the Babylonian rite in geonic times; see the article by N. Wieder in *Tarbiz* 37 (1967/8): 135f., 240f., and especially 257, n. 199.]

11. Cf. *Rivista Israelita* 4 (1907): 189; *MGWJ* 55 (1911): 595.

12. Palestinian fragments in Mann, *Palestinian*, 392. New and particularly noteworthy is the poetic introduction to the Shofar verses, which begins, as usual, with "You revealed," but is much longer and gives more attention to the midrash on the revelation at Sinai.

13. For the verses suitable for the Kingship, Remembrance, and Shofar verses, M. *R.H.* 4:6–8; B. *R.H.* 32b; Y. *R.H.* 4:7, 59c.

14. Each of three verses, as in Pal. on other festivals as well; cf. above, §23(5).

15. For the Remembrance verses, the other rites have also Ex. 6:5 (Sepharad), Ps. 105:8 (Romaniot and Rome).

16. *MGWJ* 55 (1911): 595ff.

17. R. Yose and R. Judah, M. *R.H.* 4:6–8.

18. "It is our duty" was attributed to Joshua; Frumkin, *Seder*, 1:319 still defends this idea. Further to this, cf. M. Bloch, *Shaʿare torot hataqanot* (Vienna, 1897–1906), 1:42. On the text, cf. above, §10(11).

19. For Rav's activities in connection with the liturgy, see §37(5).

20. Criticism of "You remember" and "You revealed" in the *Kohler Festschrift*, 75. It should be noted that with the words ואין שכחה, "and there is no forgetfulness," the prayer returns verbatim to a sentence near the beginning, as is usual at the end of a prayer, and that the verse quoted from Lev. 26:45 relates to all three patriarchs, not only to Abraham. [On the transition from the introduction of Remembrance to the first of the verses, L.J. Liebreich in *HUCA* 34 (1963): 163ff. expresses the exact opposite opinion, seeing it as a shining example of the author's literary skill.]

21. "And there we shall perform" (ושם נעשה) without mention of the sacrifices in Amram (Frumkin, *Seder*, 2:306); Saadia (ibid., 290); Vitry, 372, and old printed editions cited in Baer, *ʿAvodat*, 404.

22. The eulogy שומע תרועה, "Who hears the trumpeting," in Saadia (Frumkin, *Seder*, 2:290), Rome, *S.L.*, 137a.

23. Cf. B. *R.H.*, end; Ibn Ghiyath, *Shaʿare simha*, 1:38f.; Vitry, 352f.; *Siddur Rashi*, 78; Asheri to M. *R.H.* 4:14 (near the end); *S.L.*, 136a, §290.

24. The text of M. *ʿEruv.* 3, end, is cited after the edition of W. Lowe, *Mishnah* (Cambridge: University Press, 1883), 41a. In other texts the second occurrence of חדש is lacking, and *Diqduqe soferim* does not cite any variants.

25. Asheri, *R.H.*, 4:14 quotes from Y.: "Rav ordered his disciples to make reference to the New Moon sacrifice in the Additional Service," but there is no such passage.

26. *MGWJ* 55 (1911): 437f. The text of *Soferim* is cited after Vitry, 360 (*MGWJ* 55 [1911]: 430).

27. Vitry, 357f.; *Siddur Rashi*, 76; Italy: *ʿArukh*, s.v. חדש, I; *S.L.*, 136a, §290.

28. *Responsa*, ed. F. Rosenthal, nos. 43–46 (Berlin, 1898). Tosafot *ʿEruv.* 40a, s.v. זכרון; B. *Beṣ.* 16a, s.v. שהחרש; B. *R.H.* 35a, s.v. אילימא.

29. See Marmorstein in *REJ* 73 (1921): 84ff.

30. Vitry, 361, §322, end.

31. As early as B. *R.H.* 326.

32. *MGWJ* 55 (1911): 441, 595.

[33. For the conjecture that "Remember us" and other short prayers in the same quasi-piyyut style are ancient and of Palestinian origin, see J. Heinemann in the *Annual of Bar-Ilan University* 4–5 (1966–67): 132ff.]

34. Amram 44b (Frumkin, *Seder*, 2:293).

35. Rav Hai in Ibn Ghiyath, *Shaʿare simha*, 1:45.

[36. For המלך עושה השלום, "King Who makes peace," as a eulogy customary on the Days of Awe in the Babylonian rite, see N. Wieder in *Tarbiz* 37 (1967/8): 254ff.]

37. In Bondi, *Saadia*, 36 (Frumkin, *Seder*, 2:288); cf. Amram 45a; *Manhig*, "Laws of R.H.," §5.

38. To this day, Ps. 47 is recited in Ashkenaz before the blowing of the shofar; Ps. 81 because of its beginning and Ps. 29 because of the word "voice" that occurs in it repeatedly.

39. On the varying length of "Our Father, our King": Zunz, *Ritus*, 118. In no early edition of Ashkenaz is reference to martyrs found. Apparently these lines were added only after 1648; cf. Baer, ʿ*Avodat*, 111.

40. *Manhig*, "Laws of R.H.," §7.

41. On the different version, see Zunz, *Ritus*, 141ff.

42. Ibn Ghiyath, *Shaʿare simha*, 1:43f., *Manhig*, "Laws of R.H.," §1. *Manhig*, "Laws of R.H.," §3: "one prays with bent knee."

43. Amram 2:22f.; *Manhig*, "Laws of R.H.," §35; *Orhot*, 99a, §1.

44. Amram 47b; First of Elul: *Manhig*, "Laws of R.H.," §25; R. Hai Gaon in Abudarham 70c; cf. Zunz, *Ritus*, 122. Since the service was no longer said at night, a few passages were changed; Berliner, *Randbemerkungen*, 2:24. [Cf. now D. Goldschmidt, *Seder haselihot* (Jerusalem, 1964–65), intro.]

45. In France: *Manhig*, "Laws of R.H.," §24. On Ps. 37 in Ashkenaz: Berliner, *Randbemerkungen*, 1:26.

46. On the development of the liturgy, see Elbogen, *Studien*, 49f., 54f.

47. Ibid., 55; the text: *Sifra* 80d; M. *Yoma* 3:8; Y. *Yoma* 3:8, 40d; B. *Yoma* 36b; cf. Joel Müller, *Teshuvot geʾone mizrah umaʿarav*, no. 144 (Berlin, 1888).

48. "He must specify the sin": T. *Yoma* 5:14.

49. Rav, Samuel, R. Levi, R. Yohanan, R. Yehuda, and R. Hamnuna; for the text, cf. R. Hananel.

50. First in *Halakhot gedolot*, 154, 158 and Amram 47a (Frumkin, *Seder*, 2:339); Baer, ʿ*Avodat*, 414f.

51. Cf. Dan. 9:11, Job 33:27, Neh. 9:33.

52. Similar confession text in *Lev. r.* 3:3.

53. Amram 48a (Frumkin, *Seder*, 2:341) has additional sentences, apparently without manuscript authority. According to O.Z., §281, Amram originally had the alphabetic "For the sin," but the same text was not used in all services. Apparently he had the same text as in our *Vitry*, 391; for the text of Ashkenaz, cf. Baer, ʿ*Avodat*, 417.

54. Already in *Vitry*, 391. In the prayer books there are numerous variations both in text and usage, a sign that the text is very late; cf. Baer, ʿ*Avodat*, 418.

55. *Siddur Rashi*, 96. The eulogy: Cf. B. *Yoma*, 87b, "And he concludes with the confession . . . ," Saadia in Abudarham 77b. [See also N. Wieder in *Tarbiz* 37 (1967/8): 240f, 252f.]

56. In B. *Yoma* 87b.

57. Already in Amram, though it belongs to the Kingship verses customary only on the New Year; see above (§24[3]).

58. *MGWJ* 55 (1911): 443. An interesting Palestinian fragment containing all the *selihot* and the confession, *MGWJ* 55 (1911): 595f.; *JQR* NS 9 (1918–19): 294f. A Palestinian fragment in J. Mann's article in *HUCA* 4 (1927): 330; a second fragment, on p. 331, with liturgical poems between the verses.

59. Amram 47a, only on the Day of Atonement in Marx, *Untersuchungen*, 34; Frumkin, *Seder*, 2:344; and also Saadia, in Frumkin, *Seder*, 2:328; the eulogy, too, is a bit shorter in Frumkin, *Seder*, 328.

60. Evidently "And grant us" was customary at an early time (perhaps only in Palestine?), while today it is not found in any prayer book; cf. the discussion in *Vitry*, 360f.; *Manhig*, "Laws of Day of Atonement," §57, contradicting "Laws of R.H.," §2.

61. Cf. Amram 47a (Frumkin, *Seder*, 2:344); Ibn Ghiyath, *Shaʿare simha*, 1:61; *Manhig*, "Laws of Day of Atonement," §57 also on "Ascend and Come"; according to Marx, *Untersuchungen*, 35, the Amram manuscripts have the addition to the Additional Service: "And some say 'Rule.'" [Cf. N. Wieder in *Tarbiz* 37 (1967/8): 152f., 244f.]

62. [Cf. N. Wieder, *Tarbiz* 37 (1967/8): 144f.]

63. Pss. 103 and 130, because of their confidence in forgiveness of sin.

64. Marx, *Untersuchungen*, 34; Frumkin, *Seder*, 2:346f.; also in Rome and Sepharad.

65. Already in Y. *Yoma* 8:8, 45c; the variants are already in Amram.

66. In *Halakhot gedolot*, 158, "You give Your hand" is the direct continuation of "You know." Saadia too (Frumkin, *Seder*, 2:356) does not have "You give Your hand." For a discussion of the contents, see *Kohler Festschrift*, 75.

67. Already in Amram 48b; but according to Abudarham 78a, before the Afternoon Service.

68. Below, §33.

69. For the most comprehensive bibliography on "All vows," see *J.E.* 7:539f.; *Realencyklopädie*, 10:649f. Much material in Segel, *Ost und West* 19 (1919): 25f. The book *Kol Nidre* by J.S. Bloch (Vienna: R. Lowit, 1917) was rightly rejected by Poznanski. Likewise deserving of rejection is Th. Reik, *Probleme der Religionspsychologie* I 4: *Kol Nidre*.

Krauss, in *Jahrbuch der jüdischen-literarischen Gesellschaft* 19 (1928): 85f., stresses that the many carefully chosen synonyms show that "All vows" is a legal formula originally intended for the individual who appears before the court to petition for the remission of his vow. Why did it later come to be applied to the community? According to him, this was a protest against the Karaites, who rejected the remission of vows. This protest may first have arisen during the ceremonial procession around the Mount of Olives in Jerusalem and was eventually transferred from there to the synagogue. The origin of "All vows" is, in fact, obscure, and any attempt at an explanation is welcome; but against this explanation stands the problem that, despite everything that has come down to us about the procession on the Mount of Olives, no reference is made to this protest.

The objection to the prayer raised in *AfRW* 25 (1927): 328— "Anyone whose vow to God is not sacred in his own eyes can be assumed not to hold sacred his vow to his fellow man"—is an empty one; the starting point of "All vows" was in fact the extreme seriousness attached to every vow, and its purpose was to cancel vows and to clear the conscience concerning vows that one had made unintentionally and not fulfilled. In principle, the Talmud and rabbinic ethics oppose vows exactly as does the Bible; cf. B. *Ned.* 20a.

70. The first gaon to mention "All vows" is Natronai, in Amram 47a (Frumkin, *Seder*, 2:342); Ibn Ghiyath, *Shaʿare simḥa*, 1:60; opposition, ibid.

71. For the establishment of the text, *Orḥot*, 105d f., must be used. A new version that makes use of the old beginning is found in the prayer book mentioned in §46:9 (n. 50), p. 319. R. Jacob Tam in *Sefer hayashar*, §144, in the name of his father, suggests changing the tense from past to future, without taking into consideration that the text as a whole is directed to the past.

72. *J.E.* 7:542f.

73. In the prayer book for the Breslau community by Geiger, 1854; Ps. 130 is found in the Berlin prayer book and the *Union Prayerbook*.

74. By R. Meir of Rothenburg; cf. Zunz, *Ritus*, 96, and *JQR* 17 (1905): 614 for the quotation from a manuscript of Sepharad: "The custom in Ashkenaz is to pardon the sinners before the service."

§ 25   The Reading of the Torah

1. Zunz, *Haderashot*, 2f.; *J.E.* 7:648.

2. In Romaniot.

3. M. *Meg.* 4:1–3.

4. See *Meg.* 3:6: " 'And Moses told the festivals of the Lord'—[this implies] the obligation to read each one in its season." *Sifra*, 103b (to Lev. 23:43): "This teaches that Moses would tell Israel the laws of Passover on Passover, the laws of Pentecost on Pentecost, and the laws of Tabernacles on Tabernacles." *Sifre* Deut., 100b, §127 (to Deut. 16:1): "Moses said, 'Be punctilious about reciting and expounding the laws of the matter [of the festivals].' " B. *Meg.* 32a: "The sages taught, 'Moses instituted that the Jews should inquire and expound the matter of the day: of Passover on Passover. . . .' " Y. *Meg.* 4:1, 75a: "Moses instituted that the Jews should read the Torah on Sabbaths and festivals, on the New Moons and on the intermediate days of festivals, as it is said, 'Moses spoke.' "

5. Y. *Meg.* 4:1, 75a: "Ezra instituted that the Jews should read the Torah on Mondays and Thursdays and on Sabbaths at the Afternoon Service"; cf. B. *B.Q.* 82a.

6. See *Mekhilta* 45a (to Ex. 15:22): "The prophets and elders instituted that they should read the Torah on Sabbaths, Mondays, and Wednesdays." When below, §26, I call this source legendary, there is no contradiction (as claimed in *AfRW* 25 [1927]: 328), for here we are merely reporting the existence of the sources, while below we are speaking about their value. The following discussion is intended to clarify the facts independently of the tradition.

7. Cf. *J.E.* 5:321 and the literature cited there.

8. Cf. Geiger in *ZDMG* 20 (1866): 541f. (same as *Nachgelassene Schriften* [Berlin: L. Gerschel, 1875–78], 3:293); A. Büchler, "The Triennial Reading of the Law and the Prophets," *JQR* 5 (1893): 425.

9. M. *Meg.* 3:7 says: "On Passover the portion of the festivals is read . . . on the first day of Tabernacles . . . and on all the other days of Tabernacles . . ." Only T. *Meg.* 4:5 adds: "and on all the other days of Passover."

10. M. *Yoma* 7:1: "He reads 'After the death' and 'However on the tenth,' " i.e., Lev. 16:1 and 23:27.

11. M. *Meg.* 3:7.

12. *J.E.* 9:523f.; Büchler's conjecture that "Shekels" is directed against the Sadducees and "Remember" against the Hellenists is not sufficiently grounded.

13. Friedmann, *Maʾamar*, 100, where קרא מקרא (Is. 1:13) is given the same interpretation.

14. T. *Ta.* 2:4.

15. As for Hanuka, etc., no attempt is made even to rely on tradition. T. does not mention these days since it had nothing to add to the instructions in M., and there is no need to deduce, with Büchler, that it did not know of these readings.

16. Friedmann, *Ma'amar*, 101f.; other regulations below.

17. Cf. *J.E.* 3:146, ca. 300; according to Cornill, *Einleitung in das Alte Testament*, 6th ed. (Freiburg: Mohr, 1896), 282, nearly a century later.

18. The Septuagint emerged ca. 250; cf. Schürer, *History*, 3:474. This refutes the approach of R. Leszynsky, *Die Sadduzäer* (Berlin: Mayer und Müller, 1912), 133, who sees the consecutive reading of the Torah as a response to Hellenism.

19. Cf. *JQR* 19 (1907): 288.

20. *Apud* Eusebius, *Praepar. Evang.*, 8:7.

21. *Against Apion* 2.2.17.

22. Such as Luke 4:16.

23. Lev. 23:23–25.

24. Deut. 25:17–19.

25. One baraita (B. *Meg.* 21b) says: "No fewer than ten verses are read in the synagogue." Later these words were interpreted as applying to the weekday reading, but the source does not note anything of the kind. And as is usual with such prohibitions, it may be assumed that here, too, in ancient times fewer than ten verses were read; cf. Y. *Meg.* 4:2, 75a; Y. *Ta.* 4:3, 68b; Friedmann, *Ma'amar*, 106.

26. 21 = 3 × 7 verses: B. *Meg.* 23a.

27. Y. *Meg.* 4:5, 75b.

28. T. *Meg.* 4:10; B. *Meg.* 31b; cf. *Soferim* 10:4, where only the opinion of R. Judah is reported. For the calculation, Friedmann, *Ma'amar*, 100.

29. T. *Meg.* 4:18: "One does not leave over at the end of a book . . . at the end of the Torah . . . ."

30. On the triennial cycle in the midrash, cf. especially J. Theodor, "Die Midraschim und der dreijährige palästinische Cyclus," *MGWJ* 34 (1885): 420 ff.

31. Zunz, *Haderashot*, 219, n. 13; Friedmann, *Ma'amar*, 202f.

32. The list of pericopes (סדרים) in the second rabbinic Bible, Venice 1523; *Maḥberet hatijan* in *Even sapir* 2:229f. and *Journal Asiatique* 6 (1870); Finfer, *Masoret*, 39; Büchler, *Triennial*, 431.

33. 155 pericopes (קנה), *Esth. r.*, beginning. The pericopes of the triennial cycle follow also from the *qerovot* of Yannai mentioned in §40. [See §40, n. 16.]

34. The Babylonians nowhere mention the annual cycle explicitly, but it follows that it was customary from the discussion in B. *Meg.* 29b.

35. Zunz, *Haderashot*, 2; Friedmann, *Ma'amar*, 261.

36. *Benjamin of Tudela*, 98. Abraham, the son of Maimonides in Büchler, *Triennial*, 421.

37. In *Medieval Jewish Chronicles*, 1:188.

38. Cf. *Protokolle und Aktenstücke*, 127; a division of the portions, taking the Masora into account, was proposed by Herzfeld, *Tefillat*, 320f. Salomon points to the table in the prayer book of the Temple, ibid., 65. A different division is given by Geiger in his prayer book, which appeared in 1854. Geiger proposed in Frankfurt to follow the annual cycle, but beginning with the Afternoon Service of the Sabbath and continuing the reading from there (*Protokolle und Aktenstücke*, 125), but his proposal was rejected nearly unanimously. After 1863 this method was introduced in Breslau, with only one change: the new portion began at the Sabbath Morning Service. The other method was adopted in Berlin, among other places; in Munich, the first verses of the weekly portion are always read. In America the practice varies widely from place to place, as Dr. Rosenau of Baltimore has informed me; the selection printed in the *Union Prayerbook* is not at all in universal use.

39. Zunz, *Haderashot*, 2; *Ḥiluf minhagim*, 42, §48.

39*. Y. *Shab.* 17:1, 15c; the correct interpretation in Friedmann, *Ma'amar*, 170f.

39**. R. Hanina: *Lev. r.*, 3:6; *Esth. r.*, 3:6 has instead "R. Ḥanina b. R. Aha." [So in *Lev. r.*, ed. Margulies.] R. Ḥanina b. R. Aha lived only in the fourth century (Bacher, *Proömien*, 84). The verse mentioned can only be Lev. 2:10, for a pericope could not have begun with Lev. 2:3.

40. According to B. *Meg.* 29b, Num. 28:1ff. sometimes occurs together with the pericope "Shekels"; hence it must have been read in the spring; and since it belongs to the third year of the triennial cycle, which begins, according to Zunz with Num. 10, and according to Büchler with Num. 6:22, this could only happen if the cycle began in the autumn. This eliminates one of the main props of Büchler's thesis, the starting point of which is that the cycle began on the First of Nisan (Büchler, *Triennial*, 432f.). Büchler contends that the distribution of the pericopes among the various Sabbaths and festivals was determined by the consideration that the events described in them should not be read arbitrarily, but on the dates when they originally occurred, according to the traditional chronology. But the problem arises that the reading of the pericopes

could only be matched with their appropriate seasons for the current year of the cycle; thus the chronology of the flood could be matched only in the first year; that of Egypt, in the second year; that of Moses' death, in the third year. But it would be surprising if the people would accept this without opposition, especially since no one sage's opinion was followed in every case; for the flood they followed the opinion of R. Eliezer, but not for the death of Moses. The four special Sabbaths were supposed to have been instituted in order to fill the span between the Seventh of Adar, when Deut. 34 was read, and the New Moon of Nisan, when Gen. 1 was read. But this empty span occurred only in the third year, yet the four special Sabbaths were observed annually! It would have been the same for the festivals, for on each of the three years a different pericope would have been read on each one! According to the sources, the readings for festivals and the four Sabbaths are older than the fixed cycle. It has not been proved that the ancient festival pericopes were ever displaced by the cyclical ones; even according to Büchler this was done only on Passover and Pentecost, but not on the three festivals of Tishre. If the old midrash had been followed consistently, Gen 30:22 [?] should have been read on the New Year, and Ex. 40:2 and Lev. 9:22 [?] on the New Moon of Nisan. Likewise, the year-patterns assumed by him are without foundation, and he determines the length of the pericopes completely arbitrarily according to the needs of his method. Therefore, indebted as we are to Büchler, and with all the credit he deserves for demonstrating that the triennial cycle existed and that it lasted long in use, the details of his system—acute and persuasive as they are—do not stand up to exacting criticism.

41. Zunz, *Haderashot*, 2.

42. Variations in the division; cf. Loeb, *REJ* 6 (1882): 250ff.; Saadia, *Oeuvres*, 7:146ff.

43. *Halakhot gedolot*, 617f.; *Hilkhot re'u*, 132f.; Amram—see Marx, *Untersuchungen*, 20f. and Frumkin, *Seder*, 2:187; *Toratan shel harishonim*, ed. C. M. Horowitz (Frankfurt a. M., 1881), 1:38f.; Vitry, 203f., 221f.; cf. Epstein, *Hagoren* 3 (1901): 59; the principles were adopted everywhere, as is clearly attested by the fact that they were so often copied, both with and without attribution. In connection with these principles, cf. the fragment of an ancient prayer book from ca. 885 published by Marmorstein in *MGWJ* 68 (1924): 157f (see above, §12a, n. 17) and the discussion prefaced to it in the same issue, on pp. 151f.

44. M. *Meg.* 3:4. The words in parentheses in the text have no meaning; the Day of Atonement should not be included here because until now the festivals have not been mentioned, and there is no particular reason to stress them (this problem was raised already by the *Tosafot*, B. *Meg.* 29a, s.v. לכל, but their solution, "that it refers to the Afternoon Service of the Day of Atonement occurring on a Sabbath," seems unlikely) or the *ma'amadot*, for these took place each day throughout the year, so that it would not have been possible for them to be read on any day. Nor does the Talmud, 30b, deal with these words in its discussion. Thus, even though these words are found in every known manuscript, they must be dropped as spurious; they entered here through the force of association (cf. Margulies, *Rivista Israelita* 1 [1904]: 4f.; *Rivista Israelita* 2 [1905]: 3f.) from M. *Ta.*, 4:1 [cf. Albeck, *Mishnah*, 2:502].

45. B. *Meg.* 29b. Rav may have come to this opinion through consideration of *Megilat ta'anit* 1, for no other indication that Num. 28 was read on the Sabbath of "Shekels" is to be found.

46. Cf., for example, *Vitry*, 203f.

47. R. Jeremiah's opinion that "he returns to the cycle of the haftarot" (30b) already points to the amoraic opinion; *Soferim*, 17:3, 8 already shows this change. *Soferim*, 234.

48. M. *Meg.* 3:8.

49. The reading at the Afternoon Service of the Sabbath could be eliminated only on the Day of Atonement; cf. *Tosafot, Meg.* 29a, s.v. לכל.

50. *Soferim* 17:8.

51. M. *Meg.*, ibid.; T. *Meg.* 4:9; *Soferim* 17:7 rules that the "blessings and curses" be read only on a fast day for rain and on the Ninth of Av, while on other fasts, Ex. 32:11ff.

51*. See Sar Shalom in Marx, *Untersuchungen*, 16; Frumkin, *Seder*, 2:155f. (though in fact our text is different); Natronai in *Halakhot gedolot*, 623; Responsa *Hemda genuza*, no. 4. Surprising is the opinion of Rav Paltoi Gaon (cited by R. Nissim to M. *Ta.* 1) that on Monday-Thursday-Monday fasts the weekly pericope is read, and Ex. 32:11ff. only in the Afternoon Service.

52. *Soferim* 17:7; *Ekha rabati*, proem 27.

53. Only in Amram—Frumkin, *Seder* and Marx, *Untersuchungen*, ibid. O.Z. 2:161a, in the name of the geonim.

54. Since the reading required five readers, each one reading three verses.

55. B. *Meg.* 31, on each festival: "Today, since there are two days . . . ."

56. T. *Meg.* 4:5; Abaye, B. *Meg.* 31a.

57. E.g., Amram—Marx, *Untersuchungen*, 28; Frumkin, *Seder*, 2:227.

58. In accordance with *Seder 'olam*, chap. 5.

59. Huna in the name of Rav, B. *Meg.* 31a.

60. T. *Meg.* 4:5; Y. *Meg.* 3:7, 74b.

61. T. *Meg.* 4:6; B. *Meg.* 31a; Midrash; B. *R.H.* 11a.

62. On the Day of Atonement they would read Lev. 16 and 17, *Halakhot gedolot*, 619; S.L., §32.

63. M. *Meg.* 3:8; T. *Meg.* 4:8, B. *Meg.* 31a and Y. *Meg.* 3:7, 74b. [Also in Palestine itself there were various practices; on festival readings diverging from those in the Mishnah, cf. Lieberman, *Tosefta*, 5:1169f.; E. Fleischer, *Tarbiz* 36 (1956/7): 116f.; Y. Heinemann, *Tarbiz* 37 (1967/8): 344f.]

64. For the intermediate days of festivals, T. 4:8 requires the particular sacrifice of each day, i.e., Num. 29:17–19, 20–22, etc.; but already B. *Suk.* 55a requires for the Additional Service the verses of two days on each day [for the Diaspora, because of the uncertainty of the day]. *Halakhot gedolot*, 619; Amram 51a (Frumkin, *Seder*, 2:380); Rashi in *Vitry*, 442; *Manhig*, "Laws of Festival," §47; *Vitry* and *Manhig*, ibid., also on Hoshana Rabba.

65. Cf. N. Brüll, ed., *Jahrbücher für Jüdische Geschichte und Literatur* 2 (1899): 12c.

66. *Pardes*, 45b; *Vitry*, 445f.

67. For festivals Amram knows only "All firstborn" (51b).

68. Only Deut. 33 and 34 on the two days of the Eighth Day of Assembly as late as Amram 52a.

69. Judah of Barcelona, *Perush sefer yesira*, ed. S. Halberstam (Berlin, 1885), 166; Saadia, ibid.; according to Büchler, *Triennial*, 463, Saadia also pronounced against this.

70. B. *Ber.* 8b: "[he] held that one should complete all the pericopes on the eve of Yom Kippur." Cf. Halberstam to *Sefer hashetarot*, 152.

71. Cf. *Pardes*, 45b; cf. *J.E.* 11:364f.

72. M. *Meg.* 4:1; "on the Day of Atonement" in B. *Meg.* 31a seems to be a gloss. They would read Lev. 18 as a continuation of the morning pericope. Cf. *Allgemeine Zeitung des Judentums* 81, 10 (March 9, 1917).

73. B. *Shab.* 24a: "Were it not Sabbath, there would be no prophet [reading] in the Afternoon Service of festivals." And since the prophets are never read unless the Torah is read first, it follows that they read the Torah at the Afternoon Service; the absence of this is in fact noted by O.Z., 2:20b, bottom. According to *Soferim* 11:5, one continues from the pericope preceding the festival; but this may have been meant to apply to a festival that coincides with a Sabbath.

74. The baraitot know nothing of additional pericopes, but the disagreements of the amoraim reflect their existence. Cf. the system recommended by Y. *Meg.* 3:6, 74b; Y. *Ta.* 4:1, 67c; and B. *Meg.* 29b.

75. Y. *Meg.* 4:5, 75b; Y. *Yoma* 7:1, 44b; *Soferim* 11:3. In Y., ibid. it says that two Torah scrolls are brought successively, and in B. it is noted that on the New Moon of Adar and the New Moon of Tevet coinciding with a Sabbath, three scrolls are brought (B. *Meg.* 29b); but from the time of Yehudai we find this everywhere; see *Halakhot gedolot*, 618, 621, and cf. *Tosafot* to *Meg.* 30b, s.v. ושאר.

76. Cf., e.g., *Eshkol*, 2:52; *Orhot*, 1:23b, §5; against this, *Vitry*, 89f.

77. See §§28, 29.

78. M. *Meg.* 4:1–3.

79. Three verses: M. *Meg.* 4:5; ten verses: B. *Meg.* 21b.

80. Y. *Meg.* 4:2, 75a; Y. *Ta.* 4:3, 68b; *Tosafot* to *Meg.* 21b, s.v. אין פוחתין.

81. B. *R.H.* 31a, הזיו ל"ך; cf. Y. *Meg.* 3:8, 74b; for the tradition on this, *Soferim* 12:8; Frumkin, *Seder*, 2:191; Marx, *Untersuchungen*, 22; Rashi and *Tosafot*, *R.H.*, ibid.

82. T. *Meg.* 4:17; B. *Meg.* 22a.

83. In B. ibid. and B. *Ta.* 27b: "one cuts" and "one repeats"; Y. *Meg.* 4:2, 75a and Y. *Ta.* 4:3, 68b. Rava was the first to deal with dividing the New Moon readings; B. *Meg.* 21b.

84. "One must begin with something auspicious and end with something auspicious," Y. *Meg.* 3:8, 74b.

85. There are many different opinions on the division; cf. Finfer, *Masoret*, 37.

86. Cf. *Nathan the Babylonian*, 84; additional literature in Ratner, *Ahavat*, 75 to *Yoma*; Zunz, *Ritus*, 54.

87. T. *Meg.* 4:11; B. *Meg.* 23a.

88. M. *Meg.* 4:6; T. and B. ibid.

89. Y. *Meg.* 4:3, 75a.

90. See Löw, *Lebensalter*, 210f.; *J.E.* 2:509f.; this institution can be followed to the fourteenth century.

91. M. *Meg.* 4:6; Elbogen, *Studien*, 11, n. 1.

92. T. *Meg.* 4:21.

93. On the manner of going up to the Torah, see Frumkin, *Seder*, 1:396. O.Z., 2:19a already notes that the Talmud does not know of calling readers up to the Torah. On the later practice, cf. *Responsa of Maharam*, ed. Prague, no. 108; Lewysohn, *Meqore*, 57.

94. Only in this way can the talmudic expressions "one reads" and "the one who stands up to read" be understood.

95. Cf. T. *Meg.* 4:12; Y. *Meg.* 4:3, 75a.

96. T. *Meg.* 4:13. Philo, *Spec.* ii, 15, 62 (Philo[a], 5:101; Philo[b], 7:346); and Eusebius, *Praep. Evang.* 87 (same as Philo[b], 9:432).

97. Philo, *Legat.* 31 (Philo[a], 6:194; Philo[b], 10:18). Nowhere is the distortion resulting from the practice of Christian scholars of translating the word "Torah" as "Law" more evident (cf. e.g. Schürer, *Geschichte des jüdischen Volkes im Zeitalter Jesu Christi* [Leipzig, 1901–9], 2:493. [Schürer's English translators have rendered his *Gesetz* as "Torah," obscuring this point. See Schürer, *History*, 2:425—Engl. *trans.*] On this distortion, see now also T. R. Herford, *Pharisaism* (London: Williams and Norgate, 1912), 56.

98. B. *Meg.* 32a; below, §54.

99. *Ḥiluf minhagim*, 41, §41; Amram 29a (Frumkin, *Seder*, 2:67), and cf. Responsa *Shaʿare tora*, no. 59.

100. *O.Z.*, 2:20a; cf. 11a.

101. Ibid., 19b; Sepharad, cf. *ʿItim*, 264; France, *Pardes*, 8b; *Vitry*, 8; *Eshkol*, 2:68.

102. Amram 24a, MS Oxford Marx, *Untersuchungen*, 12, top; Frumkin, *Seder*, 1:397, bottom.

103. Löw, *Lebensalter*, 211f.

104. H. Graetz in *MGWJ* 18 (1869): 398 (same as *Vorträge im jüdisch-theologischen Verein*, 46). Here we may mention the custom that sometimes the congregation repeats the verses or recites them ahead of the reader; according to Saadia there are ten such verses, but doubt later arose as to their identity. Cf. *Eshkol*, 2:65; Harkavy, *Responsa*, 208.

105. Y. *Ber.* 7:2, 11b.

106. Cf. B. *Meg.* 31b, "A tanna said, 'He who commences his reading.' " This was still the practice of Rav, B. *Meg.* 22a, but our custom is already mentioned there. Waagena in *Jeschurun* 10 (1923): Hebrew section, 8f. concludes from Y. *Ber.* 7:1, 11a that in Palestine the practice even in later times followed that of the Mishnah and that the benediction of the Torah was recited only at the beginning and end of the entire reading.

107. The passages that even in early times had to be recited with a benediction in Y. *Meg.* 3:8, 74b.

108. Elbogen, *Studien*, 9f.; Saadia in *Eshkol*, 2:58; Saadia, *Oeuvres*, 9:160, top.

109. Cf. Müller, *Soferim*, 180, n. 41. *O.Z.* 2:21a, top. "Who chose us" recalls the benediction of the Haftara; the current text: Amram 24a (Frumkin, *Seder*, 1:397). [For various versions, including poetic ones, of the benediction of the Torah for special occasions, see Heinemann, *Prayer*, 105f. and the literature listed there.]

110. See above, subsection 7.

111. B. *Git.* 59b. For the effect of the absence of a Cohen on a Levite, cf. the expression "The bundle is untied," B. *Git.* 59b, and the commentaries.

112. Rav: B. *Meg.* 22b; Huna: B. *Git.* 59b.

113. See *Nathan the Babylonian*, 84.

114. *O.Z.*, 2:19a, who opposes the custom; it was likely introduced so that the rabbi, as the last, would roll the scroll. Cf. B. *Meg.*, end.

115. They were called חיובים, "obligations." Cf. Löw, *Schriften*, 5:28.

116. Löw, *Lebensalter*, 187.

117. Payments, and even auctions: Löw, *Schriften*, 5:29, bottom. These auctions did not occur everywhere, and have nothing to do with Judaism; thus, they do not demonstrate the capitalistic spirit of the Jewish religion as claimed by W. Sombart, *Die Juden und das Wirtschaftsleben* (Leipzig: Duncker und Humblot, 1911), 248f. In Cairo the right to purchase *miṣvot* in the synagogue was transmitted partially by inheritance; Zunz, *Ritus*, 56. *O.Z.*, 1:21b, §115 relates a dispute about taking out and putting away the Torah, for some wanted to restrict this rite to the precentor. It says there that some pay for the right to hand over the cover during the rolling of the Torah scroll.

118. See Lewysohn, *Meqore*, 39f.

119. Cf. Blau, *Buchwesen*, 38f. Ibid., 65 on defective copies.

120. Y. *Meg.* 3:1, 74a; this matter is discussed in B. *Git.* 60a, with Rabba and R. Joseph prohibiting.

121. M. *Yoma* 7:1; *Sota* 7:7; the סגן mentioned there later became the title of the one whose duty it was to point the place to the reader; cf. Krauss, *Synagogale*, 172, note.

122. *O.Z.*; cf. above.

123. In Riesser's periodical *Der Jude* 14 (1832); Hebrew translation by S. D. Luzzatto, *Kinor naʿim* (Warsaw, 1825–79), 2:232; cf. *MGWJ* 44 (1900): 546f.

§26 The Haftara

1. M. *Meg.* 4:3. Medieval commentary, e.g., *Manhig*, "Laws of Sabbath," §35. Rapoport, *ʿErekh*, 167,

s.v. אפטרתא; Bacher, *Terminologie* [same as ʿErkhe midrash], 2:14; additional sources on *aftarta*, though with an incorrect explanation, in Büchler, *Triennial*, 7.

2. E. Levita, *Tishbi* (Isny, 1541), s.v. פטר; earlier authors, e.g., Abudarham 47a.

3. "One may skip in the prophets": M. *Meg*. 4:5, cf. T. *Meg*. 4:18, 19; the twelve minor prophets are considered a single book and may be read out of order.

4. A single prophetic book, like the minor prophets (see above); or Isaiah, Luke 4:16 (cf. below subsection 7). It cannot be proved that originally haftarot were read only from Ezekiel, as Büchler, *Triennial*, 7, takes to be an established fact; in all the sources that have come down to us, we find haftarot from all the prophetic books. Based on the considerations cited in the body of the book, we must set the time of the institution of the prophetic reading earlier than does Büchler, *Triennial*, 2f. If such an important innovation had been introduced in the first century, it would doubtless have been mentioned somewhere in the sources. [There is reason to believe that the haftara and the following benedictions were in antiquity the end of the liturgy on Sabbaths and festivals; cf. Heinemann, *Prayer*, 143f.]

5. The amoraim instituted only a few haftarot; Rav Huna instituted a haftara on the authority of Rav, and Abaye reports on the practice that prevailed in his time (B. *Meg.*, 31a–b). Of the haftarot for the Afternoon Service, the Talmud knows only that of the Day of Atonement; for the others, cf. below (10).

6. According to Büchler's interpretation (*Triennial*, 11), Luke is speaking of a particular place that was opened for Jesus, meaning that the one called was not free to choose the place.

7. Haftarot for the Sabbath are mentioned by the Talmud only for Sabbaths coinciding with some special day, such as the New Moon of Av. Haftarot for the festivals underwent many changes, as may be deduced from the rules of Yehudai Gaon and *Vitry*.

8. Cf., e.g., B. *R.H.* 11a, "On the New Year Hanna . . . was remembered," and the relationship between Hab. 3 and the revelation at Sinai.

9. A list of haftarot for the pericopes from Gen. 5 to Lev. 4 according to the triennial cycle was first published by Büchler, *Triennial*, 39–42 (cf. ibid., 46f., 49); a different list for the pericopes from Num. 22 to Deut. 1 was studied by A. N. Adler in *JQR* 8 (1896): 528f. [Other partial lists: I. Abrahams, "Some *Triennial Haftaroth*," in *Oriental Studies Dedicated to Paul Haupt* (Baltimore: Johns Hopkins, 1926), 1–2; id., *Festskrift i anledning Professor David Simonsens 70 aarige Fodselsdag* (Copenhagen: Hertz, 1923), 77f.; N. Fried in *Textus* 3 (1963): 128f.]

10. Lists for the annual cycle are found in Maimonides, at the end of *Seder tefilot*, J.E. 6:136, and in every good edition of the Pentateuch or the Bible. It is to Büchler's great credit that he was the one who found the lists, placed them at the disposal of the scholarly community, and studied the reasons for the introduction of these particular haftarot. However, everything else in his discussion, particularly his attempt to identify the haftarot for festivals and special Sabbaths, must be rejected, along with his conjecture about the Torah readings, which is closely connected with it. R. Hai's words, below in §26(5), show that fixed haftarot were introduced only relatively late, and that the customary haftarot were often not read. For the same reason the clever attempt of L. Venetianer in his article "Ursprung und Bedeutung der Prophetenlektionen," *ZDMG* 63 (1909): 103f. must be rejected, especially in view of the additional problem that the Catholic Mass ritual can only be shown to have existed in its present form rather late. As for variations in the haftarot, cf. also Löw, *Schriften*, 4:247, 5:29.

11. See *Pardes*, 61d.

12. *ʿItim*, 279.

13. Literature on the haftarot from the Seventeenth of Tammuz on in Zunz, *Haderashot*, 83f.; Büchler, *Triennial*, 69f. H. St. Thackeray, *The Septuagint and Jewish Worship* (Milford: Oxford University Press, 1923), 100f. raised the brilliant conjecture that the book of Baruch is an example of homilies for the period from the Seventeenth of Tammuz to the New Year, but did not succeed in proving it. Nor does it seem at all likely that at the time of this book's composition fixed haftarot already existed, let alone cycles of haftarot. It seems likely that this cycle is of Babylonian origin, because the haftara lists, which are under Palestinian influence, do not mention it. [But no mention of the three haftarot of admonition or the seven of consolation in the Palestinian haftara lists should be expected, for in this rite the Torah readings and haftarot were not connected with particular dates in the cycle of the year, as mentioned above; and these special haftarot could therefore replace the fixed haftarot of any pericope in the Pentateuch.] From the sheer fact that B. does not mention the haftarot of consolation, Büchler, *Triennial*, 64, deduces that they were unknown in Babylonia and that Rav imported the haftarot of admonition Is. 1:14 and 21 from Palestine. But this *argumentum ex silentio* runs up against the special problem that Y. does not name any haftarot at all. Also, the gradual emergence of the entire cycle as Büchler sees it is not at all convincing; our information on this matter is so slight that it cannot even support conjectures. In any case it seems reasonable to assume that the formation of this haftara cycle occurred at an early time, and thus the Karaites were able to accept it without hesitation; Zunz fixes the date of the composition of the Pesiqta at ca. 700 (*Haderashot*, 86), and cf. J.E. 8:559f. [Today an early date for the redac-

tion of *Pesiqta derav kahana*, which reflects the haftarot of admonition and consolation, is accepted—some say as early as the fifth century; cf. M. Margulies's introduction to *Lev. r.*, xiii.]

14. The number of verses in the haftara is not fixed by the Mishnah; the source in T. is *Meg.* 4:18.

15. B. *Meg.* 23a; Y. *Meg.* 4:2, 75a. Surprisingly, *Soferim* 14:1 gives the number as twenty-two verses. Haftara lists always indicate the beginning and the end; often they add *fasūqain faqat*, "two verses only."

16. אפטרתא ספר: B. *Git.* 60a; cf. Blau, *Buchwesen*, 65f.; contrary opinions, e.g., Paltoi in *Eshkol*, 2:51a.

17. In Ibn Ghiyath, *Sha'are simha*, 1:105; *'Itim*, 271.

18. Cf. *S.L.*, 15b.

19. *Pardes*, 62a.

20. I have witnessed the reading of the Haftara from scrolls only in Frankfurt am Main. According to Finfer, *Masoret*, 84f., they are in use everywhere in western Russia [and also in synagogues in the state of Israel, especially in Jerusalem, that follow the practice of the Gaon of Vilna].

21. B. *Meg.* 23a, "out of respect for the Torah." Since he repeats a passage that had already been read, the question could arise whether he counts as one of the readers. In Sepharad and Rome, the *maftir* portion is read for one person, then it is read again for the *maftir*.

22. Cf. *Teshuvot hage'onim*, no. 94 (*Sha'are tora*, no. 60).

23. Such as I Sam. 1; Is. 1; Ezek. 1.

24. Cf. Löw, *Lebensalter*, 212.

25. B. *Pes.* 117b; B. *Shab.* 24a.

26. Amram 29b, but cf. Marx, *Untersuchungen*, 14 and Frumkin, *Seder*, 2:69f.

27. *Vitry*, 158.

27*. The conclusion of the third benediction, from "for in Your holy Name" to "the shield of David" is quoted first in *Midrash tehilim* on Psalms 18:25 (77b).

28. Altering the text of "Who sanctifies the Sabbath" is contrary to B. *Shab.* 24a.

29. This is the reading also in *Vitry*, 304.

30. Cf. *O.Z.*, 2:128b; *Maharil*, 20a.

31. Cf. in Amram 43b.

32. *Vitry*, 394, top.

33. For *Ber.*, cf. also *Rivista Israelita* 4 (1904) 128f.; *REJ* 57 (1909): 179.

34. J. Mann, *HUCA* 4 (1927): 283f. assumes that the custom of the Afternoon Service haftarot originated in Babylonia and that it is so ancient—perhaps even from the period of the Restoration!—that they paid no attention to the ruling of the Palestinian-edited Mishnah opposing it; according to his opinion, they continued this practice uninterrupted until the disorders about Mazdak (ca. 500), but then it was prohibited. But there is no particular reason why the gentiles objected at this time to the passages cited by Mann any more than in the nationalistic period that preceded. Here Mann's reliance on Thackeray's conjecture (p. 287) cited above (n. 13) is not much help, for Thackeray sets the place of origin of Baruch on the border of Babylonia; and besides, the lists of haftarot customary in Palestine do not include the haftarot of consolation. All the positive information that remains from these reports is simply that R. Hai Gaon knew haftara manuscripts in which the haftarot for the Afternoon Service were indicated and that in his time these haftarot were read in "Elam and the Persian isles," i.e., apparently, in the southern portion of Persia down to the Persian gulf.

35. Cf. Responsa *Hemda genuza*, no. 95; Ginzberg, *Geonica*, 2:322, no. 26; *'Itim*, 250, 289; Rashi and Maor to B. *Shab.*, 24a.

36. Such as R. Tam, *Tosafot*, 24a, s.v. שאלמלא. R. Judah b. Barzilai believed that the reading should be "Day of Atonement" instead of "festival." In Amram the haftarot for the Afternoon Service are not yet mentioned; the relevant passage in MS Oxford in Marx, *Untersuchungen*, 17 and Frumkin, *Seder*, 2:156, is certainly a late addition, for it contradicts the report of Marx, *Untersuchungen*, 17 on line 11 and Frumkin, *Seder*, 2:157: "In their Afternoon Services they read no haftara at all."

37. Ibn Ghiyath, *Sha'are simha*, 1:23.

38. "Seek" is first mentioned in *Soferim* 17:7, but the text there is not certain (cf. Müller, *Soferim*, 243, n. 26), and it is unclear whether the reference is to the morning or afternoon haftara.

39. Cf. B. *Meg.* 23a; Y. *Meg.* 4:3, 75a; *Soferim* 11:4; *Halakhot gedolot*, 622. Alfasi rules "the law is that he counts"; to the contrary, *'Itim*, 272, who even conjectures that Alfasi reversed himself. Also from *Pardes*, 8b it follows that he counts, and this is also the opinion of R. Jacob Tam, disagreeing with R. Meshulam b. Nathan; see *Responsa*, ed. S.P. Rosenthal (Berlin, 1898), 81f., no. 45c; *O.Z.*, 2:157b.

40. *Protokolle und Aktenstücke*, 137. Astonishingly, the Reform community in Berlin eliminated the reading of the prophets entirely.

§ 27 The Reading from the Hagiographa

1. See *J.E.* 3:147; there the closing of the canon is fixed at the time of John Hyrcanus; the school of Bible criticism fixes it two hundred years later; ibid., 149. Saadia already mentions the custom of letting the congregation recite a few verses along with the reader; see Marx, *Untersuchungen*, 18 and Frumkin, *Seder*, 2:178; *S.L.*, §200 gives the reason as being to please the children.

[2. On the benediction after the reading of the Scroll of Esther, see also Heinemann, *Prayer*, 65, 107.]

3. Cf. *J.E.* 3:144.

4. See Müller, *Soferim*, 201, n. 70.

5. *Soferim* 14:3.

6. E.g. *Manhig*, "Laws of Festival," §57.

7. B. *Shab.* 115a; Y. *Shab.* 16:1, 15b.

8. Rav Natronai, in *Itim*, 289, still refers to the custom of reading from the Hagiographa, and it may be conjectured that even *Itim* still knows it from its own time.

9. Rapoport, *Erekh*, 171.

10. Ed. S. Buber (Cracow, 1903); cf. Zunz, *Haderashot*, 124.

§ 28 The Translation of the Reading

1. The word *targum* is derived from the Assyrian word *targumanu*, "translator"; see Gesenius, *Handwörterbuch*, 889. The parallel verb in Greek is διερμηνεύειν; see I Corinthians 1:14, 27.

2. On the other Targumim, cf. L. Blau, *Zur Einleitung in die Heilige Schrift* (Budapest, 1894), 84, 91.

3. *S.L.*, 29a, §78; on Giuda, cf. *J.E.* 10:444.

4. For the form תרגמן, cf. Bacher, *Terminologie*, 1:206.

5. Cf. also T. *Meg.* 4:21.

6. There, it says as a criticism, "Huna stood translating and no one took his place," for the sexton's place should never be unoccupied.

7. *Nathan the Babylonian*, 84.

8. It was prohibited to read it from a book, Y. *Meg.*, 4:1, 74c; B. *Meg.* 32a.

9. Cf. T. *Meg.*, end: "R. Judah says, 'He who translates a verse literally is a falsifier, and he who adds to it is a blasphemer." See M. Friedmann, *Onkelos und Akylos* (Vienna: Israelitisch-Lehranstalt, 1896), 4f.

10. On the Septuagint's method of translation, cf. Z. Frankel, *Septuaginta*, 163f.; id., *Über den Einfluss der palästinensischen Exegese auf die alexandrinische Hermeneutik* (Leipzig: J. A. Barth, 1851), 1f.; Geiger, *Schriften*, 4:73f.

11. Geiger, *Schriften*, 106; A. Berliner, *Targum Onkelos* (Berlin, 1884), 2:105.

12. Ibid., 100; Friedmann, *Onkelos*, 60f.

13. On the time of the composition of *Onkelos*, cf. F. Rosenthal in *Bet Talmud* 2 (1882); Friedmann, ibid.

14. Geiger, ibid., 83.

15. Cf. *Pseudo-Jonathan*, ed. M. Ginsburger (Berlin, 1903), xviif. [P. Kahle, "Das Palästinische Pentateuch und Targum und das zur Zeit Jesu gesprochene Aramäisch," *ZNW* 49 (1958): 100f; id., *The Cairo Geniza* (Oxford: Blackwell, 1959), 201f.; A. Diez Macho, "The Recently Discovered Palestinian Targum: Its Antiquity and Relationship with the Other Targums," *Supplements to Vetus Testamentum*, Congress Volume (Oxford, 1959), 222–45; Y. Heinemann, "Masorot parshaniyot qedumot ba'agada uvatargumim," *Tarbiz* 35 (1965/6): 90f.]

16. Rashi to B. *Meg.* 21b, top.

17. The first to deal with the deviations in the Targum was S.D. Luzzatto in *Ohev ger.*; cf. Geiger, *Urschrift*, 16f. On the Septuagint, Frankel, *Septuaginta*, 163f.; on the Peshitta, J. Perles, *Meletemata Peschitthoniana* (Breslau: W. Friedrich, 1859), and recently, Ch. Heller, *Untersuchungen über die Peschitta* (Berlin: M. Poppelauer, 1911).

18. On "prohibited targumim," see Ginsburger in *MGWJ* 44 (1900): 1f.

[19. On the Mishnah passage "The Priestly Blessing . . . is neither read nor translated," see J. Heinemann in *Annual of Bar-Ilan University* 6 (1967–68): 33f.]

20. Saadia; cf. Harkavy, *Responsa*, 309, no. 208 [and in Saadia, *Siddur*, 368].

21. Novella 146; on the novella of Justinian, see Graetz, *Divre*, 3:398f, n. 7, and cf. Juster, *Les Juifs dans l'empire romain* (Paris: P. Gerner, 1914), 1:369f.

22. *Soferim* as well as Amram 25a (Frumkin, *Seder*, 2:49), but after the Morning Service, before the reading; cf. also *Itim*, 245.

23. Natronai in Amram 29a (Frumkin, *Seder*, 2:68) and *Itim*, 266; "Likewise R. Natronai Gaon said,

'Those that do not translate, but say "we do not need to translate into the rabbinic Targum but rather into our own language, the language that the congregation use for purpose of translation"—these do not fulfil their obligation.' "

24. Judah Ibn Quraish, *Risāla*, ed. Bargès, 1; *J.E.* 7:345.

25. See R. Hai in Harkavy, *Responsa*, no. 208; *'Itim*, 267f.

26. Cf. Ginsburger in *MGWJ* 39 (1895): 97f. He published a series of poetic introductions in *ZDMG* 54 (1900): 113 and *REJ* 73 (1921): 14f. To these publications the texts published by Kahle, *Masoreten des Westens* (Stuttgart: W. Kohlhammer, 1927–30), 2:49–62, should be compared; they contain the Palestinian Targum to Lev. 22:26–23:44, then that to the Additional Service pericope, Num. 28:16–25, Ex. 19–20:23, and that to the Additional Service pericope, Num. 28:26–31 and to Deut. 34:5–12. According to the heading, the booklet is supposed to contain "Targum for the Additional Service for all the festivals and the Targum for Hanuka." The translations diverge from that of *Vitry*.

27. By R. Meir of Worms.

28. *Orhot*, 25a, §40.

29. Ibid., 77d, §7. Arabic reworkings in North Africa: Zunz, *Ritus*, 52.

30. Thus R. Hai in *'Itim*, 278. In Mainz ca. 1050 no targum of the haftara was known; *Pardes*, 62a.

31. Cf. M. *Ḥag.* 2:1.

32. Cf. Z. Frankel, *Zu dem Targum der Propheten* (Breslau: F. W. Jugfer, 1892), 13f.; Geiger, *Urschrift*, 109.

33. See Tosafot, *Meg.* 23b, s.v. לא; 24a, s.v. ובנביא and ואם; cf. *Vitry*, 158: "On a festival when it is customary to recite the Targum of the haftara, the one saying the haftara recites three verses and then the translator recites *reshuyot*: . . . איסב רשות, 'I take permission from all of you . . .' and then the translator says על דא יתברך, 'on account of this may God's Name be blessed.' "

34. Is. 10:32–12:6.

35. By R. Jacob Tam.

36. Although the Portuguese language was no longer their vernacular, the Sepharadim, in their conservative fashion, resented deeply those who eliminated the Portuguese translation.

37. Cf. M. *Meg.* 1:8: "Even books were permitted to be written only in Greek"; and 2:1: "If he read it in translation in any language he did not fulfill his obligation." In Saragossa the Scroll of Esther was read in Spanish from 1350 on.

§29   The Sermon

1. On II Chron. 17:9, cf. H. Vogelstein in *MGWJ* 49 (1905): 427f.; Philo, *Mos.* ii, 39,216 (Philo[a], 4:250; Philo[b], 6:556).

2. Bacher, *Terminologie*, 1:103f.

3. Ibid., 1:30f.

4. Ibid., 1:25, 2:41.

5. The midrash knows homilies on the haftarot only in connection with the cycle mentioned above, §26:5, and therefore it is likely that, with this exception, they would make homilies only on the Torah reading; on the other hand, in light of Bacher's proof, *Proömien*, 9f., that the midrashic style of stringing together verses of the Torah, Prophets, and Hagiographa is characteristic of the most ancient exegesis, it seems likely that the homileticians gave due attention to the Prophets. In fact, Ginzberg published in *Ginze Schechter*, 1:302 a midrash on II Kgs. 4:1 with the conjecture that it derives from a collection of haftara midrashim.

6. Cf. W. Bousset, *Jüdisch-christlicher Schulbetrieb in Alexandria und Rom* (Göttingham, 1915), 153.

7. B. *Pes.* 70b.

8. Cf. Bacher, *Terminologie*, 1:41; 2:150.

9. The λόγος παρακλήσεως that Paul and his companions were invited to proclaim in Antioch, Acts 13:15, is not a rebuke, for it would be surprising for the community to let strangers rebuke it. Rather παράκλησις is the Greek word for consolation (E. Hatch and H. Redpath, *Concordance to the Septuagint* [Oxford, 1887], 1061); thus, the congregation expected to hear encouragement concerning the redemption.

10. Zunz, *Haderashot*, 167; Bacher, *Terminologie*, 1:25f.

11. Zunz, *Haderashot*, 174. Enough for us to point to the complaint of Agobard of Lyon (ca. 825) in his book *De Insolentia Judaeorum*, chap. 5: *ut dicant melius eis praedicare Judaeos quam presbyteros nostros*, "that they say that the Jews preach to them better than their own presbyters." Obviously only through sermons in the vernacular could the Jewish preachers make an impression on the non-Jews. But even the Jews in the Frankish kingdom did not know enough Hebrew to understand a sermon in that language.

12. Zunz, *Haderashot*, 164f., 166; Rapoport, *'Erekh*, 171f.

§ 30 Prayers Before and After the Reading of the Torah

1. It is unclear there who "begins," why the reader of the haftara appears here, and where he is to go. What is the meaning of the sentence, "Then he lifts the Torah"? The Gaon of Vilna deleted it. Apparently several sources have gotten mixed up here. [Cf. Heinemann, *Prayer*, 165, n. 18.] According to J. Mann in *HUCA* 4 (1927): 260, *Soferim* is describing the ceremony as it was practiced in Palestine (with the *Shema^c* and Kedushah) before the Byzantine government decree that led to the abridgement of the taking out of the Torah and necessitated relegating the recitation of the *Shema^c* to the haftara reader, thus limiting it to Sabbaths and festivals. But the customs were varied and diverse in different countries long before, and only with great caution can conclusions be drawn from early reports.

2. *Orhot*, 1:65a, §6; *Kol bo*, §37; and according to Mahkim, 15, generally disseminated only since Prague, 1541; cf. Berliner, *Randbemerkungen*, 1:28; 2:31.

3. Cf. O.Z., 2:19a: "And our custom in the land of Canaan . . . the precentor begins and says . . . 'There is none like You' and the congregation answer after him twice (or once) 'Your kingdom' . . . 'Father of mercy' . . . 'Hear, Israel' . . . 'One is our God' . . . 'Exalt' . . . 'Lift up' . . . 'For everything'; the people of the Rhineland do not have this custom, but they say 'Exalt.'" Rome; cf. S.L., 28b, §77. In Ashkenaz, Deut. 4:35, which in Sepharad is customary on the Sabbath, is said only on the Joy of the Torah (cf. *Manhig*, "Laws of Sabbath," §24; *Tur*, O.H., §281.)—The verses in Frumkin, *Seder*, 1:396f. are still very similar to those in *Soferim*. As for the development of the rites, which differ greatly in detail, cf. *Vitry*, 71f.; *Pardes*, 47b; *Orhot* 1:22b, §7; *Orhot* 1:65a, §6; Abudarham 35d, 46d; *Tur*, S.A., O.H., §134, 281, end.

4. Medieval sources report only that the congregation recited the verses silently. Already in 1096 it was customary in Mainz for the children to kiss the Torah during the procession; *Quellen zur Geschichte der Juden in Deutschland*, ed. A. Neubauer (Berlin: L. Simon, 1892), 2:10.

5. With some expansion of the text (Baer, *^cAvodat*, 224), said only in western Germany, and in a very solemn manner on festivals; cf. already *Vitry*, 157 [and in Yemen, during the taking out of the Torah on weekdays].—When the Torah is laid on the table before the reading, "Father of mercy" is recited in Ashkenaz; see Berliner, *Randbemerkungen*, 1:65:, 2:32; cf. O.Z., 1:39a, §106.

6. The lifting of the Torah after the reading only in Ashkenaz, according to Isserles's gloss on *Tur*, O.H., §147.

7. From the Zohar, *Vayaqhel*; on its acceptance into the prayer book, see Baer, *^cAvodat*, 122; Berliner, *Randbemerkungen*, 1:29. On the following sections, Baer, *^cAvodat*, 223; Berliner, *Randbemerkungen*, 1:46f., 60.

8. No medieval source mentions the processions on the Joy of the Torah; cf. *J.E.* 11:365.

9. *Hiluf minhagim*, §49 speaks of honoring the Torah in Palestine on taking it out and putting it back; *Soferim*'s silence about it must be due to the imperfect state of the text.—Amram 24a and Frumkin, *Seder*, 1:398.—On the psalms, see Baer, *^cAvodat*, 125; Berliner, *Randbemerkungen*, 1:25; Ps. 24:7 according to B. *Shab.* 30a; the Sephardic rite in *^cItim*, 80; *Orhot*, 65a; Abudarham 47c.

10. Mentioned first in O.Z., 2:21b; cf. Zunz, *Ritus*, 8f. [Cf. also A. Yaari, "Tefilot mi sheberakh: hishtalshelutan, minhagehen, venushe^otehen," *Qiryat sefer* 33 (1957/8): 118f.; *Qiryat sefer* 36 (1960/1): 103f; Daniel Y. Cohen, "He^carot umilu^im lemehqaro shel a. yaari ^cal tefilat 'mi sheberakh,'" *Qiryat sefer* 40 (1964/5): 542f.]

11. Already in *Pardes*, 45b, 49d; *Orhot*, 1:26b, bottom knows it as the custom of northern France and believes it to be customary in Sepharad only on the Joy of the Torah, while *Manhig*, "Laws of Festival," §56 reports exactly the same of France.

12. *J.E.* 6:238f.

13. *Reshut* recited on the day of the inauguration: *Nathan the Babylonian*, 84; for bridegroom: Zunz, *Ritus*, 15; on the Joy of the Torah: *Ritus*, 87.

14. *Manhig*, "Laws of Sabbath," §40 designates this as the place for announcements and miscellaneous prayers.

15. Amram 24a (Frumkin, *Seder*, 1:398); *Vitry*, 179 cites them for the Sabbath Afternoon Service. Amram 33b (Frumkin, *Seder*, 2:130) cites the same thing for the New Moon. Abudarham 48d knows the custom of reciting aloud Psalm 92 at the Afternoon Service of the Sabbath.

16. A blessing for those present is inserted also in Amram, 33b on the New Moon. Other, similar versions in Frumkin, *Seder*, 2:76f; Zunz, *Ritus*, 9; Berliner, *Randbemerkungen*, 1:66; *REJ* 50 (1905): 89.

17. *^cItim*, 279.

18. "May salvation arise" and similar texts: Zunz, *Ritus*, 82; Zunz, *Literaturgeschichte*, 19; Berliner, *Randbemerkungen*, 1:65f.; *J.E.* 5:293b; in manuscripts the reference to the Exilarch is often lacking: *JQR* NS 1 (1910–11): 63.

19. Philo already mentions a prayer for the Roman emperor, *Flacc.* 7, 49 (Philo[a], 6:129; Philo[b], 9:329). All manuscripts and printed editions contain the prayer for the welfare of the chief of state; the decisors explain it by reference to Jer. 29:7.

20. On how the lists of martyrs developed and how they were read in public, see S. Salfeld, *Das Martyrologium des Nürnberger Memorbuches* (Berlin: L. Simon, 1898), ix f.; on the later custom of vowing donations, *Tanya*, §17; *S.L.*, 30b, §81; on "Father of Mercy," cf. *Maharil*, 21a.

21. *Orḥot*, 1:65b, §9.

22. Marx, *Untersuchungen*, 17; Frumkin, *Seder*, 2:175; *Vitry*, 173.

23. Zunz, *Literaturgeschichte*, 670; *J.E.* 6:283; *Jüdisches Literaturblatt* 27 (1904): 21f.; Salfeld, ibid., introduction. The prayer for the dead was customary in Oriental communities ca. 1000 at latest, as proved by the many lists that have been preserved.

24. Zunz, *Ritus*, 86.

25. Already in Amram 52a (Frumkin, *Seder*, 2:385), but lacking in Marx, *Untersuchungen*, 37; Saadia's opposition: ibid. [Cf. also the text "He Who for the sake of fathers," beginning with a formal benediction, in a fragment of Saadia's prayer book published by N. Wieder, *Sefer Asaf*, ed. U. Cassuto (Jerusalem: Mossad Harav Kook, 1952/3), 241f.; also Heinemann, *Prayer*, 106f. and n. 17.]

26. The hymns, etc., are mentioned in Ibn Ghiyath, *Shaʿare simḥa*, 1:117.

27. Zunz, *Haderashot*, 67; Zunz, *Ritus*, 87f.

§31   General

1. The term *Stammgebete* ["statutory prayers"] was first used by Zunz, *Ritus*, 5.

2. Cf. J. Levy, *Neuhebräisches und chaldäisches Wörterbuch über die Talmudim und Midraschim* (Leipzig: F. A. Brockhaus, 1876–79), 3:85.

3. Cf. below, §43:3 and Zunz, *Ritus*, 3 about this practice.

4. Zunz, *Haderashot*, 183; Zunz, *Poesie*, 60; Steinschneider, *Literatur*, 421, §18.

5. Perles, *Beiträge*, 63f; for the meaning of the two words, see Krauss, *Lehnwörter*, 2:443, 262. W. Warnheim, *Qevuṣat hakhamim* (Vienna: A della Torre, 1861), 107 explains טייר as an acrostic poem.

6. Zunz, *Poesie*, 60. For *ḥizāna*, see recently Eppenstein, *Literatur*, 467f.

7. Brody, *Dichterschule*, 17; the etymology, Zunz, *Poesie*, 88, 367f.; Perles, *Beiträge*, 67.

8. Zunz, *Poesie*, 88.

9. In Joseph Ibn Megas, *Responsa*, no. 204; see Dukes, *Poesie*, 140.

10. Zunz, *Poesie*, 59, chap. 3.

§32   The Piyyut

1. Through publications of geniza materials, other terms for *piyyut* have been added. Cf. Halper, *Descriptive Catalogue of Geniza-Fragments in Philadelphia* (Philadelphia: Dropsie College, 1924) and I. Davidson, *Ginze Schechter*, vol. 3. (New York: The Jewish Theological Seminary of America, 1928).

2. Steinschneider, *Literatur*, 422.

3. Zunz, *Poesie*, 79; Steinschneider, *Literatur*, §18, n. 19; Brody, *Dichterschule*, 19.

4. See M. Hartmann, *Die hebräische Verskunst nach dem Metek Sefatajim des Immanuel Fransis und anderen werken jüdischen Metriker* (Berlin: S. Calvary, 1894), 84.

5. Zunz, *Poesie*, 80; according to J. Perles, in *Byzantinische Zeitschrift* 2 (1893): 573, from κύκλιον.

6. So J. Perles in *MGWJ* 35 (1886): 231f.

7. Zunz, *Poesie*, 61; Brody, *Dichterschule*, 35, no. 30; *muqaddima*, e.g., Amram 2:23a; Brody, *Dīwān*, 3:209f.

8. Brody, *Dichterschule*, 114; *Maḥzor yanai*, ed. I. Davidson (New York: The Jewish Theological Seminary of America, 1919), xxvii. *Gemar*: Amram 2:1a, 3b.

9. Zunz, *Poesie*, 61f.; Brody, *Dichterschule*, 23.

10. Elbogen, *Studien*, 31.

11. Steinschneider, *Literatur*, 426, 1.

12. Zunz, *Poesie*, 64f. S.D. Luzzatto, *Dīwān yehuda halevi* (Lyck, 1864), 37a; Brody, *Dichterschule*, 9; Brody, *Dīwān*, 3:5. The interrelationship between piyyutim 1–3 has not yet been fully clarified. Various objections have been raised as to the authenticity of the concluding verse of the *nishmat*, which ends "If our mouths"; see Luzzatto, ibid.; Brody, *Dichterschule*, 102, no. 92.

13. Zunz, *Poesie*, 69f.

14. Cf. Neubauer and Cowley, *Catalogue*, 2631_3, 2712_{18}, 2714_7 and many others.

15. Zunz, *Poesie*, 65f.; Berliner, *Randbemerkungen*, 2:66; Elbogen, *Studien*, 47. The word appears in the Syriac liturgy as well; see Sachs, *Poesie*, 178.

16. Possibly the interpretation in B. *Meg.* 10b to Ex. 14:20 is already based on this interpretation of the word (so Marx, *Jeschurun* 10 [1923]: 180), but it does not seem at all likely that this meaning is intended in *Sifre* Deut., §17 (*Jeschurun* 5 [1859]: 103).

17. Zunz, *Poesie*, 73; Elbogen, *Studien*, 47.

18. On the parts of the *qerova*, Zunz, *Poesie*, 65f; Brody, *Dichterschule*, 113f.; Davidson, *Yanai*, xxviii f. But recent publications listed below, §40:5, necessitate changing the division of the *qerova*.

19. Zunz, *Poesie*, 69. Cf. also Davidson, *Yannai*, 3:2–4. We now know that *qerovot* existed for the Evening Service as well.

20. In the manuscripts and old editions of Ashkenaz, as well as Romaniot and Rome, the verses may still be seen.

21. Berliner, *Randbemerkungen*, 2:66, notes that originally "O Lord" occurred already at the end of the preceding section, Ps. 22:4; also on part f., cf. Berliner, ibid. Davidson explains ואתה קדוש and "O Lord" as connectives marking the piyyutim of the third benediction, which have become confused because of copyists' errors.

22. See Zunz, *Poesie*, 69. Other compositions: Neubauer and Cowley, *Catalogue*, no. 2719₁, " 'Rain prayer' by R. Nehemiah"; the connection with ancient Babylonian conceptions was demonstrated in *MGWJ* 54 (1910): 535f.

23. The above must be changed in view of *HUCA* 3 (1926): 214 to the effect that in the piyyutim by Kallir under discussion, *shiv'ata* and *qerova* have come together.

24. Cf. Sachs, *Poesie*, 247f.; Berliner, *Randbemerkungen*, 2:62f. In Amram, and accordingly, Sepharad, "I hope" is part of the *'Amida*.

25. I no longer view the piyyutim of Yose b. Yose on the Kingdom, Remembrance, and Shofar as additions [note in second edition]; it seems that their author intended them as substitutes to the customary introductions ("It is our duty," etc.), and therefore verses are inserted into their last part, which have been eliminated only in the late editions of Ashkenaz. In Palestine, such piyyutim serving as a replacement for the traditional prayers were very common. A very artificial one for Kingdom, Remembrance, and Shofar by Mishael b. אלסטל the Precentor appears in *JQR* NS 8 (1917–18): 431f. It does not seem very old, but it shows clear signs of Palestinian influence and quotes verses that diverge from all other traditions.

26. On the *'Avoda*, see Zunz, *Ritus*, 101; Elbogen, *Studien*, 49f. On *'Avoda* poems in Sepharad, see Zunz, *Poesie*, 80.

27. Cf. *J.E.* 2:368f.; *E.J.* 3:508 and the literature cited there. A list of poets, in Jellinek, *Quntres taryag* (Vienna, 1852/5), 3; A. Neubauer, *JQR* 6 (1894): 698f.

28. *Azharot* in a secondary application, e.g., in Romaniot.

29. On the name "The Great Sabbath," see Zunz, *Ritus*, 10; *JQR* 5 (1893): 434f. The term, which (following the Christian custom) at first was applied only to the Sabbath before Passover, was eventually transferred to all the Sabbaths preceding festivals. So, e.g., R. Solomon b. Hayatom writes in his commentary to *Mo'ed qatan*, ed. Chajes, 15: "The Great Sabbath before Passover, Pentecost, the New Year, and Tabernacles." Cf. *Rivista Israelita* 7 (1910): 153.

30. אני והו is explained as a mystical formula in G. Klein, *Der älteste christliche Katechismus und die jüdische Propaganda-Literatur* (Berlin: G. Riemer, 1909), 48.

31. *Lev. r.*, 37:2.

32. B. *Suk.* 54b; Y. *Suk.* 4:1, 54b; *J.E.* 3:503b.

33. Cf. *Vitry*, 442; *O.Z.*, 2:69a, §315. On processions and versified *hosha'not*, cf. Amram 51b; *Halakhot gedolot*, 173; Ibn Ghiyath, *Sha'are simha*, 1:114f. In the quotation from Saadia there it seems that the words "one recites the Additional Service" are out of place; cf. Kohut in *MGWJ* 37 (1887): 506f., where Saadia's *hosha'not* are printed.

34. Cf. also Zunz, *Poesie*, 73f.; *J.E.* 6:161f., 476f.; *S.L.*, 166a, §369 knows processions only for the seventh day.

35. See Krauss in *Jahrbücher für jüdische Geschichte und Literatur* 22 (1919): 43f. and Mann, *Egypt*, 1:63.

36. Zunz, *Poesie*, 70, the source of the quotation at the end. "The Death of Moses": ibid., 73.

§33 The Seliḥa

1. Zunz, *Poesie*, 76f.; Berliner, *Randbemerkungen*, 2:21.

2. E.g., Num. 14:18; Joel 2:13; Nah. 1:3, Pss. 103:8, 145:8.

3. The introduction, "God, You instructed us."

4. Zunz, *Literaturgeschichte*, 17.

5. The fast-day liturgy in M. *Ta.* 2 makes use of several psalms.—Dan. 9; Ezra 9.

6. Marx, *Untersuchungen*, 28; Zunz, *Poesie*, 77, nn. 1, 2.

7. Zunz, *Ritus*, 120f.

8. Amram 35a, compared with *Vitry*, 233.

9. Two such litanies in Zunz, *Poesie*, 153. On the antiquity of most of them, see Zunz, *Literaturgeschichte*, 18. An ancient Aramaic litany from the geonic period was published by B.M. Lewin in *Ginze qedem* 4 (1930): 65f.; cf. *Qiryat sefer* 2 (1925/6): 146. The influence of such litanies on the Christian liturgy was proved by Michel, *Gebet und Bild in frühchristlicher Zeit* (Leipzig, 1902), 44f.

10. The *selihot* for the Minor Day of Atonement resemble those in Rome, hence their early character.

11. Zunz, *Poesie*, 82f, 152f.

12. Zunz, *Ritus*, 120f.

13. In Ashkenaz for the Evening Service of the New Year and the Morning Service of the Day of Atonement.

14. Zunz, *Poesie*, 77, n. 5.

15. The old type of *seliha*: Zunz, *Ritus*, 117f.

16. Zunz, *Ritus*, 33, n. 5.

17. The old *seliha*-rite for drought-fasts was in use in Babylonia as late as ca. 1000.

18. For the historical fasts, Rome has to this day the *qerovot* of Kallir; Ashkenaz and Romaniot have them for the Ninth of Av.

19. Development in the direction of the *seliha*: Zunz, *Ritus*, 125; there also, a list of fast days established after the close of the biblical period. A supplement to this list, by Simonsen, in *MGWJ* 48 (1894): 524f.; cf. *J.E.* 5:347f.

20. Amram 47b; *Manhig*, "Laws of Day of Atonement," §59 includes "A service (מעמד) that conduces to satisfaction (of God), forgiveness, praise, thanksgiving, and recalling of merit."

21. *Ma'amad* of Kallir for the Closing Service of the Day of Atonement containing *selihot* of Saadia Gaon was published by Elbogen in *HUCA* 4 (1927): 405f.—A *ma'amad* of Sepharad in Brody, *Dichterschule*, 116.—Zunz, *Poesie*, 80.—Al-Harizi, *Tahkemoni*, chap. 3, in Brody, *Dichterschule*, 175.—Al Harizi, *Tahkemoni*, chap. 3, p. 135.

22. The development and number of the days of *selihot* in Zunz, *Ritus*, 122f.; Amram 47b: "As is the custom on the days between the New Year and the Day of Atonement to stand up and recite *selihot* and words of supplication and petition."

23. *Halakhot gedolot* speaks of מעומד instead of מעמד on days of *selihot*; cf. Dukes, *Poesie*, 7; *Kerem hemed* 7 (1843): 33; Sachs, *Poesie*, 177.

24. Prayers for these dawn services in Zunz, *Ritus*, 132f.; Marx, *Untersuchungen*, 28f.; Frumkin, *Seder*, 2:308f. Tripoli: cf. Sachs, *Poesie*, 264f.; Brody, *Dichterschule*, 16, no. 13.

25. On poetic *selihot* and the manner of their inclusion, see also Berliner, *Randbemerkungen*, 2:22f, 75f.

26. All the names are in Amram 2; cf. Steinschneider, *Literatur*, §19, n. 12. *Gemar* is the name given to the first *seliha* of each day that immediately follows "Yours, O Lord," while on the Day of Atonement this name is applied to the last *selihot* preceding the reciting of the verses "Hear, O Israel," "Blessed is the name," "The Lord, He is God"; cf. Amram 2:39f., 48, 52f.

27. Zunz, *Poesie*, 88, 94, 134f.

28. Ibid., 98; Brody, *Dichterschule*, 51, no. 48.

29. Zunz, *Poesie*, 90f.

30. Ibid., 167, but cf. *Hamagid* 9 (1909): 136.

31. Zunz, *Poesie*, 95. *Qinot* on the Ten Martyrs, ibid.; 139f. *J.E.* 8:355f.

32. Zunz, *Poesie*, 135.

33. Ibid., 135, 89.

34. Amram 2:23a f., 38a f.

35. The names in Steinschneider, *Literatur*, 426; Brody, *Dichterschule*, 156.

36. Frumkin, *Seder*, 2:264.

37. Zunz, *Poesie*, 71f.; on the types and distribution of *qinot*, see Zunz, *Ritus*, 88f.

§34 The First Signs of Regular Public Worship

1. On the importance of the synagogue liturgy in the history of religion, cf. Heiler, *Das Gebet* (Munich: E. Reinhart, 1918), 474. On the importance of the synagogue, cf. also Herford, *Pharisaism*, 78f. (64f.). On the origin of the synagogue, cf. also Moore, *Judaism*, 1:283f. Finkelstein's attempt to push the synagogue back into the pre-exilic period and to demonstrate places of assembly for prayer under the direction of the

prophets, especially in the time of the Manassan reaction cannot be seen as proved (*PAAJR* 1 [1930]: 49–59). [On the origin and development of the synagogue, see also S. Krauss, *Synagogale Altertümer* (Berlin: Wien, 1922), 52f.; S. Zeitlin, in *PAAJR* 2 (1930–31): 69f.; *JQR* NS 53 (1962–63): 168f.; Y. Kaufmann, *Toledot ha'emuna hayisra'elit* (Jerusalem and Tel Aviv: Bialik Institute and the Devir Co. Ltd., 1955), 2:476f.; S. Safrai, *Hamiqdash bitequfat habayit hasheni* (Jerusalem, 1959), 1f.; Heinemann, *Prayer*, 82f.]

2. "A little sanctuary," Ezek. 11:16; one of the oldest synagogues is called this in B. *Meg.* 29a; in the late Jewish literature this expression often refers to synagogues.

3. For the gradual suppression of the sacrificial cult, see Bousset, *Judentums*, 124f.

4. On fast, cf. *J.E.* 5:347, 8:133; M. *Ta.* 2; sources in the apocryphal literature in Bousset, *Judentums*, 207.

5. Literature in Schürer, *History*, 2:426. To the argumentation in the text, there must also be added the fasts, which are stressed by Bacher, *Synagogue* (Zech. 7:5; Is. 58:3f.) and the considerations raised by Herford, *Pharisaism*, 78f. This refutes Bousset's doubts, *Judentums*, 197f. Much material in Krauss, *Synagogale*, 52f., 92f.—The status of the confession of faith in the ancient prayer-assemblies is stressed in Elbogen, *Studien*, 14. According to Blau, *J.E.* 8:133, the Shema' was introduced as a protest against dualism; thus it would have originated in the Jerusalem Temple, but even so the decisive factor would have been its status as a confession of faith.

6. On M. *Tam.* 5:1 and the Morning Service of the priests, see *Kohler Festschrift*, 77f. and B. *Ber.* 12b. [Cf. L. Ginzberg, *'Al halakha ve'agada* (Tel Aviv: Devir, 1959/60), 58 and 276, n. 63; Heinemann, *Prayer*, 80, 82f.]

7. Büchler, *Priester*, 60f., proves that the priests spoke Aramaic in the Temple.

8. We learn of the participation of laymen in the offering of sacrifices from M. *Tam.* 7:1 and Ben Sira 50:11f.

9. A. Büchler, in *ZAW* 19 (1899): 123, 133, 333; Köberle, *Tempelsänger*, esp. 100, 199; Schwaab, *Historische Einleitung*, 187.

10. On the responses, cf. Jer. 33:11; Köberle, *Tempelsänger*, 110; Büchler, *ZAW* 19 (1899): 334, and cf. Schürer, *History*, 2:303–7; Bousset, *Judentums*, 127, 418.

11. Cf. Herzfeld, *Tefillat*, 3:188, 204; Müller, *Soferim*, 236, n. 14; Büchler, *Priester*, 92ff.; Schürer, *History*, 2:293, n. 6. The truth must be deduced from M. *Ta.* 4:1f., with the help of T. *Ta.* 4:3 and Y. *Ta.* 4:2, 67d. According to these sources, each of the twenty-four districts was called a "course" (משמר); the mission of laymen of each course that was present in Jerusalem during the offering of the sacrifice was called a "delegation" (מעמד), and its leader, the "head of the delegation" (M. *Tam.* 6:6); but already in the Mishnah there is confusion about the use of these terms (e.g. M. *Bik.* 3:2). The courses divided their service into forty-eight weeks of the year; on the two festival weeks all priests could participate, and laypersons were always present as pilgrims; cf. B. *Suk.* 55b. Data in the sources give the impression that the institution was ancient, and there is no way to tell when the "later period of Judaism" (Bousset, *Judentums*, 127) occurred, in which it is supposed to have been instituted.

12. An attempt to explain the number of four services in Herzfeld, *Tefillat*, 3:188f. According to Blau, *J.E.* 8:132, the noon service was created in connection with individual sacrifices. The relationship with sacrifices is stated also in the Talmud: "The prayers were instituted parallel to the daily sacrifice" (B. *Ber.* 26b; T. *Ber.* 3:1,2), or, in another version, "They were derived from the daily sacrifice" (Y. *Ber.* 4:1, 7b); but no reason is given there for the Additional Service, and the reason for the Evening Service is tenuous. That the Additional Service was recited at midday seems likely from T. *Meg.* 4:1, where instead of the Mishnah's reading "in the Additional Service" the reading is "at midday." On the three times of prayer in Christianity and Islam, see Döller, *Gebet*, 66f.

13. This follows from "He who reads with the men of the delegation," Y. *Ber.* 1:8, 3c; B. *Yoma* 20a.

14. The great similarity between the prayers of Ezra and Daniel has been shown by Pool, *Kaddish*, 2f.

15. In our opinion the nature of the Great Assembly (cf. the literature in Schürer, *History*, 2:358f.) is irrelevant to our subject. Doubtless there were authoritative bodies of religious leadership in the centuries between Ezra and the Hasmoneans, but it was just in this period for which we have no detailed sources that the Jews underwent a great change in their religious outlooks and institutions. Cf. Herford, *Pharisaism*, 20.— The passage that we have quoted from the Talmud is cited in the name of R. Yohanan, a member of the first generation of amoraim, but it gives the impression of being ancient. But R. Yohanan is often the bearer of such traditions; cf. W. Bacher, *Agadat amora'e eres yisra'el*, trans. A. Rabinowitz (Tel Aviv: Devir, 1924–37), ii, 1, 3.

16. The importance of individual prayer for the formation of the public liturgy must be forcefully stressed (see *J.E.* 8:134f.). It may be the source of several prayers preserved in the apocrypha (A. Schlatter, *Geschichte Israels* [Stuttgart, 1906], 60f.), and it may have been the occasion for the acceptance of many psalms into the prayer book (*REJ* 73 [1921]: 148).

17. The restriction of the Additional Service to Sabbaths, etc., is apparently connected with the desig-

nation of the special sacrifice as "Additional." We do not know when this term was devised; it is not found in the Bible.

18. The readings during the week of the delegation T. *Ta.* 4:3; the institution of Torah readings on Mondays and Thursdays is attributed to Ezra; see above §25:2 and cf. T. *Ta.* 2:4.

19. Ewald, *Altertümer des Volkes Israel* (Göttingham: Dieterichschen Buchhandlung, 1848), 19; Sachs, *Poesie*, 164f.

20. Holzmann, in *AfRW* 25 (1927): 328 refers to Jer. 14:1–9, 19–22; 15:15–18; the dominant mood in these prayers certainly influenced the ancient version and may even have contributed to their formulation.—Both Ps. 119:12 and I Chron. 29:10 still lack the address "our God," typical of liturgical benedictions; likewise, Tobias 8:5, 15f.; this significant term of address to God is not mentioned by Bousset, *Judentums*, 431f. or Döller, *Gebet*, 72.—The religious vitality of these prayers, in Bousset, *Judentums*, 419f.

21. Domestic celebrations: Elbogen, *Sabbath*, vii f.

22. Day of Atonement: Elbogen, *Studien*, 54.

23. In Josephus, *Against Apion*, 1.22.210 (ed. Niese, 5:37); Th. Reinach, *Textes d'auteurs grecs et romains relatifs au judäism* (Paris: E. Leraux, 1895), 43.

24. The national petitions, cf. also *Judaica*, 669f.

§35 Prayer in the Tannaitic Period: Before the Destruction of the Temple

1. S. Funk has particularly sought to demonstrate ancient elements in the Mishnah in his *Die Entstehung des Talmuds* (Berlin: de Gruyter, 1919), §6f.

2. Ibid., 95ff., §36; many of them are included in both Talmuds.

3. Referring to the school of Hillel and Shammai (Strack, *Einleitung*, 119).

4. In Eusebius, *Praep. Evang.* 8:7 [Philo, *Hypoth.*, VII, 6—(Philo[b], 9:431)].

5. Josephus, *Antiquities*, 6.8.13.

6. E.g., B. *Ber.* 2a; Y. *Ber.* 1:5, 3b; T. *Ber.* 3:1; Maimonides, M.T., "Laws of Prayer," 1:1; *J.E.* 8:134; Elbogen, *Studien*, 39.

7. Among the disputes between Pharisees, Sadducees, and Essenes, none took place over public prayer.

8. Cf. "The time of the recitation of the *Shemaʿ*," Y. M.Q. 3:5, 83a; "Just as the time of the recitation of the *Shemaʿ* was fixed," T. *Ber.* 3:1. Cf. Luke 1:10: τὸ πλῆθος τοῦ λαοῦ ἦν προσευχόμενον τῇ ὥρᾳ τοῦ θυμιάματος, which implies the people's participation in the sacrificial rites. ("The afternoon incense," M. *Yoma* 3:5) and Acts 3:1 ἐπὶ τὴν ὥραν τῆς προσευχῆς τὴν ἐνάτην, which is about the same time; see also Acts 10:30 and Schürer, *History*, 2:303, n. 40.

9. In the street, M. *Ber.* 2:12 [sic—Engl. trans.]; on the road, ibid. 4:4f.

10. Bousset, *Judentums*, 202, 206; Herford, ibid.

11. *J.E.* 9:404f.

12. Ibid., 6:205.

13. On the influence of the Essenes on the service, cf. *J.E.* 5:225f.

14. Exegesis of the *Shemaʿ*, Sifre Deut., 74b f., §34f.; Sifre Num., 34a f., §115; considerable bibliography in Schürer, *History*, 2:479f.; cf. Elbogen, *Studien*, 16f.

15. M. *Ber.* 1–5; R.H. 4:5f.; *Ta.* 2:15, 4:1–3; *Meg.* 2:4.

16. Cf. Maimonides, Commentary to M. *Men.* 4:1, end. The Mishnah deals with synagogue institutions and prayers only in passing; e.g., in M. *R.H.* 4:5 it mentions them only because there is a disagreement as to where to insert the Kingship verses.

17. Here only such prayers are quoted as are discussed by the schools of Hillel and Shammai.

18. M. *Ber.* 1:4.

19. Ibid. 2:2 (and cf. 1:5).

20. B. *Ber.* 11b; Y. *Ber.* 1:8, 3c–d.

21. M. *Ber.* 4:1, 3.

22. T. *Ber.* 3:10 and parallels.

23. M. *Ta.* 2.

24. T. *Ber.* 3:12 f.

25. M. *Ber.* 6:1.

26. This is still the opinion of Mar Samuel, B. *Ber.* 30a–b, Y. 4:6, 8c.

27. T. *Suk.*; the text must be emended in accordance with Y. 5:2, 8c.

28. On the length of Hallel in antiquity, see A. Büchler, ZAW 20 (1900): 123f.

29. Cf. M. *Ber.* 1:4.

30. M. *R.H.*, end.
31. M. *Ber.* 4:5, 6.
32. M. *Meg.* 4:1–5.
33. The topics discussed: Zunz, *Haderashot*, 172f.; Sachs, *Poesie*, 150f.
34. Collected in Schürer, *History*, 2:448, n. 102.
35. *J.E.* 12:138f.
36. Y. *Sota* 7:1, 21b.

§36 Prayer in the Tannaitic Period: After the Destruction of the Temple

1. B. *Ber.* 26b; Y. *Ber.* 4:1, 7b; B. concludes that "The patriarchs instituted the *ʿAmidot* and the sages aligned them with the sacrifices."
2. *Avot derabi natan*, 4; cf. the discussion in Schürer, *History*, 1:521.
3. T. *Ber.* 3:1; B. and Y. *Ber.* 4, beginning.
4. B. *R.H.* 30a.
5. M. *R.H.* 4:1.
6. Ibid., 2; M. *Suk.* 3:12f.
7. Schürer, *History*, 2:293, n. 7 and Krauss, *Synagogale*, 169f. are thinking here of the priests' garments, but according to the motivation given in the Talmud, this opinion is impossible; the subject is Essene customs, many of which worked their way into nascent Christianity. Cf. *J.E.* 5:231f., 7:68.
8. For increased deification of Jesus, E. von d. Goltz, *Das Gebet in der ältesten Christenheit* (Leipzig: Hinrichs, 1901), 72f., 127.
9. In B. *Ber.* 28b הסדיר might conceivably be translated "to fix the order," and תקן, "to fix the text," and thus we would learn that in this exceptional case, a fixed text was transmitted. But the use of the expression תקנו in B. *Ber.* 33a (see above, §34[7]) shows otherwise.
10. Cf. Israel Lewy, *Über einige Fragmente aus der Mischna des Abba Saul* (Berlin: G. Bernstein, 1876), 33.
11. *Apostolic Constitutions* 6:11; other Christian prayers in Goltz, ibid., 332f.
12. As far as is known, no manuscript reads מין, "sectarian"; nevertheless I do not want to revise my opinion, as it is essentially well founded.
13. *J.E.* 5:685f. and the literature cited there.
14. "We give thanks, we give thanks": B. *Ber.* 33b; *J.E.* 5:684.—"Hear, hear": M. *Ber.* 5:3; *Meg.* 4:9; and the Talmud ad loc.
15. M. *Ber.* 2:3; *Meg.* 2:1; Levy, *Wörterbuch*, 3:202. Such strange expressions are more intelligible in light of several pagan and Christian prayers discovered in Egypt and Ethiopia.
16. M. *Ber.* 5:3; *Meg.* 4:9.
17. B. *Ber.* 33b; Y. *Meg.* 4:9, 75c; for the wording "May the good ones bless You," cf. also Simonsen in *Kaufmann Memorial Volume*, 115f.
18. M. *Ber.* 1:9: "R. Eleazar b. Azaria said." [There was no "enactment" in Palestine that the third paragraph of the *Shemaʿ* should be recited at night, and it certainly is not reported in the name of R. Gamaliel; cf. Albeck, *Mishnah*, 1:327 to Mishnah 5.]
19. For the name of Simon the Flaxworker, cf. the cognomen λινοπωλος on a gravestone discovered in Jaffa (*Palestine Exploration Fund Quarterly Studies* [1900]: 118); Schürer, *History*, 3:35.
20. M. *R.H.*, end. As early as two generations later a different reason was given: so as not to embarrass those who wish to insert here a confession for sin, B. *Sota* 32b, and cf. Rashi ad loc. It is no longer possible to ascertain how far the text of the Kedushah had developed at that time or how it was used in the public liturgy; in I Clement it is found in 34:6. It is worth mentioning that in this work, composed ca. 100, stress is laid on a definite ecclesiastical order.
21. M. *Ber.* 4:3, 5, end.
22. Explicit testimony from the amoraic period, B. *Git.* 59b.
23. Short prayers, cf. *Mekhilta*, 45b (to Ex. 15:25).—R. Akiva's conduct, T. *Ber.* 3:5.
24. E.g., M. *Ber.* 5:2; T. *Ber.* 3:10f.; M. *Ta.* 1:1; Y. *Ber.* 4:1, 7c; 4:3, 8a; 5:2, 9a; B. 29a; B. *Shab.* 24a and parallels. In all these disputes tannaim of that generation participate.
25. M. *R.H.* 4:5; T. *Yoma* 4:12; see Elbogen, *Studien*, 55.
26. Cf. above, §25(4); according to this, the cycle was not yet fixed even in the time of R. Meir.
27. B. *Meg.* 32a.
28. Zunz, *Haderashot*, 167.

29. Graetz, *Divre*, 2:250f.; *J.E.* 2:508f.

30. The Mishnah and baraita quote many disputes between R. Meir's contemporaries about the prayers.

31. E.g., Y. *R.H.* 4:6, 59c.

32. Expansion of ancient prayers: e.g., "True and Certain." Perhaps Kaddish took shape at this time.

33. Nearly all the material in Schürer, *History*, 2:481f. belongs to this period, and cannot be used for the period of which he is speaking.

34. M. *Ber.* 1:1, and T., B., and Y. thereon.

35. M. *Ber.* 2:1, 3:5; T. *Ber.* 2:6f., 3:20.

36. M. *Ber.* 2:1 and B. and Y. thereon.

37. See Bacher, *Tannaim*, 2:13, 109, 136, etc.

38. Errors: M. *Ber.* 5:5; T. 2:5; B. 21a, 29a, etc.; cf. Stössel, in *MGWJ* 56 (1912): 581f.

§ 37 Prayer in the Amoraic Period

1. Bacher, in Hastings, *Dictionary*, s.v. "Synagogue," attributes the admonition to pray in the synagogue to R. Eleazar b. Jacob, but the reading in *Pesiqta derav kahana*, 158a is not sufficiently clear. It cannot be determined when Abba Benjamin lived (B. *Ber.* 6a); nevertheless, the efforts of the amoraim to encourage prayer in the synagogue are noteworthy. The statement in *Midrash tehilim*, 27a (to Ps. 5:6) is apparently later than the talmudic statements listed here. On participation in the synagogue service in later times, see below.

2. R. Zadok: See Bacher, *Amora'e*, 2:187f. On this subject, cf. also Y. *Ber.* 5:1, 8d f.

3. On the activities of Rav and Mar Samuel on behalf of public worship, cf. Zunz, *Haderashot*, 181 and Rosenthal's note 39 to Graetz, *Geschichte*, 4:463f. of the German edition.

4. The addition that he instituted was the only distinguishing feature of the Additional Service in the Palestinian rite. Cf. §23:4.

5. Zunz, *Haderashot*, 181, 182; Bacher, *Amora'e*, 2:34f.

6. R. Papa's dictum: "Therefore let us say all of them" (B. *Sota* 40a); "Therefore let us say both of them" (B. *Ber.* 11b, according to MS Munich, 49b; 60b; B. *Meg.* 21b).

7. The order of prayer was set by the Mishnah, and was therefore unalterable.

8. Cf. Luzzatto, *Mavo*, 3f.

9. Cf., e.g., B. *Ber.* 34a; Y. 4:3, 8a; 5:3, 9c; B. *Pes.* 117b.

10. B. *Ber.* 33b; Y. 4:3, 8a; 5:2, 9b.

11. B. *Pes.* 117b. New Year: B. *R.H.* 32a–b. Day of Atonement: B. *Yoma* 87b.

12. E.g., B. *Meg.* 21b f., 29b f.; Y. *Meg.* 3:6, 74b.

13. B. *Ber.* 33b; B. *Pes.* 117b; B. *Yoma* 36b, 56b, 87b, etc.; Y. *Ber.* 1:8, 3d; *Shevu,* 1:5, 33b.

14. Elbogen, *Studien*, 31f.

15. *JQR* 10 (1898): 656.

16. Nahardea: B. *Shab.* 116b. Pumbedita: B. *Pes.* 117b. Cf. *Meg.* 22a. From a later period: Responsa of R. Isaac b. Sheshet, no. 412.

17. B. *Ber.* 16b f.; Y. *Ber.* 4:2, 7d.

18. B. *Ber.* 62b.

19. Discussion, e.g., about substitute prayers; cf. *MGWJ* 56 (1912): 700f., 714.

20. B. *Ber.* 33b; B. *Meg.* 25a. Rava: *Meg.*, 25a, and cf. Bacher, *Amoräer*, 128, n. 68; 49.

21. Cf. *Judaica*, 675.

22. Demons: e.g., B. *Ber.* 3a–b, 60a–b. Dreams: ibid., 58b, cf. stray thoughts, 60b. Magic: L. Blau, *Das altjüdische Zauberwesen* (Budapest, 1898); D. Joel, *Der Aberglaube und die Stellung des Judentum zu demselben* (Breslau, 1881–83), 1:66–105; *J.E.* 8:255f., 11:597f.

§ 38 Expansions and Embellishments of the Statutory Prayers

1. Graetz, *Divre*, 2:398f.

2. Ibid., 449f.

3. *J.E.* 10:610f.

4. Zunz, *Haderashot*, 182. Zunz attributes these expansions to the geonic period, but they must have existed earlier than that.

5. Hence, the addition of Ex. 15:19 in many prayer books cannot be ancient.

6. See König, *Stilistik*, 357.

7. *REJ* 53 (1907): 241. On this and the preceding note, cf. Zunz, *Literaturgeschichte*, 12.

[8. On the midrashic style reflected in some of the prayers in a variety of ways, cf. A. Mirsky, "Maḥṣavtan shel ṣurot hapiyut," *SRIHP* 7 (1957/8): 1f.; Heinemann, *Prayer*, 149, 152.]

9. Zunz, *Literaturgeschichte*, 17f. [Cf. Heinemann, *Prayer*, 95f.]

10. Luzzatto, *Mavo*, 6; id., *Betulat bat yehuda* (Prague: I. Landau, 1840), 11f.

11. "Men of faith" in Sepharad for Mondays and Thursdays; in Ashkenaz, for *seliḥot*; "Do not destroy us" in Ashkenaz, after the ʿ*Avoda*.

12. Sachs, *Poesie*, 177f. [On the relationship between ancient piyyut and ancient Christian liturgical poetry, see now J. Schirmann, "Hebrew Liturgical Poetry and Christian Hymnology," *JQR* 44 (1953): 123f.]

13. Elbogen, *Studien*, 56f.; the oldest one, beginning שבעת ימים, "Seven days," was first published there, 102f.

14. Ibid., 77. On the introduction, ibid., 59f.; on the prayer of the high priest, ibid., 66f.

[15. Cf. Heinemann, *Prayer*, 88f.]

16. Sentences beginning with "And so" are very common in all rites.

17. Zunz, *Literaturgeschichte*, 23f.

18. Such as "Men of faith," Zunz, *Literaturgeschichte*, 228; Sachs, *Poesie*, 176, n. 1.

19. *Azharot* are called in the manuscripts אזהרות דרבנן דמתבתא; Sachs, *Poesie*, 177, n. 1.

§ 39   *Piyyut*

1. Alphabetic acrostics, cf. *Song of Songs r.*, 1:7; *Qoh. r.*, 1:13: "This payyetan, when he makes an alphabetic acrostic. . . ."

2. On the origin of the piyyut, cf. also J. Mann in *HUCA* 4 (1927): 281f.

3. ʿ*Itim*, 252.

4. Graetz, *Divre*, 3:399; Schürer, *History*, 2:333.

5. The main source of ʿ*Itim* was Samuel the Nagid (*J.E.* 11:24f.), who himself drew considerably from R. Samuel b. Hofni (*Harkavy Festschrift*, 168f.). Also R. Benjamin b. Samuel of Constantinople [*MGWJ* 44 (1900): 295] in *Pardes*, 43d notes that the piyyut was in place of midrash ("They stopped in the place of the midrash and recited poetry on the subject").

6. See Schreiner in *MGWJ* 42 (1898): 123f.; the cited passage was translated into German by Schreiner, op. cit., 220. [English translation quoted from Moshe Perlman, "Samauʾal al-Maghribī: Ifḥām al-Yahūd: The Silencing of the Jews," *PAAJR* 32 (1964): 57.]

7. Cf. Brüll in *Jahrbücher für jüdische Geschichte und Literatur* 2 (1876): 15f.

8. See *Medieval Hebrew Chronicles* 1:33f.; Lewin, *Shrira*, 95f.

9. See G. Gottheil, in *JQR* 19 (1907): 500, 527.

10. *JQR* 18 (1906): 13.

11. Cf. I. Davidson, *Yannai*.

12. Rhyme: C. Brockelmann, *Geschichte der arabischen Literatur* (Leiden: Brill, 1937–42), 1:137. Meter: see Hartman, *Verskunst*, 41.

13. I.e., before the time of Kallir.

14. Zunz, *Ritus*, 6f.; Zunz, *Poesie*, 61.

15. Piyyutim for the Afternoon Service exist only for the Day of Atonement.

16. See Neubauer and Cowley, *Catalogue*, 2:2706$_{16}$, 2710$_{6,9}$, 2712$_4$, etc.

17. Sachs, *Poesie*, 179.

18. Zunz, *Literaturgeschichte*, Introduction, v.

19. See Neubauer and Cowley, *Catalogue*, in the index, 469f.; but the number of manuscripts in Cambridge is inestimably greater. Besides, in recent decades very late collections have come to light from Yemen and Persia; cf. W. Bacher in *REJ* 58–60 and 62 (1909–10 and 1911): 74f. W. Bacher, *Die hebräisch-arabische Poesie der Juden Yemens* (1910); also *JQR* NS 2 (1911–12): 373f. From Persia: *J.E.* 7:320; *ZHB* 14 (1910): 16f., and cf. also *REJ* 43 (1901): 101f.; *REJ* 62 (1911): 85f.

20. Sachs, *Poesie*; Zunz, *Poesie*, 126f.—On piyyut as a source for halakha, see Jeiteles in *Jahrbuch der jüdisch-literarischen Gesellschaft* 19 (1928): 293.

21. The contents of the *seliha* in Zunz, *Poesie*, 85f.—Its style: ibid., 127.

22. Sachs, *Poesie*, 204f.

23. Zunz, *Poesie*, 139f. The binding of Isaac: ibid., 136f.

24. Sachs, *Poesie*, 253, n. 1.

25. E.g., Moses Ibn Ezra in the ʿ*Avoda*: Elbogen, *Studien*, 59, discussing the imitation of a famous example from Arabic poetry. Cf. Brockelmann, ibid., 1:6.

26. Zunz, *Poesie*, 104f.

27. In this pattern, particles and the like are not taken into account; therefore, sometimes the letters of the acrostic are preceded by words like "before" or "until," etc.

28. B. *Shab.* 104a; B. *Suk.* 52a.

29. Zunz, *Poesie*, 95f., 110f.

30. The *qerova* זכור איכה, "Remember how," by Kallir is described in Zunz, *Literaturgeschichte*, 46ff.

31. Zunz, *Poesie*, 106f. Benediction formula: ibid., 108f., appendix 4, 369–72.

32. Amram 2:44a; Brody, *Dīwān*, 3:286.

33. Zunz, *Poesie*, 109f.

34. Simon and Solomon, below, §41(5); Yeḥiel: Zunz, *Poesie*, 108.

35. The rhymes in the Bible (in Zunz, *Haderashot*, 448, n. 128) are not intentional; cf. König, *Stilistik*, 356f. It is even doubtful whether the rhymes in the Talmud (Brody in his notes to Frances, *Meteq*, 33) are intentional. All medieval Hebrew writers are in agreement that rhyme was not known in Hebrew before Kallir or Yannai; cf. Hartmann, *Verskunst* and Brody, *Studien* 10.

36. Zunz, *Poesie*, 86f.

37. Ibid., 96f.

38. Ibid., 95.—*Mustajāb*: above, §33. Similar are the *rahiṭim*: Zunz, *Poesie*, 99.

39. *Maʿase efod*, 43, chap. 8.

40. Cf. the literature in König, *Stilistik*, 303f. and Steuernagel, *Lehrbuch der Einleitung in das Alte Testament* (Tübingham: J. C. B. Mohr, 1912), 108f., §30.

41. Cf. Hartmann, *Verskunst*, 47 on quantitative meter.

42. *Teshuvot talmide menaḥem*, ed. S.G. Stern (Vienna, 1870), 7, 21f.

43. *Kuzari*, chap. 4, §§70, 74, 78.

44. *Taḥkemoni*, chap. 18, cf. *Sefer ḥasidim*, §§469–70.

45. Brody, *Studien*, 17f. To the technical terminology belong also the terms מחובר and מפורד, "prose" and "poetry."

46. A list of meters, in David Rosin, *Reime und Gedichte des Abraham Ibn Esra* (Breslau: S. Schottländer, 1885–94), 1:6f., and Brody, *Studien*, 26f. Corrections to Brody, see Halper in *JQR* NS 4 (1892): 153f.

47. Hartmann, *Verskunst*, 83.

48. Zunz, *Poesie*, 114f.

49. Ibid., 117f.

50. Ibid., appendix 5, 372–75.

51. Krauss, *Lehnwörter*, 1:xxvi f.

52. Zunz, *Poesie*, 118.

53. Ibid., appendixes 6 and 7, 376–79.

54. Ibid., 119.

55. Ibid., 120f.; infinitive: ibid., appendix 8, 379f.

56. Biliteral forms: ibid., 380–83.—On ל, ב, and כ before finite verbs: 383–85; payyetanic vocabulary: 385f.; nominal forms: 386–420; new verbal forms: 420–35; particles for verbs: 436–38; obscurity: 123f., on which, appendixes 15–17; a list of special expressions typical of or peculiar to early payyetanim: 438–53. The expressions bearing on the relationship to the kingdoms ruling Israel: 457–74. The ancient covenant and the ancient help: 474–77. On the language of the payyetanim, cf. also Luzzatto, *Mavo*, 10f. [Goldschmidt, *Maḥzor*, 30f.]

57. Abraham Ibn Ezra to *Qoh.* 5:1; Zunz, *Poesie*, 117.

58. Heidenheim in his commentary to אנסיכה מלכי, "I will enthrone my King," for the Additional Service of the New Year.

59. For the modern period it suffices to mention Victor Hugo and Gabriele d'Annunzio.

60. A.A. Wolf, ʿAteret shalom veʾemet: Stimmen der ältesten glaubwürdigsten Rabbiner über die Piutim (Leipzig, 1857) and Zunz, *Ritus*, 163f., where the defenders of the piyyut are cited, but the extent of the opposition is understated.—A difference between Babylonia and Palestine: *Kerem ḥemed* 6 (1841): 247.—On the attitude toward the piyyut in its early days, cf. now the comprehensive work of Ginzberg, *Ginze*, 508f., who distinguishes not only between Babylonia and Palestine, but also between the academies of Sura and Pumbedita. In the latter, the opposition was particularly severe.—Gradual acceptance of the piyyut, cf. Eppenstein, *Literatur*, 596.

61. Ginzberg, *Geonica*, 2:51. Like him, his admirer, the author of *Pirqoi ben baboi* rejects piyyut, *REJ* 70 (1920): 130. [And cf. *Tarbiz* 2 (1930/31): 411f.]

62. Kohen-Zedek: see *S.L.*, 13a, §28.

63. See *Ḥemda genuza*, no. 50; *S.L.*, 13a, §28, and cf. *MGWJ* 54 (1910): 355.

64. ʿItim, 252, and cf. R. Hananel, *S.L.*, 12b.

65. ʿItim, 252.

66. *Vitry*, 370.

67. *S.L.*, ibid.; *Vitry*, 362f.

68. Ibid.

69. See above, note 57.

70. *Guide of the Perplexed*, 1:59 [English quoted from translation by S. Pines, *The Guide of the Perplexed* (University of Chicago Press: Chicago and London, 1963), 1:141.— *Engl. trans.*], and cf. *Qoveṣ teshuvot* 1, no. 127 and *Lewy Festschrift*, Hebrew sec., 49.

71. *Tahkemoni*, chap. 24, in Brody, *Dichterschule*, 187.

72. Wolf, ibid., 14f.; Zunz, *Ritus*, 166.

73. On *Ṭur, O.Ḥ.*, §68, 112.

74. *Maʿase rav*, no. 127.

§ 40 The Main Liturgical Poets: Up to and Including Kallir

1. On the study of medieval Hebrew poetry in the course of the nineteenth century, cf. I. Davidson, "The Study of Mediaeval Poetry in the Nineteenth Century," *PAAJR* 1 (1930): 33f. and *Madʿe hayahadut* 1 (1926): 187f.

2. To the meager sources belongs the list of ancient *seliha* poets: Zunz, *Literaturgeschichte*, appendix 1, 625f.; the list in Harkavy, *Studien*; al-Harizi, *Tahkemoni*, chap. 3 (Brody, *Dichterschule*, 170f.). On poetics: Schechter, *Saadyana*, 136, §51 and *JQR* 14 (1902): 472. A good selection of examples in Brody and Weiner, *Mivhar*.

3. Zunz, *Literaturgeschichte*, 23f.

4. Ibid., 26f; Landshuth, *ʿAmude*, 85f.; Harkavy, *Studien*, 106f.; Jawitz in the *Hoffmann Festschrift*, Hebrew sec., 74f.; Landshuth and Harkavy list all the errors of their predecessors.

5. *JQR* 14 (1902): 742.

6. See Elbogen, *Studien*, 78f., 118.

7. Rosenberg, *Qoveṣ*, 2:111f.

8. Zunz, *Literaturgeschichte*, 646f.; on Peter as author: Elbogen, *Studien*, 742.

9. Rosenberg, *Qoveṣ*, 2:1f., where it incorrectly reads נארדי.

10. Elbogen, *Studien*, 81, 118.

11. Zunz, *Literaturgeschichte*, 28.

12. Zunz, *Ritus*, 142; Landshuth, *ʿAmude*, 87; German translation: Zunz, *Poesie*, 163.

13. In Harkavy, *Studien*, 5:106ff.; Eppenstein, *Literatur*, 595.

14. Cf. Davidson, *Yannai*. Further works of his discovered since that publication: two piyyutim published by Levias in *AJSL* 15 (1898/9): 156f., correctly identified by Kahle, *Masoreten*, 24; see also Max Kober, *Zum Machzor Jannai* (Frankfurt, 1929), from *Jahrbuch der jüdischen literatur-Gesellschaft* 20 (1929): 21f.); Davidson, *Ginze*, 8–24 (cf. 1–6). Several additional items will soon appear in a Bonn dissertation. On Kober, cf. Spiegel, in *MGWJ* 74 (1930): 94f.

15. *JQR* 14 (1902): 742.

16. Harkavy, *Studien*, 5:107f.; cf. *MGWJ* 44 (1902): 377.—Davidson correctly interpreted R. Gershom's words in *S.L.*, §28 to the effect that Yannai composed piyyutim for every pericope of the triennial cycle. Some of these *qerovot* were deciphered by Davidson from palimpsests.

17. Above, §39(3).

18. Landshuth, *ʿAmude*, 103. I recall reading a similar legend about an Italian poet, but I can no longer find it. As Dr. Aldo Sorani in Florence informs me, there is a similar motif in *Morgante Maggiore* by Pulci (fifteenth century).

19. On Kallir, cf. Rapoport's biography in *Bikure haʿitim* 11 (1830): 95f.; Zunz, *Literaturgeschichte*, 29f.; Landshuth, *ʿAmude*, 27f.; Luzzatto, *Mavo*, 9f.

20. The quotation from Frankl in the *Zunz Festschrift*, 160.

21. *ʿArukh*, s.v. קלר III.

22. Zunz, *Zur Geschichte*, 168f.

23. Rapoport, *Qalir*, n. 17.

24. Jacob b. Shulam in Abraham Zacuto, *Yuhasin*, ed. Cracow (1580–81), 34b, 48b; against him, Landshuth, *ʿAmude*, 29.

25. Metaphors and symbols assumed by Rapoport, *Qalir*, n. 12; it is often objected that he greatly exaggerates here.

26. See *Mélanges Renier* (Paris: F. Vieweg, 1887), 433; Berliner, *Rom*, 15f.

27. Y. Perles, *Byzantinische Zeitschrift* 2 (1893), 582.—Northern Italy: see above.

28. In Berliner, ibid.

29. *Kerem ḥemed* 6 (1841): 7.

30. Ibid., 8; S. Krauss, *Studien zur byzantinisch-jüdischen Geschichte* (!) (Leipzig: G. Fock, 1914), 128 moves him to Constantinople.

31. Luzzatto, *Mavo*, 9. Palestine: first S. Cassel, in Frankel's *Zeitschrift für die religiösen Interessen* 2 (1846): 224f.

32. *Tosafot, Ḥagiga* 13a, s.v. ורגל. Rapoport's objections in *Qalir* (n. 1) have no force, since the congregations' uses of the piyyutim do not necessarily attest to their original purpose. Two *qerovot* for the Ninth of Av by Kallir exist, one in Ashkenaz and one in Rome; as for Purim, cf. Frankl in the *Zunz Festschrift*, 162.

33. Zunz, *Literaturgeschichte*, 33.

34. Already in Rapoport, *Qalir*, nn. 28 and 33. See Elbogen, *Achtzehngebets*, 26.

35. So, in the end, Zunz: see Zunz, *Literaturgeschichte*, 33.

36. This was already the opinion of Cassel and Perles, *OLZ* 10 (1907): 543.

37. Eppenstein, *Literatur*, 594.

38. See Landshuth, *ʿAmude*, 27; Josef Steinhardt in his book *Zikhron yosef* (Fürth, 1903) was the first to speak against this.

39. אאבין תשע מאות ועוד, "I contemplate nine hundred years," and לך ה' הצדקה, "Yours, O Lord, is the righteousness," in Rapoport, *Qalir*, n. 3; the correct interpretation in Luzzatto, *Mavo*, 10.

40. The piyyutim of Kallir are listed by Landshuth, *ʿAmude*, 31f. and Zunz, *Literaturgeschichte*, 43f.

41. E.g., in Neubauer and Cowley, *Catalogue*, index, 444; ibid., no. 2708$_1$, also some unknown piyyutim for Passover. Unknown *qerovot* for Hanukkah in Cambridge, Taylor-Schechter collection, H1.—New Kallir material was published by I. Elbogen in *HUCA* 2 and 3 (1925 and 1926); *Bericht der Hochschule für die Wissenschaft des Judentums* (1929), 47f.; *Ṣiyunim* (Y. N. Simhoni Memorial Volume), 83f. (a versified "eighteen" on the death of a scholar), 86f. (fragment of *tekiʿa* for the New Year).

42. Zunz, *Literaturgeschichte*, 32.

43. Ibid., 60.

44. Ibid., 43f.

45. Ibid., 46f.

46. Ibid., 31, 34 (n.).

47. Ibid., 29f.

48. Ibid., 603f.

49. Ibid., 35f.

50. Ibid., 33. German translations: Zunz, *Poesie*, 67, 75, 130.

51. The most ancient commentary on one of his *qinot* was published by Ginzberg, *Ginze*, 1:246f.—Quotations: Zunz, *Literaturgeschichte*, 61f.

§ 41 The Main Liturgical Poets: Kallir's Imitators

1. Cf. Zunz, *Literaturgeschichte*, 64.—For the period after 1050: ibid., 126, the source of the quotation.

2. Ibid., 64–93, 219–32.

3. H. Malter, *The Life and Works of Saadia Gaon* (Philadelphia: The Jewish Publication Society, 1921), 149f., 333–421.

4. In Rosenberg, *Qoveṣ*, 2:30f., improperly included among the *azharot* אלהים אצל (26f.) and Saadia, *Oeuvres*, 9:58f.

5. Elbogen, *Studien*, 82f.; printed in *Qoveṣ ʿal yad* 2 (1886): 10f.; the second, אלהים יה in Elbogen, *Studien*, 83f. and 122f.

6. See *MGWJ* 30 (1893): 506f.

7. Zunz, *Literaturgeschichte*, 97; Schechter, *Saadyana*, xviii; other unknown piyyutim of Saadia are published in Schechter, *Saadyana*, xvii–xxiv. A *tokheḥa* in Brody, *Mivḥar*, 51f., cf. Neubauer and Cowley, *Catalogue*, 494f.

8. See Malter, *Saadia*, 139.

9. Zunz, *Literaturgeschichte*, 100f.; Vogelstein and Rieger, *Rom*, 1:181f.

10. Ibid.; Zunz, *Literaturgeschichte*, 232f.; German translation: Zunz, *Poesie*, 167f.; Vogelstein and Rieger, *Rom*, 183.

11. Zunz, *Literaturgeschichte*, 233; but see above, §33(8).

12. Elbogen, *Studien*, 87f.

13. On the Kalonymides, see the literature in Aronius, *Regesten*, 58, §136; *J.E.* 7:424f.

14. Zunz, *Literaturgeschichte*, 104f.; Landshuth, ʿAmude, 257f.

15. Zunz, *Literaturgeschichte*, 108.

16. Ibid., 108f.; Landshuth, ʿAmude, 257f.

17. *REJ* 24 (1892): 149f.; Salfeld, *Martyrologium*, 434.

18. Elbogen, *Studien*, 85f., 126f. German translation: Zunz, *Poesie*, 130f.

19. Zunz, *Literaturgeschichte*, 111f. The epithet מלומד בנסים, "experienced with miracles," either means that he was a miracle worker or that miracles happened to him in his life.

20. See Aronius, *Regesten*, 62, §145; Salfeld, *Martyrologium*, 288.

21. Zunz, *Ritus*, 140.

22. Zunz, *Literaturgeschichte*, 235f.; German translation: Zunz, *Poesie*, 174f.

23. Zunz, *Literaturgeschichte*, 238f.; German translation: Zunz, *Poesie*, 171f.

24. See above, §41(5); on the son who apostatized, see Graetz, *Divre*, 3:378 [and 480, n. 22].

25. Zunz, *Literaturgeschichte*, 120f., 239f. Zunz, *Poesie*, 176 refers to him as the most prolific *seliha* composer of his century, "and perhaps of all the poets of France and Germany together." He gives several of his poems in German translation.

26. Zunz, *Literaturgeschichte*, 123.

27. Ibid., 123f.; Zunz, *Poesie*, 132. His piyyut was published by I. Davidson in *HUCA* 3 (1926). For an explanation of the details, see Baneth, in *MGWJ* 71 (1927): 426f.; *MGWJ* 73 (1929): 376; Barol, in *MGWJ* 73 (1929): 302f.

28. Zunz, *Literaturgeschichte*, 126f.; Landshuth, ʿAmude, 13f.

29. Rosenberg, *Qoveṣ*, 2:55f.

30. Zunz, *Literaturgeschichte*, 243.

31. See S.D. Luzzatto, *Bet haʾoṣar* (Leipzig, 1847–49), 1:48f.; Landshuth, ʿAmude, 96f.; Zunz, *Literaturgeschichte*, 129f.; *Gallia Judaica*, 308. The piyyutim mentioned are all found in Ashkenaz; explanations for אלהי הרוחות, "God of the spirits," in O.Z., 2:57c f. *Selihot*: Zunz, *Literaturgeschichte*, 243; Zunz, *Poesie*, 206f.

32. Zunz, *Literaturgeschichte*, 139, 244f.; Landshuth, ʿAmude, 17f.; German translations: Zunz, *Poesie*, 206f. Parallels in the *selihot*: Zunz, *Literaturgeschichte*, 616.

33. See Zunz, *Literaturgeschichte*, 145f., 248f.; on the name: ibid., 610; Landshuth, ʿAmude, 162. German translations: Zunz, *Poesie*, 188f.

34. Cf. the literature in *J.E.* 10:328; Zunz, *Literaturgeschichte*, 252f.; Zunz, *Poesie*, 181. On the prayer book, attributed to Rashi (Berlin, 1911), cf. the introduction by S. Buber and J. Freimann.

35. Zunz, *Literaturgeschichte*, 265f.; Landshuth, ʿAmude, 106f.

36. *Qinot* on the persecutions connected with the First Crusade are listed by Graetz, *Geschichte*, 4:436 (with considerable inaccuracy); Salfeld, *Martyrologium*, 101f.

37. Zunz, *Literaturgeschichte*, 158, 250; Landshuth, ʿAmude, 189f.; Salfeld, *Martyrologium*, 103; cf. Epstein in *MGWJ* 41 (1897): 300f.

38. Zunz, *Literaturgeschichte*, 254; Landshuth, ʿAmude, 59. The delegation to Emperor Henry IV: Aronius, *Regesten*, 71f., §170.

39. Zunz, *Literaturgeschichte*, 164f., 255.

40. Zunz, *Literaturgeschichte*, 259f.; Landshuth, ʿAmude, 20f.; *J.E.* 5:118f., cf. Zunz, *Poesie*, 246. One unknown *qina* by Kalonymos and one by Eliezer were published by Lichtenstein, in *ZGJD* 2 (1930): 237f.

41. See Zunz, *Literaturgeschichte*, 269; Landshuth, ʿAmude, 81f.; Salfeld, *Martyrologium*, 113; cf. Zunz, *Poesie*, 252.

42. Zunz, *Literaturgeschichte*, 288f., 619; Landshuth, ʿAmude, 47; *J.E.* 5:190f.; cf. Zunz, *Poesie*, 262.

43. Zunz, *Literaturgeschichte*, 274f.; Landshuth, ʿAmude, 48; cf. Zunz, *Poesie*, 254f.

44. Zunz, *Literaturgeschichte*, 294f.; Zunz, *Poesie*, 263.

45. Zunz, *Literaturgeschichte*, 357f., 623; Landshuth, ʿAmude, 160f.; cf. Zunz, *Poesie*, 312f.; *J.E.* 7:437f.

46. On later poems, see above, §39(5).

§42   The Main Poets: The Poets of Spain

[*Abraham Ibn Daud, *Sefer ha-Qabbalah: The Book of Tradition*, ed. and trans. G.D. Cohen (Philadelphia: The Jewish Publication Society of America, 1967), 102; Hebrew text, ibid., 73.]

1. General characterization in Sachs, *Poesie*; Karpeles, *Geschichte*. Kaufmann in his introduction to S. Heller, *Die echten hebräischen Melodien*, 2nd ed. (Breslau, 1893).— Dukes, Kämpf, Letteris, Edelmann, and above all, S.D. Luzzatto made particular contributions to the rediscovery of the poetry of the Jews of Spain; to its interpretation, M. Sachs, S. Sachs, A. Geiger, and, lately, H. Brody and I. Davidson have also contributed greatly.

2. See Sachs, *Poesie*, 248–55; Zunz, *Literaturgeschichte*, 178–86; Landshuth, ʿAmude, 92–94.

3. *Taḥkemoni*, chap. 3.

4. Elbogen, *Studien*, 88f.

5. *Qedusha* in Sachs, *Poesie*, 253.

6. Cf. Zunz, *Literaturgeschichte*, 179f.

7. See Sachs, *Poesie*, 255–69; Zunz, *Literaturgeschichte*, 194–200; Landshuth, ʿAmude, 111–16; Luzzatto, *Luaḥ*, 38f.; Steinschneider, *Catalogus*, 1110f.

8. Elbogen, *Studien*, 90f.

9. Distribution of the piyyutim: Zunz, *Literaturgeschichte*, 195, the source of the quotation.

10. In the *maḥzor* called *Sifte renanot* (Venice, 1648 and 1711).

11. Cf. Sachs, *Poesie*, 273f.; Zunz, *Literaturgeschichte*, 201; Landshuth, ʿAmude, 49–51; two poems were recently published at the end of the book *al-Hidāya ilā farāʾid al-qulūb*, ed. A.S. Yahuda (Leiden, 1912); cf. Brody, *Dichterschule*, 61f.

12. Zunz, *Literaturgeschichte*, 201; Landshuth, ʿAmude, 126f.; Geiger, *Jüdische Dichter*, 9–12.

13. Ibn Gabirol's sacred poems were collected in the (second) edition by H.N. Bialik and I.H. Rawnitzki (Tel-Aviv: Devir, 1927/8–1931/2).—On Ibn Gabirol, see Sachs, *Poesie*, 217–48; Zunz, *Literaturgeschichte*, 187–94; Luzzatto, *Luaḥ*, 69f.; Steinschneider, *Catalogus*, 2313f.; Geiger, *Gabirol*; S. Sachs, *Hatehiya*, 2 vols. (Berlin, 1850–57; reprint, Jerusalem, 1969). Samples of his poetry: Brody, *Dichterschule*, 39f.; *Selected Religious Poems of Solomon Ibn Gabirol*, ed. I. Davidson, trans. I. Zangwill (Philadelphia: Jewish Publication Society of America, 1928).

14. Quotation from Sachs, *Poesie*, 223.

15. Ibid., 1f., 223.

16. Heinrich Heine, "Jehuda ben Halevy" in *Romanzero* (1851). [English translation by Hal Draper, *The Complete Poems of Heinrich Heine: A Modern English Version* (Boston: Suhrkamp/Insel, 1982), 676.]

17. Steinschneider, *Catalogus*.

18. *Taḥkemoni*, trans. Victor Immanuel Reichert, 2 vols. (Jerusalem: R.H. Cohen's Press, 1965–73) 1:77.—Unknown ʿavodot: Elbogen, *Studien*, 89f., 136f.; *Haṣofe* 5 (1921): 178.

19. See Sachs, *Poesie*, 272; Zunz, *Literaturgeschichte*, 202.

20. Editions of the secular poetry of Moses Ibn Ezra: H. Brody 1–2 (Jerusalem: Schocken, 1934/5–1941/2); Bialik and Rawnitzki (Tel Aviv: Devir, 1927/8).—On his dates, Luzzatto, *Betulat*, 24; citation from Sachs, *Poesie*, 282f.; cf. also Steinschneider, *Catalogus*, 1801f.

21. Zunz, *Poesie*, 228.

22. Listing of poems: Landshuth, ʿAmude, 243–55; corrections, Zunz, *Literaturgeschichte*, 202f., 614; Luzzatto, *Luaḥ*, 54f.—On his poetics, see Steinschneider, *Arabische Literatur*, §101; Schreiner, in *REJ* 21 (1890): 98f.; 22 (1891): 68f. [; D. Pagis, *Shirat haḥol vetorat hashir lemoshe ibn ʿezra uvene doro* (Jerusalem: Bialik, 1970)].

23. Brody, *Dīwān*.—The literature on him is very rich: See Brody, *Studien*, 5, n.; *J.E.* 7:351. The new material for the poet's biography is used by Emil Bernhard Cohn, *Jehuda Halevy, Ein Dīwān* (Berlin: Erich Reiss Verlag, 1921).

24. The lines of poetry are from Heinrich Heine, "Jehuda ben Halevy." [English translation by Draper, *Complete Poems*, 672, 659 (cited in n. 16).]

25. See Sachs, *Poesie*, 303f.; Karpeles, *Geschichte*, 420f., 426.

26. Karpeles, *Geschichte*, 426.

27. Listing of sacred poems: Zunz, *Literaturgeschichte*, 203–7; Landshuth, ʿAmude, 69–77. A fuller list, though without any special order, is included in Luzzatto's introduction to his *diwan*. A new German translation with notes by Franz Rosenzweig, *Jehuda Halevi, Zweiundneunzig Hymnen und Gedichte*, 2nd ed. (Berlin: Verlag Lambert Schneider, 1926).

28. On the life of Abraham Ibn Ezra, see lately Ochs, in *MGWJ* 60 (1916): 47f.; on his sacred poetry, Sachs, *Poesie*, 310–20; Zunz, *Literaturgeschichte*, 207–14; Landshuth, ʿAmude, 5–9. Collection of his poems in Joel Egers, *Dīwān lerabi avraham ibn ʿezra* (Berlin, 1886); a list of the sacred poems not contained in the *diwan*, ibid., 186f. Samples of his poems: Zunz, *Poesie*, 238f.; Sachs, *Poesie*, 109–18; Brody, *Dichterschule*, 145f.; D. Rosin, *Reime und Gedichte des Abraham ibn Esra*, 5 vols. (Breslau, 1885–94), vol. 2, *Gottesdienstliche Poesie*.—New poems from Oriental lands: Davidson, *Ginze*.

§ 43 Prayer Books and Orders of Prayer

1. On the prohibition of writing "oral teachings," see now the detailed study B. Gerhardsson, *Memory and Manuscript*, trans. E. Sharpe (Uppsala, 1961); on the prohibition of writing prayers, see also Heinemann, *Prayer*, 12, 29f., 39f.

2. See *J.E.* 5:43f., s.v. "Education" (Güdemann).

3. Cf. H. Vogelstein, in *MGWJ* 49 (1905): 427f.

4. J. Müller, *Briefe und Responsen in der vorgeonäischen jüdischen Literatur* (Berlin: G. Bernstein, 1886).

5. Zunz, *Haderashot*, 336, n. 23.

6. Detailed discussion of *Soferim* in *Soferim* (ed. Müller); in his introduction the data on the tractate's origin and character are given.—*Soferim* speaks of the reading of the Torah and the prayers from 9:9 on, but in 12:8b–13:8 it returns to the subject of the writing of the Torah scroll; elsewhere there are digressions into aggadah.

7. Weekday prayers: *Soferim* 10:7; above, §11(4), we demonstrated that 17:11 refers to festivals.

8. Zunz, *Ritus*, 2f. Unna, in *Jeschurun* 10 (1923): 464 calls custom "the creative power of the living folk-spirit, within the limits determined by the Torah." He sees custom as a kind of religious instinct grounded not in the tradition but in the people. Carlebach goes even farther; see *Jeschurun* 14 (1927): 676f.; *Jeschurun* 15 (1928): 69f., 139f.

9. E.g., M. *Pes.* 4; *Meg.* 2; etc.

10. *Soferim* 14:18.

11. See Zunz, *Ritus*, 3f.

11*. Zunz, *Ritus*, 5, 16, 184f.; Müller, *Mafteaḥ* (the literature has grown considerably since this work).

12. For bibliography on the prayer book, cf. Krauss, *Soncino-Blätter* 2 (1927): 1f. [and *A. Freimann Festschrift* (Berlin, 1935), 125f.]. Cf. Ginzberg, *Geonica*, 1:119f.

13. Ginzberg, *Geonica*, 2:119f. His responsa in Müller, *Mafteaḥ*, 104f.

14. Ginzberg correctly stresses that prayer books were in use at that time, though his indirect proof is not valid, since the question of whether a blind person may serve as precentor relates to M. *Meg.* 4:6. But if we compare Natronai's responsum with the statement of R. Yehudai (see J. Müller, *Handschriftliche Jehudai Gaon zugewiesene Lehrsätze* [Berlin: Rosenthal and Co., 1890], 10, no. 9), it becomes clear that R. Yehudai's opposition to prayer books had been completely overcome.—The claim in Zunz, *Ritus*, 18c that Kohen-Zedek also composed a prayer book does not stand up to critical examination; cf. Müller, ibid., 17, no. 10; Ginzberg, *Geonica*, 1:123.

15. Ginzberg, *Geonica*, 1:126–54 has studied the form of this prayer book, as we have it, in detail. He, too, admits (p. 124) that various changes have occurred in the text of the prayers. But unlike Ginzberg, I doubt whether originally the full text of the prayers was given there at all. For there is no proof that סדר תפילות וברכות means the text of the prayers; it is entirely possible that this expression refers to the order of the prayers or their eulogies, as with R. Natronai. Among Amram's main sources were the practice of the two academies and that of the house of the Exilarch (that is how I explain the expression בית רבנו שבבבל, in opposition to Ginzberg, *Geonica*, 1:42f. and Krauss, *Synagogale*, 18, 221); as for his literary sources, he made particular use of the responsa of R. Natronai. Alongside the usual titles of this work, quoted below in the text, O.Z., 1:26b has also מחזורים דר׳ עמרם. On Amram, cf. the article by J. N. Epstein in *Ṣiyunim*, 122f., showing that the collection of prayers was redacted by R. Zemah b. Solomon, who was *Av bet din* under Natronai and Amram, and soon thereafter received spurious insertions. [See now Goldschmidt, *ʿAmram*.]

16. Amram's usage becomes especially clear through comparison with *ʿItim* and *Vitry*. That the piyyutim in vol. 2 of the Warsaw edition do not belong to Amram needs no proof. The *seliḥot* for the ten days of repentance are now known from Marx, *Untersuchungen*, 28 and Frumkin, *Seder*, 2:308f.

17. See Steinschneider, *Catalogus*, 2203f. and the bibliography in Malter, *Saadia*, 147f., 239, 427.

18. Ginzberg, *Geonica*, 1:166f., and *Qoves teshuvot*, 1:32.

19. E.g., R. Hai, Ginzberg, *Geonica*, 1:175. On the "prayer books" of other sages, see Zunz, *Ritus*, 19. But wherever the medieval sources cite a סדר we may think that a prayer book is intended. When the book list in E.N. Adler, *JQR* 14 (1902): 57 mentions סדר ר׳ שלמה, it is not referring to the prayer book of Rashi and the like, but to a work by Ibn Gabirol; the first line quoted there is the beginning of his long *ʿavoda* published in Elbogen, *Studien*, 143 and *Hasofe* 5 (1921): 178. Similarly, the halakhic poem of R. Josef Tov ʿElem is often called סדר; cf., e.g., *Tosafot* to B. *Pes.* 115a, s.v. והדר.

20. Halakhot of Ibn Ghiyath, first discussed by Derenburg in Geiger's *Wissenschaftliche Zeitschrift* 5 (1844): 396f. and published by S. Bamberger in 1869 with the title *Shaʿare simha*.

21. Judah al-Barceloni, cf. *J.E.* 7:340f. and Albeck, "Meḥoqeqe yehuda," in the *Lewy Festschrift*, Hebrew sec., 104f.

22. Cf. *Gallia Judaica*, 414; *J.E.* 1:110f.

23. Cf. *Qoves teshuvot*, 1:319–31.

24. Cf. above, §41(9); on *Vitry* and Zunz, *Ritus*, 20. *Quntres hapiyutim* was published by Brody in 1894.

25. The term *minhag* in its new sense of "local rite": Zunz, *Ritus*, 38.

26. Ibid., 7f.

27. Ibid., 79f.

28. Ibid., 76f.

29. Ibid., 59f.

30. Ibid., 39f.

31. Ibid., 106f., 131, 139f.

32. Ibid., 89f.

33. Ibid., 91.

34. Ibid., 95, 97.

35. Zunz, *Literaturgeschichte*, 107, 110; Berliner, *Randbemerkungen*, 2:13f. The legend of R. Amnon in Landshuth, ʿAmude, 45f. and in the old editions of the Ashkenazic-Polish prayer book for the New Year. In light of its wide distribution and language, this poem seems to come from the very beginnings of the piyyut. Cf. J.E. 1:525f.

36. Zunz, *Ritus*, 88f., 92f., 104f.

37. Ibid., 45.

38. Ibid., 131f.; in Sepharad, ibid., 132.

39. Zunz, *Ritus*, 39f. The right of different rites to exist side by side is stressed, e.g., by R. Hai Gaon in *Temim deʿim*, no. 119, end ("[There are] several prayer rites that are all pleasing").

40. Zunz, *Ritus*, 21f. Compare the very interesting work of R. Menahem Hameiri (1249–1306), *Magen avot*, ed. I. Jost (London, 1909), which deals not only with prayer rites but also contains many interesting general observations on the rites. Hameiri's position is that every person should adhere to the rite of his own land, but no one should impose his rite on another (p. 6), especially in matters of liturgy and liturgical texts (p. 101).

41. On the Worms ritual books, cf. Epstein in *Kaufmann Memorial Volume*, 288f.

42. Cf. Kassel in *Zunz Festschrift*, 122ff.; *Gallia Judaica*, 283; J.E. 1, 116ff.

43. Cf. Vogelstein and Rieger, *Rom*, 1:382.

44. Zunz, *Ritus*, 31; *Gallia Judaica*, 290, 420; J.E. 1:12, 7:538, s.v. "Kolbo."

45. Zunz, *Ritus*, 30; J.E. 1:139. The first part of the book was recently reprinted with detailed notes by Ch. L. Ehrenreich (Cluj, 1927). In al-Naqawa, *Menorat hamaʾor*, ed. Enelow (New York, 1929–32), 2:449, the name is vocalized *Abidarham*.

46. *Gallia Judaica*, 240. The text, in *Bloch Festschrift*; corrections, ZHB 9 (1905): 143f.

47. Güdemann, *Hatora*, 3:4f.

48. J.E. 7:652; quoted from the introduction of *Maharil*.

49. The exaggerated view of the value of customary practice came crudely to the fore in the strife around the Hamburg Temple (below, §55[5]); the opinions contained in *Ele divre haberit* fall back repeatedly on the immutability of custom; cf. 1a, 3, 23. They also rely on the dictum cited by R. Abraham Gumbiner in *Magen avraham* to S.A., O.Ḥ., §68 from Y. ʿEruv., chap. 3, end: "Even though we have sent you the order of prayer, do not change the customary practice of your ancestors." This dictum refers to the fixing of the calendar, and has nothing to do with prayer. Gumbiner himself relies on R. Isaac Luria.

50. Many examples of the ruining of poems in Zunz, *Ritus*, 139f. Thanks to the *Oṣar* of Davidson it is now possible to see the original form of many of these piyyutim that have been cut to pieces.

51. See Berliner, *Buchdrucks*, 2.

52. Zunz, *Ritus*, 119f.

53. Ibid., 142. Additions to the prayers of others: ibid., 144.

54. Rosanes, *Tugarma*, 1: chap. 5.

55. Zunz, *Ritus*, 145f. and Berliner, *Buchdrucks*; cf. Berliner, *Randbemerkungen*, 1:8f.

56. Zunz, *Ritus*, 147. Quotations from 148f. Examples of censorship: 222f.; cf. A. Berliner, *Censur und Confiskation hebräischer Bücher im Kirchenstaate* (Berlin: H. Itzkowski, 1891).

57. Zunz, *Ritus*, 174f.; A. Berliner, *Abhandlung über den Siddur des Schabtai ha-Sofer* (1909).

§44 The Influence of Mysticism on the Synagogue Service

1. See J.E. 4:549f.; the definition according to Maimonides is also cited there; cf. also F. Perles, *Bousset's Religion des Judentums* (Berlin: W. Peiser, 1903), 101f.; Baḥya, *Ḥovot halevavot* 8:3: "Our purpose in prayer is ... the soul's longing for God."

2. Above, §35.

3. M. *Ber.* 5:1; B. *Ber.* 23b.

4. B. *Ber.* 26a.

5. Cf. P. Bloch, in *MGWJ* 37 (1893): 18f.; quotation: ibid., 22.

6. Ibid., 73.

7. Ibid., 258.

8. Ibid., 252f. [Today opinions differ both as to the period and significance of the *yorde merkava*. See especially G. Scholem, *Jewish Gnosticism, Merkabah Mysticism, and Talmudic Tradition* (New York, 1960); also Itamar Gruenwald, "Piyute yanai vesifrut yorde hamerkava," *Tarbiz* 36 (1966/7): 257f.] Since the appearance of the first edition of this book, the approach to mysticism has changed considerably. G. Scholem's *Bibliographia Kabbalistica* (Leipzig: W. Druglin, 1927) protests our criticism of mysticism in the text. This point requires clarification. Much as we may esteem mysticism and its value for piety and the life of prayer, we must never forget that mysticism is a matter for the individual, not the community. Prayer of a mystical, ecstatic type, pursued consistently, must eventually, as in Hasidism, lead to the breakdown of the public liturgy. The failure in the development in Jewish mysticism lies in the fact that its spirit, which is exclusively a matter for the individual, became a matter for the community and regulated, public worship. But due recognition is given throughout the book to the fact that from the mystics came a strong impulse to internalize the synagogue worship.

9. In Zunz, *Literaturgeschichte*, 105, he is called a fictitious character, but now more is known about him through the book of Ahimaaz of Oria (*Medieval Jewish Chronicles*, 2:112.); cf. D. Kaufmann, in *MGWJ* 40 (1896): 465f. [same as *Gesammelte Schriften* 3:5] and Mann, *Egypt*, 56.

10. *REJ* 23 (1801): 230f.; *MGWJ* 49 (1905): 692f., with a complete bibliography on the subject.

11. On Samuel the Pious, Epstein, in *Hagoren* 4 (1903): 81f. On Judah the Pious, Zunz, *Literaturgeschichte*, 218f.; Landshuth, ʿ*Amude*, 77f.; Güdemann, *Hatora*, 1:119f.

12. A consecutive section of dicta on devotion and prayer, see *Sefer ḥasidim*, §§393–588.

13. On the Song of Unity, see Berliner, *Einheitsgesang*.

14. *Tur, O.H.*, §116, end; cf. Perles in *Graetz Festschrift*, 17f.

15. See Zunz, *Literaturgeschichte*, 317f.; Landshuth, ʿ*Amude*, 24f.; Güdemann, *Hatora*, 1:36; *J.E.* 5:100f.

16. See *J.E.* 3:456f.; Zohar: ibid., 12:689f. From the Zohar comes the prayer "Blessed is the name" for the taking out of the Torah.

17. On the subject in general, see Schechter, *Studies*, 2: 202f.; P. Bloch, in *MGWJ* 49 (1905): 129f.

18. Schechter, *Studies*, 2:209f.

19. Ibid., 2:254f.

20. Ibid., 2:242.

21. Ibid., 2:271.

22. Ibid., 2:242f.

23. Ibid., 2:249.

24. Ibid., 2:251; cf. *REJ* 58–60 (1909–10); *REJ* 62 (1911): 74f., 85f.; Rosanes, *Tugarma*, 3:309f.

25. See Schechter, Studies, 2:266f.; Landshuth, ʿ*Amude*, 64; ibid., 122 on the piyyutim of Luria.

26. Zunz, *Ritus*, 149f.; the quotations there, 150. In Ashkenaz the influence of the Kabbalah can be demonstrated since the prayer book of Thiengen (1560); cf. Berliner, *Randbemerkungen*, 1:30f.

27. *J.E.* 5:341f.

28. An idea of the great number of *tikunim* can be had from Steinschneider, *Catalogus*, 455–77; Zedner, *Catalogue*, 447f.; von Straalen, *Catalogue of the Hebrew Books in the British Museum*, index, 519f., though the list is not complete.

29. *J.E.* 11:523, no. 24.

30. Ibid., 6:465f.; Landshuth, ʿ*Amude*, 133f.

31. *J.E.* 6:220.

32. Zunz, *Ritus*, 152f.; Berliner, *Randbemerkungen*, 1:30f.

33. Schechter, *Studies*, 1:1f.; *J.E.* 6:152f.

34. Schechter, *Studies*, 1:46.

35. The quotation is from the autobiography of Solomon Maimon, *Salomon Maimon Lebensgeschichte*, ed. Karl Phillipp Moritz (Berlin: F. Koenig, 1792), 1:222.

36. In the formal opinions in *Ele divre haberit* (below, §45[5]), one may observe at every step the traces of Luria's influence. Alterations in the prayers and German translation are rejected there because they frustrate the prayers' original purpose and their influence on the supernal worlds.—As late as 1927, J. Carlebach wrote in *Jeschurun* 14 (1927): 676: "The meaning, essence, and decisive forms of the prayers have been authoritatively fixed for all eternity by our sages."

§ 45   *The First Reforms in the Synagogue Service*

1. The approach of Bendavid and David Friedländer may serve as an example of the attitude of the enlightened to the synagogue service; cf. Bernfeld, *Toledot*, 13.

2. Zunz, *Ritus*, 175; Berliner, *Randbemerkungen*, 1:9, 38f.; Lewin, *Jeschurun* 10 (1923). On his life: *MGWJ* 44 (1900): 127f.; *MGWJ* 45 (1901): 422f.; *J.E.* 6:319.

3. See Eschelbacher, *MGWJ* 52 (1908): 385f.; *J.E.* 10:613.

4. *J.E.* 2:433f.

5. Zunz, *Ritus*, 154f.; Steinschneider, *Arabische Literatur*, xvii; this list could easily be expanded.

6. Zunz, *Haderashot*, 207; Zunz, *Ritus*, 170; Philipson, *Reform*, 14f.; *J.E.* 10:172.

7. Graetz, *Divre*, 9:53f.; Philipson, *Reform*, 1:xx; *J.E.* 1:542. The polemical writings are listed by de Silva Rosa in *ZHB* 15 (1911): 107f.

8. Albert Lemoine, *Napoléon I et les Juifs* (Paris, 1900), 281; cf. Robert Anchel, *Napoléon et les Juifs* (Paris, 1928).

9. Jost, *Kulturgeschichte*, 14f.; Philipson, *Reform*, 1:29f.; Graetz, *Divre*, 9:201f. (his judgment, as well known, is most unfair); Bernfeld, *Toledot*, cf. J. R. Marcus in *Year Book of the Central Conference of American Rabbis* 38 (1928).

10. On the reforms in the kingdom of Westphalia and the attitude of the Jews toward them, see Benjamin H. Auerbach, *Geschichte der Israelitischen Gemeinde Halberstadt* (Halberstadt: H. Meier, 1860), 216f.; cf. Zunz, *Haderashot*, 211.

11. See H. Baerwald and S. Adler, *Geschichte des Realschule der Israelitischen Gemeinde (Philanthropin) zu Frankfurt am Main 1804–1904; Beilage zum Programm der Schule Ostern* (1904), 50f.

12. Zunz, *Haderashot*, 210 and Zunz, *Schriften*, 2: 214f.; *J.E.* 4:219f. Called a spurious institution by Löw, *Lebensalter*, 218f., 412.

13. *J.E.* 4:524.

14. I. H. Ritter, *David Friedländer* (Berlin: W. J. Peiser, 1871) and *J.E.* 5:514f.

15. L. Geiger, *Geschichte der Juden in Berlin* (Berlin: J. Guttenberg, 1871), 2:210f.; Friedländer's opinions in Jost, *Kulturgeschichte*, 12.

16. On Jacobsohn's public services, see Jost, *Kulturgeschichte* and Zunz, *Liberales Judentum* 9 [1917]: 114f.; Zunz, *Haderashot*, 212f., both of whom participated in it. Zunz served for a time as its preacher.

17. On the prayer books and the details of the dispute, see Geiger, ibid., 2:219f. and the corrections in Bernfeld, *Toledot*, 63f., 241f.

18. Zunz, *Haderashot*, 212, which gives the date as March 3, 1824. On the great impression made by the movement on the public, see *Liberales Judentum* (cited in n. 16).

19. On the Hamburg Temple, see Jost, *Kulturgeschichte*, 20f.; "Theologische Gutachten," in *Festschrift zum hundertjährigen Bestehen des Tempels* (Hamburg, 1842), 4f.; Graetz, *Divre*, 9:274f.; on the prayer book that first appeared in August 1919, see Bernfeld, *Toledot*, 247f.

20. Geiger's critique in his pamphlet, *Der Hamburger Tempelstreit* (1842), 37f.

21. E.g., Mannheimer; see *Theologische Gutachten*, 96; Stein, ibid., 113; Frankel in *Orient* 7–9 (1842).

22. Thomas Macaulay, *Essay and Speech on Jewish Disabilities*, ed. Abrahams and Levy (Edinburgh, 1910), 31f.

23. E.g., Graetz, *Divre*, 9:276.

24. Such as L.J. Riesser, *Sendschreiben an meine Glaubensgenossen in Hamburg oder eine Abhandlung über den Israelitischen Cultus* (Alton, 1819).

25. Altona 1819, and cf. Löwenstamm, *Şeror hahayim* (Amsterdam, 1823); cf. Jost, *Kulturgeschichte*, 22f.; Graetz, *Divre*, 9:276f.; above on §43(6) and §44(9).

26. Cf. *Ele divre haberit*, 4f., 15, 19f., 30f. and Löwenstamm, ibid., 17f.

27. The opinions included in *Noga şedeq* were collected, as correctly observed by Jost, *Kulturgeschichte*, 24f.; Bernfeld, *Toledot*, 76f., before the Hamburg dispute in order to defend the new Berlin liturgy.

28. The satire by M.J. Bresselau entitled *Ḥerev noqemet neqam berit* was reprinted in Bernfeld, *Toledot*, 254f. Other polemics in Jost, *Kulturgeschichte*.

29. Eleazar Shemen Roqeaḥ of Triesch protests abuses in the synagogue liturgy in *Ele divre haberit*, 95; cf. Zunz, *Haderashot*, 220 and 547, nn. 106f.

30. Geiger, ibid., 63f.

31. Zunz and Moser in Strodtmann, *Heinrich Heines Leben und Werke* (Berlin: F. Druckner; New York: E. Steige, 1867–69), 1:283. Heine's repeated mockery of the Temple and its preachers is well known.

32. Bresselau; see *Theologische Gutachten*, 25.

33. Zunz, *Haderashot*, 212f.; Jost, *Kulturgeschichte*, 27, 66f.; *Liberales Judentum* 9 (1917): 114f.

34. See Philipson, *Reform*, 52, 105. According to Jost, *Kulturgeschichte*, 226, Hess protested the use of any compulsion. Even S. Stern came out against him: Stern, *Geschichte*, 256.

§ 46 The Reform Movement at Its Height

1. On the period between 1820 and 1830, see Phillippson, *Geschichte*, 1:83f.

2. The internal deterioration in Geiger, *Zeitschrift für wissenschaftliche Theologie* 1 (1858): 1f.; S.R. Hirsch, *Nineteen Letters*, trans. B. Drachman, letter 1.

3. On Hirsch, see the Jubilee issue of *Der Israelit* (1908); *J.E.* 6:417.

4. On Geiger, cf. *Abraham Geiger: Leben und Lebenswerk*, ed. Ludwig Geiger (Berlin, 1910).

5. See M. Phillippson, *Geschichte* (2nd ed.), 1:245f.; Sigismund Stern, *Geschichte des Judenthums von Mendelssohn bis auf die Gegenwart* (Frankfurt a. M., 1857), 198f.

6. On the second Hamburg Temple dispute, cf. *Theologische Gutachten*, discussed above, 45:5; Jost, *Kulturgeschichte*, 193f.; *Festschrift zum hunderjährigen Bestehen des Tempels*, 26.

7. See Graetz, *Divre*, 9:282f.; *J.E.* 3:90; that he was dragged into the dispute by pressure from his congregants, Bernfeld, *Toledot*, 137 n.

8. Quotation from Geiger, *Zeitschrift für wissenschaftliche Theologie* 1 (1858), 11.

9. Zunz, *Haderashot*, 219.

10. The press became important particularly thanks to Ludwig Philipson, who published the *Allgemeine Zeitung des Judentums* from 1837 on. Besides this newspaper there also appeared in the nineteenth century in German *Der Orient* and *Der Israelit*, and, from the orthodox side, *Der treue Zionwächter*.

11. Zunz, *Haderashot*, 211, 214 names several rabbis with academic education; the innovations implemented up to 1844 are summarized by Zunz, *Schriften*, 2:216.

12. Rabbinic assemblies: See Jost, *Kulturgeschichte*, 48, 86f., 143; Geiger, *Geiger*, 45f.; the assembly in Brunswick took place thanks to Philipson's initiative; see *Allgemeine Zeitung des Judentums* 7–8 (1843 and 1844).

13. Ibid., ibid.; also Salomon Rapoport, *Tokhaḥat megula: Sendschreiben eines Rabbiner's* (Frankfurt a. M., 1845).

14. See *Protokolle*. Sharp attacks were leveled at the reliability of these protocols; cf. Jost, *Kulturgeschichte*, 237f.; D. Philipson, *Reform*, 220f.

15. *Protokolle*, 41.

16. Ibid., 99f., 45f.

17. See *Protokolle und Aktenstücke*; Jost, *Kulturgeschichte*, 249f.; Philipson, *Reform*, 233–59.

18. See *Protokolle*, 285f.; debate over formalities: ibid., 14f.; the memorandum reflects mainly the program of the ecclesiastical counselor Maier of Stuttgart (*J.E.* 7:264); see *Protokolle*, 289f.

19. Particularly demanded by Frankel: *Protokolle und Aktenstücke*, 19f.; cf. Jost, *Kulturgeschichte*, 251f.

20. *Protokolle und Aktenstücke*, 30, 54, 59f.

21. *MGWJ* 45 (1901): 234; Stern, *Geschichte*, 278.

22. *Protokolle und Aktenstücke*, 314f. Vote on the matter: ibid., 72.

23. Ibid., 106.

24. Ibid., 107.

25. Ibid., 123f.

26. Ibid., 319f.; decision: Ibid. 127, 133.

27. Ibid., 135f.

28. Ibid., 145.

29. Ibid., 151.

30. See *Protokolle der dritten Versammlung deutscher Rabbiner*.

31. Ibid., 249f.

32. Ibid., 208f.

33. Ibid., 245f.

34. See, e.g., Holdheim, *Reformgemeinde*, 139f.; Jost, *Kulturgeschichte*, 250; Geiger, *Die dritte Versammlung deutscher Rabbiner*. On the critique from the orthodox side, see Philipson, *Reform* (5th ed.), 255f., 271[5].

35. See Holdheim, *Reformgemeinde*; Stern, *Geschichte*; Lewin, *Reform*; Philipson, *Reform*, 317f. On the Berlin community, see Honigmann's sketches in *Jahrbuch für jüdische Geschichte und Literatur* 7 (1904): 177 and A. H. Heymann, *Lebenserinnerungen nach seiner Niederschrift in Auftrage seiner Kinder*, ed. H. Loewe (Berlin: M. Poppelauer, 1909), 242f. (from a conservative perspective). On the congregation's first steps: Arthur Galliner, *Sigismund Stern der Reformator und der Paedagoge* (Frankfurt a. M.: Englert und Schlosser, 1930), 56f.

36. Quotation from the proclamation "To our German co-religionists" in Holdheim, *Reformgemeinde*, 49f.

37. Ibid., 123f.; Stern, *Geschichte*, 296f.

38. Holdheim, *Reformgemeinde*, 146f.

39. Ibid., 181.

40. Ibid., 193f. Holdheim's proposals: *Reformgemeinde*, 195f. The principles of his prayer book: ibid., 204f.

41. Lewin, *Reform*, 96; dealing also with the principles on which he reworked the prayer book.—A further revision of the prayer book was done in 1927.

42. See Heymann, ibid., 278.

43. See Z.H. Chajes, *Darkhe hahora'a* (Zolkiew, 1842), 9c.

44. Government support, e.g., in Stuttgart; *Gebetbuch für die häusliche und öffentliche Gottesverehrung* by Maier appeared in 1848. On the attitude of the Bavarian government to the Reform movement around 1850, see Winter, in *Jeschurun* 16 (1929): 144f.—In most congregations, synagogue constitutions were adopted around mid-century; it would be most desirable for them to be collected and compared. Some were listed by Zunz, *Schriften*, 219 and Löw, *Schriften*, 5:24.

45. Zunz, *Haderashot*, 29; much bibliography in Philipson, *Reform*, 258; J.E. 9:433.

46. A. Geiger, *Seder tefila devar yom beyomo* (Frankfurt a. M.: H.L. Brönner, 1891) (see Geiger, *Geiger*, 146f.) appeared only in 1854, for only at the end of 1853 did the community affairs of Breslau achieve legal regulation; see M. Brann, *Die schlesische Judenheit vor und nach dem Edikt von 1812* (Breslau: Th. Schatzky, 1913), 31. Other prayer books, like that of L. Philippson, were intended for private devotion.

47. Geiger's second prayer book: *Jüdische Zeitschrift* 7 (1869): 241f.

48. 1872; cf. the polemic in *Jüdische Zeitschrift* 7 (1869): 1f., 240; also Joel, *Zum Schutz gegen "Trutz"* (Breslau: H. Skutsch, 1869).

49. Cf. *Verhandlungen der ersten Israelitischen Synode zu Leipzig* (Berlin: L. Gerschel, 1869), 185 n.

50. H. Vogelstein, *Seder tefila: Israelitisches Gebetbuch für Schule und Haus*, 2 vols. (Bielefeld, 1895–96); see the collections of opinions pro and con.

51. Cf. *Denkschrift des Oberrats der Israeliten*, and against it, D. Hoffmann's *Ein Sendschreiben an den 'Verein zur Wahrung des gesetzestreuen Judentums in Baden'* (Rödelheim, n.d.) as well as the refutation of the latter by M. Steckelmacher. Throughout the disputes on the prayer book the dictum "Whoever changes the pattern cut by the sages for benedictions . . ." plays a large role. However, as S. Serillio has correctly noted in his commentary to Y. Ber. 6:2 (ed. Mainz, 1878, 72a), this dictum refers not to prayers in general but to the Enjoyment Benedictions.

52. *Tefilot lekhol hashana: Gebetbuch für das ganze Jahr 1–2* (Frankfurt am Main, 1929) was intended as a uniform Reform prayer book for all the German congregations. It was edited by the Liberal Ritual Committee of the Prussian State Union of Jewish Communities; cf. *Jüdisches Lexikon* 2, s.v. "Einheitsgebetbuch."

§ 47   *The Reform Movement Outside of Germany*

1. See Jost, *Kulturgeschichte*, 70–77; Löw, *Schriften*, 4:331f.; J.E. 5:501. Lately many places have gone beyond the reforms mentioned in the text.

2. Cf. Zunz, *Haderashot*, 216; Philipson, *Reform*, 122f., 537f.; J.E. 8:163, 333; M. Gaster, *The Ancient Synagogue of the Spanish and Portuguese Jews* (London, 1901), 176f.

3. See J.E. 7:663.

4. Zunz, *Haderashot*, 216; Philipson, *Reform*, 461f.; B.A. Elzas, *The Reformed Society of Israelites of Charleston* (New York, 1916).

5. Philipson, *Reform*, 468f.

6. J.E. 12:541f, s.v. "Samuel Hirsch"; ibid., 6:417; on Einhorn, see Kohler, *Year Book of the CCAR* 19 (1909): 215f.—Wise's ideas about reform in Philipson, *Reform*, 477f.—On Einhorn's prayer book, ibid., 252f. On the *Union Prayerbook*, ibid., 493f.; *Year Book of the CCAR* 22 (1912): 125f., 191f.; and ibid., 38 (1928). A revised edition appeared in 1922, and new revisions are now under discussion.

7. Cf. the collection of sermons by C.G. Montefiore, *Truth in Religion* (London: Macmillan and Co., 1906). The prayer book appeared in 1903, entitled *A Selection of Prayers, Psalms and Other Passages and Hymns for Use at the Services of the Jewish Religious Union*. Passages are freely chosen during services that are held on Sabbath afternoons and on festivals, and that include the Torah reading and a sermon. Out of this organization emerged the Liberal Jewish Synagogue, which published its own prayer book, partially based on the American model but at the same time independent of it, called *Liberal Jewish Prayer Book* 1 (1926): 2 (1923): 3 (1926); cf. the introduction by the editor, Israel I. Mattuck.

8. The prayer book of the *Union Libérale Israélite* in Paris, *Kenafayim la'ares: Des aisles à la terre* (2 vols.) includes many prayers in the vernacular, but the Hebrew text for the most part is retained intact. New editions of the Paris prayer book have appeared under the title *Tefilot kol hashana: Rituel des prières journalières* (with the haftarot for the entire year in French translation), 1 (1925, with long introduction by Louis Germain Lévy), 2, 3 (1928).

9. C. Seligmann, *Israelitisches Gebetbuch*, 2 vols. (Frankfurt, 1910) and *Denkschrift*, the memorandum devoted to it that appeared in 1912.

§ 48 *Synagogues*: Name, Age, Distribution, and Location

1. Krauss, *Synagogale*, 54f., 343.
2. For the reading in B. *Shab.*, see *Diqduqe soferim*, 2:64.
3. On the various Hebrew and Greek names, see the full references in Krauss.
4. *Esnoga*: the kabbalists said that this word is Hebrew in origin and is compounded from אש plus נגה, "fire" and "gleam"; cf. S.D. Luzzatto, *Vikuah ʿal hokhmat qadmut haqabala veʿal qadmut sefer hazohar veʿal qadmut hanequdot vehateʿamim* (Gorice, 1852), 115.
5. Cf. R. Payne-Smith, *Thesaurus Syriacus*, 2 vols. (Oxford: Clarendon Press, 1879–1901), col. 497.
6. Cf. Löw, *Schriften*, 5:22.
7. *REJ* 31 (1805): 53.
8. See Berliner, *Rom*, 2:8 against Güdemann, *Hatora*, 3:75.
9. Midrash quoted by R. David Kimhi in his commentary to Jer. 39:8.
10. B. *Meg.* 29a; Epistle of R. Sherira in *Medieval Jewish Chronicles*, 1:26; the spelling in one word— שפיתיב—in *Benjamin of Tudela*, 69; cf. Krauss, *Synagogale*, 214f. and Y.N. Epstein in *Festschrift Adolf Schwarz zum siebzigste Geburtstage*, ed. S. Krauss (Berlin: R. Lowit, 1917), 326.
11. *REJ* 45 (1902): 161f.; Krauss, *Synagogale*, 263.
12. See above, §34(4) ⌊p. 189⌋.
13. In Josephus, *Antiquities*, 14.7.2, §115.
14. On synagogues in the Diaspora, see Krauss, *Synagogale*, 199–267. On the tradition preserved in the Targumim, see Bacher, *Synagogue*; Hoffmann, *Synagogen*, 5f.
15. Harnack, *Mission und Ausbreitung des Christentums*, 2 vols. (Leipzig, 1924).
16. In the meanwhile many other ancient synagogues have come to light; cf. A. L. Sukenik in *Tarbiz* 1 (1929/30). Synagogues were still being erected in the Byzantine period, as shown by the plan, mosaic, and inscription of the synagogue of Beth Alpha; cf. *E.J.* 4:388 and *Tarbiz* 1 (1929/30): 111f.
17. On synagogues near water, see the list of sources and bibliography in Krauss, *Synagogale*, 281f. and Sukenik, op. cit. (in n. 16), 146, n. 2.
18. Krauss, *Synagogale*, 282.
19. In Alexandria, according to Philo, *Flacc.*, XIV, 22: Philo(a), 6:142; Philo(b), 9:268, they would pray "at times of trouble" beside the water, just as in Palestine the fast-day prayers were held in the city square.
20. Jacob b. Asher and Palaggi in Löw, *Schriften*, 4:26. In the Letter of Aristeas, §305, to which reference is often made, it says only that the translators bathed every morning and then prayed, but it does not say whether they prayed together or where.
21. See Juster, *Juifs*, 1:458.
22. See Epstein in W. Markon, *Misifrutenu haʿatiqa* (Vilna, 1910), 48; but against them the explicit language employed by the tradition must be noted. The midrash " 'a well in the field': this refers to a synagogue" (*Gen. r.*, 70:8) adduced by Löw, *Schriften*, 4:15 and Hoffmann, *Synagogen*, 23 proves nothing, for the attention there is on the word "well" rather than "field."
23. There were also exceptions, like Mahoza, B. *Meg.* 26b, where the synagogue was in the middle of the town.
24. On the inclusion of synagogues in pictures of German cities, cf. Pinthus, in *ZGJD* 2 (1930): 283f.
25. B. ʿ*A.Z.* 43b; since Rav, Samuel, and Levi are mentioned there, it follows that the period spoken of is before the persecution by the Magians (against Hoffmann, *Synagogen*, 23).
26. See E. Renan, *Mission de Phénicie* (Paris, 1864), 774.
27. See *J.E.* 4:36f.; *JQR* NS 11 (1899): 127f.
28. See the Theodosian Code 16:8, 9, 12, 20, 21, 25–27; Juster, *Juifs*, 1:458f.
29. See Juster, *Juifs*, 462; *REJ* 44 (1902): 27.
30. See Juster I, 251, 472. *REJ* (1902), 27.
31. See *J.E.* 12:180. A detailed description of the synagogue in Toledo in *REJ* 84 (1927): 15f. The synagogue in Saragossa in *MGWJ* 69 (1925): 58.
32. Cf. Krautheimer, *Mittelalterliche*, 179 on Regensburg; on Passau, *ZGJD* 1 (1929): 135.
33. According to B. *Ket.* 105a there were 394 synagogues in Jerusalem; according to Y. *Meg.* 3:1, 73d there were 480. In Y. *Ket.* 13:1, 35c the reading is instead 460.
34. B. *Ber.* 8a.
35. Philo, *Legat.* XX, 134: Philo(b), 10:66–67.

36. See Krauss, *Synagogale*, 250f.

37. On October 20, 415, Theodosian Code 16:8, 22. For the interpretation, see the explanation of Täubler in Dubnow, *Weltgeschichte des jüdischen Volkes* (Berlin: Jüdischer Verlag, 1925–30), 571 [not in the Hebrew edition—*Hebrew trans.*].

38. See Scherer, *Rechtsverhältnisse der Juden in der deutsch-österreichischen Ländern* (Leipzig: Druckner and Humboldt, 1901), 45.

39. *J.E.* 9:396f.

40. M. *Meg.* 3:1–3 and the Talmud ad loc. According to Sukenik, the sacral character of the Beth Alpha synagogue is obvious; cf. *Tarbiz* 1 (1929/30): 111f.

41. T. *Meg.* 3:7.

42. Y. *Bik.* 3:3, 65d; Y. *Naz.* 7:1, 56a.

43. Bibliography in Krauss, *Synagogale*, 239f. His interpretation is correct.

44. Synagogue as community house: ibid., 182f.—One of the enactments of R. Gershom is directed against the interruption of the service; cf. Rosenthal in the *Hildesheimer Festschrift*, 49f.

45. On medieval synagogues, cf. Abrahams, *Jewish Life*, 7f.

§ 49 *Synagogue Construction*

1. See Krauss, *Synagogale*, 286f.

2. Ibid., 317f.; *Tarbiz* 1 (1929/30): 147f., n. 2.

3. For the text of B. *Ber.* 30a, cf. *Sifre Deut.*, 29; *Midrash tannaim*, 19.

4. Cf. H. Kohl and C. Watzinger, *Antike Synagogen in Galiläa* (Leipzig: Hinrichs, 1916); Krauss, *Synagogale*, 327; Masterman, *Studies in Galilee* (Chicago: The University of Chicago Press, 1909), 1:109f.—A. L. Sukenik is now preparing a monograph on synagogue ruins in Palestine in which he goes into all the questions of detail; cf. also Krautheimer, *Mittelalterliche*, 45f.; Ernst Cohn-Wiener, *Die jüdische Kunst* (Berlin: M. Wasservogel, 1929), 80f.—The quotation about Capernaum is quoted from *Mitteilungen der deutschen Orient-Gesellschaft*, no. 29 (1905): 14f.—The synagogue of Capernaum is in the process of being reconstructed out of its ruins (1931).

5. David Kaufmann recognized the Jewish character of these ruins; cf. *REJ* 13 (1886): 46f., where there is also a picture of the mosaic. The description follows that of Monceaux in *REJ* 44 (1902): 11f.; see Krauss, *Synagogale*, 266.

6. Cf. Y. *Suk.* 5:1, 55a; B. *Suk.* 51b.

7. Philo, *Flacc.*, VII: Philo(a), 6:129; Philo(b), 9:326.

8. *REJ* 12 (1886): 236f.; Krauss, *Synagogale*, 350.

9. Y. *Meg.* 3:4, 74a.

9*. *REJ* 34 (1897): 148; Krauss, *Synagogale*, 350.

10. *Tanhuma, Behuqotai*, 4 (3:55b); in my opinion these words are spurious.

11. E.g., in Sens, Abrahams, *Jewish Life*, 27.

12. Löw, *Schriften*, 4:27f.

12*. Kohl, *Galiläa*, 139.

13. B. *B.B.* 25a and *Tosafot*, s.v. לכל; Löw, *Schriften*, 4:39f.

14. See Rietschel, *Liturgik*, 1:88–124.

15. According to Bacher, *Synagogue*, 639, the rule that the doors must face east applies only to Babylonia, since Palestine lies to the west, but this seems unlikely. I also cannot accept his interpretation of Krauss, *Synagogale*, 323f. that T. *Meg.* 4:21–22 refers only to the opening of the synagogue and to the seating order at the fast-day ceremonies, which always occurred in the square before the synagogue. That is not the meaning of רחובה של עיר, nor do the data in the sources fit this explanation.

16. Stressed in Masterman, *Galilee*, 111, 119.

17. See *Mitteilungen der deutschen Orient-Gesellschaft*, no. 29 (1905), 25.

18. Ibid., 23.

19. *M.T.*, "Laws of Prayer," 11:2.

20. Cf. *Tosafot*, B. *Ber.* 6a, s.v. אחורי and Hagahot Maimoniyot, ibid.; *Tur, O.H.* §150.

21. *S.A., O.H.*, §150:5; Mordecai Jaffe, *Levush hatekhelet*, 94b; cf. Hatam Sofer, *Responsa*, no. 27 (Vienna, 1871), 1; Löw, *Schriften*, 4:50f.

22. Three entrances are found in ed-Dikki (Kohl, *Galiläa*, 113), Capernaum (ibid., 10), Meron (ibid., 82), and Kefar Baram (ibid., 93); cf. also Krauss, *Synagogale*, 358.

23. *Lev. r.* 22:4: תרעי מציעיא.

24. Side doors are found in Umm al-Qanāṭir, Capernaum, and Nebratein; Kohl and Watzinger, *Galiläa*, 126, 10, 103.

25. Kohl and Watzinger, *Galiläa*, 64. On the subject, cf. Löw, *Schriften*, 4:33; Elbogen, *Studien*, 34. Krauss, *Synagogale*, 372, disagrees.

26. Many synagogues having the entrance one or several steps down exist to this day—e.g., the old synagogue in Berlin; this is especially noticeable in the Altneuschul in Prague.

27. A bad floor of paving-stones in ed-Dikki and al-Qanatir (ibid., 120, 131); limestone paving-stones in Capernaum (ibid., 20); limestone mosaic in Umm el-ʿAmed (ibid., 74).

28. A very interesting mosaic showing human heads and even God's hand preventing Abraham from sacrificing Isaac, etc., is found in Beth Alpha; cf. the literature cited in §48:2.

29. See *Tosafot*, B. *Meg.* 22b, s.v. ואי בעית.

30. S.A., O.H., §131:8; cf. Lewysohn, *Meqore*, 84, §56. Cf. also Krauss, *Synagogale*, 347. The floor of the synagogue in Cochin is paved with porcelain tiles; cf. *Semitic Studies in Memory of Rev. Dr. Alexander Kohut*, ed. George A. Kohut (Berlin: S. Calvery, 1897), 416.

31. Kohl, *Galiläa*, 178; Krauss, *Synagogale*, 334f. According to Sukenik, *Tarbiz* 1 (1929/30): 148, n. 2, the basilica form is rare before the destruction of the Temple, and became widespread only thereafter.

32. Kohl, *Galiläa*, 179, in ed-Dikka, Qanatir (*Mitteilungen der deutschen Orient-Gesellschaft*, no. 29 [1905], 6f.), Miron, and Nebratain (ibid., 23, 26). Three halls in Barʿam and al-Jish (ibid., 30f.), surrounded by a colonnade in Umm el-ʿAmed (ibid., 1), Arbel, and Capernaum (ibid., 13f.).

33. See Krauss, *Synagogale*, 341.

34. Ibid., 354; Masterson, *Galilee*, 116.

35. On the style of construction of medieval synagogues, see *J.E.* 11:626; modern period, ibid., 11:631; a detailed discussion of both subjects with explanatory illustrations by Frauberger, *Mitteilungen*, vols. 1 and 2. On the construction style of medieval German synagogues, cf. the detailed data in Krautheimer, *Mittelalterliche*, and the review by Grotte, in *MGWJ* 72 (1928): 442f.

36. See Epstein, in *MGWJ* 40 (1896): 556f.

37. Ibid. 41 (1897): 29f.

38. Cf. Frauberger, *Mitteilungen*, 2:42.

39. *J.E.* 11:625f.

40. Cf. the bibliography in *J.E.* 11:262; "Zur Geschichte der Kunst in der Synagoge" in Kaufmann, *Schriften*, 1:97f.; Frauberger, *Mitteilungen*, 2:15f.; A. Grotte, *Beiträge zur Entwicklung des Synagogenbaues in Deutschland, Böhmen und im ehemaligen Königtum Polen* (Berlin: Der Zirkel, 1915). On synagogues in Poland, cf. M. Balaban, *Zabytki Histor. Zydow w Polsce* (1929); noteworthy are his remarks on synagogues in fortress form.

41. See Löw, *Schriften*, 4:34f.; Krauss, *Synagogale*, 357.

42. Zohar, *Pequde*, 251a; S.A., O.H., §90:4.

43. Epiphanius, *Haer.* 80:1.

44. *Responsa* of Maimonides (Leipzig, 1858/9), 1:139 [ed. Blau II, 380]. For the text, see Simonsen in *Festschrift zum siebzigsten Geburgstage Jacob Guttmann's* (Leipzig: G. Fock, 1915), 273f.

45. Löw, *Schriften*, 34.

46. See *Kaufmann Memorial Volume*, 129ff. and Jacob Guttmann, *Festschrift*, pp. 273ff.

47. Löw, *Schriften*, 4:5.

48. Cf. Kohl, *Galiläa*, 184f.—Masterman, *Galilee*, 121.

49. Cf. "Zur Geschichte der Kunst in der Synagoge" in Kaufmann, *Schriften*, 1:87f.

50. Cf. *A Szegedi Uj Zsinagóga* (1903), with many pictures. True artistry in both construction and furnishings can be seen in the synagogue of Essen on the Ruhr (opened in 1913) and Augsburg (opened in 1917).

51. See Löw, *Schriften*, 4:55f.; Hoffmann, *Synagogen*, 31; Krauss, *Synagogale*, 356.

52. Cf. A. Büchler, in *JQR* 10 (1898): 678.

53. E.g., B. *Ber.* 17a; B. *Sota* 22b; B. *A.Z.* 38b.

54. See Schürer, *History*, 3:857; *J.E.* 12:138f.

55. These measures are adopted for festivals when the synagogues are crowded.

56. Achelis, *Theologie*, 1:198.

57. In the Galilee there are two stories in Umm el-ʿAmed and Arbel (*Mitteilungen der deutschen Orient-Gesellschaft*, no. 29 [1905], 11), Capernaum (ibid., 15), Meron, and Nebratein (ibid., 25f.). Scholars are more and more inclined to assume that the synagogue ruins in the Galilee had women's sections. For medieval synagogues, cf. Krautheimer, *Mittelalterliche*, 138f.

58. R. Israel Isserlein, *Pesaqim*, no. 132.

59. Quoted in *Mordekhai, Shabbat*, §311.

60. See the sources above in this section, n. 36.

61. *J.E.* 10:158.

62. See Löw, *Schriften*, 4:72f.

62*. In the building of Longhena, Frauberger, *Mitteilungen*, 2:37.

63. Löw, *Schriften*, 4:72f.

64. D. Philipson, *Reform*, 468f.

65. Masterman, *Galilee*, 112, 120f.

66. See the material in Schürer, *History*, 2:443, n. 69; *Synagogale*, 336.

67. אכסדרא is equivalent to ἐξέδρα, the translation of the Hebrew לשכה.

68. Löw, *Schriften*, 5:21.

69. Philo, *Legat.*, XX, 133: Philo(b), 10:66–67. Cf. Schürer, *History*, 3:104.

70. See the explanation of Fleischer in Levy, *Wörterbuch*, 1:438.—Water installation in the Theodotius synagogue in Jerusalem, *REJ* 71 (1920): 30f.

71. In Schürer, *History*, 3:56.

72. Christian basilica in Rietschel, *Liturgik*, 1:81f. This is the simplest answer to his question (ibid., 85), "Where did the Christians get the style of the basilica?" Cf. Kohl, *Galiläa*, 227; Krauss, *Synagogale*, 337, n. 3.

§50   The Furnishing of the Synagogue

1. Cf. also Schürer, *History*, 2:446.

2. The ark was set up in its place only for the duration of the service; hence, T. *Meg.* 4:21: "And when they set the ark down"; "behind the curtain" (Y. *Yoma* 7:1, 44b).

3. Cf. Frauberger, *Mitteilungen*, 6, 11; Masterman, *Galilee*, 114 claims that he found a sanctuarium in Khorazin. See also Krauss, *Synagogale*, 329.

4. Book-scrolls were placed on the ark when being read, otherwise inside the ark, as noted above; thus there is no room for Krauss's objection, *Synagogale*, 373.

5. So already B. *Soṭa* 39b ("to strip the ark").

6. Bacher, *Synagogue*, explains קודש as an abbreviation for בית מקדש, which I regard as impossible. See above on §49:5 [n. 15].

7. Rietschel, *Liturgik*, 1:83.

8. Opposition to the use of the word ארון is due to the word's ordinary meaning being "coffin"; cf. Bacher, *Synagogue*.—The Italian word *timisia* mentioned by Krauss, *Synagogale*, 28 and 369, should be deleted; as proved by Zoller in *Freie jüdische Lehrerstimme* 1 (1912): 180, this word is a distorted form of *chinisia*, "church."—According to Krautheimer, *Mittelalterliche*, 92f., the bema held the central position in the medieval synagogue, not the ark; this changed only in the sixteenth century. I think that Krautheimer does not distinguish sufficiently between the various possibilities of combination (in the Orient) and separation (Occident) of the bema and precentor's pulpit.

9. O.Z., 2:79d.

10. On the location of the ark, see Löw, *Schriften*, 4:54f; L. Della Torre, *Scritti sparsi* (Padua, 1908), 1:162f. Maimonides actually calls it *qibla*, *JQR* NS 5 (1914/15): 15.

11. See Levy, *Wörterbuch*, 2:318. It cannot be definitely said whether כילה is identical with פריסא (B. *Meg.* 26b); Rashi and Tosafot disagree on the interpretation of the word, ibid.

12. *JQR* NS 14 (1900): 737f. Schürer, *History*, 2:445; N. Müller, *Die jüdische Katakombe am Monteverde zu Rom* (Leipzig: O. Harrasowitz, 1919), 78f; *J.E.* 2:107f.

13. For the Ten Commandments over the ark, see Abrahams in *Kohler Festschrift*, 51f. In churches in central Germany, they can be found ca. 1200; cf. M.F. Hasak, *Geschichte der deutschen Bildhauerkunst im XIII Jahrhundert* (Berlin: G. Warsmuth, 1899).

14. Löw, *Schriften*, 5:25; cf. Frauberger, *Mitteilungen*, 3–4:13f.

15. Y. *Meg.* 3:1, 74d.

16. M. *Meg.* 3:1; *Kel.* 9:3, etc. T. *Yad.* 2:12; see Bacher, *Synagogue*. It is not identical with κάλυμμα mentioned in Corinthians 3:14, as claimed by Deissmann, *Paulus: eine kultur- und religionsgeschichtliche Skizze* (Tübingham: J.C.B. Mohr, 1911), 64.

17. Bacher, ibid.; Krauss, *Synagogale*, 382.

18. Colored cloths, or more exactly, cloths embroidered with pictures (Krauss, ibid.), M. *Kel.* 28:4. זגין, T. *Kel. B.M.* 1:13; B. *Shab.* 58b.

19. *Manhig*, "Laws of Sukka," §59; cf. *Shaʿare teshuva*, no. 314; Ibn Ghiyath, *Shaʿare simha*, לולב, end.

20. Löw, *Schriften*, 5:25, with extensive bibliography; Frauberger, *Mitteilungen*, 3–4:19f. with many pictures.

21. See Löw, ibid.; Krauss, *Synagogale*, 384f.

22. M.T., "Laws of Prayer," 11:3.

23. E.g., *Vitry*, 71.

24. E.g., *'Itim*, describing the reading of the Torah.

25. *J.E.* 4:36; Krauss, *Synagogale*, 386; In *O.Z.*, 2:79d, §386, קטידרא means "a large chair." A throne of Moses is found also in synagogue ruins in Delos and Galilee; cf. the pictures in Sukenik, *Tarbiz* 1 (1929/30): 145f.

26. Berliner, *Leben*, 116.

27. Ibid.; *J.E.* 1:430.

28. כסא, e.g. in *'Itim*, but תיבה in *Manhig*, "Laws of Sabbath," §24.

29. On the different meanings of תיבה, see *Tur, O.H.*, §150 and the commentaries thereon.

30. Separate bema and precentor's pulpit, as was the former custom in Germany; together, as in the Portuguese communities.

31. Cf. *Bet yosef* to *S.A., O.H.*, §150; Isserles to *S.A., O.H.*, §150:5.

32. E.g., in Syracuse, *Corp. Inscr. Graec.* 9895; Levy, *Jahrbuch für Geschichte der Juden* 2 (1861): 273; cf. the city Sida, ibid., 272 and Schürer, *History*, 3:33.

33. See Löw, *Schriften*, 4:93f.; *J.E.* 1:431.

34. *Y. Meg.* 3:1, 73d.

35. *B. B.B.* 8b; R. Gershom, ad loc. explains this as mats spread along the synagogue walls.

36. Benches for sitting in the ruins in el-Dikka in the Galilee (Kohl, *Galiläa*, 119).—Two rows of benches in Capernaum ending with armrests (ibid., 21).

37. E.g., in Phocaea, *REJ* 12 (1886): 236f.; Schürer, *History*, 3:19.

38. Rietschel, *Liturgik*, 1:84.

39. Also the plural קתדראות: *T. Suk.* 4:6 and parallels. Because the words הספסל והקתידרא occur together in *Y. Shab.* 3:3, 6a, Bacher, *Synagogue*, 639 concluded that the unintelligible קלטירא in *Y. Meg.* 3:1, 73d should read קתידרא. The word had been formerly interpreted as lectica (?). According to Löw, *Schriften*, 5:26 (Krauss, *Lehnwörter*, 2:545a), it should be explained as κλιντήρ. P. Perles wants to read קלפטירא as κραββατάριον (Krauss, *Archäologie*, 1:66); see *OLZ* 18 (1915): 149; Asheri to *M. Meg.* 4 and *O.Z.*, ibid. . read פלטירא.

40. *O.Z.*, 2:11b, §48; cf. Löw, *Schriften*, 5:25f.

41. *T. Suk.* 4:6.

42. See Müller, *Teshuvot ge'one mizrah uma'arav*, no. 106 (Berlin, 1888) and *Ture zahav* to *S.A., O.H.*, §150 end. Sale of places: see Löw, *Schriften*, 5:33. Reading desks: ibid., 26.

43. See Krauss, *Synagogale*, 390; Berliner, *Leben*, 116 and *Zur Beleuchtung in der Synagoge* in the monthly *Jüdische Presse* (1895): p. 5.

44. *Responsa* of Maharam, ed. Budapest, no. 153c.

45. See Frauberger, *Mitteilungen*, 3:37; other devices for illumination: ibid., 39.

§51 Congregation and Synagogue

1. Cf. Krauss, *He'atid* 3 (1910/11): 17.

2. *M. Meg.* 1:3 and its explanation, *Y.* 1:6, 70b; cf. Schürer, *History*, 2:439, n. 57. According to Krauss, *Synagogale*, 103, it does not mean ten unemployed men, but the members of the council who sit in assembly and make themselves available for the service, which was held in the same place. But his source is a very doubtful medieval quotation from the Talmud.

3. *T. B.M.* 11:23. Maimonides, *M.T.*, "Laws of Prayer," 11:1; *S.A., O.H.*, §150:1.

4. *Y. Meg.* 3:1, 73d; cf. *M. Ned.* 9:2.

5. *T. Meg.* 3:5; *Y.* 3:2, 74a; *B. 'Arak.* 16b.

6. See Schürer, *History*, 3:30.

7. Like lamps or beams: *T. Meg.* 3:3,5.

8. E.g., in Aegina in Levy, ibid.; likewise Smyrna, Levy, ibid.

9. *REJ* 7 (1883): 161f.; likewise, see *T. Meg.* 3:3; *Y. Meg.* 3:2, 74a.

10. Cf. Krauss, *Synagogenruinen*.

11. The practice is not uniform everywhere. In some places they wait until the children are able to go themselves; pictures in Frauberger, *Mitteilungen*, 3:21. R. Israel Bruna (ca. 1460) speaks of a Christian donating a wimple (*Responsa*, no. 276). Dedications in antiquity: *T. Meg.* 3:2.

12. See *M. Meg.* 3:1.

13. *M. Meg.* 3:2, 3.

14. *T. Meg.* 3:6; *Y.* 3:1, 73d; *B.* 26a.

15. *B.* 26a.

16. *O.Z.*, in Asheri to M. *Meg.* 4:1; cf. Löw, *Schriften*, 5:22.

17. See Y. *Meg.* 3:1, 73d; B. 26b, 28b.

18. T. *Meg.* 3:6; B. *Meg.* 26a has instead טורסיים. According to Krauss, *Archäologie*, 2:265 the sources do not contradict each other, for the Alexandrians are called Tarsians because they were so widely occupied in manufacturing Tarsian garments.

19. Y. *Yoma* 7:1, etc.

20. B. *Meg.* 26b; it is not likely that there were Romans there, nor can the reading דרומאי be accepted, which would point to the presence of Jews from southern Palestine. Rather it seems that the reference is to Jews from the city Rumai in southern Babylonia (communication from Professor Jacob Obermeyer).

21. See Müller, *Katakombe*, 109.

22. The Vernaclesians are, according to the correct interpretation of Bormann (*Wiener Studien: Zeitschrift für Klassische Philologie und Patristik* 34 [1912]: 36³f.) Jewish slaves to the emperor born in the palace. Cf. also Krauss, *Synagogale*, 253.

23. See Schürer, *History*, 3:41, 35.

24. Ibid., 3:4, 35.

25. In *Benjamin of Tudela*, 98.

26. Berliner, *Rom*, vol. 2.

27. See Rosanes, *Tugarma* 1: chap. 5.

28. See Brann in *Graetz Festschrift*, 223.

29. See Müller, *Katakombe*, 108; Schürer, *History*, 97–98; linen merchants: see Schürer, *History*, 3:35. See above on §36, n. 19.

30. See Krauss, *Synagogale*, 182f.; Berliner, *Leben*, 114f.

31. Y. *Naz.* 7:1, 56a (for another approach, see Krauss, *Synagogale*, 210f.).

32. Schürer, *History*, 3:97–98.

33. See Masterman, *Galilee*, 121; Kohl, *Galiläa*, 103, 191.

34. See Müller, *Katakombe*, 107.

35. See Epstein, in *MGWJ* 34 (1885): 338f.; *Chwolson Festschrift*, 49.

36. So, according to Müller's correct reading.

37. Ibid.

38. See *J.E.* 11:625f.

39. E.g. in Worms; כנישתא עתיקא already in *Lev. r.* 22:4.

40. Schürer, *History*, 3:97.

§52   The Officials of the Community

1. T. *Meg.* 3:1. Probably the "scholars appointed as *parnasim* over the community" (B. *Git.* 60a) are the same as the "seven goodmen of the city" (B. *Meg.* 26a), but different from the "heads of the assemblies" (B. *Git.*, ibid.).

2. Schürer, *History*, 3:97, 2:434f.; Juster, *Juifs*, 1:440f.

3. Cf. Schürer, *History*; *J.E.* ibid. The different forms of the name in Schürer, *History*, 3:100, n. 48 and Müller, *Katakombe*, 115. It should be noted that the two inscriptions of Monteverde have inexact spellings: ἀρχισύνγωγος and ἀρχισυναγωγής.

4. *Lev. r.* 23:4.

5. M. *Yoma* 7:1; *Sota* 7:7.

6. Acts 13:15.

7. Cf. Theodoros the Archisynagogos in Aegina in Levy, *Jahrbuch für die Geschichte der Juden* 2 (1861): 272.

8. So Vogelstein and Rieger, *Rom*, 1:45 and Krauss, *Synagogale*, 119f.

9. Probably the baraita in B. *Pes.* 49a is to be preferred to the amoraic discussion B. *Git.* 60a, which goes into casuistic distinctions resulting from the influence of the baraita B. *Hor.* 13b; but the latter baraita refers to the Temple, and we may not apply it to the synagogue, as does Berliner, *Rom*, 1:68.

10. Y. *Ber.* 3:1, 6b.

11. *Theodosian Code* 16:8, 74.

12. Mark 5:22; Acts 13:15; and the inscription of Akmonia, Schürer, *History*, 3:30.

13. See Schürer, *History*, 3:100, n. 45.

14. See Chrysostom in Schürer, *History*, 3:99; according to the inscription in Berenice in Cyrenaica (Schürer, *History*, 3:94f.), the voting (ברר) would have taken place at the festival of Tabernacles. The practice of electing congregational officials just after Tabernacles may be followed up to modern times.

15. The examples are in Schürer, *History*, 3:99; Müller, *Inschriften*, 4.

16. See Ascoli, *Inscrizioni inedite o malnote greche, latine, ebraiche di antichi sepoleri giudaica de Napolitano* (Torino and Rome: E. Loescher, 1880), 49; Krauss, *Synagogale*, 118f.

17. Schürer, *History*, 2:435; Myndos: *REJ* 42 (1901): 1f. Smyrna: *REJ* 7 (1883): 161f.

18. Lampridius, *Vita Severi*, 28.

19. See Krauss, *Synagogale*, 143f.; see also Schürer, *History*, 3:98f., who believes this title to be later. On the other hand, we must bear in mind that "elders" appears very early and the identity of the two can still be seen in the equating of πρεσβύτεροι and ἀρχιφερηκῖται (ריש פירקא) in Novella 146 of Justinian.

20. προστάτης also in an inscription from Xenephyros in Lower Egypt. *REJ* 65 (1913): 137.—*Pater* and *mater synagogae* in Krauss, *Synagogale*, 166.

21. Ibid.

22. Cf. in Abrahams, *Jewish Life*, 53; Güdemann, *Hatora*, 3:73; Epstein in *Kaufmann Memorial Volume*, 308.

23. Freedom from taxation was accorded, e.g., to Moses Mendelssohn; see *MGWJ* 31 (1882): 28; ibid., 30f. also on community offices.

24. Cf. Schürer, *History*, 2:438; the meaning of νακόρος there is obscure, despite Krauss, *Synagogale*, 128.

25. See Schürer, *History*, 3:100, n. 49.

26. Y. *Ber.* 3:1, 6b. Bacher, *Synagogue*, 640 deduces from the baraita B. *Meg.* 25b that the precentor used to read the Torah; but according to the correct text in T. *Meg.*, end, R. Hanina read himself.

27. Cf. *Lewy Festschrift*, 176f.; Bacher, *Synagogue*, 640. The word comes from the Assyrian *hazzānu*, "supervisor."

28. See Bacher, in *Magazin für die Wissenschaft des Judentums* (Berliner) 17 (1890): 169; 18 (1891): 50.

29. See Juster, *Juifs*, 1:447 and Krauss, *Synagogale*, 149f. No one has noticed that the Septuagint translates the word שוטר nearly always as γραμματεύς. סופר and חזן are not yet identical in the baraita in B. *Sota* 49a, bottom.

30. See Abrahams, *Jewish Life*, 55f. For the standing and respect enjoyed by Juspas in Worms, see Epstein in *Kaufmann Memorial Volume*, 303f.

31. *Schulklopfer* (in the eighteenth century also *Umklöpper*): see Löw, *Schriften*, 5:33; Abrahams, *Jewish Life*, 9; Berliner, *Leben*, 114.

32. Krauss, *Synagogale*, 181f.

33. B. *Pes.* 50b.

34. See ʿ*Arukh*, s.v. חזן; Löw, *Schriften*, 5:31f.

35. *Pesiqta rabati*, 127a (to Prov. 3:9).

36. *J.E.* 6:284f. A. Berliner, "Entstehung des Vorbeterdienstes," in *Israelitischer Lehrer und Kantor* (supplement to *Jüdische Presse*) (1899), 4f.; Krauss, *Synagogale*, 131f. Expertise in the prayers, see B. *Ta.* 16a.

37. Cf. *Teshuvot hageʾonim*, no. 84; same as *Shaʿare teshuva*, no. 90; *O.Z.*, 2:116.

38. *Shaʿare teshuva*, no. 50, 51; Meiri, *Magen avot*, 27f., etc.; cf. also Berliner, *Vorbeterdienstes*, 30f.; *J.E.* 6:286. Extreme contempt is expressed by Joseph Zabara, *Sefer hashaʿashuim*, ed. Davidson, 48.

39. Cf. Saadia, ibid.; Moses Minz in Güdemann, *Hatora*, 77, and frequently in *Sefer hasidim*.

40. Zunz, *Haderashot*, 220f.

41. Güdemann, *Hatora*, 76f.; Zunz, *Schriften*, 2:206, 208 sees only the cantor and the religious teacher as vital officials of the Jewish community, not the rabbi.

§53 The Precentor and the Community

1. The correct meaning in Schürer, *History*, 2:429, n. 12.

2. *J.E.* 8:603; Krauss, *Synagogale*, 98f.

3. *Soferim* 10:8; cf. *Tosafot*, *Meg.* 23b, s.v. ואין; Asheri, ad loc.; Müller, *Soferim*, 151.

4. According to R. Hananel in *Tosafot*, *Git.* 59b, s.v. אבל, in his time as many people would attend synagogue services on Mondays and Thursdays as on festivals. Slightly later it was said in praise of R. Abraham b. Yom Ṭov, who died as a martyr in Trier in the persecutions of 1096, that "he would go early and stay late in the synagogue" (*Quellen der Geschichte der Juden in Deutschland*, ed. A. Neubauer [Berlin: L. Simon, 1892], 27). Also Rashi to *Meg.* 5b assumes that people were paid in order to make themselves available for public prayer; Meir of Rothenburg reflects a more satisfactory situation, *Responsa*, ed. Budapest, no. 107; Löw, *Schriften*, 5:27.

5. *Hagahot maimoniyot* to M.T., "Laws of Prayer," 11.

6. [See *Midrash shoher tov*, 209, §25:5.] The quotation is from the prayer "Be with the mouths" of the Additional Service of the Day of Atonement.

7. See Blau, in *REJ* 31 (1895): 189; Elbogen, *Studien*, 8f.

8. Cf. Leitner, *Der gottesdienstliche Vortrag*, 1906.

9. Cf. the above-mentioned article by Büchler, *Zeitschrift für Altertumswissenschaft* 20; cf. also *Tana deve eliyahu*, 65–66.

10. Elbogen, *Studien*, 3f., above §7(8). In Sepharad, where the precentor recites the *Shemaꜥ* aloud until this very day, there is an interruption after the first verse, since "Blessed be the Name" is said silently.

11. M. *Meg.* 3:4.

12. M. *R.H.* 4:8.

13. Above, §53(3).

14. Elbogen, *Studien*, 33f. Above, §8(1).

15. M. *R.H.* 4:8.

16. *Lev. r.* 23:4; Y. *Ber.* 4:4, 8b; Elbogen, *Studien*, 38; sources are given there for the rejection of the invitation.

17. T. *R.H.*, end.

18. E.g., M. *Ber.* 5; B. *Ber.* 34a f.

19. Above, §8(10), §36(2).

20. B. *Mak.* 54b; cf. Elbogen, *Studien*, 38f.

21. Above, §34(10); cf. Neh. 8:6, "with hands upraised." The Greeks, Romans, and several primitive peoples would lift their hands in prayer; cf. F. Heiler, *Das Gebet* (Munich: E. Reinhardt, 1923), 101; *MGWJ* (1916): 472.—In the amoraic period, the congregation in Palestine would stand during the reciting of the *Shemaꜥ*; cf. Y. *Ber.* 1:6, 3b; *Hiluf minhagim*, §1. During the Middle Ages on fast days and on the Days of Awe they would pray with bent knee; cf. *Manhig*, "Laws of R.H.," §3. The *ꜥAmida*, especially on fast days, was recited by scholars with clasped hands [the fingers of one hand interlaced with those of the other] in the manner of slaves; B. *Shab.* 10. On prayer gestures, see Heiler, *Das Gebet*, 101.

22. Exaggerated prostration is condemned in Y. *Ber.* 1:8, 3d; B. *Meg.* 22b.

23. R. Judah Halevi, *Kuzari*, 2:79f.; cf. *Pardes*, 58b; Berliner, *Buchdrucks*, 23; Abrahams, *Jewish Life*, 278f.; *J.E.* 11:607, s.v. "Swaying."

24. See Elbogen, *Studien*, 11; Berliner, *Vorbeterdienst*, 5.

25. Krauss in *Bloch Festschrift*, Hebrew sec., 83f.; Krauss, *Archäologie*, 1:168.

26. Cf. Berliner, *Leben*, 69f.

27. Elbogen, *Studien*, 11, n. 2. From the sources cited there, it seems that it was a special favor to the Jew that he did not have to uncover his head, since an uncovered head was considered a sign of servitude. By contrast, Paul thinks a covered head to be humiliating for a man, while he demands it of women; Corinthians 11:4f. The Romans offered their sacrifices *capite velato* (with the head covered); the Muslims, too, cover the head during prayer. See Heiler, *Das Gebet*, 104f. (cited in n. 21). On the origin of the custom of covering the head, cf. *REJ* 84 (1927): 178f. and sources therefor, *REJ* 85 (1928): 66f.; also *MGWJ* 71 (1927): 44f.

28. *Soferim* 14:15.

29. *O.Z.*, 2:43.

30. See Löw, *Schriften*, 2:251f.; on uncovered head, 311.

31. In London and Paris, too, the men sit bareheaded.

32. Quotation from Graetz, *Divre*, 9:382.

33. *J.E.* 2:532; cf. Abrahams, *Jewish Life*, 278f.; *J.E.* 2:521f. Recently, Reform synagogues in America no longer insist on the prohibition of head covering for men.

34. Zunz, *Ritus*, 6.

35. On silent and spoken prayer in the ancient world, see *ARW* 9 (1906): 185f.; on the change in Christian practice: ibid. 23 (1920): 345; Carlebach, in *Jeschurun* 14 (1927): 676 expresses himself clearly in favor of praying aloud and in opposition to choirs.

36. Cf. Rashi to *Suk.* 38b s.v. ממנהגא. In a later period, R. Abraham Gumbiner to *S.A.*, *O.H.*, §53:20 rules that everyone is thoroughly familiar with the prayers and that the precentor is needed only for the piyyutim.

37. Zunz, *Haderashot*, 220, with many sources.

§54   Synagogue Song

1. Among the few notices on this subject in Löw, *Schriften*, 5:27 is the comment: "A thankless subject." The whole literature on this subject consists merely of reworkings of Zunz, *Poesie*, 114f. Recent studies of synagogue song have been done more with high spirits and good will than with scientific rigor; Birnbaum's articles, which are based on thoroughly detailed knowledge of the history of synagogue music, are accessible

only with difficulty and ought to be collected. After his death in 1921, his collection came to Hebrew Union College in Cincinnati. Material unknown till then was published by A. Z. Idelsohn in his *Thesaurus* [Jerusalem, Berlin, Vienna]. Of this project, expected to appear in ten volumes [in three editions: German, Hebrew, and English], there have so far appeared (1) The Melodies of the Yemenite Jews, (2) Melodies of the Babylonian Jews, (3) Melodies of the Jews of Bukhara and Daghestan, (4) Melodies of the Oriental Sepharadim. [The remaining volumes that have since appeared are (5) Melodies of the Jews of Morocco, (6) Melodies of the German Jews in the Eighteenth Century, (7) Melodies of the South German Jews, (8) Melodies of the East European Jews, (9) The Folk Song of the East European Jews, and (10) Hasidic Melodies. Of these ten volumes that appeared between 1914 and 1933, only the first five have appeared in the Hebrew edition.] Especially valuable is his "Phonographierte Gesänge und Ausspracheproben des Hebräischen der jemenischen, persischen, und syrischen Juden," in the *Mitteilungen der Wiener Akademie der Wissenschaften, philos.-hist. Klasse* (1917).—Since then, [volume 1 of] Idelsohn's synthetic work, entitled *Toledot hanegina haʿivrit*, has appeared in Berlin (1924). [The manuscript of volume 2 is in the Idelsohn archive in the music department of the National and University Library in Jerusalem.] Cf. also the encyclopedia *Die Religion in Geschichte und Gegenwart*[2] 4, s.v. "Musik, Synagogale." [Idelsohn, who did not live to complete the publication of his Hebrew book on the history of Jewish music, published a summary of his research in this area in his English book, *Jewish Music in its Historic Development* (New York, 1929). A bibliography of about 10,000 entries was published by A. Sendrey, *Bibliography of Jewish Music* (New York, 1951).

Among the monographs, collections, and encyclopedia articles published after this date, the following should be noted: B. Bayer, in *Enṣiqlopedya miqraʾit* 5:755–82, s.v. "Negina vezimra"; *Yuval: qoveṣ meḥqarim shel hamerkaz leḥeqer hamusiqa hayehudit* 1 (Jerusalem, 1968); 2 (Jerusalem, 1971).

E. Werner, *The Sacred Bridge: The Interdependence of Liturgy and Music in Synagogue and Church during the First Millennium* (London and New York, 1959); id., in Grove, *Dictionary of Music and Musicians*, 5th ed., ed. Eric Bloom (New York: St. Martin's Press, 1954), 4:615–36, s.v. "Jewish Music"; S. Rosowski, *The Cantillation of the Bible* (New York, 1957); E. Gerson-Kiwi, in *Dictionnaire de la Bible*, ed. Pirot, supplement 5 (Paris, 1956), 1411–68, s.v. "Musique dans la Bible"; H. Avenari, in *Die Musik in Geschichte und Gegenwart*, ed. Friedrich Blume (Kassel, 1958), 7:224–61, s.v. "Jüdische Musik"; I. Adler, in *Encyclopédie de la musique* (Paris, 1959), 2:630–54, s.v. "Juive (musique)"; id., *La pratique musicale savante dans quelques communautés juives en Europe aux xviie et xviiie siècles*, 2 vols. (Paris, 1966). See also the musical entries in the new English *Encyclopaedia Judaica* (per the index), completed in 1971, as well as the bibliographies cited in the above publications, and the following notes.]

[2. In place of the term *recitative* it is better to use here and in the following the term *chant* to designate unmetered song in a style in which the main emphasis is on the articulation of the words, and where the melody is merely a musical overlay serving to regulate the rendering of the text and to express solemnity for public recitation. See Solange Corbin's article in *Revue de Musicologie* 47 (1961), 3f.

This problem of the origin of the melodies used in the synagogue service and the attempts to determine their nature and style in the period before the earliest notation (see below, n. 25), were among the main factors that led scholars from Idelsohn on to make use of "comparative musicology" and "ethnomusicology."

According to this method, in the absence of ancient musical notation of synagogue melodies, use must be made of oral traditions preserved till our time. The fundamental assumption is that common elements of the different Jewish traditions (especially those that are geographically distant and that have been long cut off from each other) and melodies of the ancient Christian traditions point to a common ancient source. Obviously results gained by this means cannot be as certain as those based on written sources. We cannot expect to reconstruct ancient melodies, but mainly to uncover the principles that bear on their melodic structure and performance practice. Among the main studies based on this method, the work of Idelsohn and Gerson-Kiwi mentioned in n. 1 above should be noted; R. Lachmann, *Jew, Cantillation, and Song in the Isle of Djerba* (Jerusalem, 1940). Other works on specific subjects: J. Spector, "The Significance of Samaritan Neumes and Contemporary Practice," *Studia Musicologica* 7 (1965): 141–53; A. Herzog and A Hajdu, "A la recherche du Tonus Peregrinus dans la tradition musicale juive," *Yuval* 1 (1968): 194–203 (music examples, 1–15).

Use of "documentation" uncovered at second hand by ethnomusicological means, sometimes with an attempt to verify these finds by literary sources and/or musical notations, is found also in the studies listed in n. 1 by H. Avenari, "Jüdische Musik"; E. Werner, *Bridge*; I. Adler, "Juive (musique)"; and I. Adler's article in *Revue de musicologie* 51 (1965): 19–51.]

[3. The most ancient notation of musical notes for the Day of Atonement known to us was done by Obadiah the Proselyte in the twelfth century (see below, n. 25).]

[4. As stated above (n. 2), we cannot point to "melodies that have been preserved" from the period of the Temple. It is possible to determine the means of performance, such as various types of responsive songs, archaic forms, and especially the melodic structure of psalmody. See, for example, the examples given in the studies cited in n. 1 in Gerson-Kiwi, "Musique dans la Bible"; H. Avenari "Jüdische Musik"; E. Werner, *Bridge* (esp. Part 2, chap. 5, 460–99); I. Adler, "Juive (musique)"; id., in *Encyclopédie des musiques sacrées* (Paris, 1968), 1:469–93, s.v. "Histoire de la musique juive."

As for the Priestly Blessing, there has been no study specifically dedicated to this subject and based on oral and written traditions. The earliest notation, made in connection with the dispute that broke out in Ferarra in the eighteenth century, was printed in 1715, and quotes four different versions of the melodies of the Blessing. (See Adler, *Pratique*, 1:37, 128.)]

[5. Mourning over the destruction of the Temple is mentioned in talmudic, midrashic, and rabbinic literature as one of the main reasons for the negative attitude toward music from the tannaitic period onward, but no unequivocal conclusions may be drawn, whether theoretical or practical in nature. On the one hand, a negative attitude toward music may be observed in sources earlier than the Destruction. On the other hand, it seems that only in the tannaitic period, immediately after the Destruction, was there a real connection between this religious, national mourning on the one hand, and the avoidance of all musical practice on the other. It seems that the principles of the rabbinic attitude toward music have less to do with this historical event—sporadic prohibitions of music appear also in later periods in connection with catastrophes that befell various communities—than with the functional aspect of music: Religious music is permitted, and is even desirable, while secular music is essentially prohibited, as suspect of sensuality and of being contrary to the life of sanctity to which the Jewish people are bidden. This fundamental distinction between religious music, which is permitted, and secular music, which is prohibited, is complicated by various nuances (such as the distinction between vocal and instrumental music, or between the singing of men and women), and was given more severe or more lenient interpretations in different places and times, in accordance with the musical inclinations of the rabbinic authorities. See "Attitude rabbinique envers la musique" in Adler, *Pratique*, 1:10–14, and the sources cited there.]

6. J.E. 12:139. [On the musical attestations in the writings of the Dead Sea sect and Philo's remarks about the Therapeutai, see E. Werner's article in *The Musical Quarterly* 43 (1957): 21–37 and the literature cited by B. Bayer, *Yuval* 1 (1968): 117.]

[7. Philo's description of the singing of the Therapeutai does not speak of polyphonic singing but rather of singing executed by groups, antiphonally.]

8. B. *Ta.* 16a: "With a sweet voice." [See additional sources from the talmudic period in Krauss, *Archäologie*, 3:77, 274.]

9. J.E. 1:189.

[10. It seems that the source of the tropes (as in the case of other ecphonetic systems of signs like those of the Indians, Syrians, Armenians, Copts, Byzantine Christians, and Romans) is the adaptation or graphic imitation of the cheironomic signs (i.e., hand gestures) used as a memory aid for the cantillation of the text. The first testimony for the use of cheironomy is found in the Talmud, and this method remained in use even after the graphic codification of the tropes, until today. We find evidence of its use in the eleventh century in Rashi (commentary to B. *Ber.* 62a); its use in Babylonia is mentioned in Petahia of Regensburg (*Sibuv rabi petahya* [Prague, 1594–95], 4a), and in Yemen in the nineteenth century in R. Jacob Sappir (*Sapir*, 1:56b.) In our time, this ancient tradition has been preserved in the Italian tradition of the Jews of Rome (see I. Adler in *Encyclopédie des musiques sacrées*, 1:472–73), of Yemen, Egypt, and North Africa (see S. Levin in *JBL* 87 [1968], 59–70). See also *Sefer diqduqe hate'amim lerabi aharon ben moshe ben asher*, ed. A. Dothan (Jerusalem, 1966/7), esp. part 2, 154. The literature on the tropes up to 1950 is listed in Sendrey, *Bibliography*, 82–90. On the development of scholarship on the trope systems, the relationship to ecphonetic systems, and their musical significance since Elbogen's time, see Idelsohn, *Music*, 35f.; Werner, *Bridge*, 410f.; L. Levi, in *Ensiqlopedya 'ivrit*, 18:866–72, s.v. "Ta'ame hamiqra" and the bibliography there.]

11. Ackermann, *Gesang*, 16f.; Friedmann, *Gesang*, 7f.

[12. This definition is not exact; see N. Riemann, in *Musiklexikon*12, ed. Josef Müller-Blattau (Mainz, 1939), s.v. "Tropus," who defines the various uses of the term in church liturgy and music.]

13. Berliner, *Leben*, 53. [Friedmann, *Gesang*, 13f.; H. Avenari, *Studies in the Hebrew, Syrian, and Greek Liturgical Recitative* (Tel Aviv, 1963), 21; A. Herzog, *The Intonation of the Pentateuch in the Heder of Tunis* (Tel Aviv, 1963), 6; id., in *E.J.* 12:1098–1111, s.v. "Masoretic accents (musical rendition)."]

[14. With reference to this entire section, see Idelsohn, *Music*, 35–71; likewise, his introductions to the volumes of *Osar neginot yisra'el* and the comparative tables there. Idelsohn's conclusions must be treated with caution, as he tends to exaggerate in seeing similarities when comparing melodies and cantillations; nevertheless there is today no doubt that a fundamental common line can be traced in the melodic phrasing of the reading of the Bible in the various Jewish traditions.]

15. *Soferim* 14:9.

16. Ackermann, *Gesang*, 28. [On the development of the institution of hazan and hazanut from the talmudic period on, see Idelsohn, *Music*, 101.]

17. Zunz, *Poesie*, 114.

18. *Sefer Hasidim*, §11. [See Adler, "Juive (musique)," 647.]

19. Zunz, *Poesie*, 114; Ackermann, *Gesang*, 27. [Adler, *Pratique*, 1:10–14 and n. 5 above.]

[20. On Maimonides' approach to music, see H.G. Farmer, "Maimonides on Listening to Music," *JRAS*, Series 3, 45 (1933): 867–84; B. Cohen, *The Responsum of Maimonides Concerning Music* (New York, 1953); Adler, *Pratique*, 1:12–13.]

21. Zunz, *Poesie*, 114.

22. Ibid., 115; Güdemann, *Hatora*, 76. [On this widespread phenomenon of adapting poems to melodies known by the congregation, see the literature cited in Adler, *Pratique*, 1:18–19, and the sources cited in the index there, s.v. "timbres."]

[23. See I. Adler's article in *Revue de musicologie* 51 (1965): 45–46; id., *Pratique*, 1:15f.]

24. Rietschel, *Liturgik*, 1:469.

[25. This opinion is doubtful; see n. 2, above.—At the end of this paragraph, it is appropriate to make note of the most ancient documents of synagogue melodies preserved in musical notation. The reference is to geniza fragments written by Obadiah the Proselyte between ca. 1102 and 1150, during the time of his stay in the East (Babylonia, Syria, Palestine, and Egypt). These writings include (1) the melody to the piyyut מי על הר חורב for Pentecost or Joy of the Torah (MS New York, Adler Collection, no. 4096b); (2) a fragment of the melody for a liturgical poem of which only the end is preserved, beginning with the words ואדע מה אדבר (MS Cambridge T.-S. K 5/41a); (3) cantillation of biblical verses (from Jeremiah, Proverbs, and Job), beginning with Jer. 17:7 (same MS, 41b). Numbers (1) and (2) were composed in Obadiah's time in the monodic western-Christian song style. Perhaps they were composed by Obadiah or a cantor of European origin who lived in the East. The notes in fragment 3 are certainly not a composition, but traditional cantillation that Obadiah had heard and written down in one of the Oriental communities that he visited. This cantillation has been preserved to this day in the Oriental tradition of several Jewish communities in the East and in Mediterranean lands, and it may be assumed to have been already an ancient Jewish tradition by the thirteenth century when Obadiah wrote it down. See I. Adler in *Revue de musicologie* 51 (1965): 19–51; id., "Qeta hamusiqa hehadash shel ʿovadya hager hanormands," *Divre haqongres haʿolami harevíʿi lemadaʿe hayahadut* 2 (1968/9): 395–408; H. Avenari, in *JJS* 16 (1966): 87–104; *E.J.* 12:1307–8 and the bibliography there.]

26. See also Berliner, *Leben*, 52.

27. Immanuel, *Mahbarot*, chap. 15.

28. Berliner, *Vorbeterdienstes*, 13.

29. *Kaufmann Memorial Volume*, 309f.

30. Cf. Löw, *Lebensalter*, 314.—The synod of Lithuania determined exactly how much might be sung.

[31. Against this, see Idelsohn, *Music*, 184.]

[32. To fill out this defective survey of *hazanut* from the late Middle Ages to the emancipation, see Idelsohn, *Music*, 110f., 204f.; Adler, *Pratique*, 9–38.]

33. Cf. *Medieval Jewish Chronicles*, 2:81. [See Adler, "Juive (musique)," 647.]

34. Cf. Immanuel, chap. 15.

35. See Ackermann, *Gesang*, 41f. [See below, n. 37.]

36. See A.H. Heymann, *Lebenserinnerungen* (Berlin: Eigentum der Familie, 1909), 242.

[37. The most interesting phenomenon of *meshorerim* (choir), described rather unobjectively by Elbogen, has not yet been fully studied. According to Idelsohn in "Song and Singers of the Synagogue in the Eighteenth Century," in *Hebrew Union College Volume* (Cincinnati, 1925), 401, and in his book *Jewish Music*, 204–5, this phenomenon arose under the influence of the Italian movement for the introduction of art music into the synagogue in the first half of the seventeenth century. But its roots seem to be much older. See the historical survey and musical description in the above article of Idelsohn, "Song and Singers," and in Adler, *Pratique*, 1:22–26, and the literature cited there.]

38. See Ackermann, *Gesang*, 45; *J.E.* 10486. [One of the eight part-books of] Rossi's songs was published in 1925 in a special booklet by the firm of J. Kaufmann in Frankfurt am Main.—The composer Benedetto Marcello in Venice (1686–1739) relates that he visited synagogues to get inspiration for his compositions on the psalms (*Salmidi Davids* 1). [See the literature in Adler, *Pratique*, 1:38 (n. 158).]

[39. Elbogen follows here the false notion current in his time that attributed to Salomone de' Rossi and his circle a "reform" program of introducing "organized" music into the synagogue, like the program of the reform in Germany and Austria in the first half of the nineteenth century. See Adler, *Pratique*, 1:1, 4, 237–38.]

[40. This chapter dealing with the place of art music in the synagogue in the period before the emancipation requires substantial revision. The first signs of this phenomenon appeared apparently in the second half of the sixteenth century in Italy (Padua?). After the Jews were closed into ghettos, as a result of the counter-reformation, the process began by which the activity of Jewish musicians shifted from Christian circles (especially in the ducal courts) to the circles of Jewish society within the ghetto walls, especially in and around the synagogue. This phenomenon crystallized in Italy in the first half of the seventeenth century, especially around the preeminent figures of Salomone de' Rossi, the greatest of the Jewish composers of the seventeenth century, and R. Leone Modena, who was also a musician. From the mid-seventeenth century to the end of the eighteenth century, art music in and around the synagogue was a routine phenomenon, not only in Italy but also in other Jewish centers in Europe—in southern France, Holland, and especially in the Portuguese community of Amsterdam in the eighteenth century. Art music in the seventeenth and eighteenth centuries did not enter the synagogue as an organized, fixed synagogue institution that suppressed the traditional synagogue music. There were not musical performances of certain prayers each Sabbath, but only on festivals and special Sabbaths ("on festivals and New Moons of special character" . . . and "on particular Sabbaths," as Modena says in his introduction and "ruling" appended to *Hashirim asher lishelomo* of de' Rossi), and likewise, of course, on family occasions such as circumcisions or weddings, at the dedication of a synagogue or a Torah scroll, at celebrations of societies of all kinds, on the bestowal of academic degrees, etc. See H. Schirmann, "Hate'atron vehamusiqa bishekhunot hayehudim be'italya," *Zion* 29 (1964): 61–111; Adler, *Pratique*; id., "The Rise of Art Music in the Italian Ghetto," in *Jewish Medieval and Renaissance Studies*, ed. A. Altmann (Cambridge, Mass., 1967), 321–64.]

41. See above §46, n. 45. The present position of its opponents is evident from the title of Berliner's polemic, *Zur Lehr' und Wehr: über und gegen die kirchliche Orgel im jüdischen Gottesdienst* (Berlin, 1904).

42. [The primary importance of Consolo is not in the synagogue compositions and arrangements but in the collection of traditional melodies of the Sephardic community in Leghorn that he edited and published in 1892 (see Sendrey, *Bibliography*, no. 6088), which is comparable in importance to the collection *Zimrat yisra'el keminhag karpentras*, ed. J.S. Crémieu (Marseille, ca. 1887).] On the cantors of the modern period, see Ackermann, *Gesang*, 49f.; Aron Friedmann, *Lebensbilder berühmter Kantoren* (Berlin, 1918/21); on Sulzer, J.E. 11:586 [Sendrey, *Bibliography*, nos. 5763–87]; on Lewandowski, J.E. 8:66 [Sendrey, *Bibliography*, nos. 5673–77]; on Consolo, J.E. 4:234 [Sendrey, *Bibliography*, no. 5459.—This sketch of Elbogen's on the Reform movement and its outgrowths in post-emancipation synagogue music should be compared with chapters 12–13 in Idelsohn, *Music*, 232–95; ibid., 296–315, dealing with cantors and cantorial music in Eastern Europe in the nineteenth century, and 316–36, devoted to synagogue music in the United States of America.—Bibliography of the subjects dealt with in this chapter in Sendrey, *Bibliography*, chapters "Organ in Synagogue Worship" (nos. 2537–86), "Music in the Reform Synagogue" (nos. 2587–92), and "Ḥazzan, Ḥazanut after the Emancipation" (nos. 1637–1859).]

Selected Bibliography

Abrahams, *Jewish Life*
> Israel Abrahams. *Jewish Life in the Middle Ages.* Philadelphia: Jewish Publication Society of America, 1896.

Abudarham
> David Abudarham. *Sefer Abudarham.* Prague, 1784.

Achelis, *Theologie*
> Ernst Christian Achelis. *Praktische Theologie.* 3d edition. Freiburg: Mohr, 1899.

Ackermann, *Gesang*
> A. Ackermann. "Der synagogale Gesang in seiner historischen Entwicklung." In *Die jüdische Literatur seit Abschluss des Kanons.* Edited by J. Winter and A. Wünsche. Trier: S. Mayer, 1894–96. 3:477–529.

Adler, "Juive (musique)"
> I. Adler. In *Encyclopédie de la musique.* 3 vols. Paris: Fasquelle, 1958–61. 2:630–54.

Adler, *Pratique*
> ———. *La pratique musicale savante dans quelques communautés juives en Europe aux xviie et xviiie siècles.* 2 vols. Paris: Mouton, 1966.

Agadat bereshit
> *Agadat bereshit.* Edited by Salomon Buber. Cracow: Fischer, 1902. Reprint. New York: Menora Institute, 1959.

Albeck, *Mishnah*
> Ḥanokh Albeck. *Mishnah.* 6 vols. Jerusalem: Bialik Institute, 1952–59.

Allon, *Meḥqarim*
> Gedalyahu Allon. *Meḥqarim betoledot yisra'el.* Tel Aviv: Ofek, 1957/8.

Allon, *Talmudic Age*
> ———. *The Jews in Their Land in the Talmudic Age, 70–640 C.E.* Translated and edited by Gershom Levi. 2 vols. Jerusalem: Magnes Press, The Hebrew University, 1980–84.

Amram
> *Seder rav ʿAmram Gaon.* Edited by N.N. Coronel. Warsaw, 1865. Reprint. Jerusalem: Qirya Neʾemana, 1964/5.

Aronius, *Regesten*
> Julius Aronius. *Regesten zur Geschichte der Juden im fränkischen und deutschen Reiche bis zum Jahre 1273.* Berlin: L. Simion, 1902.

ʿArukh
Nathan ben Jehiel. ʿArukh hashalem. Edited by Alexander Kohut. 8 vols. Vienna: Georg Broeg, 1878–92.

Bacher, Agada
Wilhelm Bacher. Die Agada der Tannaiten. 2 vols. Strassburg: K.J. Trubner, 1890–1913.

Bacher, Amoraʾe
———. Agadot amoraʾe ereṣ yisraʾel. Translated by A.Z. Rabinowitz. 2 vols. Tel Aviv, 1924/5–37.

Bacher, Amoräer
———. Agada der babylonischen Amoräer. Frankfurt: J. Kaufmann, 1913.

Bacher, Proömien
———. Die Proömien der alten jüdischen Homilie. Leipzig: Hinrichs, 1913.

Bacher, Synagogue
William Bacher. "Synagogue." In Dictionary of the Bible, by James Hastings. New York: C. Scribner's Sons, 1898–1904. 4:636–43.

Bacher, Tannaim
———. Agadot hatanaim. Translated by A. Rabinowitz. 2 vols. Jaffa, 1919–23.

Bacher, Terminologie
———. Die exegetische Terminologie der jüdischen Traditions-literatur. 2 vols. Darmstadt: Wissenschaftliche Buchgesellschaft, 1965.

Baer, ʿAvodat
Seligman Baer. Seder ʿavodat yisraʾel. Rödelheim: I. Lehrberger & Co., 1868.

Baer, Yisraʾel
Yitzhak Baer. Yisraʾel baʿamim. Jerusalem: Bialik Institute, 1955.

Benjamin of Tudela
The Itinerary of Rabbi Benjamin of Tudela. Translated and edited by A. Asher. 2 vols. London and Berlin: A. Asher & Co., 1840–41.

Bereshit Rabba
Midrash bereshit rabbah. Edited by Julius Theodor. Completed by C. Albeck. 4 vols. Berlin: H. Itzkowski, 1903–29.

Berliner, Buchdrucks
Abraham Berliner. Über den Einfluss des ersten hebräischen Buchdrucks. Berlin: H. Itzkowski, 1896.

Berliner, Einheitsgesang
———. Der Einheitsgesang. Berlin: Druck von H. Itzkowski, 1910. Ketavim nivḥarim. 2 vols. Jerusalem: Mossad Harav Kook, 1945–49.

Berliner, Leben
———. Aus der innern Leben der deutschen Juden im Mittelalter. Berlin: J. Benzian, 1871.

Berliner, Randbemerkungen
———. Randbemerkungen zum täglichen Gebetbuch. 2 vols. Berlin: M. Poppelauer, 1909–12.

Berliner, Rom
———. Geschichte der Juden in Rom von der ältesten Zeit bis zur Gegenwart. Frankfurt: J. Kaufmann, 1893. Reprint. Hildesheim: G. Olms, 1987.

Berliner, Vorbeterdienstes
———. "Die Entstehung des Vorbeterdienstes" in "Israelitischer Lehre und Cantor," Israelitische Monatsschrift (1889): 2–5, 13–14, 29–31, 34–35, 40.

Bernfeld, Toledot
Simon Bernfeld. Toledot hareformaṣion hadatit beyisraʾel. Warsaw: Ahiasaf, 1908.

Blau, Buchwesen
Ludwig Blau. Studien zum althebräischen Buchwesen und zur biblischen Literaturgeschichte. Strassburg: K.J. Trubner, 1902.

Bloch Festschrift
   Sefer hayovel likhvod rav moshe aryeh blokh. Edited by S. Krausz and M. Ksaweisz. Budapest, 1905.

Bloch, *Merkava*
   Philipp Bloch. "Die Yorde Merkava, die Mystiker der Gaonzeit und ihr Einfluss auf die Liturgie." *MGWJ* 37 (1893): 18–25; 49 (1905): 129–66.

Bondi, *Saadia*
   J. Bondi. *Der Siddur des Saadia Gaon.* Frankfurt: J. Kauffman, 1904.

Bousset, *Judentums*
   W. Bousset. *Die Religion des Judentums im neutestamentlichen Zeitalter.* Berlin, 1903.

Brody, *Diwan*
   Diwan yehuda halevi. Edited by Heinrich Brody. 4 vols. Berlin: Meqiṣe nirdamim, 1894–1930.

Brody, *Quntres*
   Heinrich Brody. *Quntres hapiyuṭim hanilve el hamaḥzor vitry ktav yad london.* Berlin: H. Itzkowski, 1894.

Brody, *Studien*
   ———. *Studien zu den Dichtungen Jehuda Halevis.* Berlin, 1895.

Brody and Albrecht, *Dichterschule*
   Heinrich Brody and K. Albrecht. *Die neuhebräische Dichterschule der spanisch-arabischen Epoche.* Leipzig: Hinrichs, 1905.

Brody and Wiener, *Mivḥar*
   Heinrich Brody and Meir Wiener. *Mivḥar hashira haʿivrit.* 2 vols. Leipzig: Insel-Verlag, 1922.

Büchler, *Priester*
   Adolf Büchler. *Die Priester und der Cultus im letzten Jahrzehnt des Jerusalemischen Tempels.* Vienna: Israelitisch-theologische Lehranstalt, 1895.

Büchler, *Triennial*
   ———. "The Reading of the Law and Prophets in a Triennial Cycle." *JQR* 5 (1893): 420–68; 6 (1894): 1–73.

Chwolson Festschrift
   Recueil des travaux rédigés en mémoire du jubilé scientifique de M. Daniel Chwolson. Berlin: S. Calvary, 1899.

Davidson, *Ginze*
   Israel Davidson. *Ginze Schechter.* Vol. 3. New York: The Jewish Theological Seminary of America, 1928.

Davidson, *Oṣar*
   ———. *Oṣar hashira vehapiyuṭ.* 4 vols. New York: The Jewish Theological Seminary of America, 1924–33. Reprint. New York: Ktav, 1970.

Davidson, *Yanai*
   Mahzor Yanai. Edited by Israel Davidson. New York: The Jewish Theological Seminary of America, 1919.

Diqduqe Soferim
   Raphael Nathan Rabinowitz. *Diqduqe Soferim.* 15 vols. Munich, 1867–97.

Dīwān
   Judah Halevi. *Dīwān des abū 'l-ḥasan Jehuda ha-Levi.* Edited by H. Brody. 4 vols. Berlin: Meqiṣe nirdamim, 1894.

Döller, *Gebet*
   Johann Döller. *Das Gebet im Alten Testament in religionsgeschichtlicher Beleuchtung.* Vienna, 1914.

Dukes, *Poesie*
   Leopold Dukes. *Zur Kenntnis der neuhebräischen religiösen poesie.* Frankfurt: Bach'sche Buch-und-steindruckerie, 1842.

Duschak, *Geschichte*
   M. Duschak. *Geschichte und Darstellung des jüdischen Kultus.* Mannheim, 1866.

Elbogen, *Achtzehngebets*
Ismar Elbogen. *Geschichte des Achtzehngebets*. Breslau: W. Koebner, 1903. [See also *MGWJ* 46 (1902): 330–57 and 513–30.]

Elbogen, "Eingang"
————. "Eingang und Ausgang des Sabbats." *Jewish Review* 1 (1910): 358ff.

Elbogen, *Studien*
————. *Studien zur Geschichte des jüdischen Gottesdienstes*. Berlin: Mayer und Muller, 1907.

Ele divre haberit
Ele divre haberit. Altona, 1819.

Enṣiqlopedia talmudit
Enṣiqlopedia talmudit. Edited by Shlomon Yosef Zevin and Meir Berlin. 18 vols. to date. Jerusalem: Mossad Harav Kook, 1969–present.

Eppenstein, "Literatur"
Simon Eppenstein. "Beiträge zur Geschichte und Literatur im gaonäischen Zeitalter." *MGWJ* 52 (1908): 455–72.

Eshkol
Abraham ben Isaac of Narbonne, ca. 1120–79. *Sefer ha'eshkol*. Edited by Benjamin Zevi Auerbach. Halberstadt, 1867.

Even sapir
Jacob Saphir. *Even sapir*. Lyck: Mekiṣe Nirdamim, 1866–74. Reprint. Jerusalem, 1966/7.

Finfer, *Masoret*
P. Finfer. *Masoret hatora vehanevi'im*. Vilna: Gerber, 1906.

Finkelstein, "'Amida"
Louis Finkelstein. "The Development of the 'Amida." *JQR* NS 16 (1925–26): 1–43.

Frances, *Meteq*
Immanuel Frances. *Sefer meteq sefatayim*. Edited by Heinrich Brody. Cracow: J. Fischer, 1892.

Frankel, *Einfluss*
Zacharias Frankel. *Über den Einfluss der palästinischen Exegese auf die alexandrinische Hermeneutik*. Leipzig: J.A. Barth, 1851.

Frankel, *Septuaginta*
————. *Historisch-Kritische Studien zu der Septuaginta*. Leipzig: F.C.W. Vogel, 1841.

Frankel, *Targum*
————. *Zu dem Targum der Propheten*. Breslau: F.W. Jugfer, 1892.

Frauberger, *Mitteilungen*
H. Frauberger. *Mitteilungen der Gesellschaft zur Erforschung jüdischen Kunstdenmäler*. 6 vols. Frankfurt, 1903–9. Reprinted as *Objects of Ancient Jewish Ritual Art and Illuminated Hebrew Script and Ornaments of Printed Books*. Edited by M.Z. Meyer. Jerusalem, 1970.

Friedmann, *Gesang*
Aaron Friedmann. *Die synagogale Gesang*. Berlin: C. Boas, 1904.

Friedmann, *Ma'amar*
Meir Friedmann. "Ma'amar 'al haluqat hatora." *Beit Talmud* 3 (1883): 6–10, 65–71, 100–106, 201–205, 261–70, 295–302, 323–28, 352–58.

Friedmann, *Onkelos*
————. *Onkelos und Akylos*. Vienna: Israelitisch-theologische Lehranstalt, 1896.

Frumkin, *Seder*
Aryeh Loeb Frumkin. *Seder tefila keminhag ashkenaz 'im seder rav 'amram hashalem*. 2 vols. Jerusalem, 1912.

Gallia Judaica
Heinrich Gross. *Gallia Judaica*. Paris: L. Cerf. 1897. Reprint. Amsterdam: Philo Press, 1969.

Geiger, *Gabirol*
Abraham Geiger. *Salomo Gabirol und seine Dichtungen*. Leipzig: O. Leiner, 1867.

Geiger, *Urschrift*
————. *Urschrift und Übersetzungen der Bibel in ihrer Abhängigkeit von der innern Entwicklung des Judenthums*. Breslau: J. Hainauer, 1857.

Geiger, *Geiger*
Ludwig Geiger et al. *Abraham Geiger: Leben und Lebenswerk*. Berlin, 1910.

Gesenius, *Handwörterbuch*
Wilhelm Gesenius. *Hebräisches und aramäisches Handworterbuch über das Alte Testament*. 15th edition. Leipzig: F.C.W. Vogel, 1910. 16th edition, 1915.

Ginzberg, *Geonica*
Louis Ginzberg. *Geonica*. 2 vols. New York: The Jewish Theological Seminary of America, 1909.

Ginzberg, *Ginze*
————. *Ginze Shekhter*. Vol. 2. New York: The Jewish Theological Seminary of America, 1928. Reprint. New York, 1969.

Ginzberg, *Perushim*
————. *Perushim vehidushim bayerushalmi*. 4 vols. New York: The Jewish Theological Seminary of America, 1941–61.

Ginzberg, *Seride*
————. *Seride Yerushalmi: Yerushalmi Fragments from the Genizah*. 2 vols. New York: The Jewish Theological Seminary of America, 1909.

Goldschmidt, ʿAmram
Ernst Daniel Goldschmidt. *Seder rav ʿamram gaʾon*. Jerusalem: Mossad Harav Kook, 1971.

Goldschmidt, *Hagada*
————. *Hagada shel pesah vetoledoteha*. Jerusalem: Mosad Bialik, 1960.

Goldschmidt, *Mahzor*
————. *Mahzor layamim hanoraʾim*. 2 vols. Jerusalem: H. Koren, 1970.

Goldschmidt, "Maimonides"
————. "Maimonides' Rite of Prayer According to an Oxford Manuscript" (Hebrew). *SRIHP* 7 (1958): 183–213.

Graetz, *Divre*
Heinrich Graetz. *Divre yeme yisraʾel*. Translated by Saul Phinehas Rabinowitz. 10 vols. Warsaw, 1916–?.

Graetz Festschrift
Jubelschrift zum siebzigsten Geburtstag des Professors Dr. H. Graetz. Breslau: S. Schotländer, 1873.

Graetz, *Geschichte*
Heinrich Graetz. *Geschichte der Juden von den ältesten Zeiten bis auf die Gegenwart*. Edited by F. Rosenthal. 7 vols. 3d edition. Leipzig: O. Leiner, 1873–1900.

Güdemann, *Hatora*
M. Güdemann. *Hatora vehahayim*. Translated by A. Friedberg. 3 vols. Tel Aviv, 1966–72.

Haberman, ʿAteret
Abraham Haberman. *ʿAteret renanim*. Jerusalem: Ben-Ori, 1967.

Haberman, *Beron yahad*
————. *Beron yahad*. Jerusalem: Mossad Harav Kook, 1944/5.

Haberman, *Hayihud*
————. *Shire hayihud vehakavod*. Jerusalem: Mossad Harav Kook, 1948.

Halakhot Gedolot
Halakhot Gedolot. Edited by Israel Hildesheimer. 2 vols. Berlin: H. Itzkowski, 1888–92.

Harkavy Festschrift
Zikaron le'avraham eliyahu, Festschrift zu Ehren des Dr. A. Harkavy. Edited by D. v. Gunzberg and I. Markon: St. Petersburg, 1908.

Harkavy, *Responsa*
Teshuvot hage'onim. Edited by Abraham Harkavy. Berlin: H. Itzkowski, 1887. Reprint. Jerusalem, 1966.

Harkavy, *Studien*
Studien und Mitteilungen aus der Kaiserlichen öffentlichen Bibliothek zu St. Petersburg. Edited by A. Harkavy. Berlin, 1887.

Hartmann, *Verskunst*
Martin Hartmann. *Die hebräische Verskunst.* Berlin: S. Calvary, 1894.

Hastings, *Dictionary*
James Hastings. *Dictionary of the Bible.* 5 vols. New York: C. Scribner's Sons, 1898–1904.

Heinemann, "Blessing"
Joseph Heinemann. "The Blessing 'Who Rebuilds Jerusalem' and its Metamorphoses" (Hebrew). In *Sefer ḥayim shirman.* Edited by Shraga Abramson. Jerusalem: Schocken, 1970. 93–102.

Heinemann, *Prayer*
———. *Hatefila bitequfat hatana'im veha'amora'im.* Jerusalem: The Magnes Press, 1964.

Herford, *Pharisaism*
Robert Travers Herford. *Pharisaism: Its Aim and Its Method.* London: Williams and Norgate, 1912; New York: G. P. Putnam's, 1912.

Hermann Cohen Festschrift
See *Judaica.*

Herzfeld, *Tefillat*
Levi Herzfeld. *Tefillat Jisrael: Das Israelitische Gebetbuch nach dem Braunschweiger Ritus.* Brunswick: Johann Heinrich Meher, 1855.

Hildesheimer Festschrift
Jubelschrift zum siebzigsten Geburtstag des Dr. Israel Hildesheimer. Berlin: H. Engel, 1890.

Ḥiluf Minhagim
Ḥiluf Minhagim ben bene bavel livene eres yisra'el. Edited by Joel Muller. Vienna, 1878. Reprint. Jerusalem: Makor, 1969.

Hoffmann Festschrift
Festschrift zum siebzigsten Geburgstag David Hoffmann's. Edited by S. Eppenstein et al. Berlin: L. Lamm, 1914.

Hoffman, *Synagogen*
David Hoffman. "Die Synagogen im Altertum." *Israelitische Monatsschrift* [Supplements to *Die jüdische Presse*] (1889): 5ff.

Holdheim, *Reformgemeinde*
Samuel Holdheim. *Geschichte der Enstehung und Entwicklung der jüdischen Reformgemeinde in Berlin.* Berlin: J. Springer, 1857.

Ibn Ghiyath, *Sha'are simha*
Isaac ben Judah Ibn Ghayyat. *Sha'are simha.* Edited by S. H. Bamberger. 2 vols. Furth, 1861–62.

Idelsohn, *Music*
A. Z. Idelsohn. *Jewish Music in its Historic Development.* New York: H. Holt and Co., 1929.

Idelsohn, *Oṣar*
———. *Oṣar neginot yisra'el.* 5 vols. Jerusalem, 1922–28. [Same as Idelsohn, *Thesaurus* (Hebrew).]

Idelsohn, *Thesaurus*
———. *Thesaurus of Hebrew Oriental Melodies.* 10 vols. Berlin: B. Harz, 1922–33. Vols. 1–4; New York: Ktav, 1922–32.

'Itim
Judah ben Barzilai. *Sefer ha'itim.* Edited by Jacob Schor. Cracow, 1913. Reprint. Jerusalem, 1964.

Jarden, *Sefune*
Dov Jarden. *Sefune Shirah.* Jerusalem: Privately published, 1967.

Jawitz, *Meqor*
W. Jawitz. *Meqor haberakhot.* Berlin, 1910.

Jewish Encyclopaedia (J.E.)
The *Jewish Encyclopaedia.* Edited by Isidore Singer. 12 vols. New York & London: Funk & Wagnalls Company, 1901–6.

Jost, *Kulturgeschichte*
Isaac M. Jost. *Kulturgeschichte der Israeliten der ersten Hälfte des 19 jahrhunderts.* Breslau: W. Jacobson, 1846/7.

Judaica
Judaica: Festschrift zu Hermann Cohens siebzigstem Geburtstag. Berlin: Bruno Cassirer, 1912.

Jüdisches Lexicon
Jüdisches Lexicon. Edited by Georg Herlitz and Bruno Kirschner. 4 vols. Berlin: Judischer Verlage, 1927–30.

Juster, *Juifs*
Jean Juster. *Les Juifs dans l'empire romain.* 2 vols. Paris: P. Geuthner, 1914.

Kahle, *Masoreten*
Paul Kahle. *Masoreten des Westens.* 2 vols. Stuttgart: W. Kohlhammer, 1927–30.

Karpeles, *Geschichte*
Gustav Karpeles. *Geschichte der jüdischen Literatur.* 2 vols. Berlin: R. Oppenheim, 1886.

Kaufmann, *Schriften*
David Kaufmann. *Gesammelte Schriften von David Kaufmann.* 2 vols. Edited by M. Braun. Frankfurt: J. Kaufmann, 1908–10.

Kaufmann Memorial Volume
Gedenkbuch zur Erinnerung an David Kaufmann. Edited by M. Brann and F. Rosenthal. Breslau, 1900.

Kieval, *High Holy Days*
Herman Kieval. *The High Holy Days.* 2 vols. New York: Burning Bush Press, 1959.

Köberle, *Tempelsänger*
Justus Köberle. *Die Tempelsänger im Alten Testament.* Erlangen: F. Junge, 1899.

König, *Stilistik*
E. König. *Stilistik, Rhetorik, Poetik in Bezug auf biblische Literatur.* Leipzig: T. Weicher, 1900.

Kohl and Watzinger, *Galiläa*
Heinrich Kohl and Carl Watzinger. *Antike Synagogen in Galiläa.* Leipzig: Hinrichs, 1916. Reprint. Osnabrück: O. Zeller, 1975.

Kohler Festschrift
Studies in Jewish Literature, issued in honor of Professor Kaufmann Kohler. Edited by D. Philipson et al. Berlin: G. Reimer, 1913.

Kohler, *Ursprünge*
Kaufmann Kohler. "Über die Ursprunge und Grundformen der synagogalen Liturgie." *MGWJ* 37 (1893): 441–51, 489–97.

Krauss, *Archäologie*
Samuel Krauss. *Talmudische Archäologie.* 3 vols. Leipzig: G. Fock, 1910–12.

Krauss, *Lehnwörter*
———. *Griechische und Lateinische Lehnwörter im Talmud. Midrasch und Targum.* 2 vols. Berlin: S. Calvary, 1898–99.

Krauss, *Synagogale*
———. *Synagogale Altertümer*. Berlin: Wien, 1922. Reprint. Hildesheim: G. Olms, 1966.

Krauss, *Synagogenruinen*
———. *Die galiläischen Synagogenruinen*. Leipzig: Hartmann and Wolff, 1911.

Krautheimer, *Mittelalterliche*
Richard Krautheimer. *Mittelalterliche Synagogen*. Berlin: Frankfurter Verlagsanstalt, 1927.

Landshuth, ʿ*Amude*
Leser Landshuth. ʿ*Amude haʿavoda*. 2 vols. Berlin: G. Bernstein, 1857–62.

Landshuth, *Seder*
———. *Seder biqur ḥolim*. Berlin: A. Cohn, 1867.

Landshuth, *Siddur*
———. *Siddur hegyon lev*. Königsburg: A. Samter, 1945.

Leviticus Rabbah
Midrasch wayyikra rabbah. Edited by M. Margulies. 5 vols. Jerusalem: American Academy for Jewish Research, 1953–60.

Levy, *Wörterbuch*
Jacob Levy. *Neuhebräisches und chaldäisches Wörterbuch über die Talmudim und Midraschim*. 4 vols. Leipzig: F.A. Brockhaus, 1876–89.

Lewin, *Shrira*
Benjamin Lewin. *Igeret rav shrira gaon*. Haifa, 1921. Reprint. Jerusalem: Hamaqor, 1972.

Lewin, *Reform*
M. Lewin. *Die Reform des Judenthums*. 1895.

Lewy Festschrift
Festschrift zu Israel Lewy's siebzigsten Geburtstag. Edited by M. Brann and I. Elbogen. Breslau: M. & H. Marcus, 1911.

Lewysohn, *Meqore*
A. Lewysohn. *Meqore haminhagim*. Berlin: L. Th. Kornegg, 1846.

Lieberman, *Tosefta*
Saul Lieberman. *Tosefta kifshuta*. 8 vols. New York: The Jewish Theological Seminary of America, 1955–73.

Löw, *Lebensalter*
Leopold Löw. *Die Lebensalter in der jüdischen Literatur*. Szegedin, 1875. Reprint. England: Gregg International, 1969.

Löw, *Schriften*
———. *Gesammelte Schriften*. Edited by Immanuel Löw. 5 vols. Szegedin: Alexander Baba, 1889–1900.

Luzzatto, *Betulat*
Samuele Davide Luzzato. *Betulat bat yehuda*. Prague: Landau, 1840.

Luzzatto, *Luah*
———. "Luaḥ hapayetanim." *Oṣar ṭov* 3 (1880): 1–106.

Luzzatto, *Mavo*
———. *Mavo lemahzor keminhag bene roma* (*Introduction to the Roman Mahzor*). Leghorn, 1856. [Edited by Ernst David Goldschmidt. Tel Aviv: Devir, 1966.]

Luzzatto, *Ohev*
———. *Ohev ger*. Vienna: Antonii Nebilis de Schmid, 1830.

Maʿase ephod
Maʿase ephod. Edited by S.D. Luzzatto. Vienna, 1865.

Magen avot
Menaḥem Hameiri. *Magen avot*. Edited by I. Jost. London, 1909.

Maharil
Jacob ben Moses Halevi Möllin. *Sefer maharil*. Warsaw, 1874.

Maḥzor Vitry
See *Vitry*.

Malter, *Saadia*
Henry Malter. *Saadia Gaon, His Life and Works*. Philadelphia: The Jewish Publication Society of America, 1921.

Manhig
Abraham ben Nathan Hayarhi, 12th century. *Sefer hamanhig*. Warsaw: Isaac Goldman, 1885.

Mann, *Bible*
Jacob Mann. *The Bible as Read and Preached in the Old Synagogue*. 2 vols. Cincinnati: Hebrew Union College, 1940–66.

Mann, *Egypt*
———. *The Jews in Egypt and in Palestine under the Fatimid Caliphs*. 2 vols. London: Oxford University Press, 1920–22.

Mann, *Palestinian*
———. "Genizah Fragments of the Palestinian Order of Service." *HUCA* 2 (1925): 260–328.

Marx, *Untersuchungen*
Alexander Marx. *Untersuchungen zum Siddur des Gaon R. Amram I*. Berlin: M. Poppelauer, 1908.

Masterman, *Galilee*
Ernst Masterman. *Studies in Galilee*. Chicago: The University of Chicago Press, 1909.

Medieval Jewish Chronicles
Medieval Jewish Chronicles. Edited by A. Neubauer. 2 vols. Oxford: Clarendon Press, 1895.

Megilat Taʿanit
Megilat Taʿanit. Edited by A. Neubauer. Vilna, 1925.

Mekhilta
Mekhilta derabi yishmaʿel. Edited by Meir Friedmann. Vienna, 1870. Reprint. New York, 1948.

Midrash tanaim
Midrash tanaim. Edited by David Hoffman. Berlin: H. Itzkowski, 1908–9.

Midrash tehilim
Midrash tehilim. Edited by Salomon Buber. Vilna: Romm, 1891.

Mirsky, *Yalquṭ*
Aaron Mirsky. *Yalquṭ hapiyuṭim*. Jerusalem: M. Neuman, 1958.

Moore, *Judaism*
George Foot Moore. *Judaism in the First Centuries of the Christian Era*. 3 vols. Cambridge: Harvard University Press, 1927–30.

Müller, *Briefe*
Joel Müller. *Briefe und Responsen in der vorgeonäischen jüdischen Literatur*. Berlin: G. Bernstein, 1886.

Müller, *Mafteaḥ*
———. *Mafteaḥ liteshuvot hageʾonim*. Berlin: H. Itzkowski, 1891.

Müller, *Soferim*
Masekhet Soferim. Edited by Joel Müller. Leipzig: Hinrichs, 1878.

Müller, *Inschriften*
Nikolaus Müller. *Die Inschriften der jüdischen Katakombe am Monteverde zu Rom*. Leipzig: O. Harrassowitz, 1919.

Müller, *Katakombe*
———. *Die jüdische Katakombe am Monteverde zu Rom*. Leipzig: G. Fock, 1912.

Nathan the Babylonian
    Nathan the Babylonian in *Seder ʿolam zuṭa*. See *Medieval Jewish Chronicles* 2:69–88.

Neubauer and Cowley, *Catalogue*
    Adolf Neubauer and Arthur Cowley. *Catalogue of the Hebrew Manuscripts in the Bodleian Library and in the College Libraries of Oxford*. 2 vols. Oxford: Clarendon Press, 1886–1906.

Obermeyer, *Modernes*
    Jacob Obermeyer. *Modernes Judentum in Morgen- und Abendland*. Vienna: C. Fromme, 1907.

Or zaruaᶜ
    Isaac ben Moses of Vienna, ca. 1200–70 C.E. *Or zaruaᶜ*. Edited by Akiba Lehrn. 2 vols. Zhitomer, 1862–90.

Orḥot
    Aaron ben Jacob Hakohen. *Sefer orḥot ḥayim*. Florence, 1750.

Oṣar tov
    Oṣar tov: hebräische Beilage zum Magazin für die Wissenschaft des Judenthums. Edited by Abraham Berliner and David Hoffman. 1878–93.

Pardes
    Sefer hapardes lerashi. Constantinople, 1812.

Perles, *Beiträge*
    J. Perles. *Beiträge zur Geschichte der hebräischen und aramäischen Studien*. Munich: T. Ackerman, 1884.

Pesiqta derav kahana
    Pesiqta derav kahana. Edited by Salomon Buber. Lyck, 1868.

Pesiqta rabati
    Pesiqta rabati. Edited by Meir Friedmann. Vienna, 1880. Reprint. Tel Aviv, 1963.

Philipson, *Reform*
    David Philipson. *The Reform Movement in Judaism*. Reissue of new and revised edition. Introduction by Solomon B. Freehof. New York: Ktav, 1967.

Phillippson, *Geschichte*
    Martin Phillippson. *Neuste Geschichte des jüdischen Volkes*. 2 vols. Volume 2 edited by Immanuel Bernfeld. Frankfurt: J. Kaufmann, 1922–30.

Philo(a)
    Philonis opera quae supersunt. Edited by L. Cohn and P. Wendland. 6 vols. Berlin, 1896–1930.

Philo(b)
    Philo [Loeb Classical Library]. Edited by F.H. Colson and G.H. Whitaker. 10 vols. Cambridge: Harvard University Press; London: Heinemann, 1949–62.

Pool, *Kaddish*
    David de Sola Pool. *The Old Jewish-Aramaic Prayer: The Kaddish*. Leipzig: Rudolf Haupt, 1909. Same as *The Kaddish*, 3d printing. Jerusalem: Sivan Press, 1964.

Protokolle
    Protokolle der ersten Rabbiner-Versammelung abgehalten zu Braunschweig. Brunswick, 1844.

Protokolle der dritten Versammlung deutscher Rabbiner
    Protokolle der dritten Versammlung deutscher Rabbiner, abgehalten zu Breslau, 1846. Breslau: H.E.C. Leuckart, 1847.

Protokolle und Aktenstücke
    Protokolle und Aktenstücke der zweiten Rabbiner-Versammlung abgehalten zu Frankfurt am Main. Frankfurt: E. Ullman, 1845.

Qoveṣ teshuvot
    Qoveṣ teshuvot harambam veʾigerotav. Edited by A. Lichtenberg. 3 vols. Leipzig, 1859.

R. Moses b. Maimon
    R. Moses b. Maimon: Responsa. Edited by J. Blau. 4 vols. 2d edition. Jerusalem, 1896.

Rapoport, *'Erekh*
    Salomon J.L. Rapoport. *'Erekh milin*. Prague: Landau, 1852.

Rapoport, *Qalir*
    ———. "Toledot rabbi el'azar qalir," *Biqure ha'itim* 10 (1829): 95–123.

Ratner, *Ahavat*
    Baer Ratner. *Ahavat ṣiyon virushalayim*. 12 vols. Vilna, 1901–17.

Realencyklopädie
    Realencyklopädie für protestantische Theologie und Kirche. Edited by Jakob Johann Herzog. 24 vols. Leipzig: Hinrichs, 1896–1913.

Responsa Ḥemda genuza
    Ḥemda genuza. Edited by Zeev W. Wolfensohn and Shneor Zalman Shneorsohn. Lemberg, 1864.

Rietschel, *Liturgik*
    G.C. Rietschel. *Lehrbuch der Liturgik*. 2 vols. Berlin: Reuther und Reichard, 1900–9.

Rosanes, *Tugarma*
    Salomon Rosanes. *Divre yeme yisra'el betugarma*. 6 vols. Gusyatin, 1914–45.

Rosenberg, *Qoveṣ*
    Judah Rosenberg. *Qoveṣ ma'ase yede geonim qadmonim*. 2 vols. Berlin: Friedlenders'sche Buchdruckerei, 1856.

Saadia, *Oeuvres*
    Saadia ben Joseph. *Oeuvres complètes de R. Saadiah ben Iosef al- Fayyoumi*. Edited by J. Derenbourg. 9 vols. Paris: E. Leroux, 1899.

Saadia, *Siddur*
    Siddur rav sa'adia ga'on. Edited by Israel Davidson, S. Assaf, and Y. Joel. Jerusalem: Mekiṣe Nirdamim, 1941. Second printing, 1962.

Sachs, *Poesie*
    Michael Jehiel Sachs. *Die Religiöse Poesie der Juden in Spanien*. Berlin: Veit und Co., 1845.

Salfeld, *Martyrologium*
    Siegmund Salfeld. *Das Martyrologium des Nürnberger Memorbuches*. Berlin: L. Simon, 1898.

Schechter, *Liturgy*
    Abraham I. Schechter. *Studies in Jewish Liturgy*. Philadelphia: Dropsie College, 1930.

Schechter, *Saadyana*
    Solomon Schechter. *Saadyana: Genizah Fragments of Writings of R. Saadya Gaon and Others*. Cambridge: Deighton and Bell, 1903.

Schechter, *Studies*
    ———. *Studies in Judaism*. First series. Philadelphia: The Jewish Publication Society of America, 1896. Second series, 1908. Third series, 1924.

Scheiber, *Semitic*
    Alexander Scheiber. *Semitic Studies in Memory of Immanuel Löw*. Budapest, 1947.

Schirmann, *Shirim ḥadashim*
    Hayim Schirmann. *Shirim ḥadashim min hageniza*. Jerusalem, 1965.

Schürer, *History*
    Emil Schürer. *The History of the Jewish People in the Age of Jesus Christ*. Revised and edited by Geza Vermes, Fergus Millar, and Martin Goodman. 3 vols. Edinburgh: T & T Clark Ltd, 1973–89.

Seder 'olam
    See *Medieval Jewish Chronicles* 1:163ff.

Sefer hashetarot
    Judah ben Barzilai. *Sefer hashetarot*. Edited by Solomon Halberstam. Berlin: H. Itzkowski, 1885. Reprint. Jerusalem: Makor, 1966–67.

Sefer hasidim
Ṣefer ḥasidim. Edited by Jehuda Wistenetzki. Berlin, 1891.

Sefer hashorashim
Jonah Ibn Janah. *Sefer hashorashim*. Edited by W. Bacher. Berlin: H. Itzkowski, 1893–97.

Sendrey, *Bibliography*
A. Sendrey. *Bibliography of Jewish Music*. New York: Columbia University Press, 1951.

Sha'are simha
See Ibn Ghiyath.

Sha'are teshuva
Sha'are teshuva (geonic responsa). Edited by J.J. Eliakim. Salonika, 1802.

Shibole haleqet
Zedakiah ben Abraham Anav. *Shibole haleqet hashalem*. Edited by Salomon Buber. Vilna: Romm, 1886.

Siddur Rashi
Siddur Rashi. Edited by S. Buber and J. Freimann. Berlin: Mekiṣe Nirdamim; New York: Menorah, 1911.

Sifra
Sifra. Edited by I. H. Weiss. Vienna, 1892. Reprint. New York, 1948.

Sifre
Sifre deve rav. Edited by Meir Friedmann. Vienna, 1864. Reprint. New York, 1948.

Sifre zuta
Sifre zuta. Edited by Saul Horovitz. Leipzig, 1912.

Ṣiyunim
Ṣiyunim. [Y. N. Simhoni Memorial Volume]. Berlin: Eshkol, 1928/9.

Soferim
Masekhet Soferim. Edited by Joel Müller. Leipzig: Hinrichs, 1878.

Spiegel, *Poetry*
Shalom Spiegel. "On Medieval Hebrew Poetry." In *The Jews, Their History, Culture and Religion*. Edited by Louis Finklestein. Philadelphia: Jewish Publication Society of America, 1949. 2:528–66.

Steinschneider, *Arabische Literatur*
Morris Steinschneider. *Die Arabische Literatur der Juden*. Frankfurt, 1902. Reprint. Hildesheim: G. Olms, 1964.

Steinschneider, *Catalogus*
————. *Catalogus librorum hebraeorum in bibliotheca Bodleiana*. Berlin: A. Friedlander, 1857. Reprint. Hildesheim: G. Olms, 1964.

Steinschneider, *"Literatur"*
————. "Jüdische Literatur." In *Allgemeine Encyklopädie der Wissenschaften und Künste*. Edited by J.S. Ersch and J.G. Gruber. Second section, H–N, edited by Andreas Hoffmann. Leipzig: F. A. Brockhaus, 1850: 357–471.

Stern, *Geschichte*
Sigismund Stern. *Geschichte des Judenthums von Mendelssohn bis auf die Gegenwart*. Frankfurt, 1857.

Strack, *Einleitung*
Herman Strack. *Einleitung in den Talmud*. 5th edition. Munich: Beck, 1921.

Strack, *Jesus*
————. *Jesus, die Häretiker und die Christen, nach den ältesten jüdischen Angaben*. Leipzig: Hinrichs, 1910.

Tanḥuma
Midrash Tanḥuma. Edited by Salomon Buber. Vilna, 1885.

Tanna deve eliyahu
Tanna deve eliyahu. Edited by Meir Friedmann. Vienna, 1904. Reprint. Jerusalem, 1960.

Tanna deve eliyahu zuta
    Tanna deve eliyahu zuta. Edited by Meir Friedmann. Vienna, 1900.

Teshuvot hageʾonim
    Teshuvot hageʾonim. Edited by Jacob Mussafia. Lyck, 1864.

Theologische Gutachten
    Theologische Gutachten über das Gebetbuch nach dem Gebrauch des Neuen Israelitischen Tempelsvereins in Hamburg; Festschrift zum hunderjährigen Bestehen des Tempels. Hamburg, 1918.

Tosefta
    Tosefta. Edited by M. Zuckermandel. Pasewalk, 1876. Reprint. Jerusalem: Wahrmann, 1970.

Tur
    Jacob ben Asher, ca. 1269–1340. *Arbaʿa turim.* Warsaw, 1882.

Union Prayerbook
    The Union Prayerbook for Jewish Worship. Edited by the Central Conference of American Rabbis (C.C.A.R.). Cincinnati: C.C.A.R., 1894.

Vitry
    Simḥa ben Samuel. *Maḥzor Vitry.* Edited by S. Hurwitz. Berlin: H. Itzkowski, 1893.

Vogelstein and Rieger, *Rom*
    Hermann Vogelstein and Paul Rieger. *Geschichte der Juden in Rom.* 2 vols. Berlin: Mayer und Muller, 1895–96.

Werner, *Bridge*
    Eric Werner. *The Sacred Bridge: The Interdependence of Liturgy and Music in Synagogue and Church during the First Millennium.* London: D. Dobson; New York: Columbia University Press, 1959.

Zedner, *Catalogue*
    J. Zedner. *Catalogue of the Hebrew Books in the British Museum.* London, 1867.

Zunz, *Avignon*
    Leopold Zunz. "Ritus der Synagogue in Avignon." *Allgemeine Zeitung des Judentums* 2 (1838): 580–81.

Zunz, *Haderashot*
    ———. *Haderashot beyisraʾel.* [Translated by M.A. Jacques. Edited by Ḥanokh Albeck. Jerusalem: Bialik Institute, 1954. (*Die Gottesdienstliche Vorträge der Juden historisch entwickelt.* Hebrew)].

Zunz, *Literaturgeschichte*
    ———. *Literaturgeschichte der synagogalen Poesie.* Berlin: L. Gerschel, 1865.

Zunz, *Poesie*
    ———. *Die synagogale Poesie des Mittelalters.* Vol. 1, *Die synagogale Poesie.* Edited by A. Freimann. Berlin: Louis Gerschel, 1855. Reprint. Frankfurt: J. Kauffman, 1920.

Zunz, *Ritus*
    ———. *Die synagogale Poesie des Mittelalters.* Vol. 2, *Die Ritus des synagogalen Gottesdienstes.* Berlin: J. Springer, 1859.

Zunz, *Schriften*
    ———. *Gesammelte Schriften von dr. Zunz.* Edited by Curatorium der "Zunzstiftung." 3 vols. Berlin: L. Gerschel, 1875–76.

Zunz, *Zur Geschichte*
    ———. *Zur Geschichte und Literatur.* Berlin: Veit und Co., 1845.

Zunz Festschrift
    Jubelschrift zum neunzigsten Geburtstag des Leopold Zunz. Berlin: L. Gerschel, 1884. Reprint. Hildesheim: G. Olms, 1974.

Appendix

SECTION BIBLIOGRAPHIES

§7 The Shema‹ and Its Benedictions

Rapoport, *Qalir*, 115; Zunz, *Haderashot*, 179; Landshuth, *Siddur*, 42ff.; Duschak, *Geschichte*, 189ff.; Baer, ‹Avodat, 76ff.; Schürer, *History*, 2:448–63; Jawitz, *Meqor*; Ginzberg, *Geonica*, 1:127ff.; Kohler, *Ursprünge*; id., "Shema Yisroel," *Journal of Jewish Lore* 1, 255ff.; L. Blau, "Origène et histoire de la lecture du Schema et des formules des bénédictions qui l'accompagnent," *REJ* 31 (1895): 179ff.; Elbogen, *Studien*, 3ff.

[L.J. Liebreich, "The Benediction Immediately Preceding and the One Following the Recital of the Shema‹," *REJ* 125 (1966): 151ff.; Benjamin De Pries, "Qeri›at shema‹ uvirkhoteha," *Ma‹yanot* 8 (1964): 149–54; Ḥayim Hamiel, "Ahava raba," *Ma‹yanot* 8 (1964): 113–48; Dov Rapel, "Tefilat ge›ula," *Ma‹yanot* 8 (1964): 162–69; *Jewish Encyclopaedia*, s.v. "Liturgy," "Shma," "Ahaba rabba," "Emet we-Yazzib," "Geullah"; *Realencyklopädie*, s.v. "Schema."]

§8 The ‹Amida: Composition and Structure

Rapoport, *Qalir*, 115ff.; Zunz, *Haderashot*, 179ff.; Landshuth, *Siddur*, 52; Baer, ‹Avodat, 87ff., Duschak, *Geschichte*, 196ff.; Schürer, *History*, 2:448–63; *Jewish Encyclopaedia*, s.v. "Shemoneh Esre"; *Realencyklopädie*, s.v. "Schmone-Esre"; Isidore Loeb, "Les dix-huit bénédictions," *REJ* 19 (1889): 14–40; Israel Levi, "Les dix-huit bénédictions et les Psaumes de Solomon," *REJ* 32 (1896): 161–78; David Hoffman, "Das Schmone-Eszre-Gebet," in *Israelitische Monatsschrift* (Beilage zur Jüdischen Presse, 1899), 48ff.; 1900, 2; Ismar Elbogen, *Achtzehngebets*; id., *Studien*, 33ff.; E. Schwab, *Historische Einführung in das Achtzehngebet* (*Beiträge zur Forderung christlicher Theologie*, 27, 5) (Gutersloh, 1913); Kaufmann Kohler, "The Origin and Composition of the Eighteen Benedictions," *HUCA* 1 (1924): 387ff.; Finkelstein, *Amidah*.

[Ginzberg, *Perushim*, 1:344ff.; 3:277ff.; Allon, *Talmudic Age*, 1:265–72; Lieberman, *Tosefta*, 1:53ff.; Baer, *Yisra›el*, 30ff.; S. Talmon, "Concerning the Calendar of the Judaean Desert Sect (Hebrew)," *Tarbiz* 29 (1961–62): 394–95; Heinemann, *Prayer*, 138ff.; Maurice Liber, "Structure and History of the Tefilah," *JQR* 40 (1949–50): 331ff.; Elias J. Bickermanm, "The Civic Prayer of Jerusalem," *Harvard Theological Review* 40 (1962): 163ff.; Solomon Zeitlin, "The Tefillah, the Shemoneh Esreh," *JQR* 46 (1964): 208ff.]

§9 The ‹Amida: Text

Baer, ‹Avodat, 87ff.; Frumkin, *Seder*, 2:231ff.; Joseph Dérenbourg, "Mélanges rabbiniques," *REJ* 14 (1887): 26ff.; Solomon Schechter, "Geniza Specimens," *JQR* 10 (1898): 656ff.; Gustaf Dalman, *Die Worte Jesu* (Leipzig: Hinrichs, 1898): 299ff.; Elbogen, *Achtzehngebets*, 47ff.; id., *Studien*, 43ff.; Israel Lévi, "Fragments de rituels de prières," *REJ* 53 (1907): 231–41.

§9a The Kedushah

Baer, ʿAvodat, 236ff.; Müller, Soferim, 295; Ginzberg, Geonica, 1:129ff., 2:48ff.; Jacob Mann, "Les 'chapitres' de Ben Baboi et les relations de R. Yehudai Gaon avec la Palestine," REJ 70 (1920): 122ff.; V. Aptowitzer, "La Kedouscha," REJ 87 (1950): 28ff.; Koehler, Ursprünge, 433f.; Zunz, Literaturgeschichte, 13ff.; A. Büchler, "La Kedouscha du Yocer chez les Gueonim," REJ 53 (1907): 220ff.

[Ezra Fleischer, "Lanusha haqeduma shel qedushat haʿamida," Sinai 63 (1968): 229ff.]

§9b The Priestly Blessing

Baer, ʿAvodat, 358ff.; Duschak, Geschichte, 266ff.; Berliner, Randbemerkungen, 1:40ff.; Frumkin, Seder, 1:284ff.; Jewish Encyclopaedia, s.v. "Blessing, Priestly."

§10 The Supplications

Landshuth, Siddur, 170–84; Baer, ʿAvodat, 112–52; Duschak, Geschichte, 218ff.; Zunz, Literaturgeschichte, 15ff.; Berliner, Randbemerkungen, 1:70ff.; Jawitz, Meqor, 85ff.; Realencyklopädie, s.v. "Taḥanun"; Jewish Encyclopaedia, s.v. "Taḥanun."

For §10(11): L. Scheunhaus, "Alenu Leschabbeach," Ost und West 8 (1908): 451ff.; Berliner, Einheitsgesang; Solomon Freehof, "The Origin of the Tahanun," HUCA 2 (1925): 339ff.

§11 The Morning Psalms

Landshuth, Siddur, 23ff.; Baer, ʿAvodat, 58ff.; Herzfeld, Tefillat, 198ff.; S. Margulies, "Note Liturgiche," Rivista Israelitica 4 (1907): 126ff.; Berliner, Randbemerkungen, 1:22ff.; Jawitz, Meqor, 62ff.; Realencyklopädie, s.v. "Morgengebet"; Jewish Encyclopaedia, s.v. "Baruch Sheamar."

§12 The Morning Benedictions

Zunz, Haderashot, 182ff.; Landshuth, Siddur, 23ff.; Baer, ʿAvodat, 35ff.; Berliner, Randbemerkungen, 1:11ff., 2:33ff.; Jawitz, Meqor, 5ff.; Realencyklopädie, s.v. "Benedictions"; Jewish Encyclopaedia, s.v. "Benedictions."

§12a Kaddish

Landshuth, Seder, 59ff.; Baer, ʿAvodat, 129–30, 153, 588; Kohler, Ursprünge; Berliner, Randbemerkungen, 2:4ff; Jewish Encyclopaedia, s.v. "Kaddish"; Obermeyer, Modernes, 91ff.; Pool, Kaddish; Jüdisches Volksblatt, Jahrg. I, Breslau, 1889.

§13 The Afternoon Service

Herzfeld, Tefillat, 184, 187; Jewish Encyclopaedia, s.v. "Minhah."

§14 The Evening Service

Landshuth, Siddur, 218ff.; Baer, ʿAvodat, 163ff.; Herzfeld, Tefillat, 184ff.; A. Büchler, "The Blessing 'bone yerushalayim' in the Liturgy," JQR 20 (1908): 799ff.; Israel Lévi, "Fragments de rituels de prières," REJ 53 (1907): 231–41; Jewish Encyclopaedia, s.v. "Ma'ariv."

§15   Friday Night

Landshuth, *Siddur*, 248ff.; Baer, ʿ*Avodat*, 178ff.; Herzfeld, *Tefillat*, 209ff.; Rosenthal in Graetz, *Geschichte*, 4:470; Berliner, *Randbemerkungen*, 1:43ff.; Scheiber, *Semitic*, 173ff.; Elbogen, *Eingang*, 358ff.; A. Mishcon, *Studies in the Liturgy*, vol. 2.

[Joseph Heinemann, "Tefilat shabat," *Maḥanayim* 85–86 (1963): 54ff.; D. Goldschmidt, "Qidush vehavdala," *Maḥanayim* 85–86 (1963): 48–53; Jacob Rothschild, "Tefilat shevaʿ shel yom hashabat," *Maʿyanot* 8 (1964): 181ff.]

§16   The Sabbath Morning Service

Landshuth, *Siddur*, 277ff.; Baer, ʿ*Avodat*, 206ff.

§17   The Additional Service

Landshuth, *Siddur*, 315ff.; Baer, ʿ*Avodat*, 235ff.; Herzfeld, *Tefillat*, 205ff.; Rosenthal in Graetz, *Geschichte*, 4:471.

§18   The Afternoon Service

Landshuth, *Siddur*, 338ff.; Baer, ʿ*Avodat*, 259ff.

§19   The End of the Sabbath

Landshuth, *Siddur*, 384ff.; Baer, ʿ*Avodat*, 295ff.; Elbogen, *Eingang*, 358ff.

§20   The New Moon

Landshuth, *Siddur*, 411ff.; Baer, ʿ*Avodat*, 319ff.; Abeles, *Der kleine Versöhnungstag*, 1911.

§21   Fast Days

Duschak, *Geschichte*, 310ff.; Israel Lévi, "Notices sur les jeûnes chez les Israëlites," *REJ* 47 (1903): 161.

§22   Hanukkah and Purim

Jewish Encyclopaedia, s.v. "Hanukkah," "Purim"; S. Stein, "The Liturgy of Hanukah and the First Two Books of Maccabees," *JJS* 5 (1954): 110ff., 148ff.

§23   The Three Pilgrim Festivals

Landshuth, *Siddur*, 437ff.; Baer, ʿ*Avodat*, 346ff.; Berliner, *Randbemerkungen*, 2:25ff.; Scheiber, *Semitic*, 173ff.; Elbogen, "Die Tefilla für die Festtage," *MGWJ* 55 (1911): 426ff.

§24   The Days of Awe

Landshuth, *Siddur*, 456ff.; Baer, ʿ*Avodat*, 383ff.; Friedmann, "The New Year and its Liturgy," *JQR* 1 (1889): 62ff.

[Lieberman, *Tosefta*, 5:1052ff.; Heinemann, *Prayer*, 173ff.; Naphtali Wieder, "Genizah Studies in the Babylonian Liturgy (Hebrew)," *Tarbiz* 37 (1968): 135ff., 240ff.; Joseph Heinemann, "Malkhuyot zikhronot veshofarot," *Maʿyanot* 9 (1968): 546ff.; Goldschmidt, *Mahzor*, 1:15ff., 2:9ff.; Kieval, *High Holy Days*; L.J. Liebreich, "Aspects of the New Year Liturgy," *HUCA* 34 (1963): 125ff.; id., "The Insertions in the Third Benedictions in the Holy Day ʿAmidoth," *HUCA* 35 (1964): 79f.]

§ 25 The Reading of the Torah

Zunz, *Haderashot*, chap. 1; Herzfeld, *Tefillat*, 209–15; Friedmann, *Maʾamar*, 6–10, 65–71, 100–106; J. Theodor, "Die Midraschim zum Pentateuch und der dreijährige palästinensische Cyclus," *MGWJ* 34 (1885): 420ff.; Büchler, *Triennial*, 420ff.; *Realencyklopädie*, s.v. "Vorlesung aus der Thora"; *Jewish Encyclopaedia*, s.v. "Law, Reading from the —," "Triennial Cycle"; *Protokolle und Aktenstücke der zweiten Rabbinerversammlung* (Frankfurt: E. Ullman,1845).

[I. Joel, "ʿAl ʾhasedarim' shebatora," *Qiryat sefer* 38 (1962) 12–132; J. Heinemann, "The 'Triennial' Cycle and the Calendar (Hebrew)," *Tarbiz* 33 (1963): 362–71; E. Fleischer, "Simhat tora shel bene ereṣ yisraʾel," *Sinai* 59 (1956): 210ff., A. Yaari, *Toldot hag simhat torah* (Jerusalem: Rav Kook, 1963); Mann, *Bible*; L. Morris, *The New Testament and the Jewish Lectionaries* (London: Tyndale Press, 1964); L. Crocket, "Luke IV, 16–30 and the Jewish Lectionary Cycle," *JJS* 17 (1966): 13ff.; J. Heinemann, "The Triennial Lectionary Cycle," *JJS* 19 (1968): 41ff.]

§ 26 The Haftara

Zunz, *Haderashot*, chap. 1; Rapoport, *ʿErekh*, "Afṭarta," 167ff.; Adler, "Die Haftara," *MGWJ* 11 (1862): 222ff.; A. Büchler, "The Reading of the Law and Prophets in a Triennial Cycle," *JQR* 6 (1894): 1–74; *Jewish Encyclopaedia*, s.v. "Haftarah," "Triennial Cycle."

[L. Finklestein, "The Prophetic Readings According to the Palestinian, Byzantine, and Karaite Rites," *HUCA* 17 (1942–43): 423ff.; *Ensiqlopedia talmudit*, "Haftara," 10:1–31; Heinemann, *Prayer*, 36ff.; 50, 143ff.; Mann, *Bible*.]

§ 27 The Reading from the Hagiographa

J.E., s.v. "Megillot, the five."

§ 28 The Translation of the Reading

Zunz, *Haderashot*, chap. 2; Luzzatto, *Ohev*; J.E., s.v. "Meturgeman"; Bacher, *Terminologie*, 1:204f., 2:242f.

§ 29 The Sermon

Zunz, *Haderashot*; Rapoport, *ʿErekh*, s.v. "agada," 6ff.; Bacher, *Terminologie*, 1:25f., 33f., 103f.; Bacher, *Tannaim*, 451f. (same as *JQR* 4:406): "Der Ursprung des Wortes Haggada"; Maybaum, *Homiletik*, 1f.

§ 30 Prayers Before and After the Reading of the Torah

Berliner, *Randbemerkungen*, 1:28ff., 65ff., 2:30ff. [Heinemann, *Prayer*, 158ff.]

§ 31 General

Zunz, *Haderashot*, 491, n. 141; Duschak, *Geschichte*, 24ff.; Dukes, *Poesie*; Zunz, *Literaturgeschichte*, 60ff.; Perles, *Beiträge*, 63ff.; *Jewish Encyclopaedia*, s.v. "Piyyut," "Pizmon"; H. Schirmann, "Ḥeker hashira vehapiyut," bibliographical listings appearing annually in *Qiryat sefer*.

[Spiegel, *Poetry*; S. Baron, *A Social and Religious History of the Jews* (Philadelphia: Jewish Publication Society of America, 1958), 8:62–134, 135–210, 244–80, 286–321.]

§ 32 The Piyyut

Dukes, *Poesie*; Zunz, *Literaturgeschichte*, 60ff.; *Jewish Encyclopaedia*, s.v. "Piyyut," "Pizmon," "Abodah," "Azharot," "Ḳerobot," "Yoẓerot"; Brody, *Dichterschule*.

§ 33 The Seliḥa

Dukes, *Poesie*; Zunz, *Literaturgeschichte*, 60ff.; Brody, *Dichterschule*; *Realencyklopädie*, Appendix 2, 90ff.; *Jewish Encyclopaedia*, s.v. "Seliḥah," "Ḳinah."

§ 34 The First Signs of Regular Public Worship

Zunz, *Haderashot*, 182ff.; Herzfeld, *Tefillat*, 183ff.; Graetz, *Divre*, 1:298ff.; Duschak, *Geschichte*, 183ff.; *Jewish Encyclopaedia*, s.v. "Liturgy"; Kohler, *Ursprünge*.

§ 35 Prayer in the Tannaitic Period: Before the Destruction of the Temple

Zunz, *Haderashot*, 182ff.; Herzfeld, *Tefillat*, 183ff.; Sachs, *Poesie*, 164ff.

§ 36 Prayer in the Tannaitic Period: After the Destruction of the Temple

Herzfeld, *Tefillat*, 183ff.; Graetz, *Divre*, 2; Sachs, *Poesie*, 164ff.

§ 37 Prayer in the Amoraic Period

Zunz, *Haderashot*, 182ff.; Rosenthal in Graetz, *Geschichte*, 4:463, n. 39.

§ 38 The Expansions and Embellishments of the Statutory Prayers

Zunz, *Haderashot*, 182ff.; id., *Literaturgeschichte*, 11ff.

§ 39 Piyyut

Zunz, *Literaturgeschichte*, 59ff.; Duschak, *Geschichte*, 224ff.; *Jewish Encyclopaedia*, s.v. "Piyyut"; Dukes, *Poesie*; Sachs, *Poesie*; Eppenstein, *Literatur*; Spiegel, *Poetry*; S. Baron, *A Social and Religious History of the Jews* (Philadelphia: Jewish Publication Society of America, 1958), 8:62–134, 135–210, 244–80, 286–321; A. Mirsky, "Maḥṣavtan shel surot hapiyut," *Yediʿot hamakhon leḥeker hashira haʿivrit* 7 (1957): 1–143; Werner, *Bridge*.

§ 40 The Main Liturgical Poets: Up to and Including Kallir

Rapoport, *Qalir*, 115; Zunz, *Haderashot*, 179; Landshuth, *ʿAmude*; Luzzatto, *Luaḥ*, 1–106; A. Geiger, *Jüdische Zeitschrift* 10 (1872): 262ff.; W. Bacher, "Aus einer Poetik (Schule Saadja's)," *JQR* 14 (1902): 742–44; Eppenstein, *Literatur*; H. Graetz, "Die Anfange der hebräischen Poesie," *MGWJ* 8 (1859): 401–13, 9 (1860): 19–29; Harkavy, *Studien*, 5:106ff.; Schechter, *Saadyana*.

[M. Zulay, *Zur Liturgie der Babylonischen Juden* (Stuttgart: W. Kohlhammer, 1933); id., "Contribution to the History of the Liturgical Poetry in Palestine," *Yediʿot hamakhon leḥeker hashira haʿivrit* 5 (1939): 107–80;

id., *Ben kotle hamakhon leheqer hashira ha'ivrit* (Jerusalem, 1951), 83–124; A. Mirsky, *Reshit hapiyut* (Jerusalem: Jewish Agency, 1964); Schirmann, *Shirim ḥadashim*; J. Schirmann, "The Beginning of Hebrew Poetry in Italy," in *The World History of the Jewish People*, 2nd series, vol. 2, *Medieval Period*, ed. Cecil Roth (Tel Aviv: Jewish History Publications, Ltd.; New Brunswick: Rutgers University Press, 1966), 249–60, 429–32; Efraim Urbach, *'Arugat habosem*, 4 vols (Jerusalem: Meqiṣe nirdamim, 1939–63).

After Brody's and Wiener's *Mivḥar* appeared, other anthologies containing many piyyutim were published. See Haberman, *Beron yaḥad*; id., *Hayiḥud*; id., *'Ateret*; Mirsky, *Yalkuṭ*; Jarden, *Sefune.*]

§41   The Main Liturgical Poets: Kallir's Imitators

Rapoport, *Qalir*, 115; Zunz, *Haderashot*, 179; Landshuth, *'Amude*; Luzzatto, *Luaḥ*.

§42   The Main Poets: The Poets of Spain

Zunz, *Haderashot*, 179; Landshuth, *'Amude*; Brody, *Mivḥar*; Sachs, *Poesie*; Karpeles, *Geschichte*.

[Spanish poetry receives substantial treatment in all anthologies of medieval Hebrew poetry. See the works of Brody, Haberman, Mirsky, and Jarden mentioned above (§40, notes). Also see Simon Bernstein, *'Al naharot sefarad* (Tel Aviv: Maḥbarot lesifrut, 1956).—The history of Hebrew poetry in Spain with selected texts and Spanish translation: José Maria Millas y Vallicrosa, *La poesía sagrada hebraicoespañola* (Madrid, 1940); selected sacred and secular poetry with detailed introductions and explanations: Jefim Schirmann, *Hashira ha'ivrit bisefarad uveprovans*, 2 vols. (Jerusalem: Mossad Harav Kook, 1954–56; 2d edition, 1960–62. At the end of this collection (pp. 669–700), a bibliography is provided. Lesser-known piyyutim of the poets mentioned above are published in Schirmann, *Shirim ḥadashim*. The entry for each poet contains a list of his poems published between 1935 and 1965.]

§43   Prayer Books and Orders of Prayer

Zunz, *Ritus*; *Jewish Encyclopaedia*, s.v. "Liturgy," "Prayer-Books."

§44   The Influence of Mysticism on the Synagogue Service

Zunz, *Ritus*; Phillip Bloch, "Die Yorde Merkavah, die Mystiker der Gaonzeit und ihr Einfluss auf die Liturgie," *MGWJ* 37 (1893): 18–25, 40 (1905): 129–66; Schechter, *Studies*, 1:1ff., 2:148ff.; *Jewish Encyclopaedia*, s.v. "Cabala," "Chasidism," "Prayer."

§45   The First Reforms in the Synagogue Service

Zunz, *Haderashot*, 205ff.; Graetz, *Geschichte*, vol. 7; Bernfeld, *Toledot*; *Jewish Encyclopaedia*, s.v. "Prayer," "Reform Judaism."

Philipson, *Reform*; M. Phillippson, *Geschichte*, vol. 1.

§46   The Reform Movement at Its Height

Philipson, *Reform*; Phillippson, *Geschichte*, vol. 1; Bernfeld, *Toledot*; *Jewish Encyclopaedia*, s.v. "Prayer," "Reform Judaism"; *Protokelle und Aktenstücke*.

§47   The Reform Movement Outside of Germany

Philipson, *Reform*; *Jewish Encyclopaedia*, s.v. "Prayer," "Reform Judaism."

§ 48   *Synagogues: Name, Age, Distribution, and Location*

Leopold Löw, "Der Synagogale Ritus," *MGWJ* 33 (1884): 97ff. [Löw, *Schriften*, 4:1ff.]; id., "Synagogale Altertümer, Plan und Kollektaneen," in Löw, *Schriften*, 5:21–36, 93; Hoffman, *Synagogen*; Schürer, *History*, 2:423ff., 3:87ff.; Bacher, *Synagogue*; *Jewish Encyclopaedia*, 9:618ff.; Juster, *Juifs*, 1:456ff.; Krauss, *Synagogale*; Krautheimer, *Mittelalterliche*.

[Michael Avi-Yonah and S. Yeivin, *Qadmoniyot arṣenu* (Tel Aviv: Haqibuṣ hameʾuhad, 1955); Avraham Negev, *Mavo laʾarkheʾologia shel ereṣ yisraʾel* (Jerusalem: Bet hasefer letayarut, 1967); id., *Ensiqlopedia lahafirot arkheʾologiot beʾereṣ yisraʾel* (Jerusalem: Masada, 1970); F. Kohl and C. Watzinger, *Antike Synagogen in Galiläa* (Leipzig: Hinrichs, 1916); E.L. Sukenik, *Ancient Synagogues in Palestine and Greece* (London: Oxford University Press, 1934).]

§ 49   *Synagogue Construction*

Löw, *Schriften*; Hoffman, *Synagogen*; Bacher, *Synagogue*; Samuel Krauss, *Die galiläischen Synagogenruinen* (Leipzig: Hartmann und Wolf, 1911).

§ 50   *The Furnishing of the Synagogue*

Löw, *Schriften*; Hoffman, *Synagogen*; Bacher, *Synagogue*.

§ 51   *Congregation and Synagogue*

Löw, *Schriften*, vol. 5; Bacher, *Synagogue*; Schürer, *History*; M. Weinberg, "Die Organisation der jüdischen Ortsgemeinden in der talmudischen Zeit," *MGWJ* 51 (1897): 588–95.

§ 52   *The Officials of the Community*

Löw, *Schriften*; Schürer, *History*; Bacher, *Synagogue*; Weinberg, *Die Organisation*; *Jewish Encyclopaedia*, s.v. "Archisynagogue," "Hazzan."

§ 53   *The Precentor and the Community*

Löw, *Schriften*; Schürer, *History*.

§ 54   *Synagogue Song*

Zunz, *Poesie*, 1:113–16; Berliner, *Vorbeterdienstes*, 2–5, 13–14, 29–31, 34–35, 40; Ackermann, *Gesang*, 3:477–529; Friedmann, *Gesang*; *Jewish Encyclopaedia*, s.v. "Cantillation," "Music, Synagogal."

Index of Prayers

Hebrew Incipits

English Incipits

Index of Names and Subjects